Encyclopedia of Exotic Tropical Fishes

For Freshwater Aquariums

Encyclopedia of Exotic Tropical Fishes

For Freshwater Aquariums

Glen S. Axelrod, M.S., F.Z.S., **& Brian M. Scott**

Foreword by Neal Pronek

T.F.H. Publications, Inc.
One TFH Plaza
Third and Union Avenues
Neptune City, NJ 07753

This book has been published with the intent to provide accurate and authoritative information in regard to the subject matter within. While every precaution has been taken in preparation of this book, the author and publisher expressly disclaim responsibility for any errors, omissions, or adverse effects arising from the use or application of the information contained herein. The techniques and suggestions are used at the reader's discretion and are not to be considered a substitute for veterinary care. If you suspect a medical problem consult your veterinarian.

Library of Congress Cataloging-in-Publication Data

Axelrod, G. S. (Glen S.)
Encyclopedia of exotic tropical fishes for freshwater aquariums /
        GlenS. Axelrod and Brian M. Scott. p. cm.
Includes index.
ISBN 0-7938-0570-8 (alk. paper)
1. Tropical fish. 2. Aquariums. I. Scott, Brian M. II. Title.
SF457.A896 2005
639.34--dc22
2004024501

Front cover photo: Takashi Amano
Back cover photo: M. P. & C. Piednoir

Book design and compositon by Mada Design, Inc.

Dedicated to the Memory of Alan R. Axelrod

This book is dedicated to the memory of my father, Alan R. Axelrod, without whom T.F.H. Publications would not exist today. Over 50 years ago, *Tropical Fish Hobbyist* magazine, and hence T.F.H. Publications, was founded in a small storefront in New York City near Canal Street. Two people were principally involved in the business in those days, my father, Alan, and his brother, Herbert. The business initially involved the importation and distribution of tropical fish. Small books were also written by "TFH/Axelrod" and published by companies such as Sterling Publishing Co.

In about 1954 the business was moved to a small 25 by 75 foot candy store in Jersey City, New Jersey. The neighborhood was rough, and my father carried a police nightstick with him as he walked from his car to the office. He would take a station wagon to pick up imported tropical fish at the airport, and then make rounds delivering the magazine, small aquarium hobbyist books, and the fish to pet stores and department stores such as Woolworths. Since that time, TFH has grown to be the largest publisher of pet and animal books in the world, as well as a substantial manufacturer of pet and animal products.

My father was a man of many attributes. In addition to being a beloved husband, father, grandfather, uncle, and friend of many, he was a true patriot, who loved his country and served it twice as a sergeant in the United States Army Air Corps and Air Force during the Korean War. He was an industrialist who was part of the great mid-century generation who made America what she is today. He was a natural teacher who strongly believed in education and received an MBA in the early 1950's, when graduate degrees were scarce. He was a leader who genuinely loved engaging people in constructive ways, and rose to the top of numerous social and business organizations.

My father wasn't always right, but he always tried to do the right thing. He afforded many thousands of people the opportunity of employment and as such, contributed to the support of thousands. He worked tirelessly to insure his family's security. He was always stubborn, and that is why he was able to overcome 20 years of serious hardship with his health. He did "not go gentle into that good night."

Alan R. Axelrod made many things possible, including TFH and, hence, this book.

Contents

About the Authors

Glen S. Axelrod, M.S., F.Z.S. has been an avid hobbyist for over forty years. He received his Bachelor of Arts degree in biochemistry from Rutgers College, Rutgers University, and his Masters of Science in ichthyology from the J.L.B. Smith Institute of Ichthyology, Rhodes University. Although he has had extensive experience with many types of fishes, cichlids are his personal favorite. Starting in the mid-1970's, he spent six years studying cichlids of the Great Lakes of Africa, during which time he spent three years living in Africa. During that time, he received his Masters degree in ichthyology and completed his doctoral course work, which was continued under the generous assistance and supervision of Professor Karl F. Liem, Museum of Comparative Zoology, Harvard University.

Mr. Axelrod was fortunate enough to find, describe, and name several new cichlid species, and has been a Scientific Fellow of the *Zoological Society of London* since the late 1970's, a juried honor given to those who, upon application, have made an original contribution to science. Mr. Axelrod's primary field of research dealt with the taxonomic status and ecology of African cichlids, for which he has written, or has made major contributions to, six scientific papers and over a dozen books on the subject. Mr. Axelrod's recent endeavors have included research in various areas of the pet products industry, in which he has received, and has pending, more than 50 patents on unique, new, pet-related products, including advanced aquarium filtration systems.

Mr. Axelrod is a member of a number of professional organizations, including *The American Society of Ichthyologists and Herpetologists (ASIH)*, the *Zoological Society of London (ZSL)*, and the *Society of Vertebrate Paleontology*. He is currently President and Chief Executive Officer of T.F.H. Publications, Inc. and Executive Editor of *Tropical Fish Hobbyist* magazine—The Leading Aquarium Magazine For Over Half a Century.

Brian M. Scott received his Bachelor of Science degree in biology from the Richard Stockton College of New Jersey in 2001. His primary area of research deals with cichlids but he has published extensively in other areas as well with more than three-dozen papers on various freshwater and marine fishes along with their associated care and husbandry requirements in aquariums. Recently, Mr. Scott has made major taxonomic contributions to both *Dr. Axelrod's Atlas of Freshwater Aquarium Fishes* and *Dr. Axelrod's Mini-Atlas of Freshwater Aquarium Fishes*. For these contributions, Mr. Scott was awarded co-authorship on both titles.

An avid fishkeeper since childhood, Mr. Scott currently works as the Aquatics Editor for T.F.H. Publications and Contributing Editor of *Tropical Fish Hobbyist* magazine where he proudly continues T.F.H.'s long tradition of excellence in the aquarium and publishing industries. Additionally, Mr. Scott is a member of *The American Society of Ichthyologists and Herpetologists (ASIH)*, *The Association for Tropical Biology and Conservation*, *The Society of Systematic Biologists*, and *The American Cichlid Association*.

Acknowledgements

We would like to express our sincerest gratitude to the many people who have made this book possible. A truly immense book such as this requires assistance across multiple disciplines in order to be complete and authoritative. The following acknowledgments are undoubtedly incomplete, and we must apologize in advance to those who have been inadvertently omitted.

We are especially grateful to Mr. Oliver Lucanus for his superb photography and his authoritative advice on certain families of fishes, especially the Killies of the family Aplocheilidae. Mr. Lucanus is a long-time friend and contributor to T.F.H. Publications, Inc., as well as the primary photographer for this book.

We would also like to thank Ms. Laura Muha for her work on the breeding and reproduction section of this book. Ms. Muha is a professional science writer who has completed two books for T.F.H. Publications Inc. and is a monthly columnist for *Tropical Fish Hobbyist* magazine.

Several individuals have assisted us in the completion of the species profiles in this book. They include Mr. David Boruchowitz, Editor-in-Chief of *Tropical Fish Hobbyist* magazine, Mr. Robert Hare, Mr. Frank Magallanes, Mr. Mark MacDonald, Ms. Jeni C. Tyrell, and Mr. Ed Wong. We cannot thank them enough for their contributions, and without their time and efforts, this book would not be as complete as it is. Additionally, we are forever grateful for the hard work and patience of Stan Madaloni, Peter Romeo, Alex Coroneos, Richard Giuliani, Jasmine Marcin and the rest of the design team at Mada Design, Inc. I (BMS) would also like to acknowledge my wonderful girlfriend, Lisa, for putting up with the seemingly endless hours of writing that this project required.

We would also like to thank Ms. Laura Nelson for her devotion to this project. Ms. Nelson spent many, many hours poring over the manuscript and also consulted on ways to improve the layout of the book in order to make it more understandable for novice tropical fish hobbyists.

Last, but certainly not least, we would like to give a special acknowledgement to Mr. Neal Pronek. I (GSA) have had the pleasure and great fortune of knowing Neal for 43 years. We first met in the early part of 1961, when I was a child of eight years and he became Assistant Editor of *TFH* magazine under then-Editor Bill Vorderwinkler. Neal eventually became Editor-in-Chief of TFH Publications and, although Neal officially retired from TFH several years ago after 40 years of service, we have been blessed by his willingness to stay involved in a consulting capacity. I want to express my personal thanks for his many contributions to TFH over the years and now for his help in completing this extensive tome. It would be impossible for me to separate my feelings for Neal from those of TFH, as he was such a positive influence on the organization for so many years and continues to imprint his contributions today.

Preface

With great pride we introduce to you *The Encyclopedia of Exotic Tropical Fishes for Freshwater Aquariums*. A book of this scope and magnitude did not happen overnight. It took years of research, huge amounts of resources, and above all else, experience. Real-life experiences in the field of ichthyology and aquariology are what made this book come together for its original versions and also what will hopefully help this new version to become an industry icon like its predecessors. We feel that this book will serve as a guide to all aquarists, from the novice to the seasoned professional.

T.F.H. Publications Inc. has long been an important source of literature, exploring various areas of the aquarium industry for over 50 years. We have produced books on a wide variety of subjects, ranging from Australian Rainbowfishes to Zebra Spiny Eels and including just about everything in-between. We also encourage you to read the articles and regular columns found in *Tropical Fish Hobbyist* magazine to supplement your passion for fishes. The contents of the magazine reflect the experiences and knowledge of hobbyists, aquarists, and scientists on various subjects, including, but certainly not limited to, studying fish behavior, spawning rare cichlids, and collecting popular aquarium fishes from locales all over the globe.

We take great pride in the books we publish, and this is but one of the many quality titles offered through T.F.H Publications Inc. We both sincerely hope that *The Encyclopedia of Exotic Tropical Fishes for Freshwater Aquariums* brings you closer to the world of ichthyology and gives you a better understanding of the fishes you choose to care for.

Glen S. Axelrod
President and CEO
T.F.H. Publications Inc.

Brian M. Scott
Aquatics Editor
T.F.H. Publications Inc.

Foreword

Can a brand-new book have a history? Well, this one does. Even though it's completely new in the sense that it has been re-written by some different people and presents its information in a format different from those used in T.F.H.'s four earlier all-embracive reference books, it can't escape its connection to them. Of course it wouldn't want to, because those books are the most successful aquarium books of their type ever published.

Those four books are: *Exotic Tropical Fishes, Exotic Tropical Fishes (Expanded Edition), Dr. Axelrod's Atlas of Freshwater Aquarium Fishes,* and *Aquarium Fishes of the World.* Those books all use (or, in the case of the first edition or two of the *Atlas,* used) as their textual bedrock basically the same descriptive accounts for the individual fish species. All four of them also had as their originator and co-author Dr. Herbert R. Axelrod. Glen S. Axelrod, current President and CEO of T.F.H., is the prime mover behind this new book and also is its senior author. Glen also had a hand in the writing and production of the 1979 *Exotic Tropical Fishes* in its expanded version and in *Aquarium Fishes of the World.* So the thread of continuity is there.

That explains the history of this book, but not its purpose. Its purpose is something else again. Its purpose is not to serve as just another link in the chain of aquaristic overviews that over the years have rolled off the presses of T.F.H. and other publishers. Its purpose is to be a book that will have a vital and permanent utility to people who want to learn about the fishes that form both the bedrock foundations and the penthouses of the aquarium hobby. It will not attempt to be a treatise in ichthyology or a presentation that includes photos and text about fishes completely unsuited to home aquarium care just so that it can boast about how many different species it contains. Nor will it gab on about species that appeared on a list of fishes imported in 1907 and never seen since.

No. Its focus will be on the fishes that tropical fish hobbyists definitely will (in many instances) or possibly could (in many more instances) come upon while visiting a pet shop or a pet department or a tropical fish specialty store or an auction run by an aquarium society. It will present information about fishes that many aquarists actually have a chance of being able to buy or obtain in trade. Will some readers be so situated as to be able to obtain, at least on an occasional basis, many of the fishes discussed in the book whereas others will be able to obtain only a few of them? Of course. So what? Leaving out species that are never offered in small shops in sparsely populated areas would be like leaving rare stamps out of a stamp catalog. A catalog like that might not build up false hopes, but it definitely wouldn't provide a very true picture, either.

I'm glad to be able to say that this "Encyclopedia of Tropical Aquarium Fishes" does more than just continue the tradition of T.F.H.'s tropical fish book overviews. It has improved on them. Grouping the fishes by families within their respective orders is more scientifically educational—and more educationally scientific—than just arranging them alphabetically by species name or by continent of origin. The revised arrangement adds a much greater cohesion to the book. Readers will obtain a much finer feel for how the species relate to one another in the true ichthyological sense, not just as scattered images. Also, eliminating entire sections that appeared in earlier overviews but don't really fit among the subjects related strictly to aquarium fishes performs a needed service. It leaves more room for detailed examination of many more species, species that could not have been presented in a work that necessarily has to limit its number of pages so as not to become unwieldy and overly expensive.

There are other good points about this book not shared by its predecessors. An important one in my view (and admittedly not an opinion shared by everyone connected with T.F.H.'s earlier overviews) is the elimination of assigned "popular" names to fishes that don't have any. That practice does much more harm than just cluttering up a book's index. It clutters up readers' minds as well, somehow leading many to conclude that every fish *should* have a common name and that the scientific names shouldn't be bothered with.

All in all, I think that the improvements incorporated in this book far outweigh the curtailments that have had to be made in obeisance to the great gods of book length and cost. I think that this *Encyclopedia of Exotic Tropical Fishes* and its authors can stand proudly with their forerunners and be able to say, along with Axelrod and Burgess and the late Emmens and others who have contributed to *Exotic Tropical Fishes* in its various embodiments, that they have made a good book that will be used by a good many good people for a good many years.

Part I

BLEEKER 1863

Chromobotia macracantha

Introduction

The science of ichthyology comprises our knowledge of fishes. It represents the observations and studies of scientists for over two thousand years, now organized in an orderly fashion and tested through innumerable human experiences with the scientific method, precision instruments, and mathematical analysis, and then checked and rechecked by modern experimental research techniques.

Ichthyology arose from the Greek words *ichthys*, meaning fishes, and *logos*, a discourse, by people wishing to discover the truths about fish. Ichthyology is a branch of zoology and contains many disciplines within it. Such disciplines include systematics, way of life, fisheries biology, habitat preference, distribution, reproduction, natural history, and orderly management or classifications.

Those people that dedicate their careers to researching fishes are called **ichthyologists**. Ichthyologists define fishes as those vertebrates adapted for an aquatic life, respiring by means of internal gills throughout adult life, and propelling and balancing themselves by means of fins. The latter part of the definition is frequently dropped since some fishes have highly modified fins that actually play a very minor role in their propulsion. The members of the family Anguillidae immediately come to mind, especially when compared to the members of Cichlidae.

The word **fish** is both singular and plural. When used as a plural, it is only valid as a description of more than one specimen of the same species. When there is more than one specimen and they are at least two different species, or they are thought to be two different species, then the word **fishes** is used. For example, this book contains many fishes.

This aquarium contains many *fishes*.

The role of aquarists and hobbyists in ichthyology is broad. Many master aquarists are technically referred to as **bionomic ichthyologists** while advanced aquarists are sometimes considered **amateur ichthyologists**. Bionomic ichthyologists are specialists in the care, husbandry, propagation, and general aquariology of fishes. Their publications usually consist of society journals and magazines on the subject of fishkeeping in general. Frequently, bionomic ichthyologists will publish books detailing techniques that resulted in their success with groups of fishes.

Bionomic ichthyologists usually have either a Bachelor of Science (B.S.) or a Master of Science (M.S.) degree in either biology or zoology with many credits being earned in fisheries science. In many cases, extra credits are obtained in aquaculture or other fish-related disciplines.

Amateur ichthyologists are quite common in the realm of fish-keeping. They play an important role in the industry and often have management positions with large fish shops, importers, and wholesalers. Frequently, they breed fishes at home in their spare time and usually are quite active in fish clubs where they offer their guidance to younger, less- experienced hobbyists. As far as education is concerned, amateur ichthyologists usually have a background in one of the biological sciences, but some have degrees in a completely unrelated subject such as accounting or education.

Another group of ichthyologists that you will read about quite often are the **systematic ichthyologists**. Systematic ichthyologists are usually a completely different breed of scientist. It is uncommon for an ichthyologist doing systemic research to have anything less than a Master of Science, and the vast majority either have a PhD or are working toward the completion of one. Systematic ichthyologists are the taxonomists of the fish world. They are the key individuals for naming and classifying all fishes. Often, they work closely with ecologists, microbiologists, veterinarians, and a wide assortment of other professionals. These scientists live by the rule "publish or perish" and they often do so at an astounding rate. Many of their publications are submitted for peer review in one of the several scientific journals of the field.

Fish

There are a lot of *fish* in this aquarium.

The naming of new species of fish can be quite challenging. This is mainly due to the vast amount of research that is required to name species correctly, and even then it is not always correct. When an ichthyologist thinks that they may have a new species, the work has only just begun.

To begin with, they must begin a huge search effort for that fish and all others like it. This effort involves pouring through scientific literature dating all the way back to the tenth edition of *Systema Naturae* published by Linnaeus in 1758. This is done in order to be certain that the fish was not already named, since the oldest name of a given species is always the valid one.

This is a difficult and time-consuming process that requires searching extensive libraries like those found at large universities and museums that specialize in ichthyological research. One of the best resources for such a search is the *Zoological Record*. This work has been published annually in London since 1864 and classifies natural history literature. In addition to such tools, the basic experiences of a well-seasoned ichthyologist play an important role. Generally speaking, the more experienced you are as an ichthyologist, the less likely it is that you will waste time attempting to name a species that has already been named.

Today's expert ichthyologists are continually confronted with the inadequacies of years past. Many authors have named the same fishes multiple times. This creates an astounding assortment of synonyms for each species. While there are certainly many species that do not have a single synonym, there are many more that have multiple synonyms. This troublesome affliction would be greatly improved if novices in the field submitted their "new species" to ichthyologists in the larger museums for their expert opinions before other steps were taken.

In this book, we have provided you with the most accurate scientific names that were available to us at time of publication. In order to be able to do this, we painstakingly pored through various references and resources, including many textbooks and peer-reviewed papers dealing with taxonomy. Only those works that adhere to the strict rules of *The Code of Zoological Nomenclature* have been used for the names herein. Of course, as with any substantial listing of scientific names, there will be inaccuracies. This is especially true with the dynamic taxonomy of fishes. For up-to-date, supplemental information, the *American Society of Ichthyologists and Herpetologists* (ASIH) is an invaluable source. Contact information for this society can be found in the resources section at the back of this book.

Chapter 1

A BRIEF HISTORY OF ICHTHYOLOGY

The known origins of ichthyology date back to as early as 384 B.C. in the writings of Aristotle. Aristotle was not only able to distinguish fishes from whales but also able to recognize about 120 distinct types of fishes, many of them later described as valid species. Several authors report that he was the first scientist to record fish facts in his notes and later include these in his writings on fishes.

Born in Stagirus (Stagira), on the Chalcidic peninsula of northern Greece, Aristotle was first trained in medicine and then in philosophy. After leaving the academy, it is believed that Aristotle spent several years traveling and studying biology in Asia Minor (now Turkey). He returned from his expeditions and settled in Athens where he set up a school of his own. In the chaos that followed, due to the rebellion, Aristotle fled to the island of Euboea and died a short time later.

Aristotle probably developed a fascination with fishes sometime before his travels to Asia Minor but was not able to expand his thoughts on them until that time. He went on to make important observations, such as *"Fish thrive best in the rainy season."* This may be obvious to the ichthyologists, researchers, and hobbyists of today, but in Aristotle's day such a thought almost certainly was revolutionary. Thanks to Aristotle, even thousands of years ago people recognized the effectiveness of water changes!

Aristotle's writings were more or less notes and tidbits of interesting facts and observations. Amazingly, many of his writings still provide very useful information to the hobbyists of today. Aristotle also stated,

"Fishes without exception are supplied with blood. Some of them are oviparous, and some viviparous, scaly fish are invariably oviparous, but cartilaginous fishes are all viviparous, with the single exception of the fishing-frog."

In this section, Aristotle is, of course, speaking about the modes of reproduction in fishes.

Aquariums can become a true showpiece if set up and maintained properly.

Aristotle also wrote,

"Particular places suit particular fishes; some are naturally fishes of the shore, and some of the deep sea, and some are at home in both. Some fishes will thrive in one particular spot and that spot only. As a general rule it may be said that places abounding in weeds are wholesome; at all events, fishes caught in such places are exceptionally fat: that is, fishes inhabit all sorts of habitats as well."

This was, perhaps, the beginning of ecology.

One must agree that thoughts like those of Aristotle are exceptionally refreshing. All fish hobbyists are encouraged to read the words of the premier scientists of years past. While you may not agree with all of their thoughts or theories, their writings often contain very useful pieces of information. The worst that could happen is for you to gain a little more understanding of the fishes you choose to keep.

It wasn't until the sixteenth century that others really began looking seriously at fishes. The works of prominent natural historians like P. Belon, H. Salviani, and G. Rondelet set more milestones and further expanded the role of fishes in science based on Aristotle's earlier works.

Belon is probably best known for his 1551 publication on the natural history of fishes in which he classified over 100 species based on their anatomical characteristics. Basically, Belon is responsible for the publication of the first modern systematic treatise on fishes. Salviani published sections within a broader treatise on Italian fishes, which included 92 species that he classified. This work was considered to be the first faunal work of fishes. At the same time, Rondelet was busy publishing books of the information on fishes that was already known at the time. He was responsible for bringing many areas together, and his work greatly helped to concentrate ichthyological information into one general area.

The *Natural History of Fishes of Brazil* was published in 1648. Sadly, the author, George Marcgrave, never had the opportunity to see his work since he had already passed away at the time of publication. Marcgrave was a prominent naturalist and explorer who put a lot of time and effort into his work to further expand the knowledge-base of fishes.

During these times, the knowledge of European fishes was still on the rise, and when John Ray and Francis Willoughby published their book, *Historia Piscium,* in 1686, they successfully described 420 species, 178 of them newly classified. They also managed to arrange them in a sensible and effective manner. Such works were exceptionally important since they served as the foundation for further works, such as Peter Artedi's classification system, which earned him the title of "*Father of Ichthyology*" (Moyle & Cech, 2000).

All of Artedi's works would probably have been lost after his death had his good friend Carolus Linnaeus not purchased them. Linnaeus went on to edit the material and change some of it to include his own research and experiences. The resulting work brought about the famous *Systema Naturae* in 12 editions, the first of which was published in 1735, and the work consequently became the foundation on which future classification systems were based— even today!

Since many of the world's prominent ichthyologists were based in Europe, and most of the fishes that are popular in contemporary fishkeeping are from Africa and South and Middle America, it is easy to see why the majority of ichthyological work was not begun until travel became easier and less dangerous. These researchers included people like Bloch, Schneider, Cuvier, Lecepede, Agassiz, Hubbs, Jordan, Regan, and Boulenger. There are certainly many more.

Many of the papers of the above-mentioned researchers and others are available at university libraries. It is strongly encouraged that even the most basic of hobbyists take some time to understand the roots of ichthyology and the profound impact the past has had and will continue to have on the future.

MODERN FISHES

At the time of this writing, there are between 27,000 and 28,500 known species of fishes swimming in the world's waters. It is probably not unrealistic to assume that in less than five or six years that number will be up to at least 30,000. After all, in some regions of the world, ichthyologists are discovering as many as three new species a day. Furthermore, it is not uncommon for marine biologists to collect and record as many as ten new species of fish on each deep sea excursion.

A Brief Look at the Classification of Teleosts

Subdivision Osteoglossomorpha

ORDERS
- Osteoglossoformes (bonytongues)
- Hiodontiformes (mooneyes)

Subdivision Elopomorpha

ORDERS
- Elopiformes (tarpons)
- Albuliformes (ladyfishes)
- Angulliformes (true eels)
- Notacanthiformes (spiny eels)

Subdivision Clupeomorpha

ORDER
- Clupeiformes (herrings and anchovies)

Subdivision Euteleostei (largest subdivision)

SUPERORDERS (MANY ORDERS)
- Ostariophysi
- Acanthopterygii

Nandopsis salvini Cichlids are very popular with hobbyists and researchers alike.

Many of these new species are being found in areas that were previously not known of or thought to contain fishes. Caves, caverns, springs, the deep sea, and many other unique places have proven to be full of new fish species. In general, fish occupy an extraordinarily wide assortment of habitats and fill many niches within those habitats.

In the next chapter, we will go into some detail about allopatric and sympatric speciation and the role these techniques provide in the rise of new species. More so, ecological speciation is proving to be the same as sympatric speciation, and as time goes on, this is becoming more and more evident. Sadly, even such speciation techniques are not able to produce a valid and separate species as fast as humans are altering the fish's various environments.

There are a lot more species out there than you will ever find while cruising through the isles of your local fish store. As a matter of fact, you could cruise through the isles of every local fish store on the planet and never see even a quarter of all the species that are out there. The vast majority of fishes are not suitable for keeping in aquariums for one reason or another. In addition, there are thousands of species that will never make it into the hobby due to their size, location, feeding behavior, etc.

Such species diversity reflects the long evolutionary history that consists of three major lines that have been evolving almost independently for nearly 400 million years. Of these lines, the Gnathostomata is the line of vertebrates that dominates our planet today. Within this group are the jawed fishes that are also divided into three distinct lines which are the following: Placoderms, cartilaginous fishes (Chondrichthys), and boney fishes (Osteichthyes).

Surprisingly, only about 60% of the world's fishes are marine species, while approximately 40% are freshwater species. This is very interesting, since sea water covers nearly 70% of the Earth's surface, while fresh waters only cover a little more than 1%. Such numbers may become more unbalanced in the future since the deep oceans are providing the majority of the new discoveries in marine ichthyology and biology in general. Years ago, such discoveries would mostly have occurred in the coral reefs. However, coral reefs are dominated by mostly invertebrate species, while the deep seas are proving to be dominated by fishes.

Polypterus ornatipinnis The bichirs are an interesting group of bony fishes.

Furthermore, in their book *Fishes, An Introduction to Ichthyology, Fourth Edition*, Peter Moyle and Joseph Cech list some very interesting statistics regarding the distribution of fishes in marine environments.

"Only 13% of all fish species are associated with the open ocean: 1% in the surface layer (epipelagic fishes); 5% in the unlighted sections of the water column (deepwater pelagic fishes; and 7% on the bottom (deepwater benthic fishes). A majority (78%) of marine fish species live in the narrow band of water less than 200m deep along the margins of land masses. An additional factor affecting the number of fish species is the annual temperature regime. In both fresh and salt water, a majority of the species are found in warmer environments where annual temperature fluctuations are comparatively small."

In dealing with freshwater aquariums, we mainly encounter those fishes of the group Osteichthyes. The bony fishes can be further divided into the non-teleosts (Holostei and Chondrostei) and the teleosts (Teleostei). The latter may then be further divided into such basic categories as cichlids, cyprinids (minnows, barbs, rasboras, and danios), loricarids (sucker-mouthed catfishes), characins (tetras, piranhas, and headstanders), silurids (catfishes), and so on. The non-teleosts include fishes such as the bichirs, polypterids, paddlefishes, and lungfishes.

The Teleosts

The teleosts are numerous and widespread. *Tele-osti* means "end-bone," so teleosts are best defined as having specialized bones called **uroneurals** at the end of their vertebral column. These uroneurals provide support for the symmetrical caudal fin. They are essentially the main line of fish evolution as we know and understand it today. The teleosts group contains over 40 orders, 400 families, and 24,000 species (though this number is extremely dynamic in both directions).

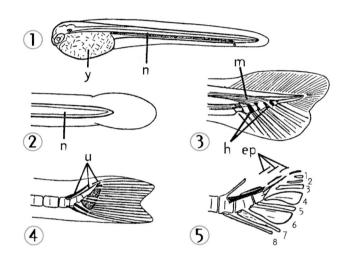

Teleosts   **Development of the homocercal tail.**
1. Clupeid larva; **y** – yolk, **n** – notochord.
2-5. Upbending of notochord and urostyle;
m – muscle fibers, **h** – hypurals, **u** –uroneurals or parts of urostyle, **ep** – epurals **1-8.** – Hypurals.

Adopted from *The Biology of Fishes*, T.F.H. Publications, Inc.

Teleosts have a wide array of designs and behaviors. If they did not, they would not be so widespread. We can basically divide them into multiple lineages, distinct in their own right. As reported by Peter Moyle and Joseph Cech in 2000, "The Present lineages were first recognized by Greenwood et al. (1966), who developed a provisional classification system that stirred up the modern debate on how teleosts are related to one another, a debate that was fueled by Lauder and Liem (1983)."

Chapter 2

SYSTEMATICS & SPECIATION

Systematics is the evolutionary classification and study of organisms with regard to their natural relationships. In modern science, systematics has become almost completely synonymous with taxonomy—the science of describing and classifying organisms.

Basically a study of relationships, systematics lies at the very foundation of the biological sciences. Such a system provides the means for developing answers to questions about the origin and evolution of life. But it's not without flaws, and many areas of systematics are highly controversial—and rightfully so. This system may provide the means for problem solving, but it does not answer all of the questions.

Scientific names were applied to plants and animals long before 1735, when Carolus Linnaeus first attempted to catalogue all known organisms. It soon became apparent to him that it was rather useless to make observations on these organisms unless they had a name. He therefore developed the binomial system of **nomenclature** and the hierarchical **classification** system for higher categories. This system proved to be very useful in organizing a constantly growing knowledgebase of plants and animals.

It is important to distinguish between "nomenclature" and "classification." The use of nomenclature is the procedure by which labels are provided for the taxonomic categories so scientists can communicate with each other using a common language. Classification is strictly a biological matter, and it is best defined as a systematic arrangement in groups or categories according to established criteria.

TAXONOMIC METHODS

One unique characteristic that many tropical fish hobbyists share is that they are, by virtue or simple curiosity, taxonomists at heart. Whether or not they actually have strict training in the science, most serious hobbyists have a basic knowledge of and a general interest in the scientific names of the organisms that are contained within their aquariums.

We often refer to fishes as having two names—a scientific name and a common name. The basic scientific name is composed of the generic name (**genus**) and specific name (**species**), while a common name is just that—a common name. An example would be the Eastern Mosquito Fish (*Gambusia affinis*). The common name is "Eastern Mosquito Fish" and the scientific name is *Gambusia affinis*.

A general rule within taxonomy is that the genus names and species names are always italicized. In some instances, we refer to a fish as having two species names. Such an example would *Chromidotilapia guentheri guentheri*. The second species name acts as a sub-specific name.

Chromidotilapia guentheri guentheri

Some fishes exhibit both a specific name as well as a subspecific name.

A sub-specific name (**subspecies**) is applied for various reasons, but the most common reason is to differentiate one population of a known species from another. Such sub-specific differentiation is required when a taxonomist thinks that one population may actually be a different species altogether but has not yet taken the proper steps to validate that belief. The most common distinguishing factor when dealing with a subspecies is a difference in coloration or pattern. Those characteristics are not really considered valid distinguishable traits alone, but in accordance with the International Code of Zoological Nomenclature they can be included as such as long as other, more reliable differences are provided in the new species description.

To arrive at such names, taxonomists must use a combination of methods that fall into six main categories. These categories are the following: morphometric measurements, meristic traits, anatomical characteristics, color patterns, karyotypes, and biochemical characteristics (Moyle & Cech, 200).

Morphometric Measurements

Simply referred to as morphometrics, these are considered to be any standard measurements that can be made on a fish. Such measurements commonly include standard length (SL), length of the snout, length of the longest ray on the dorsal fin, and the depth of the caudal peduncle. Since these measurements can, and often do, change as the fishes grow, they are best expressed as ratios to the given measurement.

Such measurements are always more useful when you are dealing with a sample of fish that are close to the same age (if known), size, and even sex. Remember that the growth of fishes in nature is not always proportional, and this will have an impact on your research if

you decide to take things further and assist in describing a fish. In reality, the growth of aquariums fishes is far more standard or able to be controlled. However, aquarium-raised specimens are not the best for use in taxonomical projects, since variables like temperature, diet, and other environmental conditions have an effect on the way fishes grow and develop.

Meristic Traits

These are the most common traits people refer to when they speak of taxonomical studies. They are also considered to be the most reliable in terms of consistency, since most of them are fairly easy to determine.

Meristic traits, or meristics, are essentially anything on a fish that is able to be counted. This includes scale rows, fin rays and spines, lateral-line pores, etc. Even the count of bones within certain areas, such as the head and lower jaw, is sometimes considered a meristic trait. The biggest potential issue when making such measurements is performing them on enough specimens. There can be considerable variation in several meristic traits even within a species, so your sample size should be as large as possible. As a general rule of thumb, at least several dozen specimens should be measured of any one species so as to get a good range of measurements.

Along with such problems as sample size and variation in the fish's measurements comes human error. Any time you have something that needs to be measured, you will inevitably run into a margin of error that is based on your measuring techniques. That is the chief reason why such techniques need to be learned and practiced over and over again, although such errors are usually reduced if standard measurements are consistently used (Moyle & Cech, 2000).

Anatomical Characteristics

Unlike the former categories, **anatomical characteristics** are difficult to actually quantify. However, they are very important in an overall description of a fish. Such characteristics include the shape of the fish's head, body, placement and length of the fins (sexual dimorphism aside), overall shape, completeness (broken or solid) and position of lateral-line, and the shape and position of the fish's internal organs. Other features such as bones and sexual characteristics are also involved in this to some extent.

Color Patterns

Of all the characteristics that may be used to describe fishes, color patterns are probably the most controversial. This is mainly due to the fact that the coloration and patterning of fishes is largely related to many outside influences. Such influences can be something as minor as the time of day to something substantially more significant such as diet or the levels of certain minerals in the environment in which the fish is found.

Regardless, coloration is something that should always be noted in the description of a new species, the revision of species within a particular genus, or in the comparison of a known species to a possible subspecies. Of course, there are other instances, such as basic articles on husbandry and care requirements, where this information could lend itself to further discussion of color variability in breeding individuals and so on.

The coloration of many popular aquarium fish species is often one of the first topics a hobbyist is drawn to when asked what they like most about having an aquarium. This is generally due to the fact that people are usually interested in coloration because it looks pretty.

Karyotypes

The chromosomal characteristics of a cell are known as **karyotypes**. These are the least likely traits to be used by the average hobbyist, since the practice necessitates the counting of chromosomes in an individual set of cells. Such a technique requires basic knowledge of and training in microbiology and cytology, as well as access to a strong microscope and all of its associated supplies (slides, cover slips, stain, etc.).

The practice of determining speciation through karyotypes analysis is often done only with fishes that are extremely similar in appearance. Another reason

Symphysodon aequifasciata Discus are known for their variation in coloration, even among members of the same locality.

The change of coloration in fishes is most dramatic during two main time periods—stress and breeding. Chapter 5 will discuss breeding coloration ranges in more detail, but stress coloration is something that is important to understand. Part of your duty as a tropical fish hobbyist is to watch and observe the daily activities of your fish. During this time, you should be taking mental notes as to how the fish look and act.

After a while, differences in mood and aggression can easily be picked up on. With these attitude differences will come a host of color and pattern changes. Solid fish may become blotched, striped fish may become spotted, and patterned fish may become solid. The coloration range depends on which species you keep.

such an analysis may be done is to serve as supportive research to other, more commonly used practices such as looking at meristic traits or taking morphometric measurements.

Biochemical Characteristics

This is another method of category of species identification that would be difficult for hobbyists to utilize correctly. Biochemical characteristics are patterns in proteins and genetic material that are typically used to identify a genetic difference between various populations (Moyle & Cech, 2000). Again, such a technique would require advanced training in such areas as biochemistry, biochemical technology, and microbiology.

The most popular technique used to translate the genetic code of an individual cell is a process known as **electrophoresis**. This process evaluates the protein similarities of a species or a range of species. The result is a range of genetic similarities or differences that can be compared to other known species. This type of testing is probably going to replace the more traditional methods in the future since it has already proven itself useful with such genera as *Cichlasoma*, *Cyphotilapia*, *Aphyosemion*, *Xiphophorus*, and *Botia*.

Cyphotilapia sp. "Burundi" Current research suggests that the "Frontosa" found off Burundi, Africa may be a new species.

In general, fishes are well-suited to systematic studies because they are abundant in species and numbers, widespread, and usually readily available. They also possess many characteristics that are especially useful for taxonomic analysis and statistical treatment. Of course, hybridization within certain species groups and complexes is common, and this is one of those areas where standard meristics and morphometrics may not be very useful, but the analysis of such things as biochemical characteristics would be.

SPECIATION

The development of new species through local adaptation and evolution best defines **speciation**. Speciation is one of the most controversial topics currently being debated among ecologists and evolutionary scientists. Whether or not you are a supporter of creationism, this subject has several areas that you will certainly find interesting as a hobbyist.

Rather than debate about where or how your fishes originated, let's discuss some of the instances where adaptability becomes paramount in the struggle for life or death in the everyday lives of tropical aquarium fishes and the role these adaptations may have had in determining their speciation.

Many species commonly kept in aquariums are generally considered to be of a small to moderate size. Such species come in a vast array of sizes and shapes, as you will read about in the next chapter, but what about other differences? What about the unique appendages and behaviors of some species? What about their sometimes cryptic coloration and ability to leap from the water? Why do some fishes survive in huge numbers while others are rare in nature? These are questions that every hobbyist asks, but few really develop solid conclusions.

Natural Selection

The role of **natural selection** is always in motion. A generic definition of natural selection is: a natural process that results in the survival and reproductive success of individuals or groups that are best adjusted to their environment and that leads to the perpetuation of genetic qualities that are best suited to that particular environment.

Nature is a collection of environments that are in a constant state of fluctuation. Therefore, the organisms within these environments are also in a constant state of fluctuation. For an organism to survive, it must be capable of adapting to these ever-changing environments. Such adaptations are often very small and do not lead to the development of a new species. Of course, there are also other factors that play a role in speciation, and while most species are generally accepted as having been valid for hundreds of thousands of years, some speciation is thought to take place at a surprisingly rapid pace (Moyle & Cech, 2000).

Geographical Isolation

The best argument for further speciation within a given species is the geographical isolation of a group of those fish. Once a group has been geographically isolated, traits that were once shared are believed to begin alteration in such a way as to favor survival in their new isolated range. This type of speciation is referred to as **allopatric** speciation.

There are many examples of this type of speciation. Sadly, most current examples deal with populations that have been divided due to the damming of rivers and waterways or because of a known species being removed and placed in a body of water that did not have them nat-

urally. Such a transplant can cause fishes to trigger their natural survival techniques instantaneously. Sometimes they work, but many times they don't.

Character Displacement

There are situations that may involve not only a change in actual meristics or morphometrics but also a fish's character (i.e. anatomical or behavioral features). The way fishes feed and what they feed on are perhaps the most common forms of character displacement observed on a regular basis. To further compound this, morphological shifts that result from competition among species are common, so expect some differences in common traits when examining specimens that are the same species but collected rather far apart from each other.

Due to the introduction of a species that is more effective at feeding on the same foods the naturally occurring fishes feed on, the naturally occurring fishes sometimes feel great pressure to shift their techniques and feeding methods to focus on other foods. If the naturally occurring fishes do not have dynamic survival

Channa micropeltes   Snakeheads cannot survive year round in most of North America.

strategies, they will usually not last long. Such thought is primarily responsible for frenzies over the introduction of non-indigenous fishes to our waterways, and perhaps no other fish has caused so much pressure on the aquarium fish industry as the fishes of *Channa*—the snakeheads.

Snakeheads naturally occur in Africa, India, and Asia. They are very efficient predatory fishes that feed on many types of animals including other fishes, amphibians, reptiles, and small mammals. An opportunistic predatory group, they have extremely dynamic feeding and survival strategies, and this is the main problem.

If snakeheads were only ravenous predators, this would not be as horrible of a situation, although still a problem. However, in addition to this trait, they are capable of surviving in cool temperatures and in waters with low dissolved oxygen content. Actually, since they are labyrinth fishes, they don't need any dissolved oxygen at all. Their gills must remain slightly moist, but as long as they don't dry out completely, snakeheads can live for some time in this state. Any species with so much flexibility is likely not one you want inhabiting waters that are not its natural home.

Snakeheads are not the first group of fishes to be transplanted, whether purposely or accidentally. As tropical fish hobbyists, never practice such foolishness with your aquarium specimens. If you need to rid yourself of some fishes for one reason or another, do it properly and responsibly. If you are unsure how to go about this, seek guidance from your local, state, or federal fish and game officials or a veterinarian.

Other Methods of Speciation

There are two other methods of speciation that are commonly accepted in the scientific community—**sympatric speciation** and **ecological speciation**. Both methods have gained popularity, especially recently, and are now almost universally accepted as being one in the same.

Essentially, sympatric speciation is described as the divergence of forms that occur within a given population without geographic isolation. Furthermore, sympatric speciation may be quite common in fishes and even more common than originally thought. There are considerable examples of sympatric speciation within many families of aquarium fishes. While a breakdown of such families is beyond the scope of this text, we can cite a few of the more common areas where sympatric speciation is thought to have taken place or is currently occurring.

African cichlids in two of the three great Rift Valley Lakes, Malawi and Victoria, are examples of fishes that make the argument for sympatric speciation possible. Of these cichlids, two genera—which have been broken up considerably in the past few years—provide the best examples. These genera are *Pseudotropheus* and *Haplochromis*.

"Pseudotropheus" sp.   Cichlids in Lake Malawi provide a great example of sympatric speciation

37

Another group of fishes that are both controversial and downright confusing are the piranhas and pirambebas. Many of the pirambebas are commonly thought to have risen through sympatric or ecological speciation. Several species are found not only in the same river system but also within the same biotope as each other. Is this ecological speciation in motion? Some say yes, others no. The truth is, several fishes that are clearly identified as separate and distinct species are found in very close proximity to each other, occasionally even in the same shoals.

Naturally Occurring Hybridization in Freshwater Fishes

In general, hybridization in freshwater fishes is relatively common. It is more common in closely related species like some of the basses (*Micropterus* spp.)

Pterophyllum sp. "domesticated" Captive-produced Angelfish are sometimes referred to as hybrids. However, they are usually crosses between various color morphs of *Pterophyllum scalare*, not actual hybrids between species.

It is thought that many species that have arisen within these genera are very young, as far as natural history goes, being less than 12,000 years old. While such a number may be incomprehensible for some, keep in mind that many species swimming in the world's oceans and lakes have remained unchanged for more than 500,000 years. Measuring the ages of species in such numbers takes an understanding of time that does not follow a traditional watch.

and sunfishes (*Lepomis* spp.), but many Central American cichlids are commonly found to interbreed in nature, as well. In some situations, hybridization is thought to be the primary cause of a new species. In other instances, it can be the single most powerful factor in the monopolization of a species.

Alternatively, there are also many species that would rarely, if ever, hybridize in nature but do so in captivity and are fairly prolific. Their young are usually also fertile,

which is one factor that leads to a strong misunderstanding and mistrust of fish systematics. Most people think that a species is unique because it is unable to reproduce with a member of it's a different species. We find that animals, fishes in particular, break this rule very often.

In aquariums, we have many examples of fishes that readily interbreed and produce viable young and then backcross with members of either parent species. Livebearers of the genera *Poecilia* and *Xiphophorus* are probably the best known, since these are the various guppies, mollies, swordtails, and platys. For years, the commonly found silver angelfish and all of its sports were thought of as hybrids between *Pterophyllum scalare* and *P. leopoldi*. There were also a host of subspecific names that went along with this, but thankfully, they are now recognized as invalid. We now know that many of these sports were actually color morphs that were the result of careful breeding techniques known as **selective breeding** and not hybrids at all.

Hybridization that results in sterility is also quite common and is probably best proven by the members of *Lepomis*. These sunfishes are very commonly used to seed new, man-made ponds and lakes and to serve as sport fish. Sadly, many local and state governments do not realize that they often stock these bodies of water with species of *Lepomis* that are not found even remotely close to where they are to be stocked. As a result, they may come in contact with local populations of various *Lepomis* species and hybridize.

The two most common *Lepomis* hybrids are the Bluegill-Green Sunfish cross (*Lepomis macrochirus* x *L. cyanellus*) and the Bluegill-Pumpkinseed Sunfish cross (*L. macrochirus* x *L. gibbosus*). Sometimes such

Lepomis marginatus Sunfishes readily hybridize in captivity but less commonly in nature.

hybrids are the result of males that quickly dart in and fertilize the female of the other species' eggs, and other times these hybrids are due to the lack of a suitable mate of the same species. When given no other option, a sunfish will usually hybridize rather than not breed at all.

Fertile hybrids typically have poor survival rates in nature. They seem to have a low amount of vigor and may have chemical imbalances as well. All the same, the actual reasons are complex and not fully understood.

Identifying a hybrid can be complex. Most researchers rely on two things—a hunch and the fish's appearance. A hunch is usually based on the researcher's knowledge of the biotope that the fish is supposed to be in and the fact that the fish may have been captured in a completely different one. A fish's appearance is suspect when more than the usual degree of color or separation is noted.

Chapter 3

ANATOMY & PHYSIOLOGY OF TROPICAL FISHES

Tropical fishes come in many shapes and sizes. Some species are quite unconventional, such as the various arowanas, while others are more traditional in design, like the predatory peacock cichlids of the genus *Cichla*. Usually a fish's body shape is very indicative of the environment that the species lives in. For example, fishes of the genus *Potamotrygon*, the river stingrays, have a body that we call dorsoventrally compressed or, simply, flattened. This design is in response to the heavy water flow and fluctuating water levels of the rivers and tributaries that they inhabit.

Other fishes that are highly modified to fit their environment are the cichlid fishes of the genus *Altolamprologus*. These cichlids, endemic to Lake Tanganyika, exhibit an extreme degree of lateral compression. This is probably due to the fact that they live among cracks in the huge boulders that make up the rubble zone of the lake.

The rubble zone in Lake Tanganyika is best defined as the gently sloping area in the lake that starts at the shore and works its way out into deeper water until the slope forms a ridge and drops off at a very steep angle. In some areas, the width of the rubble zone may only be several yards while in others it can extend several hundred yards or more. *Altolamprologus* inhabit this zone where food in the form of small fishes, crustaceans, and insect larvae is plentiful.

In addition to their highly compressed bodies, *Altolamprologus* have a relatively long snout that allows them to pick deep into the rock crevices to pluck out prey. As a side note, hobbyists wishing to keep fishes in this genus should keep their ecology in mind since these fishes tend to be shy and reclusive for long periods, often only showing themselves after the aquarium lights are turned off.

This chapter is designed to be an introduction to the external and internal parts and functions of fishes. Volumes of text could be written on nearly all aspects of the anatomy and physiology of fishes. However, this section will just touch on the basics.

EXTERNAL ANATOMY AND PHYSIOLOGY

Fishes vary widely in shape and size, but their basic external anatomy is surprisingly similar in function and form. Nearly all of the species that are considered popular in the trade of tropical fishes have the same basic characteristics, such as paired fins, unpaired fins, scales, a

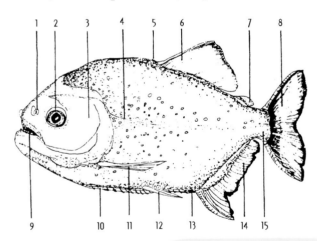

| Piranha Diagram | The Most Important External Parts of a Fish |

1. Nostril or nasal aperture. **2.** Eye. **3.** Operculum. **4.** Lateral line. **5.** The small spine(s). **6.** Dorsal fin. **7.** Adipose fin. **8.** Caudal fin. **9.** Mouth. **10.** Ventral keel. **11.** Pectoral fin. **12.** Pelvic fin. **13.** Anal pore. **14.** Anal fin. **15.** The caudal peduncle.

Adopted from *Piranhas in the Aquarium*, T.F.H. Publications, Inc.

Altolamprologus calvus — Members of the genus *Altolamprologus* show a high degree of lateral compression.

tail, a set of eyes, and a mouth. Notice we say "nearly" and not "every." This is because some fishes do not have eyes, fins, scales, or a mouth as we know them. Rather, they are modified or may even appear to be absent. In reality, most of the time they are still there but just not as we find them on more traditional fishes.

Perhaps the best example of a popular aquarium fish with a modified external anatomy is the Blind Cave Fish or *Astyanax mexicanus*. Blind Cave Fish live in areas that are so dark that they do not need their eyes in order to find food or navigate their way through the underground maze of caves. As a matter of fact, as of this writing, there is a whole new set of fishes yet to be described that are found in caves and that remain unknown to hobbyists. Some of these are fishes that have been known about for years, such as species of *Xiphophorus*, while others remain new and very exciting for the future. Imagine an aquarium full of rocky outcroppings teaming with eyeless fishes, only illuminated by a moon light-type of bulb—very unique and certainly something interesting for the future!

Fishes that are scaleless are perhaps the most common type of modified fishes available to hobbyists on

a regular basis. Scales are viewed as an integral part of a fish's anatomy. However, a surprising number of fishes are considered scaleless. This is either because they are, in fact, scaleless, or they have such small scales that they appear to be scaleless. Some very popular aquarium species that appear scaleless include, but are certainly not limited to, the following:

- Clown Loach (*Chromobotia macracantha*)
- Tiger Botia (*Syncrossus helodes*)
- Dwarf Botia (*Yasuhikotakia sidthimunki*)
- Black Ghost Knifefish (*Apteronotus albifrons*)
- Kuhli Loaches (*Pangio kuhlii* and *P. shelfordi*)
- Clown Knifefish (*Chitala chitala*)
- Smooth-skinned Catfishes (many genera and species)
- *Synodontis* species such as *S. brichardi* and *S. decorus*

Many scaleless fishes actually have very tiny scales arranged in such a way that their bodies appear smooth like skin instead of scaly. Scaleless fishes usually need special treatment during shipping and when being medicated. This is due to the fact that their small scales can easily be scraped off by overly aggressive tankmates or humans.

It is not uncommon for scaleless fishes to have negative reactions to doses of medication that are considered normal for other fishes. With some scaleless species, the lack of large protective scales allows the medication to enter the bloodstream at a faster pace, quickly reaching levels that may be toxic. Even fishes that are noticeably scaled (such as small tetras, piranhas, and silver dollars) may have adverse affects with some medications. It is necessary to be aware of what species of fishes you are keeping in order to properly treat them if they become ill.

Body Shape

The six basic categories that ichthyologists use to group fishes in terms of body shape are the following: pursuit predators (*Fusiform*), lie-in-wait, surface-oriented, bottom-dwelling, deep-bodied, and eel-like fishes.

Pursuit Predators (Fusiform)

Fishes that are said to have a fusiform shape are easily recognized and often considered to have a "traditional" shape. They have pointed head that ends with a terminal mouth and a narrow caudal peduncle that opens up to reveal a large split or forked tail. These fishes are often considered rover predators by nature and include such species as the mackerel, swordfish, tuna fishes, and some sharks.

In the hobby, fishes that are considered to have a fusiform shape include members of the family Cyprinidae (Minnows), some members of Cichlidae (Cichlids), and various species within Centrarchidae (Basses). This group is often haphazardly mixed into aquariums with other, less-demanding fishes. That is not good for the fusiform fishes as they are often more comfortable in faster-flowing waters where many of the more popular species feel less comfortable.

In nature, fusiform fishes inhabit areas with heavy water movement and agitation. In fresh water, they are often found in rivers or streams where they may have to fight strong currents or swim upstream to reach potential spawning grounds. Trout and salmon are prime examples of fusiform-shaped fishes that need to do such things. In sea water, tunas and mackerels need to battle heavy surface currents and be ready for flight at the moment's notice of a swordfish that is patiently circling their school, waiting for the perfect time to strike. Like tunas and mackerels, swordfishes need to

Gasteropelecus sternicla

Hatchetfishes are one of the most recognizable types of surface-oriented fishes

Lie-in-wait predators are not always easily recognizable by morphology alone. For example, the Cloud Cichlids look nothing like barracudas, which in turn, look nothing like the Leaffish. So you must have a general understanding of the fish's behavior in nature in order to fully appreciate, and compensate for, their surprising activity in a home aquarium.

Surface-oriented Fishes

Fishes belonging to this group are often small and exhibit an upward-pointing mouth. The best example of surface-oriented fishes would be the members of the family Poeciliidae. This family includes such popular aquarium fishes as the Swordtails and Platys (*Xiphophorus* spp.), Mollies (*Poecilia* spp.), and Mosquitofishes (*Gambusia* spp.). Other families that contain popular freshwater aquarium fishes that are also surface-oriented are Fundulidae (Killifishes), Gasteropelecidae (Hatchet Fishes) and Anablepidae (Four-eyed fishes).

The morphology of these fishes is best suited for capturing small insects and crustaceans just below the surface of the water. With their upward-pointing mouths and flat backs, these fishes cruise just below the surface and essentially gobble up anything that is edible. In aquariums, these fishes usually make excellent dither fishes for shy, bottom-dwelling species, such as loaches or *Botia* that will recognize the surface-oriented fishes as harmless and therefore be calmed by their presence above them.

be able to battle such currents and are therefore placed into the same category.

Lie-in-wait Predators

Fishes classified as lie-in-wait predators include some of the most popular game fishes in the world. Pikes, barracudas, snook, and gars are included in this group. There are also many species of popular freshwater aquarium fishes that fall into this group. Some examples are: Acestrorhynchidae (Freshwater Barracudas), those within *Nimbochromis* (Cloud Cichlids), and the Leaffishes within the families Nandidae and Polycentridae.

The vast majority of fishes placed in this category are piscivorous in nature, meaning they consume whole, live fishes as their primary source of food. On the other hand, such fishes that are popular in aquaria are often quite easily trained to accept non-living foodstuffs or, at the very least, prepared foods.

Bottom-dwelling Fishes

Bottom-dwelling species come in many shapes and sizes. Most of them have a flattened belly that is useful for "crawling" along the bottom. One very good example of such a fish that is very popular with cichlid enthusiasts is the Vampire Cichlid (*Neolamprologus furcifer*). Bottom-dwelling fishes can be classified into five overlapping subgroups: bottom-rovers, bottom-clingers, bottom-hiders, flatfishes, and rattails (Moyle & Cech, 2000). While an in-depth examination and discussion covering all five of these subgroups is out of the scope of this book, a closer look at two of these is quite important—bottom-rovers and bottom-hiders.

Bottom-rovers are best defined as those fishes that exhibit a rover predator-like body with a flattened head. Sometimes the back appears humped, and the pectoral fins are often large and fan-like in appearance. Although not tropical fishes, the members of the North American catfish family Ictaluridae are excellent representatives of this subgroup of fishes. Those species that are commonly encountered in the aquarium trade generally belong to the families Loricariidae and Pimelodidae and specifically the genera *Dianema* and *Pseudoplatystoma*.

Bottom-hiders are another group that mostly consists of catfishes. Other fishes, such as Loaches and Botias, are also well represented in this subgroup. Bottom-hiders tend to have smaller heads with elongated bodies and are often nocturnal (active at night) or crepuscular (active at twilight) in nature. In aquaria, most bottom-hiders can be trained to come out for food during daylight hours.

Deep-bodied Fishes

This group of fishes contains many that are most easily recognized by hobbyists. They are defined as having a body depth that is at least one-third of the fish's standard length. There are quite a lot of cichlids, barbs, and tetras that are included here as well as the sunfishes of the genus *Lepomis*. Deep-bodied fishes often have quite rigid spines in all of their fins with the sharpest being found in the dorsal and anal fins.

Perhaps the best-known cichlids that are considered deep-bodied are the angelfishes (*Pterophyllum*) and the discus fishes (*Symphysodon*). A lesser-known genus of deep-bodied fishes is the genus *Uaru*. Piranhas and pirambebas, of the genera *Pygocentrus* and *Serrasalmus*, are also quite deep-bodied fishes.

Deep-bodied fishes, also referred to as laterally compressed or compressiform fishes, often have very unique feeding strategies and are studied frequently in this regard. They can turn on a dime and quickly devour any food item that presents itself. Perhaps the fact that they are so interesting to watch is one reason why they are often so popular in the aquarium trade.

A subgroup within the deep-bodied fishes group is the *moderately deep-bodied* fishes. This subgroup

Uaru amphiacanthoides — Deep-bodied fishes, such as these Waroo, do best in tall and long aquariums

is mostly comprised of various herring, shad, and smelts. The presence of a rigid ventral keel differentiates these fishes from others in the group. Some species within their respective genera are more deep-bodied than others, but all are considered members of this subgroup as far as instant identifications go. This is especially true when one is sorting out a seine haul and is left with many specimens to identify. Using the group/subgroup method will at least point you in the right direction. The use of field guides will allow you to move beyond that point.

Eel-like Fishes

The last group is the eel-like fishes. The description is fairly self explanatory. These species are usually long and slender, produce a large amount of slime when removed from the water, and are often ravenous predators of smaller fishes. There are several species that have a good amount of popularity in the aquarium trade. Those that fall within the family Mastacembelidae (Spiny Eels) are probably the most popular although there are a considerable number of other species that are "eel-like" but not even closely related to eels. Weather Loaches (*Misgurnus* spp.) and Kuhli Loaches (*Pangio* spp.) are two of the best examples that come to mind.

Eel-like fishes have either blunt or wedge-shaped heads and tapering or rounded tails (Moyle & Cech, 2000). Their scales are either very small and embedded or absent entirely. Freshwater species prefer to inhabit soft substrates while marine species either live among rock or coral, or within fine sand. Their bodies scratch quite easily and open wounds may become infected. This is probably due to a high bacterial count in the slime coating, which can lead to a secondary infection.

In an aquarium, fishes within this group should be housed appropriately, because they can, and often do, outgrow even the largest of commonly available aquariums.

A good amount of research regarding their proper care, husbandry, feeding preferences, and ecology is highly recommended for even the most advanced aquarists.

Fins

A fish's fins are key to its evolution and ecology. They tell quite a lot about how a fish lives, acts, and interacts in a given environment. For example, tuna fishes have rigid fins that have a low degree of flexibility. This, combined with their body shape, allows for fast movement and good stability through swift ocean currents and heavy surf. A good example of a popular aquarium fish with fins completely opposite of those of the tuna fishes is the Siamese fighting fish (*Betta splendens*). Their fins are long and flowing and will actually fray if the movement of the water is too fast.

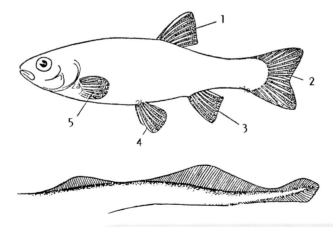

Fins

Top diagram:
1. Dorsal fin. **2.** Caudal fin. **3.** Anal fin.
4. Ventral fins. **5.** Pectoral fins.
Bottom diagram:
The simple finnage of a lamprey.

Adopted from *Illustrated Dictionary of Tropical Fishes*, T.F.H. Publications, Inc.

When ichthyologists look at a fish's fins, they look for several things. First, they look to see how many fins the fish has altogether. There are usually two sets of paired fins—the pectoral and the pelvic (ventral). The primary functions of paired fins are to provide stability in a stationary mode and braking from forward or rearward movement.

Pectoral Fins

The pectoral fins are located on the side of the fish's body. They are often paddle shaped, but in some species, especially various cichlids, they will have a slight flare to the tips. This flare is especially noticeable in males. Other fishes have highly modified pectoral fins. For example, the pectoral fins of most catfishes are rigid and often very sharp. They are also set at a different angle than the pectoral fins of most cichlids. Many of these catfishes also have small barbs on them that make removal from nets quite a challenge.

Pelvic Fins (Ventral Fins)

There are three main locations of the pelvic fins of a fish. Species that have pelvic fins along the ventral side of their body and slightly rearward are considered to have pelvic fins in the abdominal position. Species that have pelvic fins nearly in line with their pectoral fins are defined as having pelvic fins in the thoracic position. This is the most common location for the pelvic fins in most popular aquarium fishes. Finally, the third

Betta splendens

The fins of the Siamese Fighting Fish may actually fray if the current in their aquarium is too fast.

location where we find pelvic fins is the jugular position. This position is where the pelvic fins are slightly forward of the pectoral fins.

Some species are lacking pelvic fins entirely. This is most noticeable in eels. It is theorized that the eels' preference for living in tight quarters and constant rubbing against objects in their realm eventually led to the complete absence of these fins. Furthermore, in several bottom-dwelling species (none really popular in home aquariums), these fins have evolved into organs that assist the fish in holding onto the substrate or against structure.

The other fins often looked at by ichthyologists are the dorsal, anal, caudal, and adipose fins. There is quite a lot of diversity with these fins, similar to the diversity found in pectoral and pelvic fins.

Dorsal Fins

Dorsal fins are generally long and take up as much as two thirds of the entire length of the fish across the dorsum (top). They are often brightly colored or heavily patterned, as in the Pearl Gourami (*Trichogaster leeri*). In fast-swimming species, such as those within *Danio*, the dorsal fins are small and fairly rigid. The rigidness of these fins directly correlates with the environment that the species lives in. An extreme example brings us back to the tuna fishes, where the dorsal fins are almost sharp enough to cut a human hand. From this we can surmise that they require such rigidness in order to maintain stability in the harsh conditions where they are found—the upper ocean layer.

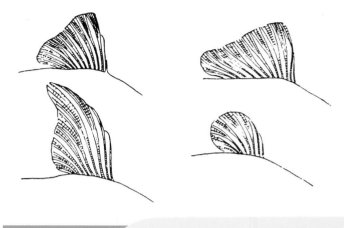

Dorsal Fins   Forms of soft-rayed dorsal fins

Adopted from *Illustrated Encyclopedia of Tropical Fishes*, T.F.H. Publications, Inc.

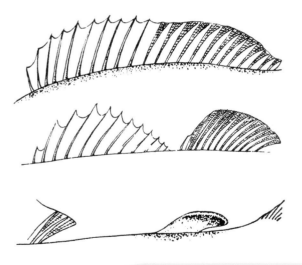

Dorsal Fins   **Top:** dorsal fin of a cichlid, with the spiny rays in front and the soft rays behind. **Center:** dorsal fins of a perch, spiny rays in the front and soft rays behind. **Below:** adipose fin as found in many characins.

Adopted from *Illustrated Encyclopedia of Tropical Fishes*, T.F.H. Publications, Inc.

The dorsal fin also serves another purpose—display. Such display is pronounced by some species when in search of a mate. Close friend and colleague Albert Connelly, editor of *Tropical Fish Hobbyist* Magazine, maintains a breeding colony of Vietnamese White Clouds (*Tanichthys micagemmae*). As of this writing, this is a very new species and hardly known in the hobby. Albert frequently speaks of the beautiful displays that are performed by his conditioned males to their potential mates. This display always involves the brilliantly colored dorsal fin. Often, males with more colorful dorsal fins are more easily able to attract the females.

Another feature of the dorsal fin is something referred to as the dorsal slot. The dorsal slot of a fish is reserved for the folding of the dorsal fin into the dorsum of the fish. This is a common feature on large pelagic fishes that swim at medium rates of speed for extended periods of time. Examples of species that have a dorsal slot are the striped bass (*Morone saxatilis*) and other fishes considered to be game or sport fishes. Peacock Cichlids of the genus *Cichla* have this feature to a lesser extent.

Anal Fins

We do not usually refer to the dorsal and anal fins as being paired. However, in some instances, it seems as if they are. Probably the best examples of this are those fishes within the genus *Channa*, referred to by hobbyists as the "snakeheads." Their anal fin is often nearly as long as their dorsal fin, but a closer look shows that they are not mirror images of each other, and so they are not paired fins.

Like dorsal fins, anal fins provide stability and prevent the fish from swaying side-to-side in the water. If you have ever kept fishes such as Discus (*Symphysodon* spp.) and they have come down with a disease that results in their fins becoming "clamped," you probably have noticed how unstable they appeared to be. Another classic example is the Livebearing Toothcarps of the family Poeciliidae. These fishes often become inflicted with external and internal protozoan pathogens that result in them exhibiting a shimmying behavior. The diseased fish will appear to rock back and forth while staying in one spot. Such behavior is sometimes believed to be due to the anal fin being clamped against the body and thus not serving the purpose of stability.

Caudal Fin (Tail Fin)

The shape of the caudal fin is directly related to the speed at which a fish swims (Moyle & Cech, 2000). In the aquarium, most hobbyists will have fishes that exhibit a rounded, forked, or squared caudal fin. As with most other parts of a fish's anatomy, ichthyologists have grouped various fishes according to the shape of their caudal fins, and there are specific names to go along with these groups.

The majority of smaller aquarium fishes fall into the category of those that have **homocercal** (forked) tails where the upper and lower lobes are equal in size. Fishes like Barbs, Rasboras, Tetras, and Danios almost always have forked tails. As a matter of fact, nearly any fish that relies on frequent or sustained swimming will have this type of caudal fin design. If you think of it, next time you are perusing the isles at the local fish shop, stop and look at the tails of the fishes that are always in motion, and see if they are forked.

The next type of tail design that may be encountered is the **heterocercal** tail design. Heterocercal tails are those where the fish's upper caudal fin lobe is larger than the lower. In a heterocercal tail, the vertebral column extends into the upper lobe of the caudal fin. Seawater fishes are more likely to have a heterocercal tail compared to freshwater species. Probably the best example is

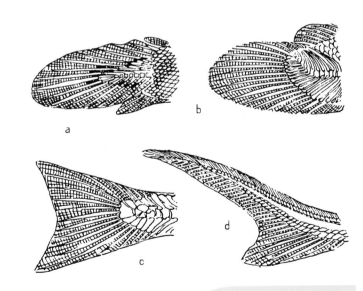

Forms of Caudal Fins: **a** – totally symmetrical; **b** and **c** – outwardly symmetrical, but inwardly of uneven structure; **d** – inwardly and outwardly unsymmetrical (after Zittel).

Adopted from *Illustrated Encyclopedia of Tropical Fishes*, T.F.H. Publications, Inc.

the tail of the Thresher Shark (*Alopias vulpinus*), a species that is totally unsuited to any marine hobbyist.

Along with fork-tailed, **round-tailed** and **square-tailed** fishes are by far the most common groups that a tropical fish hobbyist will be exposed to. The vast majority of cichlids and livebearers exhibit these types of caudal fin design as do many of the gouramis and rainbowfishes. Round-tailed fishes are usually slow-moving species that use their caudal fin more as a paddle. They usually live in areas where they do not need to swim great distances for food or shelter or to mate. The exception may only be during the rainy season in the tropics.

Square-tailed fishes are very similar to round-tailed fishes. The majority of the cichlids native to Central America have a squared caudal fin design as do the cichlids from Lake Malawi and Lake Victoria. Male Swordtails (*Xiphophorus* spp.) are best known for their square-tailed caudal fins that have a unique extension protracting from the lower lobe of the tail, hence the name Swordtail.

Adipose Fin

The adipose fin is a small, fleshy appendage that runs along the fish's dorsum between the dorsal fin and the top lobe of the caudal fin. This fin is a diagnostic trait for most tetras and closely related fishes known as Characins. Various species within several families of catfishes have adipose fins.

The true purpose of this fin is not known, other than to hypothesize that it was a useful tool of generations past. The small size and location, and lack of stiffening rays are puzzling, and the only conclusion is that perhaps it serves a useful purpose to the fishes that exhibit this fin during post larvae settlement. Other fins that are important later in life are poorly developed at this time, but the adipose fin seems to be best developed then.

50

Mouth

A fish's mouth has a lot to say—about its feeding habits, that is. By looking at the position, size, and shape of the mouth, information can be gathered to give a better idea of what the fish feeds on. There are three main categories that fishes are grouped into regarding their mouth shape, size, and location. They are inferior, superior, and terminal.

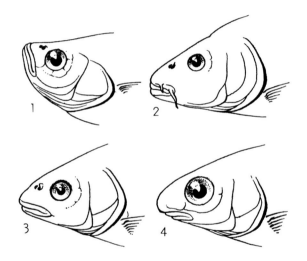

| Mouth | Various positions of the |

Various positions of the mouth in cyprinoids, from top to bottom. 1. Dorsal mouth of *Pelecus cultratus*. **2.** Terminal mouth, *Cyprinus carpio*. **3.** Inferior mouth, *Rutilus rutilus*. **4.** Ventral mouth, *Capoetobrama kuschakewitschi* (Kessl).
Adopted from *The Ecology of Fishes*, T.F.H. Publications, Inc.

Inferior

We refer to fishes with downward-pointing mouths as having inferior mouths. Fishes such as catfishes

of the genera *Corydoras* and *Synodontis* are classic examples of this group. Eartheaters of the genera *Geophagus* and *Satanoperca* are also good examples. Not surprisingly, fishes exhibiting inferior mouths are generally bottom-feeding animals.

Superior

Livebearing Toothcarps, such as those within *Xiphophorus*, *Poecilia*, and *Gambusia*, have upward-pointing mouths or superior mouths. These fishes are accustomed to feeding off of the surface of the water. Their superior mouths come in very handy when feeding on flaked foods or other prepared foods that will temporarily float at the surface of the water.

Terminal

The majority of fishes have what are called terminal mouths. This design is when the fish's head comes to a point with the mouth located at the end of the snout. Fishes exhibiting a terminal mouth structure have a widely varying array of mouth sizes and shapes. Some species, like *Cichla* and *Crenicichla,* have large gaping mouths, while *Parachromis* and *Caquetaia* have protrusible mouths, and others, like *Pterophyllum* and *Symphysodon,* have small rounded mouths. The number of examples with slight differences is nearly endless.

Geophagus brasiliensis

Having an inferior mouth allows this fish to sift through the substrate in search of food, thus giving rise to their common name of "Eartheater."

These groups are best used to categorize fishes in a broad sense. Within any one of them, there is a huge variety in terms of the size and shape of the fish's mouth. There are many species that have evolved special feeding appendages on their mouths. So, in addition to the above classifications, there are also sub-categories.

Probably the best-known subcategory regarding a fish's mouth is with the billfishes. Billfishes include the Swordfish (*Xiphias gladius*), Marlins (*Makaira* and *Tetrapturus*), Sailfish (*Istioophorus platypterus*), and the lesser-known Longbill Spearfish (*Tetrapturus pfluegeri*). These fishes are obviously not good aquarium residents, but they are an important example to illustrate just how radical some designs are.

Integument (Skin)

As in all vertebrates, the skin of a fish is made up of two parts—the **epidermis** and **dermis**. These layers are usually quite thin, especially in popular freshwater aquarium fishes, since they are commonly considered smaller species compared to, say, game fishes, which would have a considerably thicker epidermis and dermis.

Epidermis

Most species that are kept in aquariums have an epidermis that is no deeper than eight cell layers. Those hobbyists keeping Discus (*Symphysodon* spp.) probably have the most advanced understanding of the epidermis. Discus produce a whitish slime that provides nourishment for their young. They do this through their mucus glands, and both sexes take part in this method of food production.

In addition to mucus production, the epidermis is also responsible for the fish's sense of taste. It is hard to believe that fish actually taste through their skin, but it is a different kind of tasting than that of humans. These taste buds transmit impulses over branches of the facial nerve to the hindbrain. The epidermis is also often the primary layer of the skin where the fish's pigment is found.

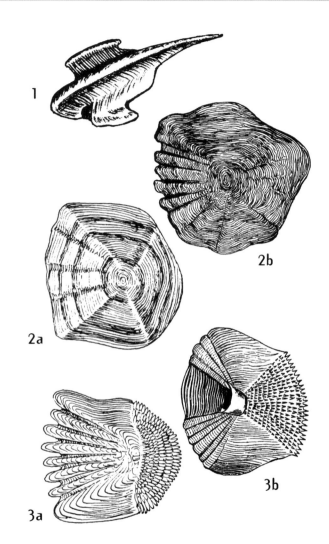

Scales **1.** Placoid scale **2a., 2b.** Cycloid scale **3a., 3b.** Ctenoid scale

Adopted from *Illustrated Encyclopedia of Tropical Fishes*, T.F.H. Publications, Inc.

Dermis

The dermis is where many blood vessels and nerves are found. Scales are grown here and lie within

Lepisosteus oculatus   Ganoid scales and the more derived elasmoid scales are responsible for the rough texture on these Spotted Gars.

Obviously, the scales are still replaced when lost but at a much slower pace.

A typical scale is composed of two primary layers: a bony surface layer that may exhibit spines, ridges, or grooves and a deeper layer known as a basal plate. Most scales are composed of concentric ridges within the surface layer. These are deposited throughout the life of the scale and are found around its margins. Several of these ridges combine to form a ring, and these rings may vary according to metabolic growth stimulation, or simply put, heavy and light feedings throughout life in an aquarium.

As with most other attributes of a fish's anatomy, something about how and where a fish lives and its niche in the environment can be determined by looking at their scales. Fishes that are constantly swimming or are fast swimmers often have smaller scales that are very smooth (Tetras, Barbs, Danios, and Rasboras). Conversely, fishes that live in slower moving waters or are slower swimmers will often have larger, courser scales (most Cichlids, Sunfishes, and Perches). Some fishes, like *Arapaima gigas*, are very slow swimmers and have huge bony scales. Gars (Lepisosteidae) are another perfect example of a very slow moving set of fishes that have large, bony scales. We can group fishes in five basic categories based on the structure and form of their scales. They are: ctenoid, cycloid, ganoid, elasmoid, and placoid.

pockets close to the surface. When a scale is lost, a new one will quickly grow and fill its place. It is important to understand that when a fish loses a scale it also loses a small portion of the epidermis. This qualifies as a wound and is certainly open to infection. Any time a fish loses a scale, it should be closely observed so as to catch any sign of trouble before it becomes a real problem.

Scales

Scales of aquarium fishes are usually thin and very flexible. They are not epidermal, but dermal. If they were epidermal, they would most likely be shed with some degree of regularity like the scales of reptiles.

Ctenoid scales are found on most **teleosts** (bony fishes) that have spiny fins. They have tiny, comb-like projections on the exposed edge of the scale that are referred to as **ctenii**. It is commonly thought that these ctenii actually improve the hydrodynamic effectiveness of these fishes as they swim through the water.

Cycloid scales are round in shape and very flat and thin. They are commonly found on fishes that live in open or fast-moving water. Fishes like herrings, trout, and various species of minnows are probably the best-known fishes that exhibit such scales.

Ganoid scales and the more derived **elasmoid** scales are found on teleosts such as Gars (Lepisosteidae). These scales resemble small bony plates more than actual scales. They are a highly effective means of protection against even the most venerable enemies. Some bowfishers claim that their arrows are actually deflected by these scales if they are not aimed at just the right angle.

The last group of scales are the placoid scales. These are small, tooth-like projections that are found on sharks and, to a lesser extent, stingrays. In some cases, these scales are found in small patches on certain areas of the fish's body, such as the head region, as in many skates and stingrays

INTERNAL ANATOMY AND PHYSIOLOGY

The external anatomy of fishes may vary widely, but it is very safe to say that the fishes most often encountered in the aquarium trade function very similarly to each other. Fortunately, hobbyists have copious numbers of resources available to them for a more in-depth look at the internal structure and function of fishes, so we will not go into much detail here. However, one area

of fishes' internal anatomy that is often noteworthy to hobbyists is the differences in swimbladder types and how they affect aquarium fishes.

Swimbladder (gas bladder)

A swimbladder allows for regulated control of buoyancy in fishes by allowing gases to be transferred in and out as necessary when the fish needs to adjust to its surrounding environment. The two main types of swimbladders are **physostomous** and **physoclistous.**

Physostomous

Physostomous swimbladders have a pneumatic duct between the gut and the swimbladder itself. Fishes with this type of swimbladder can be seen rushing toward the surface of the water to gulp air. They do this in order to inflate the swimbladder and allow for regulated buoyancy control. Fishes such as those within the genera *Corydoras* and *Hypostomus* are a prime example of these type of fishes. Do not make the mistake, however, of confusing fishes with a physostomous swimbladder with fishes that have labyrinth breathing organs. There is a huge difference, as you will see later in this chapter.

Physoclistous

Physoclistous swimbladders lack the connection that physostomous swimbladders have. This has both good and bad points. A closed swimbladder, as they are often called, is much more difficult to treat effectively if a problem arises. However, these fish are not subjected to the rigor of having to continually fill their swimbladders and then "burp" out the extra air that may have been swallowed in the process.

Perhaps the best-known fishes with this type of swimbladder are the cichlids. *Cyphotilapia* species have on-

going issues with swimbladder difficulties that date back to when they were first collected for the aquarium trade in the early 1960s. Many hobbyists report that their Frontosa (*Cyphotilapia* spp.) experience swimming problems and either float, wobble, or belly crawl. In all of these cases, the swimbladder is the chief cause of this abnormal swimming behavior and furthermore, it is damage to the swimbladder from an outside force (piercing and deflating) that most often is the underlying cause of this. While a detailed discussion of this highly controversial topic is beyond the scope of this book, it is advised that you research this topic if your Frontosa or, for that matter, any other fishes are affected by any of these ailments.

Two species that have perfect examples of swimbladder modification are *Crenicichla jegui* and *Neolamprologus furcifer*. Both of these species are basically bottom-dwelling, lie-in-wait predators. They have modified swimbladders and need to stay close to the surface at all times. This is more apparent in *N. furcifer,* because they do not just hug the bottom as *C. jegui* does but rather glide over rocks and through caverns and caves in search of new ambush sites.

Another very common species that is often associated with swimbladder difficulties is *Carassius auratus*, the common Goldfish. Due to all of the variations and exter-

Carassius auratus   The common Goldfish, in all its mutations, is a prime candidate for swimbladder disorders.

nal morphs that have been developed over the years, there has been considerable alteration to the internal features, as well, and some functions have changed.

The two largest functional problems that we see with these Fancy Goldfish variations are with their breeding and buoyancy control. Some variations, like the Pearlscale and Ryukin, are so far out of line with the fish's normal phenotype that you have to wonder how they survive at all—but they do. Within these groups of variants, we see many that simply cannot function as normal fishes do. They often do not swim well,

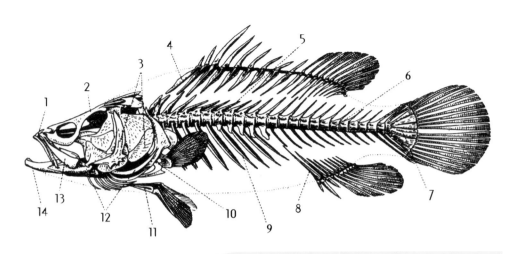

Skeletal Structure

1. Premaxillary 2. Cranium
3. Opercular bones 4. Interneural 5. Abdominal vertebra
6. Caudal vertebra 7. Hypurals 8. Interhaemal 9. Rib 10. Pectoral arch
11. Pelvic bones 12. Branchiostegal rays 13. Lower jaw 14. Maxillary

Adopted from *Illustrated Encyclopedia of Tropical Fishes*, T.F.H. Publications, Inc.

there are certainly cases that will be the result of an internal infection of the swimbladder, it is safe to say that the vast majority of these cases are the direct result of a deformed swimbladder that is not properly functioning due to morphological changes in the Goldfish's external anatomy. Simply put, the Goldfish's shape directly affects how its internal structure functions.

If you have a Goldfish with such a problem, you should not immediately rule out the use of antibiotics or any other product that is aimed at curing such an ailment. However, you should consult with a veterinarian who is

although some are still able to swim with surprising grace and effectiveness.

The buoyancy control issue is the one that will most likely affect hobbyists wishing to keep a Goldfish in a bowl, container garden pond, or other water feature. Oftentimes, hobbyists will purchase a Fancy Goldfish from their local fish store and set up a nice home for it. The fish will do fine for weeks or months but then start to wobble as it swims. One day you will find it floating upside down at the surface or bobbing up and down like a cork. The fish is very often still alive and can even right itself for some time to feed, but then it goes right back to being upside down. They may live for months or even years with this problem, but rarely do they ever become "normal" again.

The popular opinion on this problem is that it is a disease that needs to be treated with antibiotics. Although

knowledgeable about fish diseases or visit a well-known technician at your local fish store and ask them for their advice before using any such products. Of course, educate yourself by researching the subject so that you are more aware of what your options are before you make up your mind whether or not to treat the fish.

Respiration

Fishes generally live in an environment that is considered oxygen poor, at least when compared to that of their terrestrial relatives on land. Certainly oxygen is an extremely important element. Providing aquarium fishes with water rich in oxygen is vital to their health and long-term survival.

Water is generally considered to be approximately 800 times denser than air, so the energy required to

move water over the gills is therefore greater, as well. In addition, water only contains about 3 percent of the oxygen that is found in air. That means it takes a greater force to move an oxygen-poor substance over a fish's gills then it does for terrestrial animals to breathe air in and out of their lungs.

In order for fishes to obtain an adequate amount of oxygen, they must constantly move water over their gills. In most fishes, water is taken in through the mouth, passed through the buccal cavity, and then evenly pumped over the gills. However, some fishes, such as Tuna and Mackerel, use a different method of respiration called ram gill ventilation. This process allows the fishes to swim with their mouths slightly open and let the force of their forward thrust pass oxygenated water over their gills. Fishes that exhibit this method of respiration are known to be semi-warm blooded. Studies have shown that their muscles produce heat from the constant swimming, and the heat is distributed through the body via the bloodstream. Measurements have indicated that this is especially prevalent around the brain and eyes of these fishes.

In aquariums, a fish's respiration is vitally important and often directly related to its environment. Toxic substances in the water, such as ammonia, nitrite, and nitrate, can be harmful to a fish. Heavy metals can also cause fish great distress if present in the water. The damage inflicted by the presence of toxic substances is often just as harmful down the road as it is initially. If a fish has been exposed to high levels of ammonia and has managed to survive the initial poisoning, they may live for a few days even after the harmful ammonia has been removed. Unfortunately, they may still succumb to a secondary infection of a fungal or bacterial protozoan due to the lesions that result from ammonia exposure at high levels.

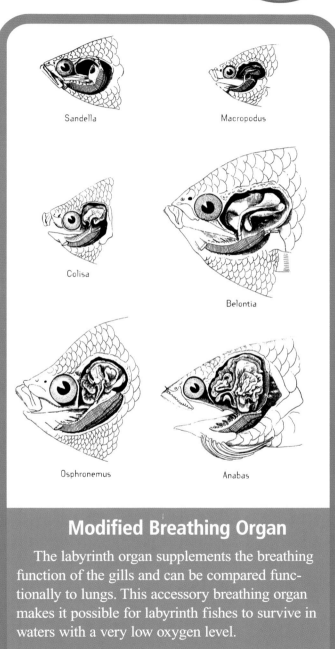

Sandella

Macropodus

Colisa

Belontia

Osphronemus

Anabas

Modified Breathing Organ

The labyrinth organ supplements the breathing function of the gills and can be compared functionally to lungs. This accessory breathing organ makes it possible for labyrinth fishes to survive in waters with a very low oxygen level.

Adopted from *Illustrated Encyclopedia of Tropical Fishes*, T.F.H. Publications, Inc.

Such instances are common with larger fishes. Smaller, less hardy species will often not survive the initial shock. It is also common for larger fishes to heal from their wounds. Permanent damage may still be present, but if the fish was in excellent health prior to exposure and has an excellent immune system that has readily fought off any invading secondary infection, their wounds are more likely to heal.

A fish's respiration is also directly related to the temperature of the environment. Water holds less oxygen as it increases in temperature, so tropical fishes need to be kept in an aquarium that has very good water circulation in order to keep the maximum amount of oxygen dissolved in it at all times. In most cases, a temperature in the mid- to upper-70s works well for tropical fishes in aquariums.

Overcrowding in an aquarium is detrimental for multiple reasons. Poor water quality, aggression, and oxygen deprivation are just a few of the reasons for not overcrowding your aquarium. In most cases of overcrowding, the fish will gather just below the surface of the water in an attempt to take in as much oxygen as possible.

In less extreme cases, an overcrowded aquarium may have sufficient water circulation but insufficient biological activity in the form of aerobic and anaerobic bacteria. Such cases will also often lead to fish gathering at the surface of the water, but rather than just being deprived of oxygen due to poor water circulation, they will be deprived of oxygen due to being slowly poisoned by an ever-increasing amount of toxic fish waste.

Under ideal conditions, fish will be able to effectively extract just over 80 percent of the oxygen in the water that passes over their gills. This is quite astonishing when you consider how rough the environment they live in actually is and even more amazing when you consider that humans only utilize approximately 20 to 25 percent of the oxygen in the air.

Such efficiency doesn't come without problems, and due to water's highly solvent nature, many impurities and other toxins will be filtered through a fish's gills, as well. This is the main reason why humans have to be careful where they buy their seafood or what they bring home after a day of fishing. Toxins can accumulate in fishes if polluted water is pumped over their gills.

Another way that toxins can build up in fish is through the fish's consumption of infected organisms. In aquariums, there is not much of a concern with this, since the fish are usually pets, not a meal for dinner one night. However, fishes that are collected as food are highly toxic due to what they have been eating. Various toxins, such as ciguatera toxin (especially prevalent in the tropics), can build up in predatory fishes seasonally. Such a buildup is directly correlated to what the predator has been feeding on.

Osmosis and Waste Reduction

Osmosis is scientifically defined as the movement of a solvent through a semipermeable membrane into a solution of higher solute concentration that tends to equalize the concentrations of solute on the two sides of the membrane. All strict freshwater fishes face two general problems with regards to osmosis, which are removing excess water and maintaining proper salt concentrations within bodily fluids. The kidneys are responsible for the removal of excess water from the fish's body. This is released as urine and is very dilute in nature compared to that of terrestrial animals.

Bony fishes will produce as much as 20 percent of their body weight in urine each day, whereas the 1.5 to

2 percent of their body weight produced by terrestrial animals. The kidneys of fish will also remove organic materials from the blood as it flows through them. Ironically, most of these organic materials are actually passed back into the blood, but the water is then released as highly diluted urine. For example, nearly all of the Na^+ in the filtrate is reabsorbed. However, less than 50 percent of the water actually passes back into the blood (Reinert, 1992).

To counter the high loss of ions due to continued urine production, ions are absorbed via the gills. Although there are many theories on how this actually takes place, the general consensus suggests that the uptake of Na^+ and Cl^- ions against a concentration gradient is mediated by a class of enzymes known as ATP-ases (Reinert, 1992).

The reactions that take place between the various compounds within the fish's gills are quite complex. However, they are not only essential to the osmoregulatory process, but also in the overall excretory function of the gills. In the end, such physiology and the osmoregulation associated with it decrease the amount of energy needed for the active transport of positively charged ions from water to the fish's blood. Thus, the fish will maintain proper salt concentrations.

The Lateral-line System

Vision, hearing, equilibrium, and lateral-line are the four basic sensory systems of fishes. The lateral-line system is thought of as having two different parts—the inner ear and the neuromast/lateral-line (Moyle & Cech, 2000). The sensory receptors of this system are called neuromast organs and are very similar to the organs found in their inner ear. Generally speaking, there are two main types of lateral-line receptors: epidermal organs and canal organs. All fishes have at least one of these types of receptors.

In modern fishes, the lateral-line system extends down the flanks of the fish and out into the head region, often encircling the eyes. This system can be seen with the naked eye and appears as a single, unbroken line running down the side of the fish. Some species have a broken lateral-line, as was discussed in more detail in chapter 2.

The lateral-line system is extremely important to all fishes. As a result, fish can sense water direction and speed as well as low-frequency vibrations, such as those made by wounded animals in the water. Piranhas use their lateral-line system very effectively to find potential prey items in the sometimes turbid waters of tropical South America.

Furthermore, fishes maintained in an aquarium probably use their lateral-line systems to sense the location of the aquarium walls. Some schooling fishes also appear to rely on their lateral-line system to maintain the integrity of the school. Movements are often made with such speed and grace that it is probably the combination of eyesight and an effective lateral-line system that make this possible.

At times you will see fishes that have the appearance of holes in their heads or along the lateral-line system. These holes are the results of degeneration of the epidermal organs within the lateral-line system itself. There are three main causes of these holes: environmental, nutritional, and pathogenic.

Both environmental and nutritional degeneration are known as head-and-lateral-line erosion or HLLE for short. While seawater fishes are more apt to suffer from these problems, there are several groups of freshwater fishes that will show HLLE.

Perhaps the most popular group of fishes to consistently suffer from this disorder is the New World cich-

Cichla temensis Fishes such as this Speckled Peacock Bass are very susceptible to HLLE if their environmental conditions are incorrect.

lids. Of these, two stand out among the rest: Oscars (*Astronotus* spp.) and Discus (*Symphysodon* spp.). The Pike cichlids (*Crenicichla* spp.) are next in order of sensitivity, but generally speaking, they are not affected as frequently as the other species mentioned.

Diagnosis of this disorder is quite easy, as the fish look as though their heads are decaying. They will have lesions or areas around the nuchal hump or eyes that appear to be dissolving. In very serious cases, the fish may show degeneration along the lateral line down the sides of their bodies.

HLLE caused by environmental conditions is common in aquariums that have not had regular maintenance. The most important aspect of proper maintenance, especially with larger fishes, is regular partial water changes. The degree and volume of water changes will be discussed in greater detail within chapter 6, but for now, realize how important they are for the health of your fish.

The nutritional requirements of fishes vary widely. Often, when a species or specimen that has been kept captive for some time does not receive the proper foods, it will show signs of HLLE. This is very common in public aquariums where the fishes are all fed the same mixture of meaty foods. Surgeonfishes (Acanthuridae) suffer the greatest harm from this, since they are vegetarians.

You will also see this with *Uaru amphiacanthoides* and *U. fernandezyepezi*. Both species are vegetarian in nature, although they relish meaty foods when they are available. A constant feeding of foods high in animal proteins will also often result in HLLE even if the aquarium is well maintained. This is a good reason to have a basic understanding of the individual nutritional requirements of your fish.

Sometimes your fish may exhibit lesions in the head area that look infected. These lesions will appear red and swollen and may have stringy matter streaming from them. Such signs are the classic symptoms of hole-in-the-head disease (HITH) disease, most often associated with Discus.

Popular opinion suggests that this disease is caused by flagellates within the genus *Hexamita*. Ironically though, *Hexamita* spp. are actually classified as intestinal flagellates and many fish pathologists have never even seen a species of *Hexamita* present in Discus. As a matter of fact, *Hexamita* outbreaks are rare in ornamental aquarium fishes.

So what is the cause of hole-in-the-head disease? The only flagellate that is similar to *Hexamita* is *Spironucleus* and neither are actually considered to be the pathogen of this disease. In actuality, many species of cichlids and other fishes have been found with holes in their heads, and any flagellates that were found among these holes were of a non-parasitic nature (Untergasser 1989).

The most widely accepted answer to this question is that lesions found among the network of organs within

the lateral-line system are caused by poor nutrition and/or poor water quality control and management. If high standards of care are maintained, the likelihood of having such a problem is very small.

Continuing Research

There are several more areas of anatomy and physiology that are not covered here simply because they are of no real concern to aquarium hobbyists. Some of these are more obvious than others. For example, you will not see sections of text devoted to vision and the structure of the eye here as well as detailed insight as to the sense of smell and the structures, both internal and external, that are associated with them. If you wish to look into these areas further, there is a large amount of material on all aspects of the anatomy and physiology of fishes available from many sources that specialize in the subject. It is always encouraged that you research as much as possible about the fishes that you care for, as many of them are quite unconventional.

Although the specific anatomical examples listed herein have a lot to do with the fish's behavior, they also show the high degree of variation in that is present in the anatomy of modern fishes. After all, a fish's anatomy allows the fish's body to carry out the command it has been given.

Chapter 4

NUTRITION & FEEDING

A comprehensive understanding of the proper dietary and nutritional needs of captive fishes is among the most important aspects of being a successful long-term hobbyist. Just as fishes come in many shapes, sizes, and colors, they also have a broad range of feeding habits and nutritional needs. This chapter is designed to give you a basic understanding of what foods to offer to your fish and also to introduce you to proper feeding techniques and overall nutrition.

Foods suitable for aquarium fishes come in various forms. Many of them have been formulated into prepared feeds that are offered for sale through pet retailers and local aquarium shops. These prepared feeds are probably the best way for a beginning hobbyist to provide a broad range of nutrients to their fishes, but there are also many other ways to do this, and that is really what this chapter is all about.

The first thing hobbyists seeking to learn about feeding fish should do, whether experienced or not, is to familiarize themselves with the various forms of fish foods that are available. It is surprising how many foods are suitable, and often of quite good quality, but are rarely used due to a lack of information on them. Another issue that concerns hobbyists is the lack of availability of many foods. This is especially true with the various live foods.

Hobbyists living in the United Kingdom often have different types of foods readily available to them than those available to hobbyists living in Australia or the United States. This does not mean they have more or less to pick from necessarily, just different. Also, hobbyists living near coastal waterways have a whole range of possibilities for live foods available to them that are not available to those who live inland. Of course, since so many of our aquarium fishes are "tropical," we are generally quite envious of those hobbyists fortunate enough to live in regions where they can collect live foods and aquarium residents on the same outing.

LIVE FOODS

In most cases, offering living foods to your fishes is the best way to supply them with a broad range of useful nutrients and vitamins. However, live foods can also be the highway for transmittable diseases, so proper precautions should always be taken to ensure that they are fresh and disease-free before offering them to your fishes. When possible, the source of these foods should be known so as to make certain that they are coming from disease-free sources. This is especially important with live *Tubifex* and black worms, since they are probably the best known live foods that regularly harbor pathogens.

Green Water

There are many organisms that are responsible for the makeup of green water, all of which are microscopic and can only be effectively observed with the use of a microscope. We recognize five genera as being those most commonly found in green water. These are: *Chlorella*, *Eudorina*, *Euglena*, *Protococcus*, and *Tetraspora*.

Green water is best used as a food for the fry of fish species that are characteristically difficult to rear due to their size at the time of hatching. Also, green water is very effective as a food source for other live foods, such as brine shrimp and water fleas. It is reported that a Mason jar filled with green water can be cleared in a few days when a small number of water fleas are added.

Green water can be purchased from a biological supply house or produced at home from an aged stock. If you wish to attempt to produce your own green water, you should obtain a small sample from a source that is

known to be clean and free of pesticides. The sample should be added to a clean, transparent container and filled with mineral or spring water and a small volume of skim milk (1 part milk to 100 parts water). Place the container in a location that receives a minimum of six to eight hours of sunlight per day, and keep it at a temperature of 65° to 70°F so the photosynthetic activity of the organisms can be maximized.

Specific cultures can be accessed at different times, depending on the quality of the stock. The most effective method of determining how long you should let your culture stand before dipping into it is best left to a culturist who specializes in these things or better yet, the advice given in a book devoted to such a topic.

Infusoria

The term infusoria is a catch-all name that includes all ciliated microscopic animals found mostly in fresh water. They often reproduce at astounding rates and are a highly valuable food source for small fishes and fish fry. As with green water, infusoria cultures can be started from a small sample of an existing stock or by purchasing a starter culture from a biological supply house.

One of the most interesting features of raising infusoria is their adaptability to various food-stuffs. They are often raised by using small portions of common household foods such as wheat germ or yeast. Small amounts are added at various times, depending on how "heavy" a population you wish to be in control of at any given time.

Infusoria are not usually picky about temperature. Standard "room temperatures" will usually suffice. Popular thought says that the warmer the water, the more infusoria will be produced. This is simply untrue. There is a point where the oxygen level in the

culture will decrease at an exponential rate, and the culture will crash if the temperature is too high. So unlike green water cultures, infusoria cultures should be kept out of the sun so as to prevent overheating as much as possible.

Hydras and Planarians

Hydras are considered too dangerous to purposely place in most aquariums, especially those containing small fishes. However, there are some fishes, such as many gouramis, that make that make hydras a large part of their diet.

Hydras are relatively large organisms compared with those in green water or infusoria cultures. They are probably best known for their ability to hunt down and completely consume small crustaceans and small young fishes. In aquariums, small fishes will often be attacked by multiple hydras. Sometimes the fish will successfully get away, but they usually have serious wounds resulting from such attacks.

On the other hand, planarians (flatworms) are usually not detrimental to aquarium inhabitants. Some hobbyists have used them as food, but their popularity as a live food has never really caught on. Many aquarists consider planarians to be pests and make every effort to remove them from their tanks at first sight, but often they simply mind their own business and add to the overall biomass of the aquarium.

Rotifers

Rotifer is the Latin word for "wheel bearer," which is what early zoologists referred to them as since the first organisms described as such looked like little wheels. They appear as little specks to the naked eye but can be seen moving about, especially on the inside surface of an aquarium's glass.

Discussions of various species of rotifers based on their taxonomy are rather difficult, because biologists do not agree on the methods to which they arrive at such conclusions. Therefore there are few standards in their nomenclature as compared with fishes or any other higher organism.

Rotifers are mainly microscopic but some species can be readily observed with the naked eye (usually as long rods or spheres). Apparently, some individuals within a given species will grow considerably larger than their conspecifics, and these are the specimens that are of particular use to hobbyists as a source of fish food.

Rotifers are commonly found at all depths of lakes, ponds, and other bodies of water. There are hardly any water-holding places on Earth where these creatures cannot be found to one degree or another. This is perhaps the reason they are considered a very important source of nutrition to the fry of most freshwater fishes.

Rotifers can be cultured very easily in either large wooden barrels that are set outdoors or smaller containers inside a garage or shed. It is strongly advised that the initial set up of the culture container include very clean water of good quality, an airstone system into which a powerful airpump can be incorporated, and a clean starter culture from a reputable supplier.

As with every cultured organism, rotifers can become infected with various bacteria and other pathogens that can cause an entire culture to die off. If you dip into your culture frequently, you will seldom see this, since you'll be using them faster then they can die, but if the disease festers it can become a serious problem, and the culture may need to be restarted.

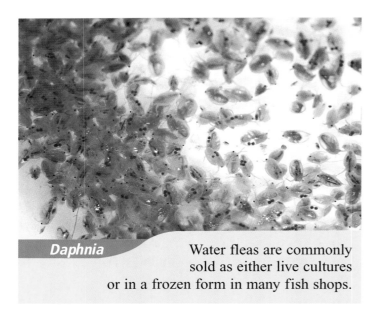

Daphnia Water fleas are commonly sold as either live cultures or in a frozen form in many fish shops.

Water Fleas (*Daphnia* and related crustaceans)

Water fleas are one of the most commonly used forms of living foods throughout the world. They are commonly found in nature and are very easily obtained from many sources, including some of the larger specialty aquarium supply houses, as live stock, frozen in cube form or flat packs. There are several organisms covering many genera that are all considered as water fleas or daphnids. Those within the genera *Daphnia* and *Bosmina* are the two most common and are frequently collected together.

Daphnia and *Bosmina* inherited the name "water fleas" from their similarity in size to the common flea. They are also referred to as "ditch fleas" on occasion, because these organisms are commonly found in ditches along roadsides. As a matter of fact, they are commonly found in many areas that you may not expect to see them, although they are not as wide-spread as infusorians. Any body of freshwater that is somewhat oxygenated and has a moderate level of organic decomposition will normally have a population of water fleas present.

Water fleas may exhibit differing colorations depending on their diet and the amount of dissolved oxygen present in their environment. Generally speaking, the lower the dissolved oxygen content in the water the higher the hemoglobin count is. Hemoglobin is red, so the higher the hemoglobin count, the redder the organism. Their diet also has an impact on their coloration, although to a lesser extent.

If you are the adventurous type and wish to collect your own water fleas, you will be most successful during the spring months. There are, however, cases in which collection during the late winter is favorable, as well. Some prefer to hunt them during winter simply because of the inaccessibility of certain waters due to a high degree of plant growth along the shores in warmer months.

The best time to actually collect water fleas is when they are just under the surface of the water. This is most common early in the morning just prior to daybreak, as they do not particularly care for bright light. As dusk approaches, particularly if it is a cloudy afternoon, the water fleas will begin to rise to the surface again.

As with most small organisms, water fleas will do best when maintained at temperatures between 60° and 70°F and in well-oxygenated water. Whether you are bringing your catch home or maintaining a supply for feeding, you should always remember that important point. For detailed information on the culturing of *Daphnia* and other water fleas, please refer to one of the many good books on the subject; if you obtain a culture from a biological supply house, they often have specific literature on the subject.

Artemia salina   Baby brine shrimp are a great starter food for newly-hatched fish fry of many popular aquarium species.

Artemia (Brine Shrimp)

For all intents and purposes, brine shrimp cultivation is only recommended for those who need to supply large numbers of the organism to fishes for the purposes of grow-out or conditioning for spawning. Years ago it was standard practice to have a small area in your fishroom or basement dedicated to the cultivation of brine shrimp. Today, this is simply not the case.

Many local fish shops have suppliers who regularly deliver freshly grown adult brine shrimp to them and they, in turn, offer them you. This is the recommended way of obtaining these organisms for a few reasons. First, purchasing brine shrimp as you need them allows your stock to be turned over frequently. Fresh stock is important since it can, and often does, foul while in holding tanks. Second, supporting your local aquarium shop is important in that it allows you, the hobbyists, to become familiar with your store's staff and this in turn allows them to become familiar with you. Familiarity often builds trust and a good partnership. That is something that the internet lacks and is, therefore, a good enough reason to support your local pet shops and aquarium stores. Third, having living brine shrimp on hand at all times requires setting up another tank for holding them in. While there are certainly many benefits to doing this, there are also always the added tasks associated with such a setup. On the other hand, having a separate aquarium properly set up to hold live brine shrimp allows you to have complete control over their nutritional value. For example, if we have a jar of green water and then add a small amount of water fleas to it, the water will become clear in a few days. Why? Well because the water fleas will have consumed the organisms that are responsible for the water turning green in the first place.

The same is true of brine shrimp. If you have a tank full of them and then add a few ounces of green water to the holding tank, the tank will take on a slight green

Artemia salina   Live adult brine shrimp are the perfect foods to be gut-loaded for small and medium-sized fishes.

This Fairy Shrimp is a closely related freshwater cousin to the brine shrimps.

haze. This haze will disappear at a rate that directly depends on the number of brine shrimp added to the tank. For example, an aquarium holding twenty gallons of water and heavily stocked with brine shrimp will consume the green water at a higher rate than the same size aquarium with a low stocking density of brine shrimp.

As a matter of fact, many breeders who have large numbers of fry will still have brine shrimp hatcheries in their fishrooms. These same breeders have come up with various methods of introducing nutrients to their brine shrimp, both adults and nauplii, so as to pass these nutrients on to the fishes. This method is called gut loading and is extremely effective when done properly.

The gut loading of live foods can be tricky. Many organisms have very high metabolisms and therefore process foods very quickly. These organisms must be gut loaded and then fed to your fishes shortly there-

after. This is especially true if the brine shrimp are kept at higher temperatures, because their metabolisms are temperature dependant.

If you purchase adult brine shrimp in bulk, you can maintain them at temperatures in the low to mid 70s. However, if you raise your own from eggs, you will have to maintain the eggs and nauplii at a higher temperature, and then, as they grow, slowly lower the temperature until you reach the recommended temperature for maintaining adults, which is 72°F.

The diet that you choose to gut load your brine shrimp with should be varied. This will allow a broader range of nutrients to be passed along to your fishes. One of the best foods is powdered Spirulina algae. These algae are very high in nutrients and provide rich color-enhancing power to the brine shrimp. Also, it is easy to see when the shrimp have consumed some of the Spirulina because they turn bright green. They are then ready to be harvested and fed to your fishes.

There are many other foods that are fantastic for your brine shrimp, too. Some include, but are certainly not limited to, powdered flake food, flour, liquid foods formulated for fish fry, and of course, green water. There are also some prepared or synthetic phytoplankton formulations that can be purchased at local pet shops that are very suitable for feeding to brine shrimp.

Whichever foods you ultimately choose to gut load your brine shrimp with, be sure to keep a close eye on water quality. The water quality of your holding aquarium is crucial. Brine shrimp are able to become infested with many types of disease-causing pathogens, and while transmission from the brine shrimp to your fishes is low, it still is possible. Also, any disease that your brine shrimp may contract will surely have a negative affect on their nutritional value.

Lumbriculus sp. Blackworms are large members of tubificids and are an excellent source of protein for many fishes.

Tubifex and Blackworms

While tubifex worms (*Tubifex*, *Limnodrilla*, and other lesser-known genera) and blackworms (*Lumbriculus variegatus*) are completely different animals from a taxonomic viewpoint, they are very similar regarding their care, culture, and feeding to aquarium fishes. Additionally, it should be noted that "tubifex" is a catch-all name for many organisms that are all closely related. In Asia, most high profile Discus breeders offer heavy feedings of tubifex worms. They do this mainly to provide their broodstock with an easy-to-use, easy-to-culture food that is exceedingly high in protein and nutrients.

In the United States, we use both tubifex worms and blackworms for much the same reasons. However, American hobbyists tend to rely on them much less than the Asian hobbyists and aquarists do. Years ago, Pierre Brichard—a world famous exporter of cichlids from Lake Tanganyika—would culture tubifex worms for use as fish food to offer the fishes awaiting export to the United States and Europe. He would offer them to the fishes in large balls once or twice daily. Brichard believed that there was no other food that could repair the damage that a fish experienced from capture the way tubifex worms could. Of course, he used a good food source, good water (from the lake itself), and expensive medications to accomplish this, but he always came back and gave the majority of the credit to the worms.

Both tubifex worms and blackworms are best purchased fresh as needed. Whether that be daily, weekly, or monthly, they can go sour very fast and need to be kept very cool and in very clean water in order to survive even a few hours. Pet shops usually have their stocks replenished twice weekly and are set up to handle these organisms, so it really is best to buy them as you need them.

Tubifex sp. There is quite a lot of controversy over whether to feed tubifex worms to aquarium fishes. If you choose to do so, make sure they are clean and come from a good source.

Microworms

Microworms are another
excellent source of vitamins
and nutrients for young fish or fry.

The proper care and handling of even a small amount of tubifex worms and blackworms that are intended for use as food for your fishes is *extremely* important. It is not uncommon to hear of hobbyists who purchased these worms and then stopped off at the grocery store to pick up dinner and at the movie rental place to pick up some entertainment, and by the time they arrived home their worms were a sloppy gray mess. Such a scenario may seem humorous, but it is far too common. What is even more shocking is the number of hobbyists who don't think anything of it and dump the entire contents of the container in their aquariums!

The almost instantaneous result is usually a very cloudy, smelly aquarium. You will know it is bad when your fishes, that usually come over to eat the worms very greedily, make a 180° turn and swim frantically to get away from the slimy gray blob that just invaded their beloved home. To combat such a situation, you will need to perform several massive water changes, and you will absolutely need to test very often for heightened levels of ammonia and nitrite. Such water changes in and of themselves can upset your aquarium in a major way, but when combined with such pollution—watch out!

Hopefully the seriousness of the responsibility of keeping these worms clean has now made itself very clear. Now we can focus on the good side of using these as an effective food source.

The addition of these worms to a solid feeding regimen is highly suggested for several reasons. First and foremost, feeding them to your fishes will offer raw animal protein in a way that they are likely to recognize immediately as food and consume with gusto. Second, the range of nutrients that these organisms offer is completely different than that offered by most other foods—not necessarily better, but certainly different. To a lesser extent, you could even suggest that by feeding live worms to your fishes, especially those maintained in a fully set-up aquarium, offers them a unique opportunity to hunt and seek out prey as if they were in nature. This is probably more beneficial to their psyche than anything else, but that is fine—fish deserve to have fun, too.

When it comes time to actually feeding the worms to your fishes, you should do so in a way that allows the fish maximum access to them. The use of a worm feeder is a very effective method or accomplishing this. Worm-feeders generally have holes that are the proper size as to allow the tubifex or blackworms easy passage through them. Most units that are commercially available through your local pet shop will have some type of attachment on them that will allow you to affix the unit to the side of the aquarium. Others may have a hollow ring around the top that holds air and allows the feeder to float freely about the water's surface.

The amount of worms that are offered to your fishes at any one time should be carefully calculated. You

should not place such a large amount in the feeder that many are allowed to free-fall to the gravel surface. Aquariums that have bare bottoms are not included in this discussion, because bare-bottomed tanks can easily be siphoned of excess worms and the worms can be recycled for use in another feeding. Blackworms are known for their ability to invade the aquarium's gravel and live for many months. They will often reproduce, and some advanced hobbyists have actually used them effectively to remove excess detritus in show tanks.

Only allow the fishes to feast on these until they have rounded off bellies, or in other words, until they reach satiation point. You may be quite surprised to learn just how many worms it takes for a small tetra to reach satiation let alone an entire school of them. You can go through a golf ball-sized amount of worms in no time with a lot of smaller fish or just a few bigger ones.

One other important note regarding feeding fishes with tubifex and blackworms is the high nutrient content of the waste. Fishes fed a steady diet high in animal matter will have waste that is very nutrient-rich. Such nutrient-rich waste fouls the water very quickly and can cause major water quality issues.

If you feel that you have overfed your fishes or may have fed them spoiled worms, the best thing to do is conduct a series of small water changes, and test for ammonia and nitrite hourly for about eight hours. The following day, you should test at least four times during the day or until you feel that the threat has subsided. If in fact you did feed your fish spoiled worms and your aquarium is starting to smell turn cloudy, you should do a series of large water changes and follow the same guidelines for testing as above. Always be sure to add water that has either been aged or conditioned with a tap-water conditioner. As with most supplies, a good conditioner should be available at your local fish shop.

Tenebrio moltor Mealworms of various sizes also make great foods to feed aquariums fishes. Feed sparingly, however, as these tend to clog a fish's digestive tract if overfed.

Insects

Most freshwater fishes consume insects at some point in their lives. Many of these insects are small, flying types that inadvertently land in the water, or in the case of archerfishes (*Toxotes* spp.), they may be shot off of low leaves hanging just above the water's surface with a small jet of water. Some fishes, such as the arowanas (*Osteoglossum* spp. and *Scleropages* spp.), are actually accomplished jumpers that are very capable of leaping several feet out of the water in order to capture a beetle or other creepy crawler walking along a leaf or branch above the surface of the water.

Either way, insects are often overlooked as suitable fare for fishes. This is unfortunate, because many species of fishes that are accused of being difficult to keep in

Various crickets are perfectly acceptable to feed to your fishes. Make sure they come from a pet shop or feed supply store so they are guaranteed to be clean and healthy.

five years in a small aquarium if it is offered a type of food that it actually likes and can derive nutrients from.

Many cichlids do very well when offered small insects on a somewhat regular basis. Those who keep larger characins such as *Distichodus*, *Myleus*, and *Metynnis* species will experience the same results. However, it all depends on the actual insects that you offer.

More experienced hobbyists may have recognized that certain wild fishes have different color intensities depending on where they were collected. This is true for one extremely popular species of cichlid, the Oscar.

Oscars are indigenous to northern South America where they inhabit rivers, lagoons, ponds, and any other body of water that is at least a few feet deep. In nature, Oscars feed on a wide variety of foods. However, their favorite food is insects, and since insects are numerous in the tropics of South America, the Oscars have quite a selection to choose from. Oscars from various regions show remarkable color differences. While coloration depends on more than just diet alone, their diet does play a crucial role in determining the overall intensity of their coloration and pattern.

For example, it is generally believed that insects are responsible for the intense red coloration of Oscars and many other cichlids in the Rio Negro, Brazil. The Rio Negro is a nutrient-poor, blackwater system that feeds into the mighty Amazon River from the northern rain-

captivity will actually do quite well if they are offered something that they actually recognize as food—bugs!

Perhaps the best example of such a species is the four-eye fishes (*Anableps* spp.). These surface-oriented fishes eat insects exclusively with the only exceptions being small fishes that may come too close. They are not built to chase down fishes like pursuit predators are, but they patrol the water's surface in search of drowning insects to gobble up. Another fish highly regarded as an insectivorous species is the Freshwater Butterflyfish (*Pantodon buchholzi*). This species, endemic to Western Africa, is a popular fish but is often hit or miss in its hardiness. If you purchase two or three specimens, you may find that only one lives for any great length of time. These numbers are discouraging for a fish that is capable of living more than

forest. Therefore, pinning this intense coloration on the presence of a mineral or some other nutrient is not possible, so we believe that such coloration is directly related to the fish's diet.

We know that coloration in certain localities is dynamic in the sense that when the fishes are removed from the environment, they lose the color very rapidly. When the fishes are placed back into their native environment and allowed to act normally, they regain this locality-specific coloration.

The only variable that we are not able to directly replicate in captivity is that of the natural nutrient range of their foods. Certain **carotenes** and **carotenoids**, the hydrocarbons directly related to coloration in fishes, are available in varying amounts and these are then able to be traced back through the food chain to much smaller organisms. In aquaria, we simply do not have the resources necessary to replicate such a broad food web.

It is insects that are believed to provide hydrocarbons to the aquatic world. In the tropics, there are vast numbers of insects that consume plant materials from the rainforest canopy. Within these plants are chloroplasts, and within the chloroplasts are the carotenes containing the crystalline hydrocarbons ($C_{40}H_{56}$) that are convertible to vitamin A. Carotenoids are also found in these plants in the form of long aliphatic polyene chains that are composed of eight isoprene units. Together, these parts make up the base compounds for the coloration of larger, more advanced organisms like fishes and reptiles.

Of all the various species of insects that are available, hobbyists really only need to be familiar with a few. To ensure that you will not add any potentially harmful chemicals to your aquarium, all insects should be purchased through your local pet shop and not collected out behind the woodpile. Pesticides and other pollutants can build up in your fish's internal organs and cause major problems that will dramatically shorten the life of your fish.

The best insects to feed most tropical aquariums fishes are probably mealworms, waxworms, and soft-shelled crickets. There are two major hurdles to overcome when feeding these organisms to your fishes— the size of the insect and blockage of the intestines. Obviously, a small fish cannot eat a cricket that is nearly the same size as it is, so you have to be prepared with alternatives. One alternative is pellet or flake food that has been formulated with insects or earthworms.

Many medium- and large-sized fishes will accept commercially available insects quite readily. These insects should be offered only a few times a week, since they are extremely high in protein and fat. They can really pack on the weight, especially in fishes that do not have a lot of swimming room in which to work off the calories. Whenever you feed insects to your fishes, you of course have to make every attempt to match them up with food that is the right size.

If you have been feeding large amounts of insects to your fish, you may notice that waste is not passing very readily. This would be evidenced by a slight bulge in the body cavity just above the vent. Usually, a blockage is the result of feeding too much of one thing. This happens a little more regularly when feeding with insects due to their chitinous exoskeletons and their tendency to sit in the gut.

Sometimes pet shops will be out of stock on certain live insects. In that case, you may want to try your local bait and tackle shop. They often carry a wide assortment of live insects, especially Waxworms, which are great for Trout and Sunfishes, and often have plenty in stock. Due to their popularity as bait, tackle shops often get regular deliveries of Waxworms, so they are usually very fresh.

Earthworms   Earthworms are probably one of the safest live foods to feed larger fishes.

Earthworms

Earthworms have been popular as fish food for decades. They are perhaps the best source of safe-to-feed animal protein for many medium and large fishes, and they can certainly be chopped up or minced for feeding to smaller fishes.

Earthworms are soft-bodied and therefore do not have the chance to build up in the fish's gut like animals having a chitinous skeleton. They are digested rather quickly, and their nutrients are able to be processed quickly, too. Fishes that consume large numbers of worms on a regular basis are usually quite chunky. Such an observation leads to the conclusion that Earthworms are high in fat as well.

Feeding only a small number of worms to your fishes daily, or even every other day or every third day, would help to lessen the possibility of obesity. Always being cautious about feeding techniques is one practice that will prove invaluable in the future. In many cases, it is better to underfeed than to overfeed.

Obtaining earthworms is fairly simple. First, nearly every bait and tackle shop in existence carries them and often in different sizes and quantities. Also, many retail fish shops carry them as well. This is especially true with full-line pet shops that may also carry birds, small animals, and fishes since earthworms make a good food source for those animals, too.

If you wish to collect your own earthworms, doing so is quite simple. The first place to look is in a compost pile or another area that contains high nutrient soil and dirt. Of course, gardens work well, too. You can also look under partially rotten wood or under slabs of rock that may be over soil. Simply take a small shovel and turn over the soil slowly and methodically. You will often see the worms trying to "worm" their way back under it.

On warm days, you may need to dig a bit deeper then on cool days. Earthworms never like the heat and if you have purchased them before at any of the above mentioned shops, you will notice that they should have removed them from the refrigerator. Early fall and spring seem to be the best times of the year to collect these animals. Be creative in your collecting techniques but always be certain to get them from areas that are not likely to have high levels of containments.

Feeder Fishes

There is perhaps no other area of feeding that has seen as much controversy as that of the feeding of live fishes. Many hobbyists dispel living food fishes as nothing more than disasters waiting to happen while others praise them and would never consider not using

also a certain degree of pleasure many hobbyists obtain while watching a predatory fish do what they were built to do—hunt!

Variation

Variety in a fish's diet is extremely important. In nature, fishes do not normally feed on the exact same thing at every feeding. They are most often opportunistic feeders that consume foods as they become available. There are some fishes, such as true piranhas (*Pygocentrus* spp.), that seasonally change the foods they eat and greatly alter their consumption during the

| **Feeder Fishes** | Only use feeder fishes that appear healthy and vibrant. |

them as a food source. Both sides are understood and respected here, so we will list both the pros and the cons of using live fishes as food, starting with the pros.

Nutrients

Live fishes contain a host of nutrients in varying amounts. Many of these nutrients are found in other foods, but in that form they may have been processed or partially broken down by bacteria, as is the case with many frozen foods. In some instances, feeding whole fishes is the only feasible way to deliver essential nutrients to predatory fishes that have not been weaned off live foods. This is especially true with new imports or during disease treatment.

Psychological

Obviously, feeding live fishes allows predators to actually hunt prey. This may sound strange to some, but believe it or not, it does serve a purpose. There is

Gut Loading Your Feeder Fishes

Just as we gut load insects, the same can be done with feeder fishes. Gut loading provides an excellent source of various nutrients that can be effectively passed along to your fishes. Begin by selecting several high-quality flake foods, and offer small amounts of each until the fishes' bellies are slightly distended. Then, wait approximately ten to fifteen minutes for digestion of the flaked food to get under way. After that, gently net out the number of feeder fishes you wish to offer your predator and feed them right away. Always be careful to only offer a few at a time so as not to cause your fish to choke. Feeding gut loaded feeder fishes has many benefits, including enhanced color, vigor, and breeding possibilities. Remember to feed your fishes responsibly.

rainy season, but usually they will feed on whatever they come across or are able to hunt down.

When feeding live fishes, it is beneficial to feed a variety of different kinds. Including various species in the diet of predatory fishes will allow a wider diversity of nutrients and minerals in different quantities to be consumed. This is very effective when you collect your own food fishes, since different species may be feeding on different organisms at that particular time of year. However, as when feeding collected insects, use extreme caution with the feeding of live fishes that you have collected from local waters. They may have pollutants in them that will cause your fishes distress.

Along with the pros come the cons. The feeding of live fishes can be harmful for the following reasons:

Diseases

The most common problem associated with the feeding of live fishes is that of disease transmission. Diseases are passed along in several ways, but the most common method is by exposure to external parasites. Some of the most common are the protozoan diseases, such as *Ichthyophthirius* (Ick / Ich) and *Chilodonella*. Infestations of these pathogens are evidenced by white spots and thickening gray mucus.

Fishes will contract such parasites more readily if they are stressed, and in some cases the outbreaks are so bad that the fishes may succumb to them or a secondary infection, usually bacterial, that takes advantage of the weakened state of the immune system. Large predatory catfishes, such as those within *Pseudoplatystoma* and *Phractocephalus,* are especially susceptible. Certainly there are other ailments that can result from the feeding of live fishes, but the majority of the time you will be dealing with parasitic infestations.

Choking

Believe it or not, fishes can choke. If a fish attempts to swallow a fish that is too large or too spiny, it runs the risk of choking to death. While this is not very common, it does happen with captive predatory fishes that are fed infrequently. When food is offered to them, they often

attempt to swallow too much at one time. Be sure to feed predatory fishes with small, easy-to-swallow feeders at regular intervals with other foods so as to help prevent such ravenous eating and, consequently, the possible choking and death of your prized show pieces.

Failure to Adapt to Other Foods

Predatory fishes that are fed exclusively on live feeders will often fail to adapt when other types of foods are offered. They get stuck in a routine of feeding exclusively on live fishes, and they become trained to eat only such as food. Of course, this failure to adapt to other foods can be broken, but it is often labor intensive on the hobbyist's part.

On the other hand, there are times when such a failure to adapt may be a good thing. This is especially true with those fishes that are known to need to eat live fishes to thrive in captivity. Most of the species that fall into such a category are marine fishes, but nevertheless, much of the information we have about them can be applied to freshwater fishes as well.

One of the best examples of fishes that are very difficult to train to accept non-living foods are the Peacock Cichlids of South America (*Cichla* spp.). These fishes are known piscivores (fish-eaters) and notoriously picky eaters. Wild-collected specimens will often refuse non-living foods until they slowly wither away and starve to death. Luckily, captive-produced specimens of all *Cichla* species seem to be more accepting of non-living foods and can be successfully maintained for long periods of time without ever eating a living fish.

Obtaining feeder fishes is best done through your local pet shop. As with nearly all other living foods, their supplies of feeder fishes are generally fresh and from good stock. The use of a quarantine aquarium is always recommended when purchasing live fishes to be used as food. This is important simply so you are able to observe the feeders prior to offering them to your predator. Also, if a disease is recognized, you will then be able to take appropriate steps with the quarantine of this group *before* you feed them to your fishes.

Crustaceans

In addition to *Daphnia* and Brine Shrimp, there are many other crustaceans that are suitable for use as fish food. Most of the time we use crustaceans that have either been cooked or frozen as food, but once in a while an offering of live ones will be accepted with gusto by your fishes. Unfortunately, many of these animals are relatively expensive or rarely available, so their use is usually quite limited anyway.

Of all the crustaceans that are out there, two types (many species within each type) come to

Procambrus clarkii Large fishes like Oscars and Red Devils will appreciate offerings of crawfishes from time to time.

mind as the best for feeding to your fishes—Crawfishes and Grass Shrimps.

Crawfishes

Other wise known as Crayfish, Crawdads, and Mud Bugs, these organisms make fantastic foods for any fish that can eat them. There are many species; only a few are really common in the aquarium trade, but certainly there are quite a number of others that you can collect yourself. They do well when maintained in an aquarium that is kept cool and dark as long as they are adequately fed. Otherwise, they will slowly cannibalize one another.

Preparing these crustaceans to feed to your fish as live food is very easy. Gut load them the same as you would gut load feeder fishes and allow them to begin digestion for approximately ten minutes or so. Remove the crustaceans from the tank and offer them to your fishes. Adequately-sized Oscars and other robust cichlids are particularly fond of Crawfishes.

Procambrus alleni Watch out for the formidable claws on those crawdads! Clip them off before feeding if you think they may cause harm to your fishes

Cherax sp. Some of the larger species of crawfish are referred to as "lobsters." For example, this species is known as the Australian Blue Lobster in many pet shops.

Grass Shrimps

The term "Grass Shrimp" is a catch-all name for many shrimps. They are characteristically transparent in nature, and their internal structures are very visible, a useful feature when gut loading them. They are not difficult to maintain, but they are nearly impossible to culture with any high degree of success.

If you live near a shoreline, you can easily collect these creatures yourself, but inlanders will have to rely on ordering them through local fish shops, since many do not regularly stock them. Those who collect their own Grass Shrimps should use clean containers and pumps that offer a good supply of vigorous circulation, as these crustaceans do not do well in oxygen-poor water. Also, when transporting them, be sure to have something for the shrimps to cling to. They are extremely reliant on structure and will stress out and die if they are forced to cling to each other.

Holding aquariums for Grass Shrimps should be simple and, like their transport containers, well oxygenated. One thing that Grass Shrimps seem to need a lot of is food. Feeding several times daily will ensure that they stay healthy and leave each other alone. Hungry shrimps often eat each other.

Grass Shrimps alone are highly nutritious but just as with other foods, they should be supplemented with a high-quality prepared food. Various flake foods are the most common supplement offered to these organisms. Since their bodies are clear, you can see the food in their gut just after it is consumed. This is very useful in determining when the shrimps are ready to be served to your fishes. All you have to do is wait until they have taken in the desired foods, in the amount that suits you, and then remove, rinse, and feed.

As with Crawfishes, feeding Grass Shrimps to your fish is relatively easy, but depending on your source from which you obtained them, they may need to have some salt added to their water to simulate a brackish-water environ-

Macrobranchium acanthurus Some freshwater shrimps make interesting display creatures as well. This Freshwater Blue Shrimp is a perfect example.

ment. If this is the case, you should consider giving them a brief rinse in clean fresh water or water from the aquarium before offering them. This is actually a good idea with any food organism, but it is not practiced very often.

FRESH FOODS

Fresh foods are generally defined as any foods that are not living, have not been frozen, and have not been processed in any way other than field dressing or cleaning. Fresh foods are perhaps the best types of food available to hobbyists today. In nearly every case, freshly collected foods offer all of the pros of live foods with hardly any of the cons.

Plant Matter

Many hobbyists will gather various fresh foods in order to formulate their own prepared foods, such as pellets or flakes. However, you can use these raw ingredients on their own.

Palaemonetes sp. Grass shrimps are an excellent source of protein and amino acids for fishes large enough to consume them.

Spirulina algae

For example, are used to gut load Brine Shrimp, which in turn are then fed to your fishes. Well, *Spirulina* is offered in various forms, and the form we feed to Brine Shrimp is only one. You can also get *Spirulina* raw, although it is costly, and this can be fed to vegetarian fishes, such as those within *Tropheus* or *Petrochromis*.

The same goes for other algae. Probably the best-known types are those used to wrap sushi. These are referred to as Nori. This alga is available through retailers who specialize in sushi. Sometimes it may be found in grocery stores and food markets, but the freshest is commonly found in oriental markets. Many fishes will relish these algae, especially seawater species.

Various other forms of fresh plant matter can be obtained and used for feeding fishes. Many tropical fish wholesalers who import the various Loricariids from South America often feed fresh zucchini, romaine lettuce, and squash to their fishes. Fresh grapes are sometimes used for the feeding of large Pacu (*Colossoma* spp.); even some piranhas will consume grapes, although it is relatively uncommon.

Red Meats

When most hobbyists think of fresh foods, they think of various types of meats. Red meats such as steak, hamburger, tenderloin, and stew meat all have their place in the diets of animals, but few fish will do well when these types of foods are offered to them. In most cases you will be far better off sticking with the tried-and-true diets that are commercially available or just sticking with known fish foods in general.

Occasional feedings of just about any red meat can be beneficial. However, a constant supply of red meats will do nothing except make your fishes obese and foul their water, particularly because of the greasiness of the meats.

These foods are very high in fat and have small blood vessels all throughout. If not drained before being added to the aquarium, the blood in these vessels will make a real mess, spreading all throughout the water and causing a horribly foul odor.

Fowl and Pork (white meats)

While white meats do not have the high number of blood vessels that red meats do, they are just as greasy. If you were to dangle a small strip of chicken in your aquarium, you would immediately notice a ring of oil radiating from it. It would appear as a bluish or rainbow-colored slick along the surface of the water.

Aquariums where white meat have been fed in large amounts will have a greasy coating on the walls. This coating is harmful and can trigger a sudden spike in the nitrogenous compounds of the aquarium, which causes water quality problems. Along with the decrease in water quality comes the increase in odor. Just as with red meats, white meats foul the water extremely fast, necessitating heavy water changes in order to get the aquarium back in balance.

Nevertheless, hobbyists still offer such foods to their beloved fishes. This is probably more out of curiosity to see whether the fishes will actually eat them then to diversify their diets. If you are going to offer such foods, make sure they have been thoroughly washed, and offer them in bite-sized pieces or smaller, so as not to allow too many chances for them to come into contact with the water. Feed white meats very sparingly.

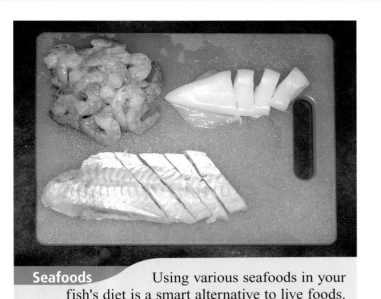

Seafoods Using various seafoods in your fish's diet is a smart alternative to live foods.

Seafoods

Out of all the groups of "fresh" foods, seafoods are by far the most useful to a tropical fish hobbyist. This group contains dozens of options. Also, many of these animals are the foundation for the majority of the well-respected and effective prepared foods currently on the market. Some are better than others, especially for freshwater fish species, and those will be outlined here.

Seafoods can be broken down into the following categories: red fish meats, pink fish meats, white fish meats, dark fish meats, shellfish, and squid. These are rough categories and the nomenclature of these may be interpreted differently by different people. What follows is a very general outline of what is contained in each category. Always explore the use of other seafoods when they become available. If you have questions or concerns about the suitability of a particular seafood, ask someone from your local fish club or pet shop.

Red Fish Meats

Tuna, Mako Shark, and Swordfish are among others included in the red fish meats category. These meats have nutritional value, but they may share some of the less attractive properties of red mammal meats. Generally, the biggest complaint is their price, since they are relatively expensive. They are also exceedingly greasy and may cause major water fouling. Use sparingly and only with fishes capable of ingesting the entire piece offered to them. Also, be sure to rinse thoroughly before offering them to your fishes.

Pink Fish Meats

The two most common types of pink fish meat are various Salmon species and Orange Roughy. Salmon are now farm-raised in good supply and can be purchased relatively inexpensively. Orange Roughy is exclusively a marine species and has good nutritional value. As with red meats, feed sparingly and offer only as much as your fish will be able to consume in one feeding.

Shrimp Shrimp provide an excellent source of vitamins and nutrients for your fish.

White Fish Meats

The largest group of fish meats is the white fish. There are many species that are generally of good quality and have significant nutritional value. Most are also cheap, which makes them that much more appealing, since most hobbyists do not wish to spend as much on dinner for the fishes as they spend on dinner for their families.

> ## Some of the best white fish meats are found in the following fishes:
>
> - Tilapia
> - Catfish
> - Trout*
> - Striped Bass
> - Flounder
> - Fluke
> - Sea Bass
> - Blackfish (Tautog)
> - Snapper
> - Grouper
> - Dolphin**
> - Walleye
>
> * Trout is perhaps one of the greasiest of all fishes even though it is considered a white fish meat. Use caution and, for best results, feed as you would red fish meats.
>
> ** Indicates the use of the fish, not the marine mammal.

Dark Fish Meats

If you have ever cleaned a Bluefish, Striped Bass, or other large gamefish, you have probably noticed a strip of dark meat just under the main fillet and along the vertebral column. This is dark fish meat, and it is an excellent source of protein and nutrients for your aquarium fishes. However, it is very similar in makeup to red fish meat and can be just as dangerous to water quality. So follow all warnings regarding the use of red fish meat, and apply them to dark fish meat, too.

Certainly such a list is just a start. Explore other fishes and see what works for you. Also, many fishes are only available seasonally, so you will have to make arrangements for a replacement species in case your staple is out of season for a while.

Shellfishes and Squid

Another broad group that encompasses many species is the shellfish group. Shellfishes are best served slightly cooked (especially crabmeat), but some are quite easy to use raw and fresh out of the sea, like clams, scallops, oysters, and mussels. The vast majority of these foods are more suitable for use with seawater fishes, but those freshwater species that accept them usually do quite well with them. Such foods round out a diet very nicely.

Shellfishes suitable for use as fish foods include, but are not limited to:

- Crabs
- Crawfishes
- Lobsters
- Shrimps
- Scallops
- Clams
- Mussels
- Oysters
- Snails
- Whelks
- Conchs
- Urchins

Shellfishes should be fed in moderation. They are very rich and will fill out a fish very fast. Many species that consume them regularly in the aquarium will put on a lot of weight, and they can even become obese on constant feedings. This is especially true with clams and scallops. Crab meat seems to be a little lighter and less likely to unduly increase obesity.

Squid (and Octopus to some extent) are used heavily in the diets of freshwater aquarium species. While

squid is moderately nutritional as a whole animal, often hobbyists are able to buy only the tough, white outer body as strips or minced up and frozen in cubes.

If possible, try to obtain fresh, whole squid and blend with some water and other seafoods to make your own fresh seafood mixture. Strain to size, and feed your fishes to satiation. Doing this once or twice a week will really add to the diet and improve the coloration and vigor of any aquarium species that will eat it.

Fresh foods should be worked into the diets of all aquarium fishes, both freshwater and marine. They are highly nutritious and have many benefits. The only real drawback is that they spoil quickly. Always buy them as fresh as possible and use immediately. You can freeze leftover portions for future use.

FROZEN FOODS

Many of the foods listed above are also available in frozen form. Generally, frozen foods have the same overall nutritional value as live or fresh foods, but they are easier to store since you can keep them in your freezer. However, the longer they are frozen, the less nutritional they become. This is primarily due to the crystalline structure of ice and the damage the ice does to the cells of the food.

Frozen foods are only good for so long. Usually it is recommended that you keep a package of frozen food no longer than one month before replacing it with another, fresher package—and even that is stretching it. Frozen foods that have been exposed to air at least twice weekly, from pulling out the package to break off a piece of food, will begin to show signs of "dry rot." This is the condition where the very cold dry air in the freezer dries out the frozen food to the point that it becomes useless.

Helpful Hints to Feeding Frozen Foods

Feeding frozen foods is highly recommended due to their diversity and freshness. Most frozen foods are easily broken into smaller pieces and can therefore be stored and thawed in individual packages so as to not expose the whole lot to air on a daily basis. They have to be fed in a way that is safe for your fishes.

To feed a piece of frozen food to your fish, simply place the piece to be fed in a small volume of water taken directly from the aquarium. Next, allow the food to thaw completely, stirring gently so as not to break up the food too much. Thawing usually takes 15 minutes or so. Then, gently strain all of the water out of the thawing container by pouring the contents of the container through an appropriately-sized net or actually removing the food by hand. In the case of larger foods like whole fish or shrimp, rinse the foods in clean tank water before offering them. Formulations should be added slowly to prevent overfeeding, as should smaller foods like Mysid Shrimp and Brine Shrimp. Only feed as much as your fish will actively consume and not let hit the bottom of the aquarium. Feed frozen foods often, but when possible, alternate them with a high-quality prepared food

Formulas

Since many types of frozen foods have already been spoken about in the two previous sections, we will now focus on the area of frozen formulations. These are foods that have undergone some form of processing and have been frozen.

Most formulas are made up of bits of raw fish, shrimp, clams, and algae. Some are made entirely up of algae and others entirely of fish. Different types are marketed for different fishes. Some are recommended only for marine angelfishes, some only for herbivores, others strictly for bottom-feeders, and so on.

Feeding these formulas is often beneficial but also quite messy. They usually have bits in them that are many different sizes. While this variation is good because it allows multiple-sized fishes to eat the same food, it is problematic because the pieces will likely end up all over the tank if the fish are too large to eat them all. Larger fishes usually ignore food particles that are too small to be worth the effort of ingesting.

When using these formulations, be sure to not only keep them in the wrapper they come in from the pet shop but also to wrap them in something else, such as a plastic sandwich bag. This will help keep the freezer burn out and the nutrients in. Even though the food is frozen, it may still have an odor. This is especially true with the formulations that are intended for use with carnivorous fishes. Sealing them in a plastic sandwich bag will help prevent any odors from being released and possibly contaminating your other foods.

Some hobbyists will break off pieces of frozen formulations and wrap them individually. Such a practice is great for preventing freezer burn, since only the packages that are going to be used for each feeding will be removed from the freezer for thawing out. Of course, trial and error will play a large part in deciphering how much food is suitable at any given feeding. When in doubt, always follow the manufacturer's directions.

If you collect your own living foods and you happen to harvest more than you think you can keep alive, freezing is a good alternative for you. To freeze extra live foods, simply rinse them appropriately and remove as much water from them as possible. Then slip them into a sturdy plastic freezer bag, flatten out the bag into what is referred to as a "flat pack," and freeze.

Many organisms are suitable for freezing for future use. Green water is especially good, since it can simply be frozen into ice cubes. To do this, siphon the Green water into a container suitable for pouring, add it to ice cube trays, and freeze. The ice cubes can then be broken out of the trays and stored in freezer bags for future use.

Unique Frozen Foods

There are many foods that are only offered frozen. These foods are often very difficult to culture or trans-

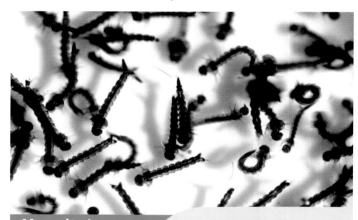

Mosquito Larvae Mosquito larvae are most commonly available to hobbyists in either the freeze-dried or frozen forms.

Bloodworms The "bloodworms" we are all familiar with are actually Chironomid Midge larvae.

Copepods Copepods can be fed to small fishes or fish fry with great success.

port alive, rare in nature, or only cultured by a select few companies or individuals. Below is a list of some unique frozen foods that are highly recommended to help vary a staple diet of more common and suitable items. Such foods include, but are not limited to the following:

- Black Mosquito Larvae
- White Mosquito Larvae / Glass Worms
- Blood Worms / Midge Larvae
- Glass Eels
- Sea Urchin
- Copepods
- *Gammarus* Shrimp
- Mysid Shrimp
- Fish Eggs (Roe)
- Beef Heart
- Brine Shrimp
- Baby Brine Shrimp
- Enriched Brine Shrimp
- *Daphnia*
- *Tubifex* Worms
- Mixed Marine Algae
- Marine Sponge

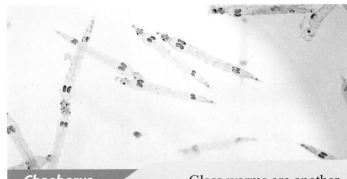

Mosquito Eggs Mosquito eggs are sometimes found in small mats or "racks."

Chaoborus Glass worms are another organism that can be used to round out a fish's diet.

Certainly there are many more frozen foods available, and a trip to the frozen food section of your local pet shop is highly recommended. Some distributors have their own packaging and unique line of foods that they offer as exclusives. These types of foods (usually mixtures) are often good and very fresh, so don't be afraid to try them.

Freeze-dried Foods

Some organisms are best stored when they go through a process known as lyophilization or "freeze drying." These organisms are preserved whole, in their original configuration and with nearly all of their essential nutrients intact. However, such foods can be expensive compared with their frozen counterparts. Nearly all foods offered as "freeze dried" are also offered as live, fresh, and frozen, so you do have options.

One species that is not offered as live, somewhat regularly offered as frozen, and very commonly offered as freeze dried is Krill. Krill are small shrimp-like creatures that inhabit the cold sub-arctic waters of both the northern and southern hemi-

Freeze-dried Foods

Many types of freeze-dried foods will stick to the glass walls of the aquarium.

spheres. They are rich in nutrients and provide outstanding color-enhancing characteristics with their potent alpha- and beta-carotenes.

Feeding a wide variety of foods to your fishes is always the best choice. If you have freezers available, perhaps you should opt to use more of the frozen foods, but if not, don't be discouraged. As with most things, each type of food has their loyal supporters, but in the end, variety is the key.

PREPARED FOODS

Nearly all of the foods available to modern hobbyists are prepared in some way or another. In actuality, even frozen and freeze-dried foods are prepared foods, but we treat them differently due to the vastness of this category. Instead, we will cover several types of foods that are traditionally considered to be prepared. Such foods are flaked foods, pelleted foods, wafers, and liquid foods.

Flaked Foods

There is perhaps no other type of fish food that comes close to flaked (or flake) foods in terms of numbers of containers produced and sold. Flake foods have been around for decades. Many brands and formulations have come and gone, with some being better in quality than others.

Flake foods are the most popular food available to hobbyists, both fresh and marine. They come in an assortment of colors, compositions, textures, and sizes. In fact, a can of flake food is often one of the first things a new hobbyist picks up.

Is flake food necessarily the best choice of food to feed your fishes? Flake foods are not bad, and many are in fact very good, but they should be fed with the same knowledge and care as all decisions about nutrition should be made.

There are two main problems with flake foods. The first problem is their ability to settle into every little nook and cranny in your aquarium and begin to decay. Such decomposition leads to poor water quality and is the basis for future disasters. This is one reason why you need to pay careful attention to how much food you are offering your fishes and make sure that too much does not hit the substrate of your aquarium.

The second problem with flake foods is their nutrient reliability. Many flake foods are quite nutritious when they are first opened, but when they are repeatedly opened day after day (sometimes multiple times daily) they lose their nutritive value rather quickly. For this reason, it is strongly recommended that you use a single flake food for no longer than two or three months. After that time, discard the can and buy a new one. Such a practice may waste some food and maybe a few dollars, but in the end it will be worth it. Furthermore, the vitamins and nutrients in flake foods are greatly diminished or lost once the flakes become waterlogged.

In addition to being of higher quality, another thing that flake foods have going for them is their diversity. There are flake foods formulated out of just about everything.

Little fishes usually have little mouths and therefore need smaller foods to feed on. Unfortunately most insects are too big for fishes such as tetras, barbs, danios, and rasboras but flake foods that are formulated with insects are the perfect size for their tiny mouths. Only with a prepared food can we add such things as earthworms, tubifex worms, and crickets to our feeding regimen.

Such foods are not often found, but when they are they should be purchased because insects are an outstanding source of natural vitamins and minerals for fishes. Just as some frozen foods fall under the unique category, we have some flake foods that deserve the same treatment. If it can be added to a paste, it can become an ingredient in flake foods. Some unique flaked foods include (with their targeted benefits):

- Earthworms
  (unique nutrients)
- Tubifex Worms
  (unique nutrients)
- Crickets (insect nutrients)
- Bee Pollen
  (color enhancement)
- *Spirulina* Powder (color and vigor enhancement)
- Beef heart
  (weight-gaining properties)
- Chicken (unique nutrients)
- Liver (iron)
- Bone Meal (extra calcium)
- Bananas (potassium)
- Blood Meal
  (color enhancement /appetite stimulant)
- Krill Meal (color enhancement)
- Marine Sponges
  (unique range of vitamins)
- Marine Algae (color enhancement)

As you can see, the list is quite long, and this just barely scratches the surface of what hobbyists and professionals alike have done with the art of making flake foods. As with all foods, variation is the key, and it is strongly recommended that you vary the diet of your fishes as often as possible. The next time you are at your local fish shop, check out the ingredients of several flake foods before you buy just one.

Pelleted Foods and Wafers

Like flake foods, pelleted foods are available in a huge assortment of colors, compositions, textures, and sizes. However, unlike flake foods, pellets seem to hold their nutritional value longer, so the fish ingests a more nutrient-packed piece of food.

Pellets can be harmful in aquariums with brisk water movement. Just like flakes, pellets have a tendency to find every possible spot to fall into and begin decaying. Watch out for this when feeding, and only feed a few at a time. After they have been consumed, add a few more. If you have very aggressive fishes, perhaps a few automatic feeders set to go off at the same time will suit you better. After all, no fish can be in two places at once. Placing one at each end of the aquarium is the best alternative in this situation. For very large aquariums (more than 8 feet in length), three or even four automatic feeders are recommended.

One very nasty trait of pellets is that they expand after ingestion. Flakes do this, too, but to a much lesser extent. Being dry, or nearly dry, pellets take in water and expand. The same happens to a piece of dog food kibble that falls into the dog's water bowl. Fish do not compensate for this expansion right away, and it can cause them great distress. So you must take such a potential problem into account. This is more reason not to overfeed your fishes!

Wafers are flattened pellets that are usually formulated for bottom-feeders, since they most often sink. There are several types on the market. One type is made out of a vegetarian-based formula and intended to provide herbivores with a quick and easy meal after the lights go

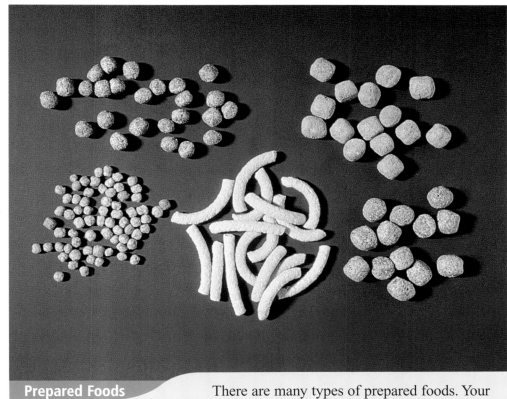

There are many types of prepared foods. Your local aquarium shop can help you pick the right types for your needs.

so, such a practice can be perhaps the most rewarding experience next to breeding your fishes. To know that you are providing a meal to your fishes that you created out of your own research and understanding of fish nutrition is something to be proud of.

To get started, you will need a blending tool (blender, grinder, chopper), the raw ingredients, a binding agent such as a gelatin-based binder, and vitamins or supplements to give your homemade food some nutritive kick.

Your raw ingredients can come from many sources. When possible, it is probably best to use organisms like squid, clams, shrimp, and other seafoods. These are generally going to give you the most value for your dollar in terms of nutritional value. The vitamins and any supplements you choose to add can come from a veterinarian or from an aquaculture supply house. In some instances they can be found at your local grocery store, but check with a board-certified veterinarian who specializes in fish medicine or an aquaculturist for the best places to obtain these additives.

out, and the others are designed for carnivorous fishes. All types are offered in multiple sizes and a few shapes. The majority are flattened, pancake-like disks, but there are also star-shaped pellets. They all serve the same purpose and add a little more variety to a fish's diet.

Homemade Foods

If you are the adventurous type and enjoy cooking or food preparation, feel free to experiment with the endless possibilities of formulating your own fish foods. Depending on just how far you want to take this endeavor and how much time you have to spend doing

Mix the contents together and strain to preferred size, if possible. This can be done with cheese cloth or strainers available in food stores. Different-sized bits are good for different sized fishes.

The mash can then be fed immediately to the fishes, or if you prepare this mixture in bulk, you should

When feeding fishes in a community aquarium, be sure to feed enough for all to eat their fair share.

from the concepts of others just as they individually differ based on our own unique experiences. (This section is a hybrid of the concepts of two hobbyists and scientists with a combined fish-base of knowledge spanning over half a century).

By now, you should have a good grasp of what foods to use in what quantities and when to feed them. Feeding your fishes is a rewarding experience. It is something that families should participate in together. Whether it is once or three times a day, young people should be included, because it is something that is educational and takes time to learn how to do properly. It is a science as well as an art.

Generally, fishes should be fed daily. However, such a generalization is marked with controversy right from the start and needs to be made more specific. So what if we said that community fishes need to be fed daily, but predatory fishes need to be fed three times weekly? This is a little better, but what if we have community of predatory fishes?

To further complicate matters, what about opportunistic predatory fishes or fishes that would not consume another animal unless it was there for the taking? Are tetras predatory? Not in the general sense, but they do prey on water fleas.

What we are getting at here is that all fish are basically predatory in one sense or another. This is an

freeze the remaining portions either in cubes or small packets for later use. Some hobbyists prefer to dry their mixtures out while others prefer to make meatballs out of them. Whatever you do, make sure the mixture stays as fresh as possible, and do not add too large of a quantity to your aquarium at any one time.

GENERAL FEEDING CONCEPTS

A concept is an abstract or generic idea that has been generalized from a particular experience or instance. The feeding concepts mentioned here will likely differ

important concept to learn and understand. The feeding of fishes has more to do with opportunity and metabolism than anything else.

The fish's opportunity to eat depends largely on you, the hobbyist, and when you are going to offer them food. More often than not, they will eat—or try to eat—whatever you put in front of them. This can be good and bad. It's especially bad when you make a conscious decision to feed them the wrong foods and less of it than their body is telling them they need. It can be good when you make a similar decision and offer them the right foods in the right amounts at the right times.

Let's break this down a little further to provide as much clarification as possible. Remember, these are guidelines to how to feed your fishes, not laws. Your results may be different, and you will need to compensate on many levels, including the temperature you keep your aquarium at, the size of the container or aquarium you have, the stocking density or overall biomass of the aquarium, and the types of fishes you are maintaining.

Communities of Fishes

Aquariums containing community fishes are probably the most popular of all aquariums in households today, but what defines a community? There are communities of peaceful fishes, there are communities of semi-aggressive fishes, and there are communities of aggressive fishes. The proper feeding techniques vary widely with regards to the kind of fish you are keeping.

Community Aquariums with Peaceful Fishes

When we think of peaceful fishes, we think of those that are generally harmless to one another or those that are simply not interested in territorial battles or fierce competition over food. While a school of tetras may be predatory against a swarm of *Daphnia*, they are not necessarily considered aggressive. As you will see, we can have many species that are predatory but not technically considered to be aggressive.

Most community aquariums contain an assortment of tetras, barbs, rasboras, or other small, peaceful fishes. Therefore, they need to be fed foods that are rather small in size. Most of the suitable foods for these fishes are either frozen formulas or flakes. Along with these, frozen or live *Daphnia* can be offered in moderate quantities.

Recommended frequency of feeding is highly variable. Many aquariums that have a high stocking density need to be fed at least once per day, but you have to be very careful not to overload the aquarium with too much food. Also keep in mind that more food equals more waste, and more fish means more food, which equals even more waste. As you can see, such a situation can be very tricky to navigate properly. In the end, it is better to offer less food and keep fewer fish in one aquarium.

Community Aquariums with Predatory Fishes

Just because you have a community aquarium does not mean you have to have peaceful fishes. Many large predatory fishes seem to almost have an unspoken truce between them. It seems as though they know how much damage they are capable of inflicting on each other. Small predatory fishes are very similar in terms of this type of behavior.

Whether you have a community aquarium full of small or large predatory fishes, you will need to offer food in much the same way. Feeding predatory fish is one of the thrills of the aquarium hobby. It is something that is both awesome and scary at the same time. This is especially true with larger predatory fishes, since

Lush aquariums containing beautiful fishes are the product of dedicated husbandry practices.

being more sensitive and finicky species. The truth is they are generally quite easy to keep.

In general, predatory fishes need to be fed at least three times per week. The young of most of the bigger species feed on insects and insect larvae, with a transition to larger foods as they grow. Smaller predatory fishes will consume foods that are relatively consistent in size throughout their lives.

The specifics of feeding predatory fishes should be decided on a case-by-case basis, but they all consume meaty foods that are high in protein and nutrients. With this diet comes an increase in the nutrients of the fish's waste. Therefore, special attention should always be paid to the water chemistry and overall quality. Always be sure to check the ammonia and other nitrogenous compounds in the aquarium's water, and take proactive steps to avoid potential problems.

their food is usually a lot larger. To see a full-grown snakehead strike a large feeder fish is something that nightmares are made of. Often, such a scene is the turning point or the point of no return for those hobbyists wishing to expand their horizons from the average everyday species. Many hard-core predator keepers can still remember the day they converted to the "dark side" of fishkeeping.

Predatory fishes often get special care in the sense that they are treated differently than those species that happily eat flaked foods and pellets with a dash of frozen foods once in a while. They are often thought of as

Species-specific Aquariums

Some hobbyists will set up aquariums with only one species of fish. Sometimes they are predatory, and other times they are not predatory. Regardless, these aquariums are usually the best in terms of ease of feeding for several reasons.

First, since all of the fishes are the same species, they can be offered all the same foods at the same times.

Second, with rare exceptions, all of the fish will have similar temperaments and share the same idiosyncrasies. This will allow them to understand each other better and hopefully lessen the risk of severe intraspecific aggression. Third, the fish should have similar growth rates. If one or more fish are not getting their fair share, it will be easy to recognize this and solve the problem before it gets out of hand.

Overall, fishkeepers should heavily research all fish foods before choosing a diet for their fishes. As a responsible hobbyist, you will need to provide a healthy and diverse diet so your fish will grow and thrive in captivity. There are multiple foods ranging from live microorganisms to freeze dried shrimps to flaked foods containing earthworms. Use as much of a variety as possible, and you will enjoy many years of happiness with your fishes.

Chapter 5

REPRODUCTION
IN FISHES

The survival of any species depends on the ability of its members to produce offspring and the ability of those offspring to continue the cycle by having progeny of their own.

Weak individuals or those or ill adapted to the rigors of their environment—whether a desert in the American Southwest or a Rift Lake in Africa—often perish before reaching maturity. Those strong and healthy enough to find food, escape predators, and resist disease will likely survive and eventually reproduce, passing on their traits to their offspring via their genetic code.

As a result, each species gradually evolves over many thousands of years, fine-tuning the physical and behavioral characteristics that help it to succeed in its environment and weeding out those that do not.

If you want to breed fish, it's important to understand the complex interplay between a fish and its surroundings, as well as the reproductive strategies that have evolved in response to it. That way, when problems arise, as they inevitably will, you will be able to think them through and come up with an array of possible solutions, something that will go a long way toward ensuring the success of your breeding program.

REPRODUCTIVE ANATOMY OF FISHES

As discussed in Chapter 3, there are many anatomical features that various species incorporate for various reasons. One of the biggest reasons that fishes develop unique features is for reproductive success. To accomplish this, fishes must not only alter the places they breed but they must also alter how they breed.

It is often not easy to determine the sex of fishes, mature or otherwise, using external anatomical features. In this instance, we say the fish does not exhibit a high degree of sexual **dimorphism** (differences in appearance) and, furthermore, does not exhibit sexual **dichromatism** (differences in coloration) either.

In many cichlids, sexual dimorphism is very apparent, as the males are usually much larger than the females. In most livebearers, the opposite is true, with the females being larger than the males. Mature female livebearers

Cryptoheros nigrofasciatus   Both sexual dimorphism and sexual dichromatism are apparent in the Convict Cichlids.

Cryptoheros nigrofasciatus   Female Convict Cichlids (background) are actually more colorful compared to males (foreground).

can be almost 40 percent larger than mature males of the same age class.

Just as with sexual dimorphism, sexual dichromatism is very apparent in most cichlids. Males are generally quite colorful and have striking displays of alternating colors. Of course, there are always exceptions, and the perfect example is the Convict Cichlid (*Cryptoheros nigrofasciatus*), as the female is brilliantly colored in an orange dress, while the male shows a striking black-and-white pattern.

Testes

The testes (typically paired structures) account for a combined weight of approximately 10 percent of the overall weight of a male fish during the spawning season. They are smooth structures and are often whitish or cream colored. Aquarium fishes that have been exposed to high amounts of medication, particularly copper-based medication, are often sterile due to the damage that has been inflicted by the medication.

Ovaries

Ovaries are also paired structures. The ovaries account for a combined weight of between 20 and 30 percent of the overall weight of the fish. They are large yellowish structures that are granular in appearance. As with the testes of male fishes, the ovaries can be harmed by too much medication.

Seminal Vesicle

In the Chondrichthyes (sharks, skates, and rays), sperm pass through a special duct that is shared with the kidneys. The sperm is then stored temporarily in the seminal vesicle until spawning has taken place. In teleosts, like cichlids, a seminal vesicle is lacking and specialized sperm ducts (in males) and ovipositors (in females) are present.

Intromittent Organs

The only popular aquarium fishes that have intromittent organs are the livebearers. With poeciliid fishes (gonopodium), the males have an altered anal fin that is penis-like in nature and is used to inseminate females. Unlike other reproductive organs, intromittent organs show a considerable degree of variation. This is probably due to their location outside of the body and since they are, after all, modified fins. The examination of intromittent organs is sometimes the only way to tell whether a fish is male or female.

METHODS OF REPRODUCTION

Almost all freshwater aquarium fishes reproduce sexually (by combining egg and sperm), but the process by which that occurs and the rearing of fry that follows vary widely from one species to another. Some fish are monogamous (at least during the course of a single breeding cycle), while others spawn repeatedly with numerous partners. Some guard their eggs or young, while others are seemingly oblivious to them—or even go so far as to eat them. Generally speaking, fish either lay eggs or give birth to live fry.

Livebearers

This is the reproductive strategy most comparable to human reproduction. Female livebearers produce eggs, which the male fertilizes by touching his gonopodium to her vent or releasing sperm in its vicinity. At the end of a gestational period (which varies in length according to light and water temperature), the female delivers fully developed fry.

There are a few key differences between human reproduction and livebearers reproduction. First of all, female livebearers are capable of having a lot more babies at one time—often 100 or more, depending on the species and size of the mother. Also unlike their human counterparts,

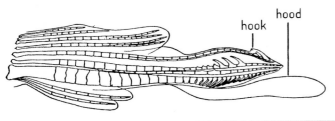

Intromittent Organ Diagrammatic representation of the gonopodium of a male Guppy (*Poecilia reticulata*).
Adopted from *Atlas of Livebearers*, T.F.H. Publications, Inc.

Xiphophorus helleri   Male Swordtails are easily recognized by the "sword" protruding outward from the ventral lobe of their caudal fin.

many female livebearers store sperm internally and, after giving birth to one batch of fry, they use the stored sperm to fertilize another batch of eggs. In fact, it's not uncommon for a female to give birth to several batches of fry over a period of several months from a single insemination. This is one of the reasons female livebearers, such as guppies and platys, sometimes have what appears to be a fatherless birth, delivering fry in tanks where there was no male present to have fathered them.

Once the fry are born, their mother's job is done. She not only does not care for the babies, but she does not even seem to recognize them as her offspring and may even try to eat them.

Some of the best-known livebearers are platys, swordtails, guppies, mollies, and the goodeids.

Egglayers

Egglaying is by far the most common means of fish reproduction. Unlike their livebearing counterparts,

egglayers do not fertilize or incubate their young internally. Rather, they release eggs and sperm into the water, and when the two come into contact with one another, fertilization takes place. Within the broad category of egg layers, however, fish employ a wide range of different reproductive strategies. Some fish scatter their eggs, while others build nests for them or deposit them on rocks, wood or plants. Other fish brood the eggs in their mouths, while a few fish even bury the eggs.

Egg Scatterers

Egg-scattering fish spawn in mid-water, where the females release eggs and the males simultaneously release a cloud of sperm, a process that can occur in less than a second, as the fish swim past one another. The breeding pair then go their separate ways, leaving their eggs to drift down through the water column and land where they may. Those that land in a protected site, such as a rock crevice, may hatch, while those

Tanichthys albonubes   White Cloud Mountain Minnows are one of the most prolific species of egg scatterers kept in aquariums today.

that land in the open are often eaten by other fish, including their own parents. To compensate for this and to ensure that some of their eggs go on to hatch and the fry grow to adulthood, fish that spawn using this strategy tend to produce large numbers of eggs, typically numbering in the hundreds or even thousands. Zebra Danios, Neon Tetras, and Bala Sharks are examples of egg-scattering fish.

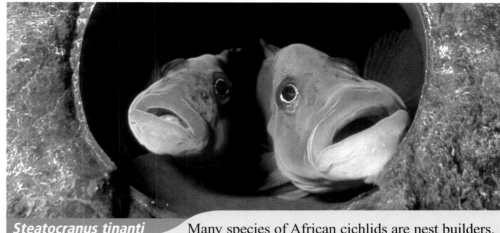

Steatocranus tinanti Many species of African cichlids are nest builders. A pair of *Steatocranus tinanti* are seen here guarding a nest.

Egg Depositors

Egg depositors deliberately seek out a site to spawn on (or in). Some are known as *plant choosers* because they spawn in clumps of vegetation, while others are called *substrate choosers* because they pick a site, such as a piece of wood or a rock, on which to lay their eggs. In the aquarium, such fish sometimes consider just about anything to be substrate, even spawning on the heater or the sides of the tank.

Males of plant-spawning species typically chase or lure the female into a clump of vegetation or a spawning mop. She then releases her eggs either all at once or a few at a time, and he simultaneously releases sperm to fertilize them. Substrate choosers frequently clean off their designated spawning site together beforehand.

Plant-spawning parents, such as rainbowfish and some species of killifish, are similar to egg scatterers in that they typically do not guard their eggs. Substrate spawners, however, sometimes do. Discus and angelfish are examples of substrate-choosing fish that guard their eggs.

Mouthbrooders

As their name indicates, mouthbrooders incubate their eggs and/or fry in their mouths to keep them safe from predators, a reproductive strategy that makes them one of the most interesting fish to breed. Typically, the process begins with the female depositing her eggs on a flat surface, such as a rock, where the male fertilizes them. One parent then gathers them in his or her mouth and incubates them.

There are several variations on this. In a few species of mouthbrooders, the female releases the eggs and picks them up immediately. The male then fertilizes them by releasing sperm into her mouth. A few species of South American cichlids allow their eggs to hatch in a nest and then gather the fry in their mouths to protect them from predators as they grow, a technique known as *delayed mouthbrooding.*

Usually, the female is the one who does the mouthbrooding. However, there are some species in which that task is relegated to the male and even a few in which both parents share the responsibility.

Cichlids are among the best-known examples of mouthbrooders, although there are other species, including a handful of bettas, which also practice this reproductive strategy.

Nest Builders

Like birds, some fish build nests in which to lay and incubate their eggs. In most cases, either the mother or father remains with them to protect them until they hatch and the fry are free swimming. Bubblenesting and pitnesting are the two different types of nesting strategies commonly employed by fish.

Bubble-nesters
These fishes construct elaborate floating nests of saliva bubbles and, in some cases, snippets of vegeta-

Betta imbellis Male Siamese Fighting Fishes construct bubble nests to assist them in attracting a mate.

tion. The breeding pair spawns directly under it, and the fertilized eggs either float into the nest or are picked up by the male and spit into it. The male then guards the nest until the fry hatch and become free swimming. Bettas and gouramis are among the best-known bubblenest builders.

Pit Nesters
Pit nesters dig holes in the substrate in which to lay their eggs. The female releases them into the nest, and the male fertilizes them there. At least one of the parents then guards the eggs, fanning fresh water over them until the fry hatch and become free swimming. Many catfish and some cichlids build pit nests in which to spawn.

Other Strategies

Some fish will only spawn in enclosed spaces, such as caves or shells. A few fish even bury their eggs to protect them. Some killifish, for instance, deposit their eggs in the mud and then die when the water dries up. The eggs remain dormant in the substrate, hatching the following year when the rainy season restores their habitat.

ENERGETICS

Similar to feeding, breeding requires a tremendous amount of energy. This is true as far as behavior but also with the production of gonadal tissue and reproductive material (eggs and sperm). Those that aren't capable of producing the required products will often perish or at least be left out of the role.

As with most living creatures, the lives of fish require a balance of the energy expended to breed, grow, swim, feed, and live in general. Such a balance is often heavily

lop-sided in aquariums but still important to be aware of, especially if you intend to breed fishes one day.

Furthermore, once fishes have spawned, their role as parents may require even more energy. Too much expulsion of vital energy resources will lead to the fishes becoming severely stressed and perhaps even perishing. Probably the best example of this is when a pair of cichlids spawns in a community setup. They are often highly devoted parents, so much so that they forget to take care of themselves. Like a human mother after giving birth to a child, female fishes need to rest and take in food after spawning so as to replace vital nutrients that were lost during egg production.

Males do not get off much easier. They also need to replace vital nutrients that were used for sperm production and mating rituals. In the end, it is common for male fishes to actually expend more energy per unit of body mass than their female partner. This is chiefly due to the attractive displays, ritualistic dances, and flutters that males of many species take part in before the actual spawning even commences.

The five general variables in the energy expenditure of reproductively active fishes are the following: reproductive effort, age of onset of reproduction, fecundity, survivorship rates, and frequency of reproduction. A key concept to understanding these factors is fitness. **Fitness** is the measurement of how likely an individual in a particular environment is to have offspring that will also reproduce successfully.

Two of the more important factors are fecundity and reproductive effort. **Fecundity** is the overall number of eggs present within the ovaries (combined) of a female fish just prior to spawning. Fecundity is the most common measurement used to determine the reproductive potential in fishes, since it is an easy measurement to make. Without going into too much detail here, fecundity increases with the size of the female fish. Consequently, a 24" long (TL) female Striped Bass (*Morone saxatilis*) is likely to produce more eggs than a smaller specimen of the same species.

The exponential relationship between the size of the fish and the fecundity count seems to hold true for many species. However, this number can be influenced by several factors, including temperature, energy exerted, egg size, frequency of spawning(s), and amount of parental care.

Reproductive effort is a measurement of the amount of energy or time put into the production of offspring. Most fisheries biologists measure the size of the reproductive organs (testes and ovaries) when they begin to investigate this index. A basic conclusion indicates that females may actually put more energy into the production of offspring based on the fact that the female's ovaries are about one third larger than male's testes at the same time in the process (Moyle & Cech, 2000).

However, as mentioned previously, it is probably the males that put more overall energy into the process. One strong argument for such a statement is the fact that the mortality of males is often considerably higher than that of females. Of course, such a factor does not include the punishment that many males exert on their females mates before, during, and after spawning periods.

THE BREEDER'S ROLE

Now that you know something about the reproductive strategies of fish, let's talk about the role that you, the hobbyist, play in getting them to reproduce. The most important thing to remember in this regard is that you don't really breed your fish. They breed themselves—as long as you provide them with a compatible mate of reproductive age, the right environment, and the diet they need to stay healthy. Let's consider these factors separately.

The Right Mate

Fish reproduce sexually, so obviously you'll need at least one male and one female of a given species in order to breed them. What's not always so obvious, however, is which fish are males and which are females.

Every species on earth, fish included, has what are known as **primary sex characteristics**, that is, body structures specific to reproduction, such as ovaries and testicles. The problem is that with some species the only way to see them is to dissect the fish.

Trichogaster leeri

Female Pear Gouramis do not show the intense red-breasted region and longer, pointed dorsal fins of the males.

That means aquarists must rely on **secondary sex characteristics**—sex-linked physical traits other than the reproductive organs—to distinguish between male and female fish. In humans, secondary sex characteristics include breasts in women and facial hair in men. In fish, secondary sex characteristics can include size, body shape, coloration, markings, fin shape, and behavior.

Some fish are dimorphic, meaning that it is easy to tell males and females apart by their secondary sex characteristics. Male pearl gouramis have red breasts and long, pointed dorsal fins, while females have shorter, more rounded dorsal fins and silvery breasts. Male Bristlenose Catfish have much larger bristles than females. And males and females of many species of livebearers can be distinguished by differences in their anal fins. Those of females (and juveniles) are fan shaped, while those of males thicken and fuse as they mature to form what is known as a gonopodium—a tube-like copulatory organ used for internal fertilization of the female.

Unfortunately, not all fish display such obvious sex-linked characteristics. In some species, males and females resemble one another so closely that even the most skilled aquarists cannot tell them apart. Neon Tetras, for example, are extremely difficult to sex, although some aquarists say they are able to tell the difference by examining the fish in profile, because the females have deeper, more rounded bellies than the males, who have a straighter line from jaw to tail. However, that's not a perfect predictor, since a well-fed male and an undernourished female could easily be confused with one another.

In other words, a certain percentage of fish fail to spawn because the aquarist has unwittingly paired two males or two females. In some such cases, the drive to reproduce is so strong that the fish court one another anyway, and in the case of two females, may even lay eggs. The poor aquarist is then left scratching his or her head, wondering why no fry resulted from what appeared to be such a vigorous courtship.

Males and females of some difficult-to-sex species, including many African cichlids, can be distinguished from one another through a process known as "venting." It involves removing the fish from the water and turning it upside down to examine the shape of its genital pore, a small pimple-like structure located between the anus and the tail. In females, the genital pore is typically shorter and wider than it is in males. However, the differences can be quite subtle and difficult to determine without repeatedly comparing fish to each other. Since being removed from the water is stressful for fish, the process must be carried out quickly and efficiently and is usually best left to experienced breeders.

An easier way to solve the problem of identifying difficult-to-sex fish is by buying a group of at least a half dozen juveniles, ensuring a better-than-90-percent chance of having a mix of both males and females as long as the group is roughly 50 percent males and 50 percent females to begin with. You can then raise the fish together, allowing them to pair off naturally. It is usually evident when they have done so, particularly in fish such as cichlids that form strong pair bonds, because the male and female stake out a territory together and drive other fish away from it.

The other thing to remember when selecting compatible breeding pairs is that the reproductive life of a fish, like that of humans, has a beginning and an end. Some loaches, for example, appear to be fully grown at about one year, but they will rarely spawn before they are two or three years old. And most bettas stop reproducing by the time they're about 14 months old.

The Right Environment

Let's examine how a fish's environment affects its likelihood of spawning. There are three elements to consider:

- The physical setup—the tank and items placed in it, such as plants or rocks
- The chemistry of the water
- Triggers or specific environmental signals that tell the fish it's time to breed.

Some fish aren't fussy about any of the above. Many livebearers, for instance, will breed just about anywhere anytime. However, other fish are so finicky that, if they're placed in a tank that makes them feel cramped or water that doesn't have just the right pH, they'll refuse to spawn. Some species also require a little extra nudge in the form of an environmental change—a sudden decrease or increase in temperature, for instance—to jump start the breeding cycle. Let's examine these elements individually.

Physical Setup

Fish, like all living creatures, are products of their environment. Over thousands of years, they have evolved physically and behaviorally to meet the demands of their surroundings. Of necessity, they've adapted their reproductive strategies to those surroundings, as well. After all, it wouldn't do any good to be a plant spawner if home were the rocky depths of Africa's Lake Tanganyika.

Keep in mind that in order to spawn fish successfully, you'll need to provide your fish with the elements that are key to the breeding process in their native habitat, whether that means thickets of plants (or their artificial equivalent), flat rocks on which to lay their eggs, substrate in which to dig nests, or caves in which to spawn.

Water Quality

Not all water is the same. If you sent samples of tap water from New York City, Des Moines, Iowa, and Pasadena, California, to a lab for analysis, the results would be very different. That's because water contains much more than just hydrogen and oxygen molecules. It can also contain varying amounts of heavy metals, dissolved minerals, gases, nitrogen compounds, gases, and chemicals such as chlorine, not to mention organic and inorganic pollutants.

The point isn't to turn this chapter into Water Quality 101. If you've been keeping fish long enough to consider breeding them, you're already aware of the important role water plays in the health and well being of your fish. But it is worth looking at the impact some properties of water can have on the breeding process, because fish that usually aren't fussy about the water you keep them in can get downright finicky when it's time for spawning. In addition, the presence of certain compounds in the water can be damaging to the eggs or fry.

Symphysodon sp. "domesticated" Discus can be very picky about where they lay their eggs. This pair has chosen the leaf of a large plant in a community aquarium for their egglaying site.

The following are some of the properties of water that can affect your success as a breeder:

Nitrogen Compounds

When organic materials, such as fish waste and uneaten food, break down in aquarium water, they produce nitrogen-based compounds, such as ammonia, nitrites and nitrates. If you've been keeping fish for even a short time, you probably already know that the presence of even small amounts of ammonia and nitrites in the water is stressful to them. What you may not know is that eggs and fry are even more sensitive than adult fish and may be stunted or die if levels are even a little bit elevated. So it's important to make sure there is no trace of ammonia or nitrite in breeding or

rearing tanks and to make sure nitrates stay within acceptable limits. The best way to reduce nitrates is to do a water change. The best way to prevent ammonia and nitrites is to use a mature filter in the tanks, do regular water changes, and test the water frequently.

pH

This is a measure of the acidity or alkalinity of water. The pH scale runs from 1 to 14, with 7.0 considered neutral. Water with a higher pH is referred to as basic or alkaline, and water with a lower pH is referred to as acidic. Each fish species has a preferred pH range it is most comfortable in, although many can adapt to a higher or lower pH. But just because they can live in it doesn't mean they'll breed in it. Because of the way fish have evolved in their native habitats, the pH at which they'll spawn is often somewhat lower than their "everyday" pH, and they're less likely to be flexible about it. In addition, pH can affect the male-to-female ratio of some species of fry. For instance, rainbowfish that breed in acidic water often produce more males, while alkaline water produces more females.

If you wish to breed fish that prefer a pH lower than that of your tap water, you can alter it using a variety of methods, such as filtering the water over peat (be sure to use aquarium-grade peat, since the peat available in garden centers may contain harmful fertilizers), bubbling carbon dioxide into the water, or using commercial compounds such as humic acid extracts, which are available at your aquarium shop.

Fish rarely require a pH higher than their normal range in which to breed. However, if you wish to keep fish that prefer water more alkaline than that of your tap, you can increase it by adding oyster shells or rocks containing limestone or by adding baking soda.

Hardness

This is a measure of the dissolved mineral salts, particularly calcium carbonate and magnesium carbonate, present in water. These salts, which occur naturally in the earth, dissolve when they come into contact with the water in underground springs. The quantity in the water depends on where it comes from and the treatment processes it undergoes. Water with a high proportion of dissolved minerals is called "hard," and water with a low proportion is called "soft."

The hardness of water is critical to breeding because it affects *osmotic pressure*—the flow of water across cell membranes. While adult fish can usually adapt to water that is harder or softer than their optimal range, their eggs and sperm often cannot. If the water is too hard, the outer membrane of a fish's eggs may toughen, hindering fertilization or preventing the eggs from hatching. If the water is too soft, the eggs and sperm may take on so much water that they literally burst.

The hardness of the water also determines its *buffering capacity*—that is, its ability to absorb acids (such as those produced by fish waste) without a drop in pH. If the buffering capacity of your water is too low, your tank may experience pH swings that could harm your fish, eggs and fry. Adding baking soda will increase the buffering capacity, but it will also raise pH. On the other hand, if your water has a high buffering capacity, you will have to go to considerable trouble to lower the pH, because the buffers will keep pushing it back up. To solve this, you can process your water through an ion exchanger that swaps magnesium carbonate and calcium carbonate for sodium (a salt that has no effect on hardness), or through a reverse osmosis unit that removes all dissolved solids from the water by filtering it through a membrane.

There are many different ways to measure and express hardness. One common scale (the one used in this book) measures it in terms of dH, or "degree of hardness," while another expresses it as gH, or "general hardness," and a third measures it in terms of parts per million, or ppm. All are equally valid. The one you use is likely to depend on which brand of test kit you purchase. Many also include conversion charts to help you switch from one to another.

Dissolved Gases

Water absorbs atmospheric oxygen and carbon dioxide through a process called *gas exchange*, which takes place at the water's surface. Fish take in oxygen as water passes across their gill membranes and give off carbon dioxide in return. The more agitation at the surface of the water, the greater the amount of oxygen that passes into the water and the greater the amount of carbon dioxide released. This is particularly critical in incubators and rearing tanks, since eggs and fry are even more sensitive to low oxygen levels than adult fish. For example, eggs will grow fungus if the oxygen level of the water is too low. Aerating the tanks with an airstone is a good way to facilitate gas exchange.

Temperature

While it's perhaps unfair to call temperature a property of water, it does play an important role, not just in inducing spawning (see spawning triggers), but also in the rate at which fry hatch.

Eggs that incubate in warmer water will hatch sooner than those kept in cooler water. Likewise, higher temperatures encourage fry to grow faster.

Other properties of water that may affect breeding include the following:

Conductivity

Conductivity is a measure of water's ability to carry an electrical current. It is related to hardness, in that water with many dissolved minerals is more conductive than extremely soft water. However, conductivity, which is measured in units known as microsiemens, measures sodium ions in addition to some other substances that do not affect the hardness of water.

Although amateur breeders traditionally have not paid much attention to conductivity, some scientists believe it may have a larger role in the spawning of some species than previously thought. For instance,

Campylomormyrus rhynchophorus Elephant noses are sensitive to the conductivity of your water. If you are constantly having problems keeping these fishes, you may want to investigate this further.

researchers have been able to prompt some fishes in the family Mormyridae to breed simply by changing the conductivity of the water in which they were kept. And some species, such as discus, also breed more readily when the conductivity falls within a particular range. Although most species that are fussy about conductivity fall outside the scope of this book, it is certainly something to keep in mind if you're interested in trying your hand with some of the species that tend to be more difficult to breed.

Heavy Metals

Tap water can also hold dissolved-metal ions such as copper, magnesium, lead, zinc, and iron. Copper is especially poisonous to fish and sometimes leaches into tap water from old copper pipes. It should go without saying that if heavy metals are present to such a degree that fish are stressed, they are unlikely to breed. Most water conditioners contain chelating agents that bind heavy metals in tap water. Alternatively, they can also be filtered out by an ion-exchange water softener.

Chlorine and/or Chloramines

These chemicals are used by utility companies to purify the drinking water supply. They are toxic to fish and must be neutralized, either by aging the water for 24 hours before adding it to the tank or by using a water conditioner. Although any experienced fishkeeper already knows this, it's worth repeating, especially since both breeding fish and raising fry often require frequent, large water changes.

SPAWNING TRIGGERS

In the wild, there are certain environmental signals, or triggers, that tell the fish it's time to spawn. Often,

Thorichthys meeki A male Firemouth Cichlid guarding his fry is an awesome sight to see.

these are linked to seasonal changes which, in turn, set off a series of environmental changes. For instance, the arrival of the rainy season in the tropics may cause the pH, hardness and temperature of lakes and rivers to drop and their depth to increase. There may also be barometric changes, higher oxygen levels in the water, and increased water flow. Some or all of these changes may stimulate physical changes necessary for the production of eggs and sperm.

Even in captivity, such environmental triggers may be required to get some species to breed, but because no obvious climate shifts take place in the home aquarium, breeders must come up with ways to simulate these environmental cues. The following is a list of some of the common triggers and ways to mimic these triggers in captivity:

- **Changes in water chemistry.** Most often the trigger is a drop in pH or hardness. The easiest way to simulate it is to do a water change (or a number of changes over a period of time), using water with the desired values.
- **Changes in depth**. The trigger can be an increase, a decrease, or both. This is simple to simulate by adding or removing tank water.
- **Changes in the light cycle.** The trigger is usually increased hours of daylight, which is easy to simulate by adjusting the tank lights. Morning sun also triggers spawning in some fish, so place their tank where it will receive natural sunlight.
- **Increased oxygenation.** The colder, faster-moving waters typical of a rainy season in the tropics carry more oxygen than warmer, slower waters. An air pump and air stone can give the same result in a breeding tank.
- **Storms.** Sudden, violent rainstorms trigger some fish to spawn. Some breeders actually simulate them for their fish, providing "rain" via watering cans, and lightening and thunder through flashing strobe lights and aluminum pans banged into microphones. Although many swear this works, to date no scientific studies have confirmed it. Rather, many scientists believe fish do not respond to the visible (and audible) aspects of the storms, but to the changes in barometric pressure that accompany them—something a bit harder to emulate in the home aquarium! Instead, try setting your fish up to spawn when you know a storm is imminent.
- **Changes in temperature:** Dropping the temperature by two or three degrees overnight and then raising it in the morning can trigger spawning in some species. Some will also respond to a water change using water with a lower temperature than that of the tank.

- **Changes in diet:** Most fish are programmed to breed at times when plenty of food will be available for their fry. From an evolutionary standpoint, that makes a lot of sense. If there weren't enough food, the fry—and ultimately the species—would be at risk of dying out. So it's no surprise that a sudden influx of food or the appearance of certain types of food (usually live foods) can serve as a trigger, telling fish it's time to spawn. Diet is such an important part of the breeding process that an entire chapter will be devoted to it elsewhere in the book. For now, just keep in mind that what you feed your fish is one of the most important factors in their ability to reproduce healthy fry.

A WORD ABOUT HYBRIDS

In nature, fish rarely seem to interbreed. Not only have they have been programmed to respond to the colors, patterns, and courtship behaviors of members of their own species, but their eggs tend to be more easily fertilized by same-species sperm. Given the opportunity, fish will almost always choose a partner of their own species. In captivity, however, such opportunities are not always available, and the drive to reproduce is so strong that males and females of closely-related species sometimes interbreed, producing hybrid offspring.

While this often occurs accidentally (the result of an aquarist innocently placing two similar species in the same tank), breeders sometimes cross species deliberately in an attempt to cash in on the public demand for new and interesting fish. Some even add hormones to the water in an attempt to induce different species to interbreed. Blood parrots and Flowerhorn cichlids — neither of which exist in the wild—are examples of

man-made hybrids that have become very fashionable among some hobbyists.

While some breeders argue that such crossbreeding contributes to scientific knowledge of fish and their reproductive strategies, others believe it is arrogant and unethical for humans to think they can improve upon nature. With more than 20,000 known fish species already out there, they say there is no need to create new ones. In addition, the exaggerated physical traits that make hybrids so unusual (and often quite popular) can also cause problems for them. Blood parrots, for example, sometimes have trouble eating because their mouths do not close normally, and their egg-shaped bodies make it difficult for them to swim rapidly.

Therefore, most responsible breeders suggest the following:

- Do not place species that crossbreed in the same aquarium.
- If fish do accidentally crossbreed, destroy the eggs or cull the young.
- Alternatively, keep the fry for your enjoyment but do not sell, trade, or give them to other hobbyists, unless you are certain they are to be used as feeder fish.
- Do not allow hybrid fish to breed, something that only perpetuates the cycle.
- Do not encourage crossbreeding by buying hybrids from pet shops or other hobbyists.

Red Parrot Cichlids

Red Parrot Cichlids are hybrids between several popular cichlid species. However, the actual species used remain a closely guarded secret.

FEEDING FRY

Would you feed a hamburger to a week-old infant? Of course not! Not only would the baby be physically unequipped to chew and digest it, but it wouldn't contain the right balance of nutrients necessary for his or her stage of development.

Like newborn humans, newborn fish need special foods, and plenty of them. Unlike adult fish, which can typically go a week or two without food, fry can starve to death within hours if they don't have enough to eat. And even if they do survive, malnourished fry probably won't grow well, and may develop problems such as curvature of the spine.

While you'll need to feed livebearer fry shortly after they're born, do not feed the fry of egg-laying species until they are *free swimming*—that is, able to swim on their own—something that usually takes a few days to a week after they hatch. Until then, the fry will remain stationary, feeding off the remnants of their *yolk* sack—a membrane-enclosed cocktail of fats, proteins, and other substances, visible as a pouch extending from their belly. But once they use this up, you will need to feed them several times a day.

From the outset, some fry, including those of most livebearers, will be big enough to eat regular flake food crushed into a powder. But fry of many other species are so small that the only things that they're able to fit in their mouths are microscopic organisms such as infusoria.

***Pterophyllum* sp. "domesticated"** Juvenile Angelfish need plenty of food as well as a considerable amount of space to grow out properly. Keep this in mind should you choose to begin breeding them.

What follows are some common first foods for fry. Many call for starter cultures, which you can obtain either from a biological supply company, from pet shops, or from other hobbyists.

- **Commercial fry food**: Comes in both liquid and powdered forms, and in formulas for livebearers and egg-layers. Fry food isn't just a ground-up version of the flakes fed to adult fish; rather, it has a nutritional balance that takes into account the accelerated growth rates of fry. Probably the easiest way to feed your fry, but some breeders claim fry fed exclusively on prepared foods will not grow as rapidly or be as robust as those fed a varied diet that includes live foods.

- **Green water:** This is just water with unicellular algae in it, often used as a first food for fry, as well

as to culture daphnia and some other live foods. To make, fill a jar with tank water and set in a sunny location until the water turns green. You can also add small, smooth rocks, which will grow a coat of algae that can be used to feed plecostomus fry and other bottom-feeding herbivores.

- **Infusoria**: This is a catch-all name for microscopic organisms such as protozoa and unicellular algae, which provide an excellent first food for tiny fry. Culturing your own is simple: Place vegetable matter, such as a couple of crumpled leaves of lettuce (make sure it's pesticide free) or a small chunk of boiled potato, in a jar and pour tank water over it. Set in a warm, dark place but do not cover, since the

spores from which infusoria grow are airborne. Within a day or two, you'll notice that the water becomes cloudy as the infusoria begin to grow. It can be added to the rearing tank with an eye dropper. Some breeders simply drop crushed lettuce leaves into the rearing tank as soon as the fry hatch; by the time they're free swimming, infusoria will have developed. The downside to this is that the decomposing lettuce leaves can pollute the water, so if you use this method, you'll need to monitor water quality carefully.

- **Baby brine shrimp (naupulii):** This is one of the most nutritious foods for fry, and can be fed to all but the smallest of them. Instructions for culturing brine shrimp can be found in Chapter 4. Make sure that you use them within 24 hours of hatching (and preferably less) since the naupulii will use up their yolk sacks after that and their nutritional value will decrease.

- **Microworms:** Another highly nutritious fry food that is easy to produce. Start by cooking a small quantity of regular unsalted oatmeal. Spread in a small plastic container such as a margarine tub to a depth of about a half inch, and cool to room temperature. Add a spoonful of worm culture and sprinkle lightly with baker's yeast. Within a few days, the culture will start to look soupy, an indication the worms are multiplying. To harvest, warm the container slightly by placing it under a lamp or on top of the tank light; within 20 minutes or so, the worms will begin climbing the sides of the container and can be scraped off with a spoon or your finger. Rinse and feed to fry with an eye dropper. One disadvantage of microworms is that they drift to the bottom of the tank, and surface-feeding fry sometimes have a hard time finding them.

- **Vinegar eels:** Despite the name, these aren't actually eels—they're nematodes that grow no larger than 1/16 of an inch. Their tiny size makes them an excellent first food for fry, and unlike microworms, they swim throughout the water column, making it easy for fry to find them. They're also easy to grow: All you have to do is fill a gallon container—a plastic milk jug, well rinsed, is fine—about two-thirds of the way with equal parts dechlorinated water and apple cider vinegar. Add half an apple sliced to fit through the neck of the bottle (it's not necessary to peel or core) and a vinegar-eel culture. Cover the mouth of the jar with cloth to let air in and keep other insects out, then store at room temperature. In about a month, if you hold the container up to a bright light and look closely, you'll see the eels, which resemble barely-visible slivers of glass. To harvest, pour the medium through a coffee filter and rinse in lukewarm tap water, then swish it in the fry tank. One advantage to feeding vinegar eels is that they can live in the tank for several days; in a pinch, you can put some in the tank in the morning and simultaneously supply your fry with breakfast, lunch and dinner without worrying about the effect of decomposing food on water quality.

- **Hard-boiled egg yolk:** Many prepared fry foods contain egg yolk. But you don't have to buy commercial foods to give your fish the benefits of this excellent protein source. Instead, wrap the yolk of a hard-boiled egg tightly in a fine-mesh cloth, dunk it in the tank and squeeze it gently under water. This forces tiny particles of the yolk through the cloth and into the tank where the fry can get them.

Chapter 6

AQUARIUM MANAGEMENT

The science of fish health management is referred to as **aquariology**. In actuality, aquariology encompasses more than just fish health management. It involves the interrelationships found within a web of many biological organisms and their environment. Aquariology is not a difficult science to master. However, there are certainly some disciplines within it that may prove more challenging than others (i.e., reefkeeping). Additionally, there are a vast number of concepts within each discipline (i.e., Berlin style of reefkeeping).

There are also different types of practices and procedures within these concepts and disciplines (many of which come as you progress in the hobby). Also, aquariology does not only deal with freshwater fishes (the main subject of this book), but also with a broader selection of animals that includes any organism, fish or otherwise, that can be maintained in the confines of an aquarium. Obviously, this includes anything from feeder guppies to the largest species of sharks, although we certainly hope that those sharks are in public aquariums. For the purpose of this book, we will refer to aquariology as dealing with fishes.

Up until now, we have only made reference to fish in aquariums, and we really have not dealt with any real topic regarding their care and husbandry, other than feeding and nutrition. If you are reading this book straight through from beginning to end, you probably think of it more as an ichthyological textbook with many pretty photos. If this is so, the book is doing for you what we have intended it to do. It is giving you a good introduction to basic ichthyology. Now let's take the focus one step further and apply what you have hopefully learned so far to actually keeping your fishes alive and well.

Hypostomus sp. Plecos and other loricariids appreciate the addition of decorations that allow them to remain hidden until the lights go out.

Most freshwater aquariums need eight primary tools for success. These tools are the following: the aquarium, a stand to support the aquarium, some type of cover, illumination, filtration, a heater and thermometer (temperature control), and test kits (water quality control). Ironically, some of the most obvious tools of the aquarium are not included among the eight primary tools. Plants, rocks, driftwood, and a background are supplementary tools and are not usually required for success with commonly kept fishes. There are exceptions, however, such as the Loricariid catfishes of the genera *Hypancistrus* and *Peckoltia*. These catfishes need cover, and live or fake plants, as well as driftwood, provide just that.

To do this, you will need to familiarize yourself with the tools of the trade. These tools, with their many forms and functions, will allow you to set up and maintain your fishes so that they thrive in their captive homes. Some of these tools are very obvious, while others are not so obvious. However, do not be fooled into thinking that tools have to be expensive and setups need to be extensive, as this is simply not true.

Throughout your experiences with aquariums, you will see that some fishes react better to an environment that offers simple yet effective means for survival. Others may not be so easily kept in captivity. These fishes need more intricate setups that can sometimes become very costly. Those of you who choose to keep large fishes, especially large predatory fishes, will see that your setups need to be drastically different from those wishing to maintain schools of tetras and barbs.

AQUARIUMS

Captive fishes can be maintained in a variety of containers. Of course, the most popular container for such an application is an **aquarium**. An aquarium is best defined as a container used for the housing of live aquatic organisms. It is important to understand that there are many variations of an aquarium. For example, an aquarium that is used to house terrestrial organisms (i.e., lizards) is still a fish tank, but we give it a fancy name—**terrarium**. Additionally, a fish tank that houses an animal that is not only terrestrial but also makes use of water, or to which water is added as a decorative feature, is referred to as an **aqua-terrarium**. Furthermore,

an aquarium that encompasses a number of organisms, both plant and animal, is considered a **vivarium**.

Aquariums were not always made of glass or acrylic, even though today nearly all of them are. Until the 1970s, aquariums were usually constructed of glass panels on all four sides with a bottom made of slate. The glass was very thick, which, combined with the slate bottom, made these aquariums extremely heavy. Almost from the beginning, people sought to make aquariums lighter, and as technology improved and people began experimenting with various types of glass, new and significantly lighter aquariums have been developed.

Acrylic Aquariums

Soon thereafter, a rather new, albeit comparatively expensive, lightweight material called acrylic plastic began to be considered for use as an aquarium material. This plastic made its popular debut in the 1980s. Acrylic plastics are often crystal clear or can be dyed various colors, including a popular gray smoke color. Additionally, these plastics are super strong; certain varieties are used for bulletproof glass in many vehicles and drive-in windows at banks.

Right away aquariums constructed of acrylic plastics were a hit, and people not only appreciated the reduced weight, but they also loved how their fishes and other animals looked behind the walls of these aquariums. The tanks were clearer and the water seemed crisper and bluer, especially in well-illuminated setups.

It is true that, even today, acrylic is clearer than most common glasses. However, there are two main problems with acrylic—expense and durability. Acrylic plastics are expensive to produce, so they are costly to purchase, as well.

Dendrobates azureus Poison Arrow Frogs are not really the best type of amphibians to include in your aqua-terrarium. They may drown if they fall into water that is too deep for them.

A lack of durability is probably the biggest problem with acrylic aquariums. While a new one is exceedingly beautiful, especially when filled with crystal clear water, they tend to lose their luster after a while. Yes, it is true that they can be buffed and polished but this involves completely breaking down the aquarium for at least a few days. Acrylic also has a nasty habit of scratching very easily. Even a small grain of sand caught between your acrylic and a cleaning sponge can terribly scratch the aquarium. If the scratch is deep, it will not usually be able to be buffed out, and these scratches may build up after time and result in poor viewing quality.

Acrylic aquariums need special care. They also need special cleaning pads that are softer and less abrasive. You have to be very cautious when moving the tank decorations. One wrong turn with a piece of lava rock just may ruin the front panel of a $2000 aquarium. While they are absolutely gorgeous, they are also in need of much TLC. This is something to consider when buying your first or next aquarium.

Caring for an acrylic aquarium is a task that some love and others hate. Many aquariums come with care recommendations for the panels. These recommendations should be closely adhered to, since following them should result in a long life for your tank. Probably the best thing you can do for the life of your acrylic aquarium is to polish the outside frequently with a polish made for such a task. Always follow the manufacturer's directions, and be sure to use a cleaner that is not only intended for acrylic plastics but specifically safe for aquariums, too.

All-glass Aquariums

As mentioned, aquariums made of glass are the most popular and commonly available type of tank today. Many manufacturers produce top-quality, all-glass aquariums. Your dealer will often carry products from one or two of these manufacturers, and most of the time, all-glass aquariums, just like acrylic aquariums, can be special ordered in various sizes to fit the needs of even the most delicate applications.

Thankfully, many materials that are often unsuitable for use with acrylic aquariums can be used on all-glass aquariums with little or no worries of damage. Those of you who keep hard water fishes, such as African cichlids or seawater fishes, will certainly appreciate the ability to scrape the salt creep and lime off of your all glass aquarium with a razor blade—something you wouldn't dare to do with an acrylic aquarium.

All-glass aquariums need some special care, as well. The best thing you can do to preserve the life of your glass tank is to wipe down the viewing panels frequently. This will prevent lime from staining the glass and should allow the panels to maintain their shine for many years.

AQUARIUM STANDS AND PLACEMENT

Even the smallest of aquaria are generally considered heavy by comparison to the weight of equally sized objects. To provide the support that your aquarium needs, you will need to make some arrangements to

Tank Placement The placement of your aquarium is perhaps the most important step in initially determining if you are to succeed or fail as a hobbyist.

have a stand that will hold the weight of the aquarium. Aquarium stands themselves can be quite heavy, which will, of course, add to the overall weight and pressure being exerted on your floor.

Before we go any further, take a look at the location where you're considering placing your tank setup. Check to see that there is an outlet with electricity being supplied to it. It is surprisingly common for someone to get everything for their new aquarium together, and after it is all placed and filled with water, they find that there isn't a plug to provide electricity to the tank's equipment. That hurts to even think about! Make sure your location has direct access to electricity.

Next, make sure there is no direct sunlight that comes in and hits the tank. You don't even want this for any amount of time, regardless of whether it's an hour or three hours. It's not advised for any fish, although "reefers" would argue this point fiercely.

Once you have chosen a spot that has electricity but no direct sunlight, you are ready to check the most important thing of all—the floor! Your floor should be solid. If you are fortunate enough to have a concrete slab under the chosen area—great; if not, make sure the floor is able to hold the combined weight of the aquarium setup. Remember, the tank and all of its equipment are going to be far heavier than what most people can readily pick up by themselves. Add water at 8.3 pounds per gallon for freshwater, and you have yourself a seriously heavy piece of furniture.

A solid floor may be first in importance in the support of your aquarium, but a solid stand is definitely a close second. Unless you are a good carpenter or know someone who is, stay away from homemade aquariums stands. In addition, many manufacturers offer warranties if you buy both an aquarium and a stand from

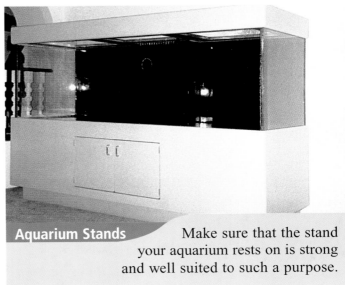

Aquarium Stands   Make sure that the stand your aquarium rests on is strong and well suited to such a purpose.

them. These combinations are by far the most highly recommended routes to take.

Regardless of the stand you choose, pay close attention to how even the aquarium is when placed on top of it. Companies that build such stands test them prior to shipping them to your local aquarium shop, but it never hurts to check for yourself. After all, sometimes the stand may have been used to support other things that are far heavier than what the stand was initially rated for, or the stand may have come in contact with excessive moisture or temperature extremes. These are factors that can significantly affect the structural integrity of the stand.

Once you have positioned your stand and placed your aquarium on it, use a level to make sure the tank sits perfectly even on all sides. Even a slight lean due to floor unevenness or the like can cause disaster to strike in the form of a cracked panel or broken seam. If there is a slight unevenness to the tank and stand, it can be fixed prior to adding water by using wooden shims or Styrofoam placed in the proper areas to offset the prob-

Leveling After the aquarium location is determined and the tank is in place, make sure it's level before you add water.

lem. Some hobbyists have used Styrofoam as a cushion placed in-between the tank and stand just in case there are small inconsistencies that cannot be readily seen with the naked eye. Such a safety is recommended, though not usually needed.

Once you have successfully placed your aquarium stand in the perfect location and have assured that the aquarium will sit evenly upon it, you can go about setting up the system. While actually filling the tank is not necessarily the next step, you can begin to add some water, so as to allow the stand some time to adjust to the eventual weight of the tank full of water. During the initial filling of the tank it is common to hear the stand creak and make some other small noises. Of course, if the creaks turn into cracks and so on, you may need to rethink your plans and adjust for whatever situation that may follow. In any instance, such noises should cause you to make draining the aquarium your first priority

and seeking the assistance of a qualified aquarium technician your second.

COVERS AND CANOPIES

One of the most disheartening situations is to awaken one morning to a beloved fish of yours dried up on the floor next to the tank. Actually, speaking from many years of experience, they are more likely to flop their way nearly across the room than stay right next to the tank. Regardless, it is certainly a sad sight.

To prevent such situations from happening, we incorporate various types of covers and canopies to be used on the aquarium. Many times, covers are plastic with a piece of thin glass running down the center from left to right. This glass strip symbolizes where the light that illuminates the aquarium is to be placed. Other types of covers are most commonly made from glass. Sometimes the more expensive glass tops are made of what is called solorized glass. This glass actually refracts and reflects the light so as to allow more of it to bounce around the inside of the aquarium. The result is better illumination without the added cost of purchasing and running additional lights.

Sometimes you will see large covers that extend up and off the tops of aquariums. These are called canopies, and they are often made of wood or plastics, such as high-grade polished ABS black plastic. Others are customized by private companies and may even include the use of stainless steel. It is very common to see large reef aquariums with large canopies on the top of them. Such large canopies are needed in order to house and hide the high-tech lighting systems that are often incorporated in such systems. Regardless, use the cover that is recommended by your local fish shop or speak with one of their knowledgeable employees, and they will be able to make further recommendations.

After filling halfway, check to be sure the aquarium has retained its levelness.

ILLUMINATION

Lighting your aquarium is only as challenging and technical as you want it to be. Nearly all of the fishes you are likely to encounter in your travels will do quite well under standard lighting systems that are marketed for average home aquariums. Once you begin to dabble in freshwater planted aquariums and seawater reef aquariums, illumination information becomes more like a college class than a quick discussion on various light bulbs.

Generally speaking, there are two main types of light bulbs that you will encounter. The first, and more popular, are the fluorescent tubular types with either one or two pins at each end. These bulbs can be found in nearly all retail pet shops and even in home and garden supply shops. They are often cheap to buy and very cheap to operate due to their energy efficiency. If you purchase an aquarium combo setup from a local fish shop, you will most likely end up with a light with a fluorescent bulb in it.

Fluorescent bulbs that are used over freshwater aquariums are often pink or yellow in color. This is due to the spectrum that the bulb is rated for. Often, quality control is not at its highest with these bulbs, so there may even be a noticeable difference in tone if you purchase multiple bulbs and view them next to each other. Regardless, they are often perfectly acceptable for doing the job they are intended to do—lighting the tank so you can watch your fish.

The other popular type of lighting is incandescent lighting. These bulbs come in a wide assortment of types and styles. The ones that freshwater fish enthusiasts most often come in contact with are those that are very cheap and are usually 15 to 25 watts each. These bulbs are great for those fishes that prefer subdued lighting or even for the hobbyist who prefers subdued lighting. Their biggest downfall is the amount of heat they produce compared to equally powerful fluorescent tubes.

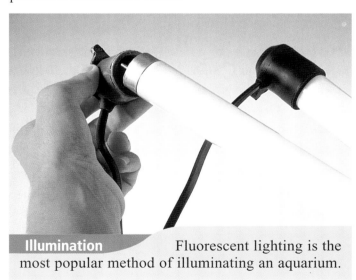

Fluorescent lighting is the most popular method of illuminating an aquarium.

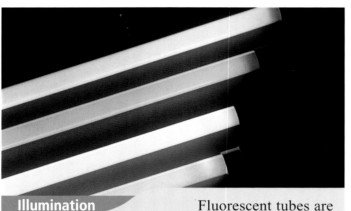

Recently there has been an increase in the use of hybrid lamps. They are fluorescent, tubular lamps that screw into sockets designed for incandescent bulbs. These are wonderful additions to the product line of illumination materials available to hobbyists, and as long as the wattage of the bulb matches or is less than that of the socket, you should have no problems incorporating them.

An average aquarium should receive no more than ten hours of overhead illumination per day, with eight hours being the median number suggested by industry professionals. Therefore, a photoperiod of eight hours on and sixteen hours off is probably the best routine you can select for your fishes. Of course, there are exceptions, but if you start your aquarium off with this photoperiod, you can always make adjustments later. Remember, fish can go about their normal daily fishy business with only the illumination from ambient sunlight. Overhead illumination (also called supplemental illumination) is so we can see them better. That said, keep the photoperiod constant unless you are attempting breeding techniques.

Regardless of the type of lighting you choose, remember that the light needs to penetrate the aquarium effectively. The higher your aquarium is the stronger the lighting system must be in order to illuminate the tank properly. This is especially true if live plants are going to be incorporated into the setup.

FILTRATION

Filtration is a large topic. It can be as simple or as intricate as you would like it to be, but one thing is certain: the need to understand what is happening on a microbiological level in your aquarium is vitally important. To begin gaining this understanding, we need to look at what the role of filtration actually is and where it begins.

Filtration is defined as a process where a substance undergoes biological, chemical, or mechanical changes in order to enhance its purity. This definition is basic and since the topic of filtration itself is rather lengthy, we will only discuss the three main types, but first we must learn a little about a very important cycle that every aquarium, whether fresh water or marine, must endure if any filtration is to be successful—the nitrogen cycle.

The Nitrogen Cycle

The nitrogen cycle is the process of converting a highly toxic nitrogen compound, usually in the form of ammonia, back to pure nitrogen and oxygen. There are several steps involved here, and each one will be touched on specifically. For now, however, it is important to understand that such a process does take place and is the primary reason that you aren't able to dump a large amount of fish into your aquarium at one time. This is especially true with new aquaria, as the "spike" of ammonia will quickly cause the fish a lot of discom-

fort and can surely kill the fish, and other organisms, should the ammonia levels become uncontrollably high.

For this reason, you should always take great care in breaking in, or cycling, your aquarium. To cycle your tank means to simply allow the proper bacterial species responsible for the breakdown of nitrogenous wastes enough time to develop and begin their duties. This time frame will vary, depending on many conditions, such as water temperature, volume of the aquarium, number of fish in the aquarium, amount of other biomass, pH and other water chemistry values of the tank's water, and the presence of a suitable substratum for the beneficial bacteria to colonize.

The estimated time frame required to properly break in an aquarium is approximately four weeks. That number is simply an average and should in no way be taken as law. However, even if your tank cycles in a week, waiting a bit longer will do absolutely no harm whatsoever. There is no punishment for moving slowly while adding live animals to your tank. Feel free to add a fish each year to the tank if you would like. On the other hand, if you dump a bunch of fish in the tank and it takes two weeks to calm down, then you must not think that you can make a habit out of continuing to dump in large amounts of fish at one time. The biological backbone of the aquarium will break, and you will lose badly.

Now you should have a good idea that the nitrogen cycle plays a huge role in the determination of your success or failure in your aquarium experiences. That

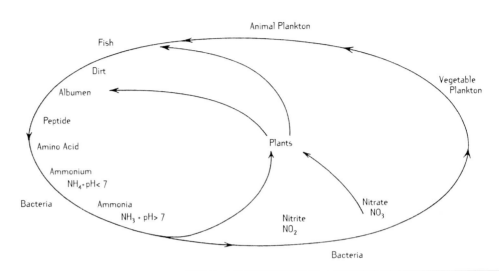

Nitrogen Cycle   A diagram of the nitrogen cycle as it occurs in nature.

Adopted from *Discus Health*, T.F.H. Publications, Inc.

said, we should attempt to get a better understanding of the inner workings of this cycle, so one will be able to identify the steps as they progress through the break-in process.

Ammonia (NH$_3$-)

The first step in the nitrogen cycle is, well, nitrogen. After all, it is a cycle, not a one-way process. However, for all intents and purposes, ammonia is where we will start. Ammonia is contained in raw fish wastes and uneaten foodstuffs, in the form of proteins, and is then excreted by the heterotrophic bacteria that consume these proteins. Proteins that are not used by the fish will be released as ammonia through the gills. In this form (usually free ammonia), it is extremely toxic and, as mentioned, can cause great suffering to your fish, should the level get too high. Ammonia is broken down

When the ammonia molecule dissolves in water, it picks up an extra hydrogen atom to form ammonium. This gives it an extra positive charge and the ammonia is considered ionized. It is now known as the ammonium ion.

$$NH_3 + H_2O <-> NH_4+ + OH-$$
(Ammonia) (Water) (Ammonium ion) (Hydroxyl ion)

into a less toxic compound, called nitrite, by nitrifying bacteria thought to be of the *Nitrosomonas* complex although there has been considerable debate about the actual genera involved with this process. This is completed by the separation of the hydrogen by the nitrogen and the binding of the nitrogen to two oxygen atoms.

Ammonia removal is fairly easy. First, you can filter your water over fresh, activated carbon that contains zeolite clay. Zeolite is an ionic-exchange substance that quickly converts harmful ammonia into non-toxic substance. One word of caution when using any ionic-exchange substance is to always make sure your water is free from any sodium. This may pose a problem with some aquariums, because people often add salt to their tanks to help prevent parasitic infestations of their fishes. These salts will react or exchange ions with ionic-exchange resins more easily, and then, any converted ammonia will revert back to its free state. This can sometimes lead to massive fish-kills in older, established aquaria that are heavily stocked (especially in public aquariums or ponds). Your best bet in preventing ammonia toxicity is to allow your aquarium to cycle for several weeks, allowing the beneficial bacteria to slowly take hold.

Nitrite (NO$_2$)

Nitrite should be taken very seriously, for it is a highly toxic substance, albeit not as harmful as ammonia in the same concentrations, but it can still easily kill koi and other fishes. The nitrite compound is made up of one nitrogen atom and two oxygen atoms. In their lone states, neither element is toxic at a normal atmospheric pressure. However, when combined in the right amounts, they become a new substance—one that can kill your fish very quickly. Remember that polluted water may be crystal clear but can still hold a high concentration of harmful substances. With this combination of oxygen and nitrogen, certain nitrifying bacteria, possibly of the genus *Nitrobactor*, are able to convert the nitrite into a less-toxic nitrogen compound called nitrate. Nitrite is odorless, so don't be fooled into believing that you can smell your water to see if it is bad.

The best defense against nitrite poisoning is to feed sparingly, remove any uneaten foodstuffs, perform regular water changes, and make all adjustments slowly to

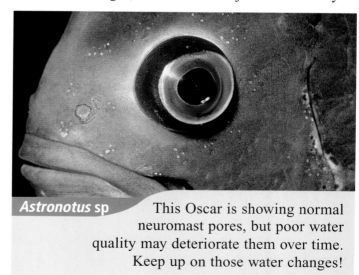

Astronotus sp   This Oscar is showing normal neuromast pores, but poor water quality may deteriorate them over time. Keep up on those water changes!

prevent the beneficial bacteria bed from stressing out and dying off. If you find that your aquarium is showing a high nitrite reading, you can perform all of the same functions you would perform if your aquarium were suffering from a high ammonia concentration.

Nitrate (NO₃)

Nitrate is the last breakdown and least harmful product in the nitrogen cycle. From here, any nitrate that is not converted back to free nitrogen and oxygen will be used to provide nutrients to any type of photosynthetic organism that your water comes in contact with. These include all species of plants and algae in your Aquarium. As a matter of fact, old tank water is often used to water house plants or a garden, due to the high levels of nitrate and other metabolites that are often found in it. Anaerobic bacteria will also consume nitrate, in which case nitrogen will be liberated, and then the cycle will be completed.

Nitrate is not usually found in high concentration in natural bodies of water. Needless to say, many fish, even the hardy Oscar (*Astronotus* spp.), will only tolerate so much. Keeping the overall nitrate level below 50mg/L is best, as anything higher than that may cause acute toxicity over long periods of time. Remember to perform partial water changes and not to overfeed.

Another conversion that takes place in an aquarium is denitrification. This process is not as common as nitrification but still very important. **Denitrification** is the process in which a nitrogen-based compound, such as nitrate (NO₃), is broken down into free nitrogen and oxygen.

Denitrification most often takes place in the hypoxic or anoxic areas of the aquarium, or the areas with low or no dissolved oxygen. These areas are largely barren of life, but certain strains of anaerobic bacteria thrive there,

and these are the primary organisms responsible for the breakdown of nitrate.

Biological Filtration

Biological filtration is the breakdown of organic and non-organic compounds into less toxic and/or simpler substances. The nitrogen cycle is only one of several cycles that take place within an ecosystem—yes, your aquarium is a mini-ecosystem. The carbon cycle is, perhaps, the next most important cycle in environmental

Biological Filtration Wet-dry filters provide excellent biological filtration, but their end product is nitrate, so be sure to keep up on your regular water changes to maintain a healthy environment overall.

sciences. The carbon cycle is basically the flow of carbon in an ecosystem, specifically within the associated food web. Carbon is another substance that can sometimes be considered a metabolite, but more commonly, carbon must be chemically adhered to another element to form a molecule, such as in carbon dioxide.

Efficient biological filtration is best achieved by having tank water flowing over a medium that is suitable for the colonization of beneficial bacteria species, such as those responsible for the breakdown of nitrogenous compounds. Some examples of good-quality media for positive recruitment of these beneficial bacteria include course foam, lava rock, tufa rock, coral rock, plastic bio-balls, plastic pipe pieces, Japanese filter matting, filter brushes, flint gravel, and porcelain pieces. All of these materials and more are widely available at many local fish shops.

The velocity of the water flowing over your biological filter should be moderate, not so rapid that no build-up can take place. Conversely, the water flow need not be too slow, as this will encourage sediment to settle and prevent the materials from becoming colonized with beneficial bacteria. Many ready-made filter/pump kits address these problems by providing the right water pump with the filtration unit that you are purchasing. Figuring out the flow rate that is required to properly filter your aquarium can be tricky and demanding. That is one more reason to not only purchase a pump/filter kit, but also to seek the advice of professionals that work with these units on a regular basis. They will be able to help you answer questions that will certainly arise, especially if they involve custom setups.

Biological filtration takes place in all areas of your aquarium but is concentrated more heavily in certain ones. Areas with good water flow and a higher level of dissolved oxygen are certainly the most productive areas of nitrification. These areas tend to be within a filtration unit, such as a wet-dry filter or a fluidized bed filter. Certainly, any commercial filter system is capable of providing the proper surface area that is needed for nitrification to begin. However, some do it more effectively than others.

Chemical Filtration

Chemical filtration has three basic types: chemicals to neutralize or detoxify harmful chemicals, absorption materials such as activated carbon, and ionic-exchange

Bio Media Bits of lava rock serve as excellent media for beneficial bacteria to colonize in your biological filter.

Hoplarchus psitticus Some fishes, such as this True Parrot Cichlid, seem to thrive when provided with water that is filtered over carbon.

resins such as zeolite clay. All three have their own uses in the aquarium, but perhaps none is as popular as the use of activated carbon.

Activated carbon is available in many different grades. Many of the grades are just about as close in absorptive value as the next one. The only grade that is universally considered worthless is the "raw" grade. This grade has almost no pores on the surface of each bit and therefore does not have a very high surface area, which translates into a low absorptive value. The higher grades of carbon are very porous and have a high absorptive value. That can work to your advantage sometimes and against it at other times, because high-grade activated carbon will absorb toxins and contaminants so quickly that the carbon becomes "spent" and will need to be replaced more often than lesser grades.

There are assorted types of chemical additives that may or may not be helpful in an aquarium. Many of these will neutralize heavy metals or toxins, such as chlorine and/or chloramines. They have a limited use,

however, due to the fact that they usually produce either precipitates or other by-products that will, in turn, cause acute toxicity if allowed to build up. There are also several chemical additives that can be associated with biological filtration because they contain products that stimulate the beneficial bacteria populations that are required for a well-balanced tank. Lumping them into the chemical filtration group, however, may be a stretch.

Mechanical Filtration

Mechanical filtration is the physical process of removing suspended debris from the water column. Good quality mechanical filters will make the water in your tank appear polished. Often, mechanical filtration materials are the first materials that the raw water from the tank comes in contact with. This helps to reduce the possibility of the decomposition of solids on the biological filter material and within the chemical filtering media.

Materials that are suitable for mechanical filtration usage are so-called "angel hair," fine foam rubber, fil-

Bio Media Bits of lava rock serve as excellent media for beneficial bacteria to colonize in your biological filter.

ter felt, poly fiber, cotton (no longer common), micron cartridges (many canister filters use these), and sand. All of these materials are commonly available through your local fish shop and are often in the form of replaceable cartridges that are easily disposed of when soiled.

Another type of mechanical filtration is known as foam fractionation. This is the process of attaching air molecules to hydrophobic materials. These materials are often inorganic in nature and are not capable of dissolving in water or any other liquid environment. Foam fractionators are tall, cylindrical pieces of equipment that afford the longest possible contact time between water and tiny air bubbles that are injected into the system via a venturi air valve or an airstone attached to an outside air source. These air valves draw in a certain amount of air based on the water that is flowing through them. The more water flow you have, the more air will be injected into the reaction chamber, where the air bubbles attach themselves to the hydrophobic particles. Once air has attached to particles, the particles begin to rise while the clean water is denser and flows out of the system into the aquarium. The particles will be pooled in a collection cup located at the top of the reaction chamber. The product is usually very clean and crystal-clear aquarium water. Foam fractionators are more commonly used in very large commercial setups or in aquaculture facilities. Their suitability for use on average-sized home aquariums is being explored and

Paracheirodon axelrodi Cardinal Tetras need very warm water in order to thrive in captivity. Having a low nitrate level won't hurt, either.

developed, so we may see units for sale to the public in the future.

TEMPERATURE CONTROL

Water temperature has both direct and indirect effects on the health and vitality of your fish. If you are maintaining fish that are more comfortable in temperate waters along with your tropical species, the stress induced by the higher water temperature is a direct effect. Conversely, if the fishes are stressed due to water quality being poor and the poor water quality is, in turn, due to a temperature-related issue, that is an indirect effect.

For most tropical species, a water temperature maintained between 70° and 78°F is suitable. Higher temperatures are needed for some species, such as Discus (*Symphysodon* spp.) and Cardinal Tetras (*Paracheirodon axelrodi*). Also, as discussed in the previous chapter on

reproduction, many species will need a slight rise in temperature in order for spawning to be induced.

In order to establish a suitable temperature, you will need to use a combination of a heater and a thermometer. At this point, it is also important to bring up one other piece of equipment—a chiller. Chillers are not commonly used in freshwater aquariums containing tropical fishes unless the lighting over the aquarium is very intense. Intense lighting is used over reef aquariums and sometimes when dealing with live plants.

Heaters come in a vast array of sizes and wattages. They are constructed of materials such as glass, stainless steel, and titanium. For heavy-duty jobs, the use of a pass-through design heater is also an option, albeit an expensive one. Pass-through heaters are units where water from the aquarium is passed through it before returning to the aquarium. Most hobbyists use the more traditional glass heaters, which come in hang-on and submersible styles. Of these, both types are good, but submersibles seem to function slightly more efficiently.

Regardless of the style of heater you are using, their applications are basically the same. The purpose, above all else, is to maintain a desired temperature that is as close to steady and non-fluctuating as possible, unless, of course, you wish to induce seasons in your aquarium where the water will be cooler for a few months then warm up for the next few months and so on. Regardless, there will always be some fluctuation, but a really good heater will keep it to an absolute minimum. Furthermore, a good heater will bring your water as close to the desired temperature as possible. Sometimes the temperature of the aquarium will be different than what the heater is set for. This gap becomes smaller as a quality heater is continually used.

The placement of the heater is also important. Placing a heater is very simple—think moderate flow. You don't want to place the heater in an area that has slow flow, because this can actually form a warm zone, and it may tell the thermostat in the heater that the water is warmer than it really is.

Larger aquariums (over 75 gallons) may need multiple heaters incorporated into the system. To do this you should find as many moderate flow areas as you can, and then pick two that are about equidistant from each other, and place the two heaters there. Of course, if you wish to add three heaters, follow the same steps, but pick out three spots with moderate water flow and so on.

In almost all situations, you should have at least two thermometers. Multiple thermometers are better for two main reasons. The first reason is so you can check the temperature of the water in multiple areas of the aquarium. The second reason is so you can check to make sure that your heater(s) are not totally off balance, or in some cases, one of your other thermometers may be faulty. It is not uncommon for many hobbyists to incorporate two thermometers for every three to four feet of aquarium.

The placement of the thermometers should be close to a heater but not right next to it. Inevitably, even in an area of the aquarium with moderate flow, you will have a warm-zone around the heaters. These areas may mislead you into thinking that the water is warmer then it really is overall, and while such a case may never bother you or your fishes, there are species that need their temperatures to be right on. Of course, you probably don't want thermometers stuck all over the sides of your aquariums, so be creative in incorporating them into the aquascaping.

WATER QUALITY CONTROL

Water is essentially a fish's atmosphere. If the water is of poor quality, the fish will soon be of poor quality. Understandably, the quality of the water in your aquarium is of highest importance.

What constitutes good water quality? That is an open-ended question. What may be regarded as high quality water for one species may not be so for another. That said, we need to set standards, although we will not be harping on every particular detail of water chemistry. To do so would be changing the scope of this book. We will give you guidelines—a foundation of sorts—to help you to make and develop your own conclusions and solve the problems you may experience.

General Water Chemistry

Water can be tested for many things. Some of these are more important to the average hobbyist than others. Seawater enthusiasts will be more bent on REDOX (oxidation and reduction) and ORP (oxidation and reduction potential) readings than, say, a hobbyist wishing to breed a new species of Rift Lake cichlid. Since this book is focused primarily on the ichthyology of freshwater fishes, we will talk about what a freshwater hobbyist should be aware of regarding the chemistry of their aquariums.

pH

The test most commonly performed on water is a pH test. The pH of a liquid is a measure of the relative amounts of hydrogen ions (H^+) and hydroxyl ions (OH^-) that are present in a solution. The pH scale is an attempt to quantify these readings and make a universal language similar to that of the role that scientific names play when discussing particular species with people from other countries.

The pH scale runs from 1 through 14. A pH value of 7.0 is referred to as being neutral, since there are the same number of H^+ ions as OH^- ions present at that reading. Any reading over 7.0 is considered alkaline (basic) and results from OH^- ions predominating, while

a pH reading of under 7.0 is considered acidic and signifies a dominance of H^+ ions.

Most freshwater fishes inhabit waters with a pH measuring close to 7.0 in general. Of course, there are extremes. Many of the small tetras and other characins that inhabit the tannin-stained blackwaters of the Amazon River and its thousands of tributaries can be found in water with a pH measurement as low as 3.9. Conversely, the waters of Africa's Great Rift Valley contain many species of popular freshwater fishes and sometimes they are found in waters with a pH measuring as high 9.2. It is not difficult to see that freshwater fishes can significantly vary in their water chemistry preferences, but they really don't have much of a choice in nature.

Fish do not suddenly get to decide which pH value they would like when they are imported into the aquarium trade. That is why you, the hobbyist *must* do your homework and research the needs of the fishes you intend to stock in your aquariums *before* you bring them home.

Many species of freshwater fishes that are captive produced in fish farms and breeder's basements all over the world will usually be more adaptable to varying pH requirements and water chemistry fluctuations on the whole. Support your local fish clubs and captive breeding whenever possible. It's better for you and certainly better for the fish.

Nitrogen Compounds

The testing of nitrogenous compounds is the most popular water test next to pH. These compounds include, but are not limited to, ammonia (NH_4), ammonium (NH_3), nitrite (NO_2), and nitrate (NO_3).

Ammonia and ammonium are concentrated into one test while nitrite and nitrate are tested independently. More detailed descriptions of these compounds can be found on the previous pages of this chapter.

Water Hardness

The degree of water's hardness is directly proportional to the concentrations of various dissolved minerals in it. Of all of the minerals that could possibly be dissolved in water, two are most dominant—calcium (Ca) and magnesium (Mg). Therefore, hardness is commonly expressed in terms of the amount of calcium carbonate ($CaCO_3$) that is present in a solution.

Measurements of water hardness are expressed either by the German scale, which uses the term "DH," or in straight parts per million (ppm). One DH is equivalent to 17 ppm. A generalized scale of various classifications of hardness is listed in the following table:

Water Hardness and its Relation to Water Quality

Soft:	0 to 75 ppm
Moderately Hard:	76 to 150 ppm
Hard:	151 to 300 ppm
Very Hard:	301+ ppm

The most important thing hobbyists must remember about water hardness in general is that the lower the hardness, or softer the water, the poorer the buffering capacity. If your buffering capacity is low, you will have a difficult time maintaining a good pH. The pH of an aquarium is more stable in aquaria with a higher buffering capacity.

Carbon Dioxide

While measuring carbon dioxide is not something that most freshwater hobbyists do on a regular basis, those of you who have or would like to have a planted aquarium will become intimately acquainted with its importance. Carbon dioxide (CO_2) is a byproduct of aerobic respiration and is released not only by fish and plants, but also by bacteria. It is utilized by both plants (for photosynthesis) and fish.

Unlike oxygen, carbon dioxide is highly soluble in water, where it forms carbonic acid. But, as with ammonia, the dissolved carbon dioxide is in equilibrium with carbonic acid and the bicarbonate ion. This is represented below:

$$CO_2 + H_2O <\!\!> H_2CO_3 <\!\!> HCO_3 + H+$$

carbon dioxide · water · carbonic acid · bicarbonate ion · hydrogen ion

Notice the free hydrogen ion at the other end of the equation. This is why carbon dioxide has such a significant effect on the pH of water. Carbon dioxide produced from respiration is exhaled from the gills. If there are high levels of carbon dioxide in the water, the pH will fall due to the high number of free H+ ions produced by this respiration. This also reduces the fish's ability to remove carbon dioxide from its body, so its tissues become too acidic. This is known as an acidosis, and it affects a wide range of normal body fluids. In extreme cases, an anesthetic-like narcosis develops, and the fish will become very sluggish and may die. Prolonged exposure to carbon dioxide levels greater than 10–20mg/l has been linked to nephrocalcinosis, a condition where mineral deposits form in the kidneys.

Using Test Kits

Now that you are totally aware of what you should be testing for, it's time to discuss how to perform the tests and at what frequency. Test kits can be purchased from one of many sources. Retail outlets are perhaps the best option, since they often keep a steady flow of merchandise coming through their doors. One thing

Poor Buffering Capacity

A buffer is a compound that protects against any temporary swings in pH. In aquaria, the most important buffers are in the bicarbonate-carbonate system. Dissolved bicarbonate is usually in chemical equilibrium with carbonate, typically present as calcium carbonate found in calcareous rocks and gravel.

$$HCO_3 <-> H+ \ + \ CO_{32}$$

Bicarbonate ion   Hydrogen ion   Carbonate ion
(Usually as calcium carbonate)

With the above buffering system, if we add more acid (H^+) to the water, it will combine with spare carbonate ions to form bicarbonate ions, removing the extra H^+ from the solution and preventing it from becoming more acidic. Carbonate ions can be recruited from calcium carbonate-containing materials if necessary.

Conversely, if there is a rise in pH due to a loss of hydrogen ions, more can be released from the bicarbonate ions, with the extra carbonate ions formed by that process deposited as calcium carbonate. This effect will help to counter a rise in pH.

Many aquaria with high pH rely on the use of buffering materials to help counteract the acidifying processes described above. Typically, these are calcium carbonate based and include such materials as tufa rock, coral sand, and oyster shells. To counteract the increasing levels of hydrogen ions, they rely on compounds dissolving from them. Over time, the buffering capacity of such materials can be exhausted, so regular changing of these materials is recommended (roughly every one to two years). Alternatively, specific buffering solutions to add to your pond or aquarium are marketed. To prevent pH crashes, the pH must be monitored closely and the instructions for these preparations followed.

you don't want is a test kit that has been sitting around for a while, since, like any other chemicals, their effectiveness will expire and they will begin to give you false readings.

Certain tests should be done regularly, but the term "regularly" is open-ended, since what is regular for one person may not be regular for another. As a general guideline, pH tests should be done about once or twice a week, while others can be performed once per week or even once every other week. However, these guidelines are only for established aquariums. Those

aquariums that are not yet established will need appropriate testing more frequently. This is especially true with the big four tests, which are pH, NH_4, NO_2, and NO_3. One of the best things you can do for your aquarium inhabitants is to keep a watchful eye on the aquarium's parameters through proper and regular testing.

When it comes time to do a water test, it is a good idea to read over the directions *before* you actually begin the test. This is a good habit to develop, even if you have a good idea of exactly how the test is done.

Doing the tests the same way each time will help you to consistently obtain the most accurate results possible.

Before and after each test, be sure to rinse the test tube(s) and any other pieces that may come in contact with the aquarium water. If possible, do this using water that is pure (reverse osmosis or de-ionized water is best). Also be sure to shake the reagents as thoroughly as possible to bring them into full suspension.

Once the tests have been taken, you may wish to dry any piece of equipment that has been rinsed off. This will help to ensure that any residual testing reagents have been wiped away and will not be able to interrupt your results next time. Always store these kits in a cool dry location to assist in preserving their shelf life.

Maintenance

Plants will assist you in maintaining high water quality in your aquarium.

Maintaining Good Water Quality

Most fishes that are common in the aquarium trade are rather tough and do well in a broad range of water chemistry parameters. This is especially true of those fishes that are healthy and adapted to life in the confines of a tank. However, even hardy fishes can succumb to poor water quality if it remains poor over a long period of time.

Water quality encompasses several things. First, it can refer to a specific property of water. For example, the quality of water can be considered poor due to the lack of dissolved minerals. Thus, this water will be overly soft and may be harmful to some fishes.

Second, water quality may be considered poor due to its temperature. Water temperature is a huge factor in determining overall water quality, as water at higher temperatures is more apt to have stabilization problems with regard to the bacteria count and algae blooms. Therefore, temperature is often considered when determining overall water quality.

However, when one thinks of water quality, it is more commonly in reference to the amount of dissolved metabolites that are contained in the water. Metabolites can most simply be thought of as by-products of metabolic processes. For example, when fish breathe, they release carbon dioxide, and in that case, carbon dioxide is a metabolite. Fish also excrete nitrogenous wastes in the form of ammonia and urea. Both of these are by-products of digestion and are considered metabolites as well. Since metabolites are always being produced, they must be controlled in such a way as to prevent them from building up to the point where they have a negative affect on your water quality.

The most effective method for the removal of metabolites in tank water is performing partial water changes on a regular basis—about once every two or three weeks. Water changes should become an integral part of your maintenance routine with your aquarium, like feeding and skimming the surface of the water to remove debris.

Some of the signs that your fish may be suffering from metabolite toxicity are labored breathing at the water's surface, head and lateral line degeneration, chronic disease outbreaks (especially bacterial infections), listlessness or lazy behavior, and feeding irregularity. Generally, when conditions are corrected and brought back to more favorable parameters, the signs and symptoms rapidly reverse. Again, always try to perform regular partial water changes, and do not over feed your fishes.

Importance of Water Changes

There is one husbandry practice that is above all else in terms of importance—water changes. Yes, routinely testing your water is important, as are regular feedings and filter maintenance, but regular partial water changes are key to keeping successful aquariums.

Years ago, water changes were basically considered taboo. Why fix it if it isn't broken, right? Wrong! Water changes have proven to be vitally important, and hobbyists who haven't been doing them are inadvertently causing their fishes harm.

What makes water changes so effective? This is the most common question, next to "why are water changes so vitally important?" The answers are fairly simple.

In nature, all bodies of water rely on a constant flow of water. This water has to come from somewhere, of course. Simply, if you look at a basic pond, there is generally an input and an output. Both are usually in the form of streams. Water enters from one area and fills the pond to the brim. Then, it overflows and runs out through another stream to another body of water until it eventually ends up flowing into one of the world's oceans. Under ideal conditions, there is a constant supply of clean, fresh water to replenish the older water as it flows out of the pond.

An aquarium does not have this constant flow of water, unless you have taken the time to set up an automatic water-changing system. Without such a system, you must become the constant flow of water for the tank. To do this, you must partially change the water in your tank on a regular basis.

How Much and How Often?

Unfortunately, there is no magical equation to determine how often you should change the water in your tank. It's just plain foolish to assume that such an equation exists. Why? Because of the term we refer to as biomass.

Biomass is the amount of living matter within a given area or volume. This includes fish, plants, and any other critter that you may have swimming or walking about the tank. Also, don't forget about all the beneficial bacteria that are in your system, which are alive, as well. How much biomass is in your system dictates how much water should be changed and how often.

How? Well the most common way is through a modified version of the nitrogen cycle. This is quite common in all closed systems where fishes are

Vibrantly colored fishes and plants are just one beneficial product of performing regular partial water changes in your aquarium.

the schedule for water changes that best suits you and the health of your aquarium.

As a general rule, it is a good idea to perform at least a 10-percent water change weekly on aquariums with very low biomass. Some will argue that this is too much, while others will say that it is too little. The latter is especially true of those hobbyists who focus on breeding species such as Discus or Angelfish. These hobbyists are accustomed to performing large water changes daily.

Water changes of about 50 percent weekly are better yet. The biggest concern with doing water changes on such a grand scale is that the change will shock the tank's inhabitants. This is true not only with the fish, but also with the beneficial bacteria. You will find that an aquarium that has received frequent, large-scale water changes will eventually be more stable. If your tank has not had a water change in two months, and you go and change half the water that you're going to have a major problem on your hands.

housed. Instead of the ammonia being converted into nitrite and then into nitrate, only to be broken into free nitrogen and oxygen, the modified version leaves the end product as nitrate. This buildup of nitrate is one way you can determine the quality of your water and when it is time for a water change.

This buildup is the result of what is referred to as bioactivity. **Bioactivity** is activity that has an effect on living organisms. In this case, the effect is a buildup of nitrate and the result is poor water quality. So how can we determine when the buildup is too high? By testing the nitrate. That's why it's so important to regularly test your water.

As your overall biomass increases (from adding fishes, etc.), the time between water changes increases. This is also true in large, complex systems, although not as much as in smaller systems. You will have to determine

Remember to conduct regular, significant water changes and to test the water frequently. You should really attempt to get into a steady routine, regardless of how experienced you are or how many tanks you have cared for over the years. It doesn't matter if you are a novice and you have only a small aquarium with a few fish or you are an aquarist caring for a 1000-gallon Amazonian setup in a public aquarium. In both instances, and every situation in-between, it is important to develop a routine and stick with it.

Part II

Acestrorhynchus falcirostris

ACESTRORHYNCHIDAE
FRESHWATER BARRACUDAS

Northern South America is home to thousands of species of freshwater fishes. One group, above all others, has gained a lot of attention in the past few years and deservingly so. These fishes are sleek, nicely colored, and present a unique showpiece for the serious fish collector who is looking for something truly different. They are the freshwater barracudas of the family Acestrorhynchidae.

There are 15 described species that are considered valid within this small and highly specialized group of piscivorous fishes and possibly ten or more nominal species that are waiting for proper description. They prove quite a challenge for ichthyologists, since not a lot is known about their biology or breeding habits in nature. Therefore, we cannot reliably or comfortably say how many species there actually (or nominally) are.

Acestrorhynchus species are indigenous to South America, and the greatest species diversity within the genus is, not surprisingly, found within the Orinoco and Amazon River drainages. Three species are found farther south within the drainages of the Sao Francisco, Parana, Paraguay, and La Plata rivers, where they mostly inhabit lakes, lagoons, and even small streams, although most are inhabitants of large bodies of water.

Acestrorhynchus altus

MENEZES 1969

Natural Range: Amazon and Paraguay River basins, South America.

Size: Commonly from 5" to 6," but some adults can exceed 8" TL (15–35 cm).

Water Chemistry: Neutral to slightly acidic is best.

Behavior: Non-aggressive towards fishes they cannot swallow.

Dietary Requirements: Meaty foods such as bloodworms and shrimp will suffice, supplemented by regular feedings of live or freshly dead whole fishes.

Remarks: Nearly all of the freshwater barracudas have the same care and husbandry requirements. They're a relatively undemanding species that do their best in aquariums that have a neutral to slightly acidic pH. Filtering over peat will not only allow the hobbyist to achieve this but will give the water a slightly tea-stained appearance. *Acestrorhynchus altus* is one of the rarer species within the genus and anyone wishing to collect these fishes should jump at the chance to add one of this species to their collection.

Acestrorhynchus britskii

MENEZES 1969

Natural Range: Rio Sao Francisco basin, Brazil.

Size: 6" (15 cm) TL; usually smaller.

Water Chemistry: Neutral to slightly acidic is best.

Behavior: Non-aggressive towards fishes they cannot swallow.

Dietary Requirements: Smaller fishes such as guppies and fry of other livebearers in addition to other meaty foods will provide the best results.

Remarks: *Acestrorhynchus britskii* is a smaller species within the genus and is one of the least common. This species is usually available once per year in large numbers with smaller imports occurring infrequently throughout the year. Recently, exports of *Pygocentrus piraya* and *Serrasalmus brandtii* from this region have increased, so perhaps the export of *A. britskii* will, too.

Acestrorhynchus falcatus

BLOCH 1794

Natural Range: Rio Amazonas and Orinoco drainages in northern South America and rivers in Guyana, Suriname, and French Guiana.

Size: 10" (30 cm) TL with some adults reaching nearly 12" (35 cm) TL.

Water Chemistry: Neutral to slightly acidic is best.

Behavior: Predatory; may intimidate smaller species in aquariums.

Dietary Requirements: Strictly carnivorous with the majority of their diet consisting of small, live fishes.

Remarks: This species is often listed as the red-tailed barracuda in pet shops or aquarium stores. They are probably the most common species of the genus available to hobbyists both in Europe and North America and are certainly one of the largest. *A. falcatus* does best in larger aquariums measuring at least 48" x 24" x 24" with even larger sizes being preferred. Tankmates should be large as well because these fish have a remarkable ability to swallow fishes close to half their length.

Acestrorhynchus sp. aff. *altus* freshly caught

Acestrorhynchus dentition

Acestrorhynchus sp. aff. *britskii*

Acestrorhynchus sp.

Acestrorhynchus falcatus juvenile

Acestrorhynchus falcatus adult

Acestrorhynchus falcirostris

CUVIER 1819

Natural Range: Amazon and Orinoco Rivers and various rivers in Guyana.

Size: This is the largest species in the genus with adults occasionally measuring 14" to 16" (35 to 40 cm) TL.

Water Chemistry: Neutral to slightly acidic is best, but slightly alkaline should be fine, too.

Behavior: Flighty and reclusive in aquariums; sometimes hard to adapt to captive life.

Dietary Requirements: Bold predator with an insatiable appetite for whole fishes.

Remarks: Adult *Acestrorhynchus falcirostris* are quite an awesome sight in an aquarium. They are often very large as far as aquarium fishes go and are quite heavy bodied as well. Of all the species within the genus *Acestrorhynchus*, *A. falcirostris* is probably the hardest to train to eat other foods besides whole, live fishes.

Acestrorhynchus isalineae

MENEZES & GERY 1983

Natural Range: Rio Madeira basin of Brazil.

Size: Most specimens range from 3" to 4" (7.5 to 10 cm) with some measuring up to 6" (15 cm) TL.

Water Chemistry: Neutral to slightly acidic is best.

Behavior: Occasional fin nippers but otherwise harmless to fishes they cannot eat; prefer to be in small schools of three to four fish.

Dietary Requirements: Live, small fishes such as livebearer fry seem to be best, but as juveniles thesefish will accept live insect larvae.

Remarks: This small, striped species is quite beautiful in planted aquariums where its colors are most pronounced. They appreciate the cover offered by these plants which is something that does not often matter with most other species of *Acestrorhynchus*. Similar to *A. falcatus*, *A. isalineae* have red in their tails. However, the red is isolated to the upper lobe of the caudal fin only and not on both lobes as in *A. falcatus*.

Acestrorhynchus microlepis / Pike Characin

SCHOMBURGK 1841

Natural Range: Northern South America.

Size: Adults measure close to 8" (20 cm) with some exceeding 10" (25 cm) TL.

Water Chemistry: Neutral to slightly acidic is best. Moderate hardness is reported to be acceptable as well.

Behavior: A larger schooling species that does well in large aquariums.

Dietary Requirements: Strict piscivores that are capable of consuming fishes nearly half of their own length.

Remarks: *Acestrorhynchus microlepis* are unique in that they show a high degree of regional color variation. This is probably due to vitamin and mineral differences that start off in the lower organisms but work their way up the food chain. They are a relatively slender species that does not exhibit a bulbous nose or heavy build that may be characteristic of other species within *Acestrorhynchus*. This species is exported infrequently despite its inclusion on suppliers' lists on a regular basis.

Acestrorhynchus falcirostris juvenile

Acestrorhynchus falcirostris adult

Acestrorhynchus isalineae juvenile

Acestrorhynchus isalineae adult

Acestrorhynchus sp. aff. *microlepis*

Acestrorhynchus sp.

141

Phenacogrammus interuptus

ALESTIDAE
AFRICAN TETRAS

Africa is home to many species of freshwater fishes that are suitable for keeping in aquaria. Many of these resemble the tetras of South America, which is why members of Alestidae are referred to as the African tetras. In fact, these fishes were once a subfamily of Characidae. Their sizes and shapes vary from the three inch deep-bodied *Alestopetersius caudalis* to the four-foot, torpedo-shaped *Hydrocynus goliath*.

Their care and husbandry in captivity are also very varied, but egglaying is one thing they all have in common. Many species, such as the smaller members, will scatter their eggs in and among roots and submerged vegetation. Larger species, such as the tiger fishes, have such a high fecundity level that they are more accurately labeled as broad cast spawners.

Currently, there are 109 species of African tetras with new ones being added frequently. There is little doubt among professionals in the field that there is actually twice this number still waiting to be discovered or scientifically described. As we plow deeper and deeper into the jungles of Africa, we should see this family grow, and with it, the popularity of many of these species in the aquarium trade should grow, as well.

Alestopetersius caudalis / Yellowtail Tetra

BOULENGER 1899

Natural Range: Small bodies of water in the Democratic Republic of the Congo, Africa.
Size: 3" TL (6.2 cm).
Water Chemistry: Prefers pH to be slightly alkaline with a hardness of ~20 dH.
Behavior: A small shoaling fish that prefers to be in groups. They may nip fins.
Dietary Requirements: Small shrimps and insect larvae offered with dry foods are best.

Remarks: Yellowtail tetras are a small and highly prized species for the hobbyist who appreciates small fishes. These tetras do wonderfully in a planted aquarium that has many hiding spaces. They will often do better in larger schools so an aquarium measuring at least 36" x 18" is recommended, but they may do well in smaller aquaria, too. Provide frequent feedings of plant matter to help prevent the tetras from nibbling at the tender new growth that will sprout in your tank.

Arnoldichthys spilopterus / African Red-eyed Tetra

BOULENGER 1909

Natural Range: Tropical West Africa.
Size: Adults measure about 3" (7.5 cm) TL.
Water Chemistry: pH should measure from 6.0 to 7.5 with a dGH of no more than 15, while the temperature should be maintained in the high 70s to low 80s F.
Behavior: These fish are a small, peaceful schooling species.
Dietary Requirements: Small crustaceans such as *Daphnia* or *Artemia* should be fed in small amounts in addition to staple dried foods for color enhancement and diet stability. Juveniles should be fed with *Cyclops*.

Remarks: African Red-Eyed Tetras are a beautiful and hardy species of characin. They are relatively long-lived with specimens living more than three years being common. They need plenty of swimming room despite their small size. Their water should be filtered through peat so as to not only soften the water's hardness but also to darken the water's color. These fish seem to appreciate water with natural tannins in it, and the light will reflect off of their red eyes, giving the tank an interesting look.

Brycinus nurse / Nurse Tetra

RUPPELL 1832

Natural Range: African rivers including the Nile, Chad, Niger, Volta, Gambia, and Sénégal.
Size: Nurse Tetras grow to approximately 8" (20 cm).
Water Chemistry: pH 6.5 to 7.8, hardness to 35 dGH, and temperature range from low 70s to mid 80s F.
Behavior: Juveniles and small adults less than 4" TL can be kept with other schooling tetras; larger adults should be housed with similarly sized, but peaceful fishes.
Dietary Requirements: Small invertebrates along with worms and commercial diets.

Remarks: Nurse tetras are rare treats in the ornamental aquarium trade. They are a peaceful schooling fish, suitable for larger aquariums since they grow to nearly 8" in total length. They are often found in association with bottom structure but will inhabit a wide diversity of biotopes. Males are distinct from females by having a concave anal fin whereas the female's anal fin is straight.

Alestopetersius caudalis

Alestopetersius caudalis

Arnoldichthys spilopterus

Arnoldichthys spilopterus

Brycinus nurse adult

Brycinus nurse juvenile

Hydrocynus forskahlii / Forskahlii African Tiger Fish

CUVIER 1819

Natural Range: Sierra Leone, Ghana, Congo, Liberia, Cameroon, Senegal, and Volta.

Size: Males attain a TL of approximately 30" (75 cm) while females remain slightly smaller.

Water Chemistry: Tropical; Otherwise not critical.

Behavior: Aggressive; keep alone in very large aquariums.

Dietary Requirements: Feed mostly on smaller fishes but will consume snails, crabs, and shrimps as well. Feed a varied diet with some plant matter when possible.

Remarks: The Forskahlii African Tiger Fish does not grow as large as some other species within *Hydrocynus,* but they are equally aggressive. This species is an open water shoaling fish in nature that needs a lot of swimming room in order to thrive in captivity. They are best identified by their sleek, slender profile and the bright red color of the anterior end of the anal fin.

Hydrocynus vittatus / Vittatus African Tiger Fish

CASTELNAU 1861

Natural Range: Most common in the Senegal, Nile, Omo, and Congo Rivers and Lake Tanganyika, Africa.

Size: A large fish growing to nearly 36" (90 cm) TL.

Water Chemistry: Tropical; othewise not critical.

Behavior: As with other species of Tiger Fishes, this species is a ravenous predator in open waters. This species will show intraspecific aggression with congeners.

Dietary Requirements: Meaty foods such as whole fishes and shrimps. Feed to satiation two or three times weekly.

Remarks: Vittatus African Tiger Fish are very similar to their larger cousins, the Goliath African Tiger Fish. Use caution when selecting tankmates, as some specimens are more intolerable of co inhabitants than others. Provide plenty of open swimming room and sparse decorations, as these fish may bang into large rocks or bogwood and cause damage to their large scales. As with many species of Tiger Fishes, this species is an important food fish in its native waters.

Phenacogrammus altus

BOULENGER 1899

Natural Range: Democratic Republic of the Congo (Zaire).

Size: 3" (6.5 cm) TL.

Water Chemistry: Soft, slightly acidic water will be best for this species. Be sure to maintain very high water quality.

Behavior: Very peaceful schooling fish.

Dietary Requirements: Live and prepared foods supplemented with frozen foods.

Remarks: This species is one of those "must-have" species for characin fanatics. They are small yet very active and super attractive when they are set against a background of lush plant growth. Unfortunately, *P. altus* is not as commonly available as they should be, although this could be because they are not yet demanded by hobbyists. Hopefully this will change in the since they are such a strikingly beautiful species.

Hydrocynus forskahlii freshly caught

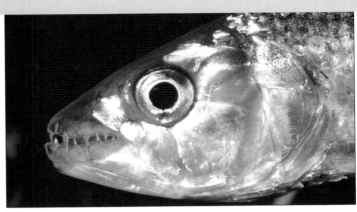

Hydrocynus sp. profile

Hydrocynus vittatus

Hydrocynus vittatus small adult

Phenacogrammus altus adult

Alestopetersius caudalis for comparison

147

Phenacogrammus interruptus / Congo Tetra

BOULENGER 1899

Natural Range: Democratic Republic of the Congo.

Size: Males grow to 4" (10 cm) TL while females grow to about 3" (7.5 cm) TL.

Water Chemistry: Tropical; slightly acid with moderate to soft hardness.

Behavior: A peaceful fish that enjoys equally peaceful tankmates.

Dietary Requirements: Small crustaceans such as *Daphnia* should make up a considerable portion of their diet along with prepared foods containing plant matter.

Remarks: Congo tetras are one of the aquarium hobby's most recognizable and popular species of tetra. They need rather spacious aquariums due to their continuous swimming behavior; however, hobbyists have kept and bred this species in smaller aquariums ranging from 20 to 40 gallons. Even so, aquariums in the 50-gallon range should be considered a minimum for this schooling species. Try to keep at least three with larger schools being preferred.

Phenacogrammus major

BOULENGER 1903

Natural Range: Africa: Rio Muni, Cameroon.

Size: 4" (10 cm) TL.

Water Chemistry: These fish do best in a tropical climate with a pH that is slightly alkaline. Hardness should be moderate.

Behavior: *P. major* is a medium-sized species that also does best in larger schools. They are relatively harmless to all but the smallest of fishes.

Dietary Requirements: Normal prepared foods supplemented with small shrimps, insect larvae, and live *Daphnia* will suit this species very well.

Remarks: As with most species within *Phenacogrammus*, *P. major* appreciates plenty of swimming space in addition to a fair amount of root tangles and caves to hide in and swim among. These fish serve as an attractive and effective dither species for larger fishes such as African dwarf cichlids of the genus *Pelvicachromis*. However, do not make the mistake of thinking this species is a good target species for aggressive African or Middle American cichlids such as *Hemichromis* or *Cryptoheros* respectively.

Phenacogrammus interuptus group

Phenacogrammus sp.

Phenacogrammus major

Alestopetersius caudalis juvenile for comparison

Microctenopoma ansorgii

ANABANTIDAE
CLIMBING GOURAMIES

There is no fish family that can approach the labyrinth fishes when it comes to the multiplicity of interesting behavior. Even the cichlids, the favorite subjects of behavioral research, fall short in comparison with the labyrinth fishes. This family includes species that can leave their natural habitat—water—and travel short distances over land. It also include species that can bury themselves in order to survive the dry season in their natural habitat (usually dry savannah).

The climbing gouramis are distributed widely over Africa, India, and the Philippines. They are rarely found in brackish water but can tolerate some salt added to the aquarium water. In addition, there are very different and often highly distinctive reproductive habits that vary from species to species. There are non-brooding labyrinth fishes, bubblenest builders, cave or hole brooders, and mouthbrooders. These are all good reasons, besides their often attractive coloration, for their continually increasing popularity among tropical fish hobbyists.

Anabas testudineus / Climbing Perch

BLOCH 1792

Natural Range: India to China.

Size: 10" (25 cm) TL.

Water Chemistry: Not picky, avoid extremes.

Behavior: They exhibit a high degree of interspecific aggression with congeners.

Dietary Requirements: Almost anything edible, from small fishes and invertebrates to plant matter and prepared foods such as pellets and large flaked foods.

Remarks: The climbing perch is one of those species that we refer to as "grandfathers" in the aquarium hobby. This species and its close relative *A. oligolepis* were among the first species to be kept by aquarists many years ago. What is most interesting about this species is its ability to remain buried under mud for many months during the dry season only to emerge when conditions are again favorable.

Ctenopoma acutirostre / Leopard Ctenopoma

PELLEGRIN 1899

Natural Range: Congo basin, Africa.

Size: 6" (15 cm) TL.

Water Chemistry: Wide pH range from 6.0 to 8.0; dH of no more than 15 is preferred.

Behavior: Only keep with fishes not able to be swallowed.

Dietary Requirements: Meaty foods such as fish, or live insects, or bits of earthworms are best.

Remarks: This species is a model citizen in aquariums containing a community of fishes—as long as the tankmates cannot be swallowed. In nature, they are often subjected to water conditions far worse than those allowed by all but the laziest of aquarists. Feeding is usually no problem, since they are opportunistic predators and have a hardy appetite for nearly anything that smells like food. Spawning is an awesome sight with the pair showing colors that are vibrant and certainly not present on many of the other members of the family.

Ctenopoma ocellatum / Eyespot Ctenopoma

PELLEGRIN 1899

Natural Range: Lower Congo basin, Africa.

Size: 6" (15 cm) TL.

Water Chemistry: They do best in tropical temperatures with a pH range that is best kept at 6.0 to 7.5 with a moderate hardness.

Behavior: Strikingly similar to that of *C. acutirostre*.

Dietary Requirements: The diet described for *C. acutirostre* is also appropriate for this species.

Remarks: This species is best identified by the dark-colored ocellus at the base of the tail. This ocellus gives rise to the specific name of *ocellatum*. Other than differences in meristic measurements and coloration, *C. ocellatum* are nearly identical to their close cousin—*C. acutirostre*.

Anabas testudineus

Anabas testudineus

Ctenopoma acutirostre adult

Ctenopoma acutirostre pair

Ctenopoma ocellatum adult

Ctenopoma ocellatum profile

Ctenopoma oxyrhynchum / Mottled Ctenopoma

BOULENGER 1902

Natural Range: Lower Congo basin, Africa.

Size: 4" (10 cm) TL.

Water Chemistry: Do best in a tropical climate with a neutral pH and moderate hardness.

Behavior: Generally quite peaceful and less territorial compared with other congeners.

Dietary Requirements: Meaty foods such as insect larvae and small fishes are best with regular supplementation of prepared foods.

Remarks: This species is easily spawned in moderately-sized aquariums of 20 gallons or larger. They do not provide any brood care, and the young will chase live *Artemia* nauplii after only a few days. As with nearly all other *Ctenopoma*, *C. oxyrhynchum* does best with larger tankmates. This species seems to especially relish live earthworms and should be offered them somewhat regularly.

Microctenopoma ansorgii / Ornate Ctenopoma

BOULENGER 1912

Natural Range: Congo basin, Africa and Tropical West Africa.

Size: 3.5" (8 cm) TL.

Water Chemistry: Does best in tropical climates with a neutral pH and moderate to soft on the hardness scale.

Behavior: Very peaceful.

Dietary Requirements: Does especially well on a diet of live insects. Dry food is often inadequate for the long term.

Remarks: Ironically, this *Ctenopoma* can suffer the exact opposite fate of their big brothers—they can be the ones getting bullied and harassed or even eaten by tankmates! Due to their small size and very peaceful nature, *C. ansorgii* are best kept in a planted aquarium with other shy or reclusive species. They will not do well in aquariums that contain fast-moving or overly active fishes such as tiger barbs *Puntius tetrazona* or any large *Danio* species.

Microctenopoma nanum / Dwarf Ctenopoma

GUNTHER 1896

Natural Range: Southern Cameroon, Gabon, and Congo basin, Africa.

Size: 2.5" (8 cm) TL.

Water Chemistry: A tropical climate with a pH in the range of 6.0 to 7.0 and a moderate hardness is probably best for this species.

Behavior: Usually peaceful with some interspecific aggression taking place occasionally.

Dietary Requirements: Same as *M. ansorgii*.

Remarks: *M. nanum* seem to appreciate the cover that a well-planted aquarium provides. As with most other *Ctenopoma*-type fishes, this species may nibble on plants, so keep an eye on them when they are in association with soft-leaved species. Many hobbyists have reported successful spawnings of these fish, but apparently the young are quite difficult to rear. Perhaps this species should have a dedicated aquarium when attempting to spawn.

Ctenopoma oxyrhynchum

Ctenopoma oxyrhynchum adult

Microctenopoma ansorgii non-breeding color

Microctenopoma ansorgii displaying male

Microctenopoma nanum non-breeding color

Microctenopoma nanum on display

Anguilla anguilla

ANGUILLIDAE
FRESHWATER EELS

There are approximately 21 species of eels in the family Anguillidae. Of these, only three are profiled here, since many are unavailable to the average hobbyist, and even if you were to obtain specimens, they all grow to very large sizes in aquariums.

Anguilla species are usually catadromous by nature and live most of their lives in freshwater or brackish water environments until they become sexually mature. At this time, they move out to the open ocean and to great depths in order to reproduce. The young (elvers) will slowly make their way back to the same general area that their parents originated from. The adults die after spawning has been accomplished.

As with many groups of fishes, Anguillidae has its share of confusion, and many ichthyologists doubt the validity of all species currently recognized. In time, and as DNA analysis is perfected, their validity will be determined.

Anguilla anguilla / European Eel

LINNAEUS 1758

Natural Range: Atlantic Ocean: Baltic, Sargasso (breeding), and Mediterranean.

Size: 36 – 48" (90 – 120 cm) TL.

Water Chemistry: Temperate, demersal, and catadromous. Avoid extremes.

Behavior: Harmless unless tankmates can be readily swallowed.

Dietary Requirements: A meaty diet consisting of various seafoods and pellets is best.

Remarks: A fairly hardy species, European eels spend much of their time hiding amongst tank décor. They are not usually aggressive except on rare occasions and provide interesting behavior for those who are patient enough to sit and observe them. Due to their large-growing size, they are really only suitable for those hobbyists with aquariums measuring at least 72" in length and 18–24" deep.

Anguilla rostrata / American Eel

LESUEUR 1817

Natural Range: East coast of North America from Canada south to Trinidad.

Size: 48–60" (120 – 150 cm) TL.

Water Chemistry: Subtropical, demersal, and catadromous. Avoid extremes.

Behavior: Generally harmless to anything that cannot easily be swallowed whole.

Dietary Requirements: A meaty diet consisting of seafoods and pellets is best.

Remarks: The American eel grows rather large. They should be kept in large aquariums and provided with plenty of hiding spaces. American eels have been known to be a little more aggressive with their tankmates, so it would be a good idea to only keep them with other fishes that are capable of defending themselves.

Anguilla anguilla elvers

Anguilla anguilla adult

Anguilla rostrata

Anguilla rostrata

159

Leporinus fasciatus

ANOSTOMIDAE
HEADSTANDERS

The headstanders are a large and very interesting group of fishes. Twelve species are featured here, but do be fooled, as there are over 110 species within the family and probably all of them would do well in most large aquariums. They are easy to feed and keep, provided they have clean water and plenty of space.

Feeding can be a challenge, since many are omnivorous and need some plant matter, usually in the form of algae, in their diets. In nature, those species that require the intake of plant proteins are commonly seen grazing on aquatic vegetation and scraping submerged wood and roots. Although some ecologists believe this to be a seasonal dietary shift, many hobbyists with experience keeping these fishes can attest to their acceptance of plant matter on a continual basis.

The name "Headstander" is given to this group of fishes due to their odd behavior of swimming with their heads in a downward position. This is probably due to their constant lookout for small worms and crustaceans that they feed on in addition to any plant matter that is grazed upon. There are species of Headstanders in nearly every major body of water in South America except for the upper regions of the Andes Mountains.

Abramites hypselonotus / Marbled Headstander

GUNTHER 1868

Natural Range: Widely distributed over much of South America.

Size: 6" (15 cm) TL.

Water Chemistry: Tropical, soft water with a neutral pH.

Behavior: A harmless species that prefers to live among vegetation and roots. They may become very aggressive toward each other if visual barriers are not provided.

Dietary Requirements: Small insects, worms, and prepared foods that are enriched with plant matter are best.

Remarks: A long-time resident of the aquarium trade, *A. hypselonotus* has been very popular for nearly 60 years. They tend to nibble on plants so even though they appreciate the cover such decorations provide, be aware of this behavior when taking their décor into account. This is an interesting and active species that needs plenty of room to swim about.

Anostomus anostomus / Striped Headstander

LINNAEUS 1758

Natural Range: Amazon and Orinoco River basins, northern South America.

Size: 6 – 8" (15–20 cm) TL.

Water Chemistry: Tropical, soft and slightly acidic.

Behavior: Shy and peaceful, should have plenty of hiding spaces. Usually observed standing motionless with heads pointed downward toward the aquarium's gravel.

Dietary Requirements: They seem to do best on prepared foods but relish feedings of small living foods, as well. Supplement with plant matter.

Remarks: A small, pointed head with a mouth that points upward characterizes this handsome species. They are often very shy and need to be kept with other less boisterous fishes. Those tankmates that are overly territorial will often compete with them for food and may stress them to the point of illness and eventual death.

Abramites hypselonotus dark var.

Abramites hypselonotus normal var.

Anostomus anostomus

Anostomus anostomus

163

Leporinus affinis

GUNTHER 1864

Natural Range: Amazon River basin, South America.
Size: 10" (25 cm) TL.
Water Chemistry: Tropical, prefers soft acidic water with a pH around 6.5.
Behavior: Usually peaceful but may nip on the fins of other fishes. Use caution when keeping them with small species.
Dietary Requirements: Need plant matter in their diet, so use prepared foods that have been enriched with algae or another source of plant matter.

Remarks: This species tends to be hardy and very forgiving in aquariums. They need plenty of room to swim, since they grow rather large by aquarium standards. Additionally, *L. affinis* prefers a strong current, so the use of strong filtration and even additional powerheads is advised to keep them happy.

Leporinus arcus / Lipstick Leporinus

EIGENMANN 1912

Natural Range: Northern South America.
Size: 18" (40 cm) TL max. Usually much smaller.
Water Chemistry: Tropical, prefers soft acidic water with a pH around 6.5.
Behavior: Usually peaceful but may nip on the fins of other fishes. Use caution when keeping them with small species.
Dietary Requirements: Similar to *L. affinis* but may take more animal matter, including small fishes.

Remarks: *L. arcus* is one of the largest growing species within *Leporinus*. They are often collected in fast-moving waters but sometimes bite a baited hook. In aquariums, this species can be a bully with members of its own genus but is usually harmless to other fishes. This species makes an excellent dither fish in tanks containing other large fishes.

Leporinus fasciatus / Banded Leporinus

BLOCH 1794

Natural Range: Amazon River basin.
Size: 12" (30 cm) TL. Usually much smaller.
Water Chemistry: Tropical, prefers soft acidic water with a pH of around 6.5.
Behavior: Usually peaceful but may nip at the fins of other fishes, particularly smaller specimens.
Dietary Requirements: Highly omnivorous, taking equal amounts of plant and animal matter.

Remarks: *L. fasciatus* is probably the most easily recognized member of the genus *Leporinus*. They are a colorful species that tends to swim in small schools. Just as with other members of the genus, *L. fasciatus* make excellent dithers for large or overly shy species. In some instances, they also serve as a target fish for more aggressive species.

Leporinus affinis adult

Leporinus affinis profile

Leporinus arcus

Leporinus arcus var.

Leporinus fasciatus adult

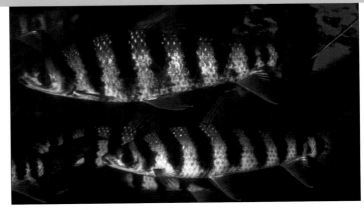

Leporinus fasciatus group

Leporinus maculatus / Spotted Leporinus

MULLER & TROSCHEL 1844

Natural Range: North Eastern South America.
Size: 6" (18 cm) TL.
Water Chemistry: Tropical, prefers moderately soft water with a pH range of 6.5 to 7.2.
Behavior: An active swimmer that hunts down small invertebrates with incredible effectiveness.
Dietary Requirements: More carnivorous than its close cousins. Feed a diet high in shrimp and worms.

Remarks: As with most other species within *Leporinus*, this species occurs in sandy areas where the water current is strong. It may be beneficial to attempt to recreate this environment using driftwood and rockwork along the sides and back of the aquarium, but leave the center open to form a sand flat. They will usually be seen living in this sandy area, awaiting their next meal.

Leporinus striatus

KNER 1858

Natural Range: South America: Orissanga, Parana, and Paraguay River basins.
Size: 10" (25 cm) TL.
Water Chemistry: Tropical, prefers soft water with a nearly neutral pH and moderate hardness.
Behavior: Found in open, fast-flowing water. Peaceful in aquariums, but watch for fin-nipping behavior.
Dietary Requirements: Mainly vegetarian but feeds actively on prepared foods and small living fishes.

Remarks: While this species is considered to be a tropical one, studies indicate that *L. striatus* is capable of living quite well in cooler water also. This species is still rare in the aquarium trade, but since the market for fishes from southern South America is increasing, *L. striatus* is sure to gain popularity in the near future.

Leporinus friderici / Threespot Leporinus

BLOCH 1794

Natural Range: South America: Suriname, Amazon basin.
Size: 18" (40 cm) TL max. Usually much smaller.
Water Chemistry: Tropical, wide range of pH and hardness is accepted, avoid extremes.
Behavior: This large-growing species is surprisingly peaceful but may nip the fins of any fish in the aquarium, big or small, so keep an eye out for that.
Dietary Requirements: Omnivorous, eats insects as well as nuts, fruits, and leafy greens.

Remarks: A food fish in its native lands, this attractive species apparently has a wonderful taste. *L. friderici* lives among tangled roots and vegetation in slightly deeper waters compared with other members of the genus. Provide large pieces of driftwood in a tangled fashion so as to provide a home that is suitable.

166

Leporinus maculatus

Leporinus maculatus profile

Leporinus striatus

Leporinus striatus var.

Leporinus friderici

Leporinus friderici profile

Pseudanos gracilis

KNER 1858

Natural Range: South America: Guapore, Negro, and Orinoco River basins.

Size: 6" (15 cm) TL.

Water Chemistry: Tropical, prefers acidic to neutral pH with moderate hardness.

Behavior: Generally peaceful but may nip at fins and scales of smaller fishes.

Dietary Requirements: Feeds predominantly on small invertebrates and plant matter.

Remarks: *P. gracilis* is a harmless species that lives in the crevices of root tangles. They prefer areas of higher water flow and dash out of their hiding spots at the first sign of a potential meal. Offer plenty of cover in their aquariums.

Pseudanos trimaculatus / Threespot Headstander

KNER 1858

Natural Range: Amazon River basin, South America.

Size: 5" (12 cm) TL.

Water Chemistry: Tropical, soft acidic water is best.

Behavior: A deepwater species that prefers to be in schools. Peaceful with most other fishes.

Dietary Requirements: Mainly vegetarian but will greedily accept living worms and insect larvae.

Remarks: This hardy species is most comfortable in large schools, among roots and tangles of wood and rocks. They also prefer a dimly lit aquarium and will show their best coloration and pattern in such a setting. Provide good circulation and plenty of vegetable-based foods, and these fish should do very well for years in captivity.

Pseudanos gracilis

Pseudanos trimaculatus for comparison

Pseudanos trimaculatus

Pseudanos trimaculatus pair

169

Aphyosemion australe

APLOCHEILIDAE

KILLIFISHES

While members of Aplocheilidae are found in many areas around the world, only African and Asian species normally appear in the aquarium trade. This is probably due to the brilliant colors and patterns that are associated with them.

Killies are often not difficult to keep and breed in aquariums, but some are easier than others. Many species are only available through specialists, and this is probably due to the higher prices that are usually associated with them. Some fish shops have reported that while these fishes are beautiful to look at, they are often outside the price range of what one is willing to pay for a very small fish (usually less than 3" TL).

While that may be the case, it is important to know that when their aquariums are properly set up and maintained, Killies make wonderful and very interesting pets.

Aphyosemion australe / Lyretail Panchax

RACHOW 1921

Natural Range: Northwestern Gabon southward to parts of Angola and western Congo (Zaire).
Size: 2.5" (6 cm) TL.
Water Chemistry: Tropical, soft and slightly acid water is best.
Behavior: A very peaceful fish that does very well in captivity.
Dietary Requirements: Insects, worms, and various small crustaceans. Prepared foods that are high in protein are taken quite readily, as well.

Remarks: Various color morphs are available to hobbyists, but the chocolate and the gold are probably the most popular. *A. australe* is not reported as being a seasonal killifish, so a lifespan of several years can be expected.

Aphyosemion ahli / Ahl's Lyretail

MYERS 1933

Natural Range: Tropical West Africa.
Size: 2" (5 cm) TL.
Water Chemistry: Tropical; prefers soft, acidic water.
Behavior: Peaceful in a community aquarium.
Dietary Requirements: Small living foods such as *Daphnia* and *Artemia* are preferred.

Remarks: *Aphyosemion ahli* is one of the most strikingly beautiful members of the genus. They are sometimes available in specialty shops, but more often than not you will need to locate a breeder in order to find them. They breed easily, but pairs need a rest once in a while to prevent egg infertility. This is actually a good practice to follow with all Killies.

Aphyosemion bitaeniatum / Two-striped *Aphyosemion*

AHL 1924

Natural Range: Southern regions of Togo, Benin, and Nigeria (Niger River), Africa.
Size: 2" (5 cm), females slightly smaller.
Water Chemistry: Tropical; neutral pH and low hardness are best.
Behavior: Peaceful, keep with other gentle fishes.
Dietary Requirements: Small living foods and prepared foods taken readily.

Remarks: Another super-brilliantly colored species of *Aphyosemion*. As with others within the genus, keep these fish in a quiet, peaceful community setting that has plants and driftwood to accent their colors. Breeding is in normal Killie-fashion with eggs deposited among plants or roots.

Aphyosemion australe

Aphyosemion australe

Aphyosemion ahli

Aphyosemion ahli

Aphyosemion bitaeniatum

Aphyosemion bitaeniatum

Aphyosemion bivittatum / Twostripe Lyretail

LONNBERG 1895

Natural Range: Southern Nigeria and Cameroon, Africa.
Size: 2" (5 cm) TL.
Water Chemistry: Tropical, prefers soft acidic water best.
Behavior: Generally peaceful in community aquariums. Males may be aggressive among each other.
Dietary Requirements: Probably best to feed a diet of small crustaceans and water fleas.

Remarks: As with many other species within *Aphyosemion*, *A. bivittatum* will appreciate a well-planted aquarium with a limited number of other fishes to share it with. While they are generally very peaceful, males may fight if more than one is placed in the same tank. Usually, they deposit their eggs in fine-leaved plants close to the surface, although they have been seen burying their eggs in the substrate, as well.

Aphyosemion bualanum / African Swamp Killie

AHL 1924

Natural Range: Eastern Cameroon and the Central African Republic.
Size: To 2.5" (6 cm), females slightly smaller.
Water Chemistry: Tropical, prefers soft and slightly acidic water.
Behavior: Peaceful when kept with fish its own size.
Dietary Requirements: Readily accepts small live foods as well as prepared fare.

Remarks: Found in a wide range of habitats, *A. bualanum* can tolerate varying degrees of water chemistry and temperatures but does best in soft and slightly acidic water that is tropical in temperature. Ironically, their colors are said to be much richer if they are kept on the cooler side. This species spawns in plant thickets or floating bunches near the surface.

Aphyosemion calliurum / Blue Lyretail

BOULENGER

Natural Range: Liberia to northern Angola.
Size: 2" (5 cm) TL; may grow a bit larger in nature.
Water Chemistry: Tropical; prefers soft, acidic water.
Behavior: Peaceful.
Dietary Requirements: Small living organisms are greedily taken.

Remarks: *Aphyosemion calliurum* is one of the easiest plant-spawning Killies to keep and is highly recommended for beginners that are fortunate enough to find them. Unfortunately, the popularity of this species among killifish fanciers is limited at best. This is probably due to their lack of brilliant colors when compared to so many other available choices.

Aphyosemion bivittatum

Aphyosemion bivittatum

Aphyosemion bualanum

Aphyosemion bualanum

Aphyosemion calliurum

Aphyosemion calliurum var.

175

Aphyosemion cameronense / Cameroon Killie

BOULENGER 1903

Natural Range: Cameroon, Congo, Equatorial Guinea, and Gabon, Africa.
Size: 2" (5 cm) TL.
Water Chemistry: Tropical, neutral pH with moderate hardness.
Behavior: Peaceful.
Dietary Requirements: Prefers small living foods but will switch to prepared foods in aquariums.

Remarks: This species prefers to be in aquariums that are dimly illuminated. In nature, they live where there is a dark forest cover over the water. They do not like a swift current and may become overly stressed if forced to live in aquaria with a heavy water flow. Filter water over peat to darken water more naturally.

Aphyosemion caudofasciatum / Caudal-stripe Killie

HUBER & RADDA 1979

Natural Range: Southern Congo, Africa.
Size: 2" (5 cm) TL, females slightly smaller.
Water Chemistry: Tropical, neutral pH and moderate hardness.
Behavior: Peaceful with small tankmates.
Dietary Requirements: Small living foods and prepared foods are best.

Remarks: This species has a tendency to be difficult to keep in aquariums, so they should only be attempted after having kept other Killie species first. Once a group has been established, place spawning mops both just below the surface of the water and rooted in the gravel. Juveniles may show different color patterns than adults. Keep in a dimly lit aquarium.

Aphyosemion celiae / Celia's Killie

SCHEEL 1971

Natural Range: Mungo drainage system, western Cameroon, Africa.
Size: 2" (5 cm) TL, females may be smaller.
Water Chemistry: Tropical, neutral to slightly acidic water with moderate hardness is best.
Behavior: Peaceful.
Dietary Requirements: Small living foods preferred but will readily accept prepared foods that are occasionally supplemented with frozen bloodworms.

Remarks: A great fish for beginners, *A. celiae* is hardy and presents no problems when kept in a community aquarium with other peaceful species. It is not uncommon for the beginner to breed this species in the aquarium. A darkened, well-planted aquarium will be best for them.

Aphyosemion cameronense male

Aphyosemion cameronense female

Aphyosemion caudofasciatum

Aphyosemion caudofasciatum profile

Aphyosemion celiae winfredi

Aphyosemion celiae

177

Aphyosemion christyi / Christy's Lyretail

BOULENGER 1915

Natural Range: Central Congo drainage, Africa.
Size: 2" (5 cm) TL, females slightly smaller.
Water Chemistry: Tropical; neutral pH and moderate hardness are best.
Behavior: Completely peaceful.
Dietary Requirements: Small living and frozen foods.

Remarks: The various color strains and geographical races of this species cross readily, but the young are often sterile. This is due in part to the fact that different populations differ in chromosome numbers. The hobbyist interested in propagating this species is urged to use peat moss on the tank bottom instead of sand. In addition to lowering the pH, peat moss seems to put several other substances in the water that may trigger a spawning response in several fishes.

Aphyosemion cognatum / Red-spotted Lyretail

MEINKEN 1951

Natural Range: Lower Congo River.
Size: 2" (5 cm) TL. Females may not get as large.
Water Chemistry: Tropical; soft, acidic, and aged water is preferred.
Behavior: Peaceful but best kept alone.
Dietary Requirements: Small, living foods will provide best all-around health and vigor.

Remarks: Males have an oddly-shaped dorsal fin that has the longest rays toward the tail, making it look as if it had been stuck on backwards. Although this species is not quite as hardy as some of the other species within the genus, they are still able to tolerate fluctuations in water quality and temperature as long as extremes are avoided.

Aphyosemion christyi

Aphyosemion christyi

Aphyosemion cognatum

Aphyosemion australe for comparison

Aphyosemion geryi / Gery's Killie

LAMBERT 1958

Natural Range: Sierra Leone.
Size: 3" (7.5 cm) TL, females slightly smaller.
Water Chemistry: Well aged water with an acidic pH and soft to moderate hardness.
Behavior: Peaceful, better kept in pairs in a small aquarium.
Dietary Requirements: Small living foods preferred.

Remarks: Gery's Killies are extremely hardy and can tolerate a wide range of water chemistry and temperatures. Furthermore, they do not seem to be susceptible to many diseases. This, along with the male's bright red coloration, makes this species an excellent aquarium fish.

Aphyosemion filamentosum / Togo Lyretail

MEINKE 1933

Natural Range: Tropical West Africa.
Size: 2" (5 cm), males may get slightly larger in nature.
Water Chemistry: Tropical; soft and slightly acidic water is preferred.
Behavior: Peaceful but mature males may be bullies.
Dietary Requirements: Will accept all standard aquarium fare, but living foods are preferred.

Remarks: There are few other species of *Aphyosemion* that can rival the finnage produced by a male *A. filamentosum* in full breeding dress. Most pictures do not do them justice, and just when you think you have seen an extra-nice specimen you'll see an even more beautiful one. Since males may be quarrelsome amongst themselves, it is best to provide one male with multiple females instead of keeping several pairs in one container, as is recommended with several other Killies.

Aphyosemion hera

HUBER 1998

Natural Range: Gabon.
Size: 1.5" (3.1 cm) TL.
Water Chemistry: Tropical; soft and slightly acidic water is best.
Behavior: Peaceful with other small fishes.
Dietary Requirements: Small, living foods preferred. Prepared foods accepted.

Remarks: *A. hera* is a fairly new addition to the family Aplocheilidae. They are a small species growing to just about 1.5" in total length and seem to prefer aquariums with a lot of cover. Providing them with a dense growth of plants certainly will not do them any harm. Tankmates should be less boisterous species such as small *Corydoras* catfishes or small tetras.

Aphyosemion geryi

Aphyosemion geryi

Aphyosemion filamentosum

Aphyosemion filamentosum profile

Aphyosemion hera

Aphyosemion hera profile

181

Aphyosemion ogoense / Ogowe Killie

PELLEGRIN 1930

Natural Range: Gabon and Congo.
Size: 2" (5 cm) TL.
Water Chemistry: Tropical; neutral and slightly soft water are best.
Behavior: Peaceful; does best with small fishes.
Dietary Requirements: Small, living foods are taken with gusto; may be picky with prepared foods.

Remarks: *A. ogoense* is a typical plant-spawning Killie that deposits its eggs in bunched plants at all levels. While they are nothing new to science, you may find it difficult to find this species as they seem to have been more popular several years ago. As with most Killies, breeding groups are kept going by many hardcore Killie breeders.

Aphyosemion primigenium / Douano Killie

RADDA & HUBER 1977

Natural Range: Southwestern Gabon.
Size: 2" (5 cm) TL.
Water Chemistry: Tropical; neutral to slightly acidic pH with a moderate hardness is best.
Behavior: Generally peaceful but difficult to maintain.
Dietary Requirements: Small, living foods, shrimps, and water fleas.

Remarks: This species is only suitable for the more advanced aquarists and hobbyists. Conflicting reports indicate that this species is easy to keep and can be maintained by beginners, however, others say quite the opposite. Perhaps the best remedy to this conflict is to obtain your specimens from a known Killie-expert who will be able to guide you in the proper direction with this species.

Aphyosemion schioetzi / Schiotz's Killie

HUBER & SCHEEL 1981

Natural Range: Congo.
Size: 2" (5 cm) TL.
Water Chemistry: Tropical; neutral to slightly acidic pH with moderate hardness.
Behavior: Generally peaceful; keep with slightly larger fishes of same disposition.
Dietary Requirements: Small living foods such as Daphnia and brine shrimp are best.

Remarks: This is another species that some describe as easy and some describe as difficult. Again, it may be best to refer to someone with a lot of experience with this species to get their notes. As with almost all fishes, the experience will differ some from one hobbyist to another.

Aphyosemion ogoense

Aphyosemion ogoense

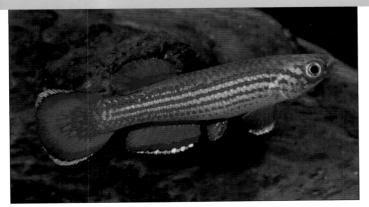

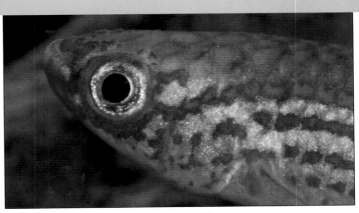

Aphyosemion primigenium

Aphyosemion primigenium profile

Aphyosemion schioetzi

Aphyosemion schioetzi

183

Aphyosemion striatum / Five-lined Killie

BOULENGER 1911
Natural Range: Guinea to Gabon, Africa.
Size: 3" (7.5 cm) TL, females smaller.
Water Chemistry: Tropical; soft and acidic water is best.
Behavior: Better to keep by themselves, may be aggressive toward tankmates of a similar size.
Dietary Requirements: Live foods, frozen foods, and prepared foods.

Remarks: Not a large species, *A. striatum* is considered large compared to many other Killies. They also tend to be a little more aggressive and may nip at the fins of other fishes. Keep in a roomy enclosure with plenty of visual barriers in the form of bogwood and plants. This species should be very easy both to keep and to spawn.

Aplocheilus blocki / Dwarf Panchax

ARNOLD 1911
Natural Range: Sri Lanka and India.
Size: 2" (5 cm) TL, females slightly smaller.
Water Chemistry: Tropical; aged water that is soft and slightly acidic is best for them.
Behavior: Peaceful; do not keep with large fishes.
Dietary Requirements: Will eat dried foods but prefer small living and frozen foods.

Remarks: *Aplocheilus blocki* is generally considered to be the smallest member of the genus. Although adults can reach two inches in total length, they average only about one and a half. It was named after Captain Block of Hamburg, Germany, who brought in a great many Bettas around 1909 and included this species in one of his importations. This species does best in a small aquarium with plenty of live plants and bogwood for them to hide among.

Aplocheilus lineatus / Striped Panchax

VALENCIENNES 1846
Natural Range: India and Sri Lanka.
Size: 4" (10 cm) TL.
Water Chemistry: Tropical; neutral to slightly acidic and soft is best.
Behavior: Will not harm anything it can't swallow; may be kept with larger fishes as well.
Dietary Requirements: Small, living foods supplemented with dry prepared foods.

Remarks: These are best kept in an aquarium all to themselves even though they can co-exist with other fishes. The tank should be planted and have at least some floating plants to provide cover. Large specimens will readily accept live Guppies, White Clouds, and livebearer fry as food. Use caution when selecting tankmates.

Aphyosemion striatum

Aphyosemion striatum var.

Aplocheilus blocki female

Aplocheilus blocki male

Aplocheilus lineatus

Aplocheilus lineatus

Aplocheilus panchax / Blue Panchax

HAMILTON 1822

Natural Range: Pakistan, India, Bangladesh, Burma, and the Indo-Malaysian archipelago.
Size: 4" (10 cm) TL.
Water Chemistry: Tropical; not critical; avoid extremes.
Behavior: May swallow small fishes; otherwise peaceful.
Dietary Requirements: Should be given a diet rich in meaty foods.

Remarks: The Blue Panchax is a gorgeous fish that is perfect for the community aquarium containing large, slow-moving fishes. There have been several controversies over the taxonomy of this species, as with nearly all Killies. Today, we recognize one species with several color morphs, some of which are more popular within the aquarium industry than others.

Callopanchax occidentalis / Golden Pheasant Panchax

CLAUSEN 1966

Natural Range: Sherboro Island and Sierra Leone along the coastal lowlands, Africa.
Size: 3.5" (8 cm) TL.
Water Chemistry: Tropical; soft and slightly acid conditions are best.
Behavior: Not a peaceful species. Better kept in species-specific aquaria.
Dietary Requirements: Small living foods and prepared foods.

Remarks: Although this fish has been in the hobby for many years, it was only first recognized as a distinct species in 1966. The first account of this fish was on June 9th, 1908. Grote, a German aquarist from Hamburg who was serving on a ship returning from West Africa, caught three specimens of this species on Sherboro Island near Sierra Leone. At the time, these specimens were thought to be in the genus *Fundulus*.

Epiplatys annulatus / Banded Panchax (Clown Killie)

BOULENGER 1915

Natural Range: Sierra Leone to Liberia.
Size: 2" (5 cm) TL, females slightly smaller.
Water Chemistry: Soft acidic water filtered over peat is best.
Behavior: Peaceful but very small; may be eaten by other fishes.
Dietary Requirements: Small living and frozen foods are best.

Remarks: First described by BOULENGER in 1915, this species was not brought alive into Europe until 40 years later, but the water they were placed in was of improper chemistry, and they all died. E. Roloff made an expedition into Sierra Leone in 1965, providing for much of the hobbyist-oriented information we have on this species. The information he collected has made this species much easier to keep and breed in aquariums today.

Aplocheilus panchax var. Java

Aplocheilus panchax

Callopanchax occidentalis

Callopanchax occidentalis

Epiplatys annulatus

Epiplatys annulatus

Epiplatys chaperi / Chaper's Panchax

SAUVAGE 1882
Natural Range: Sierra Leone to Ghana, Africa.
Size: 2" (5 cm) TL.
Water Chemistry: Tropical; prefer soft acidic water.
Behavior: Peaceful; should not bother anything it cannot swallow.
Dietary Requirements: Small living foods are best.

Remarks: Taxonomic work has indicated that the fish most commonly known as *E. chaperi* is actually *E. dageti*. Chaper's Panchax is actually a distinct but little-seen species. One pair can be kept successfully in a small aquarium and are often quite peaceful with other fishes as long as they cannot swallow them.

Epiplatys dageti / Redchin Panchax

POLL 1953
Natural Range: Southwestern Liberia to southwestern Ghana.
Size: 2" (5 cm) TL.
Water Chemistry: Tropical; soft and slightly acidic water is preferred.
Behavior: May be aggressive towards fishes its own size and smaller; an active and energetic swimmer.
Dietary Requirements: Live, frozen, and prepared are all usually accepted.

Remarks: This beautiful fish has several subspecies and color morphs that are all occasionally available to hobbyists. It first became known to hobbyists in a shipment of aquarium fishes from West Africa in 1908. These pretty fish, regardless of their complicated historical origins and troublesome taxonomic considerations, require relatively uncomplicated aquarium maintenance procedures.

Epiplatys duboisi / Dubois' Panchax

POLL 1952
Natural Range: Congo, Africa.
Size: 1.5" (3.5 cm) TL.
Water Chemistry: Tropical, neutral pH and moderate hardness.
Behavior: Peaceful.
Dietary Requirements: Small living foods preferred.

Remarks: This is one of the smallest aquarium fish most hobbyists will come in contact with. This species will get lost in many larger aquariums. For this reason, *E. duboisi* really deserve an aquarium all their own. In nature, they live in weedy parts of brooks, small streams, and swamps, so their aquarium décor should reflect a similar environment.

Epiplatys chaperi

Epiplatys chaperi

Epiplatys dageti

Epiplatys dageti

Epiplatys duboisi

Epiplatys duboisi

189

Epiplatys olbrechtsi

POLL 1941

Natural Range: Liberia and Guinea.
Size: 3.5" (8.5 cm) TL.
Water Chemistry: Tropical; soft acidic water is preferred.
Behavior: Generally peaceful; may nip at fins of similar-sized fishes.
Dietary Requirements: Small living fishes and similar-sized prepared foods.

Remarks: While most Killies are rather small, *E. olbrechtsi* is one species that actually grows to a suitable size to be placed among other common fishes in a community aquarium. The only problem is that they tend to be a little nippy and may harass similarly sized fishes, so care must be taken to avoid behavioral problems. In the end, it's probably best to keep them in a species-specific aquarium.

Epiplatys sexfasciatus / Six-banded Panchax

GILL 1862

Natural Range: West coast of Africa from southern Liberia to the mouth of the Congo River.
Size: 4" (10 cm) TL, average is smaller.
Water Chemistry: Tropical; soft and slightly acidic water is best.
Behavior: Fairly peaceful with fishes its own size.
Dietary Requirements: All kinds of living foods that can be swallowed whole.

Remarks: This attractive little fish is not quite as brightly colored as others in the "panchax" group and is therefore not seen as frequently. Specialists often have broodstock from many generations available, and these are the perfect specimens to obtain. In community aquariums, they tend to shy away from bright lights and prefer a dimly lit aquarium.

Fundulopanchax arnoldi / Arnold's Lyretail

BOULENGER 1908

Natural Range: Niger River.
Size: 2" (5 cm) TL. May grow slightly larger.
Water Chemistry: Tropical; prefer soft, acidic water.
Behavior: Peaceful.
Dietary Requirements: Small, living foods preferred over dried and frozen.

Remarks: Females of this species do not have the lyre-shaped caudal fins and are comparatively dull brown in color, with some red spots on the fins and body. This species is not easily kept and is best suited to those with some Killie experience under their belts. As with all species of *Aphyosemion*, this species must eat regularly or their health will be compromised.

Epiplatys olbrechtsi   *Epiplatys olbrechtsi*

Epiplatys sexfasciatus   *Epiplatys sexfasciatus* var.

Fundulopanchax arnoldi   *Fundulopanchax arnoldi* var.

Fundulopanchax gardneri / Blue Lyretail

BOULENGER 1911

Natural Range: Coast of Nigeria to the Republic of the Congo.
Size: 2" (5 cm) TL.
Water Chemistry: Tropical; aged soft water with a low pH is ideal.
Behavior: Males may fight; keep alone or in pairs.
Dietary Requirements: Small, living foods.

Remarks: This is another bottom-spawner. An aquarium for spawning them may be prepared by putting a layer of peat moss about 1 cm thick on the bottom of a 10-gallon aquarium. The eggs are best removed by gently stirring the peat moss and siphoning them out with an eyedropper. Eggs will hatch in about six weeks.

Nothobranchius eggersi

SEEGERS 1982

Natural Range: Rufiji River drainage, eastern Tanzania.
Size: 2" (5 cm) TL.
Water Chemistry: Tropical; prefer soft acidic water.
Behavior: Generally peaceful.
Dietary Requirements: Small, living foods and prepared foods supplemented with plant matter will give best results.

Remarks: *Nothobranchius eggersi* occur in small pools and swampy areas in nature. They are a gorgeous species of Killie and should be kept in a species-specific aquarium where they can often be observed courting and breeding.

Nothobranchius guentheri / Redtail Notho

PFEFFER 1893

Natural Range: East Africa.
Size: 2" (5 cm) TL.
Water Chemistry: Tropical; soft and slightly acidic.
Behavior: Somewhat pugnacious; should be kept in pairs in their own tank.
Dietary Requirements: Do best on live foods.

Remarks: The adaptability of animal life to its surroundings is very graphically illustrated by the *Nothobranchius* group from eastern Africa. These fishes make their home in shallow pools which are filled in the rainy months and then become gradually smaller and shallower as the dry season progresses, finally drying out altogether. This is an annual fish which is survived by its eggs only for the cycle to repeat itself at the start of the next rainy season.

Fundulopanchax gardneri

Fundulopanchax gardneri var.

Nothobranchius eggersi

Nothobranchius eggersi

Nothobranchius guentheri

Nothobranchius guentheri

193

Nothobranchius rachovii / Bluefin Notho

AHL 1926

Natural Range: Mozambique and South Africa.
Size: 2" (5 cm) TL.
Water Chemistry: Tropical; soft and slightly acidic conditions are best.
Behavior: May be quarrelsome, should be given their own tank.
Dietary Requirements: Small, living and frozen foods.

Remarks: Any hobbyist who sees a beautiful male specimen of this endearing species in his full dress will never deny that they are one of the most strikingly colored freshwater fishes in the world. A jewel such as this deserves its own setting, and it is best to give them a tank with only their own kind.

Nothobranchius rubripinnis

SEEGERS 1986

Natural Range: Tanzania, Africa.
Size: 2" (5 cm) TL, may grow larger.
Water Chemistry: Tropical; prefer soft acidic water.
Behavior: Generally peaceful.
Dietary Requirements: Small, living foods preferred.

Remarks: These beautiful little Killies are not the most popular species, but those who are fortunate enough to obtain them rave about how easy they are to care for in aquariums. These bottom-spawners can be kept in much the same fashion as other Killies, but they may grow slightly larger than their cousins. For best results, keep alone or in pairs in a 10-gallon or larger aquarium.

Pachypanchax playfairi / Golden Panchax

GUNTHER 1866

Natural Range: Seychelles, Africa.
Size: 4" (10 cm) TL.
Water Chemistry: Tropical; neutral to slightly alkaline water of moderate hardness.
Behavior: May be "bossy" with smaller fishes.
Dietary Requirements: All standard aquarium fair is commonly accepted with little hesitation.

Remarks: The Golden Panchax is sometimes found for sale among the various African barbs or characins in local pet shops. They are a rare treat among average hobbyists, but this species has been known to the hobby for many decades. They do best in a brightly illuminated and well-planted aquarium. *P. playfairi* has an unusual trait which is worth mentioning: the scales, especially along the back, stand out instead of lying close to the body. This is natural and must not be diagnosed as a disease symptom.

Nothobranchius rachovii

Nothobranchius rachovii

Nothobranchius rubripinnis male

Nothobranchius rubripinnis female

Pachypanchax playfairi young male

Pachypanchax playfairi pair

Pachypanchax omalonotus / Green Panchax

DUMERIL 1861
Natural Range: Western and northern Madagascar and adjacent islands.
Size: 4" (10 cm) TL.
Water Chemistry: Tropical, soft acidic water with moderate hardness is best. May tolerate salt in small concentrations.
Behavior: Peaceful with fishes too large to be swallowed.
Dietary Requirements: Live, frozen, and freeze-dried foods accepted.

Remarks: This name of this species is often the victim of a serious misspelling—*"P. homalonatus."* It is much less common than its cousin *P. playfairi* but equally beautiful. The first record of this species being kept in an aquarium appeared in 1951, but it was not generally made available until sometime in 1953. Spawning usually occurs in the morning among fine-leaved plants, but the adults may eat the eggs if they are not hidden well. For this reason, they are sometimes very difficult to obtain.

Pachypanchax sakaramyi

HOLLY 1928
Natural Range: Northern Madagascar.
Size: 4" (10 cm) TL.
Water Chemistry: Tropical; neutral pH with moderate hardness.
Behavior: Generally peaceful with similar-sized fishes.
Dietary Requirements: Small, living foods and prepared foods accepted.

Remarks: This species prefers water a little cooler (70°–72°F), albeit still within the tropical range. They occur in brooks and fast-flowing creeks in the mountainous region of Madagascar. As with nearly all fishes in Madagascar, *P. sakaramyi* is listed as a vulnerable species in threat of extinction due to habitat destruction. One day, it is likely that the only specimens left in the world will be those in hobbyists' aquariums.

Scriptaphyosemion bertholdi / Berthold's Lyretail

ROLOFF 1965
Natural Range: Liberia.
Size: 2" (5 cm) TL; females may be slightly smaller.
Water Chemistry: Tropical; prefers soft, acidic water.
Behavior: Peaceful.
Dietary Requirements: Small living foods accepted.

Remarks: We can always depend on a great number of brilliantly colored fishes in the *"Aphyosemion"* group, and *S. bertholdi* is no exception. This species was found in Totoba, Liberia by E. Roloff of Germany. Mr. Roloff discovered many of our most attractive Killies, and like the rest of the *"Aphyosemion"* group, there are several color variations with this species, as well.

Nothobranchius rachovii

Nothobranchius rachovii in display

Nothobranchius rubripinnis male

Nothobranchius rubripinnis female

Pachypanchax playfairi young male

Aphyosemion cognatum for comparison

Apteronotus albifrons

APTERONOTIDAE
GHOST KNIFEFISHES

There are approximately 64 species within the family Apteronotidae. However, the taxonomic status of several of these is questionable. Here we discuss three of them in some detail: *Apteronotus albifrons*, *A. leptorhynchus*, and *A. rostratus*. Unfortunately, some of the most interesting species are simply unavailable to hobbyists due to locality restrictions and lack of general interest.

All species within the family are highly predacious on insect larvae and sometimes even small fishes. Feeding should be done either in the early morning hours or just after the aquarium lighting is turned out. With some time, patience, and training, these fishes can become accustomed to making appearances in the daylight. Otherwise, they will often remain hidden in the crevices and caves of your aquarium.

Apteronotids have their highest degree of species diversity in the Amazonian floodplain, where many are commonly found deep within the river channels. These species tend to be highly aggressive piscivores while many of the other species are opportunistic piscivores and consume planktonic foods more commonly.

Apteronotus albifrons / Black Ghost Knifefish

LINNEAUS 1766

Natural Range: Widely distributed over much of South America.

Size: Commonly around 12" (30 cm) but may grow considerably larger.

Water Chemistry: Tropical; wide range of pH is acceptable with a moderate hardness.

Behavior: Peaceful with most other fishes but may battle with other knifefishes (especially males).

Dietary Requirements: Highly predacious on worms and insect larvae. May eat small fishes.

Remarks: The Black Ghost Knifefish possesses a weakly discharging electric organ and ampullary electro receptors that enable it to find food in its natural range. These fish prefer to have aquariums with various crevices and caves to hide in during the day. Sometimes hobbyists use special tubes that are made of transparent plastic. These tubes afford the Knifefish a home while still allowing the hobbyist to see it. Repeated feedings during the day may make these fish more apt to come out during daylight hours.

Apteronotus leptorhynchus / Brown Ghost Knifefish

ELLIS 1912

Natural Range: Northern South America.

Size: 10" (25 cm) TL.

Water Chemistry: Tropical; prefer soft acidic water.

Behavior: Will not harass fishes they cannot swallow.

Dietary Requirements: Meaty items, worms, insect larvae, and prepared foods.

Remarks: Brown Ghost Knifefishes are not quite as popular among hobbyists as their close relative, the Black Ghost Knifefish. Regardless, they continue to find their way into the hobby, and those that enjoy the rare or unusual will certainly want one of these. Care is exactly the same as with the Black Ghost Knifefish only they do not grow as large. In addition to providing caves and crevices to hide in, heavy water flow will be appreciated by this species.

Apteronotus albifrons

Apteronotus albifrons pair

Apteronotus leptorhynchus

Apteronotus leptorhynchus var.

Bunocephalus coracoideus

ASPREDINIDAE

BANJO CATFISHES

The family Aspredinidae is a small family of rather small catfishes indigenous to South America. They inhabit freshwater, brackish water, and even the marine littoral zone on occasion. The anterior portion of their body and head is wide and flattened, and the tail is often long and slender. Such attributes have given rise to the common name of Banjo Catfishes.

The Banjo Catfishes are not of any significant economic importance other than their suitability as aquarium residents. Some of the larger members of the family are occasionally used as food fishes when caught, but this is purely opportunistic on the part of the fishermen, and as of this writing, no fishery for Banjo Catfishes has been established.

The majority of the species within Aspredinidae are in the subfamily Bunocephalinae and are commonly found in the coastal lowlands throughout their range where they inhabit small streams and other areas of slow moving water. They are considered primary freshwater fishes, and none are known to enter estuaries or other brackish waters.

Aspredo aspredo / Banjo Catfish

LINNAEUS 1758

Natural Range: Coastal northeastern South America.
Size: 16" (40 cm) TL.
Water Chemistry: Tropical; soft water with moderate hardness is best.
Behavior: Peaceful with fishes that are not able to be swallowed.
Dietary Requirements: Prefer whole, large food items such as shrimps and small fishes but will accept a wide variety of meaty foods.

Remarks: This is one of the largest-growing species of Banjo Catfishes available to hobbyists today. There have been reports of this species reaching two feet in length, but they remain unverified. Regardless, this fish needs plenty of room to swim and roam about. Feed sparingly, as they grow very fast if overfed.

Bunocephalus knerii / Ecuador Banjo Catfish

STEINDACHNER 1882

Natural Range: Western Amazon River basin.
Size: 6" (15 cm) TL. May grow slightly larger.
Water Chemistry: Tropical; prefer acidic water with a moderate hardness.
Behavior: Peaceful; will eat small fishes that are easily swallowed.
Dietary Requirements: Meaty foods.

Remarks: This species is not quite as common as other *Bunocephalus* species but should be mentioned here due to the increasing popularity and availability of fishes out of Ecuador. They need a spacious aquarium with plenty of hiding places and darkened areas to feel comfortable. Some amount of training will be needed to bring this fish out of seclusion during daylight hours.

Bunocephalus coracoideus / Two-colored Banjo Catfish

COPE 1874

Natural Range: Amazonia.
Size: 6" (15 cm) TL; may grow larger.
Water Chemistry: Tropical; prefer soft, acidic water.
Behavior: Peaceful but will swallow small fish whole.
Dietary Requirements: Accepts living and frozen foods as well as prepared diets specifically designed for bottom-dwellers.

Remarks: Some fish are famous for their beauty and some for their ugliness. This species—all species in this family, as a matter of fact—happens to be the latter case. This species is so unlike the "typical" fish that it is difficult to tell where exactly the eyes and mouth are located. Interestingly, this species incubates its eggs like a chicken—by sitting on them.

Aspredo aspredo

Aspredo aspredo profile

Bunocephalus sp. aff. *knerii*

Bunocephalus sp. aff. *coracoideus* for comparison

Bunocephalus coracoideus

Bunocephalus coracoideus

Platystacus cotylephorus / Banded Banjo Catfish

BLOCH 1794

Natural Range: Along the coast from Venezuela to Northern Brazil.

Size: 12" (30 cm) TL; may get slightly larger in nature.

Water Chemistry: Tropical; prefer salt in their water and neutral to alkaline pH with moderate hardness.

Behavior: Peaceful but may swallow small fish whole.

Dietary Requirements: Meaty foods; can be trained to accept dead small fishes and shrimps.

Remarks: This species mainly occurs in brackish water estuaries where it can be found over a soft mud bottom. They are reported to migrate from estuaries into rivers and streams leading to fresh water to breed. The females will carry the eggs on their undersides, which is thought to be a method of oxygenating the eggs in muddy waters.

Pterobunocephalus depressus

HASEMAN 1911

Natural Range: Amazon, Orinoco, and Paraguay River basins.

Size: 4" (10 cm) TL.

Water Chemistry: Subtropical and tropical; soft and slightly acidic water is preferred.

Behavior: Peaceful but may eat small fishes.

Dietary Requirements: Meaty foods; insect larvae and live worms.

Remarks: This small Banjo Catfish is sometimes encountered in shipments from Bolivia and Paraguay, since their species diversity is not as high as that of northern, more tropical regions. As with most other Banjo Catfishes, this species tends to be shy and reclusive and prefers to explore the aquarium after the lights go out. Use a substrate that is fine and rounded, as coarse substrate will irritate their soft underside.

Xyliphius kryptos

TAPHORN & LILYSTROM 1983

Natural Range: Lake Maracaibo basin.

Size: 4" (10 cm) TL; may grow slightly larger in nature.

Water Chemistry: Tropical; prefer water with a neutral pH and moderate hardness.

Behavior: Generally peaceful but may eat small fish whole.

Dietary Requirements: Meaty foods. Strips of squid, clams, and shrimp are accepted greedily.

Remarks: This somewhat rare species is quite a treasure should you be fortunate enough to find one. Catfish fanciers, especially those interested in Banjo Catfishes, will be quite happy when this species becomes available. It is usually a seasonal import.

Platystacus cotylephorus

Platystacus cotylephorus var.

Pterobunocephalus depressus

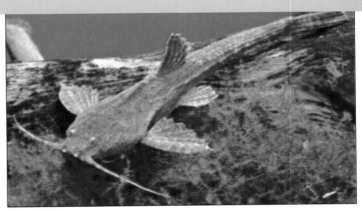

Pterobunocephalus depressus

Xyliphius kryptos

Xyliphius kryptos profile

Liosomadoras oncinus

AUCHENIPTERIDAE
DRIFTWOOD CATFISHES

Auchenipteridae is a moderate-sized family of naked catfishes inhabiting the fresh waters of South and Central America from Argentina to Panama. They are generally nocturnal catfishes, commonly found beneath submerged logs and other debris with many other types of fishes spanning multiple families (Burgess, 1989).

The driftwood catfishes generally prefer slow-moving water that is tropical in temperature and neutral to slightly acidic in pH. They appreciate bogwood as tank décor, as this provides them with a more realistic and natural setting.

Reproduction has occurred with many species, but the fry are apparently difficult to rear successfully. Some hobbyists have reported that microworms and copepods were used as initial food for the fry, but actual published accounts of success stories are few and far between.

Ageneiosus pardalis / Bottlenose Catfish

LUTKEN 1874

Natural Range: Northern South America.
Size: 16" (40 cm) TL.
Water Chemistry: Tropical; neutral pH with moderate hardness.
Behavior: Males may quarrel; otherwise peaceful.
Dietary Requirements: Insect larvae, worms, small fishes, and other meaty foods.

Remarks: These catfishes are very interesting in aquariums if you can get past their love of hiding deep within roots and other décor in your aquarium. Just as with most apteronotids, Bottlenose Catfish can easily be trained to come out of hiding and show their whiskers during daylight hours—especially if food is involved.

Liosomadoras oncinus / Jaguar Catfish

JARDINE 1841

Natural Range: Rio Branco.
Size: 8" (20 cm) TL.
Water Chemistry: Tropical; soft and acidic is preferred.
Behavior: Generally peaceful; males may fight.
Dietary Requirements: Worms, insect larvae, small fishes, and other meaty foods.

Remarks: *Liosomadoras oncinus* is a medium-sized catfish that is popular among catfish fanciers. They are often imported as small adults or large juveniles and apparently do well in shipping. As with all woodcats, this species does best in aquariums that are decorated with bogwood and plants. Lighting should be dim at best. Juveniles have a much different pattern than adults.

Pseudauchenipterus nodosus / Cocosada Catfish

BLOCH 1794

Natural Range: Venezuela to northern Brazil and Bahia region.
Size: 8" (20 cm) TL.
Water Chemistry: Tropical; soft and acidic.
Behavior: Generally peaceful; males may fight.
Dietary Requirements: Worms, insect larvae, small fishes, and other meaty foods.

Remarks: Cocosada catfish are found over muddy bottoms mostly in brackish water mouths of rivers and streams. Their bodies are thick compared to *Auchenipterus*, their close relative. Although they are listed as being omnivores, these cats love their meat, too. Regardless, be sure to provide dried foods that have been supplemented with plant matter occasionally.

Ageneiosus pardalis juvenile

Ageneiosus pardalis adult

Liosomadoras oncinus dark var.

Liosomadoras oncinus normal var.

Pseudauchenipterus nodosus

Pseudauchenipterus nodosus profile

Tatia perugiae

STEINDACHNER 1882

Natural Range: Upper Amazon River basin.
Size: 2" (5 cm) TL; may grow slightly larger.
Water Chemistry: Tropical; soft and acidic.
Behavior: Generally peaceful; males may fight.
Dietary Requirements: Worms, insect larvae, small fishes, and other meaty foods.

Remarks: This little woodcat is a wonderful addition to any community aquarium that contains fishes that are too large to be swallowed. They have an interesting pattern that makes them all but disappear when looked at from above. They inhabit larger rivers where the water is swift, and they prefer to be over sandy or slightly rocky bottoms.

Trachelyopterichthys taeniatus / Striped Woodcat

KNER 1858

Natural Range: Upper Amazon River basin.
Size: 6" (15 cm) TL.
Water Chemistry: Tropical; soft and acidic.
Behavior: Generally peaceful; males may fight.
Dietary Requirements: Worms, insect larvae, small fishes, and other meaty foods.

Remarks: This interesting species does not grow as large as some of the other woodcats in the family Auchenipteridae. They prefer soft and acidic water but can tolerate a wide range of parameters as long as extremes are avoided. Use caution when placing smaller fishes in any aquarium that contains woodcats.

212

Tatia perugiae

Tatia perugiae profile

Trachelyopterichthys taeniatus

Trachelyopterichthys taeniatus

213

Badis badis

BADIDAE

CHAMELEON FISHES

Years ago, these fish were more popular than they are now. While they do not have much going for them regarding color, they have quite a lot going for them in terms of behavior. Their reproduction is particularly interesting, and they often prove to be very easy to breed.

Members of Badidae are most often found in lowland swamps and other areas of slow-moving water. They currently number about 15 valid species, although there are several suspected subspecies that may be elevated to species-status in the future. This has already happened with many subspecies of *Badis badis*. For example, years ago we saw two very prominent subspecies: *B. badis badis*, and *B. badis burmanicus*. Today, we treat the latter species as *B. ruber* while the former species is lumped into *B. badis*.

Badis badis / Dwarf Chameleon Fish

HAMILTON 1822
Natural Range: India.
Size: 4" (10 cm) TL.
Water Chemistry: Not critical.
Behavior: Peaceful but will hide in a community aquarium.
Dietary Requirements: Will eat almost anything, especially meaty foods.

Remarks: These interesting little nandids have all of the characteristics of the dwarf cichlids. When kept by themselves in a small aquarium, they breed readily. A rock or a leaf surface, or even the inside of a flowerpot, will be cleaned scrupulously by the male. The female is then coaxed to the spot and mating proceeds with the hanging of between 50 to 60 eggs on the surface. Eggs hatch in 2 to 3 days and infusoria should be fed several times daily until sufficient growth allows the feeding of larger foods.

Badis ruber / Burmese Chameleon Fish

SCHREITMULLER 1923
Natural Range: Burma.
Size: 2" (5 cm) TL; may grow slightly larger in nature.
Water Chemistry: Tropical; otherwise not critical.
Behavior: Peaceful but may hide a great deal if placed in a community aquarium.
Dietary Requirements: Small, live foods are best, but many captive bred specimens will take prepared foods, too.

Remarks: Formerly known as *Badis badis burmanicus*, this small species of Chameleon Fish has been given full species status. *B. ruber* has been around the tropical fish hobby for more than 80 years! Unfortunately, they are not particularly colorful or else they would probably be more popular. Care and breeding are the same as for *B. badis*.

Dario dario

HAMILTON 1822
Natural Range: India.
Size: 1" (2.5 cm) TL; may grow slightly larger in nature.
Water Chemistry: Tropical; otherwise not critical.
Behavior: Peaceful.
Dietary Requirements: Small, live foods are best.

Remarks: This tiny fish is just starting to become available in the aquarium trade in significant numbers despite being known about for decades. Those hobbyists who are looking for something truly different will appreciate the uniqueness of this species. Keeping them is rather simple provided they are given their own aquarium. Otherwise, keep according to the Killifishes.

Badis badis adult male

Badis badis profile

Badis ruber juvenile

Badis ruber juvenile profile

Dario dario

Badis badis juvenile for comparison

Bagrichthys sp.

BAGRIDAE
BAGRID CATFISHES

The family Bagridae is a large group of fresh and brackish water catfishes with approximately 210 described species. Their range extends from Africa and Syria through Pakistan, India, Bangladesh, Sri Lanka, Burma, Thailand, Cambodia, Laos, Vietnam, and Malaya to the East Indies, China, Taiwan, Korea, and Japan.

They reside mostly in rivers, pools, and lakes where they are either crepuscular or nocturnal. Bagrids may be active during daylight hours if they inhabit waters that are laden with dirt and silt. Most species are voracious predators on anything that they can fit in their mouths and are reported to be some of the most ill-tempered catfishes one can keep in an aquarium.

The family Bagridae is said to be the Old World equivalent of the South American Pimelodidae family of catfishes. More importantly, the bagrids have often been cited as being the basic ancestral catfish family, and other families have undoubtedly been derived from it (Burgess, 1989).

Auchenoglanis occidentalis / Giraffe Catfish (Bubu)

VALENCIENNES 1840

Natural Range: Lake Chad, Nile River, Congo-Lualaba River system.

Size: 32" (70 cm) TL.

Water Chemistry: Tropical; otherwise not critical but avoid extremes.

Behavior: Generally peaceful but very active; large males may be aggressive.

Dietary Requirements: Omnivorous; will take everything from small feeder fishes to clams to seeds. Feed small amounts frequently.

Remarks: This beautiful, large catfish grows to huge proportions. In nature, males will guard nests of eggs. Apparently, these nests may also be invaded by the young of *Dinotopterus cunningtoni*, which takes advantage of the parental care these fish provide only to eat all of the young *A. occidentalis*. So in the end, the adult A. occidentalis has raised a group of D. cunningtoni instead of their own. Keep in a large aquarium with other large, peaceful fishes.

Bagrichthys macracanthus / Black Lancer Catfish

BLEEKER 1854

Natural Range: Thailand to Indonesia.

Size: 10" (25 cm) TL.

Water Chemistry: Tropical; otherwise not critical.

Behavior: Specimens vary; some are very peaceful while others are aggressive. Generally peaceful with larger fishes.

Dietary Requirements: Meaty foods such as crabmeat, squid, clams, and a good-quality staple diet will be best.

Remarks: Black Lancers are one of the old favorites of the hobby. They are an absolutely gorgeous fish with a strikingly beautiful white stripe that starts approximately one-third down from the head and runs to the caudal peduncle. The author (Scott) has found this species to be quite calm when multiple hiding places are provided. Feed frequently.

Hemibagrus nemurus / Asian Redtail Catfish

VALENCIENNES 1840

Natural Range: Mekong, Chao Phraya, and Xe Bangfai basins and Sumatra, Java, and Borneo.

Size: 26" (65 cm) TL.

Water Chemistry: Tropical; otherwise not critical, avoid extremes.

Behavior: Aggressive; will eat anything it can swallow; best kept alone.

Dietary Requirements: Not picky, all foods accepted; voracious feeder.

Remarks: The Asian Redtail Catfish is one of the more commonly available bagrids found in the hobby today. While not nearly as aggressive as some other members of the family, their temperament is highly variable and best thought of as aggressive so proper precautions are taken from the start. Some individuals may become very tame.

Auchenoglanis occidentalis

Auchenoglanis occidentalis profile

Bagrichthys macracanthus

Bagrichthys hypselopterus for comparison

Mystus nemurus

Mystus nemurus

Hemibagrus wyckii / Wyckii Catfish

BLEEKER 1858

Natural Range: Thailand to Indonesia, Asia.
Size: 32" (70 cm) TL; usually half this size at best.
Water Chemistry: Tropical; otherwise not critical.
Behavior: Very aggressive; keep alone.
Dietary Requirements: Not picky, meaty foods are best; voracious feeder.

Remarks: The Wyckii Catfish is probably the most aggressive catfish that can be kept in an aquarium. They are often very intolerant of any other aquarium residents. It is not uncommon to hear reports that these fish become very tame and approach the glass when people come in the room. Strangely, one specimen in particular was able to recognize only the one who fed it; otherwise, it would ignore anyone else. Perhaps it recognized the owner's footsteps?

Mystus micracanthus / Twospot Catfish

BLEEKER 1846

Natural Range: Mekong basin, Malaysia, and Indonesia.
Size: 6" (15 cm) TL.
Water Chemistry: Tropical; otherwise not critical. Avoid extremes.
Behavior: Generally peaceful; may eat small fish.
Dietary Requirements: Feed mainly meaty foods including their favorite, insect larvae.

Remarks: These small catfish are very handsome and active. While they enjoy having hiding places available to them just like other catfishes, they can often be seen roaming about the aquarium at all times of the day and night. As with other bagrids, feed small amounts frequently so as to curb unnecessary aggression.

Phyllonemus typus / Spatula-barbeled Catfish

BOULENGER 1906

Natural Range: Lake Tanganyika.
Size: 4" (10 cm) TL.
Water Chemistry: Tropical; hard, alkaline water is best.
Behavior: Generally peaceful; may eat small fishes.
Dietary Requirements: Prefer shrimps and other crustaceans but will accept most standard aquarium fish fare.

Remarks: This unique little catfish prefers a dark aquarium and plenty of hiding places—usually in the form of rocky caves. They have modified maxillary barbels that enable them to search out food deep in the rocky crevices of Lake Tanganyika's littoral zone. They are oviparous and practice bi-parental mouthbrooding.

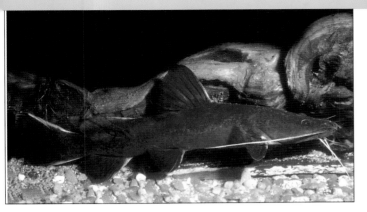

Hemibagrus wyckii

Bagrichthys macropterus for comparison

Mystus micracanthus

Mystus cf. *vittatus*

Phyllonemus typus

Phyllonemus typus profile

Gastromyzon punctulatus

BALITORIDAE
RIVER LOACHES

There are approximately 500 species of River Loaches. Many of these are never seen in the aquarium trade, therefore, only three will be discussed here. By far, the most popular of these is *Psuedogastromyzon myersi*, which is often referred to as the "Stingray Pleco." Actually, these fish are not even remotely related to any "Pleco" or any other member of Loricariidae.

Ironically, some of these fishes will consume bits of algae and other plant matter, although most are dedicated detritivores. This behavior is really what caused the name "Pleco" to be applied in the first place.

In order to successfully keep these fishes alive and well in captivity, you must be willing to provide them with a cooler environment, plenty of food, and highly oxygenated water. Even the species listed as being tropical will do best with a temperature on the cooler side. A range of 66° to 74°F is probably about right for all species.

Gastromyzon punctulatus / Hillstream Loach

INGER & CHIN 1961

Natural Range: Borneo.
Size: 2" (5 cm) TL; may grow slightly larger.
Water Chemistry: Tropical; prefer strong currents with high dissolved oxygen level.
Behavior: Generally peaceful; males may fight amongst themselves.
Dietary Requirements: Feed on algae and other matter that coats the rocks and wood in their native habitat.

Remarks: Sometimes referred to as the "spotted stingray pleco," these small loaches are both interesting and unique to care for. They are quite a devil to catch in aquariums since they have such incredible suction and are able to scurry along at a very high speed. This species is excellent to keep with other species that prefer a strong current.

Jinshia sinensis / Chinese Hillstream Loach

SAUVAGE & DABRY DE THIERSANT 1874

Natural Range: Yangtze and Jinsha-jiang drainages, China.
Size: 3" (7.5 cm) TL.
Water Chemistry: Temperate; prefer cooler water that is rich in dissolved oxygen.
Behavior: Peaceful; males may become quarrelsome with age.
Dietary Requirements: Feed on algae and other matter that covers the rocks in their native habitat.

Remarks: These unique little fish are somewhat rare in the hobby, and when they are imported they often go unnoticed. Provide an aquarium that has several hiding places in the form of rocks and caves as well as a strong current. They will often be seen near the outflows of filters and powerheads where the current is at its greatest.

Psuedogastromyzon myersi / "Stingray Pleco"

HERRE 1932

Natural Range: China.
Size: 2" (5 cm); may grow slightly larger.
Water Chemistry: Subtropical; prefer cooler water with a heavy current.
Behavior: Peaceful.
Dietary Requirements: Feed on algae and detritus on rocks and in crevices.

Remarks: The famous "stingray pleco" is actually a loach and a cool water species. Just as the previously described species, *P. myersi* prefers as much current as it can get. They inhabit rapids and the stronger section of streams and rivers in their homelands and therefore should only be housed in aquariums where such a habitat is recreated. This is a very easy species to keep when conditions are correct.

Gastromyzon cf. *punctulatus*

Gastromyzon punctulatus

Jinshia sinensis

Gastromyzon ctenocephalus for comparison

Pseudogastromyzon myersi adult

Pseudogastromyzon myersi in action!

Corydoras barbatus

CALLICHTHYIDAE

CALLICHTHYID ARMORED CATFISHES

The members of this large family of relatively small, heavily armored catfishes come from many tropical regions of South America and Trinidad. These are the famous "Cory Cats" that are sold in pet shops as "janitors," because they clean up the excess food along the substrate of the aquarium. A community aquarium is just not a community aquarium without one of these fishes.

In aquaria, callichthyids are adaptable to a wide variety of conditions and as such are probably the most used of any of the catfish families in a community aquarium. They are generally peaceful, except for battles between rival males, and their armor allows them to survive attacks from all but the most aggressive fishes. This armor also assists them in preventing parasitic attacks, but in severe cases, the parasites often prevail.

The aquarium size for these fishes can vary considerably. They do best in small groups and all too often they are placed in the aquarium to clean up after the real fishes. Such a mentality will certainly lead to their demise. They are active swimmers and need plenty of food themselves. Food should be varied and sufficient.

Aspidoras menezesi

NIJSSEN & ISBRUCKER 1976

Natural Range: Brazil.
Size: 2" (5 cm) TL.
Water Chemistry: Tropical; soft and acidic.
Behavior: Peaceful.
Dietary Requirements: Worms and other small live foods as well as prepared.

Remarks: The original specimens of this species were collected in the Rio Granjeiro, Brazil by R.S. de Menezes. They are not suitable for the larger community aquarium due to their hiding behavior. Provide a small aquarium that is nicely decorated with plants and bogwood for best results. Provide strong filtration.

Aspidoras pauciradiatus / Six-ray Corydoras

WEITZMAN & NIJSSEN 1970

Natural Range: Rio Araguaia, Brazil.
Size: 2" (5 cm) TL.
Water Chemistry: Tropical; soft and acidic.
Behavior: Peaceful.
Dietary Requirements: Worms and other small live foods are greedily accepted.

Remarks: This small catfish has been found in two major locations—the Rio Negro and Rio Araguaia systems. Because of their wide distribution, *A. pauciradiatus* is perhaps the best known and most widely available of the *Aspidoras* genus.

Aspidoras virgulatus

NIJSSEN & ISBRUCKER 1980

Natural Range: Brazil.
Size: 2" (5 cm) TL.
Water Chemistry: Tropical; soft and acidic is preferred.
Behavior: Peaceful.
Dietary Requirements: Small living foods such as Daphnia and tubificid worms are best.

Remarks: *Aspidoras virgulatus* exhibit a very unique and often dramatic coloration. There is a dark stripe extending along the upper and lower lateral plates from behind the head to the base of the tail.

Aspidoras menezesi

Aspidoras sp.

Aspidoras pauciradiatus adult

Aspidoras pauciradiatus

Aspidoras virgulatus

Aspidoras sp. "Phantom"

Brochis britskii / Britski's Catfish

NIJSSEN & ISBRUCKER 1983

Natural Range: Upper Rio Paraguay, Brazil.
Size: 4" (10 cm) TL.
Water Chemistry: Tropical; soft and acidic.
Behavior: Peaceful.
Dietary Requirements: Small, live foods and prepared foods accepted greedily.

Remarks: *Brochis britskii* is most closely related to *B. multiradiatus*. Like the other species in *Brochis*, *B. britskii* is a peaceful bottom-dwelling species that happily forages among the décor and substrate of the aquarium.

Brochis multiradiatus / Hognosed Brochis

ORCES 1960

Natural Range: Ecuador and Peru.
Size: 3" (7.5 cm) TL.
Water Chemistry: Tropical; soft and slightly acidic.
Behavior: Peaceful.
Dietary Requirements: Worms, insect larvae, and prepared foods will suffice.

Remarks: As the name "*multiradiatus*" implies, members of this species have a high number of dorsal fin rays (17), which immediately distinguishes them from *B. splendens*. Furthermore, they are distinguishable from *B. britskii*, which also have a high number of dorsal fin rays (15–18), by their longer snout, smaller eye, and smaller overall size. This is a peaceful species that appreciates a medium-coarse gravel to search through for foodstuffs.

Brochis splendens / Emerald Catfish

CASTELNAU 1855

Natural Range: Amazon basin, Brazil.
Size: 2" to 4" (7–9 cm) TL; females larger than males.
Water Chemistry: Tropical; soft and acidic.
Behavior: Peaceful.
Dietary Requirements: Small, live foods and prepared foods are best.

Remarks: *Brochis splendens* is the most commonly available of all the *Brochis* species. It has a fairly wide distribution where it seems to inhabit slowly moving or sluggish waters. The light metallic green to bluish color gives rise to its specific name of "*splendens*."

Brochis britskii adult male

Brochis britskii adult female

Brochis multiradiatus adult male

Brochis multiradiatus

Brochis splendens

Brochis splendens

233

Corydoras adolfoi

BURGESS 1982

Natural Range: Rio Negro, Brazil.
Size: 2" (5 cm), females slightly larger.
Water Chemistry: Tropical; soft and acidic.
Behavior: Peaceful.
Dietary Requirements: Small, live foods such as *Daphnia*, *Tubifex* worms, and blackworms are best. Prepared foods accepted as well.

Remarks: *C. adolfoi* was discovered at Sao Gabriel da Cachoeira, a small tributary of the upper Rio Negro in Brazil, by Dr. Herbert R. Axelrod. As a social species, they should be kept in groups numbering at least six specimens but preferably more. Weekly water changes of no less than 25% should be performed to maintain high water quality standards.

Corydoras aeneus / Common Cory Cat

GILL 1858

Natural Range: Northern South America.
Size: 3" (7.5 cm) TL.
Water Chemistry: Tropical; soft and acidic.
Behavior: Peaceful.
Dietary Requirements: Dry foods supplemented with live and frozen foods.

Remarks: *Corydoras aeneus* is by far the most popular "Cory" cat available to hobbyists today. They do best in small schools, but single specimens can thrive for years by themselves, even in small tanks. Most of the albino Cory cats that are seen in pet shops are the *C. aeneus*.

Corydoras agassizi

STEINDACHNER 1876

Natural Range: Upper Amazon basin.
Size: 3" (7.5 cm); females slightly larger.
Water Chemistry: Tropical; soft and acidic.
Behavior: Peaceful.
Dietary Requirements: Small, live foods are best but will readily accept prepared and frozen foods, too.

Remarks: Being more tropical than some of the other species of *Corydoras*, *C. agassizi* prefer water with a temperature in the upper 70s to low 80s F. This species is recognizable by the rows of spots, many of which are horizontally rectangular, on the body, the band through the eye, and the dark band through the pectoral fin base that extends upward to include the spine and anterior rays of the dorsal fin (Burgess 1992).

Corydoras adolfoi adult

Corydoras adolfoi Adult

Corydoras aeneus

Corydoras aeneus

Corydoras agassizi pair

Corydoras agassizi

Corydoras amapaensis

NIJSSEN 1972

Natural Range: French Guiana and Brazil.
Size: 2" (5 cm) TL; females slightly larger.
Water Chemistry: Tropical; soft and acid conditions are best but can tolerate a high pH.
Behavior: Peaceful.
Dietary Requirements: Small, live foods are best.

Remarks: *Corydoras amapaensis* is one of the less commonly available species of *Corydoras*. They have a strikingly beautiful pattern complemented by a metallic coloration.

Corydoras araguaiaensis

SANDS 1989

Natural Range: Rio Araguaia, Brazil.
Size: 2" (5 cm) TL.
Water Chemistry: Tropical; soft and acidic.
Behavior: Peaceful.
Dietary Requirements: Small, live foods are best.

Remarks: This recently described and controversial species is very similar to *C. haraldschultzi*. It is thought to differ in the details of the head pattern. Unfortunately, such distinctions are hard to make—especially by those not well versed in the science of taxonomy. Future research on this species is badly needed.

Corydoras arcuatus

ELWIN 1939

Natural Range: Rio Ucayali, Peru.
Size: 2" (5 cm) TL.
Water Chemistry: Tropical; soft and acidic.
Behavior: Peaceful.
Dietary Requirements: Small, live foods.

Remarks: *Corydoras arcuatus* are quite distinctive Cory cats with a dark band running through the eye then extending to, and including, the lower edge of the caudal fin. This species has been bred numerous times in captivity. Aquarists report that they do so in a manner that is in standard Cory cat fashion.

Corydoras amapaensis

Corydoras amapaensis Profile

Corydoras araguaiaensis female

Corydoras araguaiaensis

Corydoras arcuatus adult

Corydoras arcuatus

237

Corydoras atropersonatus

WEITZMAN & NIJSSEN 1970
Natural Range: Northern Peru and Ecuador.
Size: 2" (5 cm) TL. Females slightly larger.
Water Chemistry: Tropical; soft and acidic.
Behavior: Peaceful.
Dietary Requirements: Standard prepared foods supplemented with small, live foods will be best.

Remarks: This is a very peaceful and friendly species of *Corydoras* that does best in smaller aquariums with many hiding places. Tankmates should be peaceful as well. As with nearly all Cory cats, *C. atropersonatus* is a diurnal catfish that will be seen rooting around the tank for food all day long.

Corydoras axelrodi / Axelrod's Cory

ROSSEL 1962
Natural Range: Rio Meta, Colombia.
Size: 2" (5 cm) TL; females may grow slightly larger.
Water Chemistry: Tropical; soft and acidic.
Behavior: Peaceful.
Dietary Requirements: Small, live foods, such as *Tubifex* worms and *Daphnia*, as well as prepared foods are accepted.

Remarks: Axelrod's Cory is easily identified by the eye bar and the dark band that extends from the origin of the lateral line to the lower tip of the caudal fin, combined with a secondary band below the anterior part of this band that extends posteriorly only a relatively short distance. No concise reports are yet available on its reproduction in aquaria, but this may only be because the species is not particularly common. in the aquarium trade.

Corydoras barbatus

QUOY & GAIMARD 1824
Natural Range: Southern Brazil.
Size: 5" (12.5 cm) TL. Usually smaller in captivity.
Water Chemistry: Tropical; soft and acidic.
Behavior: Peaceful.
Dietary Requirements: Standard prepared foods supplemented with small, live foods are best.

Remarks: This unusual *Corydoras* comes from southeastern Brazil. In addition to being one of the prettiest species of the genus, it is also the largest. This species does not often reach its full potential size in captivity, with most specimens growing to about half the maximum length. They make a great addition to aquariums containing other peaceful species.

238

Corydoras atropersonatus

Corydoras atropersonatus pair

Corydoras sp. aff. *axelrodi*

Corydoras axelrodi

Corydoras barbatus

Corydoras barbatus

Corydoras blochi / Spotback Cory

NIJSSEN 1971

Natural Range: Northern Brazil and Southern Venezuela.
Size: 2" (5 cm) TL.
Water Chemistry: Tropical; soft and acidic.
Behavior: Peaceful.
Dietary Requirements: Standard prepared foods supplemented with small, live foods will be best.

Remarks: This species has been divided into two subspecies—*C. blochi blochi* and *C. blochi vittatus*. They differ in their coloration, with *C. blochi vittatus* having a horizontal stripe along the posterior part of the body and *C. blochi blochi* having vertical stripes in the caudal fin.

Corydoras bondi

GOSLINE 1940

Natural Range: Suriname and Venezuela.
Size: 2" (5 cm) TL.
Water Chemistry: Tropical; soft and acidic.
Behavior: Peaceful.
Dietary Requirements: Standard prepared foods supplemented with small, live foods will be best.

Remarks: These small *Corydoras* do well in a community aquarium that houses other small, peaceful fishes, such as Rasboras and Tetras. Their unique head shape allows them to be readily identified. If you look closely, you will also see bright blue coloration under their faces close to their mouth. These rare beauties are occasionally imported when fishes are allowed out of Venezuela.

Corydoras burgessi / Burgess's Cory

AXELROD 1987

Natural Range: Brazil.
Size: 2" (5 cm) TL.
Water Chemistry: Tropical; soft and acidic.
Behavior: Peaceful.
Dietary Requirements: Standard prepared foods supplemented with small, live foods will be best.

Remarks: Named for Dr. Warren Burgess, *C. burgessi* is another truly beautiful *Corydoras* species. They are perfectly adapted to poking through the tank décor in search of edibles and will be very peaceable with their tankmates. This species is highly recommended for the aspiring Cory Catfish collector.

Corydoras blochi adult

Corydoras blochi

Corydoras bondi

Corydoras bondi Juvenile

Corydoras burgessi

Corydoras burgessi

Corydoras caudimaculatus

ROSSEL 1961

Natural Range: Bolivia and Brazil.
Size: 2" (5 cm) TL.
Water Chemistry: Tropical; soft and acidic.
Behavior: Peaceful.
Dietary Requirements: Standard prepared foods supplemented with small, live foods will be best.

Remarks: This small attractive species originates from the Rio Guapore on Brazil's boarder with Bolivia. They are uncommon in the hobby but highly sought after by those looking for something a little different. While still tropical in nature, these little catfishes are able to tolerate temperatures slightly cooler than other species.

Corydoras cervinus

ROSSEL 1962

Natural Range: Brazil.
Size: 2" (5 cm) TL; may grow slightly larger.
Water Chemistry: Tropical; soft and acidic.
Behavior: Peaceful.
Dietary Requirements: Standard prepared foods supplemented with small, live foods are best.

Remarks: This species was described from only two specimens that were imported for the aquarium hobby in the early 1960s. Since then, their status has been validated, but some serious hobbyists and amateur ichthyologists remain unconvinced. Regardless, it is treated as a species herein.

Corydoras cochui

MYERS & WEITZMAN 1961

Natural Range: Brazil.
Size: 1" (2.5 cm) TL.
Water Chemistry: Tropical; soft and acidic.
Behavior: Peaceful.
Dietary Requirements: Standard prepared foods supplemented with small, live foods are best.

Remarks: First collected on the Rio Araguaia in Brazil, these small Cory catfishes are one of the smallest species known to exist. In aquaria, they need to be fed very small, live foods, such as baby brine shrimp or microworms. They will live several years if maintained in a small, species-specific aquarium.

Corydoras caudimaculatus adult

Corydoras caudimaculatus

Corydoras cervinus

Corydoras cf. *cervinus*

Corydoras cochui pair

Corydoras cochui

Corydoras concolor

WEITZMAN 1961
Natural Range: Venezuela.
Size: 2" (5 cm) TL; may grow slightly larger.
Water Chemistry: Tropical; soft and acidic.
Behavior: Peaceful.
Dietary Requirements: Standard prepared foods supplemented with small, live foods are best.

Remarks: This uniquely-colored species was first collected in a tributary of the Rio Parguaza, Venezuela. Later, it was collected in the Rio Parguaza itself. These rare fish are not often available in the hobby due to Venezuela's strict fishing seasons and limits, but when they are available they should be snapped up at once. You won't regret the price once they are adults.

Corydoras condiscipulus

NIJSSEN & ISBRUCKER 1980
Natural Range: French Guiana.
Size: 2" (5 cm) TL.
Water Chemistry: Tropical; soft and acidic.
Behavior: Peaceful.
Dietary Requirements: Standard prepared foods supplemented with small, live foods will be best.

Remarks: As with other *Corydoras*, the confirmation of this species is being questioned by some. Further taxonomic studies are needed to figure out if this is a true species or just a variant of another species.

Corydoras davidsandsi

BLACK 1987
Natural Range: Brazil.
Size: 2" (5 cm) TL; females may grow slightly larger.
Water Chemistry: Tropical; soft and acidic.
Behavior: Peaceful.
Dietary Requirements: Small live, foods are best for this species.

Remarks: Once again we find ourselves in controversy. This "Skunk Cory" is probably closely related to *C. metae* or *C. melini*, since they look very similar. As with many other *Corydoras* species, DNA analysis will be needed to tell what we are actually looking at. Their care is identical to that of other Cory catfishes of similar size and from the same locality.

Corydoras concolor female

Corydoras concolor pair

Corydoras condiscipulus

Corydoras condiscipulus

Corydoras davidsandsi pair

Corydoras davidsandsi adult

245

Corydoras delphax / False Blochi Cory

NIJSSEN & ISBRUCKER 1983
Natural Range: Colombia.
Size: 2" (5 cm) TL.
Water Chemistry: Tropical; soft and acidic.
Behavior: Peaceful.
Dietary Requirements: Standard prepared foods supplemented with small, live foods are best.

Remarks: Besides the usual sexual differences in size and girth, males usually have a stronger pattern. This is evident at an early age, and many experienced Cory keepers can differentiate the sex of this species by simply looking at a group of them. This is a great Cory when it's available.

Corydoras elegans

STEINDACHNER 1876
Natural Range: Central Amazon region, Brazil.
Size: 2" (5 cm) TL.
Water Chemistry: Tropical; soft and acidic.
Behavior: Peaceful.
Dietary Requirements: Standard prepared foods supplemented with small, live foods are best.

Remarks: This species of small *Corydoras* is one of the more inconspicuous species that is not as commonly kept by aquarists as many of the others. They are very peaceful little fish that enjoy the company of others of their own kind. Interestingly, they are also the only species of the non-dwarfs that seem to enjoy swimming in the middle water layers of the tank.

Corydoras ellisae

GOSLINE 1940
Natural Range: Paraguay.
Size: 2" (5 cm) TL.
Water Chemistry: Tropical; soft and acidic.
Behavior: Peaceful.
Dietary Requirements: Standard prepared foods supplemented with small, live foods are best.

Remarks: Another species that prefers cool water. These little Cory catfish come from the Rio Paraguay system, which is much cooler than the majority of the mighty Amazon. They are easily recognized by their pointed snout and roughly diamond-shaped dark marking just behind their head.

Corydoras delphax

Corydoras delphax pair

Corydoras elegans

Corydoras elegans

Corydoras ellisae juvenile

Corydoras ellisae adult

Corydoras eques / Golden-eared Cory Catfish

STEINDACHNER 1876

Natural Range: Brazilian Amazon.
Size: 2" (5 cm) TL; females slightly larger.
Water Chemistry: Tropical; soft and acidic.
Behavior: Peaceful.
Dietary Requirements: Standard prepared foods supplemented with small, live foods are best.

Remarks: The brilliant emerald-green gill covers and iris are very attractive. Like other Cory cats, they do better in a group of at least six individuals. They are beefy little fish that need a medium-sized aquarium and good circulation in order to thrive. Just as with other Cory cats, their pH should be slightly acidic, and moderate to soft hardness is best.

Corydoras esperanzae

CASTRO 1987

Natural Range: Colombia.
Size: 2" (5 cm) TL; females slightly larger.
Water Chemistry: Tropical; soft and acidic.
Behavior: Peaceful.
Dietary Requirements: Standard prepared foods supplemented with small, live foods are best.

Remarks: As with other fishes from Colombia, this species' availability is at the mercy of geopolitics. Since shipments coming from the country are steady from only a few sources, new exporters are rare and when they do export, only occasionally do they export *C. esperanzae*.

Corydoras evelynae / Evelyn's Cory Catfish

ROSSEL 1963

Natural Range: Brazil.
Size: 2" (5 cm) TL; females slightly larger.
Water Chemistry: Tropical; soft and acidic.
Behavior: Peaceful.
Dietary Requirements: Standard prepared foods supplemented with small, live foods are best.

Remarks: Described from a single specimen in 1966, *C. evelynae* was named so in honor of Evelyn Axelrod, the wife of Dr. Herbert R. Axelrod. The color pattern of this beautiful Cory is distinct, particularly the row of spots that form a line along the fish's dorsum. To this day, few are imported and there is almost no information on their care and husbandry.

Corydoras eques

Corydoras eques

Corydoras esperanzae

Corydoras esperanzae

Corydoras evelynae

Corydoras evelynae profile

Corydoras fowleri / Fowler's Cory Catfish

BOHLKE 1950

Natural Range: Peru.
Size: 2" (5 cm) TL; females slightly larger.
Water Chemistry: Tropical; soft and acidic.
Behavior: Peaceful.
Dietary Requirements: Standard prepared foods supplemented with small live foods will be best.

Remarks: The pattern of *C. fowleri* is quite distinctive and should not be confused with other *Corydoras*. Unfortunately, this species is very rare in the hobby, and just as with others that are rare, they should be purchased and kept in an aquarium by themselves. This way they may be able to be spawned and subsequently enjoyed by many hobbyists.

Corydoras gossei

NIJSSEN 1972

Natural Range: Brazil.
Size: 2" (5 cm) TL; females slightly larger.
Water Chemistry: Tropical; soft and acidic.
Behavior: Peaceful.
Dietary Requirements: Standard prepared foods supplemented with small, live foods are best.

Remarks: This plain-bodied species resembles *C. aeneus* in many ways. Until recently, this species was almost never available in the hobby, but thankfully specimens have slowly been making their way into Europe and the United States. Captive care is similar to other species from Northern Brazil.

Corydoras gracilis

NIJSSEN & ISBRUCKER 1976

Natural Range: Brazil.
Size: 1" (2.5 cm) TL; females slightly larger.
Water Chemistry: Tropical; soft and acidic.
Behavior: Peaceful.
Dietary Requirements: Standard prepared foods supplemented with small, live foods will be best.

Remarks: This is an interesting species that grows to only about one inch in length. Additionally, it differs from all other species by its unique pattern. No particular conditions are known for this species, but they seem to do well as long as extremes are avoided.

Corydoras fowleri adult

Corydoras fowleri

Corydoras gossei adult

Corydoras gossei

Corydoras gracilis

Corydoras gracilis adult

Corydoras habrosus

WEITZMAN 1960
Natural Range: Venezuela.
Size: 1" (2.5 cm) TL for females, males slightly smaller.
Water Chemistry: Tropical; soft and acidic.
Behavior: Peaceful.
Dietary Requirements: Small, live foods are best.

Remarks: The size and color pattern of this small species are enough to distinguish it from all others in the genus. They will do their best in a small aquarium that has been dedicated to them. Any tankmates should be very small tetras or rasboras.

Corydoras haraldschultzi / Harold Schultz's Cory Catfish

KNAACK 1962
Natural Range: Widely distributed over Brazil.
Size: 2" (5 cm); females slightly larger.
Water Chemistry: Tropical; soft and acidic.
Behavior: Peaceful.
Dietary Requirements: Standard prepared foods supplemented with small, live foods are best.

Remarks: This peaceful social species is happiest when living in small groups. Often, they don't even need to be part of a group of their own species, as any other species seems to adopt them into their own. Of course, if given the choice, *C. haraldschultzi* will choose their own kind to swim with. Feed small live foods and/or prepared foods daily for best results with this peaceful, active species.

Corydoras hastatus

EIGENMANN & EIGENMANN 1888
Natural Range: Amazon basin and Southern Brazil.
Size: 1" (2.5 cm) maximum; males smaller.
Water Chemistry: Tropical; soft and acidic.
Behavior: Peaceful.
Dietary Requirements: Standard prepared foods supplemented with small, live foods are best.

Remarks: *Corydoras hastatus* has the distinction of being one of the two smallest species (*C. cochui* is the other) within the genus. By the time this book goes to print, it may have been separated into its own genus, however, so watch for the different name. These little catfish are actually a free-swimming species that remains nearly motionless in the water column. They appreciate a slightly stronger current than other smaller fishes, so don't be afraid to add a powerhead for circulation.

Corydoras habrosus

Corydoras habrosus

Corydoras haraldschultzi

Corydoras haraldschultzi

Corydoras hastatus

Corydoras hastatus

Corydoras imitator / Imitating Cory Catfish

NIJSSEN & ISBRUCKER 1983

Natural Range: Brazil.

Size: 2" (5 cm) TL; females slightly larger and heavier than males.

Water Chemistry: Tropical; soft and acidic.

Behavior: Peaceful.

Dietary Requirements: Standard prepared foods supplemented with small, live foods are best.

Remarks: The long-snouted form of *C. adolfoi*, this is a peaceful, schooling species that does well in small groups. All conditions that apply for *C. adolfoi* apply for *C. imitator*.

Corydoras julii

STEINDACHNER 1906

Natural Range: Lower Amazon basin, Brazil.

Size: 2" (5 cm) TL; females slightly larger and heavier than males.

Water Chemistry: Tropical; soft and acidic.

Behavior: Peaceful.

Dietary Requirements: Standard prepared foods supplemented with small, live foods are best.

Remarks: It has been suggested that this species requires more swimming room around the bottom of the aquarium as compared to other species. Few demands are placed on the condition of the water as long as extremes are avoided. It should also be noted that the true *C. julii* is very infrequently imported, and most specimens sold as *C. julii* are actually *C. trilineatus*.

Corydoras latus

PEARSON 1924

Natural Range: Brazil.

Size: 2" (5 cm) TL; females slightly larger and heavier than males.

Water Chemistry: Tropical; soft and acidic.

Behavior: Peaceful.

Dietary Requirements: Standard prepared foods supplemented with small, live foods are best.

Remarks: This species has almost certainly been sold has *C. aeneus* due to their close resemblance. They are also similar in many other aspects, such as size, shape, and husbandry requirements. Occasionally, *C. latus* is also sold as *C. concolor*, although this is only so as juveniles, because adult *C. concolor* are very easy to distinguish from most other Cory cats. They can be kept under the same conditions as *C. aeneus*.

Corydoras imitator pair

Corydoras imitator

Corydoras julii adult group

Corydoras julii

Corydoras latus

Corydoras sp.

Corydoras leucomelas / Leopard Cory Catfish

EIGENMANN & ALLEN 1942

Natural Range: Peru, Ecuador, and Colombia.
Size: 2" (5 cm) TL; females slightly larger and heavier than males.
Water Chemistry: Tropical; soft and acidic.
Behavior: Peaceful.
Dietary Requirements: Standard prepared foods supplemented with small, live foods are best.

Remarks: This is an ideal community tank species that can be housed in a 15- to 20-gallon aquarium with small tetras, dwarf cichlids, and other peaceful species. The females are more rounded in the belly region, and males haves more elongate, pointed fins.

Corydoras melanistius / Bluespotted Cory Catfish

REGAN 1912

Natural Range: Northern South America.
Size: 2" (5 cm) TL; females slightly larger and heavier than males.
Water Chemistry: Tropical; soft and acidic.
Behavior: Peaceful.
Dietary Requirements: Standard prepared foods supplemented with small, live foods are best.

Remarks: There has been some published confusion about the validity of this species as well as the validity of one or more subspecies. As of this writing, we recognize only one as being valid and that is the original combination of Regan in 1912. *C. melanistius* requires the same care as other similar-sized Cory cats.

Corydoras melini / Bandit Cory Catfish

LONNBERG & RENDAHL 1930

Natural Range: Brazil.
Size: 2" (5 cm) TL; females slightly larger and heavier than males.
Water Chemistry: Tropical; soft and acidic.
Behavior: Peaceful.
Dietary Requirements: Standard prepared foods supplemented with small, live foods are best.

Remarks: The care and breeding of this species is typical for the genus. *C. melini* is most often confused with *C. metae* but differs from that species by having black only at the base of the dorsal fin and a black stripe extending onto the lower edge of the caudal fin (Burgess 1992). Care and breeding are of normal Cory fashion.

Corydoras leucomelas juveniles

Corydoras leucomelas adult

Corydoras melanistius

Corydoras melanistius

Corydoras melini adult

Corydoras melini

257

Corydoras metae / Masked Cory Catfish

EIGENMAN 1914

Natural Range: Colombia.

Size: 2" (5 cm) TL; females slightly larger and heavier than males.

Water Chemistry: Tropical; soft and acidic.

Behavior: Peaceful.

Dietary Requirements: Standard prepared foods supplemented with small, live foods are best.

Remarks: This omnivorous species of *Corydoras* will eat a variety of foods but prefers small live ones such as *Daphnia*, *Tubifex* worms, and insect larvae. Again, the care and husbandry for *C. metae* is nearly identical to other closely related Cory cats. Spawning is said to occur in a 14-day rhythm.

Corydoras nanus

NIJSSEN & ISBRUCKER 1967

Natural Range: Surinam.

Size: 2" (5 cm) TL; females slightly larger and heavier than males.

Water Chemistry: Tropical; soft and acidic.

Behavior: Peaceful.

Dietary Requirements: Standard prepared foods supplemented with small, live foods are best.

Remarks: This species was once more popular than it is now due to restrictions imposed by the government of Surinam on exports of wild life. For many years, this species has been captive bred in many parts of the world, and specimens obtained now are probably from broodstock that has been kept going for several decades. They thrive in standard conditions for other Cory cats. Wild-collected specimens may still come from suppliers in neighboring Guyana.

Corydoras napoensis

NIJSSEN & ISBRUCKER 1986

Natural Range: Peru and Ecuador.

Size: 2" (5 cm) TL; females slightly larger and heavier than males.

Water Chemistry: Tropical; soft and acidic.

Behavior: Peaceful.

Dietary Requirements: Standard prepared foods supplemented with small, live foods are best.

Remarks: Although the species name indicates that it hails from the Rio Napo in Peru, *C. napoensis* is not restricted to that system. Rather, they are found over a broad area that includes the Rio Napo and many of its tributaries, as well as the Rio Aguarico in Ecuador.

Corydoras metae

Corydoras metae

Corydoras nanus juvenile

Corydoras nanus

Corydoras napoensis

Corydoras napoensis

259

Corydoras narcissus

NIJSSEN & ISBRUCKER 1980

Natural Range: Brazil.

Size: 2" (5 cm) TL; females slightly larger and heavier than males.

Water Chemistry: Tropical; soft and acidic.

Behavior: Peaceful.

Dietary Requirements: Standard prepared foods supplemented with small, live foods are best.

Remarks: *C. narcissus* appears to be the long-snouted version of the sympatric *C. arcuatus*. The patterns are the same, as are the keeping and breeding conditions (Burgess 1992).

Corydoras nattereri / Blue Cory Catfish

STEINDACHNER 1876

Natural Range: Brazil.

Size: 2" (5 cm) TL; females slightly larger and heavier than males.

Water Chemistry: Tropical; soft and acidic.

Behavior: Peaceful.

Dietary Requirements: Standard prepared foods supplemented with small, live foods are best.

Remarks: This is an old favorite in the aquarium industry. Its care and breeding are in normal Cory cat fashion, and water conditions are not critical as long as extremes are avoided. They are commonly available in many pet shops and fish dealers and are usually very reasonably priced.

Corydoras notatus

NIJSSEN & ISBRUCKER 1976

Natural Range: South America.

Size: 2" (5 cm) TL.

Water Chemistry: Tropical; soft and acidic.

Behavior: Peaceful.

Dietary Requirements: Standard prepared foods supplemented with small, live foods are best.

Remarks: This interesting little Corydoras is easily recognized by its dark horizontal pattern and short, blunt snout. They are active and peaceful and do best in a small community aquarium with fishes of a similar temperament.

Corydoras narcissus

Corydoras narcissus

Corydoras nattereri adult

Corydoras nattereri juvenile

Corydoras notatus

Corydoras notatus

Corydoras oiapoquensis / Oyapok Cory Catfish

SANDS 1989

Natural Range: French Guiana.
Size: 2" (5 cm) TL; females slightly larger and heavier than males.
Water Chemistry: Tropical; soft and acidic.
Behavior: Peaceful.
Dietary Requirements: Standard prepared foods supplemented with small, live foods are best.

Remarks: The type locality, the Oyapok River, French Guiana, provided the name for this species. This is the short-snouted form associated with the long-snouted *C. condiscipulus*. Information given for that species also applies to this one (Burgess 1992).

Corydoras paleatus / Peppered Cory Catfish

JENYNS 1842

Natural Range: Brazil.
Size: 2" (5 cm) TL; females slightly larger and heavier than males.
Water Chemistry: Tropical; soft and acidic.
Behavior: Peaceful.
Dietary Requirements: Standard prepared foods supplemented with small, live foods are best.

Remarks: There are several well-known and easily recognized species of *Corydoras* and this is one of them. *C. paleatus* is probably the easiest to keep and breed out of all of the species within the genus. Standard aquarium fare will suffice for feeding and a small- to moderate-sized aquarium with peaceful tank-mates will do.

Corydoras panda / Panda Cory Catfish

NIJSSEN & ISBRUCKER 1971

Natural Range: Peru.
Size: 2" (5 cm) TL.
Water Chemistry: Tropical; soft and acidic.
Behavior: Peaceful.
Dietary Requirements: Standard prepared foods supplemented with small, live foods are best.

Remarks: *C. panda* seems to be restricted to the Pachitea River system, Peru. This unique and very popular Cory catfish has won the hearts of many tropical fish hobbyists over the years, and the demand for them is still very high compared to other species. This species does well when treated as *C. adolfoi*.

Corydoras oiapoquensis adult

Corydoras oiapoquensis juvenile

Corydoras paleatus

Corydoras paleatus blue var.

Corydoras panda

Corydoras panda

Corydoras polysticta

REGAN 1912
Natural Range: Brazil.
Size: 2" (5 cm) TL; females slightly larger and heavier than males.
Water Chemistry: Tropical; soft and acidic.
Behavior: Peaceful.
Dietary Requirements: Standard prepared foods supplemented with small, live foods are best.

Remarks: Known to come from the tributaries of the Rio Guapore (Mato Grosso, Brazil), this medium-sized Cory cat does best in small groups of similar-sized specimens. They are a peaceful species that will spend a good portion of the day searching out food that has fallen in the various cracks and crevices of the aquarium's décor. This species seems to do particularly well when maintained on fine sand as a substrate.

Corydoras pulcher

ISBRUCKER & NIJSSEN 1973
Natural Range: Brazil.
Size: 2" (5 cm) TL.
Water Chemistry: Tropical; soft and acidic.
Behavior: Peaceful.
Dietary Requirements: Standard prepared foods supplemented with small, live foods are best.

Remarks: *C. pulcher* is specifically found in the Rio Purus, which is part of the Rio Amazonas system, Brazil. This small species is exceedingly peaceful and may be bullied if kept with fishes that are too active or aggressive for it. Their aquarium should be set up with very clear water that is well filtered and aerated. Filtering over peat may help induce spawning since they react well to tannins in their water.

Corydoras punctatus

BLOCH 1794
Natural Range: Surinam.
Size: 2" (5 cm) TL; may grow slightly larger.
Water Chemistry: Tropical; soft and acidic.
Behavior: Peaceful.
Dietary Requirements: Standard prepared foods supplemented with small, live foods are best.

Remarks: This small species prefers to live in small, shallow creeks with overhanging vegetation. Populations of *C. punctatus* that live over darker substrates apparently have larger and darker spotting. Captive care and husbandry are in normal *Corydoras* fashion.

Corydoras polysticta female

Corydoras polysticta male

Corydoras pulcher

Corydoras pulcher

Corydoras punctatus

Corydoras punctatus profile

Corydoras pygmaeus / Pygmy Cory Catfish

NIJSSEN & ISBRUCKER 1980

Natural Range: Brazil, Peru, and Ecuador.
Size: 1" (2.5 cm); females may grow slightly larger.
Water Chemistry: Tropical; soft and acidic.
Behavior: Peaceful.
Dietary Requirements: Standard prepared foods supplemented with small, live foods are best.

Remarks: This diminutive Cory inhabits the Calama at the mouth of the Rio Jiparana or Machado in the Rio Madeira, Brazil, Loreto, Peru, and the Rio Aguarico system in Ecuador. Females may grow as large as 3.5 cm TL, but the males are usually smaller. Of course, due to their small size, only the smallest and most peaceful of species should be housed with them (Burgess 1992).

Corydoras rabauti

LA MONTE 1941

Natural Range: Brazil and Peru.
Size: 2" (5 cm) TL; females slightly larger and heavier than males.
Water Chemistry: Tropical; soft and acidic.
Behavior: Peaceful.
Dietary Requirements: Standard prepared foods supplemented with small, live foods are best.

Remarks: This species should be kept in a 15- to 20-gallon aquarium with soft, slightly acidic water that is warm and filtered over peat for best results. Well-conditioned specimens will spawn readily.

Corydoras reticulatus

FRASER-BRUNNER 1938

Natural Range: Amazon basin.
Size: 2" (5 cm) TL; females slightly larger and heavier than males.
Water Chemistry: Tropical; soft and acidic.
Behavior: Peaceful.
Dietary Requirements: Standard prepared foods supplemented with small, live foods are best.

Remarks: Under normal conditions for most Cory catfishes, *C. reticulatus* breed regularly in captivity. Similar to *C. sodalis*, they differ by the black blotch or similar marking on their dorsal fin. In *C. sodalis*, the dorsal fin may be banded but has no blotch. As the name implies, the body markings are more reticulate than with other *Corydoras*.

Corydoras pygmaeus

Corydoras pygmaeus

Corydoras rabauti adult

Corydoras rabauti small adult

Corydoras sp. aff. *reticulatus*

Corydoras reticulatus

267

Corydoras robinae / Flagtailed Cory Catfish

BURGESS 1983
Natural Range: Brazil.
Size: 2" (5 cm) TL.
Water Chemistry: Tropical; soft and acidic.
Behavior: Peaceful.
Dietary Requirements: Standard prepared foods supplemented with small, live foods are best.

Remarks: This unusual species of *Corydoras* was described by Dr. Warren Burgess in 1983 and named for Robina Schwartz. They are quite peaceful and sociable little fish that do well in a group. It is suggested that due to their locality in nature, they should have very warm, clean water that has been filtered over peat. After realizing that it's not the closely related Flagtailed Porthole Catfish (*Dianema urostriatum*), one glance at the caudal fin should leave no doubt as to which species of *Corydoras* this is (Burgess 1992).

Corydoras schwartzi

ROSSEL 1963
Natural Range: Brazil.
Size: 2" (5 cm) TL; females slightly larger and heavier than males.
Water Chemistry: Tropical; soft and acidic.
Behavior: Peaceful.
Dietary Requirements: Standard prepared foods supplemented with small, live foods are best.

Remarks: This species was discovered near the mouth of the Rio Purus in Brazil (Burgess 1992). Captive conditions are basically the same as for most other species, but *C. schwartzi* prefer water with some vigorous movement. Good filtration, and possibly even supplemental circulation, will be beneficial in keeping this species long term.

Corydoras septentrionalis

GOSLINE 1940
Natural Range: Venezuela.
Size: 2" (5 cm) TL; females slightly larger and heavier than males.
Water Chemistry: Tropical and subtropical; soft and acidic.
Behavior: Peaceful.
Dietary Requirements: Standard prepared foods supplemented with small, live foods are best.

Remarks: *Corydoras septentrionalis* prefer water that is slightly on the cooler side, so they can be kept with species that originate from mountainous or subtropical regions. Aside from their temperature preferences, this species is very easily cared for and bred in home aquariums.

Corydoras robinae

Corydoras robinae

Corydoras schwartzi

Corydoras schwartzi

Corydoras septentrionalis adult

Corydoras septentrionalis profile

269

Corydoras simulatus

WEITZMAN & NIJSSEN 1970
Natural Range: Rio Meta system, Colombia.
Size: 2" (5 cm) TL; females slightly larger and heavier than males.
Water Chemistry: Tropical; soft and acidic.
Behavior: Peaceful.
Dietary Requirements: Standard prepared foods supplemented with small, live foods are best.

Remarks: When available, this peaceful species makes a perfect addition to a peaceful community aquarium. They are robust and hardy and may accept a wide variation in water chemistry, provided that extremes are avoided. *C. simulatus* very closely resemble the longer-snouted *C. septentrionalis*.

Corydoras sodalis

NIJSSEN & ISBRUCKER 1986
Natural Range: Boarder of Brazil and Peru.
Size: 2" (5 cm) TL; females slightly larger and heavier than males.
Water Chemistry: Tropical; soft and acidic.
Behavior: Peaceful.
Dietary Requirements: Standard prepared foods supplemented with small, live foods are best.

Remarks: *Corydoras sodalis* are peaceful and sociable Cory catfish that do well in a small aquarium where they can search the caves and crevices of bogwood and plants for food. They are not as colorful or interesting to look at as many of the other *Corydoras*. However, they make a wonderful addition to the collector's aquarium.

Corydoras stenocephalus

EIGENMANN & ALLEN 1942
Natural Range: Peru.
Size: 2" (5 cm) TL; females slightly larger.
Water Chemistry: Tropical; soft and acidic.
Behavior: Peaceful.
Dietary Requirements: Standard prepared foods supplemented with small, live foods are best.

Remarks: This medium-sized Cory catfish is closely related to *C. acutus*. This rare and unusual species presents no difficulties when kept in an aquarium.

Corydoras simulatus adult

Corydoras simulatus

Corydoras sodalis juvenile

Corydoras cf. *sodalis adult*

Corydoras stenocephalus small adult

Corydoras stenocephalus

Corydoras sterbai

KNAACK 1962

Natural Range: Brazil and Bolivia.
Size: 2" (5 cm) TL; females slightly larger and heavier than males.
Water Chemistry: Tropical; soft and acidic.
Behavior: Peaceful.
Dietary Requirements: Standard prepared foods supplemented with small, live foods are best.

Remarks: A beautifully attractive species of *Corydoras*, *C. sterbai* is a true prize. They are still quite pricy, as far as Cory cats go, but well worth the expense. Healthy individuals will often live for many years when properly cared for.

Corydoras pastazensis

WEITZMAN 1963

Natural Range: Pastazensis River basin.
Size: 2" (5 cm) TL; females slightly larger and heavier than males.
Water Chemistry: Tropical; soft and acidic.
Behavior: Peaceful.
Dietary Requirements: Standard prepared foods supplemented with small, live foods are best.

Remarks: Although *C. pastazensis* has been known to science for many years, there are quite a few "imitator" species that come from the same region—or close by—that appear to be very closely related. Their care and husbandry are of normal Cory fashion.

Corydoras trilineatus / Threestripe Cory Catfish

WEITZMAN 1964

Natural Range: Peru.
Size: 2" (5 cm) TL; females slightly larger and heavier than males.
Water Chemistry: Tropical; soft and acidic.
Behavior: Peaceful.
Dietary Requirements: Standard prepared foods supplemented with small, live foods are best.

Remarks: *Corydoras trilineatus* is no newcomer to the aquarium hobby, although under this name it may appear so. Actually, it has been incorrectly referred to as *C. julii* in much of the older aquarium literature—even older versions of this text. This species does well using standard Cory care.

Corydoras sterbai pair

Corydoras sterbai adult

Corydoras pastazensis rare variety

Corydoras pastazensis profile

Corydoras trilineatus

Corydoras trilineatus

Corydoras xinguensis / Rio Xingu Cory Catfish

NIJSSEN 1972

Natural Range: Rio Xingu, Brazil.
Size: 2" (5 cm) TL max.; usually much smaller.
Water Chemistry: Tropical; slightly soft and acidic.
Behavior: Peaceful.
Dietary Requirements: Standard prepared foods supplemented with small, live foods are best.

Remarks: As the name implies, this *Corydoras* is native to the Rio Xingu in Brazil. They are small-sized and do very well in small aquariums with clear, well-oxygenated water.

Dianema longibarbus / Porthole Catfish

COPE 1872

Natural Range: Amazon River basin.
Size: 4" (10 cm) TL.
Water Chemistry: Tropical; soft and acidic.
Behavior: Peaceful.
Dietary Requirements: Standard prepared foods supplemented with small, live foods are best.

Remarks: This peaceful species of small catfish was very popular at one time but seems to have lost its flare. Exporters have claimed that they are not as common as once thought, and the areas where they originate are no longer fished with any regularity. Regardless, this interesting species makes a great addition to a community aquarium with other peaceful fishes.

Dianema urostriatum / Flagtail Catfish

MIRANDA-RIBEIRO 1912

Natural Range: Amazon River basin.
Size: 4" (10 cm) TL.
Water Chemistry: Tropical; soft and acidic.
Behavior: Peaceful.
Dietary Requirements: Standard prepared foods supplemented with small live foods will be best.

Remarks: Unlike its close cousin *D. longibarbus*, *D. urostriatum* is widely available and frequently imported into the trade via many suppliers. This species prefers slow-moving water and dark hiding areas where it can sit on the substrate or scurry around to find bits of food.

Corydoras xinguensis small adult

Corydoras xinguensis

Dianema longibarbus

Dianema longibarbus

Dianema urostriatum

Dianema urostriatum

Hoplosternum littorale / Armored Catfish

HANCOCK 1828

Natural Range: Mid to northern South America.
Size: 10" (25 cm) TL.
Water Chemistry: Subtropical; neutral pH with moderate hardness.
Behavior: Peaceful.
Dietary Requirements: Standard prepared foods supplemented with small, live foods are best.

Remarks: In nature, *H. littorale* inhabit swamps and other stagnant areas that are high in vegetative detritus. This is most probably due to their love of chironomids that are associated with the decaying matter. In aquaria, feed them heavily on sinking foods with a high chitinous content, such as brine shrimp and other crustaceans. Be sure to include some type of insect in their diet as well.

Lepthoplosternum pectorale

EIGENMANN 1913

Natural Range: Paraguay River basin.
Size: 2" (5 cm) TL; may grow larger in nature.
Water Chemistry: Subtropical; neutral pH with moderate hardness.
Behavior: Peaceful.
Dietary Requirements: Standard prepared foods supplemented with small, live foods are best.

Remarks: A small species of catfish that prefers cooler water, *L. pectorale* is perfect for the aquarium containing mountainous fishes. Just like their larger cousins, this species feeds heavily on the organisms that are associated with detritus. Feed small amounts frequently for best results.

Megalechis thoracata

MEEK & HILDEBRAND 1916

Natural Range: Northern South America.
Size: 6" (15 cm) TL; may grow slightly larger.
Water Chemistry: Tropical; neutral pH with moderate hardness.
Behavior: Peaceful.
Dietary Requirements: Standard prepared foods supplemented with small, live foods are best.

Remarks: *M. thoracata* is an old fish with a brand new name. Previously known as *Hoplosternum thoracatum*, this species has been around the hobby for decades. Care and husbandry should be similar to those of other "Hoplo Cats."

Hoplosternum littorale adult

Hoplosternum littorale juvenile

Lepthoplosternum pectorale large adult

Lepthoplosternum pectorale juvenile

Megalechis thoracata small adult

Megalechis thoracata adult

Lepomis marginatus

CENTRARCHIDAE
SUNFISHES AND BASSES

The 30 or so members of Centrarchidae are indigenous to the freshwaters of North America only. However, many species, like the Largemouth Bass (*Micropterus salmoides*), have been introduced in many parts of the United States where they did not occur naturally, as well as other countries worldwide. Included in this family are the various sunfishes, basses, and crappies that are very popular with anglers and native fishkeepers alike. Members of Centrarchidae are laterally compressed, having two dorsal fins, the first with sharp spines and the second with soft rays, and they are joined in such a way that they appear as one. With only one exception, the Sacramento Perch, centrarchids build nests and guard their young. The males can be seen, often in early spring, constructing circular pits in the substrate or vegetation by fanning their fins very rapidly over the spot. The male will often chase the female away from his nest and remain with the eggs and young after spawning.

Enneacanthus chaetodon / Blackbanded Sunfish

BAIRD 1855

Natural Range: Eastern United States, from New Jersey south to central Florida.
Size: 4" (10 cm) TL.
Water Chemistry: Temperate; soft and acidic conditions are preferred.
Behavior: Peaceful in most cases.
Dietary Requirements: Small insects and fishes. In the aquarium, this species will accept most all common foods.

Remarks: This small sunfish is easily kept in small aquariums. Be sure to provide ample structure, such as bogwood and live plants, for them to hide in and among. For years, people living in the Pine Barrens of New Jersey called them "Pines Angelfish" due to their similar coloration to *Pterophyllum scalare*, the Silver Angelfish.

Enneacanthus obesus / Banded Sunfish

GIRARD 1856

Natural Range: Southern New Hampshire to southern Florida.
Size: 4" (10 cm) TL.
Water Chemistry: Temperate; avoid extremes.
Behavior: Peaceful in most cases.
Dietary Requirements: Small insects and fishes. In the aquarium, this species will accept most all common foods.

Remarks: A small sunfish that is easily kept in small aquariums. As with *E. chaetodon*, provide ample structure, such as bogwood and live plants, for them to hide in and among. This species is very easily confused with less common *E. gloriosus*, the Bluespotted Sunfish.

Lepomis auritus / Redbreast Sunfish

LINNEAUS 1758

Natural Range: Widespread over much of North America.
Size: 12" (30 cm) TL.
Water Chemistry: Temperate; avoid extremes.
Behavior: Aggressive; keep with larger tankmates.
Dietary Requirements: Insects and snails; may also prey on smaller fish.

Remarks: A sandy and rocky substrate is ideal. Tankmates must be of equal size for best compatibility. This is one of the most beautiful of the sunfish species. Males may become intolerant of other fishes in early spring, so pay special attention to their behavior at this time of the year.

Enneacanthus chaetodon juvenile

Enneacanthus chaetodon adult

Enneacanthus obesus female

Enneacanthus obesus male

Lepomis auritus juvenile

Lepomis auritus adult

Lepomis cyanellus / Green Sunfish

RAFINESQUE 1819

Natural Range: Widespread over much of the United States and Canada; introduced elsewhere worldwide.
Size: 12" (30 cm) TL.
Water Chemistry: Temperate; avoid extremes.
Behavior: Aggressive.
Dietary Requirements: Insects and snails; will prey on smaller fish.

Remarks: This species is found in backwaters and quiet pools of rivers, often in and among vegetation. In the aquarium, this species should be provided with structure and live plants. Tankmates should be half the size or larger with mild aggression. During breeding, the males will become very aggressive. The female should be provided with ample cover, or a divider can also be used. Green Sunfish are excellent game fish, as well.

Lepomis gibbosus / Pumpkinseed

LINNEAUS 1758

Natural Range: New Brunswick in Canada to South Carolina in the United States; also introduced elsewhere worldwide.
Size: 10" (25 cm) TL.
Water Chemistry: Temperate; avoid extremes
Behavior: Mildly aggressive compared with their larger cousins.
Dietary Requirements: Small fish, crustaceans, insects, and worms are best.

Remarks: Easily kept in aquariums if provided with live/artificial plants and rock. This species can be a pest to tankmates by constantly fluttering around them. While such behavior is interesting, and the Pumpkinseed normally shows gorgeous coloration, this displaying becomes stressful on the tankmates and may lead to a failed immune system and then disease.

Lepomis megalotis / Longear Sunfish

RAFINESQUE 1820

Natural Range: Northeastern Mexico and north to the Great Lakes, United States.
Size: 10" (25 cm) TL.
Water Chemistry: Temperate; avoid extremes.
Behavior: Docile compared to its close cousins but may still be aggressive during spawning.
Dietary Requirements: Small aquatic invertebrates, insects, and small fish.

Remarks: This species is found in shallow, heavily vegetated areas in lakes, ponds, and rivers. Provide ample plants and low current.

Lepomis cyanellus

Lepomis cyanellus adult male

Lepomis gibbosus female

Lepomis gibbosus male

Lepomis megalotis juvenile

Lepomis megalotis adult male

Micropterus dolomieu / Smallmouth Bass

LACEPEDE 1802

Natural Range: Widespread in cooler rivers and lakes of North America.
Size: 24" (60 cm) TL; may grow larger.
Water Chemistry: Temperate; cooler waters preferred, otherwise not critical.
Behavior: Somewhat aggressive toward other Small Mouths.
Dietary Requirements: Fish, crayfish, and insects are best; may accept prepared foods after some time in captivity.

Remarks: This species occurs in areas that are shallow and rocky. Most often found in deep channels of rivers. In the aquarium, provide a gravel substrate and rockwork as décor. Powerheads should be used for better water circulation.

Micropterus salmoides / Largemouth Bass

LACEPEDE 1802

Natural Range: Widespread over much of North America, from Canada to Mexico.
Size: 30" (75 cm) TL; may grow larger.
Water Chemistry: Temperate to subtropical; avoid extremes.
Behavior: Somewhat aggressive.
Dietary Requirements: Whole fish, crayfish, insects, and frogs.

Remarks: This species is often found in lakes, ponds, and other areas with plenty of vegetation and wood structure. In the aquarium, provide bogwood and plants. Largemouth Bass grow very large in both length and girth.

Pomoxis nigromaculatus / Black Crappie

LESUEUR 1829

Natural Range: Widely introduced all over North America, including Canada and Mexico.
Size: 18" (45 cm).
Water Chemistry: Temperate and subtropical; avoid extremes.
Behavior: Mildly aggressive.
Dietary Requirements: Fish, worms (especially mealworms and grubs), and prepared foods.

Remarks: This species is a nocturnal feeder and prefers the backwaters and ponds associated with large rivers or lakes. In the aquarium, provide them with plants and a sandy or gravel substrate for the ultimate Crappie setup.

Micropterus dolomieu

Micropterus dolomieu adult

Micropterus salmoides large tank-raised specimen

Micropterus salmoides small adult

Pomoxis nigromaculatus

Pomoxis nigromaculatus

Channa bleheri

CHANNIDAE

SNAKEHEADS

Snakeheads have received a lot of very bad press recently, due to their ability to survive and often out-compete nearly all competition. There are approximately 21 valid Snakehead species worldwide. They are indigenous to tropical Africa and southern Asia where they are fished both commercially and for sport. They also are popular in aquaculture, and their meat is sold in many different countries.

Unfortunately, they are all but too effective at surviving with some species able to slither over very short bridges of land between water holes. More often than not, the truth about these fish is wildly exaggerated, which is unfortunate because they make great aquarium residents, provided the hobbyist has plenty of room.

We cover nine of the most commonly encountered species of Snakeheads here. Most of these are no longer available in the United States, due to the ban on their importation because of ill-informed or ill-intentioned hobbyists releasing them into local waterways where this apex predator of the Asian rice fields completely dominates their new homes. If you are fortunate enough to be a hobbyist still allowed to house these fish, do not release them!

Channa argus / Snakehead

CANTOR 1842

Natural Range: China and western Korea, Asia.
Size: 34" (85 cm) TL.
Water Chemistry: Tropical; otherwise not critical.
Behavior: Aggressive and highly predatory.
Dietary Requirements: Accept all types of live foods, such as fish, shrimp, and crayfish. They may also be trained to accept non-living and prepared foods.

Remarks: This species is one of the moderately-sized snakeheads. They commonly grow to about two feet in length and may weigh several pounds. In the aquarium, they will do best if supplied with a constant supply of live foods although they appear to be quite easy to train to accept dead and prepared foods as well. Make sure you have a tight-fitting lid to prevent them from jumping out.

Channa barca / Barca Snakehead

HAMILTON 1822

Natural Range: India; Asia.
Size: 36" (90 cm) TL.
Water Chemistry: Tropical and subtropical; otherwise not critical.
Behavior: Aggressive and highly predatory.
Dietary Requirements: Accept all types of live foods such as fish, shrimp, and crayfish. They may also be trained to accept non-living and prepared foods.

Remarks: This species is both subtropical and tropical, meaning that their range is in both climates. Therefore, *C. barca* are able to tolerate cooler waters than many of their cousins. This does not mean that they can reproduce and thrive in cooler conditions, however. In aquariums, keep as a tropical fish in warmer waters.

Channa bleheri / Dwarf Snakehead

VIERKE 1991

Natural Range: India; Asia.
Size: 6" (15 cm) TL; usually much smaller.
Water Chemistry: Tropical; otherwise not critical.
Behavior: Aggressive and highly predatory.
Dietary Requirements: Accept all types of live foods such as fish, shrimp, and crayfish. They may also be trained to accept non-living and prepared foods.

Remarks: These small snakeheads are perfect aquarium inhabitants for those who want all the aggression with a fraction of the size. They do well in normal-sized aquariums and may even reproduce. Reproduction occurs after a brief courtship where the males display to a female under their bubble nest. After the young are free-swimming, they can be offered newly hatched brine shrimp and Daphnids. As with all snakeheads, make sure you have a tight-fitting cover on the tank.

Channa argus

Channa sp. aff. *argus* adult

Channa barca

Channa barca profile

Channa bleheri

Channa bleheri

289

Channna gachua

HAMILTON 1822

Natural Range: Sri Lanka, Indonesia, and India; Asia.
Size: 8" (20 cm) TL.
Water Chemistry: Tropical; otherwise not critical.
Behavior: Aggressive and highly predatory.
Dietary Requirements: Accept all types of live foods such as fish, shrimp, and crayfish. They may also be trained to accept non-living and prepared foods.

Remarks: *C. gachua* is yet another "dwarf" species of snakehead—the term "dwarf" being relative, of course. They do well in most aquariums that have a neutral pH and other water parameters that are not extreme. In nature, they are found in streams and other rapid-flowing bodies of water as well as those that are stagnant.

Channa marulius / Great Snakehead

HAMILTON 1822

Natural Range: India to China; Asia.
Size: May grow to more than 3' (100 cm+) in TL; usually much smaller.
Water Chemistry: Tropical; otherwise not critical.
Behavior: Aggressive and highly predatory.
Dietary Requirements: Accept all types of live foods such as fish, shrimp, and crayfish. They may also be trained to accept non-living and prepared foods.

Remarks: This is a true tankbuster—literally. The emphasis on safety cannot be high enough with a species such as *C. marulius*. If frightened, they can plow right through sidewalls of aquariums if they have enough room to build up speed. This species is best left for public aquarium displays or the dinner table—not a good aquarium fish.

Channa micropeltes / Giant Snakehead

CUVIER 1831

Natural Range: Sumatra, Borneo, and the Malay Peninsula; Asia.
Size: 52" (130 cm) maximum size TL.
Water Chemistry: Tropical; otherwise not critical.
Behavior: Aggressive and highly predatory.
Dietary Requirements: Accept all types of live foods such as fish, shrimp, and crayfish. They may also be trained to accept non-living and prepared foods.

Remarks: Just like the Great Snakehead, Giant Snakeheads are really best suited for public aquarium displays. They are absolutely beautiful as juveniles with bright red coloration, but this red color quickly fades as they seem to grow in front of your eyes and turn into a bland grayish and white background color with dark or black markings.

Channa gachua

Channa pleurophthalmus Indonesia

Channa marulius juvenile

Channa marulius young adult

Channa micropeltes juvenile

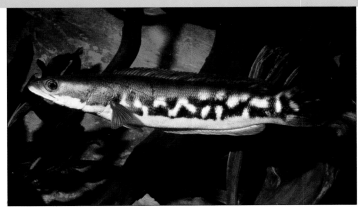

Channa micropeltes adult

Channa orientalis / Walking Snakehead (Oriental Snakehead)

BLOCH & SCHNEIDER 1801

Natural Range: Afghanistan, Sri Lanka, Indonesia; Asia.
Size: 14" (35 cm) TL.
Water Chemistry: Tropical; otherwise not critical.
Behavior: Aggressive and highly predatory.
Dietary Requirements: Accept all types of live foods such as fish, shrimp, and crayfish. They may also be trained to accept non-living and prepared foods.

Remarks: This small species of snakehead is quite popular among hobbyists fortunate enough to find them. They are a highly adaptive species that lives in rivers, lakes, ponds, and any other body of water deep enough for them to submerge into. Similar to other snakeheads, this species is able to "walk" from one water hole to another in times of dry weather, using their pelvic fins.

Channa striata / Striated Snakehead

BLOCH 1793

Natural Range: Pakistan to southern China; Asia.
Size: 40" (100 cm) TL.
Water Chemistry: Tropical; otherwise not critical.
Behavior: Aggressive and highly predatory.
Dietary Requirements: Accept all types of live foods such as fish, shrimp, and crayfish. They may also be trained to accept non-living and prepared foods.

Remarks: This large snakehead inhabits ponds and streams in nature where they actively hunt down anything they can swallow. Although not listed as subtropical, this species—as well as many others—can tolerate temperatures in the low 60s for short periods of time. Temperatures any lower usually cause death within a short period of time. *C. striata* is probably best left to public aquariums as well.

Parachanna obscura

GUNTHER 1861

Natural Range: Nile, Senegal, and the Congo River systems; Africa
Size: 20" (50 cm) TL.
Water Chemistry: Tropical; otherwise not critical.
Behavior: Aggressive and highly predatory.
Dietary Requirements: Accept all types of live foods such as fish, shrimp, and crayfish. They may also be trained to accept non-living and prepared foods.

Remarks: Once known as "*Channa obscura*," this medium-sized African species does well in a large, well-filtered aquarium with tankmates that are too large to be swallowed. It has been reported that these fish have a particular fondness for frogs. In nature, they inhabit vegetated areas of marshes and plains.

Channa orientalis adult

Channa orientalis profile

Channa striata juvenile

Channa striata adult

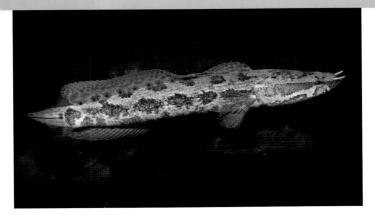

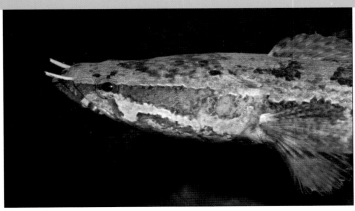

Parachanna obscura

Parachanna obscura profile

Paracheirodon axelrodi

CHARACIDAE
CHARACINS

Characidae is made up of no less than 700 species with nearly that many more awaiting description or discovery. Recently, this family has been subdivided several times. This is mainly due to improved species diagnostic practices and a better understanding of the taxonomy of fishes in general. Even today, this large and diversified family includes many of the most popular and easily recognized members of the aquarium community.

The range of species within Characidae is just as broad as the fishes that comprise it. Members can be found in the southern United States, Mexico, and nearly every country in both Central and South America. Some have even been accidentally released into the waterways of southern Florida and have developed into full breeding populations.

There is little doubt that much work remains to be done on a phylogenetic level with certain areas of this family. Recently, the African members have been split out of Characidae into their own family—Alestidae. The potentially dangerous piranhas as well as the South American tetras and Blind cave fish still remain in Characidae.

Acnodon normani / Sheep-pacu

GOSLINE 1951

Natural Range: Rio Xingu and Tocantins, Brazil.
Size: 6" (15 cm) TL.
Water Chemistry: Tropical; neutral and moderate hardness preferred.
Behavior: Generally peaceful but may nip fins and scales of tankmates.
Dietary Requirements: Plants, fish scales, insects, and snails.

Remarks: The species is not sexually dimorphic, and behavior in the aquarium can be problematic as they are primary plant eaters. Not commonly seen in the home aquarium.

Aphyocharax anisitsi / Bloodfin Tetra

EIGENMANN & KENNEDY 1903

Natural Range: Rio Parana, Argentina.
Size: 2" (5 cm) TL.
Water Chemistry: Subtropical to Tropical; neutral with moderate hardness.
Behavior: Active species that schools if kept in a large group; excellent community fish.
Dietary Requirements: Omnivorous; plants, live food, blood worms, brine shrimp, and prepared foods are accepted.

Remarks: The males are sexually dimorphic and slightly more brilliant in coloration than the females. Males have a small hook on the anal fin and a more slender body. The female is fuller in girth. They are egg layers and are known to leap from the aquarium during this process, while dropping eggs. *A. anisitsi* is usually a very hardy species.

Aphyocharax erythurus / Flametail Tetra

EIGENMANN 1912

Natural Range: Essequibo River basin, Guyana.
Size: 3" (7.5 cm) TL.
Water Chemistry: Tropical; avoid extremes.
Behavior: Peaceful species.
Dietary Requirements: Small, live foods and prepared foods are best.

Remarks: These small tetras make a great addition to the community aquarium containing peaceful fishes. They do best in groups where they prefer to live among plants and other décor. Provided with fluorescent illumination, their red tails will be very noticeable as they swim about the aquarium.

Acnodon normani juvenile

Acnodon normani adult

Aphyocharax anisitsi

Aphyocharax anisitsi gold form

Aphyocharax erythurus

Aphyocharax erythurus

Aphyocharax paraguayensis

EIGENMANN 1915

Natural Range: Paraguay basin, Paraguay.
Size: 2" (5 cm) TL.
Water Chemistry: Tropical but can take cooler water temperatures; otherwise not critical.
Behavior: Very peaceful.
Dietary Requirements: Small, live and prepared foods will work well.

Remarks: There are about a dozen species within Aphyocharax, some colorful, many not so colorful. What this species lacks in color it makes up for in its suitability for aquarium living. This is one "tetra" that will do well in aquariums that are on the cooler side, such as those containing goldfish or other cool water species.

Aphyocharax rathbuni / Red Flank Bloodfin

EIGENMANN 1907

Natural Range: Paraguay River Basin, Paraguay.
Size: 2" (5 cm) TL.
Water Chemistry: Subtropical and tropical; avoid extremes.
Behavior: Peaceful.
Dietary Requirements: Small, live foods and prepared foods are best.

Remarks: Similar in shape and appearance to other *Aphyocharax*, *A. rathbuni* is also a very good addition to those aquariums containing peaceful community fishes. They are easily identified by their gold bodies and the bright red patch of coloration that extends along the ventral side of their bodies from the anal pore to the lower lobe of the caudal fin.

Astyanax fasciatus / Banded Astyanax

CUVIER 1819

Natural Range: Widely distributed over much of North America and South America.
Size: 4" (10 cm) TL.
Water Chemistry: Tropical; avoid extremes.
Behavior: Generally aggressive; use caution when adding tankmates; will eat small fish.
Dietary Requirements: Regular aquarium food and small, live feeders.

Remarks: They inhabit slow-moving rivers without strong currents and streams. *A. fasciatus* can be caught on meat and are sometimes eaten by humans. Not recommend as a community fish, but perhaps as a single-species display.

Aphyocharax paraguayensis

Aphyocharax paraguayensis

Aphyocharax rathbuni

Aphyocharax rathbuni

Astyanax fasciatus pair

Astyanax fasciatus albino

299

Astyanax mexicanus / Mexican Tetra

DE FILIPPI 1853

Natural Range: Southern United States; eastern and central Mexico.
Size: 4" (10 cm) TL.
Water Chemistry: Tropical; otherwise not critical.
Behavior: Generally peaceful but may nip at fins.
Dietary Requirements: Small, live foods and prepared foods are best.

Remarks: This interesting species comes in two forms: the regular, colored form and the blind, colorless form. The latter is referred to as the "Blind Cave Fish" by most hobbyists and retailers. Watch this species in the community aquarium as it has a tendency to nip at the fins of other fish.

Axelrodia stigmatias / Ruby Tetra

FOWLER 1913

Natural Range: Amazon River basin, Brazil.
Size: 2" (5 cm) TL.
Water Chemistry: Tropical; prefers soft, acidic conditions.
Behavior: Very peaceful.
Dietary Requirements: Small, live foods and prepared foods are best.

Remarks: These intriguing little fish are very interesting to watch in heavily planted aquariums. The bright, leading edges of their dorsal and anal fins really stand out under fluorescent illumination. In sparsely decorated aquariums, you will not be able to fully witness their beauty. Keep in groups for best results.

Catoprion mento / Wimple Piranha

CUVIER 1819

Natural Range: Widespread over South America, including the Amazon, Orinoco, Essequibo, and upper Paraguay River basins.
Size: 6" (15 cm) TL.
Water Chemistry: Tropical; soft and acidic conditions are preferred.
Behavior: Best kept alone; not suited for community aquariums.
Dietary Requirements: Scales, some fin nipping, shrimp is taken greedily.

Remarks: Males are characterized by the bilobed anal fin. Unusual dentition, tubercle in formation. Best suited for well planted aquariums where it hides, waiting for prey to approach. Be prepared to offer plenty of larger fish for this fish to de-scale.

Astyanax mexicanus blind

Astyanax mexicanus

Axelrodia stigmatias

Axelrodia stigmatias

Catoprion mento juvenile

Catoprion mento

Chalceus macrolepidotus / Pinktail Chalceus

CUVIER 1818

Natural Range: Rio Negro and Orinoco River basins and coastal rivers of Northern South America.
Size: 10" (25 cm) TL.
Water Chemistry: Tropical; otherwise not critical.
Behavior: Peaceful but jumpy; very active swimmer.
Dietary Requirements: Small, live foods supplemented with prepared diets including shrimp pellets and the like.

Remarks: This species needs a long, low aquarium in order to fully adjust to life in captivity. They are often long-lived when given the proper setup but they really need their space. *C. macrolepidotus* do well as dither fish for larger, peaceful fishes.

Charax gibbosus / Glass Headstander

LINNAEUS 1758

Natural Range: Essequibo River basins and coastal rivers of Suriname: Guyana and Suriname.
Size: 6" (15 cm) TL.
Water Chemistry: Tropical; otherwise not critical.
Behavior: May be a fin nipper; best to keep with other active, larger fishes.
Dietary Requirements: Small, live foods and other meaty foods are best.

Remarks: In most literature where this species is profiled, we see it listed as "peaceful." This is usually the case; however, when placed in aquariums with smaller fishes, the smaller fishes often end up as a meal. Hobbyists report mixed results with this and other *Charax* species not profiled here.

Colossoma macropomum / Tambaqui

CUVIER 1818

Natural Range: Amazon and Orinoco basins; South America.
Size: 40" (100 cm) TL.
Water Chemistry: Tropical; otherwise not critical.
Behavior: Young ones cannot be trusted with smaller fish. Adults are more docile but will eat anything small enough to fit in their mouths.
Dietary Requirements: Adults tend to feed on fruits and grains. Young ones are opportunistic feeders and will eat small fish and prepared foods.

Remarks: Species has been introduced in Bolivia, Brazil, Colombia, Peru, and Venezuela in South America and Cuba, Dominican Republic, Honduras, Jamaica, and Panama in Central America. Some hobbyists have released this species in the United States. Not recommended for the home aquarium as you will need a fairly large pool to keep them in when they are adults.

Chalceus macrolepidotus eating a cricket

Chalceus macrolepidotus adult

Charax gibbosus adult

Charax gibbosus juvenile

Colossoma macroponum

Colossoma macroponum profile

Exodon paradoxus / Bucktooth Tetra

MULLER & TROSCHEL 1844

Natural Range: Amazon River basin and Tocantins River basin, Brazil and Guyana.
Size: 6" (15 cm) TL; usually much smaller.
Water Chemistry: Tropical; broad range of water chemistry is acceptable; avoid extremes.
Behavior: Notorious scale eater. Not a good community fish.
Dietary Requirements: Scales, small live fish, and prepared foods.

Remarks: These are hardy fish, but they quarrel amongst themselves. As a single species kept in a large group they school magnificently. Young fish have beautiful coloration, but tend to become rather drab with age.

Gymnocorymbus ternetzi / Black Tetra

BOULENGER 1895

Natural Range: Paraguay and Guapore River basins: Argentina, Brazil, and Bolivia.
Size: 2" (5 cm) TL.
Water Chemistry: Tropical; very tolerant of wide shifts in pH and hardness; avoid sudden extremes.
Behavior: Peaceful; excellent for community aquarium; adults tend to nip fishes that have long flowing fins.
Dietary Requirements: Insects, flake food, and small shrimp.

Remarks: This species has been introduced in Colombia. They are best kept in groups of five or more and are ranked as being one of the easiest fishes to breed in the home aquarium. Use of a substrate with marbles is recommended, since this will allow the eggs to fall through and remain safe from the parent fishes. There seem to be several genetically altered varieties of this species that are commonly referred to as "skirt" tetras.

Hasemania nana / Silvertip Tetra

LUTKEN 1875

Natural Range: Sao Francisco River basin, Minas Gerias, Brazil.
Size: 2' (5 cm) TL.
Water Chemistry: Tropical; prefer soft and acidic conditions.
Behavior: Very peaceful.
Dietary Requirements: Small, live foods and prepared foods are best.

Remarks: This strikingly beautiful species really stands out among many other tetras when housed in a planted aquarium. Their bright silver-tipped fins make them very easy to follow throughout the aquarium, even while observing the tank from a distance. This species is highly recommended for both beginner and advanced hobbyists.

Exodon paradoxus adults

Exodon paradoxus juvenile

Gymnocorymbus ternetzi

Gymnocorymbus ternetzi

Hasemania nana

Hasemania nana

Hemigrammus bleheri / True Rummynose Tetra

GERY & MAHNERT 1986

Natural Range: Negro and Meta River basins, Brazil and Columbia.
Size: 2" (5 cm) TL.
Water Chemistry: Tropical; prefer soft and acidic conditions.
Behavior: Very peaceful.
Dietary Requirements: Small, live foods and prepared foods are best.

Remarks: This species and the Cardinal Tetra (*Paracheirodon axelrodi*) are probably the most commonly kept species in true planted aquariums. Their brilliance is hard to beat in other freshwater fishes of a similar peaceful nature, and they are usually long-lived while never growing too large. This species was named in honor of its discoverer, Mr. Heiko Bleher.

Hemigrammus erythrozonus / Glowlight Tetra

DURBIN 1909

Natural Range: Essequibo River, Guyana.
Size: 1.5" (3.5 cm) TL.
Water Chemistry: Tropical; prefer soft and acidic conditions.
Behavior: Very peaceful.
Dietary Requirements: Small, live foods and prepared foods are best.

Remarks: Glowlight Tetras are very difficult to see unless there is good lighting over the aquarium. This will make their coloration really stand out, and like the Silvertip Tetras (*Hasemania nana*), they are then easy to watch—even from a distance.

Hemigrammus ocellifer / Head-and-Taillight Tetra

STEINDACHNER 1882

Natural Range: Rivers of Guyana, Suriname, French Guiana, and the Amazon basin in Peru and Brazil.
Size: 2" (5 cm) TL.
Water Chemistry: Tropical; prefer soft and acidic conditions.
Behavior: Very peaceful.
Dietary Requirements: Small, live foods and prepared foods are best.

Remarks: Another beautiful small characin is the Head-and-Taillight Tetra. This small tetra is native to a wide range of habitats and is very tolerant of fluctuating water parameters as long as extremes are avoided.

Hemigrammus bleheri adult

Hemigrammus bleheri

Hemigrammus erythrozonus adult

Hemigrammus erythrozonus

Hemigrammus ocellifer

Hemigrammus ocellifer

Hemigrammus rhodostomus / Rummy-nose Tetra

AHL 1924

Natural Range: Lower Amazon River basin and Orinoco River basin, Brazil and Venezuela.
Size: 3" (7.5 cm) TL.
Water Chemistry: Tropical; prefer soft and acidic conditions.
Behavior: Very peaceful.
Dietary Requirements: Small, live foods and prepared foods are best.

Remarks: There are actually three species of "Rummynose" tetras, and this is one is sometimes available when the other species are not. The most significant difference in this Rummynose compared to the others is the purplish hue that colors the dorsal side of the body. Additionally, their bodies are not as elongated as their cousins', and they appear to be heavier built.

Hemigrammus ulreyi

BOULENGER 1895

Natural Range: Paraguay River basin, Paraguay.
Size: 2" (5 cm) TL.
Water Chemistry: Tropical but can tolerate lower water temperatures; avoid extremes.
Behavior: Very peaceful.
Dietary Requirements: Small, live foods and prepared foods.

Remarks: These little "glass tetras" are easily identified by the black horizontal stripe that runs from their nose through the eye and down to their tail. As with other small tetras, keep this species in a group—preferably of a dozen or more individuals—for best results.

Hyphessobrycon columbianus / Colombian Red and Blue Tetra

ZARSKE & GERY 2002

Natural Range: Colombia.
Size: 2" (5 cm) TL; may grow slightly larger.
Water Chemistry: Tropical; otherwise not critical.
Behavior: Generally peaceful with larger species of community fishes; may be a fin nipper so watch with small fishes.

Remarks: These brutes are a heavy-bodied tetra that may, at times, become aggressive, although we list them as generally peaceful. Some specimens are more aggressive than others. Keep in a small group of five to ten individuals for best results and behavior.

Hemigrammus rhodostomus adult pair

Hemigrammus rhodostomus young pair

Hemigrammus ulreyi

Hemigrammus ulreyi group

Hyphessobrycon columbianus

Hyphessobrycon columbianus profile

Hyphessobrycon eques / Serpae Tetra

STEINDACHNER 1882

Natural Range: Amazon, Guapore, and Paraguay River basins: Brazil, Bolivia and Paraguay.
Size: 2" (5 cm) TL.
Water Chemistry: Tropical but may tolerate cooler temperatures; prefer soft and acidic conditions.
Behavior: Generally peaceful but may quarrel among other tetras.
Dietary Requirements: Small, live foods and prepared foods.

Remarks: Red Phantom Tetras are a beautiful small species of tetra that do well in community aquariums containing other peaceful fishes. Watch their behavior as they have a tendency to bully smaller fishes. Tankmates for this species should be slightly larger than the Red Phantom Tetras.

Hyphessobrycon erythrostigma / Bleeding-heart Tetra

FOWLER 1943

Natural Range: Upper Amazon River basin, Brazil, Columbia, and Peru.
Size: 3" (7.5 cm) TL.
Water Chemistry: Tropical; prefers soft and acid conditions.
Behavior: Very peaceful.
Dietary Requirements: Small, live foods and prepared foods are best.

Remarks: Bleeding-heart Tetras are one of the old standbys—almost everyone who has been keeping fish for even a little while knows of them. These fish are very easy to care for and should be experienced by everyone. Even long-time hobbyists tend to go back to this species at some point in their lives.

Hyphessobrycon flammeus / Flame Tetra

MYERS 1924

Natural Range: Coastal areas of Rio de Janeiro State, Brazil.
Size: 2" (5 cm) TL; usually smaller.
Water Chemistry: Tropical; prefer soft and acidic conditions.
Behavior: Very peaceful.
Dietary Requirements: Small, live foods and prepared foods are best.

Remarks: These interesting little fish closely resemble the Black Tetra (*Gymnocorymbus ternetzi*) but are more colorful. Their ease of maintenance makes them one of the top tetras to buy for beginners when available.

Hyphessobrycon eques normal variant

Hyphessobrycon eques super red variant

Hyphessobrycon erythrostigma adult

Hyphessobrycon erythrostigma adult

Hyphessobrycon flammeus

Hyphessobrycon flammeus

Hyphessobrycon herbertaxelrodi / Black Neon Tetra

GERY 1961

Natural Range: Paraguay River basin, Brazil.
Size: 1.5" (3 cm) TL.
Water Chemistry: Tropical; prefer soft and acidic conditions.
Behavior: Very peaceful.
Dietary Requirements: Small, live foods and prepared foods are best.

Remarks: Black Neon Tetras are a perfect addition to a peaceful community aquarium containing some of the brighter species. They are shy and will keep to themselves, rarely harassing anything in the aquarium. Of course, buy a group of them as they feel safer in schools.

Hyphessobrycon heterorhabdus / Flag Tetra

ULREY 1894

Natural Range: Lower Amazon River basin, Brazil.
Size: 2" (5 cm) TL.
Water Chemistry: Tropical; prefer soft and acidic conditions.
Behavior: Very peaceful.
Dietary Requirements: Small, live foods and prepared foods are best.

Remarks: Flag Tetras are uncommonly seen in the hobby, but when they are, they're worth grabbing. Of course, such rarity is relative to where in the world you reside. In the United States, many of the Flag Tetras that are available are only available seasonally. That just gives you one more reason to stroll through the isles of your favorite aquarium store from time to time.

Hyphessobrycon megalopterus / Black Phantom Tetra

EIGENMANN 1915

Natural Range: Upper Paraguay and Guapore River basins, Bolivia and Brazil.
Size: 2" (5 cm) TL.
Water Chemistry: Tropical; prefer soft and acidic conditions.
Behavior: Very peaceful.
Dietary Requirements: Small, live foods and prepared foods are best.

Remarks: Black Phantom Tetras have been in the hobby for decades. They are considered one of the top tetras for beginners, and many hobbyists who keep planted aquariums will have a few of these swimming around. They breed easily but may become aggressive during spawning.

Hyphessobrycon herbertaxelrodi

Hyphessobrycon herbertaxelrodi profile

Hyphessobrycon heterorhabdus male

Hyphessobrycon heterorhabdus female

Hyphessobrycon megalopterus male

Hyphessobrycon megalopterus

Hyphessobrycon pulchripinnis / Lemon Tetra

AHL 1937

Natural Range: Tapajos River system, Brazil.
Size: 2" (5 cm) TL.
Water Chemistry: Tropical; prefer soft and acidic conditions.
Behavior: Peaceful, excellent community fish.
Dietary Requirements: Small, live foods and prepared foods are best.

Remarks: Lemon Tetras make excellent tankmates for many of the popular smaller aquarium fishes. When introduced as a group, they can often be observed schooling tirelessly around the aquarium. Just like other small tetras, Lemon Tetras are susceptible to disease if their water quality is poor, so be sure to do those water changes!

Hyphessobrycon peruvianus / Peruvian Tetra

LADIGES 1938

Natural Range: Upper Amazon River basin, Peru.
Size: 2" (5 cm) TL.
Water Chemistry: Tropical; prefer soft and acidic conditions.
Behavior: Very peaceful.
Dietary Requirements: Small, live foods and prepared foods are best.

Remarks: Peruvian Tetras are a beautiful small species of characin that have gained popularity in the recent years. Their blue coloration sometimes gives them the common name of "Blue Tetra," although this name is not really correct. Adults have a dark red color along the dorsal side of their eyes.

Hyphessobrycon sweglesi / Red Phantom Tetra

GERY 1961

Natural Range: Orinoco River basin, Colombia.
Size: 2" (5 cm) TL; usually slightly smaller.
Water Chemistry: Tropical; prefer soft and acidic conditions.
Behavior: Very peaceful.
Dietary Requirements: Small, living foods and prepared foods are best.

Remarks: There is some confusion as to the differences between this species and the Serpae Tetra (*H. eques*). Both species look remarkably similar. However, they originate from different localities and have differences on the meristic level. Otherwise, the care and maintenance required in captivity for these two species are identical.

Hyphessobrycon pulchripinnis

Hyphessobrycon pulchripinnis

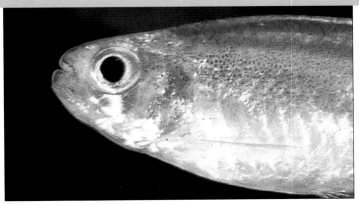

Hyphessobrycon peruvianus

Hyphessobrycon peruvianus profile

Hyphessobrycon sweglesi

Hyphessobrycon sweglesi

Inpaichthys kerri / **Royal Tetra**

GERY & JUNK 1977

Natural Range: Aripuana River, upper Madeira River basin, Brazil.
Size: 2" (5 cm) TL; may grow slightly larger.
Water Chemistry: Tropical; prefer soft and acidic conditions.
Behavior: Very peaceful.
Dietary Requirements: Small, live foods and prepared foods are best.

Remarks: Although not as hardy as many other tetras, Royal Tetras are one of the most beautiful and desirable of the small characins. They are peaceful and rarely bother anything in their aquariums but are very susceptible to disease. Always watch for Ich outbreaks, and be sure to keep their water fresh and clean.

Metynnis hypsauchen / **Silver Dollar**

MULLER & TROSCHEL 1844

Natural Range: Amazon and Paraguay River basins, Brazil and Paraguay.
Size: 6" (15 cm) TL.
Water Chemistry: Tropical; prefer soft, acidic conditions.
Behavior: Moderately peaceful; keep with larger peaceful species.
Dietary Requirements: Omnivorous; will take both meat- and plant-based foods.

Remarks: Young specimens are very colorful, but adults become dull in coloration. They may easily consume smaller fishes if given the opportunity. Keep this species in a spacious aquarium in small groups numbering about four to six individuals.

Metynnis luna

COPE 1878

Natural Range: Amazon River basin, Peru.
Size: 8" (20 cm) TL.
Water Chemistry: Tropical; prefer soft and acidic conditions.
Behavior: Usually very peaceful but may be intimidating; very active swimmers.
Dietary Requirements: Mainly vegetarian but will also take all types of small, live foods and prepared foods.

Remarks: As with other "silver dollars," this species is a very active swimmer that needs plenty of room to move about the aquarium. They are best kept in large schools, but fin nipping may occur. Overall, these fish are very nice in the aquarium but are somewhat difficult to keep in pristine shape.

Impaichthys kerri

Impaichthys kerri

Metynnis hypsauchen

Metynnis sp. aff. *hypsauchen* "barred"

Metynnis sp. aff. *luna*

Metynnis sp. aff. *luna*

317

Metynnis maculatus / Spotted Metynnis

KNER 1858

Natural Range: Amazon and Paraguay River basins, Brazil and Paraguay.
Size: 8" (20 cm) TL.
Water Chemistry: Tropical; prefer soft and acidic conditions.
Behavior: Usually very peaceful but may be intimidating; a very active swimmer.
Dietary Requirements: Mainly vegetarian but will take all types of small, live foods and prepared foods.

Remarks: The Spotted Metynnis is a very attractive species of silver dollar tetra. Their care and husbandry are the same as for others of the genus.

Moenkhausia oligolepis / Glass Tetra

GUNTHER 1864

Natural Range: Amazon River basin; Brazil, French Guiana, Guyana, Peru, Suriname, and Venezuela.
Size: 4" (10 cm) TL.
Water Chemistry: Tropical; prefer soft and acid conditions.
Behavior: Very peaceful.
Dietary Requirements: Small, live foods and prepared foods.

Remarks: This interesting species is easily confused with *M. sanctaefilomenae*, another tetra with red in their eyes. While their distribution does not overlap, their care and husbandry in captivity are identical.

Moenkhausia pittieri / Diamond Tetra

EIGENMANN 1920

Natural Range: Lake Valencia basin, Venezuela.
Size: 3" (7.5 cm) TL.
Water Chemistry: Tropical; prefer soft and acidic conditions.
Behavior: Very peaceful; some may nip fins.
Dietary Requirements: Small, live foods and prepared foods.

Remarks: The Diamond Tetra is one of the flashiest tetras around. Their speckles seem to sparkle as the lighting reflects off of them. Breeding Diamond Tetras are a sight to behold with their highly reflective scales showing hues of purples, greens, and blues. This species is a must-have for the tetra fanatic.

318

Metynnis maculatus

Metynnis sp. aff. *maculatus*

Moenkhausia oligolepis female

Moenkhausia oligolepis male

Moenkhausia pittieri female

Moenkhausia pittieri male

319

Moenkhausia sanctaefilomenae / Redeye Tetra

STEINDACHNER 1907

Natural Range: Paraiba, Sao Francisco, upper Parana, Paraguay and Uruguay River basins; Brazil and Paraguay.
Size: 3" (7.5 cm) TL.
Water Chemistry: Tropical but may tolerate cooler temperatures; prefer soft and acidic conditions.
Behavior: Very peaceful.
Dietary Requirements: Small, live foods and prepared foods.

Remarks: Redeye Tetras are probably one of the top most commonly available species of tetra currently in the hobby. They are captive produced in huge numbers today—as are many tropical fishes—as compared with years past when all of them were wild collected. Their care and husbandry in aquariums is the same as for others in the genus.

Myleus pacu

JARDINE & SCHOMBURGK 1841

Natural Range: Essequibo River, Guyana.
Size: 8" (20 cm) TL.
Water Chemistry: Tropical; otherwise not critical, avoid extremes.
Behavior: Generally peaceful; keep with other larger peaceful species.
Dietary Requirements: Feed principally on plants, more rarely on seeds.

Remarks: *M. pacu* grow too large for the average home aquarium, and they possess powerful teeth that can cause serious bites. Use caution when dealing with this species, as if you are handling piranhas.

Myleus rubripinnis / Redhook Silver Dollar

MULLER & TROSCHEL 1844

Natural Range: Amazon and Orinoco River basins; Brazil and Venezuela.
Size: 12" (30 cm) TL; usually far smaller.
Water Chemistry: Tropical; neutral pH with moderate hardness is preferred.
Behavior: Largely non-aggressive species.
Dietary Requirements: Feed on leaves of river plants in nature, but a diet high in plant matter will suffice in the aquarium.

Remarks: Large species that requires huge aquariums for proper growth and development. This species needs to swim quite a lot to remain calm. When frightened, they will often bash their heads into the walls of the aquarium and knock themselves unconscious.

Moenkhausia sanctaefilomenae

Moenkhausia sanctaefilomenae

Myleus pacu

Myleus maculatus for comparison

Myleus rubripinnis

Myleus rubripinnis var

321

Myleus schomburgkii / Blackband Silver Dollar

JARDINE 1841

Natural Range: Middle and lower Amazon basin, Nanay River, upper Orinoco River basin; Brazil, Peru, and Venezuela.
Size: 14" (35 cm) TL; usually far smaller.
Water Chemistry: Tropical; avoid extremes.
Behavior: A peaceful but very active swimmer that may cause calmer fishes to hide.
Dietary Requirements: Largely vegetarian in nature, this species will accept most standard fare in aquariums.

Remarks: Unfortunately, this beautiful species requires the same amount of room as *M. rubripinnis* and is best left for aquariums that can fully accommodate them.

Myleus ternetzi

NORMAN 1929

Natural Range: East and northeast South America.
Size: 10" (25 cm) TL.
Water Chemistry: Tropical; avoid extremes.
Behavior: Harmless, a good community fish.
Dietary Requirements: Feeds on leaves of river plants. During the flooded zones, its diet consists of flowers and seeds that it finds in the flood zones of the forest.

Remarks: This large-growing species is not for the average home aquarium. While peaceful, they may intimidate other fishes and cause them to hide. In large public aquaria, this species is very active and constantly moving about the tank. They may also become quite social as adults.

Nematobrycon palmeri / Emperor Tetra

EIGENMANN 1911

Natural Range: Atrato and San Juan River basins, Colombia.
Size: 2" (5 cm) TL.
Water Chemistry: Tropical; prefer soft and acidic conditions.
Behavior: Very peaceful.
Dietary Requirements: Small, live foods and prepared foods.

Remarks: Emperor Tetras are not the hardiest of tetras available from suppliers. They have a tendency to come in from Colombia somewhat rough, and even today many are not captive produced. Of course, there are some fish farmers who are breeding these by the thousands. To keep this species alive, you will need to keep your water quality very high. Not for beginners.

Myleus schomburgkii var.

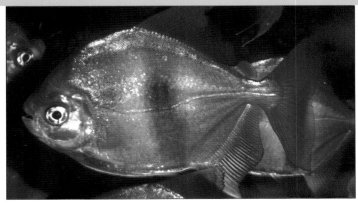

Myleus schomburgkii

Myleus ternetzi

Myleus ternetzi profile

Nematobrycon palmeri

Nematobrycon palmeri

323

Ossubtus xinguense

JEGU 1992

Natural Range: Rio Xingu River basin, Brazil.
Size: 6" (15 cm) TL.
Water Chemistry: Tropical; avoid extremes.
Behavior: Seem to be generally peaceful, but watch for fin nipping and scale biting.
Dietary Requirements: Highly herbivorous but will take snails (see photo) and meaty foods as well.

Remarks: This unique characin is a fairly new addition to the tropical fish hobby. They are not very colorful, but their unique appearance and inquisitive behavior make them a new and exciting addition to your aquarium. There is much to be learned about this species and its care in captivity.

Paracheirodon axelrodi / Cardinal Tetra

SCHULTZ 1956

Natural Range: Upper Orinoco and Negro River basins; Brazil, Colombia, and Venezuela.
Size: 2" (5 cm) TL.
Water Chemistry: Tropical; prefer soft and slightly acidic conditions.
Behavior: Peaceful.
Dietary Requirements: Small, live foods and prepared foods are best.

Remarks: This species was named in honor of Dr. Herbert R. Axelrod. There is perhaps no other fish that looks as good moving through a nicely planted aquarium. They feel most comfortable in large groups and with other peaceful and slow-moving species. Additionally, they make excellent tankmates for Discus.

Paracheirodon innesi / Neon Tetra

MYERS 1936

Natural Range: Tributaries of Solimos River, Brazil.
Size: 2: (5 cm) TL.
Water Chemistry: Tropical; prefer soft and slightly acidic conditions.
Behavior: Peaceful.
Dietary Requirements: Small, live foods and prepared foods are best.

Remarks: The Neon Tetra is currently number one in species recognition of all tetras. Ironically, this species can be difficult to care for and is not a good fish for beginners. Just as with the Emperor Tetra (*Nematobrycon palmeri*), Neons will need excellent water quality and a good diet of live or frozen crustaceans, such as Brine Shrimp or *Daphnia*.

Ossubtus xinguensis juvenile

Ossubtus xinguensis eating a snail

Paracheirodon axelrodi

Paracheirodon axelrodi pair

Paracheirodon innesi

Paracheirodon innesi

Paracheirodon simulans / Green Neon Tetra

GERY 1963

Natural Range: Upper Negro and Orinoco River basins; Brazil, Colombia, and Venezuela.
Size: 2" (5 cm) TL.
Water Chemistry: Tropical; prefer soft and slightly acidic conditions.
Behavior: Peaceful.
Dietary Requirements: Small, live foods and prepared foods are best.

Remarks: While not as commonly available as their cousins, the Cardinal Tetra and Neon Tetra, the Green Neons are a rarity among imports. Their care and husbandry requirements are identical to those for the other members of the genus. Not a fish for beginners.

Petitella georgiae / False Rummynose Tetra

GERY & BOUTIERE 1964

Natural Range: Upper Amazon River basin.
Size: 3" (7.5 cm) TL.
Water Chemistry: Tropical; prefer soft, acidic conditions.
Behavior: Peaceful.
Dietary Requirements: Small, live foods and prepared foods are best.

Remarks: The False Rummynose Tetra is an absolutely striking species of tetra that does very well in captivity. Of course, unless you are very observant, this species is commonly sold as the Rummynose Tetra, while the True Rummynose Tetra (*Hemigrammus bleheri*) is not as common as many may think. Recently, captive breeding has made both species somewhat more available than in years past.

Pristella maxillaris / X-ray Tetra

ULREY 1894

Natural Range: Amazon and Orinoco River drainages; Brazil, Colombia, and Venezuela.
Size: 2" (5 cm) TL.
Water Chemistry: Tropical; prefer soft and slightly acidic conditions.
Behavior: Peaceful.
Dietary Requirements: Small, live foods and prepared foods are best.

Remarks: These fish are sometimes referred to as "Pinktailed Tetras" in local fish shops. They are small, peaceful tetras that have requirements identical to others in their family of similar size. This species is also quite striking when a group is maintained in a heavily planted aquarium.

Paracheirodon simulans   *Paracheirodon simulans*

Petitella georgiae   *Petitella georgiae*

Pristella maxillaris male   *Pristella maxillaris* female

Pygocentrus cariba / Orinoco Red-bellied Piranha

HUMBOLT & VALENCIENNES 1821

Natural Range: Widely distributed in the Orinoco River basin lowlands and tributaries throughout Venezuela and into Columbia.

Size: 15" (38 cm) TL.

Water Chemistry: Tropical; avoid extremes.

Behavior: Extremely aggressive; cannibalistic; may be shy and very skittish.

Dietary Requirements: Whole fish (live and/or dead) and meat products.

Remarks: Potentially dangerous to humans. Do not handle with hands, as severe bites or loss of fingers can occur. Strong musculature and razor sharp teeth can cut into human flesh even at small sizes. Many myths about the ferocity of this species are written in serious scientific literature and public documents. *P. cariba* are prohibited in some States.

Pygocentrus nattereri / Red-bellied Piranha

KNER 1858

Natural Range: Widely distributed over much of tropical South America.

Size: 14" (35 cm) TL.

Water Chemistry: Tropical; wide degree of variation in chemistry; avoid extremes.

Behavior: Extremely aggressive.

Dietary Requirements: Whole fish, and other meats.

Remarks: Potentially dangerous to humans, particularly during handling; otherwise, same care and husbandry as *P. cariba*. Prohibited in some States.

Pygocentrus piraya / Piraya

CUVIER 1819

Natural Range: Restricted to the Rio Sao Francisco, Brazil.

Size: 18" (45 cm) TL, the largest in the genus.

Water Chemistry: Tropical; neutral to slightly alkaline with moderate hardness is preferred.

Behavior: Extremely aggressive.

Dietary Requirements: Whole fish and other meats.

Remarks: *P. Piraya* are often difficult to keep in groups. Space seems to be the biggest requirement. They are not meant for small show tanks commonly found in the home and are even prohibited in some States.

Pygocentrus cariba juvenile shoal

Pygocentrus cariba adult

Pygocentrus nattereri juvenile

Pygocentrus nattereri adult

Pygocentrus piraya juvenile shoal

Pygocentrus piraya adult

Pygopristis denticulata / Lobetoothed Pirambeba

CUVIER 1819

Natural Range: Orinoco River basin, north and eastern Guiana Shield rivers; tributaries of the lower Amazon River; northern South America.

Size: 8" (20 cm) TL.

Water Chemistry: Temperatures between 75–82°F; pH: 6.0–74; dGH: 6.

Behavior: One of the few piranha species that can be kept with other fishes (ie., silver dollars or pacus).

Dietary Requirements: Whole fish, fruit, and seeds.

Remarks: The silvery scales and yellow trimming on the fins make this one of the prettiest of the pirambebas. They are prohibited in some states.

Serrasalmus brandtii / Pirambeba

LUTKEN 1875

Natural Range: Rio Sao Francisco and its tributaries, Brazil.

Size: 8" (20 cm) TL.

Water Chemistry: Tropical; neutral pH with moderate hardness.

Behavior: Solitary species; aggressive and a fin biter.

Dietary Requirements: Whole fish and fins.

Remarks: Rather shy species that tends to flee when approached. Keep alone to avoid damage to other fishes. They are prohibited in some states.

Pygopristis denticulata juveniles

Pygopristis denticulata adult

Serrasalmus brandtii

Serrasalmus brandtii Profile

Serrasalmus eigenmanni / Eigenman's Piranha

NORMAN 1929

Natural Range: Brazil, Venezuela, French Guiana, Suriname, and Guyana.
Size: 8" (20 cm) TL.
Water Chemistry: Tropical; soft and slightly acidic conditions are best.
Behavior: An aggressive fin biter that is best kept as a solitary species.
Dietary Requirements: Insects, crustaceans, fruits, seeds, and fish fins.

Remarks: Species looks very similar to those in the genus *Pristobrycon* (*P. humeralis* and *P. serrulatus*). If kept, a heavily planted tank is recommended. Though the fish have small teeth, they can cause a severe bite, so use caution, especially when netting. They are prohibited in some states.

Serrasalmus elongatus / Elongated Piranha

KNER 1858

Natural Range: Amazon and Orinoco River basins; Brazil, Colombia, and Venezuela.
Size: 12" (30 cm) TL.
Water Chemistry: Tropical; avoid extremes.
Behavior: Solitary species; bites the fins of other fishes.
Dietary Requirements: Whole fishes and fins; may accept other meaty foods as well.

Remarks: This is basically a river fish and requires good filtration and strong circulation. Its torpedo-shaped body and strong tail allow it to move swiftly to bite the fins of prey fishes in the open river. *S. elongatus* are prohibited in some states.

Serrasalmus geryi / Violet-line Piranha

JEGU & SANTOS 1988

Natural Range: Rio Araguaia and Tocantins River basins; Brazil.
Size: 10" (25 cm) TL.
Water Chemistry: Tropical; may experience wide temperature shifts during the night; otherwise neutral pH and moderate hardness.
Behavior: Shy and very inquisitive species.
Dietary Requirements: Very little is known about the dietary requirements of *S. geryi*. Aquarium accounts relate the fish dines on small live fishes, shrimp, and even regular pelleted foods.

Remarks: A very rare and attractive species in nature, this species is considered harmless. Their natural habitat is being altered by human intervention. They are prohibited in some states.

Serrasalmus eigenmanni

Serrasalmus eigenmanni adult profile

Serrasalmus elongatus

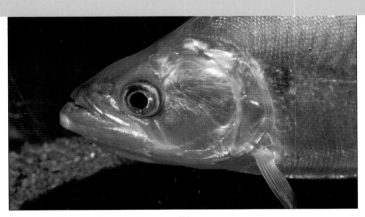

Serrasalmus elongatus profile

Serrasalmus geryi juvenile

Serrasalmus geryi adult

Serrasalmus gouldingi

FINK & MACHADO-ALLISON 1992

Natural Range: Amazons and Orinoco River basins; Brazil and Venezuela.

Size: 12" (30 cm) TL.

Water Chemistry: Tropical; prefer soft acidic conditions.

Behavior: Little is known about the aquarium behavior of *S. gouldingi*.

Dietary Requirements: Fruits, seeds, whole small fish, and fish scales.

Remarks: *S. gouldingi* and *S. manueli* are very similar in appearance and are physically separated by minimal measurements. The only obvious difference between them that is observed during growth is the eye color— *S. gouldingi* has brownish-orange eyes and *S. manueli* has red eyes. When fully grown, *S. gouldingi* resembles *S. rhombeus* based on their dark color and black eyes. They are prohibited in some states.

Serrasalmus manueli

FERNANDEZ-YEPEZ & RAMIREZ 1967

Natural Range: Amazon and Orinoco River basins; Brazil and Venezuela.

Size: 18" (45 cm) TL; may grow larger in nature.

Water Chemistry: Tropical; prefer soft, acidic conditions.

Behavior: Appear to be solitary and intolerant of tankmates.

Dietary Requirements: Diet is very similar to that of *S. gouldingi*. Aside from whole fishes, diet includes fruits and seeds.

Remarks: Not meant for small aquariums less than 200 gallons. Their prominent, oversized humeral spot, greenish reflective overtones, and striking red belly give them a most attractive appearance. Requirements include heavy oxygenation of the tank water. *S. manueli* are prohibited in some states.

Serrasalmus rhombeus / Black Piranha

LINNAEUS 1766

Natural Range: Wide-spread species found over much of northern South America.

Size: 20" (50 cm) TL; may grow larger.

Water Chemistry: Tropical; otherwise not critical; avoid extremes.

Behavior: Aggressive, solitary species in most cases.

Dietary Requirements: Mainly meat but is known to eat some plants, fruit and seeds.

Remarks: Occurs in the rapids, but is also captured in deep zones of main rivers. They are sometimes found in association with *S. manueli*. This species has the dubious distinction of being the only *Serrasalmus* species creating a population in United States waters (Florida). They are prohibited in some states.

Serrasalmus gouldingi juvenile

Serrasalmus gouldingi adult

Serrasalmus manueli juvenile

Serrasalmus manueli adult

Serrasalmus rhombeus "Xingu"

Serrasalmus rhombeus

335

Serrasalmus spilopleura / Speckled pirambeba

KNER 1858

Natural Range: Guapore River basin; Brazil.
Size: 10" (25 cm) TL.
Water Chemistry: Tropical; prefer soft and acidic conditions.
Behavior: Solitary and aggressive species.
Dietary Requirements: Mostly fins; will also eat whole, small fishes.

Remarks: *S. spilopleura* is a complex species. Their main characteristic is a dark band on the midline of the tail. They share some common characteristics with *S. maculatus*, a species found in Rio Parana, Paraguay. In some localities, they is being decimated by the introduction of *S. marginatus* due to human intervention. They are prohibited in some states.

Serrasalmus sanchezi / Red-throated Diamond Pirambeba

GERY 1964

Natural Range: Ucayali River basin, Peru.
Size: 6" (15 cm) TL.
Water Chemistry: Tropical; neutral pH and moderate hardness.
Behavior: Aggressive, solitary species that tends to hide among plants.
Dietary Requirements: Fins and whole fish.

Remarks: This species is most similar in coloration to *P. nattereri*. According to some field collectors, the fish is often found with *P. nattereri* in their Peru catches. The fish is also commonly found along fish docks, where it feeds on fish entrails tossed into the water. Juvenile forms are difficult to delineate from *S. rhombeus* of equal juvenile size. They are prohibited in some states.

Thayeria boehlkei / Penguin Tetra

WEITZMAN 1957

Natural Range: Upper Amazon River basin in Peru and Araguaia River in Brazil.
Size: 3" (7.5 cm) TL; may grow slightly larger.
Water Chemistry: Tropical; prefer soft and slightly acidic conditions.
Behavior: Very peaceful.
Dietary Requirements: Small, live foods and prepared foods are best.

Remarks: Penguin Tetras are very popular but not as common as they used to be. Their unique pattern, a black line that runs from the head through the lower lobe of the caudal fin, has earned them another common name—the Hockey Stick Tetra. This species does well when cared for as other tetras of their kind.

Serrasalmus spilopleura "Gold"

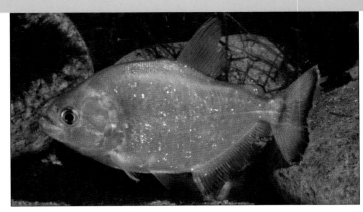

Serrasalmus spilopleura

Serrasalmus sanchezi juvenile

Serrasalmus sanchezi adult

Thayeria boehlkei "gold"

Thayeria boehlkei

Cichla orinocensis

CICHLIDAE
THE CICHLID FISHES

Overall, members of Cichlidae are probably the most commonly kept fishes of any group on Earth. There are approximately 1,300 valid species and at least several hundred that are yet to be officially described. They range in size from the small *Gobiocichla* to the huge *Boulengerochromis* and are found naturally in more areas than nearly any other family of fishes in the world.

Cichlids are widely distributed over much of Central and South America, the West Indies, Africa, Madagascar, and even have smaller distribution in places such as Syria, Israel, Iran, Sri Lanka, coastal southern India, and one species is indigenous to Texas (USA).

The family Cichlidae was erected in 1801 by SCHNEIDER based on one species, today known as *Cichla ocellaris*, from Guyana. After a short period of time, it became evident to taxonomists of the day that this family was actually composed of many more fishes than originally thought. Between then and just a few years ago, the taxonomy of many groups and subgroups of cichlids was poorly understood.

Acarichthys heckelii / Threadfin Acara

MULLER & TROSCHEL 1849

Natural Range: Amazon basin, Brazil, Guyana, and Peru.

Size: 8" (20 cm) TL.

Water Chemistry: Tropical; soft and acidic conditions preferred.

Behavior: Generally peaceful among similar-sized fishes.

Dietary Requirements: Prepared diets that are supplemented with meaty foods.

Remarks: This species was originally placed in the genus *Acara* and was occasionally listed in scientific literature as *Geophagus heckelii*. Today, we recognize this species as something completely different, resulting in its placement in *Acarichthys*.

Acaronia nassa

HECKEL 1984

Natural Range: Amazonia region, northern South America.

Size: 8" (20 cm) TL.

Water Chemistry: Tropical; soft, slightly acidic conditions are preferred.

Behavior: Generally peaceful, but is highly predatory on fishes it can swallow.

Dietary Requirements: Small live fishes and other meaty foods.

Remarks: While considered monotypic for many years, we now see that the genus has two distinct and valid species—*A. nassa* and *A. vultuosa*. Both species have the same basic captive care and husbandry. They do differ in distribution, with *A. nassa* being more widespread over Amazonia, and *A. vultuosa* hailing from the Orinoco drainage in Venezuela.

Aequidens coeruleopuntcatus

KNER & STEINDACHNER 1863

Natural Range: Costa Rica and Panama.

Size: 6" (15 cm) TL.

Water Chemistry: Tropical; prefers moderately hard and alkaline conditions.

Behavior: Generally peaceful with other fishes of a similar size.

Dietary Requirements: Small live and prepared foods.

Remarks: This species is the only representative of *Aequidens* to be found in Central America. They are a robust cichlid that does well in a medium to large community tank with mixed fishes of a similar size. Their color is an emerald green, and males have a distinct forehead and long-flowing fins.

Acarichthys heckelii

Acarichthys heckelii

Acaronia nassa female

Acaronia nassa

Aequidens coeruleopuntcatus female

Aequidens coeruleopuntcatus male

Aequidens diadema

HECKEL 1840

Natural Range: Orinoco River basin, Colombia and Venezuela.
Size: 6" (15 cm) TL.
Water Chemistry: Tropical; slightly acid with moderate hardness.
Behavior: Generally peaceful, but may bully smaller tankmates.
Dietary Requirements: Small live and prepared foods.

Remarks: This small, colorful cichlid is native to the Orinoco River basin. Like other small to medium-sized *Aequidens* species, they do well in a peaceful community tank with other fishes of similar size and habits. Of course, be sure to keep an eye out for pair bonding and associated aggression on tankmates.

Aequidens patricki

KULLANDER 1984

Natural Range: Peru.
Size: 6" (15 cm) TL.
Water Chemistry: Tropical; slightly acid with moderate hardness.
Behavior: Generally peaceful, but may bully smaller tankmates.
Dietary Requirements: Small live and prepared foods.

Remarks: *A. patricki* is easily identifiable by the large semi-circular dark-colored blotch on its flanks and its bright, rust-colored head. They are commonly seen for sale by cichlid specialists, and like their close relatives, they breed rather easily.

Aequidens pulcher / Blue Acara

GILL 1858

Natural Range: Trinidad and northern Venezuela.
Size: 6" (15 cm) TL.
Water Chemistry: Tropical; slightly acid with moderate hardness.
Behavior: Generally peaceful, but may bully smaller tankmates.
Dietary Requirements: Small live and prepared foods.

Remarks: The Blue Acara is perhaps the oldest and best-known species within *Aequidens* that is still in the hobby. Years ago, this species and the true Green Terror were easily obtainable, but today, only the Blue Acara remains common. Their colors are considerably more pronounced when a pair is kept in an aquarium that provides a lot of caves and rockwork for them to build a nest and spawn. This species is an excellent beginner's cichlid.

Aequidens diadema male

Aequidens diadema pair

Aequidens patricki

Aequidens metae for comparison

Aequidens pulcher male

Aequidens pulcher pair

Aequidens rivulatus / Green Terror

GUNTHER 1859

Natural Range: Remote areas of western Ecuador.
Size: 8" (20 cm) TL.
Water Chemistry: Tropical; slightly acid with moderate hardness.
Behavior: Moderately aggressive.
Dietary Requirements: Small live and prepared foods.

Remarks: Only recently has this species become available to hobbyists after many, many years of being absent. The fishes currently called "Green Terrors" in the hobby are actually two separate and distinct species that remain undescribed. Ironically, the true Green Terror is not all that aggressive when you compare it to fishes such as *Parachromis dovii* or the slightly smaller *Parachromis managuensis*.

Aequidens sapayensis

REGAN 1903

Natural Range: Colombia.
Size: 6" (15 cm) TL.
Water Chemistry: Tropical; slightly acid with moderate hardness.
Behavior: Generally peaceful, but may bully smaller tankmates.
Dietary Requirements: Small live and prepared foods.

Remarks: This small *Aequidens* is often confused with *A. pulcher* as being the Blue Acara. While they are bluish, they are usually not comparable to the real Blue Acara that we all know and recognize. Their care and husbandry are identical, however.

"Aequidens" sp. *"gold saum"* / Gold-edged Terror

UNDESCRIBED TO DATE

Natural Range: Ecuador.
Size: 10" (25 cm) TL.
Water Chemistry: Tropical; slightly acid with moderate hardness.
Behavior: Moderately aggressive.
Dietary Requirements: Small live and prepared foods.

Remarks: Erroneously called the Green Terror for years, the Gold-edged Terror is a closely related species of it in the *"Aequidens"* complex. Their care and husbandry in aquariums is much like others of the genus, only this species grows an average of approximately two inches larger in total length.

344

Aequidens rivulatus

Aequidens rivulatus

Aequidens sapayensis

Aequidens sapayensis

"*Aequidens*" sp. "gold saum"

"*Aequidens*" sp. "gold saum"

345

"Aequidens" sp. "silver saum" / Silver-edged Terror

UNDESCRIBED TO DATE

Natural Range: Western Peru and possibly Ecuador.
Size: 10" (25 cm) TL; usually slightly smaller.
Water Chemistry: Tropical; slightly acid with moderate hardness.
Behavior: Moderately aggressive.
Dietary Requirements: Small live and prepared foods.

Remarks: Also still in the *Aequidens* complex is this fish, called the Silver-edged Terror or Silver Saum by hobbyists. This is a beautiful species that, like the Golden-edged Terror (its close cousin), remains undescribed. Its care and husbandry is the same as the Golden-edged Terror.

Altolamprologus calvus / Calvus

POLL 1978

Natural Range: Lake Tanganyika.
Size: 6" (15 cm) TL.
Water Chemistry: Tropical; hard, alkaline water is best.
Behavior: Generally peaceful, but may swallow smaller tankmates.
Dietary Requirements: Small shrimps and other crustaceans.

Remarks: This unique cichlid shows an exaggerated degree of lateral compression. They live among rocks and wood in their native habitat and feed heavily on aquatic invertebrates. In the aquarium, feed them heavily on zooplankton, brine shrimp, and mysis shrimps. Provide large shells or small caves for them to live and spawn in.

Altolamprologus compressiceps / Compressiceps

BOULENGER 1898

Natural Range: Lake Tanganyika.
Size: 8" (20 cm) TL.
Water Chemistry: Tropical; hard, alkaline water is best.
Behavior: Generally peaceful, but may swallow smaller tankmates.
Dietary Requirements: Small shrimps and other crustaceans.

Remarks: Another cichlid species that exhibits a high degree of lateral compression. *A. compressiceps* lives deep within the crevices of rocks and boulders in Lake Tanganyika. As with *A. calvus*, Compressiceps will feed heavily on aquatic invertebrates and even small fishes when the opportunities present themselves.

"Aequidens" sp. "silver saum" female

"Aequidens" sp. "silver saum" male

Altolamprologus calvus female

Altolamprologus calvus male

Altolamprologus compressiceps female

Altolamprologus compressiceps male

Amphilophus alfari

MEEK 1907

Natural Range: Honduras to Panama.
Size: 6" (15 cm) TL.
Water Chemistry: Tropical; slightly alkaline with moderate hardness.
Behavior: Generally peaceful; watch for aggression in males.
Dietary Requirements: Small live foods and prepared foods of all types are accepted.

Remarks: There are many color variations of *A. alfari*. In the aquarium trade, we tend to see only a few of these, since this species is only collected from a small number of locations, and those are used as the broodstock to supply the hobby with. Generally peaceful, this moderate-sized cichlid is best kept with other fishes of equal or slightly greater size.

Amphilophus altifrons

KNER & STEINDACHNER 1863

Natural Range: Pacific slope of Costa Rica and Panama.
Size: 6" (15 cm) TL.
Water Chemistry: Tropical; slightly alkaline with moderate hardness.
Behavior: Generally peaceful among similar-sized fishes; watch for aggression in males.
Dietary Requirements: Small live foods and prepared foods of all types are accepted.

Remarks: This interesting cichlid is not always available to hobbyists but is certainly more common today than in years past. They are, as with most similar species of cichlids, very easy to care for. *A. altifrons* is generally peaceful but will often harass smaller, weaker fishes. Use caution in a community aquarium.

Amphilophus atromaculatus / Black-spot Amphilophus

REGAN 1912

Natural Range: Ecuador.
Size: 10" (25 cm) TL.
Water Chemistry: Tropical; slightly acidic with moderate hardness.
Behavior: Generally peaceful, but may bully smaller tankmates.
Dietary Requirements: Small live and prepared foods.

Remarks: These beautiful cichlids are sexually dichromatic—it is possible to distinguish their sexes by coloration. Females are more brightly colored compared to males and may retain some coloration even when not conditioned to spawn. They are a robust cichlid and can sometimes have a nasty attitude. Use caution with tankmates.

Amphilophus sp. aff. *alfari*

Amphilophus alfari

Amphilophus altifrons

Amphilophus altifrons small adult

Amphilophus atromaculatus

Amphilophus atromaculatus

349

Amphilophus calobrensis

MEEK & HILDEBRAND 1913

Natural Range: Pacific slope of Panama.
Size: 12" (30 cm) TL; usually far smaller.
Water Chemistry: Tropical; slightly alkaline with moderate hardness.
Behavior: May be very aggressive towards tankmates; use caution.
Dietary Requirements: Meaty foods such as shrimp and worms as well as prepared foods.

Remarks: This robust cichlid is absolutely gorgeous as an adult. Juveniles are distinctive, with their bright green iridescence and dark horizontal stripe that runs from their gill operculum to the caudal peduncle. This species does well in very large aquariums with ample swimming room and good circulation.

Amphilophus citrinellus / Midas Cichlid

GUENTHER 1864

Natural Range: Atlantic slope of Nicaragua and Costa Rica.
Size: 12" (30 cm) TL.
Water Chemistry: Tropical; slightly alkaline with moderate hardness.
Behavior: Usually very aggressive; best kept alone or in a very large aquarium with other big, robust fishes.
Dietary Requirements: Shrimp and other meaty foods.

Remarks: The Midas Cichlid is very often confused with its close cousin, the Red Devil (*A. labiatus*). While their coloration is often very similar, their morphometrics characters are completely different. Years ago, wild-collected specimens were in good supply, but over the last few years, they have been scarce. Because of this, many specimens in the hobby today are hybrids between the two species.

Amphilophus diquis

BUSSING 1974

Natural Range: Pacific slope of Costa Rica and Panama.
Size: 6" (15 cm) TL is average for adults.
Water Chemistry: Tropical; slightly alkaline with moderate hardness.
Behavior: Generally peaceful, but may be pushy with smaller or weaker fishes.
Dietary Requirements: All forms of meaty and prepared foods.

Remarks: This is closely related species to *A. alfari*, but is just as pretty. Some have stated that *A. diquis* is aggressive in the aquarium. The author (B.M. Scott) does not find this to be valid when they are kept with fishes of a similar size and ample space is afforded for territorial boundaries. Regardless, keep an eye on them, especially males.

Amphilophus calobrensis female

Amphilophus calobrensis male

Amphilophus citrinellus male

Amphilophus citrinellus female

Amphilophus diquis male

Amphilophus diquis female

Amphilophus festae / Festae

BOULENGER 1899

Natural Range: Ecuador.
Size: 20" (50 cm) TL; usually far smaller.
Water Chemistry: Tropical; otherwise not critical, avoid extremes.
Behavior: Generally very aggressive; males may be punishing on tankmates.
Dietary Requirements: All types of meaty and prepared foods.

Remarks: The Festae Cichlid is probably the most easily recognizable of the large cichlids that are commonly available to hobbyists today. Their large size and striking orange to red coloration makes them a must-have for the cichlid enthusiast. They, of course, come with their downfalls: size and aggression. This species does best alone in very large aquariums.

Amphilophus labiatus / Red Devil

GUENTHER 1864

Natural Range: Atlantic slope of Nicaragua.
Size: 10" (25 cm) TL.
Water Chemistry: Tropical; slightly alkaline with moderate hardness.
Behavior: Often very aggressive, especially males.
Dietary Requirements: Shrimp and other meaty foods.

Remarks: The Red Devil is a must-have for those hobbyists who are cichlid nuts. When properly set up and cared for, this long-lived cichlid makes quite a showpiece. They do best in large aquariums with good filtration and stable rock structure. Feed a lot of shrimp-based foods.

Amphilophus longimanus / Redbreast Cichlid

GUENTHER 1869

Natural Range: Pacific slope of southern Guatemala to Costa Rica.
Size: 6" (15 cm) TL.
Water Chemistry: Tropical; slightly alkaline with moderate hardness.
Behavior: Generally peaceful, but may be pushy in community cichlid aquariums.
Dietary Requirements: All types of meaty and prepared foods; not picky.

Remarks: This interesting moderate-sized cichlid is not much to look at when young. However, as adults, they are quite striking with their deep red breast area and bright blue-green spangles. Provide plenty of caves and caverns for this species to hide among.

Amphilophus festae female

Amphilophus festae male

Amphilophus labiatus young male

Amphilophus labiatus older male

Amphilophus longimanus

Amphilophus longimanus

Amphilophus lyonsi / Lyon's Cichlid

GOSSE 1966

Natural Range: Pacific slope of Costa Rica and Panama.

Size: 8" (20 cm) TL; males may grow slightly larger.

Water Chemistry: Tropical; slightly alkaline with moderate hardness.

Behavior: Moderately aggressive; watch with smaller tankmates.

Dietary Requirements: Many types of meaty and prepared foods; not picky.

Remarks: Lyon's Cichlids are gorgeous both as adults and juveniles. Their shades of reds are hard to match even in other naturally beautiful fishes. For this reason, they are often kept in large cichlid community aquariums to add a shade of color other than the normal range of blues and greens. Adult males may be punishing on tankmates.

Amphilophus macracanthus

GUENTHER 1864

Natural Range: Pacific slope of southern Mexico to El Salvador.

Size: 10" (25 cm) TL; usually far smaller.

Water Chemistry: Tropical; slightly alkaline with moderate hardness.

Behavior: Moderately aggressive; watch adult males.

Dietary Requirements: All types of meaty and prepared foods.

Remarks: *A. macracanthus* is rather drab when young, but the black and white contrast of the adults somewhat resembles the coloration of *Cyphotilapia* species from Lake Tanganyika (Conkel 1993).

Amphilophus rhytisma

LOPEZ 1983

Natural Range: The Atlantic slope of Costa Rica and Panama.

Size: 6" (15 cm) TL; may grow slightly larger.

Water Chemistry: Tropical; slightly alkaline with moderate hardness.

Behavior: Moderately aggressive; watch with smaller tankmates.

Dietary Requirements: All types of meaty and prepared foods.

Remarks: For years—more accurately, decades—this species was unavailable since it is rare in nature and hardly collected. Recently, however, with the rise in interest among cichlid fanciers of Central American cichlids, this species has now been imported on multiple occasions and is now being bred successfully by many people. Provide this species with plenty of circulation and strong filtration.

Amphilophus lyonsi female

Amphilophus lyonsi male

Amphilophus macracanthus young female

Amphilophus macracanthus adult male

Amphilophus rhytisma

Amphilophus rhytisma

Amphilophus robertsoni / Emerald Cichlid

REGAN 1905

Natural Range: Mexico to Honduras.
Size: 8" (20 cm) TL.
Water Chemistry: Tropical; slightly alkaline with moderate hardness.
Behavior: Moderately aggressive; watch with smaller tankmates.
Dietary Requirements: All types of meaty and prepared foods.

Remarks: Adult male Emerald Cichlids are truly unbelievable in coloration. They often show a light turquoise green or blue that rivals that of some Discus (*Symphysodon* spp.). Keeping them in aquaria is not often a problem, but these fish may harass smaller tankmates, especially during spawning.

Amphilophus rostratum

GILL & BRANSFORD 1877

Natural Range: Nicaragua and Costa Rica (Atlantic slope).
Size: 8" (20 cm) TL; usually smaller.
Water Chemistry: Tropical; slightly alkaline with moderate hardness.
Behavior: Moderately aggressive; watch with smaller tankmates.
Dietary Requirements: All types of meaty and prepared foods.

Remarks: The longer snout of this species gives it the specific name of *rostratum*. They are generally peaceful, but will swallow smaller tankmates if allowed to do so. Keep with similar-sized species and watch for aggression in males.

Amphilophus trimaculatum / Trimac

GUENTHER 1869

Natural Range: El Salvador and Southern Mexico.
Size: 16" (40 cm) TL; usually far smaller.
Water Chemistry: Tropical; slightly alkaline with moderate hardness.
Behavior: Adult males are very aggressive; females and juveniles should be watched carefully for excessive aggression on all tankmates.
Dietary Requirements: All types of meaty and prepared foods.

Remarks: There are some cichlids that have sex appeal, and the Trimac is definitely one of them. These boldly marked cichlids are big and often very aggressive. The males are intolerant of other fishes when a female is present. Recently, this species has been, and continues to be, used to produce various hybrids called Flowerhorns. Because of this, and the very infrequent importation of wild-collected stock, pure-blood Trimacs are becoming difficult to find.

Amphilophus robertsoni young female

Amphilophus robertsoni young male

Amphilophus rostratum

Amphilophus rostratum

Amphilophus trimaculatum adult male

Amphilophus trimaculatum pair

Amphilophus tuyrense

MEEK & HILDEBRAND 1913

Natural Range: Panama.
Size: 8" (20 cm) TL; sometimes slightly larger.
Water Chemistry: Tropical; slightly alkaline with moderate hardness.
Behavior: Moderately aggressive; watch with smaller tankmates.
Dietary Requirements: Accepts most types of meaty and prepared foods, but will also eat large amounts of plant matter.

Remarks: Many Central American cichlids are decidedly carnivorous; however, this species is completely omnivorous. Any plants that are in the aquarium when *A. tuyrense* is introduced will not be there for long. They appreciate regular offerings of plant matter in their diet. Feed accordingly for best results.

Amphilophus uropthalmus / Red Terror

GUENTHER 1862

Natural Range: Coastal areas of Central America.
Size: 12" (30 cm) TL.
Water Chemistry: Tropical; slightly alkaline with moderate hardness. May adjust to full-strength seawater for short periods.
Behavior: Usually aggressive, and may be intolerant of tankmates that are close in appearance.
Dietary Requirements: All types of meaty and prepared foods.

Remarks: It is rare to find a cichlid from the New World that is able to tolerate saline conditions, let alone full-strength seawater. Although we officially say that this species is able to tolerate living in a marine environment for short periods, recently we have discovered that many hobbyists have been fishing in the Gulf of Mexico and caught this species on hook and line many miles off shore. Such would then indicate that the Red Terror may be able to tolerate marine environments for longer periods of time than we once thought.

Amphilophus zaliosus / Arrow Cichlid

BARLOW 1976

Natural Range: Nicaragua.
Size: 8" (20 cm) TL.
Water Chemistry: Tropical; slightly alkaline with moderate hardness.
Behavior: Moderately aggressive; watch with smaller tankmates.
Dietary Requirements: All types of meaty and prepared foods.

Remarks: Lately, the Arrow Cichlid has gained immense popularity among those dedicated to Central American cichlid keeping. The actual reason is unclear, but many that have been interviewed indicate a preference for the fish's unique shape and dramatic, albeit bland, coloration and pattern. Regardless, this easy-to-keep species does best when cared for the same way as their close cousins—the Red Devil.

Amphilophus tuyrense adult

Amphilophus tuyrense juvenile

Amphilophus uropthalmus adult

Amphilophus uropthalmus juvenile

Amphilophus zaliosus

Amphilophus nourissati for comparison

Anomalochromis thomasi

BOULENGER 1915

Natural Range: Guinea, Sierra Leone, and Nigeria.
Size: 3" (7.5 cm) TL
Water Chemistry: Tropical; slightly acidic with moderate hardness is preferred.
Behavior: Generally peaceful; may breed in a community aquarium.
Dietary Requirements: Small live and prepared foods.

Remarks: *A. thomasi* is a little-known dwarf cichlid from western Africa. They are best kept in a medium-sized community aquarium with other peaceful fishes of similar size. Their normal coloration is quite different from their rather cryptic breeding dress, and these are a must-keep cichlid for those interested in dwarfs. As of this writing, *Anomalochromis* remains monotypic.

Apistogramma agassizi

STEINDACHNER 1875

Natural Range: Amazon basin, Brazil, and Peru.
Size: 3" (7.5 cm) TL; females smaller.
Water Chemistry: Tropical; soft, acidic conditions are best.
Behavior: Generally peaceful.
Dietary Requirements: Small live and prepared foods.

Remarks: These slender dwarf cichlids rank high among the world's most popular cichlids. *A. agassizi* comes in many color forms, and generally speaking, aquarists recognize blue, yellow, and red varieties. Of course, there are fancier names associated with locality points that need to be mastered should you choose to speak the language of true dwarf cichlidophile.

Apistogramma bitaeniata

PELLEGRIN 1936

Natural Range: Several localities in Brazil, Colombia, and Peru.
Size: 3" (7.5 cm) TL; females smaller.
Water Chemistry: Tropical; soft, acidic conditions are best.
Behavior: Generally peaceful.
Dietary Requirements: Small live and prepared foods.

Remarks: After a taxonomic debate spanning many years, this small cichlid is finally referred to as *A. bitaeniata* on an official basis. Their care and husbandry are quite similar to other species within *Apistogramma*.

Anomalochromis thomasi pair

Anomalochromis thomasi

Apistogramma agassizi

Apistogramma agassizi

Apistogramma bitaeniata

Apistogramma bitaeniata

Apistogramma borellii

REGAN 1906

Natural Range: Argentina, southern Brazil, and Paraguay.
Size: 3" (7.5 cm) TL; females smaller; usually smaller in general.
Water Chemistry: Tropical, but may tolerate slightly cooler temperatures; soft, acidic conditions are best.
Behavior: Generally peaceful.
Dietary Requirements: Small live and prepared foods.

Remarks: This small species of *Apistogramma* is a great dwarf cichlid for community aquariums that contain other peaceful coolwater fishes. While they do best in tropical aquariums, they are certainly capable of tolerating cooler waters, as found in Argentina and southern Brazil. Otherwise, their care is identical to other species of the genus.

Apistogramma cacatuoides / Cockatoo Dwarf Cichlid

HOEDEMAN 1951

Natural Range: Peru.
Size: 3" (7.5 cm) TL; females smaller.
Water Chemistry: Tropical; soft, acidic conditions are best.
Behavior: Generally peaceful.
Dietary Requirements: Small live and prepared foods.

Remarks: This is one of the most popular of all dwarf cichlids—Old World or New World. Many hobbyists, as well as ornamental aquaculture facilities, commonly breed them. Because of their unique dorsal fins, they have earned the name of "Cockatoo Dwarf Cichlid," after the Cockatoo parrot. *A. cacatuoides* is probably the best dwarf cichlid for new hobbyists to test their skills on.

Apistogramma cf. agassizi

UNDESCRIBED TO DATE

Natural Range: Amazonas region.
Size: 3" (7.5 cm) TL; females smaller.
Water Chemistry: Tropical; soft, acidic conditions are best.
Behavior: Generally peaceful.
Dietary Requirements: Small live and prepared foods.

Remarks: There are actually many fishes that fall into the category of *A.* cf. *agassizi*. This is because the taxonomy of these little fishes is still in its infancy. Dr. Kullander of the Swedish Museum of Natural History is spearheading efforts to further sort out these species, but it is a monumental task, and such a project is likely to take many, many years.

Apistogramma borellii

Apistogramma borellii

Apistogramma cacatuoides

Apistogramma cacatuoides

Apistogramma cf. *agassizi*

Apistogramma agassizi for comparison

Apistogramma diplotaenia

KULLANDER 1987

Natural Range: Rio Negro, Brazil.
Size: 3" (7.5 cm) TL; females smaller.
Water Chemistry: Tropical; soft, acidic conditions are best.
Behavior: Generally peaceful.
Dietary Requirements: Small live and prepared foods.

Remarks: This newer species of *Apistogramma* comes from the Rio Negro and its associated tributaries. It is sometimes referred to as the "Double-banded Apisto" and is commonly found in similar habitats as the Cardinal Tetra (*Paracheirodon axelrodi*).

Apistogramma elizabethae

KULLANDER 1980

Natural Range: Upper Rio Negro, Brazil.
Size: 3" (7.5 cm) TL; usually smaller.
Water Chemistry: Tropical; soft, acidic conditions are best.
Behavior: Generally peaceful.
Dietary Requirements: Small live and prepared foods.

Remarks: As with all species within *Apistogramma*, the males grow slightly larger than the females. Also, much of the size data that is reported in popular literature does not reflect the actual sizes many of these cichlids reach in aquariums. In some instances, the sizes are smaller; more commonly, they are larger. Regardless, this species is still a dwarf cichlid and should be treated as such.

Apistogramma eunotus

KULLANDER 1981

Natural Range: Western Brazil and Peru.
Size: 3" (7.5 cm) TL; females smaller.
Water Chemistry: Tropical; soft, acidic conditions are best.
Behavior: Generally peaceful.
Dietary Requirements: Small live and prepared foods.

Remarks: While this species is not one of the most colorful dwarf cichlids available, they make an interesting addition for the hobbyist who has acquired all the others. As with most other *Apistogramma* species, they are wonderful additions to those community aquariums that contain peaceful fishes.

Apistogramma diplotaenia

Apistogramma diplotaenia profile

Apistogramma elizabethae

Apistogramma elizabethae var.

Apistogramma eunotus

Apistogramma eunotus

Apistogramma gibbeceps

MEINKEN 1969

Natural Range: Amazon River basin.
Size: 3" (7.5 cm) TL.
Water Chemistry: Tropical; soft and slightly acidic is preferred.
Behavior: Generally peaceful.
Dietary Requirements: Small live and prepared foods.

Remarks: This interesting dwarf cichlid is sometimes available in the hobby. Collection seems to be sporadic, but the highest numbers for sale within the trade seem to occur between August and October.

Apistogramma juruensis

KULLANDER 1986

Natural Range: Rio Jurua, Brazil.
Size: 4" (10 cm) TL, usually smaller.
Water Chemistry: Tropical; soft, acidic conditions are best.
Behavior: Generally peaceful.
Dietary Requirements: Small live and prepared foods.

Remarks: This species is a prime example of how localized some *Apistogramma* species are. *A. juruensis* is only known to exist in the remote Rio Jurua, a small river in Brazil. Of course, they are probably also found in tributaries and the like, but no other localities have been reported as of yet.

Apistogramma macmasteri

KULLANDER 1979

Natural Range: Colombia.
Size: 3" (7.5 cm) TL; females smaller.
Water Chemistry: Tropical; soft, acidic conditions are best.
Behavior: Generally peaceful.
Dietary Requirements: Small live and prepared foods.

Remarks: As with many species of *Apistogramma*, this species is sexually dichromatic: the males are more colorful than the females. They also have longer, more pointed dorsal, anal, and ventral fins. The species' care and husbandry in aquariums is similar to that of others from a similar locality.

Apistogramma gibbeceps female guarding eggs

Apistogramma gibbeceps male

Apistogramma juruensis

Apistogramma sp.

Apistogramma macmasteri

Apistogramma macmasteri

Apistogramma nijsseni

KULLANDER 1979

Natural Range: Western Brazil and Peru.
Size: 3" (7.5 cm) TL; females smaller.
Water Chemistry: Tropical; soft, acidic conditions are best.
Behavior: Generally peaceful.
Dietary Requirements: Small live and prepared foods.

Remarks: These little dwarfs are rather thick and bulky compared to other *Apistogramma*. They are also one of the most strikingly colored fish out there. Males have a gorgeous red-edged caudal fin that seems to glow under fluorescent illumination. Some specimens, both male and female, also appear lavender under such illumination.

Apistogramma norberti

STAECK 1991

Natural Range: Peruvian Amazon.
Size: 3" (7.5 cm) TL; females smaller.
Water Chemistry: Tropical; soft, acidic conditions are best.
Behavior: Generally peaceful.
Dietary Requirements: Small live and prepared foods.

Remarks: Upon close examination, you will see a dark, circular blotch in the posterior portion of this species' caudal fin. This unique characteristic is a diagnosable feature of the species. Additionally, the red "lipstick" that this species exhibits makes their mouths appear larger than they really are. This interesting species should be a part of all cichlid collections.

Apistogramma trifasciata

EIGENMANN & KENNEDY 1903

Natural Range: Argentina, Bolivia, Southwestern Brazil, and Paraguay.
Size: 3" (7.5 cm) TL; females smaller.
Water Chemistry: Tropical; soft, acidic conditions are best.
Behavior: Generally peaceful.
Dietary Requirements: Small live and prepared foods.

Remarks: Apparently, breeding conditions have a direct and somewhat suspect influence on the overall appearance of this small cichlid. There is questionable validity to such claims, but such a topic is worth mentioning. Otherwise, this species seems to do well under normal conditions for other, more common *Apistogramma* species.

Apistogramma nijsseni

Apistogramma nijsseni

Apistogramma norberti

Apistogramma sp.

Apistogramma trifasciata

Apistogramma trifasciata

Apistogramma uaupesi

KULLANDER 1980

Natural Range: Upper Rio Negro, Brazil.
Size: 3" (7.5 cm) TL; females smaller.
Water Chemistry: Tropical; soft, acidic conditions are best.
Behavior: Generally peaceful.
Dietary Requirements: Small live and prepared foods.

Remarks: A slender species of dwarf cichlid, *A. uaupesi* is not commonly available to hobbyists. Occasionally, specialists in the sale and breeding of cichlids will have young fish from a single spawn available, but this is one of those rare jewels that should be purchased when available.

Apistogramma viejita

KULLANDER 1979

Natural Range: Colombia.
Size: About 2" to 3" (5 – 7.5 cm) TL.
Water Chemistry: Tropical; soft, acidic conditions are best.
Behavior: Generally peaceful.
Dietary Requirements: Small live and prepared foods.

Remarks: There are three known variations of this species. They are all close variations and differ only in locality and coloration. These differences are apparent when the variations are placed next to each other or when looking at pictures side-by-side; otherwise, they are undoubtedly *A. viejita*.

Archocentrus centrarchus / Flier Cichlid

GILL & BRANSFORD 1877

Natural Range: Honduras and Costa Rica.
Size: 5" (12.5 cm) TL.
Water Chemistry: Tropical; slightly alkaline with moderate hardness.
Behavior: Generally peaceful with similar-sized fishes.
Dietary Requirements: Small live and prepared foods of all types.

Remarks: The Flier Cichlid is not as popular as it should be. These small but interesting cichlids are quite comical and prolific in home aquariums. Large males can be downright grumpy at times, but they are otherwise safe for community aquariums that contain other fishes of equal size. Provide plenty of hiding places for them to retire to.

Apistogramma uaupesi

Apistogramma sp. for comparison

Apistogramma viejita female

Apistogramma panduroi female for comparison

Archocentrus centrarchus

Archocentrus nanoluteus for comparison

371

Archocentrus octofasciatus / Jack Dempsey

REGAN 1903

Natural Range: Mexico to Belize.
Size: 6" (20 cm) TL; may grow larger in captivity but rarely in nature.
Water Chemistry: Tropical; slightly alkaline with moderate hardness.
Behavior: Wild specimens are highly aggressive, while captive-raised ones are moderately aggressive.
Dietary Requirements: Small live and prepared foods of all types.

Remarks: The Jack Dempsey is so named due to the somewhat pugnacious attitude of wild-collected specimens. Ironically, many hobbyists keep this species with peaceful community fishes of a similar size. If they are provided with plenty of hiding places, they will usually guard only those spots and allow the other fishes to go about their business. Always keep an eye on them, though, just in case.

Astronotus crassipinnis / Southern Oscar

HECKEL 1840

Natural Range: Southern Brazil and Paraguay.
Size: 14" (35 cm) TL; may grow larger.
Water Chemistry: Tropical, but may tolerate cooler temperatures; otherwise, not critical.
Behavior: Moderately aggressive; will swallow small fishes whole.
Dietary Requirements: Meaty, live, and prepared foods of all types.

Remarks: These Oscars are part of a larger group of fishes that are currently in desperate need of reclassification. This species is supposed to have a tiger-type pattern on a bland and very drab background. They are a big fish that has a large, blunt head. Otherwise, they are very Oscar-like in all other aspects, including care and husbandry in aquariums.

Astronotus ocellatus / Oscar

AGASSIZ 1831

Natural Range: Northern South America.
Size: 14" (35 cm) TL; may grow larger.
Water Chemistry: Tropical, but may tolerate cooler temperatures; otherwise, not critical.
Behavior: Moderately aggressive; will swallow small fishes whole.
Dietary Requirements: Meaty, live, and prepared foods of all types.

Remarks: Aside from the Silver Angelfish (*Pterophyllum scalare*), the Oscar is by far the most popular and easily recognized species of cichlid. Oscars are big brutes and need big tanks—far larger than most people think. In nature, Oscars feed heavily on aquatic invertebrates and small fishes. In captivity, their diet should resemble their wild one. Additionally, be sure to perform frequent water changes and provide good, strong filtration.

Archocentrus octofasciatus blue var.

Archocentrus octofasciatus adult

Astronotus crassipinnis juvenile

Astronotus crassipinnis

Astronotus ocellatus juvenile

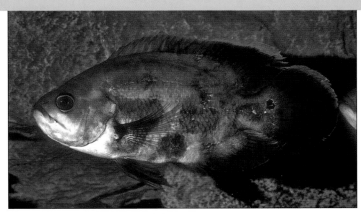

Astronotus ocellatus adult

Aulonocara baenschi / Yellow Peacock Cichlid

MEYER & RIEHL 1985

Natural Range: Lake Malawi.

Size: 6" (15 cm) TL.

Water Chemistry: Tropical; hard and alkaline.

Behavior: Generally peaceful; males may quarrel in the presence of females.

Dietary Requirements: Small live and prepared foods.

Remarks: Bright yellow fishes are rare in freshwater aquariums, but luckily we have this species available to us. *A. baenschi* is a beautiful African cichlid that comes from Lake Malawi in eastern Africa. Males can grow to about 6" (15 cm) in total length, although they more commonly grow to around 4" (10 cm) TL. They are easily cared for, provided that their diet consists of both plant and animal matter.

Aulonocara ethelwynnae / Chitande Peacock Cichlid

MEYER, RIEHL, & ZETZSCHE 1987

Natural Range: Lake Malawi.

Size: 4" (10 cm) TL.

Water Chemistry: Tropical; hard and alkaline.

Behavior: Generally peaceful; males may quarrel in the presence of females.

Dietary Requirements: Small live and prepared foods.

Remarks: A smaller species of *Aulonocara,* the Chitande Peacock Cichlid is a popular species among hobbyists that want a peacock cichlid that does not grow to the proportions of their close relatives. This species commonly displays large, brilliant blue dorsal and anal fins. Males exhibit large, yellow pseudo-eggs or false egg spots. These fish are a great addition to the Rift Lake community aquarium.

Aulonocara hansbaenschi

MEYER, RIEHL, & ZETZSCHE 1987

Natural Range: Lake Malawi.

Size: 6" (15 cm) TL.

Water Chemistry: Tropical; hard and alkaline.

Behavior: Generally peaceful; males may quarrel in the presence of females.

Dietary Requirements: Small live and prepared foods.

Remarks: Not quite as small as reported in previous texts, *A. hansbaenschi* is a wonderful addition to the Rift Lake community aquarium that contains larger fishes. As with all *Aulonocara,* watch males among each other in the presence of females, as they may become overly aggressive. Feed a varied diet with some plant material included.

Aulonocara baenschi

Aulonocara baenschi

Aulonocara ethelwynnae

Aulonocara sp. "Walteri" is closely related

Aulonocara hansbaenschi

Aulonocara hansbaenschi

Aulonocara hueseri

MEYER, RIEHL, & ZETZSCHE 1987

Natural Range: Lake Malawi.
Size: 4" (10 cm) TL.
Water Chemistry: Tropical; hard and alkaline.
Behavior: Generally peaceful; males may quarrel in the presence of females.
Dietary Requirements: Small live and prepared foods.

Remarks: These beautiful fish have multiple color variations. They are most commonly colored in a turquoise-blue dress with a brilliant yellow or gold underside. Their eyes are large and their fins small compared with other *Aulonocara* species. These fish appreciate a large amount of crustaceans in their diet. Females have a distinctive barring along their sides.

Aulonocara jacobfreibergi

MEYER, RIEHL, & ZETZSCHE 1987

Natural Range: Lake Malawi.
Size: 6" (15 cm) TL.
Water Chemistry: Tropical; hard and alkaline.
Behavior: Generally peaceful; males may quarrel in the presence of females.
Dietary Requirements: Small live and prepared foods.

Remarks: Perhaps one of the most variable and often brilliantly colored species within the genus is *A. jacobfreibergi*. This species has such drastic coloration differences between populations that they are often mistakenly thought of as a new species. Once, the author (BMS) observed an aquarium that had many different color variations in the tank. All the specimens were males, and they tolerated each other with few problems. This was probably due to the absence of females to compete over.

Aulonocara maylandi / Sulfurhead Peacock

TREWAVAS 1984

Natural Range: Lake Malawi.
Size: 4" (10 cm) TL.
Water Chemistry: Tropical; hard and alkaline.
Behavior: Generally peaceful; males may quarrel in the presence of females.
Dietary Requirements: Small live and prepared foods.

Remarks: Sometimes referred to as the Sulfurhead Peacock, *A. maylandi* is a strikingly colored peacock cichlid. They are a smaller species of *Aulonocara,* and males only grow to about 4" (10 cm) TL in nature. In aquariums, they may grow slightly larger. Feed a varied diet, but always be sure to offer them a staple prepared food for regularity.

376

Aulonocara hueseri

Aulonocara hueseri

Aulonocara jacobfreibergi sunburst var.

Aulonocara jacobfreibergi

Aulonocara maylandi female

Aulonocara maylandi male

Aulonocara saulosi

MEYER, RIEHL, & ZETZSCHE 1987

Natural Range: Lake Malawi.
Size: 6" (15 cm) TL.
Water Chemistry: Tropical; hard and alkaline.
Behavior: Generally peaceful; males may quarrel in the presence of females.
Dietary Requirements: Small live and prepared foods.

Remarks: Another relatively new species of *Aulonocara* is *A. saulosi*. They are a moderately-sized peacock cichlid that attain a total length of approximately 6" (15 cm) in aquariums. Their care and husbandry in aquariums are identical to that of others of the genus.

Aulonocara steveni

MEYER, RIEHL, & ZETZSCHE 1987

Natural Range: Lake Malawi.
Size: 6" (15 cm) TL.
Water Chemistry: Tropical; hard and alkaline.
Behavior: Generally peaceful; males may quarrel in the presence of females.
Dietary Requirements: Small live and prepared foods.

Remarks: *Aulonocara steveni* are easily recognized by the light blue stripe that travels along the dorsal edge. Additionally, they have a nearly-solid-yellow-to-rusty flank and metallic blue head.

Aulonocara stuartgranti

MEYER & RIEHL 1985

Natural Range: Lake Malawi.
Size: 6" (15 cm) TL.
Water Chemistry: Tropical; hard and alkaline.
Behavior: Generally peaceful; males may quarrel in the presence of females.
Dietary Requirements: Small live and prepared foods.

Remarks: Here is another cichlid that has multiple color variations. Each color morph may have a different name, giving the impression of being multiple species or subspecies.

Aulonocara saulosi

Copadichromis cf. *cyaneus* for comparison

Aulonocara steveni

Aulonocara steveni

Aulonocara stuartgranti

Aulonocara stuartgranti

379

Bathybates ferox

BOULENGER 1898

Natural Range: Lake Tanganyika.
Size: 14" (35 cm) TL.
Water Chemistry: Tropical; hard and alkaline.
Behavior: Generally peaceful, except with smaller fishes.
Dietary Requirements: Live or dead meaty foods.

Remarks: *Bathybates* is a unique genus among the family Cichlidae. Generally, they are elongated predatory fishes that require regular feedings of meaty foods, including whole live or dead fishes. This species is one of the more common within the genus. but nevertheless, they are still quite rare in the hobby.

Bathybates vittatus

BOULENGER 1914

Natural Range: Lake Tanganyika.
Size: 10" (25 cm) TL; may grow slightly larger.
Water Chemistry: Tropical; hard and alkaline.
Behavior: Generally peaceful, except with smaller fishes.
Dietary Requirements: Live or dead meaty foods.

Remarks: As with all *Bathybates*, *B. vittatus* is a predatory cichlid that feeds on small fishes. In aquariums, this species will often accept other meaty foods, although live small fishes are relished with gusto. *B. vittatus* differs from other *Bathybates* because of their scales. Two types of scales can be distinguished in this species. Each normal scale supports an edge of small scales, giving *B. vittatus* a checkered appearance (Konings 1988).

Benitochromis batesi

BOULENGER 1901

Natural Range: Cameroon and north Gabon.
Size: 4" (10 cm) TL.
Water Chemistry: Tropical; neutral to slightly acidic with moderate hardness.
Behavior: Generally peaceful with other similar-sized fishes.
Dietary Requirements: Small live and prepared foods.

Remarks: *B. batesi* are generally good parents should you be fortunate enough to have yours spawn for you. They lay their eggs in caves or covered areas where other fishes will have difficulty accessing them. The male does the primary area guarding, while the female stays with the eggs and subsequent young when they hatch. The pair may remain with the young for an additional month after they become free swimming.

Bathybates ferox

Bathybates ferox

Bathybates vittatus

Bathybates minor for comparison

Benitochromis batesi male

Benitochromis batesi female

381

Benitochromis conjunctus

LAMBOJ 2001

Natural Range: Western Cameroon.
Size: 4" (10 cm) TL.
Water Chemistry: Tropical; slightly acidic with moderate hardness.
Behavior: Generally peaceful with other similar-sized fishes, but high intraspecific aggression may be a problem.
Dietary Requirements: Small live and prepared foods.

Remarks: Apparently, this species dislikes members of its own kind. That said, a large, well-decorated aquarium is a must should you choose to keep these fish together. If you want to breed this species, it is advised that you purchase a group of juveniles and allow them to form their own pairs by placing them all in a large tank and raising them to maturity. As pairs form, isolate them in their own tanks.

Benitochromis finleyi

TREWAVAS 1974

Natural Range: Western Cameroon.
Size: 4" (10 cm) TL.
Water Chemistry: Tropical; slightly acidic with moderate hardness.
Behavior: Generally peaceful with other similar-sized fishes.
Dietary Requirements: Small live and prepared foods.

Remarks: The care and husbandry is similar to *B. conjunctus,* but with less intraspecific aggression (Lamboj 2004).

Benitochromis nigrodorsalis

LAMBOJ 2001

Natural Range: Coastal areas of western Cameroon.
Size: 4" (10 cm) TL; perhaps slightly larger.
Water Chemistry: Tropical; slightly acidic with moderate hardness.
Behavior: Generally peaceful with other similar-sized fishes.
Dietary Requirements: Small live and prepared foods.

Remarks: Named *"nigrodorsalis"* for its black-colored dorsal fin, *B. nigrodorsalis* is an interesting and rather peaceful species. Their care and husbandry is essentially the same as *B. conjunctus*.

Benitochromis conjunctus

Benitochromis conjunctus

Benitochromis finleyi

Chromidotilapia finleyi for comparison

Benitochromis nigrodorsalis

Benitochromis nigrodorsalis profile

Benthochromis tricoti

POLL 1948

Natural Range: Lake Tanganyika.
Size: 8" (20 cm) TL; females smaller.
Water Chemistry: Tropical; hard and alkaline.
Behavior: Generally peaceful, except when males are courting females.
Dietary Requirements: Small live and prepared foods.

Remarks: While this species is not the most aggressive of Lake Tanganyika's cichlids, they are not the most peaceful either. Most hobbyists report that this fish is only really considered aggressive when males are competing for females. However, a few hobbyists indicate trouble when they are housed with smaller fishes. Keep a close eye on them in a community setting.

Biotodoma cupido

HECKEL 1840

Natural Range: Brazil.
Size: 4" (10 cm) TL; may grow slightly larger.
Water Chemistry: Tropical; slightly acidic with moderate hardness.
Behavior: Generally peaceful with other similar-sized fishes.
Dietary Requirements: Small live and prepared foods.

Remarks: This peaceful small cichlid is often seen for sale in specialty shops dealing with rare fishes. While *B. cupido* itself is not exceedingly rare, they do not seem to have a huge demand, and their sales have been restricted to only those hobbyists who may be looking for something truly different and don't want to have to break the bank to get it.

Boulengerochromis microlepis / Emperor Cichlid

BOULENGER 1899

Natural Range: Lake Tanganyika.
Size: 40" (100 cm) TL; usually far smaller (world's longest cichlid).
Water Chemistry: Tropical; hard and alkaline.
Behavior: Aggressive; keep alone or with other very large fishes.
Dietary Requirements: Small live fish and other meaty foods.

Remarks: The title of the world's longest cichlid belongs to *B. microlepis*. These giants are basically unsuitable for any but the largest of all aquariums. Additionally, the author (BMS) reports that they become exceedingly aggressive with conspecifics, and occasionally even with other fishes that are not related. This species cannot be trusted and is best to keep in a species aquarium.

Benthochromis tricoti male

Benthochromis tricoti pair

Biotodoma cupido

Biotodoma cupido

Boulengerochromis microlepis adult with fry!

Boulengerochromis microlepis adult pair

Buccochromis lepturus

REGAN 1922

Natural Range: Lake Malawi.
Size: 16" (40 cm) TL; usually much smaller.
Water Chemistry: Tropical; hard and alkaline.
Behavior: Generally peaceful, except with other males or fishes small enough to be swallowed.
Dietary Requirements: Small live fishes, meaty foods, and large prepared foods.

Remarks: *B. lepturus* is a predator that hunts over sandy or rubble areas in Lake Malawi. Not much is known about their breeding in aquariums. It is thought that pairs nest in the open or in close proximity to rocky outcroppings. Provide a large aquarium for this robust cichlid.

Buccochromis rhoadesii

BOULENGER 1908

Natural Range: Lake Malawi.
Size: 14" (35 cm) TL.
Water Chemistry: Tropical; hard and alkaline.
Behavior: Generally peaceful, except with small fishes and other males.
Dietary Requirements: Small live fishes, meaty foods, and large prepared foods.

Remarks: This piscivorous species hunts fishes in the open sandy areas of Lake Malawi. Their care and husbandry in aquariums is generally the same as other large predatory cichlids, with good filtration, high-quality foods, a large aquarium, and frequent water changes being the most important aspects of their aquariology.

Burjurquina mariae

EIGENMANN 1922

Natural Range: Colombia.
Size: 6" (15 cm) TL.
Water Chemistry: Tropical; slightly acidic with moderate hardness.
Behavior: Moderately aggressive.
Dietary Requirements: Small live and prepared foods.

Remarks: These highly underestimated cichlids are not very common in the hobby, and that is unfortunate, since mature specimens in good health are gorgeously colored. They appear as a species of *Aequidens,* but with a longer body and rounded snout. Their colors are highly varied and may include blues, greens, and even reds.

Buccochromis lepturus male

Buccochromis lepturus young male

Buccochromis rhoadesii female

Buccochromis rhoadesii male

Burjurquina mariae

Burjurquina mariae

387

Burjurquina vittata / Banded Cichlid

HECKEL 1840

Natural Range: Bolivia.
Size: 6" (15 cm) TL; females slightly smaller.
Water Chemistry: Tropical; slightly acidic with moderate hardness.
Behavior: Moderately aggressive.
Dietary Requirements: Small live and prepared foods.

Remarks: Bolivia holds many treasures that are unknown to the aquarium hobby. This species is one of them. Sure to gain popularity as time progresses, *B. vittata* is already seeing a following in certain areas where fishes from Bolivia are being exported regularly.

Callochromis melanostigma

BOULENGER 1906

Natural Range: Lake Tanganyika.
Size: 6" (15 cm) TL.
Water Chemistry: Tropical; hard and alkaline.
Behavior: Best kept in species-specific groups of one male to multiple females.
Dietary Requirements: Small live and prepared foods.

Remarks: These sexually dichromatic cichlids are recognized by their long slender bodies, terminal mouths, and large eyes. They inhabit sandy areas that are in close proximity to bottom cover, where they feed on small insect larvae and crustaceans.

Caquetaia kraussii

STEINDACHNER 1878

Natural Range: Northern South America.
Size: 16" (40 cm) TL; usually much smaller.
Water Chemistry: Tropical; slightly acidic with moderate hardness.
Behavior: Moderately aggressive; watch carefully in community aquariums.
Dietary Requirements: Small live fishes and other meaty foods.

Remarks: These big, bold cichlids are not for the average hobbyist. They are rather temperamental and require excellent water quality. Aggression is highly variable, with some specimens being outwardly aggressive, while others are very peaceful (except with small fishes, of course).

Burjurquina vittata pair guarding fry!

Burjurquina vittata

Callochromis melanostigma

Callochromis melanostigma profile

Caquetaia kraussii

Caquetaia kraussii

Caquetaia myersi / Myersi

SCHULTZ 1944

Natural Range: Colombia and Ecuador.
Size: 12" (30 cm) TL; usually far smaller.
Water Chemistry: Tropical; slightly acidic with moderate hardness.
Behavior: Moderately aggressive; watch carefully in community aquariums.
Dietary Requirements: Small live fishes and other meaty foods.

Remarks: Another big and bold cichlid is *C. myersi*. They are a very beautiful cichlid with their gold to chartreuse coloration. Years ago, this species was virtually impossible to obtain. Today, although prices are still high, they can be found with little difficulty. Keep with large, peaceful fishes and provide excellent water quality for best results.

Caquetaia spectabilis

STEINDACHNER 1875

Natural Range: Lower course of the Amazon River system.
Size: 12" (30 cm) TL.
Water Chemistry: Tropical; slightly acidic with moderate hardness.
Behavior: Moderately aggressive; watch carefully in community aquariums.
Dietary Requirements: Small live fishes and other meaty foods.

Remarks: This beautiful cichlid is rather difficult to keep healthy in aquariums. They need large aquariums with warm, acidic water that is free of excessive bacteria. Even the slightest scrapes and scratches will become infected should their aquarium's water become too sour. Be sure to use good filtration and use activated carbon to remove excessive pollutants if necessary.

Caquetaia umbrifera / Umbie

MEEK & HILDEBRAND 1913

Natural Range: Panama to Colombia.
Size: 20" (50 cm) TL; may grow larger, but usually far smaller.
Water Chemistry: Tropical; slightly alkaline with moderate hardness.
Behavior: Aggressive, large-growing species.
Dietary Requirements: Meaty foods and prepared foods of all types.

Remarks: *Caquetaia umbrifera*, or the Umbie, directly competes with *Parachromis dovii* for the largest "*Cichlasoma*" award. This robust fish is an open-water species that feeds primarily on whole, live fishes and aquatic invertebrates in nature. Their aquariums should be the largest possible, and filtration, as well as circulation, should be strong and efficient.

Caquetaia myersi female

Caquetaia myersi male

Caquetaia spectabilis

Caquetaia spectabilis profile

Caquetaia umbrifera

Caquetaia umbrifera

Chalinochromis brichardi

POLL 1974

Natural Range: Lake Tanganyika.
Size: 6" (15 cm) TL.
Water Chemistry: Tropical; hard and alkaline.
Behavior: Aggressive toward conspecifics; otherwise, generally peaceful.
Dietary Requirements: Small live and prepared foods.

Remarks: Both males and females of these cave-spawning cichlids will defend their young. They are not very colorful, and even less colorful as juveniles, but they make a wonderful and interesting addition to the Tanganyikan cichlid community aquarium.

Champsochromis caeruleus

BOULENGER 1908

Natural Range: Lake Malawi.
Size: 14" (35 cm) TL.
Water Chemistry: Tropical; hard and alkaline.
Behavior: Generally peaceful, except with smaller fishes and other males.
Dietary Requirements: Small live fishes and other meaty foods are best.

Remarks: Very few cichlids have naturally long, flowing finnage, but *C. caeruleus* is one of them. In many respects, *C. caeruleus* resembles several other large cichlid species from Lake Malawi. However, *C. caeruleus* may be somewhat grumpier, so be sure to watch their behavior closely in the community aquarium.

Chilotilapia rhoadesii

BOULENGER 1908

Natural Range: Lake Malawi.
Size: 12" (30 cm) TL.
Water Chemistry: Tropical; hard and alkaline.
Behavior: Generally peaceful, but males will quarrel among themselves.
Dietary Requirements: Meaty foods—especially snails—and most prepared foods accepted equally.

Remarks: As a juvenile, *C. rhoadesii* is barely distinguishable from the closely related *C. euchilus*. Both species do well in large aquariums with other peaceful fishes of equal size and temperament. Many of the cichlids endemic to Lake Malawi are some of the most colorful and beautiful fishes available to tropical fish hobbyists, and *C. rhoadesii* is no exception.

Chalinochromis brichardi

Chalinochromis brichardi

Champsochromis caeruleus female

Champsochromis caeruleus male

Chilotilapia rhoadesii

Chilotilapia rhoadesii

Chromidotilapia guntheri

SAUVAGE 1882

Natural Range: Western and central African coastal countries.

Size: 6" (15 cm) TL.

Water Chemistry: Tropical; slightly alkaline with moderate hardness.

Behavior: Generally peaceful with other fishes of similar size and temperament.

Dietary Requirements: Small crustaceans, other meaty foods, and prepared foods rich in plant matter are all equally appreciated.

Remarks: Recently, we have seen some serious controversy over the correct spelling of this fish's name. In actuality, it is *Chromidotilapia guntheri*, not *C. guentheri* (Lamboj 2004). Regardless, there are two distinct subspecies that are nearly impossible to distinguish with the naked eye. The care and husbandry of these interesting cichlids are remarkably similar to many of the Central American cichlids of equal size.

Chuco godmanni

GUENTHER 1862

Natural Range: Guatemala.

Size: 8" (20 cm) TL; may grow slightly larger.

Water Chemistry: Tropical; slightly acidic with moderate hardness.

Behavior: Moderately aggressive; may bully smaller tankmates.

Dietary Requirements: Meaty foods and all types of prepared foods.

Remarks: *Chuco godmanni* is easily identifiable by the bold black mark that resembles a check. This mark is present throughout their lives and is very apparent on wild-collected individuals. Provide a sizable aquarium with plenty of hiding places and peaceful tankmates of similar size.

Chuco intermedius

GUENTHER 1862

Natural Range: Belize, Guatemala, and southern Mexico.

Size: 8" (20 cm) TL.

Water Chemistry: Tropical; slightly acidic with moderate hardness.

Behavior: Moderately aggressive; may bully smaller tankmates.

Dietary Requirements: Meaty foods and all types of prepared foods.

Remarks: This distinctive cichlid is identifiable by the black marking that closely resembles an "L" on its side. This mark, similar to *C. godmanni*'s, is present throughout their lives at all stages, and furthermore, the mark is more apparent in wild-collected individuals, just as in *C. godmanni*.

Chromidotilapia guntheri pair

Chromidotilapia guntheri female

Chuco godmanni juvenile

Chuco godmanni adult male

Chuco intermedius female

Chuco intermedius male

Chuco microphthalmus

GUENTHER 1862

Natural Range: Southern Guatemala and northern Honduras.
Size: 10" (25 cm) TL.
Water Chemistry: Tropical; slightly acidic with moderate hardness.
Behavior: Moderately aggressive; may bully smaller tankmates.
Dietary Requirements: Meaty foods and all types of prepared foods.

Remarks: This big, bold, and beautiful cichlid is now much more available in the aquarium trade than it was in years past. Their metallic gold speckles make them very visible in the aquarium under proper illumination, even at a distance. They are a mild-mannered fish that seems to do well in the presence of other cichlids of equal size and temperament.

Cichla monoculus / Amazonian Peacock Bass

SPIX & AGASSIZ 1831

Natural Range: Amazon basin, Brazil and Peru.
Size: 24" (60 cm) TL.
Water Chemistry: Tropical; soft and acidic conditions are best.
Behavior: Aggressive pursuit predator.
Dietary Requirements: Small live fishes; often accepts non-living foods.

Remarks: Most of the *Cichla* that are available in aquarium shops are this species. This is mostly due to them being pond-bred in the Far East in huge numbers. Amazonian Peacock Bass grow to huge proportions and need large aquariums. Generally, this species is peaceful to fishes they cannot swallow. Strong, efficient filtration is a must for this species, as well as all *Cichla*.

Cichla ocellaris / Butterfly Peacock Bass

BLOCH & SCHNEIDER 1801

Natural Range: Northeastern Brazil, Guyana, and Surinam.
Size: 24" (60 cm) TL.
Water Chemistry: Tropical; soft and acidic conditions are best.
Behavior: Aggressive pursuit predator.
Dietary Requirements: Small live fishes; often accepts non-living foods as a long-term captive.

Remarks: Adult Butterfly Peacock Bass are distinguishable by their glaring red eyes and single eyespot where the third vertical bar was as a juvenile. Unfortunately, juveniles and sub-adults are very similar in appearance to *C. monoculus* to the south and *C. orinocensis* to the west.

Chuco microphthalmus

Chuco microphthalmus

Cichla monoculus juvenile

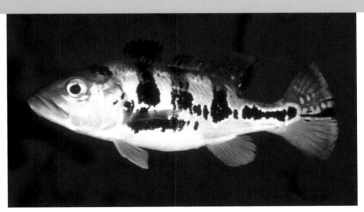

Cichla monoculus young adult

Cichla ocellaris adult

Cichla ocellaris adult

Cichla orinocensis / Orinoco Peacock Bass

HUMBOLDT 1821

Natural Range: Colombia, northern Brazil, and Venezuela.
Size: 30" (75 cm) TL; may grow even larger.
Water Chemistry: Tropical; soft and acidic conditions preferred.
Behavior: Aggressive pursuit predator.
Dietary Requirements: Small live fishes, may accept non-living foods as a long-term captive.

Remarks: This species is very scarce in the hobby, but regular shipments are being brought into the United States, Europe, and Japan, with this species often included in them. As with all *Cichla*, this species grows too large for all but the largest of aquariums. Large, peaceful tankmates, such as *Uaru*, *Hypselacara*, and *Hoplarchus*, are best to keep with them.

Cichla temensis / Speckled Peacock Bass

HUMBOLDT 1821

Natural Range: Bolivia, Brazil, Colombia, and Venezuela.
Size: 30" (75 cm) TL; may grow larger (heaviest cichlid in the world).
Water Chemistry: Tropical; soft and acidic conditions are preferred.
Behavior: *Cichla temensis* is a predatory pursuit predator in nature and needs large aquariums with excellent water quality in order to thrive in captivity.
Dietary Requirements: Whole live fishes.

Remarks: In captivity, this species best when offered large aquariums with regular feedings of live or otherwise meaty foods. *C. temensis* is not particularly fussy about water chemistry as long as extremes are avoided. Their eventual adult size limits their popularity among hobbyists. However, for those who are extremely dedicated and able to offer larger-than-normal aquariums, *C. temensis* proves to be a long-lived and fascinating species of predatory cichlid.

Cichla sp. "Rio Jau"

UNDESCRIBED TO DATE

Natural Range: Rio Jau, Brazil.
Size: Probably close to 20" (50 cm) TL; may grow slightly larger.
Water Chemistry: Tropical; soft and acidic is preferred.
Behavior: Aggressive pursuit predator.
Dietary Requirements: Small live fishes.

Remarks: This species is yet to make a presence in the tropical fish hobby. However, its arrival is highly anticipated.

Cichla orinocensis

Cichla orinocensis

Cichla temensis juvenile

Cichla temensis non-breeding adult male

Cichla sp. "Rio Jau"

Cichla ocellaris for comparison

Cichla sp. "Venezuela"

UNDESCRIBED TO DATE

Natural Range: Rio Orinoco basin, Venezuela.
Size: Unknown, but probably more than 20" (50 cm) TL.
Water Chemistry: Tropical; slightly soft and acidic.
Behavior: Aggressive pursuit predator.
Dietary Requirements: Small live fishes; may accept nonliving foods.

Remarks: Only recently (2004) has this fish become available to hobbyists. Their care and husbandry is identical to that of *C. orinocensis*.

Cichla sp. "Xingu"

UNDESCRIBED TO DATE

Natural Range: Rio Xingu basin, Brazil.
Size: Unknown, but probably more than 20" (50 cm) TL.
Water Chemistry: Tropical; slightly soft and acidic.
Behavior: Aggressive pursuit predator.
Dietary Requirements: Small live fishes; may accept nonliving foods.

Remarks: *C.* sp. "Xingu" is available in the hobby, but not with any regularity. As adults, most of these fish are bright chartreuse green with a row of broken spots that extends from their gill operculum to their caudal peduncle. As with all species of *Cichla*, this nominal species is highly variable in coloration.

Cichlasoma amazonarum / Amazonian Cichlid

KULLANDER 1983

Natural Range: Amazon River basin.
Size: 4" (10 cm) TL; may grow slightly larger.
Water Chemistry: Tropical; slightly soft and acidic.
Behavior: Generally peaceful with fishes of equal size and temperament.
Dietary Requirements: Small live and prepared foods.

Remarks: This small cichlid is one of the only members of *Cichlasoma* that remains valid. Years ago, so many species were placed in the genus that is has been referred to as a catchall group. When an ichthyologist wasn't sure where a fish belonged, he or she would just lump the fish into *Cichlasoma*. Thankfully, through the tireless work of Dr. Sven Kullander and many others, they have succeeded in splitting this genus into many others and thus making the fishes much easier to identify.

Cichla sp. "Venezuela"

Cichla sp. "Venezuela"

Cichla sp. "Xingu"

Cichla sp. "Xingu"

Cichlasoma amazonarum

Cichlasoma boliviense a closely related species

Cichlasoma bimaculatum / Black Acara

LINNAEUS 1758

Natural Range: Northern South America (Venezuela).
Size: 6" (15 cm) TL.
Water Chemistry: Tropical; slightly soft and acidic.
Behavior: Generally peaceful with fishes of equal size and temperament.
Dietary Requirements: Small live and prepared foods.

Remarks: These interesting small cichlids are named the Black Acara because of their dark appearance as adults. Occasionally, we do see nearly jet-black specimens, but it is thought that these are breeding adults. Their care and husbandry in aquariums is remarkably similar to that of the *Aequidens* groups of fishes.

Cichlasoma faceatum / Chameleon Cichlid

JENYNS 1842

Natural Range: Argentina and southern Brazil.
Size: 7" (18 cm) TL.
Water Chemistry: Tropical; slightly soft and acidic.
Behavior: Generally peaceful with fishes of equal size and temperament.
Dietary Requirements: Small live and prepared foods.

Remarks: A little larger than their close cousins, *C. faceatum* is a popular aquarium fish and has been so for many decades. They can be slightly on the belligerent side, especially when spawning, but otherwise they make wonderful inhabitants for the community aquarium that contains similar-sized fishes.

Cleithracara maroni / Keyhole Cichlid

STEINDACHNER 1881

Natural Range: French Guiana.
Size: 6" (15 cm) TL.
Water Chemistry: Tropical; slightly soft and acidic.
Behavior: Generally peaceful with fishes of equal size and temperament.
Dietary Requirements: Small live and prepared foods.

Remarks: The Keyhole Cichlid is one of the most popular and widely-kept species of cichlid in the world. Many years ago, there were very few cichlid species available, and this was one of them. They are easy to breed and rear in captivity and therefore come as a highly recommended species for beginners and advanced hobbyists alike.

Cichlasoma bimaculatum

Cichlasoma bimaculatum

Cichlasoma sp. aff. *faceatum*

Cichlasoma faceatum

Cleithracara maroni

Cleithracara maroni

403

Copadichromis chrysonotus

BOULENGER 1908

Natural Range: Lake Malawi.
Size: 6" (15 cm) TL; may grow larger.
Water Chemistry: Tropical; hard and alkaline conditions preferred.
Behavior: Generally peaceful, but males will quarrel with each other in competition for females.
Dietary Requirements: Small live and prepared foods.

Remarks: *C. chrysonotus* live in the open water of sheltered bays, where they are commonly found over rocks. The rocks can be some distance below them, with depths of over 10 meters not being uncommon. They can be identified by three large, black spots on the flanks. Of course, several other species have this type of pattern, but *C. chrysonotus* are more commonly available. Therefore, if your specimen has such features, it has a good chance of being this species.

Copadichromis cyaneus

TREWAVAS 1935

Natural Range: Lake Malawi.
Size: 6" (15 cm) TL; may grow larger.
Water Chemistry: Tropical; hard and alkaline conditions preferred.
Behavior: Moderately aggressive; males may fight amongst themselves.
Dietary Requirements: Small live and prepared foods.

Remarks: Unlike their congeners, *C. cyaneus* is only found in clear water over sediment-free rocks. Otherwise, their care and husbandry in aquariums is identical to others in the group.

Copadichromis jacksoni

ILES 1960

Natural Range: Lake Malawi.
Size: 8" (20 cm) TL; may grow slightly larger.
Water Chemistry: Tropical; hard and alkaline conditions preferred.
Behavior: Moderately aggressive; males may fight amongst themselves.
Dietary Requirements: Small live and prepared foods.

Remarks: Large schools of *C. jacksoni* can be observed in the deeper waters of sheltered bays throughout the lake. They are commonly associated with aufwuchs-covered rocks. Unlike other *Copadichromis*, this species prefers slightly darker aquariums.

Copadichromis chrysonotus male

Copadichromis chrysonotus female

Copadichromis cyaneus male

Copadichromis cyaneus profile

Copadichromis jacksoni male

Copadichromis jacksoni note blunt nose

405

Copadichromis mloto

ILES 1960

Natural Range: Lake Malawi.
Size: 6" (15 cm) TL.
Water Chemistry: Tropical; hard and alkaline conditions preferred.
Behavior: Moderately aggressive; males may fight amongst themselves.
Dietary Requirements: Small live and prepared foods.

Remarks: In nature, you can find *C. mloto* over sandy bottoms in shallow water. Under actinic lighting, this species—as well as many others from Lake Malawi—seems to fluoresce a deep, metallic blue color. They are stunning fish that do well with other species of similar size and behavior.

Copadichromis pleurostigma

TREWAVAS 1935

Natural Range: Lake Malawi (northern portion).
Size: 6" (15 cm) TL.
Water Chemistry: Tropical; hard and alkaline conditions preferred.
Behavior: Moderately aggressive; males may fight amongst themselves.
Dietary Requirements: Small live and prepared foods.

Remarks: Not too long ago, this species was impossible to obtain, with the only exceptions being those specimens that came in either as special orders, those that were collected by hobbyists visiting the lake, or in mixed bags of miscellaneous cichlids. Today, we enjoy the rarity of this species, but thankfully, they are more commonly available than they used to be. Their care and husbandry is identical to others of the genus.

Crenicara punctulatum

GUENTHER 1862

Natural Range: Brazil.
Size: 4" (10 cm) TL.
Water Chemistry: Tropical; slightly soft and acidic.
Behavior: Generally peaceful.
Dietary Requirements: Small live and prepared foods.

Remarks: An interesting dwarf cichlid, *C. punctulatum* only grows to about 4" in total length. They seem to do very well when placed in a medium-sized community aquarium where they have places to hide from more active tankmates. Feed small live foods such as *Artemia*, *Daphnia*, or *Tubifex* worms along with a good staple dry food.

Copadichromis mloto male

Copadichromis mloto note large eye

Copadichromis pleurostigma male

Copadichromis pleurostigma female

Crenicara punctulatum female

Crenicara punctulatum male

Crenicichla cincta

REGAN 1905

Natural Range: Amazonian region, western Brazil and Peru.
Size: 16" (40 cm) TL.
Water Chemistry: Tropical; slightly soft and acidic.
Behavior: Very aggressive.
Dietary Requirements: Small live fishes and other meaty foods; may accept prepared foods.

Remarks: Many Pike Cichlids grow large by aquarium standards, and this fish is no exception. Growing to about 16" (40 cm) in total length, *C. cincta* needs an aquarium that is both long and wide. Their tankmates should be selected with care, since they don't like competition. A pair can be housed together, but only with sufficient visual barriers and plenty of room to move about freely.

Crenicichla compressiceps

PLOEG 1986

Natural Range: Northeast Brazil.
Size: 4" (10 cm) TL; usually slightly smaller.
Water Chemistry: Tropical; slightly soft and acidic.
Behavior: Aggressive.
Dietary Requirements: Small live fishes and other meaty foods; may accept prepared foods.

Remarks: Some Pike Cichlids do not grow so large, and *C. compressiceps* is a perfect example of one that only grows to about 4" (10 cm) in total length. This species feeds primarily on the fry of other fishes, cichlids in particular, so if you maintain them in a community aquarium with other fishes, you may want to rule out any young from living very long. These dwarfs will seek them out wherever they try to hide. Otherwise, these interesting fish make excellent aquarium fishes.

Crenicichla geayi

PELLEGRIN 1903

Natural Range: Orinoco system.
Size: 8" (20 cm) TL.
Water Chemistry: Tropical; slightly soft and acidic.
Behavior: Aggressive.
Dietary Requirements: Small live fishes and other meaty foods; may accept prepared foods.

Remarks: As with so many other fishes from the Orinoco River system, this species' availability is directly dependent on the exporters of the region. Usually collected seasonally, you may not be able to find specimens all the time. Check with specialists who deal in cichlids for their availability. Their care in captivity is similar to other Pike Cichlids of comparable size.

Crenicichla cincta pair

Crenicichla cincta note very blunt snout

Crenicichla compressiceps adult

Crenicichla compressiceps note sharp snout

Crenicichla geayi

Crenicichla gaucho another interesting species

Crenicichla jegui

PLOEG 1986

Natural Range: Northeast Brazil.
Size: 8" (20 cm) TL, sometimes larger.
Water Chemistry: Tropical; slightly soft and acidic.
Behavior: Aggressive.
Dietary Requirements: Small live fishes and other meaty foods; may accept prepared foods.

Remarks: This interesting Pike Cichlid is a bottom-dwelling species. They are commonly found living in submerged structures such as roots and bogwood. In aquariums, they are a sedentary species that will only move if provoked or when food is placed in their tank. They are somewhat intolerant of each other, and as of this writing, there are no published accounts of captive breeding.

Crenicichla johanna

HECKEL 1840

Natural Range: Amazonian region.
Size: 16" (40 cm) TL.
Water Chemistry: Tropical; slightly soft and acidic.
Behavior: Aggressive.
Dietary Requirements: Small live fishes and other meaty foods; may accept prepared foods.

Remarks: This big, bold, and beautiful species is best left to those dedicated hobbyists with extra large aquariums. They are often grumpy aquarium residents that are rather intolerant of tankmates. Of course, they will do best in aquariums with many visual barriers, and if tankmates are to be added, be sure they are large and have a similar disposition.

Crenicichla lenticulata

HECKEL 1840

Natural Range: Northern Brazil, Colombia, and Venezuela.
Size: 16" (40 cm) TL.
Water Chemistry: Tropical; slightly soft and acidic.
Behavior: Aggressive.
Dietary Requirements: Small live fishes and other meaty foods; may accept prepared foods.

Remarks: The heavy spotting on the head is an unmistakable trait of *C. lenticulata*. They are a large-growing fish that needs big tanks with excellent water quality. Nearly all species of jumbo Pike Cichlids will show signs of head and lateral line erosion should their environment become too polluted. Frequent, large-scale water changes, along with a good and varied diet, will help prevent this disorder from happening.

Crenicichla jegui

Crenicichla jegui

Crenicichla johanna female adult

Crenicichla lugubris adult female for comparison

Crenicichla lenticulata

Crenicichla lenticulata

411

Crenicichla lepidota

HECKEL 1840

Natural Range: Brazil.
Size: 4" (10 cm) TL; may grow slightly larger.
Water Chemistry: Tropical; slightly soft and acidic.
Behavior: Aggressive.
Dietary Requirements: Small live fishes and other meaty foods; may accept prepared foods.

Remarks: This is one of the original Pike Cichlids; the species is one of the oldest and most widely available species of Pike Cichlids that hobbyists are likely to come in contact with. In aquariums, they often do quite well, provided that they are kept well fed and their water remains stable. This long-lived species may live for many years under the proper conditions.

Crenicichla lugubris

HECKEL 1840

Natural Range: Amazonas area, Brazil.
Size: 16" (40 cm) TL; usually smaller.
Water Chemistry: Tropical; slightly soft and acidic.
Behavior: Aggressive.
Dietary Requirements: Small live fishes and other meaty foods; may accept prepared foods.

Remarks: There are many color varieties of *C. lugubris*. Some appear striated, especially as juveniles, while others exhibit large red to green blotches randomly spread over their bodies. Such color variability is generally related to the fish's diet or possibly even the water chemistry of the area they live. Like other large *Crenicichla*, keep this species in an extra large aquarium with large tankmates, or preferably in a large species-specific aquarium.

Crenicichla marmorata

PELLEGRIN 1904

Natural Range: Rio Tapajos, Brazil.
Size: 14" (35 cm) TL.
Water Chemistry: Tropical; slightly soft and acidic.
Behavior: Aggressive.
Dietary Requirements: Small live fishes and other meaty foods; may accept prepared foods.

Remarks: This highly sought after species of jumbo Pike Cichlid is not always as colorful as many published pictures present. They are most easily distinguished by their eight to nine light pink to reddish-orange blotches that run horizontally down their flanks. The underside of the female is pink, while the male's underside remains a somewhat dull cream. Occasionally, males may appear to be a completely different species, but closer examination usually reveals their true identity. Juveniles go through dramatic color changes and are difficult to identify.

Crenicichla lepidota

Crenicichla lepidota

Crenicichla lugubris pair

Crenicichla lugubris pair arguing!

Crenicichla marmorata

Crenicichla marmorata stress coloration

Crenicichla notophthalmus / Northern Pike Cichlid

REGAN 1913

Natural Range: Orinoco system, Colombia, and Venezuela.
Size: 6" (15 cm) TL.
Water Chemistry: Tropical; soft and acidic conditions preferred.
Behavior: Generally peaceful, except towards fishes they can swallow.
Dietary Requirements: Small live and meaty foods are best.

Remarks: Females of this species are easily recognized by the ocellus that is present in the fish's dorsal fin. In line with normal Pike Cichlid characteristics, the males are noticeably less colorful than the females. Overall, their coloration may vary, but members of both sexes that are not in breeding form always seem to have a dark horizontal stripe that runs from their snout through their caudal fins. Care and husbandry in aquariums is remarkably similar to that of *C. compressiceps*.

Crenicichla percna

KULLANDER 1991

Natural Range: Rio Xingu, Brazil.
Size: 14" (35 cm) TL.
Water Chemistry: Tropical; slightly soft and acidic.
Behavior: Aggressive.
Dietary Requirements: Small live fishes and other meaty foods; may accept prepared foods.

Remarks: A large, sedentary Pike Cichlid, *C. percna* is easily recognized by the three large circular blotches that are commonly black to dark green. This is an aggressive Pike Cichlid that does not often tolerate others of its own species. They are best left to those hobbyists who can keep them alone.

Crenicichla regani

PLOEG 1989

Natural Range: Northeast Brazil.
Size: 4" (10 cm) TL.
Water Chemistry: Tropical; slightly soft and acidic.
Behavior: Aggressive.
Dietary Requirements: Small live fishes and other meaty foods; may accept prepared foods.

Remarks: Dwarf Pike Cichlids make interesting and active additions to those aquariums that contain fishes tough enough to live with them. Many species will do fine with them as long as they are large enough to avoid being swallowed. Regardless, these fish will always be somewhat aggressive, and that may cause harmless fishes to become overly stressed. Use caution, and always ask a reputable dealer for his or her advice *before* adding these fish to your tank.

Crenicichla notophthalmus male

Crenicichla notophthalmus female

Crenicichla percna freshly collected

Crenicichla percna note underslung lower jaw

Crenicichla regani pair

Crenicichla regani female

415

Crenicichla saxatilis

LINNAEUS 1758

Natural Range: Guyana and Surinam.
Size: 8" (20 cm) TL.
Water Chemistry: Tropical; slightly soft and acidic.
Behavior: Aggressive.
Dietary Requirements: Small live fishes and other meaty foods; may accept prepared foods.

Remarks: Probably one of the most easily recognized species within *Crenicichla*, *C. saxatilis* has been known in the hobby since the early 1900s, when fishes were first being imported for the hobby in very small amounts. Their care and husbandry in aquariums is very similar to others of the same size and temperament.

Crenicichla sp. "Tapajos Red"

UNDESCRIBED TO DATE

Natural Range: Rio Tapajos, Brazil.
Size: Unknown, but estimated at more than 12" (30 cm) TL.
Water Chemistry: Tropical; slightly soft and acidic.
Behavior: Aggressive.
Dietary Requirements: Small live fishes and other meaty foods; may accept prepared foods.

Remarks: This is another Pike Cichlid that has gained considerable popularity in the last few years. They are still quite expensive, but more regular imports are slowly bringing the price down. This species does not seem to grow too large, with 10" (25 cm) in total length being about as large as the author (BMS) has seen them. Of course, they could still be babies, but we don't know much about them yet.

Crenicichla sp. "Xingu I"/ Orange Pike Cichlid

UNDESCRIBED TO DATE

Natural Range: Rio Xingu, Brazil.
Size: Unknown, but estimated at more than 12" (30 cm) TL.
Water Chemistry: Tropical; slightly soft and acidic.
Behavior: Aggressive.
Dietary Requirements: Small live fishes and other meaty foods; may accept prepared foods.

Remarks: Juvenile Orange Pike Cichlids are brightly colored and active little creatures. They are sensitive to overly aggressive tankmates, which is ironic when you consider the monstrous beasts they turn into as adults. They are best purchased in a small group and allowed to pair off. Pairs will stake out a significantly large territory where other inhabitants will not be allowed. At this time, you may wish to give them their own aquarium.

Crenicichla saxatilis

Crenicichla saxatilis

Crenicichla sp. "Tapajos red"

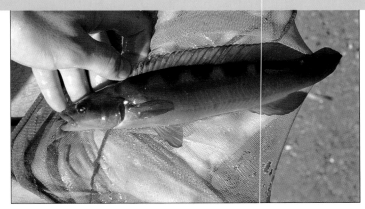

Crenicichla sp. "Tapajos red"

Crenicichla sp. "Xingu" I

Crenicichla sp. "Xingu" I juvenile

Crenicichla sp. "Xingu II"

UNDESCRIBED TO DATE

Natural Range: Rio Xingu, Brazil.
Size: Unknown, but estimated at more than 12" (30 cm) TL.
Water Chemistry: Tropical; slightly soft and acidic.
Behavior: Aggressive.
Dietary Requirements: Small live fishes and other meaty foods; may accept prepared foods.

Remarks: This species of large, aggressive Pike Cichlid is only rarely available in the hobby. Their care and husbandry in captivity is identical to that of the Orange Pike Cichlid.

Crenicichla sp. "Xingu III" / Black Pike Cichlid

UNDESCRIBED TO DATE

Natural Range: Rio Xingu, Brazil.
Size: Unknown, but estimated at more than 12" (30 cm) TL.
Water Chemistry: Tropical; slightly soft and acidic.
Behavior: Aggressive.
Dietary Requirements: Small live fishes and other meaty foods; may accept prepared foods.

Remarks: The holy grail of Pike Cichlids, *C.* sp. "Xingu III" is one of the most sought-after of all species (next to *C. tigrina*). Juveniles and males are nothing special to look at, but watch out for the females; they're like nothing you've seen before. Often, the females are solid satin black, with a slight orange tinge in the eyes and a large patch of brilliant red or fiery orange on the belly. Unfortunately, many photos of these fish seem to be of very rare or special individuals. Regardless, they are amazing fish to observe and care for.

Crenicichla strigata / Striated Pike Cichlid

GUENTHER 1862

Natural Range: Rio Tapajos and Tocantins, Brazil; probably elsewhere.
Size: 14" (35 cm) TL.
Water Chemistry: Tropical; slightly soft and acidic.
Behavior: Aggressive.
Dietary Requirements: Small live fishes and other meaty foods; may accept prepared foods.

Remarks: The Striated Pike Cichlid is probably distributed over a wide area, or else there are several species within a complex that all look very similar to the Striated Pike Cichlid. There care in aquariums is similar to other large-growing Pike Cichlids, and they are better suited to species-specific aquariums.

Crenicichla sp. "Xingu" II

Crenicichla cametana a very rare species

Crenicichla sp. "Xingu" III

Crenicichla missioneira a newly discovered species

Crenicichla strigata juvenile

Crenicichla strigata young adult

419

Crenicichla vittata

HECKEL 1840

Natural Range: Argentina and Paraguay.
Size: 14" (35 cm) TL.
Water Chemistry: Subtropical; slightly soft and acidic.
Behavior: Aggressive.
Dietary Requirements: Small live fishes and other meaty foods; may accept prepared foods.

Remarks: Another species where the males are more brilliantly colored than the females, *C. vittata* is a must-have species for the cool-water cichlid aquarium. Their bold behavior and interesting coloration makes them pleasant to look at. Provided with a large aquarium, good water quality, and a varied diet of meaty foods, this species does well and is long-lived.

Cryptoheros nigrofasciatus / Convict Cichlid

GUENTHER 1869

Natural Range: Guatemala, Honduras, Costa Rica, and Panama.
Size: 4" (10 cm) TL.
Water Chemistry: Tropical; slightly alkaline with moderate hardness.
Behavior: Moderately aggressive.
Dietary Requirements: All types of prepared foods.

Remarks: The Convict Cichlid is probably the most commonly kept cichlid species besides the angelfishes (*Pterophyllum* spp.) and the Oscars (*Astronotus* spp.). They are said to be so prolific that they will actually breed in the plastic bag on the way home from the fish shop. While such claims are slightly far-reaching, it's true that these little cichlids are very prolific and are probably easier to have spawn for you than many livebearers.

Cryptoheros sajica

BUSSING 1974

Natural Range: Costa Rica.
Size: 4" (10 cm) TL.
Water Chemistry: Tropical; slightly alkaline with moderate hardness.
Behavior: Moderately aggressive.
Dietary Requirements: All types of prepared foods.

Remarks: Only the older males of this species possess a nuchal hump. They are quite distinctive, with their bluish fins and a broad dark-colored center transverse bar. Juveniles are rather peaceful, while adults can be aggressive but still maintained in a cichlid community aquarium.

Crenicichla vittata small adult

Crenicichla vittata freshly collected adult

Cryptoheros nigrofasciatus female pink var.

Cryptoheros nigrofasciatus male normal var.

Cryptoheros sajica female with fry

Cryptoheros sajica male

Cryptoheros septemfasciatus

REGAN 1908

Natural Range: Costa Rica, Nicaragua, and Panama.
Size: 4" (10 cm) TL.
Water Chemistry: Tropical; slightly alkaline with moderate hardness.
Behavior: Moderately aggressive.
Dietary Requirements: All types of prepared foods.

Remarks: This species is barely even moderately aggressive, but we still classify them as such because they can inflict serious damage to peaceful fishes. As with most other cichlids, there are a few color variations. Dealers will often label them by locality, so you may wish to investigate their variations in color before you purchase them.

Cryptoheros spilurus

GUENTHER 1862

Natural Range: Belize and Honduras.
Size: 4" (10 cm) TL.
Water Chemistry: Tropical; slightly alkaline with moderate hardness.
Behavior: Moderately aggressive.
Dietary Requirements: All types of prepared foods.

Remarks: These prolific spawners are easy to keep in the aquarium. Similar to other members of the genus, *C. spilurus* will use any type of crevice or cave to lay their eggs in. When keeping this cichlid in a community aquarium, be sure to house it with only those fishes that are capable of swimming fast. Additionally, make sure to feed them varied diet for best success.

Cyanthopharynx furcifer

BOULENGER 1898

Natural Range: Lake Tanganyika.
Size: 8" (20 cm) TL max.
Water Chemistry: Tropical; hard and alkaline conditions preferred.
Behavior: Generally peaceful; males will quarrel amongst themselves. Keep one male with multiple females.
Dietary Requirements: Small live and prepared foods.

Remarks: Take care when netting this species out of aquariums, as they have a tendency to bruise easily. Their care is remarkable easy as long as proper steps have been taken to ensure their acclimatization has been performed properly. Several geographical variations occur, and some are more striking compared to others, but males of the northern race seem to be most popular with hobbyists due to their dark blue, metallic scales.

Cryptoheros septemfasciatus male

Cryptoheros septemfasciatus female

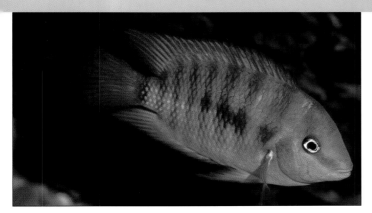

Cryptoheros spilurus

Cryptoheros spilurus

Cyanthopharynx furcifer

Cyanthopharynx furcifer

Cynotilapia afra

GUENTHER 1894

Natural Range: Lake Malawi.
Size: 4" (10 cm) TL.
Water Chemistry: Tropical; hard and alkaline conditions preferred.
Behavior: Moderately aggressive.
Dietary Requirements: Primarily herbivorous, but will greedily accept most prepared foods as well.

Remarks: An avid grazing cichlid, *C. afra* feeds primarily off the biocover on rocks. In aquariums, feed this species many types of prepared foods that are high in plant materials. Often, foods that are marketed for marine fishes such as angelfishes and surgeonfishes are best. They are quite aggressive little devils that need to be monitored closely.

Cyphotilapia frontosa / Kigoma Frontosa (7-bar Frontosa)

BOULENGER 1906

Natural Range: Kigoma region of Lake Tanganyika.
Size: 12" (30 cm) TL; may grow larger.
Water Chemistry: Tropical; hard and alkaline conditions preferred.
Behavior: Moderately aggressive; males often intolerant of one another.
Dietary Requirements: Meaty foods and large pellets.

Remarks: The bulbous nuchal region of this species combined with their highly contrasting bluish-white and black barring makes the Frontosa one of the hobby's most distinctive and desirable fishes. Recently, there has been considerable taxonomic revision done to this genus, which was once thought to be monotypic. We now know that there are actually no fewer that two valid species, with several more nominal species still under investigation.

Cyphotilapia gibberosa / Southern Frontosa (Blue Frontosa)

TAKAHASHI ET AL 2003

Natural Range: Southern half of Lake Tanganyika.
Size: 12" (30 cm) TL; may grow larger.
Water Chemistry: Tropical; hard and alkaline conditions preferred.
Behavior: Moderately aggressive; males often intolerant of one another.
Dietary Requirements: Meaty foods and large pellets.

Remarks: This newly described species is made up of several populations that are well known to hobbyists the world over. Names such as "Mpimbwe Blue," "Samazi," "Bismarck Blue," and "Ikola Blue" are all local or common name descriptions of this species, which is highly variable in coloration. Their care and husbandry in aquariums is nearly identical to that of *C. frontosa*, with the only exception being that males are said to be more aggressive than their calmer cousins.

Cynotilapia afra

Cynotilapia afra yellow var.

Cyphotilapia frontosa male

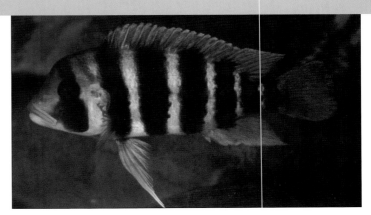

Cyphotilapia frontosa female

Cyphotilapia gibberosa female

Cyphotilapia gibberosa male

425

Cyphotilapia sp. "Burundi" / Burundi Frontosa (6-bar Frontosa)

UNDESCRIBED TO DATE

Natural Range: Burundi region of Lake Tanganyika.
Size: 12" (30 cm) TL; may grow larger.
Water Chemistry: Tropical; hard and alkaline conditions preferred.
Behavior: Moderately aggressive; males often intolerant of one another.
Dietary Requirements: Meaty foods and large pellets.

Remarks: For years, photos of the mighty Frontosa have actually been of this nominal species. Unfortunately, many texts are misleading and refer to this fish as the original Frontosa when, in actuality, the holotype and paratypes of *Cyphotilapia frontosa* are of the 7-bar variety found east of this population. *C.* sp. "Burundi" is a 6-bar Frontosa that grows to a very large size. Specimens of nearly 16" (40 cm) in total length have been recorded in aquariums on many occasions.

Cyphotilapia sp. "Zaire Blue" / Zaire Frontosa (6-bar Frontosa)

UNDESCRIBED TO DATE

Natural Range: Congo coastline of Lake Tanganyika.
Size: 12" (30 cm) TL, probably larger.
Water Chemistry: Tropical; hard and alkaline conditions preferred.
Behavior: Moderately aggressive; males are often intolerant of one another.
Dietary Requirements: Meaty foods and large pellets.

Remarks: There is speculation that the *Cyphotilapia* found in the deeper waters off the Congo coastline, are yet another species. While there is little disagreement that these fish are generally bluer (some even a violet purple), standard meristic and morphometrics techniques have provided no data that suggests these fish to be something new. Perhaps with use of DNA analysis, we may one day provide the hobby with a new species of Frontosa from this region. For now, though, we will still treat it as a possibility and list it separately herein.

Cyprichromis leptosoma

BOULENGER 1898

Natural Range: Lake Tanganyika.
Size: 4" (10 cm) TL; may grow slightly larger depending on the variation.
Water Chemistry: Tropical; hard and alkaline conditions preferred.
Behavior: Generally peaceful; males may fight amongst themselves.
Dietary Requirements: Small live and prepared foods.

Remarks: These interesting little cichlids live in the open water of Lake Tanganyika. They feed primarily on plankton, so their diet in aquariums should consist of small live foods such as guppy fry and brine shrimp, but they will readily take all types of fare, including frozen meaty foods and even pellets.

Cyphotilapia sp. "Burundi" female

Cyphotilapia sp. "Burundi" male

Cyphotilapia sp. "Zaire Blue" pair

Cyphotilapia sp. "Zaire Blue" adult male

Cyprichromis leptosoma

Cyprichromis leptosoma "blue flash"

Cyrtocara moorii / Blue Dolphin

BOULENGER 1902

Natural Range: Lake Malawi.
Size: 8" (20 cm) TL; may grow slightly larger.
Water Chemistry: Tropical; hard and alkaline conditions preferred.
Behavior: Generally mild mannered, but adult males may be belligerent.
Dietary Requirements: Small live and prepared foods.

Remarks: The Blue Dolphin is one of the most easily identifiable cichlids of Lake Malawi. They resemble a solid blue Frontosa with their large, pronounced nuchal hump. Their care and husbandry in aquariums is similar to that of the closely related *Copadichromis* species.

Dicrossus filamentosus

LADIGES 1958

Natural Range: Rio Negro, Brazil and surrounding area.
Size: 3" (7.5 cm) TL.
Water Chemistry: Tropical; slightly soft and acidic.
Behavior: Generally peaceful, except during spawning.
Dietary Requirements: Small live and prepared foods.

Remarks: Not all dwarf cichlids belong to the genus *Apistogramma*, although you may think so because of their overwhelming popularity. These little treasures are not commonly available through most pet shops, but they are easily obtained through private breeders. Of course, your local pet shop could contact these breeders for you and arrange for you to purchase them through their store.

Dicrossus maculatus

STEINDACHNER 1875

Natural Range: Rio Tocantins, Brazil and surrounding area.
Size: 3" (7.5 cm) TL.
Water Chemistry: Tropical; slightly soft and acidic.
Behavior: Generally peaceful, except during spawning.
Dietary Requirements: Small live and prepared foods.

Remarks: Another unique dwarf cichlid is *Dicrossus maculatus*. This species does well in most small to medium-sized aquariums with other peaceful fishes. They can get rather territorial when breeding, but otherwise they do well and are long-lived.

Cyrtocara moorii male

Cyrtocara moorii female

Dicrossus filamentosus

Dicrossus filamentosus

Dicrossus maculatus

Dicrossus maculatus

Dimidiochromis compressiceps / Malawi Eye-biter

BOULENGER 1908

Natural Range: Lake Malawi.
Size: 10" (25 cm) TL; usually much smaller.
Water Chemistry: Tropical; hard and alkaline conditions preferred.
Behavior: Ambush predator of smaller fishes, otherwise generally peaceful.
Dietary Requirements: Meaty and prepared foods of all types.

Remarks: The Malawi Eye-biter is an interesting species endemic to Lake Malawi. They earned the name of "eye-biter" due to their somewhat infrequent behavior of plucking the eyes out of tankmates. There are conflicting reports by hobbyists as to whether this nickname has any validity. The author (BMS) has kept many specimens, both male and female, of this species without such incidents. Perhaps a steady diet of high-quality foods influences them against such behavior.

Etia nguti

SCHLIEWEN & STIASSNY 2003

Natural Range: Western Cameroon.
Size: 8" (20 cm) TL.
Water Chemistry: Tropical; neutral to slightly alkaline with moderate hardness.
Behavior: Generally peaceful; males may quarrel.
Dietary Requirements: Small live foods and all types of prepared foods. They are detritivores in nature.

Remarks: Treating this species as an eartheater is probably not a bad idea, since they act like them in nature. In aquariums, however, they do well on a diet that is varied and consists of all types of prepared foods. There is a heightened level of intraspecific aggression between males, although sometimes females will quarrel as well.

Etroplus canarensis / Canara Pearlspot

DAY 1877

Natural Range: South Karnataka, India.
Size: 4" (10 cm) TL; may grow slightly larger.
Water Chemistry: Tropical; neutral to slightly alkaline with moderate hardness; may tolerate a low level of salt in their water.
Behavior: Generally peaceful; males may quarrel.
Dietary Requirements: Small live foods and all types of prepared foods.

Remarks: Recently, this rare cichlid has been imported from suppliers in India. There are no accounts of regular spawnings; however, it is quite possible that in a few more years, we will see this species for sale in local pet shops occasionally. For now, you will probably have to purchase them through specialists who import their own fishes.

Dimidiochromis compressiceps male in breeding dress   *Dimidiochromis compressiceps* female mouthbrooding

Etia nguti pair   *Etia nguti* profile of female

Etroplus canarensis   *Etroplus canarensis*

Etroplus maculatus / Orange Chromide

BLOCH 1795

Natural Range: India and Sri Lanka.
Size: 4" (10 cm) TL; possibly larger.
Water Chemistry: Tropical; neutral to slightly alkaline with moderate hardness; may tolerate a low level of salt in their water.
Behavior: Generally peaceful; males may quarrel.
Dietary Requirements: Small live foods and all types of prepared foods.

Remarks: In nature, this cichlid inhabits small streams and lagoons, where it feeds on fish fry, insects, and other small organisms. They occasionally move into estuaries where they will be subjected to tidal influences and brackish water. Orange Chromides do well in aquariums with other peaceful cichlids and fishes large enough to fend for themselves.

Etroplus suratensis / Green Chromide

BLOCH 1790

Natural Range: India and Sri Lanka.
Size: 16" (40 cm) TL; usually far smaller.
Water Chemistry: Tropical; neutral to slightly alkaline with moderate hardness; may tolerate a low level of salt in their water.
Behavior: Generally peaceful; males may quarrel.
Dietary Requirements: Omnivorous; small live foods and all types of prepared foods are accepted with gusto.

Remarks: The Green Chromide has been observed breeding in both fresh and brackish water conditions. They are found in large rivers, reservoirs, lagoons, and estuaries. In captivity, they need large aquariums with peaceful but large tankmates. Many hobbyists keep large Scats or Monos with them as dither fishes.

Geophagus brasiliensis / Brazilian Eartheater

QUOY & GAIMARD 1824

Natural Range: Brazil.
Size: 10" (25 cm) TL.
Water Chemistry: Tropical; slightly soft and acidic.
Behavior: Generally peaceful with similar-sized fishes.
Dietary Requirements: Small sinking foods of all types.

Remarks: This large-growing Eartheater is a great addition to cichlid community aquariums that contain large, peaceful species such as Chocolate Cichlids, Waroo, True Parrot Cichlids, and/or Severums. They eat quite a lot and may become aggressive during feeding time, but then again, so can all cichlids. Keep an eye on them to make sure that all tankmates get their faire share of food.

Etroplus maculatus

Etroplus maculatus

Etroplus suratensis

Etroplus suratensis

Geophagus brasilliensis young male

Geophagus brasilliensis older male

433

Geophagus proximus

CASTELNAU 1855

Natural Range: Amazonas area.
Size: 8" (20 cm) TL.
Water Chemistry: Tropical; slightly soft and acidic.
Behavior: Generally peaceful with similar-sized fishes.
Dietary Requirements: Small sinking foods of all types.

Remarks: As with so many other types of eartheaters, *Geophagus proximus* is often misidentified. Their care and husbandry is identical to others like *G. altifrons*, but you may need to consult one of the many good sources for cichlids to get actual specimens.

Geophagus steindachneri / Red Hump Eartheater

EIGENMANN & HILDEBRAND 1910

Natural Range: Colombia.
Size: 10" (25 cm) TL.
Water Chemistry: Tropical; slightly soft and acidic.
Behavior: Generally peaceful with similar-sized fishes.
Dietary Requirements: Small sinking foods of all types.

Remarks: This is one of the most popular species of eartheaters. They are easily recognized by their red hump (in males) and red patch of color in the nuchal region (in females). Sometimes their lips are red as well. Their care in aquariums is simple, and since so many are produced commercially now, there is little need to provide special water conditions for them. Of course, avoid extremes.

Geophagus surinamensis / Surinam Eartheater

BLOCH 1791

Natural Range: Surinam and northern South America.
Size: 8" (20 cm) TL; may grow slightly larger.
Water Chemistry: Tropical; slightly soft and acidic.
Behavior: Generally peaceful with similar-sized fishes.
Dietary Requirements: Small sinking foods of all types.

Remarks: Yet another species that is hardly ever correctly identified in the trade. These fishes (there is certainly more than one species in the complex) look very similar to each other. Their care and husbandry in aquariums is identical to *G. altifrons*.

Geophagus proximus

Geophagus proximus

Geophagus steindachneri young pair

Geophagus steindachneri femaie with fry!

Geophagus surinamensis male

Geophagus surinamensis female

Gobiocichla ethelwynnae

ROBERTS 1982

Natural Range: Western Cameroon.
Size: 4" (10 cm) TL; may grow slightly larger.
Water Chemistry: Tropical; hard and alkaline conditions are best.
Behavior: Generally peaceful.
Dietary Requirements: Small live and prepared foods that are high in plant matter.

Remarks: *Gobiocichla ethelwynnae* are easily kept in aquariums as long as they have good water quality and peaceful tankmates. These small cichlids will take up residency in places that are secluded and dark. They are not very aggressive and may be kept with large African Barbs and other peaceful fishes.

Gobiocichla wonderi

KANAZAWA 1951

Natural Range: Niger River system.
Size: 4" (10 cm) TL; may grow slightly larger.
Water Chemistry: Tropical; hard and alkaline conditions are best.
Behavior: Generally peaceful.
Dietary Requirements: Small live and prepared foods.

Remarks: Care and husbandry in aquariums is identical to that of its congener; *G. ethelwynnae.*

Guianacara sp. "Caroni"

UNDESCRIBED TO DATE

Natural Range: Rio Caroni, Venezuela.
Size: 6" (15 cm) TL.
Water Chemistry: Tropical; slightly soft and acidic.
Behavior: Generally peaceful with similar-sized fishes.
Dietary Requirements: Small live and prepared foods.

Remarks: This undescribed species of *Guianacara* is now starting to make a presence in the hobby—albeit a small presence. Their care and husbandry in aquariums is identical to others of the genus.

Gobiocichla ethelwynnae

Gobiocichla ethelwynnae note dark eye

Gobiocichla wonderi

Gobiocichla wonderi note clear eye

Guianacara sp. "Caroni"

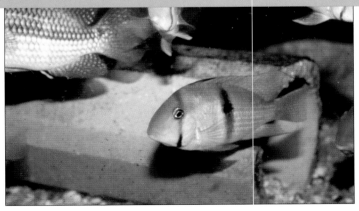

Guianacara geayi for comparison

Gymnogeophagus australis

EIGENMANN 1907

Natural Range: Southern Brazil.
Size: 6" (15 cm) TL.
Water Chemistry: Subtropical and tropical; slightly soft and acidic.
Behavior: Generally peaceful with similar-sized fishes.
Dietary Requirements: All types of prepared foods.

Remarks: This small species is a rarity in the hobby, although those hobbyists wishing to obtain them can do so with a good degree of regularity. As with so many other cichlids, a quick call to someone who specializes in this group can make all the difference in the world. Sometimes you can find this species in pet shops, but they are more commonly special ordered.

Gymnogeophagus balzanii

PERUGIA 1891

Natural Range: Argentina, Paraguay, and southern Brazil
Size: 8" (20 cm) TL; possibly larger.
Water Chemistry: Subtropical and tropical; slightly soft and acidic.
Behavior: Generally peaceful with similar-sized fishes.
Dietary Requirements: All types of prepared foods.

Remarks: The bulbous nuchal region is a distinguishing feature of the adult *G. balzanii*. They are a subtropical species that prefers water on the slightly cooler side, as compared to many other fishes. Since Argentina and southern Brazil are now open to regular fishing, this and other subtropical cichlids are commonly available, albeit slightly expensive due to transport fees.

Gymnogeophagus gymnogenys

HENSEL 1870

Natural Range: Southern Brazil.
Size: 8" (20 cm) TL.
Water Chemistry: Subtropical and tropical; slightly soft and acidic.
Behavior: Generally peaceful with similar-sized fishes.
Dietary Requirements: All types of prepared foods.

Remarks: Some specimens of *G. gymnogenys* are gorgeous, with their bright red fins and nearly metallic yellow and lime green nuchal region and flanks. The contrast is perfect for those who want to add something truly different to their cool-water aquarium. Many hobbyists have been exploring the different tankmates that are suitable with this and other *Gymnogeophagus* species and are finding that many fishes that are native to the United States make good tankmates for them. This is surely true because of their temperature requirements.

Gymnogeophagus australis male

Gymnogeophagus sp. aff. *australis* female

Gymnogeophagus balzanii male

Gymnogeophagus balzanii female

Gymnogeophagus gymnogenys female

Gymnogeophagus gymnogenys male

Gymnogeophagus labiatus

HENSEL 1870

Natural Range: Southern Brazil and surrounding areas.
Size: 8" (20 cm) TL; may grow slightly larger.
Water Chemistry: Subtropical and tropical; slightly soft and acidic.
Behavior: Generally peaceful with similar-sized fishes.
Dietary Requirements: All types of prepared foods.

Remarks: No other species of eartheater is quite like *G. labiatus*; they are more elongated and have a distinctive look that's all their own. In the aquarium, they make great additions to tanks that are set up for southern South American fishes.

Gymnogeophagus meridionalis

REIS & MALABARBA 1988

Natural Range: Southern Brazil and surrounding areas.
Size: 6" (15 cm) TL.
Water Chemistry: Subtropical and tropical; slightly soft and acidic.
Behavior: Generally peaceful with similar-sized fishes.
Dietary Requirements: All types of prepared foods.

Remarks: Many species of eartheater are gorgeous, and this is one of them. They are generally peaceful with other fishes within the cichlid community aquarium as long as they are of similar size. Additionally, males are rather quarrelsome, so it is recommended that only one male be kept per aquarium. There may also be some aggression on males of similar-looking species, so watch them closely. Otherwise, this is a must-have species of rare cichlid.

Gymnogeophagus rhabdotus

HENSEL 1870

Natural Range: Brazil.
Size: 6" (15 cm) TL; usually smaller.
Water Chemistry: Subtropical and Tropical; slightly soft and acidic.
Behavior: Generally peaceful with similar-sized fishes.
Dietary Requirements: All types of prepared foods.

Remarks: Similar in appearance to *G. meridionalis*, *G. rhabdotus* is a brilliantly-colored species with good, peaceful habits in the cichlid community aquarium. Of course, males may become intolerant of each other during spawning. Keeping them is easy, provided the water temperature does not get too warm. They, like other southern Brazilian species, prefer cooler water temperatures.

Gymnogeophagus labiatus female

Gymnogeophagus labiatus male

Gymnogeophagus meridionalis female

Gymnogeophagus meridionalis male

Gymnogeophagus rhabdotus male

Gymnogeophagus rhabdotus female

Haplochromis nubilis

BOULENGER 1906

Natural Range: Lake Victoria.
Size: 4" (10 cm) TL.
Water Chemistry: Tropical; hard and alkaline conditions preferred.
Behavior: Moderately aggressive.
Dietary Requirements: Small live and prepared foods.

Remarks: As with so many cichlids from Lake Victoria, *H. nubilis* is in serious danger of becoming extinct. Recently, there have been major efforts geared toward building captive breeding stock of this and similar species, since someday in the not too distant future, they may be the only ones on Earth.

Haplochromis nyererei

WITTE-MAAS & WITTE 1985

Natural Range: Lake Victoria.
Size: 4" (10 cm) TL.
Water Chemistry: Tropical; hard and alkaline conditions preferred.
Behavior: Moderately aggressive.
Dietary Requirements: Small live and prepared foods.

Remarks: This colorful *Haplochromis* is often found in specialty shops where their prices vary. They exhibit their best colors when they are offered a color-enhancing food on a regular basis.

Haplochromis obliquidens / Obliquidens

HILGENDORF 1888

Natural Range: Lake Victoria.
Size: 4" (10 cm) TL.
Water Chemistry: Tropical; hard and alkaline conditions preferred.
Behavior: Moderately aggressive.
Dietary Requirements: Small live and prepared foods.

Remarks: Two fishes are both referred to as *Haplochromis obliquidens*. One is less colorful than the other, but both are identical in their care and husbandry in aquariums. Many hobbyists keep these fish in community aquariums with other Rift Lake cichlids such as Mbuna or Peacocks.

Haplochromis nubilis

Haplochromis nubilis

Haplochromis nyererei

Haplochromis sp. "flameback"

Haplochromis obliquidens female "zebra"

Haplochromis obliquidens male "zebra"

Hemichromis fasciatus

PETERS 1858

Natural Range: Widely distributed in remote regions of western Africa.
Size: 8" (20 cm) TL; possibly larger.
Water Chemistry: Tropical; slightly alkaline with moderate hardness.
Behavior: Very aggressive; keep alone.
Dietary Requirements: Small live and all types of prepared foods.

Remarks: This aggressive and antisocial species forms long-lasting pair bonds. The territory of these pairs sometimes covers as much as 25 square meters, and anything that attempts to take up residency within this area is probably going to come under heavy assault. Keep this species alone. If a pair does form in a large community setting, separate them from the other fishes, and use an incomplete divider to allow the female to get away from the male.

Hemichromis frempongi

LOISELLE 1979

Natural Range: Endemic to Lake Bosumtwi in central Ghana.
Size: 6" (15 cm) TL.
Water Chemistry: Tropical; slightly alkaline with moderate hardness.
Behavior: Moderately aggressive to aggressive, depending on the specimen.
Dietary Requirements: Small live and prepared foods.

Remarks: In general, if you are experienced with *H. elongatus* and *H. fasciatus*, you will have no difficulty keeping this species either.

Hemichromis gutattus

GUENTHER 1862

Natural Range: Cameroon, Ghana, Ivory Coast, and Nigeria.
Size: 4" (10 cm) TL.
Water Chemistry: Tropical; slightly alkaline with moderate hardness.
Behavior: Moderately aggressive to aggressive, depending on the specimen.
Dietary Requirements: Small live and prepared foods.

Remarks: This is probably the species of Jewel Cichlid that hobbyists today are most familiar with, though it is commonly mislabeled (Lamboj 2004). The care and husbandry of *H. guttatus* is typical of the group.

Hemichromis fasciatus

Hemichromis fasciatus

Hemichromis frempongi

Hemichromis frempongi

Hemichromis guttatus

Hemichromis guttatus

Hemichromis lifalli

LOISELLE 1979

Natural Range: Congo and Ubangi Rivers.
Size: 4" (10 cm) TL.
Water Chemistry: Tropical; slightly alkaline with moderate hardness.
Behavior: Moderately aggressive to aggressive, depending on the specimen.
Dietary Requirements: Small live and prepared foods.

Remarks: Another red-colored Jewel Cichlid, *H. lifalli* is not quite as readily available in the hobby. This species is usually only available through cichlid dealers that specialize in the rare and unusual species. Their care and husbandry is identical to others in the group.

Herichthys carpintis / Carpintis

JORDAN & SNYDER 1899

Natural Range: Mexico.
Size: 8" (20 cm) TL.
Water Chemistry: Tropical; slightly alkaline with moderate hardness.
Behavior: Aggressive.
Dietary Requirements: All types of meaty and prepared foods.

Remarks: This cichlid is also known as the Green Texas Cichlid among hobbyists. They are a robust cichlid that does well in most large aquariums. Tankmates should be of a similar size and temperament. For best results, provide plenty of caves and crevices for them to hide in and among.

Herichthys cyanoguttatus / Texas Cichlid

BAIRD & GIRARD 1854

Natural Range: Mexico and Texas (United States).
Size: 8" (20 cm) TL.
Water Chemistry: Subtropical and tropical; slightly alkaline with moderate hardness.
Behavior: Aggressive.
Dietary Requirements: All types of meaty and prepared foods.

Remarks: The Texas Cichlid is a well-known species that is similar in coloration, size, and captive care as the Carpitis, a close cousin. This species does especially well in cooler aquariums and can be kept with various species of bass (*Micropterus* spp.) and sunfishes (*Lepomis* spp.).

Hemichromis lifalli

Hemichromis lifalli pair

Herichthys carpintis

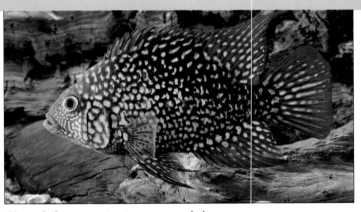

Herichthys carpintis young adult

Herichthys cyanaguttatus male

Herichthys cyanaguttatus female

Herichthys labridens

PELLEGRIN 1903
Natural Range: Mexico.
Size: 8" (20 cm) TL.
Water Chemistry: Tropical; slightly alkaline with moderate hardness.
Behavior: Aggressive.
Dietary Requirements: All types of meaty and prepared foods.

Remarks: This is one of the most colorful of all Central American cichlids. In recent years, this species has gained much popularity due to the importation of wild-collected specimens, which has resulted in captive breeding projects and the availability of juveniles. Provided with warm water of good quality, this species will do well in captivity for many years.

Herichthys minckleyi / Pearl Cichlid

KORNFIELD & TAYLOR 1983
Natural Range: Mexico.
Size: 8" (20 cm) TL; may grow slightly larger.
Water Chemistry: Tropical; slightly alkaline with moderate hardness.
Behavior: Moderately aggressive.
Dietary Requirements: All types of prepared foods supplemented with meaty foods.

Remarks: Pearl Cichlids are now available with a much better degree of regularity than in years past. They are a moderately aggressive species that does well in a large cichlid community aquarium with other large fishes. Adults show a wide degree of variation in both color and pattern.

Herichthys pearsei

HUBBS 1936
Natural Range: Guatemala and Mexico.
Size: 8" (20 cm) TL; may grow slightly larger.
Water Chemistry: Tropical; slightly alkaline with moderate hardness.
Behavior: Moderately aggressive.
Dietary Requirements: All types of prepared foods supplemented with plant matter.

Remarks: This big, bold cichlid is one of the most interestingly-colored species available. They are somewhat rare in the hobby, with their popularity coming in intervals, followed by many months or years of sporadic sales. They complement a collection of similar-sized cichlids in a community aquarium very well. Feed large amounts of plant matter.

Herichthys labridens

Herichthys labridens

Herichthys minckleyi

Herichthys minckleyi

Herichthys pearsei

Herichthys pearsei profile

449

Herichthys steindachneri / Steindachner's Cichlid

JORDAN & SNYDER 1899

Natural Range: Northern Mexico.
Size: 10" (25 cm) TL.
Water Chemistry: Tropical; slightly alkaline with moderate hardness.
Behavior: Moderately aggressive.
Dietary Requirements: All types of prepared foods supplemented with meaty foods.

Remarks: Steindachner's Cichlid is a robust species that does well in aquariums that have good filtration, strong water current, and moderate hardness. When breeding, this species takes on a completely different dress and may become surprisingly aggressive. Watch for pair bonding in your aquarium as a precursor to heightened aggression.

Heros appendiculatus / Green Severum

CASTELNAU 1855

Natural Range: Upper Amazon River drainage.
Size: 10" (25 cm) TL.
Water Chemistry: Tropical; slightly soft and acidic.
Behavior: Moderately aggressive; keep with other fishes of equal size.
Dietary Requirements: Omnivorous; feed equal amounts of plant and animal matter.

Remarks: This beautiful medium-sized cichlid is native to a broad expanse of water, ranging from the Rio Ucayali through the lower sections of the Nanay, Napo, and Ica Rivers. They are often referred to as the "Turquoise" Severum because of their intense blue-green coloration. Their care in the aquarium is basic, and unless you wish to breed them, there is no need to monitor specific water parameters. Avoid extremes.

Heros efasciatus

HECKEL 1840

Natural Range: Lower course of Rio Negro, Brazil.
Size: 10" (25 cm) TL.
Water Chemistry: Tropical; slightly soft and acidic.
Behavior: Moderately aggressive, keep with other fishes of equal size.
Dietary Requirements: Omnivorous; feed equal amounts of plant and animal matter.

Remarks: A beautiful and fairly peaceful species, *H. efasciatus* does best in large community aquariums of equally-sized fishes. They are moderately aggressive and may bully smaller tankmates. This species, and all species within *Heros*, need sufficient plant matter in their diet, since they are omnivorous in nature.

Herichthys steindachneri

Herichthys steindachneri

Heros appendiculatus Female

Heros appendiculatus male

Heros efasciatus young

Heros efasciatus adult male

451

Heros notatus

JARDINE 1843

Natural Range: Guyana.
Size: 12" (30 cm) TL.
Water Chemistry: Tropical; slightly soft and acidic.
Behavior: Moderately aggressive; keep with other fishes of equal size.
Dietary Requirements: Omnivorous; feed equal amounts of plant and animal matter.

Remarks: Unfortunately, this beautiful species of severum does not often hold up well after shipping. They seem to be extremely sensitive to stress, and many shippers pack this species far too tightly, and they end up tearing each other up while in transit. Otherwise, those that do live will often thrive in aquariums, as long as their water quality is well maintained and they are provided with a balanced and varied diet.

Heros sp. "Rotkeil" / Redheaded Severum

UNDESCRIBED TO DATE

Natural Range: Peru.
Size: 10" (25 cm) TL.
Water Chemistry: Tropical; soft and acidic is preferred.
Behavior: Generally peaceful, except when spawning.
Dietary Requirements: Omnivorous; feed equal amounts of plant and animal matter.

Remarks: This new cichlid on the block is highly recognizable with beginners and experienced aquarists alike. They are probably one of the most beautiful *Heros*, with their bright red heads and blue-green spangles. Aquarium care is identical to others in the genus.

Herotilapia multispinosa / Rainbow Cichlid

GUENTHER 1866

Natural Range: Costa Rica and Honduras.
Size: 4" (10 cm) TL; usually slightly smaller.
Water Chemistry: Tropical; slightly alkaline with moderate hardness.
Behavior: Generally peaceful.
Dietary Requirements: Small live and prepared foods.

Remarks: Although Rainbow Cichlids are quite small, they may still be somewhat aggressive. Usually they are fine in community aquariums that house fishes that are similar in size. When breeding, they may stake out an unusually large territory, so watch for that in your tank. A very colorful and personable species.

Heros notatus

Heros notatus

Heros sp. "Rotkeil" female

Heros sp. "Rotkeil" male

Herotilapia multispinosa female

Herotilapia multispinosa male

Heterochromis multidens

PELLEGRIN 1922

Natural Range: Upper Congo system.
Size: 12" (30 cm) TL; usually smaller.
Water Chemistry: Tropical; otherwise not critical.
Behavior: Moderately aggressive.
Dietary Requirements: Small live foods and all types of prepared foods.

Remarks: As of this writing, there are no published accounts of successful spawnings with this species. They are large, maybe up to one foot in length, and require large aquariums with good filtration. Feeding is easy, since they are not picky, and will accept nearly all prepared foods.

Hoplarchus psitticus / True Parrot Cichlid

HECKEL 1840

Natural Range: Northern Brazil, Colombia, and Venezuela.
Size: 12" (30 cm) TL.
Water Chemistry: Tropical; slightly soft and acidic.
Behavior: Moderately aggressive.
Dietary Requirements: Small live foods and all types of prepared foods.

Remarks: The True Parrot Cichlid is a rare and often expensive species that is only seasonally available from selected importers. Reproduction is only reported in very old specimens in captivity, and apparently, they are known to be poor parents, with egg cannibalism being a common problem, especially in young parents.

Hypselacara coryphaenoides / Coryphaenoides

HECKEL 1840

Natural Range: Brazil and Venezuela.
Size: 10" (25 cm) TL.
Water Chemistry: Tropical; slightly soft and acidic.
Behavior: Moderately aggressive; keep with other fishes of equal size.
Dietary Requirements: Small live foods and all types of prepared foods.

Remarks: This is one of those must-have species of rare cichlids. They are not often available, and when they are, they're surprisingly cheap compared to other rare cichlids from the same localities. It is best to provide a large aquarium with ample hiding places—usually in the form of bogwood or artificial plants. *Coryphaenoides* are a long-lived species that do very well with other moderately-sized cichlids.

Heterochromis multidens small adult

Heterochromis multidens adult male

Hoplarchus psitticus

Hoplarchus psitticus adult male

Hypselacara coryphaenoides juvenile

Hypselacara coryphaenoides adult

Hypselacara temporalis / Chocolate Cichlid

GUENTHER 1862

Natural Range: Brazil and Peru.
Size: 12" (30 cm) TL.
Water Chemistry: Tropical; slightly soft and acidic.
Behavior: Moderately aggressive.
Dietary Requirements: Small live foods and all types of prepared foods.

Remarks: The Chocolate Cichlid is an excellent species for the peaceful community aquarium of large cichlids. They are normally only aggressive when breeding, and even this aggression is only directed at those fishes that wish to disrupt the nest. This large-growing fish is highly recommended for the hobbyist who likes big fish with a small attitude.

Hypsophrys nicaraguensis / Nicaraguensis

GUENTHER 1862

Natural Range: Costa Rica and Nicaragua.
Size: 10" (25 cm) TL.
Water Chemistry: Tropical; neutral with moderate hardness.
Behavior: Moderately aggressive.
Dietary Requirements: Small live foods and all types of prepared foods.

Remarks: The Nicaraguensis is a moderately aggressive but outrageously colorful species that needs water with some hardness and a neutral to slightly alkaline pH. They do well in small harems of one male to three or four females. Provide plenty of hiding places for the females to seek shelter from the male.

Iodotropheus sprengerae / Rusty Cichlid

OLIVER & LOISELLE 1972

Natural Range: Lake Malawi.
Size: 5" (12 cm) TL.
Water Chemistry: Tropical; hard and alkaline.
Behavior: Moderately aggressive.
Dietary Requirements: Omnivorous; feed prepared foods supplemented with plant matter.

Remarks: Very few cichlids are actually colored like a well-conditioned Rusty Cichlid. As the name implies, this species is, well, rusty-colored. They are also occasionally purple, and this especially true of wild-collected males. Care and husbandry in aquariums is simple, and these fish do well under normal conditions for fishes from Lake Malawi.

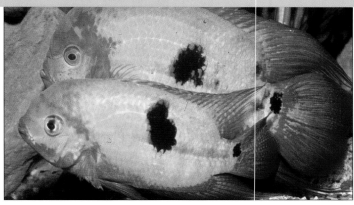

Hypselacara temporalis

Hypselacara temporalis pair

Hypsophrys nicaraguensis

Hypsophrys nicaraguensis

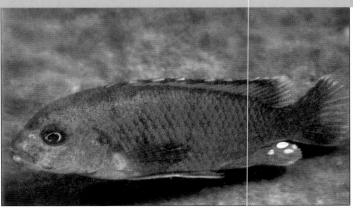

Iodotropheus sprengerae

Iodotropheus sprengerae

457

Julidochromis dickfeldi

STAECK 1975

Natural Range: Lake Tanganyika.
Size: 4" (10 cm) TL.
Water Chemistry: Tropical; hard and alkaline.
Behavior: Generally peaceful.
Dietary Requirements: Small live foods and all types of prepared foods.

Remarks: These fish are best kept in pairs in medium-sized aquariums where they can breed among the rocks and the tank's décor. Be sure to provide many caves and crevices.

Julidochromis marlieri

POLL 1956

Natural Range: Lake Tanganyika.
Size: 4" (10 cm) TL; females slightly larger than the males.
Water Chemistry: Tropical; hard and alkaline.
Behavior: Generally peaceful.
Dietary Requirements: Small live foods and all types of prepared foods.

Remarks: These cave brooders lays their eggs on the ceiling of caves. Provide ample shelter and keep in small groups.

Julidochromis ornatus

BOULENGER 1898

Natural Range: Lake Tanganyika.
Size: 4" (10 cm) TL.
Water Chemistry: Tropical; hard and alkaline.
Behavior: Generally peaceful.
Dietary Requirements: Small live foods and all types of prepared foods.

Remarks: Do not keep this species with *J. transcriptus*. Otherwise, their care and husbandry is the same as others of the genus. A small aquarium of about 15 to 20 gallons is suitable for each pair.

Julidochromis dickfeldi

Julidochromis dickfeldi

Julidochromis marlieri

Julidochromis marlieri

Julidochromis ornatus

Julidochromis ornatus

Julidochromis regani

POLL 1942

Natural Range: Lake Tanganyika.
Size: 4" (10 cm) TL; female slightly larger than males.
Water Chemistry: Tropical; hard and alkaline.
Behavior: Generally peaceful.
Dietary Requirements: Small live foods and all types of prepared foods.

Remarks: This species of *Julidochromis* is commonly found in the intermediate habitat in relatively shallow water. They are best kept as pairs in small aquariums. Just as other species within the genus do, *J. regani* does well in smaller aquariums with plenty of rockwork.

Julidochromis transcriptus

MATTHES 1959

Natural Range: Lake Tanganyika.
Size: 3" (7.5 cm) TL.
Water Chemistry: Tropical; hard and alkaline.
Behavior: Generally peaceful.
Dietary Requirements: Small live foods and all types of prepared foods.

Remarks: The smallest species of the genus, *J. transcriptus* is an inhabitant of rocky areas between 15 and 75 feet. They do well in small, dimly illuminated aquariums with plenty of rockwork in which to hide and breed.

Konia eisentrauti

TREWEVAS 1962

Natural Range: West Cameroon.
Size: 4" (10 cm) TL.
Water Chemistry: Tropical; slightly acidic with moderate hardness.
Behavior: Moderately aggressive.
Dietary Requirements: Small live foods and all types of prepared foods.

Remarks: *Konia eisentrauti* is endemic to Lake Barombi-Mbo in Western Cameroon. They live in small groups or alone in shallows, where they prefer to stay close to the bottom over sandy, open areas. They are easy to keep and even breed in most aquarium setups.

Julidochromis regani

Julidochromis regani Kipili race

Julidochromis transcriptus

Julidochromis transcriptus

Konia eisentrauti

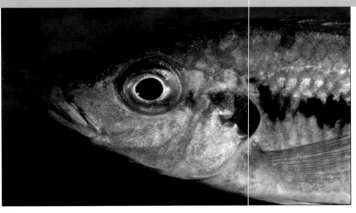

Konia eisentrauti

461

Krobia guianensis / Guyana Cichlid

REGAN 1905

Natural Range: Guyana.
Size: 8" (20 cm) TL.
Water Chemistry: Tropical; slightly soft and acidic.
Behavior: Moderately aggressive.
Dietary Requirements: Small live foods and all types of prepared foods.

Remarks: This interesting cichlid from Guyana is occasionally imported with other cichlids from Guyana. They do not ship well and are often in poor condition upon arrival, so they need some time to acclimatize to aquarium conditions. After they are properly adjusted, they prove to be a tough and hardy species that will live quite a long time in large aquariums.

Labeotropheus fuelleborni

AHL 1926

Natural Range: Lake Malawi.
Size: 6" (15 cm) TL.
Water Chemistry: Tropical; hard and alkaline.
Behavior: Moderately aggressive.
Dietary Requirements: Prepared foods high in plant matter.

Remarks: *L. fuelleborni* is always deeper bodied and fuller than its close cousin *L. trewavasae*. They graze from sediment-free rocks in their native habitat, where they leave scrape marks as if they were peeling an orange. *L. fuelleborni* do well in aquariums, but males are often intolerant of one another, so it is best to keep them either as a single specimen or in groups of one male to multiple females.

Labeotropheus trewavasae

FRYER 1956

Natural Range: Lake Malawi.
Size: 6" (15 cm) TL.
Water Chemistry: Tropical; hard and alkaline.
Behavior: Moderately aggressive.
Dietary Requirements: Prepared foods high in plant matter.

Remarks: This species, as well as *L. fuelleborni*, are easily distinguished from other Rift Lake cichlids by their blunt noses. They have a more elongated body when compared to *L. fuelleborni*, and when the two species are housed together, such differences in body shape are clear. Their care in aquariums is identical to that of *L. fuelleborni*.

Krobia guianensis

Krobia sp.

Labeotropheus fuelleborni

Labeotropheus fuelleborni

Labeotropheus trewavasae

Labeotropheus trewavasae

463

Labidochromis caeruleus / Yellow Lab

FRYER 1956

Natural Range: Lake Malawi.
Size: 4" (10 cm) TL.
Water Chemistry: Tropical; hard and alkaline.
Behavior: Generally peaceful.
Dietary Requirements: Small live foods and all types of prepared foods.

Remarks: In nature, this species can be observed feeding off the ceilings of caves and deep within rock crevices. Aquarium specimens are not picky about the foods they consume, with most standard prepared foods being suitable. Round out their diet to include both plant and animal matter in somewhat equal quantities.

Labidochromis chisumulae

LEWIS 1982

Natural Range: Lake Malawi.
Size: 4" (10 cm) TL.
Water Chemistry: Tropical; hard and alkaline.
Behavior: Generally peaceful.
Dietary Requirements: Small live foods and all types of prepared foods.

Remarks: *Labidochromis chisumulae* is found in many different habitats, but is always associated with rocks (Konings 1990). They are not quite as common as *L. caeruleus*, but many cichlid specialists have access to broodstock or sometimes even wild stock. Their care and husbandry is identical to that of *L. caeruleus*.

Laetacara dorsigerus

HECKEL 1840

Natural Range: Paraguay.
Size: 3" (7.5 cm) TL.
Water Chemistry: Tropical; slightly soft and acidic.
Behavior: Generally peaceful.
Dietary Requirements: Small live foods and all types of prepared foods.

Remarks: Just like *L. curviceps*, this species does well in a community aquarium with other peaceful fishes with similar habits. However, unlike *L. curviceps*, *L. dorsigerus* prefers slightly cooler water.

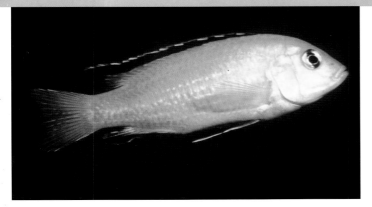

Labidochromis caeruleus

Labidochromis caeruleus

Labidochromis chisumulae

Labidochromis "pearlmutt" for comparison

Laetacara dorsigerus

Laetacara dorsigerus

Laetacara thayeri

STEINDACHNERI 1875

Natural Range: Western Amazonia.
Size: 5" (12 cm) TL.
Water Chemistry: Tropical; slightly soft and acidic.
Behavior: Generally peaceful.
Dietary Requirements: Small live foods and all types of prepared foods.

Remarks: This is the larger cousin to the ever-popular *L. curviceps*. For those hobbyists who would like to keep a *Laetacara* species in their aquarium with larger species, this one's for you. Otherwise, their care and husbandry are identical to their smaller cousins.

Lamprologus callipterus

BOULENGER 1906

Natural Range: Lake Tanganyika.
Size: 6" (15 cm) TL.
Water Chemistry: Tropical; hard and alkaline.
Behavior: Moderately aggressive.
Dietary Requirements: Small live foods and all types of prepared foods.

Remarks: This is generally a poor aquarium species, but a truly fascinating one nonetheless, due to its variety of behaviors. It has a voracious appetite and is a perennial roamer; it is a species that, because of this last feature, puts to rest the theory that substrate-spawning cichlids are territorial and only mouthbrooders are roamers.

Lamprologus congoensis

SCHILTHUIS 1891

Natural Range: West Africa.
Size: 6" (15 cm) TL.
Water Chemistry: Tropical; hard and alkaline.
Behavior: Moderately aggressive.
Dietary Requirements: Small live foods and all types of prepared foods.

Remarks: *Lamprologus congoensis* is the only riverine species of *Lamprologus* that is commonly available. They are very hardy and easily kept as long as extremes in water chemistry are avoided. Keep with similar-sized species, and be sure to provide plenty of sheltered crevices and caves.

Laetacara thayeri

Laetacara thayeri

Lamprologus callipterus adult

Lamprologus callipterus juvenile

Lamprologus congoensis male

Lamprologus congoensis female

467

Lamprologus lemairii

BOULENGER 1899

Natural Range: Lake Tanganyika.
Size: 6" (15 cm) TL; may grow larger.
Water Chemistry: Tropical; hard and alkaline.
Behavior: Moderately aggressive.
Dietary Requirements: Small live foods and all types of prepared foods.

Remarks: This is another highly predatory cichlid that is only suitable for large aquariums that contain other aggressive species. They are best kept alone, but due to their rather drab coloration, they don't make very good show specimens unless coloration is not important to the hobbyist.

Lamprologus ocellatus

STEINDACHNERI 1909

Natural Range: Lake Tanganyika.
Size: 2" (5 cm) TL.
Water Chemistry: Tropical; hard and alkaline.
Behavior: Moderately aggressive.
Dietary Requirements: Small live foods and all types of prepared foods.

Remarks: This small shell-dweller is often confused with a close relative—*Neolamprologus brevis*. They can be distinguished from *N. brevis* by the concave outline of the snout, which appears slightly caved in. The colors are not unattractive, but are altogether drab. As with other shell dwellers, it is best to keep only one male with multiple females and provide plenty of shells for them to hide in and among.

Lepidiolamprologus cunningtoni

BOULENGER 1906

Natural Range: Lake Tanganyika.
Size: 8" (20 cm) TL; sometimes larger.
Water Chemistry: Tropical; hard and alkaline.
Behavior: Aggressive.
Dietary Requirements: Small live and other 3meaty foods.

Remarks: As a rule, *L. cunningtoni* prefers to swim close to the sand bottom, though the others in this genus seem to prefer hovering over the substrate. They make good tankmates for large aquariums with other predatory cichlid species.

Lamprologus lemairii adult

Lamprologus lemairii juvenile

Lamprologus ocellatus

Lamprologus ocellatus

Lepidiolamprologus cunningtoni pair

Lepidiolamprologus cunningtoni male

469

Lepidiolamprologus elongatus

BOULENGER 1898

Natural Range: Lake Tanganyika.
Size: 8" (20 cm) TL; sometimes larger.
Water Chemistry: Tropical; hard and alkaline.
Behavior: Aggressive.
Dietary Requirements: Small live and other meaty foods.

Remarks: *L. elongatus* is the most common of the six species within the genus. The others have been exported only sporadically at best, although captive-bred young are sometimes available from specialists.

Lepidiolamprologus kendalli

POLL & STEWERT 1977

Natural Range: Lake Tanganyika.
Size: 8" (20 cm) TL; sometimes larger.
Water Chemistry: Tropical; hard and alkaline.
Behavior: Aggressive.
Dietary Requirements: Small live and other meaty foods.

Remarks: This species is similar in habit and relation to *L. elongatus* and another, less common species, *L. profundicola*. Out of all of the fishes in the group, this one is probably the most colorful and interesting to look at.

Lepidiolamprologus nkambae

STAECK 1978

Natural Range: Lake Tanganyika.
Size: 6" (15 cm) TL; sometimes larger.
Water Chemistry: Tropical; hard and alkaline.
Behavior: Aggressive.
Dietary Requirements: Small live and other meaty foods.

Remarks: *Lepidiolamprologus nkambae* is slightly smaller than other members of the genus. In nature, they can usually be found hiding deep within the crevices of rocks. Their aquariums should contain caves constructed of rocks or anything else that will provide suitable cover. This species is native to the southern end of Lake Tanganyika.

Lepidiolamprologus elongatus

Lepidiolamprologus elongatus

Lepidiolamprologus kendalli

Lepidiolamprologus kendalli

Lepidiolamprologus nkambae

Lepidiolamprologus kendalli for comparison

471

Maylandia barlowi

MCKAYE & STAUFFER 1986

Natural Range: Lake Malawi.
Size: 5" (12 cm) TL.
Water Chemistry: Tropical; hard and alkaline.
Behavior: Moderately aggressive.
Dietary Requirements: Algae, aufwuchs, and prepared foods high in plant matter.

Remarks: For some time, this Mbuna was referred to as *Pseudotropheus fusco*. While this name is no longer valid, the fish is obviously the same. Their care in aquariums is identical to others in the genus, with no special exceptions.

Maylandia estherae / Red Zebra

KONINGS 1995

Natural Range: Lake Malawi.
Size: 5" (12 cm) TL.
Water Chemistry: Tropical; hard and alkaline.
Behavior: Moderately aggressive.
Dietary Requirements: Algae, aufwuchs, and prepared foods high in plant matter.

Remarks: The Red Zebra is a very popular species that has recently experienced a revitalized popularity with the introduction of the "Super" Red Zebra. Of course, as the name implies, the Super Red Zebra is a very red version of the common Red Zebra. Regardless, their care in aquariums is identical to others in the genus, with no special exceptions.

Maylandia hajomaylandi

MEYER & SCHARTL 1984

Natural Range: Lake Malawi.
Size: 5" (12 cm) TL.
Water Chemistry: Tropical; hard and alkaline.
Behavior: Moderately aggressive.
Dietary Requirements: Algae, aufwuchs, and prepared foods high in plant matter.

Remarks: Endemic to the Chizumulu Island, *M. hajomaylandi* prefers the sediment-rich rocky biotope and is frequently found over sand of intermediate habitat (Konings 1990). Their care in aquariums is identical to others in the genus, with no special exceptions.

Maylandia barlowi

Maylandia barlowi

Maylandia estherae male

Maylandia estherae female

Maylandia hajomaylandi

Maylandia hajomaylandi

Melanochromis auratus

BOULENGER 1897

Natural Range: Lake Malawi.
Size: 5" (12 cm) TL.
Water Chemistry: Tropical; hard and alkaline.
Behavior: Moderately aggressive.
Dietary Requirements: Algae, aufwuchs, and prepared foods high in plant matter.

Remarks: The color pattern of this cichlid remains identical throughout their range, but the intensity of the yellow in the females and the brown in the males varies among populations (Konings 1990). Konings further reports that the most intensely colored individuals are found around Mbenji, Maleri, and Mumbo Islands. Their care in aquariums is identical to others in the genus, with no special exceptions.

Melanochromis chipokae

JOHNSON 1975

Natural Range: Lake Malawi.
Size: 5" (12 cm) TL.
Water Chemistry: Tropical; hard and alkaline.
Behavior: Moderately aggressive.
Dietary Requirements: Micropredator of small fishes and invertebrates.

Remarks: *M. chipokae* is characterized by its large size and lively coloration (Konings 1990). Their care in aquariums is identical to others in the genus, with no special exceptions. Use caution when adding this fish to cichlid community aquariums, as they tend to be outwardly aggressive, even to fishes they would never be able to swallow.

Melanochromis johannii

ECCLES 1973

Natural Range: Lake Malawi.
Size: 5" (12 cm) TL.
Water Chemistry: Tropical; hard and alkaline.
Behavior: Moderately aggressive.
Dietary Requirements: Algae, aufwuchs, and prepared foods high in plant matter; will also eat plankton.

Remarks: This is an interesting fish that belongs to an interesting genus. Rarely do we see a genus with fishes exhibiting so much variability in behavior and aggression. Of all the members of *Melanochromis*, *M. johannii* is probably the most peaceful. They make wonderful additions to the Rift Lake community aquarium, as long as the tank does not already contain fishes that will harm them.

Melanochromis auratus female

Melanochromis auratus male

Melanochromis chipokae female

Melanochromis chipokae male

Melanochromis johannii female

Melanochromis johannii male

475

Mesonauta festivus / Flag Cichlid

HECKEL 1840

Natural Range: Amazonia.
Size: 8" (20 cm) TL; may grow slightly larger.
Water Chemistry: Tropical; slightly soft and acidic.
Behavior: Generally peaceful.
Dietary Requirements: Small live foods and all types of prepared foods.

Remarks: The Flag Cichlid has had limited popularity over the years. Many of these fish are still wild collected, and they do not ship well unless they are caught and transported when they are very small. Small ones suitable for shipping are only available for a very limited time each year. Ironically, many pet shops that stock these fish when they're available seem to sell them very quickly.

Mesonauta insignis / Netback Flag Cichlid

HECKEL 1840

Natural Range: Rio Orinoco and Rio Negro basins.
Size: 8" (20 cm) TL.
Water Chemistry: Tropical; slightly soft and acidic.
Behavior: Generally peaceful.
Dietary Requirements: Small live foods and all types of prepared foods.

Remarks: The care and husbandry of *M. insignis* is identical to that of *M. festivus*.

Metriaclima callainos / Cobalt Blue Zebra

STAUFFER, BOWERS, KELLOGG, & MCKAYE 1997

Natural Range: Lake Malawi.
Size: 5" (12 cm) TL.
Water Chemistry: Tropical; hard and alkaline.
Behavior: Moderately aggressive.
Dietary Requirements: Algae, aufwuchs, and prepared foods high in plant matter.

Remarks: Another highly variable species is the relatively new *M. callainos*. While many specimens are deep cobalt bluish, there also is a white form that is sometimes referred to as the "Platinum" Zebra. Regardless, their care in aquariums is identical to others in the genus, with no special exceptions.

Mesonauta festivus

Mesonauta festivus

Mesonauta insignis

Mesonauta insignis note red eye

Metriaclima callainos pearl var.

Metriaclima callainos

Metriaclima greshakei / Ice Blue Zebra

MEYER & FOERSTER 1984

Natural Range: Lake Malawi.

Size: 5" (12 cm) TL.

Water Chemistry: Tropical; hard and alkaline.

Behavior: Moderately aggressive.

Dietary Requirements: Algae, aufwuchs, and prepared foods high in plant matter.

Remarks: Konings reports that breeding males are very territorial and, in nature, will defend a cave excavated between rocks. More than likely, this is common in the aquarium as well. Their care in aquariums is identical to others in the genus, with no special exceptions.

Metriaclima mbenjii

STAUFFER, BOWERS, KELLOGG, & MCKAYE 1997

Natural Range: Lake Malawi.

Size: 5" (12 cm) TL.

Water Chemistry: Tropical; hard and alkaline.

Behavior: Moderately aggressive.

Dietary Requirements: Algae, aufwuchs, and prepared foods high in plant matter.

Remarks: Probably the most notable attribute of this species is its brilliant color. The care of this species in aquariums is identical to that of others in the genus, with no special exceptions.

Metriaclima zebra / Malawi Zebra

BOULENGER 1899

Natural Range: Lake Malawi.

Size: 5" (12 cm) TL.

Water Chemistry: Tropical; hard and alkaline.

Behavior: Moderately aggressive.

Dietary Requirements: Algae, aufwuchs, and prepared foods high in plant matter.

Remarks: Malawi Zebras are often referred to as the "original" mbuna. Many years ago, when we first saw shipments of this species, they were mixed with many other mbuna from various regions. At that time, they were all lumped into one genus (*Pseudotropheus*) and a single species (*zebra*). Today, after tireless efforts by several notable ichthyologists, we have split this genus into many genera with many more species. Regardless, their care in aquariums is identical to others in the genus, with no special exceptions.

Metriaclima greshakei OB var.

Metriaclima greshakei

Metriaclima mbenjii

Pseudotropheus williamsi for comparison

Metriaclima zebra common var.

Metriaclima zebra OB var.

479

Mikrogeophagus ramirezi / Blue Ram

MYERS & HARRY 1948

Natural Range: Colombia and Venezuela.
Size: 3" (7.5 cm) TL.
Water Chemistry: Tropical; slightly soft and acidic.
Behavior: Generally peaceful.
Dietary Requirements: Small live and all types of prepared foods.

Remarks: Perhaps the most popular dwarf cichlid next to *Apistogramma cacatuoides*, *M. ramirezi* is a colorful and peaceful resident for the community aquarium. They are very easy to care for, and hobbyists have several forms to choose from. There are wild-collected specimens, long-finned specimens, and even gold-colored ones, too. Provide them with plenty of places to seek shelter from more active and boisterous species in the aquarium. Also, many hobbyists keep them with discus or angelfishes.

Myaka myaka

TREWAVAS 1972

Natural Range: Western Cameroon.
Size: 4" (10 cm) TL.
Water Chemistry: Tropical; soft and slightly acidic or neutral is best.
Behavior: Moderately aggressive.
Dietary Requirements: Small live insects and all types of prepared foods.

Remarks: This easy-to-keep species is, unfortunately, impossible to obtain. It is mentioned herein because a few importers in North America are beginning to import this species in small numbers, and since they breed readily in captivity, they should be on the scene in great numbers relatively soon. They are an interesting species with big clear eyes and an awkwardly upturned mouth. They use this mouth to feed on phytoplankton and insects off the surface.

Nandopsis beani

JORDAN 1888

Natural Range: Pacific slope of Mexico.
Size: 12" (30 cm) TL.
Water Chemistry: Tropical; slightly alkaline with moderate hardness.
Behavior: Aggressive.
Dietary Requirements: All types of meaty and prepared foods.

Remarks: This large cichlid is highly sought-after in the aquarium trade. They are not outrageously colorful, but their pleasing pattern of eight to nine blotches arranged along their flanks makes them intriguing and different. They are often kept in large cichlid community aquariums, with varying degrees of success.

Mikrogeophagus ramirezi normal var.

Mikrogeophagus ramirezi gold var.

Myaka myaka

Myaka myaka

Nandopsis beani juvenile

Nandopsis beani adult male

481

Nandopsis grammodes

TAYLOR & MILLER 1980

Natural Range: Southern Mexico.
Size: 12" (30 cm) TL.
Water Chemistry: Tropical; slightly alkaline with moderate hardness.
Behavior: Aggressive.
Dietary Requirements: Small live foods and all types of prepared foods.

Remarks: This beautiful and robust cichlid has enjoyed popularity for many years among those hobbyists interested in Central American cichlids. They can be rather temperamental, and adults often need to be kept alone. Many hobbyists eventually attempt to breed these fish, and in doing so, inadvertently lose the female to outright aggression from the males. To avoid this, use the incomplete divider method or a complete divider method of spawning.

Nandopsis haitiensis / Black Nasty

TEE-VAN 1935

Natural Range: Dominican Republic and Haiti.
Size: 12" (30 cm) TL.
Water Chemistry: Tropical; slightly alkaline with moderate hardness.
Behavior: Aggressive.
Dietary Requirements: Small live foods and all types of prepared foods.

Remarks: This large and popular cichlid has only recently earned the name of "Black Nasty." Such a name is unique, to say the least. Apparently, this fish is very temperamental and outrageously aggressive to tankmates. The author (BMS) has observed this fish living in large communities of Central American cichlids without much aggression. Of course, the addition of a female changes the tone quite a bit, especially if they are set up for spawning.

Nandopsis istlanum

JORDAN & SNYDER 1899

Natural Range: Mexico.
Size: 12" (30 cm) TL.
Water Chemistry: Tropical; slightly alkaline with moderate hardness.
Behavior: Aggressive.
Dietary Requirements: Small live foods and all types of prepared foods.

Remarks: It is rare for any mature specimen of this species to be ugly; they are some of the most underestimated cichlids out there. Of course, their popularity seems to be on a roller coaster ride, with its ups and downs alternating every few years. They breed very easily when provided with good water, plenty of space, and a good diet.

Nandopsis grammodes

Nandopsis grammodes

Nandopsis haitiensis female with fry

Nandopsis haitiensis male

Nandopsis istlanum male

Nandopsis istlanum male

Nandopsis ramsdeni

FOWLER 1938

Natural Range: Cuba.
Size: 14" (35 cm) TL.
Water Chemistry: Tropical; slightly alkaline with moderate hardness.
Behavior: Aggressive.
Dietary Requirements: Small live foods and all types of prepared foods.

Remarks: A rare cichlid, to say the least. Close friend and colleague Jeff Rapps has kept several pairs of this species for some time. He reports that they are very aggressive with each other, and therefore, he must use the complete divider method in order to keep them from killing each other. Otherwise, their care and husbandry in aquariums is the same as other *Nandopsis* species.

Nandopsis salvini / Salvini

GUENTHER 1862

Natural Range: Belize, Guatemala, and Mexico.
Size: 6" (15 cm) TL.
Water Chemistry: Tropical; slightly alkaline with moderate hardness.
Behavior: Aggressive.
Dietary Requirements: Small live foods and all types of prepared foods.

Remarks: Of all the *Nandopsis* out there, none are close in coloration to the brilliance of *N. salvini*. They have all the tenacity of larger congeners at less than half the size, though, and are only recommended for the hobbyist who is planning to keep them in a tank with larger, aggressive cichlids. These fish are even more beautiful—and aggressive—when they are in spawning dress.

Nandopsis tetracanthus / Cuban Cichlid

VALENCIENNES 1831

Natural Range: Cuba.
Size: 14" (35 cm) TL.
Water Chemistry: Tropical; slightly alkaline with moderate hardness.
Behavior: Aggressive.
Dietary Requirements: Small live foods and all types of prepared foods.

Remarks: Another cichlid endemic to Cuba, *N. tetracanthus* is considerably more available than *N. ramsdeni*. They are a large-growing species that can be very aggressive should a pair set up to spawn. Pairs are best kept in a species-specific aquarium.

Nandopsis ramsdeni

Nandopsis ramsdeni adult male

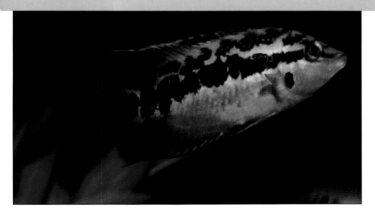

Nandopsis salvini

Nandopsis salvini

Nandopsis tetracanthus

Nandopsis tetracanthus

Nannacara adoketa

KULLANDER & PRADA-PEDREROS 1993

Natural Range: Rio Negro, Brazil.
Size: 5" (12 cm) TL.
Water Chemistry: Tropical; slightly soft and acidic.
Behavior: Generally peaceful.
Dietary Requirements: Small live foods and all types of prepared foods.

Remarks: While not overly colorful, *N. adoketa* are a nice addition to the community aquarium if you can find them. They are not common but are included herein since they make such great additions to peaceful cichlid aquariums.

Nannacara anomala

REGAN 1905

Natural Range: Western Guyana region.
Size: 3" (7.5 cm) TL.
Water Chemistry: Tropical; slightly soft and acidic.
Behavior: Generally peaceful.
Dietary Requirements: Small live foods and all types of prepared foods.

Remarks: The more popular species within *Nannacara* is this one, *N. anomala*. Just as others in the genus, this species does well in cichlid community aquariums. Keep an eye on their behavior because pairs may become outwardly aggressive towards tankmates.

Nanochromis dimidiatus

PELLEGRIN 1900

Natural Range: Congo.
Size: 2.5" (7 cm) TL.
Water Chemistry: Tropical; soft and acidic.
Behavior: Moderately aggressive with congeners.
Dietary Requirements: Small live foods and all types of prepared foods.

Remarks: This is one of the smallest members of the genus at only 2.5" (7 cm) in total length. They are a moderately aggressive species that can be seen chasing one another around their aquarium. Rarely, however, is there any real damage. Keep in a community aquarium with barbs, or other active yet peaceful species, as dithers.

Nannacara adoketa

Nannacara adoketa

Nannacara anomala

Nannacara anomala profile

Nanochromis dimidiatus

Nanochromis dimidiatus

Nanochromis parilus

ROBERTS & STEWART 1976

Natural Range: Congo.
Size: 4" (10 cm) TL.
Water Chemistry: Tropical; soft and acidic.
Behavior: Moderately aggressive with congeners.
Dietary Requirements: Small live foods and all types of prepared foods.

Remarks: Unlike other members of *Nanochromis*, *N. parilus* seems to be tolerant of higher pH levels. They do best, however, at a lower pH of around neutral. Otherwise, their care and husbandry is identical to others in the genus.

Nanochromis transvestitus

STWERT & ROBERTS 1984

Natural Range: Congo.
Size: 2" (5 cm) TL; may grow slightly larger.
Water Chemistry: Tropical; soft and acidic.
Behavior: Moderately aggressive.
Dietary Requirements: Small live foods and all types of prepared foods.

Remarks: This is probably the smallest of the genus (Lamboj 2004). Otherwise, their care is identical to the previous species profiled.

Neolamprologus brevis

BOULENGER 1899

Natural Range: Lake Tanganyika.
Size: 2" (5 cm) TL.
Water Chemistry: Tropical; hard and alkaline.
Behavior: Moderately aggressive.
Dietary Requirements: Small live foods and all types of prepared foods.

Remarks: These little shell-dwellers are fascinating to observe in the home aquarium. For the best show, keep two or three males with a small harem of females in a 20-gallon long aquarium. Provide a shell for each fish and watch the males battle harmlessly over which one gets more of the shells. Obviously, the male that gets more shells gets more of the females, and thus is able to reproduce and spread his genes on to future generations.

Nanochromis parilus male

Nanochromis parilus female

Nanochromis transvestitus

Nanochromis transvestitus

Neolamprologus brevis

Neolamprologus brevis

Neolamprologus brichardi / Brichardi

POLL 1974

Natural Range: Lake Tanganyika.
Size: 5" (12 cm) TL.
Water Chemistry: Tropical; hard and alkaline.
Behavior: Moderately aggressive.
Dietary Requirements: Small live foods and all types of prepared foods.

Remarks: One of the most famous fish to come from the lake, along with *Julidochromis* and *Tropheus*, *N. brichardi* was introduced to the market in 1971 and, although perhaps one of the easiest cichlids to breed in captivity, it is still a favorite wild-caught fish. Because of its qualities, this could be the fish used to introduce hobbyists to the world of African lake cichlids.

Neolamprologus buescheri

STAECK 1983

Natural Range: Lake Tanganyika.
Size: 5" (12 cm) TL.
Water Chemistry: Tropical; hard and alkaline.
Behavior: Moderately aggressive.
Dietary Requirements: Small live foods and all types of prepared foods.

Remarks: Mr. Buscher discovered this species during trips to the southern shores of Lake Tanganyika in August 1982 and in February 1984. They are a deep-water species that is, of course, difficult to bring to the surface alive because of their need for a slow decompression period. They are unmistakable, with their horizontal stripes, crescentic caudal fin, and a shape reminiscent of *N. furcifer*.

Neolamprologus caudopunctatus

POLL 1978

Natural Range: Lake Tanganyika.
Size: 4" (10 cm) TL.
Water Chemistry: Tropical; hard and alkaline.
Behavior: Moderately aggressive.
Dietary Requirements: Small live foods and all types of prepared foods.

Remarks: *L. caudopunctatus* is a midwater microorganism feeder that does very well in aquariums. Unfortunately, they are not very colorful, and are often overlooked as a bland and drab species. They live and breed in normal *Neolamprologus* species fashion.

Neolamprologus brichardi

Neolamprologus brichardi

Neolamprologus buescheri

Neolamprologus buescheri

Neolamprologus caudopunctatus

Neolamprologus caudopunctatus

491

Neolamprologus cylindricus

STAECK & SEEGERS 1986

Natural Range: Lake Tanganyika.
Size: 6" (15 cm) TL.
Water Chemistry: Tropical; hard and alkaline.
Behavior: Moderately aggressive.
Dietary Requirements: Small live foods and all types of prepared foods.

Remarks: Very closely related to *N. leleupi*, *N. cylindricus* is a long, torpedo-shaped species that does well in aquariums that contain other fishes of similar disposition. As with all types of *Neolamprologus*, rocks are the preferred decorating tools, and hard, alkaline water chemistry is preferred.

Neolamprologus falcicula

BRICHARD 1989

Natural Range: Lake Tanganyika.
Size: 5" (12 cm) TL.
Water Chemistry: Tropical; hard and alkaline.
Behavior: Moderately aggressive.
Dietary Requirements: Small live foods and all types of prepared foods.

Remarks: The entire body of *N. falcicula* (meaning a sickle from the shape of the caudal fin) is a drab beige color, including the unpaired fins, which are devoid of any markings. Due to its lackluster appearance, this species is only exported rarely, but is a favorite among those who collect Tanganyikan cichlids.

Neolamprologus fasciatus

BOULENGER 1898

Natural Range: Lake Tanganyika.
Size: 4" (10 cm) TL; may grow slightly larger.
Water Chemistry: Tropical; hard and alkaline.
Behavior: Moderately aggressive.
Dietary Requirements: Small live foods and all types of prepared foods.

Remarks: Not rare in the south, much rarer in the northern basin, and never seen on the northeastern coast in Burundi, *N. fasciatus* has the same adaptations as *Altolamprologus compressiceps* with the way it feeds and in its diet. The body is streamlined and cylindrical, although the fish is normally never seen darting here and there, as one would expect with such anatomy (Brichard 1989).

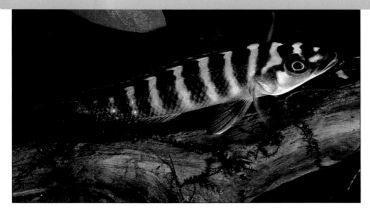

Neolamprologus cylindricus

Neolamprologus cylindricus

Neolamprologus falcicula

Neolamprologus cygnus for comparison

Neolamprologus fasciatus juvenile

Neolamprologus fasciatus adult

493

Neolamprologus furcifer / Vampire Cichlid

BOULENGER 1898

Natural Range: Lake Tanganyika.
Size: 6" (15 cm) TL.
Water Chemistry: Tropical; hard and alkaline.
Behavior: Moderately aggressive.
Dietary Requirements: Small live foods and all types of prepared foods.

Remarks: The name *furcifer* is Latin for "carrying a fork." This species carries a forked tail and is therefore aptly named *Neolamprologus furcifer*. They are a cave-dwelling cichlid that is quite spooky looking, with a sharply-pointed snout and big round eyes. They often are referred to as the "Vampire Cichlid" because of their unwillingness to come out into open water during daylight. Of course, once they understand that feeding usually takes place with the aquarium's lights on, they often change their habits.

Neolamprologus leleupi / Leleupi

POLL 1956

Natural Range: Lake Tanganyika.
Size: 6" (15 cm) TL.
Water Chemistry: Tropical; hard and alkaline.
Behavior: Moderately aggressive.
Dietary Requirements: Small live foods and all types of prepared foods.
Remarks: The males of this species exhibit a unique coloration during spawning. Their lips appear dark, almost black, and they look as if they have lipstick on. *N. leleupi* is one of the most famous cichlids to have ever been exported from the lake. The first specimens were exported from Burundi back in 1961, although they were collected from the northwestern shore. The entire body of this species, including the fins, is bright yellow and appears as if it has been dipped in tempera. Their care and husbandry in aquariums is of the standard fashion of the group.

Neolamprologus longior

POLL 1948

Natural Range: Lake Tanganyika.
Size: 5" (12 cm) TL.
Water Chemistry: Tropical; hard and alkaline.
Behavior: Moderately aggressive.
Dietary Requirements: Small live foods and all types of prepared foods.

Remarks: This species was described by a single specimen caught by Max Poll. From its morphology, one would believe that it belongs to the same line as *N. caudopunctatus* (Brichard 1989).

Neolamprologus furcifer juvenile

Neolamprologus furcifer adult

Neolamprologus leleupi juvenile

Neolamprologus leleupi adult

Neolamprologus longior

Neolamprologus leleopi

Neolamprologus mustax

POLL 1978

Natural Range: Lake Tanganyika.
Size: 6" (15 cm) TL.
Water Chemistry: Tropical; hard and alkaline.
Behavior: Moderately aggressive.
Dietary Requirements: Small live foods and all types of prepared foods.

Remarks: A typical rubble-dweller like so many others of the genus, *N. mustax* is found only on the southern shores of the lake, especially in Cameroon Bay (Brichard 1989). The care and husbandry of this species is in the typical fashion of the genus.

Neolamprologus niger / Black Cichlid

POLL 1956

Natural Range: Lake Tanganyika.
Size: 4" (10 cm) TL.
Water Chemistry: Tropical; hard and alkaline.
Behavior: Moderately aggressive.
Dietary Requirements: Small live foods and all types of prepared foods.

Remarks: Apparently *N. niger* belongs to the same species group as *N. leleupi*. It lives on the northwestern shores of the lake and is not found in the southern half (Brichard 1989).

Neolamprologus olivaceous

BRICHARD 1989

Natural Range: Lake Tanganyika.
Size: 4" (10 cm) TL.
Water Chemistry: Tropical; hard and alkaline.
Behavior: Moderately aggressive.
Dietary Requirements: Small live foods and all types of prepared foods.

Remarks: Endemic to the Bay of Luhanga, *N. olivaceous* was once thought to be synonymous with *N. brichardi*. Their care and husbandry are identical to that complex of species.

Neolamprologus mustax

Neolamprologus mustax

Neolamprologus niger

Neolamprologus nigriventris for comparison

Neolamprologus olivaceous

Neolamprologus marunguensis a similiar species

Neolamprologus pulcher / Daffodil Cichlid

TREWAVAS & POLL 1952

Natural Range: Lake Tanganyika.
Size: 6" (15 cm) TL.
Water Chemistry: Tropical; hard and alkaline.
Behavior: Moderately aggressive.
Dietary Requirements: Small live foods and all types of prepared foods.

Remarks: This species was at first considered to be a subspecies of *N. savoryi*, but was set apart as a distinct species by Max Poll. The fish is known to be a rock dweller and is probably microphagus like *N. brichardi*, to which it seems to be closely related (Brichard 1989).

Neolamprologus savoryi

POLL 1949

Natural Range: Lake Tanganyika.
Size: 6" (15 cm) TL.
Water Chemistry: Tropical; hard and alkaline.
Behavior: Moderately aggressive.
Dietary Requirements: Small live foods and all types of prepared foods.

Remarks: Not at all a bad looking fish, *N. savoryi* has a nasty temper that makes it a poor aquarium fish unless it is housed with larger fishes (Brichard 1989). Their color is a dark-blue to black body with darker bands. The fins are elongated into filaments—they are not as long, however, as those of *N. brichardi*.

Neolamprologus sexfasciatus / Six-bar Cichlid

TREWAVAS & POLL 1952

Natural Range: Lake Tanganyika.
Size: 8" (20 cm) TL.
Water Chemistry: Tropical; hard and alkaline.
Behavior: Moderately aggressive.
Dietary Requirements: Small live foods and all types of prepared foods.

Remarks: *N. sexfasciatus* is, without a doubt, one of the most spectacular species of cichlid in Lake Tanganyika. It is distinguished from its close relatives by the fact that it has six dark bands, whereas *N. tretocephalus* has only five bands. The two species have peculiar flat molar teeth on the center and rear pharyngeal bone, which has a different shape in *N. tretocephalus*—and an unusual one at that. Their care and husbandry in aquariums is identical to that of others in the genus.

498

Neolamprologus pulcher

Neolamprologus pulcher note yellow around eye

Neolamprologus savoryi

Neolamprologus savoryi

Neolamprologus sexfasciatus normal var.

Neolamprologus sexfasciatus gold var.

Neolamprologus tetracanthus

BOULENGER 1899

Natural Range: Lake Tanganyika.
Size: 8" (20 cm) TL.
Water Chemistry: Tropical; hard and alkaline.
Behavior: Moderately aggressive.
Dietary Requirements: Small live foods and all types of prepared foods.

Remarks: This is one of the least specialized forms of *Neolamprologus*, found mainly on the sandy bottom all around the lake without any noticeable local races. Of all the sand-dwelling species in the lake, this species is one of the better-looking ones, and it is popular with hobbyists. They are prolific spawners, and it is not uncommon for hobbyists to raise many more fry than they will ever be able to give away or sell back to their local pet shop.

Neolamprologus toae

POLL 1949

Natural Range: Lake Tanganyika.
Size: 6" (15 cm) TL.
Water Chemistry: Tropical; hard and alkaline.
Behavior: Moderately aggressive.
Dietary Requirements: Small live foods and all types of prepared foods.

Remarks: On the western coast of the lake, *L. toae* is common all the way south to Kalemie. They are very easy to care for in aquariums, and their care and husbandry are identical to others of the genus.

Neolamprologus tretocephalus / Five-bar Cichlid

BOULENGER 1899

Natural Range: Lake Tanganyika.
Size: 6" (15 cm) TL.
Water Chemistry: Tropical; hard and alkaline.
Behavior: Moderately aggressive.
Dietary Requirements: Small live foods and all types of prepared foods.

Remarks: Five-bar Cichlids are very popular due to their unique bluish coloration. Adult males in good condition are sometimes purple along the edges of their fins. Their care and husbandry in aquariums are similar to other species in the genus.

Neolamprologus tetracanthus female

Neolamprologus tetracanthus male

Neolamprologus toae juvenile

Neolamprologus toae adult

Neolamprologus tretacephalus

Neolamprologus tretacephalus

Nimbochromis linni

BURGESS & AXELROD 1975

Natural Range: Lake Malawi.
Size: 12" (30 cm) TL.
Water Chemistry: Tropical; hard and alkaline.
Behavior: Moderately aggressive.
Dietary Requirements: Small live foods and all types of prepared foods.

Remarks: *N. linni* is a piscivore that ambushes its prey in a peculiar manner. It rests its chin on a rock and watches the juvenile fishes that are hiding in cracks and crevices just over the edge of this rock. Waiting patiently, the fish may sit there for many minutes before one of the juveniles ventures out a little too far. When this happens, *N. linni* rapidly extends its highly protrusible mouth and sucks up the juvenile fish (Konings 1990). Occasionally offer this species some small feeder fishes, so as not to lose this highly adaptive and natural behavior.

Nimbochromis livingstoni / Livingstoni

GUENTHER 1893

Natural Range: Lake Malawi.
Size: 10" (25 cm) TL.
Water Chemistry: Tropical; hard and alkaline.
Behavior: Moderately aggressive.
Dietary Requirements: Small live foods and all types of prepared foods.

Remarks: *N. livingstoni* hunts its food in an interesting way. The fish is a highly predatory piscivore, just like others in the genus. It will approach a sandy area next to a rock where smaller fishes normally travel, and actually lie flat on its side, motionless. When a small fish swims over *N. livingstoni*'s head, it instantly grabs it with a quick sideways stroke of the head and mouth.

Nimbochromis polystigma

REGAN 1922

Natural Range: Lake Malawi.
Size: 8" (20 cm) TL; possibly larger.
Water Chemistry: Tropical; hard and alkaline.
Behavior: Moderately aggressive.
Dietary Requirements: Small live foods and all types of prepared foods.

Remarks: *N. polystigma* is a predator that hunts its prey in several ways. Sometimes, single specimens can be observed actually chasing small fishes throughout weed beds, but they have also been observed hunting in a similar fashion to *N. livingstoni*. Regardless, they are an effective predator, and such efficiency does not end in the wild. Captive specimens will make short work of fishes they can swallow in your aquarium, too.

Nimbochromis linni

Nimbochromis linni profile

Nimbochromis livingstoni

Nimbochromis livingstoni

Nimbochromis polystigma

Nimbochromis linni (top) and *N. polystgma* (bottom)

503

Nimbochromis venustus

BOULENGER 1908
Natural Range: Lake Malawi.
Size: 8" (20 cm) TL.
Water Chemistry: Tropical; hard and alkaline.
Behavior: Moderately aggressive.
Dietary Requirements: Small live foods and all types of prepared foods.

Remarks: *N. venustus* is commonly encountered over sandy areas where they hunt small invertebrates and fishes by ambushing them. As with many other Rift Lake cichlids, juveniles and subadults are found in the rocky biotope from about 5 meters in depth to around 20 meters in depth. Their care in aquariums is identical to others in the genus, with no special exceptions.

Ophthalmotilapia boops

BOULENGER 1901
Natural Range: Lake Tanganyika.
Size: 6" (15 cm) TL.
Water Chemistry: Tropical; hard and alkaline.
Behavior: Moderately aggressive towards conspecifics.
Dietary Requirements: Small live foods and all types of prepared foods high in plant matter.

Remarks: All species within *Ophthalmotilapia* are nearly identical regarding their care and husbandry in aquariums. While they are not large cichlids, they do need plenty of room to swim. They seem to prefer living over open substrate, so a heavily decorated aquarium may not make them comfortable. Males excavate huge spawning nests in the sand or sometimes on a large, free-standing boulder.

Ophthalmotilapia nasuta

POLL & MATTHES 1962
Natural Range: Lake Tanganyika.
Size: 8" (20 cm) TL.
Water Chemistry: Tropical; hard and alkaline.
Behavior: Moderately aggressive towards conspecifics.
Dietary Requirements: Small live foods and all types of prepared foods high in plant matter.

Remarks: Three races are commonly found in the hobby: Magara race, west coast northern basin race, |and the Chipimbi southern race. Each one is slightly different in color and form. Their care and husbandry in aquariums is identical to that of others of the genus.

Nimbochromis venustus adult male

Nimbochromis venustuss adult male in breeding dress

Ophthalmotilapia boops

Ophthalmotilapia sp.

Ophthalmotilapia nasuta

Ophthalmotilapia nasuta

Ophthalmotilapia ventralis

BOULENGER 1898

Natural Range: Lake Tanganyika.
Size: 6" (15 cm) TL.
Water Chemistry: Tropical; hard and alkaline.
Behavior: Moderately aggressive towards conspecifics.
Dietary Requirements: Small live foods and all types of prepared foods high in plant matter.

Remarks: Previously, two distinct subspecies were recognized—*O. ventralis ventralis* and *O. ventralis heterodontus*. Their validity is still questioned as of this writing, but many ichthyologists consider them one and the same. Regardless of their taxonomic standing, they have the same requirements in the aquarium.

Oreochromis mossambicus

PETERS 1852

Natural Range: Lower Zambezi and Shire River system; widely introduced elsewhere.
Size: 12" (30 cm) TL.
Water Chemistry: Tropical; freshwater and brackish; otherwise not critical.
Behavior: Moderately aggressive.
Dietary Requirements: Not picky; will consume almost anything edible, but has a preference for algae.

Remarks: Unfortunately, this species has been widely introduced in many parts of the world where it should not have been (this is actually true for many *Tilapia* species). They are a robust species that does exceedingly well in a variety of habitats and water conditions. Provide a large aquarium, peaceful companions, and plenty of food, and your *O. mossambicus* may live for many years,

Oreochromis niloticus

LINNAEUS 1758

Natural Range: Widely distributed over western Africa; introduced elsewhere.
Size: ~12" (30 cm) TL.
Water Chemistry: Tropical; otherwise not critical.
Behavior: Moderately aggressive.
Dietary Requirements: Feeds mainly on algae and detritus, but will readily accept nearly all prepared foods.

Remarks: There are currently seven subspecies described under *Oreochromis niloticus*. All of these are very easy to care for in the aquarium and are tolerant of varying water conditions. They are best kept in large tanks with strong filtration. Just as with other large cichlids, they have a tendency to foul their water very quickly. Feed small amounts of food frequently throughout the day for the best results.

Ophthalmotilapia ventralis

Ophthalmotilapia ventralis

Oreochromis mossambicus

Oreochromis mossambicus

Oreochromis niloticus

Oreochromis niloticus

Oreochromis tanganicae

GUENTHER 1894

Natural Range: Lake Tanganyika; introduced elsewhere.
Size: 16" (40 cm) TL.
Water Chemistry: Tropical; hard and alkaline.
Behavior: Moderately aggressive.
Dietary Requirements: Detritus and phytoplankton.

Remarks: As with other species of the genus, this fish needs a very large aquarium, and males can become aggressive with each other—especially in the presence of females. Other fishes are generally ignored

Otopharynx heterodon

TREWAVAS 1935

Natural Range: Lake Malawi.
Size: 6" (15 cm) TL.
Water Chemistry: Tropical; hard and alkaline.
Behavior: Moderately aggressive.
Dietary Requirements: Small live foods and all types of prepared foods.

Remarks: *O. heterodon* is a rather small cichlid that will not usually be confused with others. Juveniles exhibit three small blotches along the flanks. Additionally, this species is more deep-bodied than others of the genus. They do well in most aquariums that are properly set up to house them.

Otopharynx lithobates

OLIVER 1989

Natural Range: Lake Malawi.
Size: 6" (15 cm) TL.
Water Chemistry: Tropical; hard and alkaline.
Behavior: Moderately aggressive.
Dietary Requirements: Small live foods and all types of prepared foods.

Remarks: It might come as a surprise to many hobbyists already familiar with the outstanding appearance of this species that it is in fact a cave dweller. Rarely are *O. lithobates* in breeding dress observed outside their secluded hideaways. They are a micropredator of fish fry and small invertebrates, and their diet in captivity should include some plant matter. Males are intolerant of one another during spawning.

Oreochromis tanganicae juvenile

Oreochromis tanganicae adult

Otopharynx heterodon female

Otopharynx heterodon male

Otopharynx lithobates female

Otopharynx lithobates male

Parachromis dovii / Wolf Cichlid

GUENTHER 1864

Natural Range: Costa Rica, Honduras, and Nicaragua.
Size: 20" (50 cm) TL.
Water Chemistry: Tropical; slightly alkaline with moderate hardness.
Behavior: Very aggressive.
Dietary Requirements: All types of meaty and live foods.

Remarks: The Wolf Cichlid is one of the giant guapotes. They can attain such a large size that they can make a meal of many other fishes. Watch this species in cichlid community tanks. If a pair forms, you will have a bad situation on your hands, since the pair will likely systematically remove each fish from the tank. This species is best kept in a species-specific aquarium.

Parachromis friedrichsthalii / Monarch Cichlid

HECKEL 1840

Natural Range: Atlantic slope of Mexico to Belize (yellow morph is found in Guatemala).
Size: 12" (30 cm) TL.
Water Chemistry: Tropical; slightly alkaline with moderate hardness.
Behavior: Aggressive.
Dietary Requirements: All types of meaty and prepared foods.

Remarks: This species is both lacustrine (lake inhabiting) and riverine (river inhabiting) in nature, where it prefers slower-moving waters. In aquariums, it is imperative that *P. friedrichsthalii* is given a large aquarium with good filtration and moderate current. They can be kept in a cichlid community tank with good results, as long as their cohabitants are of equal size and aggression.

Parachromis managuensis / Jaguar Cichlid

GUENTHER 1867

Natural Range: Costa Rica, El Salvador, southern Mexico, and Nicaragua
Size: 18" (45 cm) TL.
Water Chemistry: Tropical; slightly alkaline with moderate hardness.
Behavior: Very aggressive.
Dietary Requirements: All types of meaty and prepared foods.

Remarks: The Jaguar Cichlid is popular with hobbyists, who inadvertently purchase this species without knowing what they are in for down the road. This species needs a huge aquarium and plenty of food. Good-quality filtration is essential, since they are susceptible to head-and-lateral-line erosion.

Parachromis dovii

Parachromis dovii

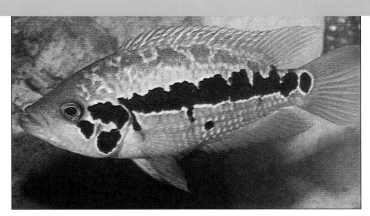

Parachromis friedrichsthalii

Parachromis friedrichsthalii

Parachromis managuensis gold var.

Parachromis managuensis

Parachromis motaguensis

GUENTHER 1867

Natural Range: Guatemala and Honduras.
Size: 12" (30 cm) TL.
Water Chemistry: Tropical; slightly alkaline with moderate hardness.
Behavior: Aggressive.
Dietary Requirements: All types of meaty and prepared foods.

Remarks: The care and husbandry of *P. motaguensis* is identical to that of *P. managuensis*, except this species remains slightly smaller. Perhaps they are a better choice for those who want to add a guapote to their collection.

Paracyprichromis nigripinnis

BOULENGER 1901

Natural Range: Lake Tanganyika.
Size: 4" (10 cm) TL; possibly larger in long-term captives.
Water Chemistry: Tropical; hard and alkaline.
Behavior: Generally peaceful.
Dietary Requirements: Small live foods and all types of prepared foods.

Remarks: This interesting species should be maintained in groups. Males can be quarrelsome amongst one another, but overall, *P. nigripinnis* is a beautiful and peaceful species that does well in large aquariums with other peaceful tankmates.

Parananochromis longirostris

BOULENGER 1903

Natural Range: Cameroon and Gabon.
Size: 6" (15 cm) TL; maybe slightly larger.
Water Chemistry: Tropical; slightly acidic and soft conditions preferred.
Behavior: Moderately aggressive.
Dietary Requirements: Small live foods and all types of prepared foods.

Remarks: Dr. Anton Lamboj, a well-respected ichthyologist and authority on West African fishes, has observed this species as a cave spawner, not a mouthbrooder (as previously thought). Otherwise, their care and husbandry in aquariums is reported to be easy and trouble-free as long as extremes are avoided.

Parachromis motaguensis

Parachromis motaguensis

Paracyprichromis nigripinnis mouthbrooding female

Paracyprichromis nigripinnis

Parananochromis longirostris

Parananochromis longirostris

Paraneetroplus bulleri

REGAN 1905

Natural Range: Southern Mexico.
Size: 10" (25 cm) TL, usually smaller.
Water Chemistry: Tropical; slightly alkaline with moderate hardness.
Behavior: Generally peaceful, but males may bully smaller fishes.
Dietary Requirements: All types of prepared foods; supplement with large amounts of plant material.

Remarks: This large species of Central American cichlid needs a big tank with good filtration and circulation. They feed heavily on algae and aufwuchs in nature and should have their diets supplemented with a plant-based food regularly.

Paratilapia polleni

BLEEKER 1868

Natural Range: Madagascar.
Size: 10" (25 cm) TL.
Water Chemistry: Tropical; neutral with moderate hardness.
Behavior: Moderately aggressive.
Dietary Requirements: Small live foods and all types of prepared foods.

Remarks: *Paratilapia polleni* is probably still the most popular of all the Malagasy cichlids. Often, they are considered the Oscar of Madagascar due to their personality and willingness to surface when you approach their aquarium. This is a good species for those who are new to cichlids of that region.

Paretroplus damii

BLEEKER 1868

Natural Range: Madagascar.
Size: 6" (15 cm) TL.
Water Chemistry: Tropical; prefers neutral pH with moderate hardness.
Behavior: Moderately aggressive towards congeners.
Dietary Requirements: Accepts all types of prepared foods, as well as small live and frozen foods.

Remarks: *Paretroplus damii* is native to the northwestern region of Madagascar. They do well in aquariums that contain other large, peaceful fishes, but during spawning, males may become intolerant of each other. Large adults are best kept in very large aquariums with excellent water quality.

Paraneetroplus bulleri

Paraneetroplus bulleri

Paratilapia polleni

Paratilapia polleni

Paretroplus damii juvenile

Paretroplus damii adult

Paretroplus kieneri

ARNOULT 1960

Natural Range: Madagascar.
Size: 6" (15 cm) TL.
Water Chemistry: Tropical; otherwise not critical.
Behavior: Moderately aggressive, especially towards other males.
Dietary Requirements: Small live and prepared foods are readily accepted.

Remarks: Calico in color, *P. kieneri* is distinctive in appearance. They act in a similar fashion as others of the genus, and their care and husbandry are similar as well. Be sure to place these fish in an aquarium that has a lot of visual barriers, especially if more than one male is present.

Paretroplus maculatus

KIENER & MAUGE 1966

Natural Range: Northwestern Madagascar (Kamoro area).
Size: 6" (15 cm) TL; may grow slightly larger in aquariums.
Water Chemistry: Tropical; neutral to slightly acidic with moderate hardness.
Behavior: Moderately aggressive; males intolerant of each other.
Dietary Requirements: Omnivorous; feed equal amounts of plant and animal matter.

Remarks: *P. maculatus* is critically endangered. They will not be able to make a comeback unless major changes are made to policies concerning the export of Madagascar's natural resources. Wild-collected specimens are growing increasingly rare, and hobbyists who have extra tank space are encouraged to keep these beautiful fish while they still have the chance.

Paretroplus menarambo

ALLGAYER 1996

Natural Range: Madagascar.
Size: 6" (15 cm) TL.
Water Chemistry: Tropical; prefers soft and acidic conditions, but avoid extremes.
Behavior: Moderately aggressive; males are intolerant of each other.
Dietary Requirements: Omnivorous; feed equal amounts of plant and animal matter.

Remarks: This damba may be more common than many of its cousins, but that doesn't mean that it is any safer from a conservation standpoint. Keeping a tankful of these brutes will be a rewarding experience. They are very interesting to observe, but keep in mind that mature males may battle terribly.

Paretroplus kieneri

Paretroplus kieneri

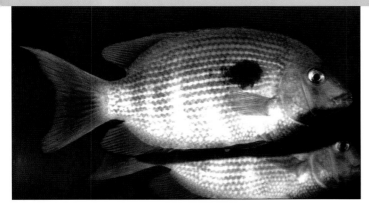

Paretroplus maculatus

Paretroplus maculatus

Paretroplus menarambo

Paretroplus menarambo profile

Paretroplus nourissati

ALLGAYER 1998

Natural Range: Madagascar.
Size: 5" (12 cm) TL.
Water Chemistry: Tropical; otherwise not critical; avoid extremes.
Behavior: Territorial; watch the males very closely.
Dietary Requirements: Omnivorous in captivity, but prefers meaty foods such as frozen bloodworms.

Remarks: This is not a species that you would want to lose due to hobbyist error. These fish, and all cichlids in the genus *Paretroplus*, are recommended only for those hobbyists who have some experience in keeping cichlids. Their behavior seems to change at the flip of a switch, and one day all will be fine, while the next day, you may have a very aggressive specimen to deal with. Large tanks with plenty of visual barriers in the form of bogwood and tough-leaved plants are recommended.

Pelmatochromis ansorgii

BOULENGER 1901

Natural Range: Ivory Coast, Ghana, Togo, Benin, Nigeria, and Gabon.
Size: 5" (12 cm) TL.
Water Chemistry: Tropical; neutral to slightly acid pH with moderate hardness.
Behavior: Generally peaceful, except during spawning.
Dietary Requirements: Small live foods and all types of prepared foods.

Remarks: *Thysochromis* are pair-bonding cichlids that do not seem to use small-entranced caves for breeding. They will often lay their eggs on overhanging broad leaves or stones, where the male will guard them until hatching. Both parents guard the free-swimming fry (Lamboj 2004).

Pelvicachromis humilis

BOULENGER 1916

Natural Range: Guinea, Sierra Leone, and the western regions of Liberia.
Size: 5" (12 cm) TL.
Water Chemistry: Tropical; slightly acidic with soft to moderate hardness.
Behavior: Generally peaceful, except when spawning; males may quarrel.
Dietary Requirements: Small live foods and all types of prepared foods.

Remarks: There is little factual data concerning this species in captivity. What is generally thought throughout the hobby is that they differ little from the care and husbandry of *P. pulcher*.

Paretroplus nourissati

Paretroplus nourissati profile

Pelmatochromis ansorgii

Pelmatochromis ansorgii

Pelvicachromis humilis

Pelvicachromis humilis

519

Pelvicachromis pulcher

BOULENGER 1901

Natural Range: Benin, Nigeria, and Cameroon.
Size: 5" (12 cm) TL.
Water Chemistry: Tropical; slightly acidic with soft to moderate hardness.
Behavior: Generally peaceful, except when spawning; males may quarrel.
Dietary Requirements: Small live foods and all types of prepared foods.

Remarks: Often referred to as "Kribs," these small cichlids make wonderful additions to the community aquarium that houses other peaceful fishes. They may become considerably territorial when brooding, but otherwise are generally harmless. Of course, don't keep them with small fishes that they could easily harass or make a meal out of, because in the end, they're still cichlids.

Pelvicachromis rubrolabiatus

LAMBOJ 2004

Natural Range: The Kolente region of Guinea.
Size: 4" (10 cm) TL.
Water Chemistry: Tropical; slightly acidic with soft to moderate hardness.
Behavior: Generally peaceful, except when spawning; males may quarrel.
Dietary Requirements: Small live foods and all types of prepared foods.

Remarks: For years, this undescribed cichlid has been referred to as *Pelvicachromis* sp. "Bandi 2," for the river (Bandi) that it is native to. Only this year (2004) has it finally been officially named by expert ichthyologist Anton Lamboj. The author (BMS) had the honor and privilege of meeting Dr. Lamboj during an American Cichlid Association's annual convention, where he gave several presentations on cichlids, and other fishes, from western Africa. The care and husbandry of this small cichlid is generally the same as for others of the genus.

Pelvicachromis suboccelatus

GUENTHER 1872

Natural Range: Gabon to the Congo.
Size: 3" (7.5 cm) TL.
Water Chemistry: Tropical; slightly acidic with soft to moderate hardness.
Behavior: Generally peaceful, except when spawning; males may quarrel.
Dietary Requirements: Small live foods and all types of prepared foods.

Remarks: This small species of *Pelvicachromis* is more slender-bodied and has a rounder head than others of the genus. Otherwise, their care and husbandry is remarkably similar.

Pelvicachromis pulcher

Pelvicachromis pulcher

Pelvicachromis rubrolabiatus

Pelvicachromis rubrolabiatus

Pelvicachromis suboccelatus

Pelvicachromis suboccelatus

521

Pelvicachromis taeniatus

BOULENGER 1901

Natural Range: Benin, Nigeria, and Cameroon.
Size: 4" (10 cm) TL.
Water Chemistry: Tropical; slightly acidic with soft to moderate hardness.
Behavior: Generally peaceful, except when spawning; males may quarrel.
Dietary Requirements: Small live foods and all types of prepared foods.

Remarks: Occasionally, this small cichlid is available through larger pet shops or those that specialize in cichlids from western Africa. They make great additions to heavily-planted aquariums, where they will take up residency in a sheltered area. As with others in the genus, be sure to watch them when spawning—they may get aggressive with tankmates.

Petenia splendida / Snook Cichlid

GUENTHER 1862

Natural Range: Belize, Guatemala, and Mexico (Atlantic slope).
Size: 20" (50 cm) TL; usually far smaller.
Water Chemistry: Tropical; slightly alkaline, with moderate hardness preferred.
Behavior: Aggressive; will eat small fishes.
Dietary Requirements: Live fishes, shrimps, and crawfishes; may be trained to accept non-living foods as well.

Remarks: The Snook Cichlid is available in two color variations: red and normal. Their red coloration ranges from a washed-out pinkish color to an intense red, while their normal coloration is a greenish-bronze background, with six to eight spots along their flanks. This species needs a very large aquarium to thrive in captivity. These are popular as a food fish in their native waters.

Petrochromis polydon

BOULENGER 1898

Natural Range: Lake Tanganyika.
Size: 10" (25 cm) TL.
Water Chemistry: Tropical; hard and alkaline conditions preferred.
Behavior: Very aggressive.
Dietary Requirements: Aufwuchs, algae, and any prepared foods that contain algae or plant matter.

Remarks: This species is only available in small numbers and is reported to be fiercely aggressive. Such behavior is odd, given that *P. polydon* is basically a vegetarian. Regardless, it is recommended that this species be given a large aquarium with only fishes of similar size and temperament.

Pelvicachromis taeniatus

Pelvicachromis taeniatus

Petenia splendida

Petenia splendida

Petrochromis polydon

Petrochromis polydon

Petrochromis trewavasae

BRICHARD 1989

Natural Range: Lake Tanganyika.
Size: 6" (15 cm) TL; may grow slightly larger.
Water Chemistry: Tropical; hard and alkaline conditions preferred.
Behavior: Very aggressive intraspecifically; avoid putting two males in the same aquarium.
Dietary Requirements: Aufwuchs, algae, and any prepared foods that contain algae or plant matter.

Remarks: *P. trewavasae* is one of the few species of the group that are actually suitable for the aquarium. Provided with a large tank and plenty of rockwork, this species will be long-lived and provide the hobbyist with years of enjoyment. Occasionally, spawning occurs, and the hobbyist will find small *P. trewavasae* swimming about the rockwork and décor of the aquarium.

Petrotilapia tridentiger

TREWAVAS 1935

Natural Range: Lake Malawi.
Size: 6" (15 cm) TL; possibly larger.
Water Chemistry: Tropical; hard and alkaline.
Behavior: Moderately aggressive; watch with other mbuna species.
Dietary Requirements: Algae, aufwuchs, and all types of prepared foods that are high in plant matter.

Remarks: Like all *Petrotilapia* species, *tridentigers* use their tricuspid teeth and large mouth to feed from the sediment-free biocover on rocks in their native habitat (Konings 1990). In aquariums, this species may become very aggressive during breeding, so be sure to keep a careful eye on them in cichlid community aquariums.

Placidochromis electra

BURGESS 1979

Natural Range: Lake Malawi.
Size: 6" (15 cm) TL.
Water Chemistry: Tropical; hard and alkaline.
Behavior: Moderately aggressive.
Dietary Requirements: Small live foods and all types of prepared foods.

Remarks: This is not usually a shy fish, and they are frequently found over sandy substrates. While they are routinely observed in shallow waters, *P. electra* was initially collected at a depth greater than 15 meters, giving rise to its common name of Deep Water Hap. Their care and husbandry in aquariums is similar to that of other *Haplochromis*-type fishes.

Petrochromis trewavasae adult

Petrochromis trewavasae juvenile

Petrotilapia tridentiger female

Petrotilapia tridentiger male

Placidochromis electra female

Placidochromis electra male

525

Placidochromis milomo / VC-10

OLIVER 1989

Natural Range: Lake Malawi.
Size: 10" (25 cm) TL.
Water Chemistry: Tropical; hard and alkaline.
Behavior: Moderately aggressive, especially toward conspecifics.
Dietary Requirements: Small live invertebrates and all types of prepared foods.

Remarks: The VC-10 is distributed lakewide. They exhibit a unique coloration that is quite difficult to confuse with any other species in the lake. Feeding consists of pressing their fleshy lips, which act as a plunger, over small holes or crevices that contain shrimps or other invertebrates and then sucking the animals out whole.

Plecodus straeleni

POLL 1948

Natural Range: Lake Tanganyika.
Size: 6" (15 cm) TL.
Water Chemistry: Tropical; hard and alkaline.
Behavior: Aggressive scale and fin nipper.
Dietary Requirements: Small live foods, scales, fins, and all types of prepared foods.

Remarks: This Frontosa look-alike is actually a predator of fish scales and fins. It seems to prefer to live over sandy areas where it can approach other fishes in a peaceful, non-threatening manner. After swimming with these fishes for a short time, *P. straeleni* dashes over to the unsuspecting victim and bites off what it can. Sometimes a large chunk of fin is torn off, but more commonly, a small patch of scales is removed. This species needs to be kept singly, or else they will literally tear your fishes apart.

Protomelas fenestratus

TREWAVAS 1935

Natural Range: Lake Malawi.
Size: 8" (20 cm) TL.
Water Chemistry: Tropical; hard and alkaline.
Behavior: Moderately aggressive.
Dietary Requirements: Small live and all types of prepared foods.

Remarks: Unless the locality is known, *P. fenestratus* is quite difficult to distinguish from its close cousin *P. taeniolatus*. The race with the largest individuals is reported to occur at Taiwan Reef, and this is the same locality in which many specimens in the aquarium industry originally came from. Their care and husbandry in captivity is very basic, and as long as they are provided with good quality water and a large aquarium, they will do very well for many years.

Placidochromis milomo juvenile

Placidochromis milomo adult

Plecodus straeleni juvenile

Plecodus straeleni adult

Protomelas fenestratus female

Protomelas fenestratus male

527

Protomelas similis

REGAN 1922

Natural Range: Lake Malawi.
Size: 6" (15 cm) TL.
Water Chemistry: Tropical; hard and alkaline.
Behavior: Moderately aggressive.
Dietary Requirements: Small live foods, and all types of prepared foods that are high in plant matter.

Remarks: We mainly find *P. similis* in shallow areas that are heavily vegetated. Konings reports that they are abundant in some places but completely absent in others. Males will use their sharp teeth to crop the weeds just above the sand's surface. Here a nest will be made and a female will be tempted into spawning with him. After spawning has commenced, the mouthbrooding females move into deep cover within the weeds and guard the fry while the male lures in another mate

Pseudotropheus demasoni

KONINGS 1994

Natural Range: Lake Malawi.
Size: 3" (7.5 cm) TL.
Water Chemistry: Tropical; hard and alkaline.
Behavior: Moderately aggressive; males are intolerant of one another in small aquariums.
Dietary Requirements: Prefers all types of prepared foods that are high in plant matter.

Remarks: These little beauties are perhaps the most brilliantly colored dwarf mbuna commonly available in the trade. Generally, they are peaceful with other cichlids, as long as they are smaller than their tankmates. It is quite a sight to sit back in front of your aquarium and watch *P. demasoni* dart in and out of the rockwork. Additionally, the females are even more brightly colored, which is something that is rather uncommon in African cichlids.

Pseudotropheus livingstoni

BOULENGER 1899

Natural Range: Lake Malawi.
Size: 5" (12 cm) TL.
Water Chemistry: Tropical; hard and alkaline.
Behavior: Moderately aggressive; males are intolerant of one another in small aquariums.
Dietary Requirements: Prefers all types of prepared foods that are high in plant matter.

Remarks: This species is currently thought to be synonymous with *P. lanisticola*, even though they may appear as a distinct species on some dealers' price lists. In nature, non-breeding individuals are commonly encountered over sandy areas. Of course, females holding eggs or young will be well-hidden deep within the recesses of the boulders in the lake. In aquariums, this species is distinctive, but never seems to get the attention we think it deserves. Hobbyists looking for something interesting may want to consider this fish.

Protomelas similis female

Protomelas similis male

Pseudotropheus demasoni

Pseudotropheus demasoni

Pseudotropheus livingstoni

Pseudotropheus lanisticola for comparison

Pseudotropheus lombardoi

BURGESS 1977

Natural Range: Lake Malawi.
Size: 5" (12 cm) TL; may grow slightly larger.
Water Chemistry: Tropical; hard and alkaline.
Behavior: Moderately aggressive; males are intolerant of one another in small aquariums.
Dietary Requirements: Prefers all types of prepared foods that are high in plant matter.

Remarks: Also known as the "Kenyi," *P. lombardoi* is a large, moderately aggressive mbuna that does very well in aquariums. It should be pointed out that males and females look like two different species; the male is a bright orange, and the female is a deep blue. Like *P. crabro*, this species may grow larger than its recorded size for wild individuals.

Pseudotropheus saulosi

KONINGS 1990

Natural Range: Lake Malawi.
Size: 3" (7.5 cm) TL.
Water Chemistry: Tropical; hard and alkaline.
Behavior: Moderately aggressive; males are intolerant of one another in small aquariums.
Dietary Requirements: Prefers all types of prepared foods that are high in plant matter.

Remarks: Just as with *P. lombardoi*, the sexes of this small mbuna are dichromatic. However, unlike *P. lombardoi*, it is the males that are blue in color, with dark black bars, and the females are a brilliant yellow. Their care in aquariums is identical to that of others of the genus.

Pseudotropheus socolofi

JOHNSON 1974

Natural Range: Lake Malawi.
Size: 5" (12 cm) TL.
Water Chemistry: Tropical; hard and alkaline.
Behavior: Moderately aggressive; males are intolerant of one another in small aquariums.
Dietary Requirements: Prefers all types of prepared foods that are high in plant matter.

Remarks: Sometimes referred to as the Ice Blue Mbuna due to their light color, *P. socolofi* is a distinct species with a dark edge to its dorsal fin. Additionally, their heads are broad and rounded, giving them a bullish appearance. Watch them in the aquarium; they sometimes are quite pushy, but beautiful all the same.

Pseudotropheus lombardoi female

Pseudotropheus lombardoi male

Pseudotropheus saulosi female

Pseudotropheus saulosi male

Pseudotropheus socolofi

Pseudotropheus socolofi

531

Pterophyllum altum / Altum Angel

PELLEGRIN 1903

Natural Range: Brazil, Colombia, and Venezuela.
Size: 8" (20 cm) TH (total height).
Water Chemistry: Tropical; slightly soft and acidic.
Behavior: Moderately aggressive among conspecifics, otherwise generally peaceful.
Dietary Requirements: Small live foods and all types of prepared foods.

Remarks: As with so many other cichlids, there is considerable confusion among the actual taxonomic standing of the species within *Pterophyllum*. There are at least three species within the Altum complex, however, today we only recognize one. Hopefully in the near future we will be better able to distinguish the others and as more and more work is being done with DNA analysis, this should prove to be very interesting indeed. Aside from this, their care and husbandry in aquariums is generally the same as with Pterophyllum scalare but many Altum angels need a little more attention paid to the quality of their water. Since nearly all of them are still wild collected, it is best to make sure their water is very warm, soft, acid, and has a low bacterial count. This species is not recommended for beginners.

Pterophyllum leopoldi / Leopold's Angel

GOSSE 1963

Natural Range: Brazil and Peru.
Size: 6" (15 cm) TH.
Water Chemistry: Tropical; slightly soft and acidic.
Behavior: Generally peaceful, males may quarrel and all will eat small fishes.
Dietary Requirements: Small live foods and all types of prepared foods.

Remarks: Previously known as *Pterophyllum dumerilii*, Leopold's Angels are hardy and robust angelfishes that do very well in aquariums provided that they have been properly acclimated to captive conditions. Like the various Altum angels, Leopold's Angels are almost always wild collected and care must be taken to ensure that their water remains very warm, acidic, slightly soft, and has a low bacterial count. Also like the Altum Angels, this species is not recommended for beginners.

Pterophyllum altum

Pterophyllum altum

Pterophyllum leopoldi

Pterophyllum leopoldi

Pterophyllum scalare / Silver Angel

LICHTENSTEIN 1823

Natural Range: Brazil and maybe Peru.
Size: 6" (15 cm) TH.
Water Chemistry: Tropical; slightly soft and acidic.
Behavior: Generally peaceful but spawning males may quarrel amongst themselves.
Dietary Requirements: Small live foods and all types of prepared foods.

Remarks: Aside from the Discus, the Silver Angel is the King of the Aquarium. They are probably the most recognizable freshwater aquarium fish throughout the world. As a matter of fact, many people who know very little about tropical fishes can tell you which fish is an angelfish in an aquarium containing them. Another interesting fact is that many hobbyists can hardly believe that Angelfishes are actually cichlids and more closely related to Oscars (*Astronotus* spp.) then say, many large disk-shaped tetras. There are many, many books and excellent magazine articles that go very deep into the care and husbandry of these beautiful fish. It is the author's recommendation that you research this fish and see what is available to you in terms of color varieties and fin choices. There are literally dozens to choose from.

Pungu maclareni

TREWAVAS 1962

Natural Range: Endemic to Lake Barombi-Mbo in western Cameroon.
Size: 5" (12 cm) TL.
Water Chemistry: Tropical; otherwise not too critical; avoid extremes.
Behavior: Generally peaceful, but males may quarrel.
Dietary Requirements: Small live and all types of prepared foods; supplement with plant matter for best coloration.

Remarks: *P. maclareni* is reported to be a peaceful community fish that does well in aquariums containing other fishes of similar temperament and size. They are an oddly colored species, with some specimens being mottled in coloration. This species' muscular jaws are a result of a specialized feeding preference (sponges) in the river and its tributaries.

Pterophyllum scalare

Pterophyllum scalare black var.

Pungu maclareni

Pungu maclareni

Retroculus lapidifer

CASTELNAU 1855

Natural Range: Araguaia and Tocantins Rivers, Brazil.
Size: 10" (25 cm) TL; usually far smaller.
Water Chemistry: Tropical; slightly soft and acidic.
Behavior: Moderately aggressive.
Dietary Requirements: Small live foods and all types of prepared foods.

Remarks: This odd and unique species of bottom-dwelling cichlid is quite a prize to obtain. They are not readily available but if you are fortunate enough to have the opportunity to get a hold of a specimen or two then it is highly agreed that you do so. Their care in captivity is somewhat unknown although a quick visit to any of the various cichlid on-line forums usually turn up some invaluable information on keeping this species, as well as nearly everything else rare and unusual, in aquariums.

Retroculus xinguensis

GOSSE 1971

Natural Range: Rio Xingu, Brazil.
Size: 10" (25 cm) TL; usually far smaller.
Water Chemistry: Tropical; slightly soft and acidic.
Behavior: Moderately aggressive.
Dietary Requirements: Small live foods and all types of prepared foods.

Remarks: You will need to be determined and steadfast should you wish to successfully keep these absolutely gorgeous cichlids in the average aquarium. The author (BMS) has attempted many and succeeded with few. The general thought among cichlid fanatics is that they, like Altum Angels and Long-finned Waroo, do not do well in aquariums with a high bacterial count. Regardless, as with any fish, a good, strong filtration system combined with a varied diet and plenty of water changes should improve your chances of success with *R. xinguensis*.

Rhamphochromis ferox

REGAN 1922

Natural Range: Lake Malawi.
Size: 18" (45 cm) TL.
Water Chemistry: Tropical; hard and alkaline.
Behavior: Moderately aggressive; will swallow small fishes and invertebrates.
Dietary Requirements: Meaty foods of all types.

Remarks: This awesome open-water-roaming predatory cichlid is probably the closest thing to a barracuda you could find—unless you're an *Acestrorhynchus* fan, of course. They need very, very large aquariums with extremely clean water and strong filtration in order to thrive for extended periods in captivity.

Retroculus lapidifer

Retroculus lapidifer

Retroculus xinguensis

Retroculus xinguensis

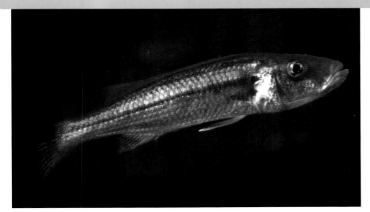

Rhamphochromis ferox

Rhamphochromis macrophthalmus

Sarotherodon linnelli

LONNBERG 1903

Natural Range: Endemic to Lake Barombi-Mbo in West Cameroon.

Size: 10" (25 cm) TL.

Water Chemistry: Tropical; otherwise not critical; avoid extremes.

Behavior: Generally peaceful, and not usually aggressive towards other species.

Dietary Requirements: Omnivorous; feed plenty of plant and animal matter equally.

Remarks: It is deeper-bodied as a juvenile, but when fully grown, *S. linnelli* is a slender species that exhibits a high degree of color variation and a pointed snout. As with all "Tilapia," smaller foods are preferred over larger ones, but regardless, this species seems to do well and is robust in most cases. Since they grow to be relatively large, be sure to provide them with a large aquarium.

Sarotherodon lohbergeri

HOLLY 1930

Natural Range: Lake Barombi-Mbo and the surrounding waters near Kumba, Cameroon (Lamboj 2004).

Size: 6" (15 cm) TL.

Water Chemistry: Tropical; otherwise not critical; avoid extremes.

Behavior: Generally peaceful, and not usually aggressive towards other species.

Dietary Requirements: Omnivorous; feed plenty of plant and animal matter equally, but always as small flakes or bits.

Remarks: This specie prefers to feed on small particles whenever possible. Their care and husbandry in aquariums is otherwise the same as many of the others in the genus *Sarotherodon*.

Satanoperca acuticeps

HECKEL 1840

Natural Range: Santerem region, Brazil.

Size: 10" (25 cm) TL.

Water Chemistry: Tropical; slightly soft and acidic.

Behavior: Generally peaceful.

Dietary Requirements: Small live foods and all types of prepared foods.

Remarks: You can easily distinguish this species by their four dark circular blotches that run almost in a perfect line down the middle of their flanks from just posterior to their gill opercula to the base of their tail. Their heads are sharply pointed and mouths terminal in standard Eartheater fashion.

Sarotherodon linnelli

Sarotherodon linnelli profile

Sarotherodon lohbergeri

Sarotherodon lohbergeri profile

Satanoperca acuticeps using terminal mouth

Satanoperca acuticeps

Satanoperca daemon

HECKEL 1840

Natural Range: Rio Orinoco region, Colombia and Venezuela.
Size: 10" (25 cm) TL.
Water Chemistry: Tropical; slightly soft and acidic.
Behavior: Moderately aggressive.
Dietary Requirements: Small live foods and all types of prepared foods.

Remarks: Like *S. acuticeps*, *S. daemon* is easily distinguishable by its row of spots that run down their flanks. However, unlike *S. acuticeps*, *S. daemon* has only three of them instead of the four that the former species exhibits. Additionally, young *S. daemon* are easily recognizable by their camouflaged pattern and very long and ornate finnage.

Satanoperca jurupari

HECKEL 1840

Natural Range: Santerem region, Brazil.
Size: 10" (25 cm) TL.
Water Chemistry: Tropical; slightly soft and acidic.
Behavior: Moderately aggressive.
Dietary Requirements: Small live foods and all types of prepared foods.

Remarks: Easily the most common and recognizable species of South America cichlid, *S. jurupari* has been a hit for many years. Until recently, many species where known under this name but thanks to Dr. Sven Kullander and many devoted hobbyists, we now have a much better understanding of the taxonomy of this group of large Eartheaters. Their care in aquariums is very simple and undemanding as long as extremes are avoided.

Satanoperca leucosticta

MULLER & TROSCHEL 1848

Natural Range: Colombia and Venezuela.
Size: 8" (20 cm) TL.
Water Chemistry: Tropical; slightly soft and acidic.
Behavior: Generally peaceful.
Dietary Requirements: Small live foods and all types of prepared foods.

Remarks: While this species has been known to science for more than a century, hobbyists have been erroneously referring to it as *S. jurupari*. While *S. jurupari* and *S. leucosticta* are clearly related they differ dramatically in coloration and pattern. Otherwise, their care and husbandry in aquariums is identical.

Satanoperca daemon juvenile

Satanoperca daemon adult

Satanoperca jurupari young adult

Satanoperca jurupari

Satanoperca leucosticta

Satanoperca leucosticta note head pattern

Steatocranus casuarius / Buffalo Head Cichlid

POLL 1939

Natural Range: West Africa.

Size: 6" (15 cm) TL.

Water Chemistry: Tropical; neutral to slightly alkaline with moderate hardness.

Behavior: Generally peaceful; best kept in pairs in a medium to large aquarium.

Dietary Requirements: Small live foods and all types of prepared foods.

Remarks: Good filtration and strong circulation is a must for this fish. They are probably the best known of all the *Steatocranus* species and are commonly sold in pet shops under the name of Buffalo Head Cichlid. Unfortunately, quite a lot of these do not live very long because they are housed with other cichlids that are too aggressive, and this causes a great deal of stress for the Buffalo Heads. They are best kept in pairs in a moderately-sized aquarium

Steatocranus irvinei

TREWAVAS 1943

Natural Range: West Africa.

Size: 6" (15 cm) TL; possibly larger.

Water Chemistry: Tropical; neutral to slightly alkaline with moderate hardness.

Behavior: Generally peaceful; best kept in pairs in a medium to large aquarium.

Dietary Requirements: Small live foods and all types of prepared foods.

Remarks: Reports of this species in aquariums indicate that this species exhibits a high degree of inter- and intraspecific aggression. This is unique, because so many of its congeners do not show this behavioral characteristic. This aggressiveness, combined with a somewhat large size, makes this species suitable only for the larger species-specific aquarium.

Steatocranus mpozoensis

ROBERTS & STEWART 1976

Natural Range: Congo system, West Africa.

Size: 5" (12 cm) TL.

Water Chemistry: Tropical; neutral to slightly alkaline with moderate hardness.

Behavior: Generally peaceful; best kept in pairs in a medium to large aquarium.

Dietary Requirements: Small live foods and all types of prepared foods.

Remarks: Similar to *S. irvinei*, this species exhibits an overlapping upper lip, although it is not quite as noticeable as it is with the other species. Apparently, there are multiple variations within this genus that may turn out to be new species. More research is needed to determine the validity of that statement; however, multiple reports have indicated this. Their care and husbandry is the same as others described herein, with the most important aspect being filtration and circulation.

Steatocranus casuarius female

Steatocranus casuarius male

Steatocranus irvinei

Steatocranus irvinei

Steatocranus mpozoensis

Steatocranus mpozoensis

543

Steatocranus tinanti

POLL 1939

Natural Range: West Africa.
Size: 6" (15 cm) TL.
Water Chemistry: Tropical; neutral to slightly alkaline with moderate hardness.
Behavior: Generally peaceful; best kept in pairs in a medium to large aquarium.
Dietary Requirements: Small live foods and all types of prepared foods.

Remarks: While only a handful of this species has ever been exported for the aquarium hobby, their care and husbandry in captivity seems to be remarkably similar to others in the genus. Perhaps in the near future, we will see more of these fish become available to hobbyists worldwide.

Stigmatochromis woodi

REGAN 1922

Natural Range: Lake Malawi.
Size: 12" (30 cm) TL; usually much smaller.
Water Chemistry: Tropical; hard and alkaline.
Behavior: Moderately aggressive.
Dietary Requirements: Small live foods and all types of prepared foods.

Remarks: There are many different races of this large cichlid found throughout the lake. Some are said to have smaller mouths, while others have better coloration. Regardless, this species is not common in the aquarium trade, and those who seek it will probably have to contact a cichlid specialist, or else special order them from your local aquarium shop.

Stomatepia pindu

TREWAVAS 1972

Natural Range: Lake Barombi-Mbo, Cameroon.
Size: 5" (12 cm) TL.
Water Chemistry: Tropical; neutral to slightly acidic pH with moderate hardness.
Behavior: Generally peaceful with other fishes, but conspecifics may quarrel.
Dietary Requirements: Small live foods and all types of prepared foods.

Remarks: *Stomatepia* are not very colorful fishes in general. They are almost unheard of in the aquarium hobby, with the only exceptions being a handful of specimens that are occasionally exported. Now that people are more aware of this, and of other West African cichlids, then perhaps the demand for them will grow, and the supply will flow a little heavier. This is an excellent species to add to the collection of rare and unusual species.

Steatocranus tinanti

Steatocranus tinanti

Stigmatochromis woodi

Stigmatochromis woodi

Stomatepia pindu

Stomatepia pindu

Symphysodon aequifasciatus / Blue Discus

PELLEGRIN 1904

Natural Range: Northern Brazil.
Size: 8" (20 cm) TL.
Water Chemistry: Tropical; slightly soft and acidic.
Behavior: Generally peaceful; males may quarrel.
Dietary Requirements: Small live foods and all types of prepared foods.

Remarks: The King of the Aquarium. There are only a few other species that are able to be housed in freshwater aquariums that have coloration as spectacular as the Discus. Of course, over the years there have been numerous color varieties or sports that have been developed. Some of these have been improvements on the fish's coloration while many have not been. The most important aspect of keeping Discus in home aquariums is to provide them with very warm water that is slightly acidic and very soft. Feeding should be frequent and of small amounts as Discus are slow feeders and need to be housed with other fishes of similar temperament. This species seems to benefit highly from frequent, large-scale water changes.

Symphysodon discus / Heckle Discus

HECKEL 1840

Natural Range: Northern Brazil.
Size: 8" (20 cm) TL.
Water Chemistry: Tropical; slightly soft and acidic.
Behavior: Generally peaceful.
Dietary Requirements: Small live foods and all types of prepared foods.

Remarks: Like the Blue Discus, the Heckle Discus requires similar care and husbandry in aquariums. Unlike the Blue Discus, this species is rarely bred in home aquariums and they do not have nearly the number of man-made color varieties available either. The most distinguishing feature of the Heckle Discus is their broad center bar, which extends from the base of the dorsal fin down to the ventral region at about the middle of the body.

Symphysodon aequifasciatus

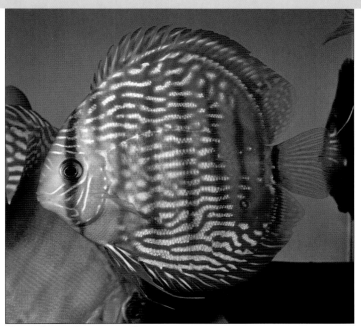

Symphysodon aequifasciatus

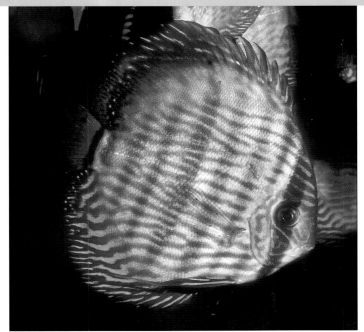

Symphysodon discus

Symphysodon discus

Taenicara candidi / Torpedo Cichlid

MYERS 1935

Natural Range: Amazonas region, Brazil.
Size: 3" (7.5 cm) TL.
Water Chemistry: Tropical; slightly soft and acidic.
Behavior: Generally peaceful.
Dietary Requirements: Small live foods and all types of prepared foods.

Remarks: These little cichlids do very well in most aquariums that have ample hiding places for them to dart in and out of. If you choose to keep other small cichlids with this species, be sure they are not able to swallow the Torpedo Cichlids. These small fish are also a good candidate for inclusion in community aquariums that contain other peaceful fishes, too.

Tanganicodus irsacae

POLL 1950

Natural Range: Lake Tanganyika.
Size: 2" (5 cm) TL; may grow slightly larger.
Water Chemistry: Tropical; hard, alkaline conditions preferred.
Behavior: Generally peaceful, especially compared to *Spathodus* species.
Dietary Requirements: Small live foods and all types of prepared foods.

Remarks: This small cichlid is a good tankmate for many of the smaller *Neolamprologus* species, as well as *Julidochromis* and *Lamprologus* species. They need very clean water with a high dissolved oxygen content. Their aquariums should be at least 30 gallons in volume.

Teleocichla cinderella

KULLANDER 1988

Natural Range: Rio Tocantins, Brazil.
Size: 3" (7.5 cm) TL; may grow slightly larger.
Water Chemistry: Tropical; slightly soft and acidic.
Behavior: Moderately aggressive.
Dietary Requirements: Small live foods and all types of prepared foods.

Remarks: These small cichlids are very popular with hobbyists who keep the rare and unusual. They require excellent water quality and some current as they are primarily found in the faster moving shallow waters of rivers and tributaries throughout their range.

Taenicara candidi

Taenicara candidi

Tanganicodus irsacae

Spathodus marlieri a closely related species

Teleocichla cinderella

Teleocichla cinderella

Teleogramma brichardi

POLL 1959

Natural Range: Congo.

Size: 5" (12 cm) TL.

Water Chemistry: Tropical; moderately alkaline and acidic conditions are best, but may tolerate a broad range of parameters, as long as extremes are avoided.

Behavior: Generally peaceful, except towards conspecifics.

Dietary Requirements: Small live foods and all types of prepared foods.

Remarks: Larger aquariums that contain plenty of hiding places and visual barriers are a must in order to achieve success with this cichlid. They can be very aggressive towards one another, but interspecific aggression seems to be mild. Spawns are fairly small and number only about 30 eggs. Females are particularly striking in their coloration, as are males, but good water and a balanced diet are needed for proper conditioning.

Theraps irregularis

GUENTHER 1862

Natural Range: Atlantic slope of southern Mexico to Guatemala.

Size: 8" (20 cm) TL; possibly larger.

Water Chemistry: Tropical; slightly alkaline with moderate hardness.

Behavior: Moderately aggressive.

Dietary Requirements: Small live foods and all types of prepared foods.

Remarks: Easily identified by their long, slender bodies with irregular patchwork along their flanks, *T. irregularis* is a bold cichlid that does well in a cichlid community aquarium with others of similar size and temperament.

Theraps lentiginosus

STEINDACHNER 1864

Natural Range: Southern Mexico to Guatemala.

Size: 10" (25 cm) TL.

Water Chemistry: Tropical; slightly alkaline with moderate hardness.

Behavior: Moderately aggressive.

Dietary Requirements: Small live foods and all types of prepared foods.

Remarks: *T. lentiginosus* is similar in shape and overall appearance to that of *T. irregularis*. However, the main difference is the height of the body and adult coloration compared with *T. irregularis*. Their heads are distinctively Theraps in shape and size. The care and husbandry of them in aquariums is remarkably similar to that of the species within *Vieja*.

Teleogramma brichardi

Teleogramma brichardi

Theraps irregularis

Theraps wesseli for comparison

Theraps lentiginosus adult female

Theraps lentiginosus male

Thoracochromis brauschi

POLL & THYS VAN DEN AUDENAERDE 1965

Natural Range: Congo region.
Size: 6" (15 cm) TL.
Water Chemistry: Small live foods and all types of prepared foods.
Behavior: Generally peaceful, but males may quarrel.
Dietary Requirements: Mainly vegetarian, but when supplemented with small crustaceans, this species will exhibit remarkable coloration.

Remarks: This robust species belongs to a genus of fishes that are rarely kept in aquariums. There is little data on their care and husbandry, but it is likely that they are similar to fishes of the genus *Haplochromis*, since they were originally described as such.

Thorichthys aureus / Aureum

GUENTHER 1862

Natural Range: Belize, Guatemala, and Honduras.
Size: 6" (15 cm) TL; usually smaller.
Water Chemistry: Tropical; slightly alkaline with moderate hardness.
Behavior: Moderately aggressive.
Dietary Requirements: Small live foods and all types of prepared foods.

Remarks: Aside from *T. meeki*, *T. aureus* are perhaps the next in line for the most brilliantly-colored *Thorichthys*. Otherwise, their care and husbandry is identical to that of others within the genus.

Thorichthys ellioti

MEEK 1904

Natural Range: Widely distributed over much of southern Mexico.
Size: 6" (15 cm) TL; usually smaller.
Water Chemistry: Tropical; slightly alkaline with moderate hardness.
Behavior: Moderately aggressive.
Dietary Requirements: Small live foods and all types of prepared foods.

Remarks: Please see the profile for *T. meeki* regarding their similar care and husbandry in aquariums.

Thoracochromis brauschi

Thoracochromis brauschi

Thorichthys aureus

Thorichthys aureus

Thorichthys ellioti

Thorichthys ellioti

Thorichthys meeki / Firemouth

BRIND 1918

Natural Range: Guatemala and southern Mexico.
Size: 6" (15 cm) TL; usually smaller but males occasionally grow even larger.
Water Chemistry: Tropical; slightly alkaline with moderate hardness.
Behavior: Moderately aggressive.
Dietary Requirements: Small live foods and all types of prepared foods.

Remarks: The Firemouth Cichlid ranks in the top ten of easy-to-keep and recognizable cichlids that are available to hobbyists worldwide. They are a relatively undemanding cichlid that do best in an aquarium with good filtration and plenty of hiding spots. A pair will normally seek out a small cave and guard it vigorously. After some time, the female may emerge with a cloud of free-swimming fry. Normally, the colors of the Firemouth Cichlid will become strikingly beautiful before and during spawnings.

Thorichthys pasionis

RIVAS 1962

Natural Range: Guatemala and southern Mexico.
Size: 6" (15 cm) TL; usually smaller.
Water Chemistry: Tropical; slightly alkaline with moderate hardness.
Behavior: Moderately aggressive.
Dietary Requirements: Small live foods and all types of prepared foods.

Remarks: Many hobbyists love cichlids but simply cannot afford to offer them the space that they need. Similarly, those same hobbyists may not really want dwarf cichlids. Well look no further, the members of *Thorichthys* are perfect candidates for small to medium-sized aquariums from about 30 gallons on up. With them, *T. pasionis* is one of the more unique species that are available through cichlid specialists.

Tilapia busumana

GUENTHER 1903

Natural Range: West Africa.
Size: 10" (25 cm) TL.
Water Chemistry: Tropical; otherwise not critical; avoid extremes.
Behavior: Moderately aggressive.
Dietary Requirements: Omnivorous; feed equal amounts of plant and animal matter.

Remarks: This typical *Tilapia* species is both an open-substrate spawner and a plant eater. They generally hold large territories and are only suitable for the largest of aquariums.

Thorichthys meeki

Thorichthys meeki

Thorichthys pasionis

Thorichthys helleri for comparison

Tilapia busumana

Tilapia busumana

Tilapia buttikoferi / Hornet Cichlid

HUBRECHT 1881

Natural Range: West Africa.
Size: 16" (40 cm) TL.
Water Chemistry: Tropical; otherwise not critical; avoid extremes.
Behavior: Moderately aggressive, although some specimens seem to be very aggressive.
Dietary Requirements: Omnivorous; feed equal amounts of plant and animal matter; this species is particularly fond of snails.

Remarks: Here is a very easy-to-keep and robust species for the largest of aquariums. They are normally very aggressive, but some specimens seem to be quite placid, as long as there are no other members of the same species in the same tank. They make great tank-mates for large predatory catfishes and cichlids from Central and South America, as well as native fishes of the United States such as the various *Lepomis* species.

Tilapia bythobates

STIASSNY, SCHLIEWEN, & DOMINEY 1992

Natural Range: West Africa.
Size: 6" (15 cm) TL.
Water Chemistry: Tropical; otherwise not critical; avoid extremes.
Behavior: Moderately aggressive.
Dietary Requirements: Omnivorous; feed equal amounts of plant and animal matter.

Remarks: These fish are relatively easy to keep and are reported to be quite peaceful when not spawning. Aquariums of 50 to 75 gallons will suffice for a single pair. Filtration should be strong, and regular partial water changes are a must.

Tilapia deckerti

THYS VAN DEN AUDENAERDE 1967

Natural Range: West Africa.
Size: 8" (20 cm) TL.
Water Chemistry: Tropical; otherwise not critical; avoid extremes.
Behavior: Moderately aggressive.
Dietary Requirements: Omnivorous; feed equal amounts of plant and animal matter.

Remarks: There is no published information on the long-term care and husbandry of this cichlid. If you have such information, please report it in *Tropical Fish Hobbyist* magazine!

Tilapia buttikoferi

Tilapia buttikoferi

Tilapia bythobates

Tilapia bythobates

Tilapia deckerti

Tilapia deckerti

557

Tilapia discolor

GUENTHER 1903

Natural Range: West Africa.
Size: 10" (25 cm) TL.
Water Chemistry: Tropical; otherwise not critical; avoid extremes.
Behavior: Moderately aggressive.
Dietary Requirements: Omnivorous; feed equal amounts of plant and animal matter.

Remarks: This fairly slender species is reported to be simple to keep in aquariums. They have no special care, and breeding is typical of the genus. Large aquariums are a must, as are good filtration and circulation. STIASSNY et al. (1992) observed pairs defending juveniles collectively, which might be an indication of cooperative broodcare (Lamboj 2004).

Tilapia guineensis

TREWAVAS 1936

Natural Range: West Africa.
Size: 10" (25 cm) TL.
Water Chemistry: Tropical; otherwise not critical; avoid extremes.
Behavior: Moderately aggressive.
Dietary Requirements: Omnivorous; feed equal amounts of plant and animal matter.

Remarks: Although rarely imported into the United States, European hobbyists report that this fish is easy to keep and breed under normal conditions for others of the genus.

Tilapia joka

THYS VAN DEN AUDENAERDE 1969

Natural Range: West Africa.
Size: 6" (15 cm) TL.
Water Chemistry: Tropical; otherwise not critical; avoid extremes.
Behavior: Moderately aggressive.
Dietary Requirements: Omnivorous; feed equal amounts of plant and animal matter.

Remarks: *T. joka* is more common in the hobby than once believed. Hobbyists all over the world enjoy this species in their cichlid community aquariums. While not very large, they still need quite a bit of space, so be sure to provide a large aquarium with good water quality. Juveniles of this species are strikingly beautiful.

Tilapia discolor

Tilapia discolor note moderately sharp snout

Tilapia guineensis

Tilapia guineensis note sharp snout

Tilapia joka

Tilapia joka note blunt snout

Tilapia mariae

BOULENGER 1897

Natural Range: West Africa.
Size: 14" (35 cm) TL.
Water Chemistry: Tropical; otherwise not critical; avoid extremes.
Behavior: Moderately aggressive.
Dietary Requirements: Omnivorous; feed equal amounts of plant and animal matter.

Remarks: While certainly not considered a rare species, *T. mariae* is not as common in the hobby as it is in the canals of southern Florida (USA). Their care and husbandry in aquariums is simple. Keep in a similar fashion to *T. buttikoferi*.

Tilapia zillii

GERVAIS 1848

Natural Range: West Africa.
Size: 12" (30 cm) TL.
Water Chemistry: Tropical; otherwise not critical; avoid extremes.
Behavior: Moderately aggressive.
Dietary Requirements: Omnivorous; feed equal amounts of plant and animal matter.

Remarks: Both parents of this species will actively guard their eggs and young. They are a large *Tilapia* that needs an equally large aquarium with strong filtration and frequent partial water changes. Sometimes, this species is referred to as the "Red Breasted Tilapia" by hobbyists because of their brilliant red throat and ventral regions. Females are heavily striated during spawning and may look as if they are a completely different species altogether.

Tropheus duboisi

MARLIER 1959

Natural Range: Lake Tanganyika.
Size: 6" (15 cm) TL.
Water Chemistry: Tropical; hard and alkaline.
Behavior: Moderately aggressive; very aggressive towards conspecifics.
Dietary Requirements: Mainly herbivorous; feed plenty of algae-enriched foods.

Remarks: There are two main types of *T. duboisi*, a broad yellow band variety and the "Maswa" variety. This species has a discontinuous distribution in the northern part of the lake and is found in the Congo as well as Tanzania (Konings 1996). They seem to be more tolerant of meaty foods in their diet than *T. moorii*.

Tilapia mariae

Tilapia mariae note unique eye pattern

Tilapia zillii

Tilapia zillii

Tropheus duboisi juvenile

Tropheus duboisi subadults

561

Tropheus moorii

BOULENGER 1898

Natural Range: Lake Tanganyika.
Size: 4" (10 cm) TL.
Water Chemistry: Tropical; hard and alkaline.
Behavior: Moderately aggressive; very aggressive towards conspecifics.
Dietary Requirements: Mainly herbivorous; feed plenty of algae-enriched foods.

Remarks: The most important thing that a hobbyist needs to know about this species is their intolerance of diets that are too high in animal proteins. This is probably due to the fact that their gut is so long that animal matter begins to decay in the intestines and causes a die-off of the natural flora and fauna that is important for the digestion of plant material. The end result is an infection commonly known as bloat. If the disorder is not treated immediately by internal medication, the infected fish will usually succumb rather quickly.

Tropheus polli

AXELROD 1977

Natural Range: Lake Tanganyika (eastern coast).
Size: 6" (15 cm) TL.
Water Chemistry: Tropical; hard and alkaline.
Behavior: Moderately aggressive; very aggressive towards conspecifics.
Dietary Requirements: Mainly herbivorous; feed plenty of algae-enriched foods.

Remarks: While there is much controversy over the validity of this species as compared with *T. annectens*, both authors support *Tropheus polli* as being valid, and both authors have firsthand experience with them. Glen S. Axelrod discovered the fish and named it in honor of Max Poll, and Brian M. Scott has bred the fish in captivity and has many years of experience with their care and husbandry in aquariums. This species is more capable of ingesting meaty foods than others of the genus, but take care to provide them with a rounded-out diet.

Uaru amphiacanthoides / Waroo

HECKEL 1840

Natural Range: Brazil.
Size: 12" (30 cm) TL.
Water Chemistry: Tropical; soft and slightly acidic.
Behavior: Generally peaceful, but males may be pushy.
Dietary Requirements: Mainly herbivorous; feed plenty of algae-enriched foods.

Remarks: Waroo are large, generally peaceful cichlids that relish feedings of plant-based materials such as leaves of romaine lettuce or blanched spinach. They do well with other large cichlids of similar size and temperament. Adults may become quite belligerent if they pair up and look to spawn.

Tropheus moorii

Tropheus moorii var.

Tropheus polli juvenile

Tropheus polli adult

Uaru amphiacanthoides young adult

Uaru amphiacanthoides clear water var.

Uaru fernandezyepezi / Long-finned Waroo

STAWIKOWSKI 1989

Natural Range: Rio Orinoco and Atabapo basins, Colombia, and Venezuela.
Size: 12" (30 cm) TL.
Water Chemistry: Tropical; soft and slightly acidic.
Behavior: Generally peaceful, but males may be pushy.
Dietary Requirements: Mainly herbivorous; feed plenty of algae-enriched foods.

Remarks: This rather new and exciting cichlid comes from two main river systems; the Rio Atabapo in Colombia and the Rio Orinoco in Venezuela and Colombia. They can be aggressive when they have to be, but are generally peaceful when kept with similar-sized fishes. *U. fernandezyepezi* seem to be very sensitive to dissolved metabolites in their water. Be sure to have good filtration and perform frequent water changes.

Vieja argentea / Silver Vieja

ALLGAYER 1991

Natural Range: Southern Mexico to Guatemala.
Size: 14" (35 cm) TL.
Water Chemistry: Tropical; slightly alkaline with moderate hardness.
Behavior: Moderately aggressive; may bully smaller tankmates.
Dietary Requirements: Small live foods and all types of prepared foods.

Remarks: These large, beautiful cichlids are very popular with hobbyists looking for something large and different. They are being bred both commercially and by hobbyists alike and are often available from cichlid specialists or sometimes even your local pet shop. Provide a large aquarium and make sure to perform routine partial water changes.

Vieja bifasciata

STEINDACHNER 1864

Natural Range: Southern Mexico and surrounding areas.
Size: 14" (35 cm) TL.
Water Chemistry: Tropical; slightly alkaline with moderate hardness.
Behavior: Moderately aggressive; may bully smaller tankmates.
Dietary Requirements: Small live foods and all types of prepared foods.

Remarks: One of the more colorful large-growing cichlids, *V. bifasciata* is a good tankmate for large Oscars (*Astronotus* spp.) and other fishes that are robust but overly aggressive. This species exhibits a high degree of interspecific aggression so be careful and keep an eye out for fights amongst themselves.

Uaru fernandezyepezi juvenile

Uaru fernandezyepezi adult pair

Vieja argentea juvenile

Vieja argentea

Vieja bifasciata "xanthic"

Vieja zonatum for comparison

Vieja fenestrata

GUENTHER 1860

Natural Range: Southern Mexico.
Size: 16" (40 cm) TL, usually far smaller.
Water Chemistry: Tropical; slightly alkaline with moderate hardness.
Behavior: Moderately aggressive; may bully smaller tankmates.
Dietary Requirements: Small live foods and all types of prepared foods.

Remarks: While not as common as the others within *Vieja*, *V. fenestratus* is a bold cichlid that does well in community aquariums with other large, peaceful fishes. Be sure to provide plenty of rockwork or drift wood for them to hide in and among.

Vieja guttulata

GUENTHER 1864

Natural Range: Atlantic slope of Mexico.
Size: 14" (35 cm) TL.
Water Chemistry: Tropical; slightly alkaline with moderate hardness.
Behavior: Moderately aggressive; may bully smaller tankmates.
Dietary Requirements: Small live foods and all types of prepared foods.

Remarks: Juveniles and small adults are easily identified by the black stripe that runs from just posterior to their gill opercula to the base of their tail. Otherwise, their care in aquariums is the same as for the others in the genus.

Vieja hartwegi

TAYLOR & MILLER 1980

Natural Range: Southern Mexico and Guatemala.
Size: 12" (30 cm) TL.
Water Chemistry: Tropical; slightly alkaline with moderate hardness.
Behavior: Moderately aggressive; may bully smaller tankmates.
Dietary Requirements: Small live foods and all types of prepared foods.

Remarks: This species is remarkably similar in many ways to *V. guttulata*.

Vieja bifasciata

Vieja melanurus for comparison

Vieja guttulata

Vieja guttulata

Vieja hartwegi

Vieja hartwegi adult male

Vieja heterospilus

HUBBS 1936
Natural Range: Mexico to Guatemala.
Size: 10" (25 cm) TL.
Water Chemistry: Tropical; slightly alkaline with moderate hardness.
Behavior: Moderately aggressive; may bully smaller tankmates.
Dietary Requirements: Small live foods and all types of prepared foods.

Remarks: A bold cichlid that does well is cichlid community aquariums as long as their tankmates are too large to be swallowed. Provide plenty of caves for this species hide out in. as they grow older they will usually become quite tame.

Vieja maculicauda / Black Belt Cichlid

REGAN 1905
Natural Range: Southern Mexico, Nicaragua, and Panama.
Size: 14" (35 cm) TL, usually far smaller.
Water Chemistry: Tropical; slightly alkaline with moderate hardness.
Behavior: Moderately aggressive; may bully smaller tankmates.
Dietary Requirements: Small live foods and all types of prepared foods.

Remarks: The Black Belt Cichlid has enjoyed years of popularity among Central American cichlid enthusiasts. Provided with a large aquarium and plenty of food they will do quite well for many years.

Vieja regani

MILLER 1974
Natural Range: Southern Mexico.
Size: 14" (35 cm) TL.
Water Chemistry: Tropical; slightly alkaline with moderate hardness.
Behavior: Moderately aggressive; may bully smaller tankmates.
Dietary Requirements: Small live foods and all types of prepared foods.

Remarks: A very popular and colorful cichlid, *V. regani* is an excellent Central American cichlid to add to your large cichlid community aquarium. They are large-growing, colorful beasts that are surprisingly peaceful for their size.

Vieja heterospilus female

Vieja heterospilus male

Vieja maculicauda

Vieja maculicauda

Vieja regani adult female

Vieja regani small male

Vieja synspila / Fire Head Cichlid

HUBBS 1935

Natural Range: Mexico south through Guatemala and Belize.
Size: 16" (40 cm) TL, usually smaller.
Water Chemistry: Tropical; slightly alkaline with moderate hardness.
Behavior: Moderately aggressive; may bully smaller tankmates.
Dietary Requirements: Small live foods and all types of prepared foods.

Remarks: It is rather difficult to beat the intense red coloration of an adult Fire Head Cichlid. This species is very popular among hobbyists who fancy big fishes, not just cichlids, and their popularity among Asian hobbyists has never been greater. This species is suspected in being involved with the making of Flowerhorns.

Xenotilapia flavipinnis

POLL 1985

Natural Range: Lake Tanganyika.
Size: 3" (7.5 cm) TL; sometimes slightly larger.
Water Chemistry: Tropical; hard and alkaline.
Behavior: Generally peaceful.
Dietary Requirements: Small live foods and all types of prepared foods.

Remarks: This small Tanganyikan cichlid does best on a sandy substrate in small groups. They are a biparental mouthbrooding species where the female broods the eggs and fry for approximately 9 days after which the male takes over for the remaining time, usually about 5 to 6 days.

Vieja synspila

Vieja synspila

Xenotilapia flavipinnis

Xenotilapia flavipinnis

Distichodus lusosso

CITHARINIDAE
DISTICHODUS

Citharinidae includes about 100 species of African characins. Formerly belonging to Characidae, these fishes have been split into their own designated family. They are made up of mostly medium-sized fishes, although some do grow to considerable proportions, both in nature and in the aquarium.

Here, we will be discussing three of the members of the genus *Distichodus*. These fishes are big, bold, and beautiful and make fantastic additions to aquariums that contain larger fishes, but beware that they are no pushovers. *Distichodus* can very easily turn the tables on a bully and may even become bullies themselves sometimes.

Some hobbyists prefer to house these fish with other members of their genus, thus making genus-specific aquariums. While such a sight is quite beautiful and unique, it is not recommended. As *Distichodus* grow, they become less and less tolerant of one another—especially males—and may fight terribly. For this reason alone, it is best to keep one per aquarium.

Distichodus affinis / Silver Distichodus

GUNTHER 1873

Natural Range: Congo basin, Africa.
Size: 8" (20 cm) TL.
Water Chemistry: Tropical; prefer hard, alkaline conditions.
Behavior: Generally peaceful but may nip fins and scales.
Dietary Requirements: Omnivorous; feed equal amounts of plant and animal matter.

Remarks: This moderately-sized African characin does best in large, filtered aquariums. Tankmates should be equal in size and temperament to the Silver Distichodus, since this species can be aggressive toward smaller cohabitants. Feed small amounts of food frequently to avoid scale and fin nipping.

Distichodus lusosso / Longsnout Distichodus

SCHILTHUIS 1891

Natural Range: Congo basin, Africa.
Size: 16" (40 cm) TL.
Water Chemistry: Tropical; prefer hard, alkaline conditions.
Behavior: Moderately aggressive to aggressive as adults.
Dietary Requirements: Omnivorous; feed equal amounts of plant and animal matter.

Remarks: The Longsnout Distichodus is a large, nicely-colored species of Africa characin that needs a large tank with plenty of swimming room. Peaceful as juveniles, these brutes grow very large, very fast. As they grow, their temperament becomes ill and they will cause major headaches in aquariums containing small fishes. Use caution with this species.

Distichodus sexfasciatus / Sixbar Distichodus

BOULENGER 1897

Natural Range: Congo basin and Lake Tanganyika.
Size: 30" (75 cm) TL.
Water Chemistry: Tropical; prefer hard, alkaline conditions.
Behavior: Aggressive as adults.
Dietary Requirements: Omnivorous; feed equal amounts of plant and animal matter.

Remarks: Sixbar Distichodus live in shoals in nature but seem to be rather intolerant of one another in all but the largest of aquariums. They are brightly colored as juveniles, and even adults that have been fed good amounts of foods with carotenes will show bright colors. This species is best kept alone or with other very large fishes.

Distichodus affinis juvenile

Distichodus affinis adult

Distichodus lusosso

Distichodus lusosso

Distichodus sexfasciatus small adult

Distichodus sexfasciatus juvenile

575

Yasuhikotakia morleti

COBITIDAE

LOACHES

The family Cobitidae represents a group of about 130 species of tropical or sometimes temperate fish, which are known as Loaches, along with species of the family Balitoridae. Species of the family Cobitidae are distinguished by two main features: their complex respiration method and the presence of suborbital spines.

Loaches have tiny scales, but only a few species are correctly described as "scaleless." The minute scales allow them to absorb oxygen (and other elements) directly through the skin. They are also able to gulp air at the surface of the water and process it in their intestine. Unused air is then passed through the anus. Some loaches, like the Weather Loach (*Misgurnus anguillicaudatus*), are able to endure oxygen-depleted water because of this adaptation. At the same time, their fine scales make them highly sensitive to pollutants and impurities in the water, so when kept in an aquarium, the water must be changed frequently and devoid of ammonia or nitrates.

All members of the family Cobitidae possess defensive spines, which are present between the eye and the snout. When not erect, these are hidden in a small pouch beneath the skin.

Loaches inhabit waters from Europe to Indonesia, with a few species present in North Africa. They live in rivers and can have complex seasonal migrations for spawning and feeding. Cobitids are also omnivorous, scavenging fish, and should be offered a varied diet.

Very few species have been successfully bred in captivity—that is, they are nearly all wild caught. Many popular species will arrive with diseases or parasites, so every species should undergo a period of quarantine before they are added to the community aquarium.

Acantopsis choirorhynchos / Horseface Loach

BLEEKER 1854

Natural Range: Indochina and Malaysia, Borneo. Found throughout the Mekong River Basin, in Laos, Thailand, Cambodia and Vietnam.
Size: 8" (20 cm) TL.
Water Chemistry: Tropical; clean water is essential.
Behavior: Very peaceful.
Dietary Requirements: A varied diet of meaty foods or high quality flake food. Bloodworms, brine shrimp, and *Daphnia* should be rotated and offered in small amounts.

Remarks: *A. choirorhynchos* are burrowing loaches and should be provided with a substrate of rounded sand or fine gravel for this purpose. The Horseface Loach siphons fine sand through its gills in search of microorganisms and other food particles. Because of their burrowing nature and peaceful disposition, they make excellent additions to the community tank.

Botia almorhae / Yoyo Loach

GRAY 1831

Natural Range: Sub-Himalayan India and Bangladesh.
Size: 6" (15 cm) TL.
Water Chemistry: Tropical; clean water is essential.
Behavior: Peaceful.
Dietary Requirements: A mixed diet of flake food, live or frozen invertebrates, and raw or blanched vegetables. Sinking wafers and pellets are also relished. Do not overfeed.

Remarks: The markings on this loach alternate between a spot at the median line and forked "Y" shapes, giving the appearance of the word "YOYO" along its length. This social fish should be kept in groups of no less than three, and it mixes particularly well with other species of *Botia*, although it seems to be less sensitive to light conditions and may be seen out in the open more frequently.

Botia dario / Bengal Loach

HAMILTON 1822

Natural Range: Northern India, Bangladesh, and tributaries of the Ganges River.
Size: 6" (15 cm) TL.
Water Chemistry: Tropical; clean water is essential.
Behavior: Peaceful but inquisitive and active.
Dietary Requirements: A mixed diet of flake food, live or frozen invertebrates, and raw or blanched vegetables. Sinking wafers and pellets are also relished. Do not overfeed.

Remarks: *Botia dario* is a social fish. Like all Botia species, it should be kept in groups of no less than three. Dark, sheltered hiding spots are critical. Raw slices of seedless cucumber seem to be a favorite food. They can be staked into the substrate with a wooden skewer or held in place with a specialized vegetable clip. No ammonia or nitrates should be present in their tanks. Frequent, large water changes can minimize this effect.

Acantopsis choirorhynchos adult

Acantopsis choirorhynchos profile

Botia almorhae

Botia almorhae

Botia dario adult

Botia dario juvenile

579

Botia histrionica / Burmese Loach

BLYTH 1860

Natural Range: Northeastern India to Myanmar (Burma).
Size: 6" (15 cm) TL.
Water Chemistry: Tropical; clean water is essential.
Behavior: Peaceful.
Dietary Requirements: A mixed diet of flake food, live or frozen invertebrates, and raw or blanched vegetables. Sinking wafers and pellets are also relished. Do not overfeed.

Remarks: This peaceful and gregarious loach makes an excellent companion for other *Botia* species but should be kept in groups of at least three to provide for its social nature. Raw slices of seedless cucumber seem to be a favorite food. These can be staked into the substrate with a wooden skewer or held in place with a specialized vegetable clip. Excess food is turned into excess waste and can pollute their water.

Botia striata / Zebra Loach

NARAYAN RAO 1920

Natural Range: Central India in clear, mountain streams.
Size: 3" (8 cm) TL.
Water Chemistry: Tropical; clean water is essential.
Behavior: Peaceful.
Dietary Requirements: A mixed diet of flake food, live or frozen invertebrates, algae wafers, and vegetable matter.

Remarks: *Botia striata* is an attractive loach that doesn't get too big for most community tanks. They are peaceful and social fish that should be kept in groups of at least three and mix well with other *Botia* species and Clown Loaches (*C. macracanthus*). This species spends a lot of time out in the open, foraging for food and shoaling. As with all loaches, the water should be kept very clean through regular, large water changes in order to simulate their river habitats and to prevent buildup of toxins.

Chromobotia macracanthus / Clown Loach

BLEEKER 1852

Natural Range: Sumatra and Borneo, Indonesia. Also found in Malaysian Borneo.
Size: Can exceed 12" (30 cm) TL.
Water Chemistry: Tropical; clean water is critical to the health of this loach.
Behavior: Peaceful.
Dietary Requirements: An omnivorous creature, they require a minimum mixture of live or frozen invertebrates, vegetable matter, and prepared foods.

Remarks: By far the most popular and available loach in the hobby, *C. macracanthus* should not be purchased on a whim without first considering their demanding needs and longevity. The Clown Loach can live for as long as 35 years and attain a size that requires a very large aquarium. Their water must be kept pure with a slightly acidic, soft chemistry. These fish have extremely small scales and depend on their skin for part of their respiration. Clown Loaches are beautiful and brightly colored inhabitants, suitable for a larger, peaceful aquarium.

Botia histrionica

Botia histrionica

Botia striata

Botia striata group

Chromobotia macracantha juvenile

Chromobotia macracantha adult

Misgurnus anguillicaudatus / Weather Loach or Dojo

CANTOR 1842

Natural Range: Mekong River Basin, Indochina. Also found in China, North Korea, Japan, and Taiwan.
Size: 10" (25 cm) TL.
Water Chemistry: Subtropical to tropical; avoid extremes.
Behavior: Peaceful.
Dietary Requirements: Flake food, small invertebrates, snails.

Remarks: These widespread and ancient loaches are found in Asia, in muddy waters and rice paddies, and have evolved a number of interesting features. Their swim bladders have shrunken and adapted over time so that they are highly sensitive to barometric pressure. The Weather Loaches (or Dojos, as they are known in Japan) will generally become more active as the atmospheric pressure drops before storms, for instance. They are active grazers of the gravel or pebble substrate and can reduce a snail population very quickly.

Pangio kuhlii / Coolie Loach

VALENCIENNES 1846

Natural Range: Java, Indonesia.
Size: 4.75" (12 cm) TL.
Water Chemistry: Tropical.
Behavior: Peaceful.
Dietary Requirements: High quality flake food, frozen bloodworms, algae wafers.

Remarks: These representatives of the so-called "eel loaches" give their generic name Coolie (or Kuhli) Loach to several species of similar fish that show regional distinctions. *Pangio malayana* and *Pangio semi-cincta* may be very hard to differentiate from *P. kuhlii* without knowing their exact collection data. That said, *P. kuhlii* bear nine to thirteen dark brown bars along their otherwise golden length. When stressed, the fish may turn a salmon pink or even gray for a short time.

Pangio myersi / Giant Kuhli

HARRY 1949

Natural Range: Mekong River and its tributaries, Indochina.
Size: 4" (10 cm) TL.
Water Chemistry: Tropical.
Behavior: Peaceful.
Dietary Requirements: High quality flake food, frozen bloodworms, algae wafers.

Remarks: Sometimes referred to as Myer's Slimy Loach, this variation of the "eel loach" has a heavier set body and a distinctly thick slime coat that it uses to protect its minute scales. Clean water is essential to the health of these loaches, as part of their respiration takes place through the skin. They can be identified by the ten to fourteen thick black bands that run the length of their orange body, nearly to the belly.

Misgurnus anguillicaudatus profile

Misgurnus anguillicaudatus var.

Pangio kuhlii var.

Pangio kuhlii normal form

Pangio myersi juvenile

Pangio myersi adult

Pangio shelfordii / Borneo Loach

POPTA 1903

Natural Range: Kapuas and Mahakam River Basins, Borneo.
Size: 3" (8 cm) TL.
Water Chemistry: Cooler tropical waters.
Behavior: Peaceful.
Dietary Requirements: High quality flake food, frozen bloodworms, algae wafers.

Remarks: These "eel loaches" bear a series of saddle-like, dark stripes that do not extend to the belly area. The background color of the fish is pinkish-yellow. It is important to note that *P. shelfordii* come from cooler waters, and will experience discomfort at temperatures higher than 79°F (26 C). Like the other *Pangio* species, *P. shelfordii* are found in leaf litter at the edges of slow moving streams. They should be housed in tanks with relatively dim lighting and soft, acidic water (pH 6.0 – 6.5), and given ample spots to hide.

Syncrossus helodes / Tiger Loach

SAUVAGE 1876

Natural Range: Chao Phraya and Mekong Rivers, Indochina. Also found in Tonle Sap Lake, Cambodia, during flooding.
Size: 12" (30 cm) TL.
Water Chemistry: Tropical; clean water is essential.
Behavior: Somewhat aggressive; nocturnal.
Dietary Requirements: A varied diet of snails, invertebrates, flake food, and vegetable matter.

Remarks: *Syncrossus helodes* grow to be very large loaches. Their territorial nature and combative attitude toward smaller tank mates should be considered. If a large tank is provided, with many sheltered hiding spots, and the water is kept very clean, these loaches can live for decades. A species tank may be preferable. They can be kept with other loaches of significant size, such as the Clown Loach (*Chromobotia macracanthus*).

Yasuhikotakia lecontei / Orange-finned Purple Botia

FOWLER 1937

Natural Range: Mekong River and Chao Phraya River, Indochina.
Size: 6" (15 cm) TL.
Water Chemistry: Tropical; clean water is essential.
Behavior: Semi-aggressive.
Dietary Requirements: Mixed diet of flake food, live or frozen invertebrates, or live snails.

Remarks: These are territorial loaches and, like other members of the genus *Yasuhikotakia*, their territorial nature will diminish somewhat if numerous hiding spots are offered in the tank setting. In their natural habitat, *Y. lecontei* are found in areas of the river with fast-flowing water amid boulders and large gradient gravel. For this reason, the water should be kept very clean and extra circulation should be considered.

Pangio shelfordi adult

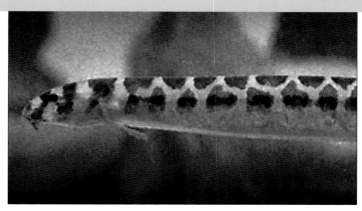

Pangio shelfordi profile

Syncrossus helodes young adult

Syncrossus helodes profile

Yasuhikotakia lecontei

Yasuhikotakia lecontei

585

Yasuhikotakia modesta / Redtail Loach

BLEEKER 1865

Natural Range: Chao Phraya and Mekong Rivers, Indochina. Also found in Tonle Sap Lake, Cambodia, during flooding.
Size: 10" (25 cm) TL.
Water Chemistry: Tropical; clean water is essential.
Behavior: Somewhat aggressive and very active.
Dietary Requirements: Mixed diet of flake food, live or frozen invertebrates, or live snails.

Remarks: Robust and social loaches, *Y. modesta* should only be considered for a large aquarium, as they require ample space in which to swim and explore. A substrate of fine gravel should be used because these loaches spends much of their time digging for food particles and may uproot plants. A diet rich in carotene will bring out the colors on the dorsal and caudal fin, so bloodworms and brine shrimp should included. Avoid overfeeding.

Yasuhikotakia morleti / Hora's Loach or Skunk Loach

TIRANT 1885

Natural Range: Common along the Mekong River from Laos to Vietnam. Also present in the Tonle Sap Lake in Cambodia and Chao Phraya River, Thailand.
Size: 4" (10 cm) TL.
Water Chemistry: Tropical; clean water is essential.
Behavior: Very aggressive; should not be mixed with peaceful, long-finned, or timid fish.
Dietary Requirements: Mixed diet of flake food, live or frozen invertebrates, or live snails. Do not overfeed.

Remarks: Like most species in the genus *Yasuhikotakia*, this is an aggressive and territorial loach. One way of minimizing this behavior (though it will always be present) is to provide eight or more hiding spots per fish. Despite their territorial nature, Skunk Loaches are attractive fish, and can be kept with hardy tankmates, such as Rasboras. Be warned that these loaches will root through the substrate in search of food to the point of uprooting plants.

Yasuhikotakia sidthimunki / Dwarf Loach

KLAUSEWITZ 1959

Natural Range: Mekong River, Kwai River, and Chao Phraya River, Indochina.
Size: 2.25" (5.5 cm) TL.
Water Chemistry: Tropical; clean water is essential.
Behavior: Peaceful.
Dietary Requirements: A mixed diet of flake food, algae wafers, bloodworms, and brine shrimp.

Remarks: *Y. sidthimunki* are very attractive and tiny loaches that should be kept in groups of five or more. These fish are endangered in their natural habitat and must only be considered by aquarists willing to provide for their needs. Weekly water changes of up to 50 percent will prevent any buildup of ammonia or nitrates, both of which are very toxic to this loach. Kept in groups in medium to large aquariums, they will hunt for food in packs and spend much time shoaling socially.

Yasuhikotakia modesta   *Yasuhikotakia modesta*

Yasuhikotakia morleti   *Yasuhikotakia morleti*

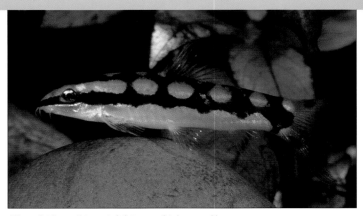

Yasuhikotakia sidthimunki adult   *Yasuhikotakia sidthimunki* juvenile

Coius microlepis

COIIDAE

SIAMESE TIGERFISHES

These large, moderately aggressive species make excellent additions to aquariums devoted to the maintenance of large, predatory fishes. Datnoides will not hesitate to swallow smaller fishes if they feel they can fit them in their mouth—and often they think more can fit in their mouth than actually can.

There are currently five species within the family, but only three of them are profiled here: *Coius campbelli*, *C. microlepis*, and *C. quadrifasciatus*. They are considered to be the latest and greatest of the *feng shui* fishes (Sung, 2004).

Aquarium care of these individuals is rather easy, provided they have space and good water. Many hobbyists report that only *C. campbelli* are overly aggressive with each other, and the other species seem to do well as long as there is enough room for each individual to have their own space. These fishes make outstanding display creatures in large, Asian-influenced show aquariums where the combination of their beauty and decorative lore makes them fascinating to observe.

Coius campbelli / New Guinea Tigerfish

WHITLEY 1939

Natural Range: Irian Jaya, Indonesia, and Papua New Guinea.
Size: 18" (45 cm) TL.
Water Chemistry: Tropical; tolerant of either fresh or brackish conditions.
Behavior: Generally peaceful toward fish too big to swallow; extremely aggressive toward each other.
Dietary Requirements: Feed meaty foods including shrimp, krill, silversides, fish meat, and feeder fish.

Remarks: New Guinea Tigerfish are rarely available in the hobby and as a result command a high price. They are easily distinguished from other *Coius* species by the intense gold body color and the indistinct margins of the black bars that exhibit an irregular and variegated appearance. Their unique appearance and vibrant colors make them a very desirable fish for the aquarium.

Coius microlepis / Indonesian Tigerfish, Finescale Tigerfish

BLEEKER 1853

Natural Range: Chao Phraya, Mekong, Kapuas, and Musi basins, and Sumatra and Borneo.
Size: 18" (45 cm) TL.
Water Chemistry: Tropical; otherwise not critical.
Behavior: Semi-aggressive, particularly toward conspecifics.
Dietary Requirements: Prefer live feeder fish but will accept other meaty foods including shrimp, krill, silversides, fish meat, and sinking pellets.

Remarks: A handsome, deep-bodied fish. Multiple vertical bars make it a very popular aquarium fish particularly in Asian countries. A commonly available and affordable species of *Coius*, *C. microlepis* can be shy and timid when first introduced into new surroundings, so provide ample cover and subdued lighting. Once comfortable in their environment, they regain their confident and outgoing personalities.

Coius quadrifasciatus / Silver Tigerfish, Four-barred Tigerfish

SEVASTIANOF 1809

Natural Range: India to Indonesia and New Guinea.
Size: 12" (30 cm) TL.
Water Chemistry: Tropical; thrive in brackish conditions.
Behavior: Semi-aggressive, particularly toward conspecifics.
Dietary Requirements: Prefer live feeder fish but will accept other meaty foods including shrimp, krill, silversides, fish meat, and sinking pellets.

Remarks: Silver Tigerfish are distinguished from other *Coius* species by their silver body coloration and unique "bullet"-shaped body. They feature up to 7 full vertical bars, often with 1 to 4 partial bars between the full bars. One of the original species first available to the hobby, they are readily available and inexpensive. The fact that they occur naturally in brackish waters has led to the common misconception in the hobby that all Tigerfish species are brackish.

Coius campbelli

Coius campbelli note distictive stripe

Coius microlepis

Coius microlepis

Coius quadrifasciatus

Coius quadrifasciatus profile

591

Boulengerella maculata

CTENOLUCIDAE
PIKE-CHARACIDS

Ctenolucidae contains approximately seven species, of which three are profiled herein. The genera included in the family are *Ctenolucius* and *Boulengerella*. Representatives from these both of these genera are common in the aquarium trade, but *Boulengerella* seem to be more prevalent year around.

Boulengerella is widely distributed over much of northern South America, including the Rio Negro, Orinoco, and Tocantins basins. They are common throughout this range and collected frequently for export to countries worldwide.

Boulengerella species are all highly piscivorous and feed frequently throughout the day. In the aquarium, they should be fed small live fishes frequently. Some hobbyists have reported that they have had some success with training their *Boulengerella* to accept non-living and prepared foods. They do best in species-specific aquariums, since they have a tendency to be harassed by more aggressive tankmates.

Boulengerella lateristriga / Striped Pike-characin

BOULENGER 1895

Natural Range: Brazil and Venezuela.
Size: 12" (30 cm) TL.
Water Chemistry: Tropical; soft, acidic conditions are preferred.
Behavior: Aggressive with smaller fishes.
Dietary Requirements: Small, live fishes; may accept non-living foods.

Remarks: This interesting fish is a very efficient predator of smaller fishes. Any tankmate should be large enough to keep the Pike Characin from swallowing it. The best situation for this species, as well as all *Boulengerella*, is to not have tankmates. They do best in large aquariums by themselves.

Boulengerella lucius / Golden Pike-characin

CUVIER 1816

Natural Range: Rio Amazonas and Rio Orinoco basins; Brazil and Venezuela.
Size: 18" (45 cm) TL.
Water Chemistry: Tropical; avoid extremes.
Behavior: Aggressive with smaller tankmates.
Dietary Requirements: Small, live fishes; may accept non-living foods.

Remarks: The Golden Pike-characin is the largest of the genus. They can reach more than 18" in total length but are more commonly encountered at less than half that size. Aside from their larger size, their care and husbandry in aquariums is the same as with *B. lateristriga*.

Boulengerella maculata / Spotted pike-characin

VALENCIENNES 1850

Natural Range: Widely distributed over much of northern South America.
Size: 16" (40 cm) TL.
Water Chemistry: Tropical; prefer soft, acidic conditions.
Behavior: Aggressive toward small fishes.
Dietary Requirements: Small, live fishes; may accept non-living foods.

Remarks: Another interesting Pike Characin is the Spotted Pike-characin *Boulengerella maculata*. This species is broadly distributed over the northern regions of South America. Their care and husbandry in captivity is identical to that of other members of the genus.

594

Boulengerella lateristriga adult

Boulengerella maculata for comparison

Boulengerella lucius

Boulengerella sp. "Colombia"

Boulengerella maculata juvenile

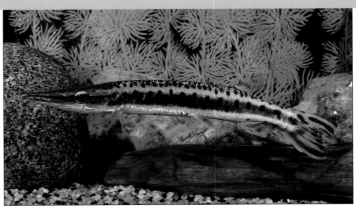

Boulengerella maculata adult

Puntius tetrazona

CYPRINIDAE

BARBS, RASBORAS, AND SHARKS

With more than 2000 valid species, Cyprinidae is one of the largest families of freshwater fishes on Earth. They are distributed in regions of Canada south through Mexico in North America, many regions of Africa, and certain systems in Eurasia.

One of the most distinctive features of the members of this family is the presence of barbels, although they may also be absent. However, most fishes that are common in the aquarium trade will have them. These barbels are used much in the same way as the barbels on catfishes, although some people speculate that the catfish's barbels are more sensitive. This is probably true for two reasons: catfishes normally have more than just two barbels (one on either side of the mouth) as the cyprinids do, and catfishes normally live in turbid water and may rely on only their barbels to find food, whereas many cyprinids live in relatively clear water where their eyesight could assist them in finding food.

In the aquarium, most of these fishes can be kept very easily. Generally, they do well when offered small amounts of live foods, such as blackworms, tubifex worms, and *Daphnia*, along with a staple diet of normal aquarium-type prepared foods such as flake foods or small granules. Since they are widely distributed over much of the planet, their temperature requirements will vary, so be sure that you keep only those with similar requirements together.

Balantiocheilos melanopterus / Bala Shark (Tri-colored Shark)

BLEEKER 1951

Natural Range: Mekong and Chao Phraya basins, Malay Peninsula, Sumatra, and Borneo.
Size: 16" (40 cm) SL.
Water Chemistry: Tropical; otherwise not critical.
Behavior: Peaceful schooling fish.
Dietary Requirements: Normal aquarium fare; should have some vegetable foods.

Remarks: These large fish should be kept in groups of five or more in a very large aquarium. They are generally compatible with fishes too small to ingest. Many are sold at small sizes, then languish in tiny tanks.

Barbonymus schwanenfeldii / Tinfoil Barb

BLEEKER 1853

Natural Range: Mekong and Chao Phraya basins, Malay Peninsula, Sumatra and Borneo.
Size: 16" (40 cm) TL.
Water Chemistry: Tropical; adaptable; prefer moderately hard, slightly acidic water.
Behavior: Peaceful for such a large barb.
Dietary Requirements: Largely herbivorous; will eat algae and plants.

Remarks: Another schooling fish for a very large tank. The black submarginal stripe along each lobe of the caudal fin is diagnostic; *B. altus* lacks these stripes. The red fins and shiny silver body make this an impressive species for large displays. An albino morph is established in the hobby.

Barbus arcislongae

KEILHACK 1908

Natural Range: Endemic to Lake Malawi.
Size: 2.75" (6.8 cm) TL.
Water Chemistry: Tropical, hard, basic.
Behavior: Unknown.
Dietary Requirements: Omnivorous.

Remarks: Even though African barbs are less known in the hobby than Asian species, this one is even rarer—and even more unusual in that it is endemically sympatric with mbuna.

Balantiocheilos melanopterus juvenile

Balantiocheilos melanopterus adult

Barbonymus schwanenfeldii gold var.

Barbonymus schwanenfeldii adult group

Barbus arcislongae pair

Barbus arcislongae profile showing barbels

Barbus camptacanthus / African Redfin Barb

BLEEKER 1863

Natural Range: Area of Cameroon and Gabon into the Congo.
Size: 6" (15.5 cm) TL.
Water Chemistry: Tropical; otherwise not critical.
Behavior: A typical large schooling barb.
Dietary Requirements: Will take most aquarium fare.

Remarks: These African barbs are found in small, forested rivers.

Barbus caudovittatus

BOULENGER 1902

Natural Range: Congo River system into Lake Tanganyika.
Size: 32" (80 cm) TL.
Water Chemistry: Tropical; moderate pH and hardness.
Behavior: Unknown.
Dietary Requirements: Omnivorous.

Remarks: Now, here's a barb! At three feet long apiece, a school of these fish would require a house-sized aquarium. These are good candidates for dither fish in a Tanganyika biotope tank with *Boulengerochromis microlepis*.

Barbus dorsalis / Long-snouted Barb

JERDON 1849

Natural Range: India and Sri Lanka
Size: 10" (25 cm) TL.
Water Chemistry: Tropical.
Behavior: A typical large schooling barb.
Dietary Requirements: Largely herbivorous; eat algae and plants.

Remarks: These are detritivores that prefer flowing water. Provide plenty of current and aeration, and feed a largely vegetarian diet.

Barbus camptacanthus

Barbus camptacanthus pair

Barbus caudovittatus

Barbus caudovittatus profile

Barbus dorsalis

Barbus sajadrensis for comparison

601

Barbus eutaenia / Orangefin Barb

BOULENGER 1904

Natural Range: Widespread in Africa, including the Congo system and Lake Tanganyika.
Size: 6" (16 cm) TL.
Water Chemistry: Tropical; adaptable.
Behavior: A typical large schooling barb.
Dietary Requirements: Will take most aquarium fare.

Remarks: These fish are found in clear, rocky streams and occasionally in Lake Tanganyika.

Barbus fasciolatus / African Banded Barb

GÜNTHER 1868

Natural Range: Widespread in African river systems, including the Congo and Zambezi.
Size: 2.75" (7 cm) TL.
Water Chemistry: Tropical; fairly soft, slightly acid conditions.
Behavior: Shy and crepuscular; need planted tank.
Dietary Requirements: Omnivorous, with a strong preference for small invertebrates.

Remarks: This barb is found in well-oxygenated but vegetated areas such as floodplain rivers.

Barbus greenwoodi

POLL 1967

Natural Range: Angola.
Size: 1.5" (4.1 cm) TL.
Water Chemistry: Tropical.
Behavior: Benthopelagic, like most barbs.
Dietary Requirements: Omnivorous.

Remarks: This species is at the lower extreme of the vast size spectrum for its genus.

Barbus eutaenia adult

Barbus miolepis miolepis for comparison

Barbus fasciolatus pair

Barbus fasciolatus group

Barbus greenwoodi adults

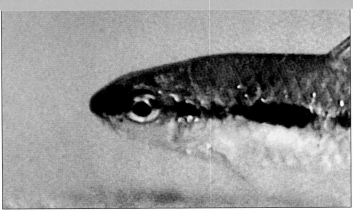

Barbus greenwoodi profile

603

Barbus jae / Jae Barb

BOULENGER 1903

Natural Range: Southern Cameroon, Gabon, Equatorial Guinea.
Size: 1.5" (3.8 cm) TL.
Water Chemistry: Tropical; this barb comes from extremely soft, very acid water.
Behavior: Peaceful and schooling.
Dietary Requirements: Omnivorous; especially fond of small live invertebrates.

Remarks: Although known to science for a century, these fish have only recently become regularly available in the hobby. They make an extremely beautiful display as a large school in a planted tank.

Barbus kerstenii kerstenii / Redspot Barb

PETERS 1868

Natural Range: Widespread in Southern Central and East Africa to Lake Victoria.
Size: 4.25" (11 cm) TL.
Water Chemistry: Tropical; midrange on pH and hardness.
Behavior: A typical barb.
Dietary Requirements: Omnivorous.

Remarks: In the wild, this barb is found in streams and along vegetated shores of large rivers.

Barbus miolepis miolepis / Zigzag Barb

BOULENGER 1902

Natural Range: Congo and Zambezi River systems.
Size: 5" (12.5 cm) TL.
Water Chemistry: Tropical.
Behavior: A typical medium-sized barb.
Dietary Requirements: Omnivorous.

Remarks: Not regularly encountered in the trade, these barbs are a bit large for most community tanks, especially since they are best kept in schools.

Barbus jae male

Barbus jae pair

Barbus kerstenii kerstenii

Barbus macrops for comparison

Barbus miolepis miolepis

Barbus miolepis miolepis pair

Barbus narayani / Narayan Barb

HORA 1937

Natural Range: India.
Size: 3" (7.8 cm) TL.
Water Chemistry: Tropical.
Behavior: Generally peaceful but may nip at the fins of larger fishes.
Dietary Requirements: Omnivorous; will accept most types of prepared foods.

Remarks: These barbs are endemic to Indian and are found in hill streams. They resemble a pinkish-tan tiger barb with incomplete bars.

Barbus sylvaticus

LOISELLE & WELCOMME 1971

Natural Range: Benin and Nigeria.
Size: 1" (2.5 cm) TL.
Water Chemistry: Tropical
Behavior: Timid and peaceful.
Dietary Requirements: Omnivorous; food must be of sufficiently small size for their tiny mouths.

Remarks: These barbs are about as small as they come. A school could be kept in a 10-gallon planted tank.

Barbus viviparus / Bowstripe Barb

WEBER 1897

Natural Range: East African coastal rivers and lakes.
Size: 2.75" (7 cm) TL.
Water Chemistry: Tropical; quite adaptable.
Behavior: Typical for barbs.
Dietary Requirements: In the wild, these fish primarily eat small invertebrates. They will take any aquarium foods.

Remarks: Despite the name, these are typical egg scatterers. In form and color, they are reminiscent of the Cherry Barb.

Barbus narayani

Barbus narayani

Barbus sylvaticus

Puntius sp. for comparison

Barbus viviparus

Barbus viviparus

Boraras brigittae

VOGT 1978

Natural Range: Borneo, Indonesia.
Size: 1.25" (3.5 cm) TL.
Water Chemistry: Tropical.
Behavior: Small, peaceful, schooling.
Dietary Requirements: In nature, they eat small invertebrates; most aquarium fare accepted.

Remarks: Like other related small, red rasboras, this species can be positively brilliantly colored when conditions are to its liking—a school in a planted tank, no big tankmates, perhaps slightly acidic water.

Boraras maculata / Dwarf Rasbora

DUNCKER 1904

Natural Range: Malay Peninsula to Indonesia.
Size: 1" (2.5 cm) TL. One of the smallest cyprinids in the world.
Water Chemistry: Tropical, prefer soft, acidic water, which will best bring out their color.
Behavior: Very small, very peaceful, timid schooling fish.
Dietary Requirements: In nature, they eat small invertebrates; most aquarium fare accepted.

Remarks: One of the interesting things about many rasboras, which this one takes to the extreme, is how they school in place. The fish are about equally spaced from each other, and they can be in any orientation relative to the rest. They will occasionally make short, jumpy, movements, but the school remains in one spot. Add their gorgeous color, and these fish are a true joy to observe.

Carassius auratus auratus / Goldfish

LINNAEUS 1758

Natural Range: Widespread over much of Asia; introduced elsewhere.
Size: 24" (60 cm) TL.
Water Chemistry: Temperate to subtropical; otherwise not critical.
Behavior: Generally peaceful but may swallow small fishes as adults.
Dietary Requirements: Consumes almost anything edible; not a picky feeder.

Remarks: In all of its unique and often shocking forms, the Goldfish is still the most popular species in the aquarium industry. They are usually quite easy to care for, being rather undemanding in terms of water chemistry and feeding requirements. Of course, as with any fish, you still want to provide them with as much space as possible, good filtration, and a well-balanced diet.

Boraras brigittae

Boraras brigittae

Boraras maculata

Boraras maculata pair

Carassius auratus

Carassius auratus var. "red oranda"

Chela dadyburjori / Dadio

MENON 1952

Natural Range: India.
Size: 1" (3 cm) TL.
Water Chemistry: Tropical.
Behavior: A peaceful, schooling fish.
Dietary Requirements: Will take all aquarium fare.

Remarks: The fishes in the genus *Chela* seem intermediate between danios and other cyprinids like barbs. Some species, in fact, are commonly called barbs.

Crossocheilus siamensis / Siamese Algae Eater

SMITH 1931

Natural Range: Thailand, Cambodia, Malay Peninsula.
Size: 6.25" (16 cm) TL.
Water Chemistry: Tropical; very adaptable to almost any pH and hardness.
Behavior: A peaceful, active, schooling fish.
Dietary Requirements: Feed naturally on plankton and algae. Must have algae in their diet.

Remarks: The Holy Grail for many aquatic gardeners, this fish is prized as the best algae eater for planted tanks. Its appetite includes red and black algae that most other algae-eating species will ignore.

Cyprinus carpio carpio / Common Carp (Koi)

LINNAEUS 1758

Natural Range: Western Europe through eastern Eurasia; throughout Asia.
Size: 48" (120 cm) TL; usually smaller.
Water Chemistry: Temperate to subtropical; otherwise not critical.
Behavior: Generally peaceful except during spawning; will eat small fishes.
Dietary Requirements: Feed mainly on detritus in nature, but any staple pond food is suitable otherwise.

Remarks: While the Goldfish is the king of the aquarium, the Carp (Koi) is the king of the pond. Koi are sold in many, many different color varieties and fin types. There are many good books on these fish sold at local pet shops. It is recommended that you read about these beautiful fishes *before* purchasing one.

Chela dadyburjori pair

Chela dadyburjori

Crossocheilus siamensis

Crossocheilus siamensis

Cyprinus carpio carpio

Cyprinus carpio carpio "butterfly" sanke

Danio albolineatus / Pearl Danio

BLYTH 1860
Natural Range: Burma to Laos and Sumatra.
Size: 2.75" (7 cm) TL.
Water Chemistry: Tropical; otherwise not critcal.
Behavior: A typical danio—peaceful, always active, extremely hardy.
Dietary Requirements: Will take any foods.

Remarks: The demeanor of these fish and their mother-of-pearl iridescence have made them perennial favorites for close to a century. Although not bearing spots or stripes like many of their congeners, they have a subtle beauty that is emphasized when a large school is kept in a well-lit, planted tank.

Danio choprae / Glowlight Danio

HORA 1928
Natural Range: Northern Burma.
Size: 1" (3 cm) TL.
Water Chemistry: Tropical.
Behavior: A typical danio.
Dietary Requirements: Any foods are taken; occasionally nibble on algae.

Remarks: As Burmese collections for the aquarium trade have increased, this beautiful little species has become fairly consistently available.

Danio kerri / Blue Danio

SMITH 1931
Natural Range: Malay Peninsula.
Size: 2" (5 cm) TL.
Water Chemistry: Tropical.
Behavior: A typical danio.
Dietary Requirements: Any aquarium foods.

Remarks: These colorful little minnows are very suitable for inclusion in small- to medium-sized aquariums where they will readily form tight schools. The requirements for their care and husbandry in aquariums are identical to those for *Danio rerio*.

Danio albolineatus

Danio albolineatus

Danio choprae

Danio sp. for comparison

Danio kerri

Danio kerri spawning

Danio nigrofasciatus / Dwarf Danio

DAY 1870

Natural Range: Northern Burma.
Size: 2" (5 cm) TL.
Water Chemistry: Tropical.
Behavior: A typical danio.
Dietary Requirements: Any foods of appropriate size.

Remarks: Dwarf Danios are probably one of the smallest species within *Danio*. They thrive in aquariums that have lush plant growth and slightly alkaline conditions. In nature, they can be found living in schools in the faster-moving waters of streams and creeks, as well as in some larger rivers.

Danio rerio / Zebra Danio

HAMILTON 1822

Natural Range: India, Pakistan, Bangladesh, Nepal, and Burma.
Size: 2.25" (6 cm) TL.
Water Chemistry: Tropical.
Behavior: The quintessential danio.
Dietary Requirements: Any aquarium foods.

Remarks: One of the first aquarium fish and still immensely popular, *D. rerio* have been developed in various color morphs and long-fin varieties, though the original wild-type fish can't be beat for temperament, hardiness, color, and action. The first transgenic aquarium fish, the Glo Fish™, is a zebra danio with transgenically acquired red coral pigment. Like the fruit fly and the white rat, this fish has been extensively used in laboratory studies—everything from genome mapping to environmental bioassay.

Devario aequipinnatus / Giant Danio

MCCLELLAND 1839

Natural Range:
Size: 6" (15 cm) TL.
Water Chemistry: Tropical.
Behavior: Typical schooling danios, only larger.
Dietary Requirements: Any foods will be taken; in nature eat mostly insects.

Remarks: This species provides the flashy activity of a school of danios for larger tanks with larger tankmates. As with all danios, keep a tank containing these jumpers well covered.

614

Danio nigrofasciatus

Danio nigrofasciatus

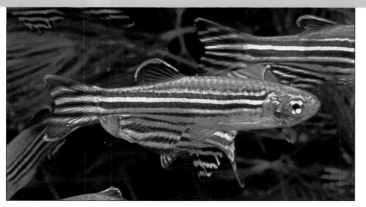

Danio rerio

Danio rerio var. "longfin"

Devario aequipinnatus

Devario aequipinnatus

Devario devario / Sind Danio

HAMILTON 1822

Natural Range: India, Nepal, Pakistan, Bangladesh, and reportedly Afghanistan.
Size: 4" (10 cm) TL.
Water Chemistry: Subtropical.
Behavior: Large danios.
Dietary Requirements: Like all danios, these fish eat mainly small invertebrates, and they will take any prepared foods.

Remarks: This species is very similar to the Giant Danio but will tolerate an unheated tank.

Eirmotus octozona / Eight-banded False Barb

SCHULTZ 1959

Natural Range: Thailand, western Borneo.
Size: 1.5" (4 cm) TL.
Water Chemistry: Tropical.
Behavior: Unknown.
Dietary Requirements: Small, live foods and prepared foods are suitable.

Remarks: Appearing much like several Asian barb species, these small fish require the same kind of setup and diet.

Epalzeorhynchos bicolor / Red-tailed Black Shark

SMITH 1931

Natural Range: Thailand.
Size: 4.75" (12 cm) TL.
Water Chemistry: Tropical.
Behavior: Primarily a bottom feeder. As they mature, they become more territorial and aggressive.
Dietary Requirements: Omnivorous; must have some plant matter in their diet.

Remarks: Although very popular because of their striking black and red color pattern, these fish are too large and too nasty for most community tanks. Do not house more than one per aquarium, as they are particularly nasty toward conspecifics. These cyprinids are believed to be extinct in the wild, but tens of thousands are raised every year in captive ponds in Asia.

Devario devario female

Devario devario male

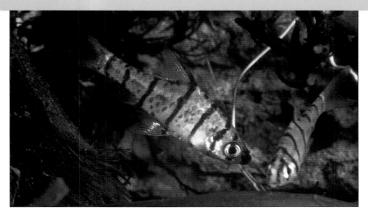

Eirmotus octozona pair

Eirmotus octozona profile

Epalzeorhynchos bicolor adult

Epalzeorhynchos bicolor juvenile

617

Epalzeorhynchos frenatum / Ruby Shark (Rainbow Shark)

FOWLER 1934

Natural Range: Cambodia; Thailand.
Size: 6" (15 cm) TL.
Water Chemistry: Tropical.
Behavior: Can be territorial and aggressive.
Dietary Requirements: Largely herbivorous.

Remarks: Another very popular fish that probably shouldn't be. An albino morph is established, and this is often dyed and sold in assorted colors. This practice is injurious to the fish and should be avoided.

Epalzeorhynchos kalopterus / Siamese Flying Fox

BLEEKER 1851

Natural Range: Malay; Thailand; Indonesia
Size: 6.25" (16 cm) TL.
Water Chemistry: Tropical.
Behavior: A solitary, territorial species.
Dietary Requirements: Omnivorous; must have plant matter.

Remarks: Another Flying Fox, this one is definitely not a schooling fish. It also is not going to keep your tank free of algae, though it may eat some of your plants.

Labeo chrysophekadion / Black Shark

BLEEKER 1850

Natural Range: Thailand; Cambodia; Malay Peninsula; Sumatra; Java; Borneo.
Size: 36" (90 cm) TL; 15 pounds (7 kg).
Water Chemistry: Tropical.
Behavior: Fairly peaceful but solitary—one per tank.
Dietary Requirements: Detritivorous carp; eat anything.

Remarks: A major food fish in its native lands, these are more cyprinids that are popular and sold by the thousands as streamlined, shark-shaped, black juveniles. Unfortunately, these fish soon lose their color and gain enormous size. Some cichlid keepers use them as tankmates for their fish, but even they rarely have an aquarium large enough for a 3-foot fish to even turn around in.

Epalzeorhynchos frenatum adult

Epalzeorhynchos frenatum juvenile

Epalzeorhynchos kalopterus adult

Epalzeorhynchos kalopterus juvenile

Labeo chrysophekadion adult

Labeo chrysophekadion juvenile

Labeo forskali

RÜPPEL 1836

Natural Range: The Nile drainage basin.
Size: 14" (36 cm) TL.
Water Chemistry: Tropical.
Behavior: Fairly peaceful.
Dietary Requirements: Absolutely omnivorous.

Remarks: More manageable at about a foot than some other *Labeo*, this rather drab fish is not very common in the hobby.

Microrasbora rubescens

ANNANDALE 1918

Natural Range: Burma.
Size: 1.75" (3 cm) TL.
Water Chemistry: Tropical.
Behavior: Timid and peaceful.
Dietary Requirements: Very small invertebrates or their equivalent.

Remarks: A tiny baitfish in its native land, this pale red rasbora is more common in the hobby in Europe than in the United States.

Puntioplites bulu

BLEEKER 1851

Natural Range: Indonesia; Cambodia; Thailand.
Size: 14" (35 cm) TL.
Water Chemistry: Tropical.
Behavior: Unknown.
Dietary Requirements: Largely herbivorous.

Remarks: This fish is uncommon the wild, and may be extinct. Aquarium specimens can be sometimes found through private breeders.

Labeo forskali

Labeo forskali

Microrasbora rubescens var.

Microrasbora rubescens

Puntioplites bulu pair

Puntioplites bulu profile showing their unique mouth

Puntius arulius

JERDON 1849

Natural Range: Southern India
Size: 5" (12 cm) TL.
Water Chemistry: Tropical; moderately soft and acid preferred.
Behavior: A typical large schooling barb.
Dietary Requirements: Will take most aquarium fare.

Remarks: These barbs from large rivers and lakes are distinctive with the male's long dorsal fin and the colorful pattern (which improves with age). They should be kept in schools, which should also minimize nippiness.

Puntius conchonius / Rosy Barb

HAMILTON 1822

Natural Range: Afghanistan; India; Pakistan; Bangladesh; Nepal.
Size: 5.5" (14 cm) TL.
Water Chemistry: Subtropical; very adaptable to water chemistry.
Behavior: Peaceful, schooling.
Dietary Requirements: Omnivorous; should have algae in their diet.

Remarks: Longfin and "neon" morphs have been established, but the original fish are true beauties. When ready to spawn, males become truly rosy in color. This is a very popular and long-appreciated aquarium species, extremely hardy, even for a barb.

Puntius denisonii / Red-lined Torpedo Barb

DAY 1865

Natural Range: Endemic to India.
Size: 6" (15 cm) TL.
Water Chemistry: Subtropical; moderate pH and hardness.
Behavior: An active and fairly peaceful large barb, though some specimens are nippy.
Dietary Requirements: Will take regular aquarium fare.

Remarks: Since it started being widely available recently, this fish has gained quite a following. Currently, hobbyists are rushing to be the first to breed this species, but it is apparently hard to get any females. Since it comes from very fast, cool mountain streams, oxygenation is of particular importance, especially if you are keeping the fish in warmer water. They are happiest at temperatures between 60° and 75°F.

Puntius arulius

Puntius arulius pair spawning

Puntius conchonius pair

Puntius conchonius male

Puntius denisonii

Puntius denisonii group

Puntius fasciatus / Melon Barb

JERDON 1849

Natural Range: India.
Size: 6" (15 cm) TL.
Water Chemistry: Tropical; quite soft and acidic.
Behavior: Unknown.
Dietary Requirements: Unknown.

Remarks: Prefer flowing rivers in which considerable seasonal migration appears to take place.

Puntius pentazona / Five-banded Barb

BOULENGER 1894

Natural Range: Malay peninsula to Sumatra, Indonesia
Size: 3.5" (8.8 cm) TL.
Water Chemistry: Tropical.
Behavior: A typical small barb.
Dietary Requirements: Omnivorous; accept all aquarium foods.

Remarks: Although not quite as common as the Tiger Barb *P. tetrazona*, this species is very popular due to its beauty, hardiness, and adaptability. As with all small barbs, keep them in groups of five or more, both to elicit natural schooling behaviors and to keep any rambunctiousness within the school.

Puntius rhombooccelatus

KOUMANS 1940

Natural Range: Borneo.
Size: 3.5" (8.8 cm) TL.
Water Chemistry: Tropical.
Behavior: A typical barb.
Dietary Requirements: Omnivorous.

Remarks: Very flashy little fish, the typical barb splotches along the body are ocelli, but not round ones; instead, they are close to rhomboid in shape.

624

Puntius fasciatus

Puntius fasciatus young pair

Puntius pentazona

Puntius nigrofasciatus for comparison

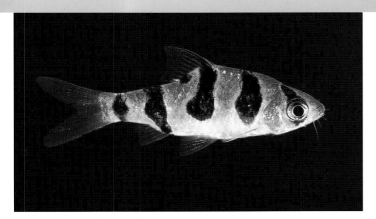

Puntius rhomboocelatus

Puntius rhomboocelatus

Puntius semifasciolatus / Chinese Barb

GÜNTHER 1868

Natural Range: Southeast China.
Size: 2.75" (7 cm) TL.
Water Chemistry: Subtropical; adaptable to just about any non-extreme pH and hardness.
Behavior: A typical barb.
Dietary Requirements: Omnivorous; will take any aquarium foods.

Remarks: The extremely common Gold Barbs are believed to be either domesticated versions of these fish or hybrids of these with another barb.

Puntius tetrazona / Tiger Barb (Sumatra Barb)

BLEEKER 1855

Natural Range: Sumatra; Borneo.
Size: 2.75" (7 cm) TL.
Water Chemistry: Tropical; extremely adaptable.
Behavior: Typical small barbs; will definitely nip at long-flowing fins.
Dietary Requirements: Omnivorous; will eat anything offered.

Remarks: Quintessential aquarium fish, these barbs enliven and beautify the tank of almost every aquarist at some time in their fishkeeping career. Easily kept, easily spawned, and easily one of the most beautiful barbs, their popularity is continuous. Many different color morphs have been established, including albino and green. The color pattern of gold background, black bars, and red fins, is shared with several unrelated species, such as the Asian Clown Loach *Chromobotia macracanthus* and species in the African genus *Distichodus*.

Puntius ticto

HAMILTON 1822

Natural Range: India; Pakistan; Bangladesh; Burma; Thailand.
Size: 4" (10 cm) TL.
Water Chemistry: Subtropical, fresh, and brackish.
Behavior: Typical barbs.
Dietary Requirements: Prefer meaty foods, such as small invertebrates. Will take any aquarium food.

Remarks: These barbs from still, shallow waters in Asia have a domesticated variant called the Odessa Barb, the males of which have brilliant red coloration.

Puntius semifasciolatus

Puntius nigrofasciatus for comparison

Puntius tetrazona var. "green"

Puntius tetrazona normal var.

Puntius ticto group

Puntius ticto pair

Puntius titteya / Cherry Barb

DERANIYAGALA 1929
Natural Range: Sri Lanka
Size: 2" (5 cm) TL.
Water Chemistry: Tropical; very adaptable.
Behavior: Very peaceful barb.
Dietary Requirements: Omnivorous with a heavy leaning toward herbivorous; must have algae or other plant material.

Remarks: These barbs are real old timers in the hobby. They are very hardy and very easy to spawn. They do best (and look best) in a planted tank. For the most color, get mixed sex groups. The males take on a burgundy maroon glow when courting, so the presence of females will ensure an almost continuous show. An albino morph is established in the hobby.

Rasbora borapotensis / Blackline Rasbora (Redtail Rasbora)

SMITH 1934
Natural Range: Cambodia, Thailand, Malay Peninsula
Size: 1.5" (4 cm) TL.
Water Chemistry: Tropical.
Behavior: Peaceful, timid, schooling.
Dietary Requirements: In nature, they eat small invertebrates; most aquarium fare accepted.

Remarks: A wonderful choice for schooling fish in a planted tank.

Rasbora dorsioccelata / Eyespot Rasbora

DUNCKER 1904
Natural Range: Malay Peninsula, Indonesia
Size: 2.5" (6 cm) TL.
Water Chemistry: Tropical; prefer acidic water.
Behavior: Small, peaceful, schooling.
Dietary Requirements: In nature, they eat small invertebrates; most aquarium fare accepted.

Remarks: In form, these rasbora are similar to scissortail *R. trilineata*, but that species lacks the dorsal spot that gives these fish their specific name. *R. dorsioccelata* are fine schooling fish for a peaceful community tank.

Puntius titteya male

Puntius titteya female

Rasbora borapotensis

Rasbora borapotensis

Rasbora dorsioccelata

Rasbora dorsioccelata

629

Rasbora dusnensis / Yellowtail Rasbora

BLEEKER 1851

Natural Range: Cambodia; Thailand; Malay Peninsula; Borneo; Sumatra.
Size: 5.5" (14 cm) TL.
Water Chemistry: Tropical.
Behavior: Peaceful, schooling.
Dietary Requirements: In nature, they eat small invertebrates; most aquarium fare accepted.

Remarks: These larger rasbora are less brilliantly colored than most fish in this group, being mostly silver with a hint of color in the fins. Their caudal fins often have a black posterior margin.

Rasbora kalochroma / Clown Rasbora

BLEEKER 1851

Natural Range: Malay Peninsula to Indonesia.
Size: 4" (10 cm) TL.
Water Chemistry: Tropical.
Behavior: Peaceful.
Dietary Requirements: In nature, they eat small invertebrates; most aquarium fare accepted.

Remarks: These large rasboras have both color and distinctive markings—two dark spots on the side. They are good schooling fish for a larger community setup.

Rasbora trilineatus

STEINDACHNER 1870

Natural Range: Thailand; Cambodia; Malay Peninsula; Borneo; Sumatra.
Size: 5" (13 cm) TL.
Water Chemistry: Tropical; quite adaptable to water chemistry.
Behavior: Large but peaceful schooling fish.
Dietary Requirements: In nature, they eat small invertebrates; most aquarium fare accepted.

Remarks: These rasboras lack colors, but they make up for this by having intriguing silver and black markings. The two ends of the forked tail have a black spot on them, and as the fish swims, it opens and closes its tail in a scissoring motion, causing the spots to wink. Although they get large for rasboras, they are peaceful and good community fish.

Rasbora dusnensis

Rasbora dusnensis

Rasbora kalochroma

Rasbora kalochroma

Rasbora trilineatus male

Rasbora trilineatus female

Rasbora vaterifloris / Pearly Rasbora

DERANIYAGALA 1930

Natural Range: Sri Lanka.
Size: 1.5" (4 cm) TL.
Water Chemistry: Tropical, soft, acidic water.
Behavior: Peaceful, small rasboras.
Dietary Requirements: In nature, they eat small invertebrates; most aquarium fare accepted.

Remarks: These fish come from heavily shaded jungle streams, so they prefer subdued lighting. They have longer fins than most other rasboras.

Sawbwa resplendens / Inle Barb

ANNANDALE 1918

Natural Range: Endemic to Inle Lake in Burma
Size: 1" (2.5 cm) TL.
Water Chemistry: Tropical.
Behavior: Peaceful; prefer large schools.
Dietary Requirements: In nature, they eat small invertebrates; most aquarium fare accepted.

Remarks: Found only in this one lake, these fish, although still numerous, are endangered by the rapid destruction of their habitat. They are more commonly found in the hobby in Europe than in the United States.

Sundadanio axelrodi

BRITTAN 1976

Natural Range: Borneo; Sumatra.
Size: 1" (2.5 cm) TL.
Water Chemistry: Tropical.
Behavior: Tiny, peaceful, schooling rasboras.
Dietary Requirements: Standard aquarium fare in small sizes.

Remarks: Found only in this one lake, these fish, although still numerous, are endangered by the rapid destruction of their habitat. They are more commonly found in the hobby in Europe than in the United States.

Rasbora vaterifloris   *Rasbora vaterifloris*

Sawbwa resplendens   *Sawbwa resplendens*

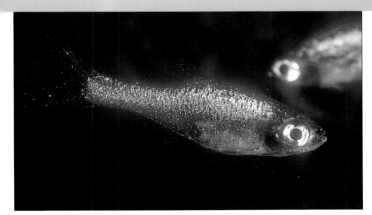

Sundadanio axelrodi female   *Sundadanio axelrodi* male

633

Tanichthys albonubes / White Cloud Mountain Minnow

LIN 1932

Natural Range: China. Probably extinct in the wild.
Size: 1.5" (4 cm) TL.
Water Chemistry: Temperate to subtropical to tropical with any water chemistry.
Behavior: Absolutely peaceful.
Dietary Requirements: Will eat anything of the appropriate size.

Remarks: A thoroughly domesticated species, this fish is available in longfin and gold varieties. They were originally known in the hobby as the poor man's neon for their green fluorescent stripe, which is exceptionally bright in juvenile fish. Extremely hardy, they have been known to survive in water under ice. Usually, the adults will not eat the fry, so a species tank will soon have a population increase.

Tanichthys micagemmae / Blue White Cloud

FREYHOF & HERDER 2001

Natural Range: Vietnam.
Size: 1" (2.5 cm) TL.
Water Chemistry: Tropical.
Behavior: Absolutely peaceful.
Dietary Requirements: Will eat anything of the appropriate size.

Remarks: These "new white clouds" have taken the hobby by storm since their introduction a few years ago. Slightly smaller, tropical cousins of White Clouds, these fish share the same hardiness (except for temperature tolerances) and ease of spawning. Therefore, they are becoming ever more available and less expensive.

Trigonostigma espei / Lambchop Rasbora

MEINKEN 1967

Natural Range: Thailand and Cambodia.
Size: 1.25" (3 cm) TL.
Water Chemistry: Tropical; prefer slightly acidic water.
Behavior: Very peaceful and schooling.
Dietary Requirements: In nature, they eat small invertebrates; most aquarium fare accepted.

Remarks: The lambchop-shaped dark marking distinguishes this species from the harlequin rasbora, which has a more triangular splotch. This is a timid fish, hailing from heavily vegetated swamps, so a planted tank will make them feel secure and bring them out of hiding.

Tanichthys albonubes

Tanichthys albonubes var. "longfin"

Tanichthys micagemmae juvenile

Tanichthys micagemmae adult

Trigonostigma espei

Trigonostigma espei

Trigonostigma hengeli / Glowlight Rasbora

MEINKEN 1965

Natural Range: Sumatra and Borneo.
Size: 1.5" (3 cm) TL.
Water Chemistry: Tropical; prefer slightly acidic water.
Behavior: Small, timid, peaceful.
Dietary Requirements: In nature, they eat small invertebrates; most aquarium fare accepted.

Remarks: *T. heteromorpha* have the triangle dark spot and *T. espei* have the lambchop spot, both against a bronze background. *T. hengeli* concentrates the reddish bronze in a strip above the narrower triangle spot.

Trigonostigma heteromorpha / Harlequin Rasbora

DUNCKER 1904

Natural Range: Thailand to Sumatra.
Size: 2" (5 cm) TL.
Water Chemistry: Tropical.
Behavior: Peaceful, timid, schooling.
Dietary Requirements: In nature, they eat small invertebrates; most aquarium fare accepted.

Remarks: A mainstay of the hobby for almost a century, to many people these fish are *the* rasboras. A school of a dozen or more in a well-planted tank with dark gravel can rival any neon tetra tank. Their unusual breeding behavior of sticking eggs on the undersides of leaves is one reason this genus was erected, removing several species from *Rasbora*.

Zacco platypus / Freshwater Minnow (Blue Zacco)

TEMMINCK & SCHLEGEL 1846

Natural Range: Northern China and Vietnam.
Size: 8" (20 cm) TL.
Water Chemistry: Subtropical.
Behavior: Unknown.
Dietary Requirements: Detritivore and omnivore; will eat anything that will fit in their mouths.

Remarks: These medium-sized cyprinids live in well-oxygenated waters. Sometimes they are ice fished and eaten raw—the cause of parasitic infections in the people who consume them.

Trigonostigma hengeli

Trigonostigma hengeli pair

Trigonostigma heteromorpha

Trigonostigma heteromorpha

Zacco platypus

Zacco platypus profile

Agamyxis pectinifrons

DORADIDAE
THORNY CATFISHES

These primitive catfishes are most commonly found throughout northern South America, specifically Brazil, Peru, and the Guianas. They can be easily identified by the row of lateral bony plates that runs along their body (similar in fashion to the lateral line system of the fish).

In nature, they usually inhabit slow-moving water such as that found in small rivers, lakes, and ponds. Doradids are efficient scavengers that will eat nearly anything that is capable of fitting in their mouths. Their primary interest is small fishes, shrimps, and insect larvae, but in aquariums, they will eat whatever is put in front of them—including waste from their tankmates. For this reason, they are often referred to as the vacuum cleaners of the aquarium.

Most species within Doradidae grow to rather large proportions by aquarium standards. They do best in dimly illuminated aquariums that contain many hiding places for them to stay out of the way. After the lights go out, they can usually be seen cruising around the aquarium in search of foodstuffs. Of course, these are not fishes you should include in aquariums that contain small or flighty species, since their nighttime endeavors may spook their tankmates and cause them great stress.

Agamyxis pectinifrons / Spotted Raphael Catfish

COPE 1870

Natural Range: Amazon River basin.
Size: 6" (15 cm) TL.
Water Chemistry: Tropical; otherwise not critical.
Behavior: Peaceful, but will swallow small fishes.
Dietary Requirements: Scavenger; eats almost anything that is edible.

Remarks: The Spotted Raphael Catfish is a very popular medium-sized species that does well in most aquariums as long as there are ample hiding places. They prefer to squeeze themselves into the tightest crevices and cracks of bogwood, where their spines hold them in place and prevent potential predators from prying them out. They do, however, grow to about six inches in total length and can fit a lot in their mouths, so watch tankmates closely.

Leptodoras juruensis

BOULENGER 1898

Natural Range: Amazon River basin.
Size: 12" (30 cm) TL.
Water Chemistry: Tropical; otherwise not critical.
Behavior: Moderately aggressive; will consume anything able to fit in its mouth.
Dietary Requirements: Scavenger; meaty foods are relished, but they will consume anything edible.

Remarks: This long, slender catfish species is an excellent display animal in large, well-filtered aquariums with peaceful tankmates of equal size. They should be target fed several time weekly to ensure that they have received enough food. Large species such as this cannot be left to find their own food in an aquarium, regardless of the tank's size. There just simply won't be enough of it.

Megalodoras sp. "Irwini"

UNKNOWN TO DATE

Natural Range: Amazon River basin.
Size: Greater than 12" (30 cm) TL.
Water Chemistry: Tropical; otherwise not critical.
Behavior: Generally peaceful, but will swallow anything it can fit into its mouth.
Dietary Requirements: Scavenger; meaty foods are best, but anything edible is usually consumed.

Remarks: This interesting species is not known to science under *Megalodoras irwini*. Regardless, hobbyists know it under that name, and you will find it listed as such on many availability lists. Their care and husbandry is identical to the various "Raphael Cats."

Agamyxis pectinifrons

Agamyxis pectinifrons

Leptodoras juruensis

Leptodoras juruensis

Megalodoras sp. "Irwini" adult

Megalodoras sp. "Irwini" juvenile

Oxydoras niger / Ripsaw Catfish

VALENCIENNES 1821

Natural Range: Widely distributed over much of northern South America.
Size: 40" (100 cm) TL.
Water Chemistry: Tropical; otherwise not critical.
Behavior: Moderately aggressive; will eat anything able to be swallowed whole.
Dietary Requirements: Meaty foods are best, although the species is a scavenger in nature. Target feeding is recommended.

Remarks: Formerly known as *Pseudodoras niger*, the Ripsaw Catfish has been given a new genus that it currently shares with two other species: *O. kneri* and *O. sifontesi*. This big brute of a species needs a huge aquarium with good water quality in order to thrive in captivity. Additionally, they are long-lived, and 20-year-old specimens are not uncommon in public aquariums.

Platydoras armatulus

VALENCIENNES 1840

Natural Range: Parana River basin.
Size: 8" (20 cm) TL.
Water Chemistry: Subtropical; otherwise not critical.
Behavior: Generally peaceful, but will swallow tankmates able to fit in its mouth.
Dietary Requirements: Scavenger; meaty foods and other edibles are greedily accepted.

Remarks: With the exports from southern South America becoming larger and more frequent, there is a push for geographically correct aquariums. For those of you wishing to recreate the look and feel of a subtropical Rio Parana aquarium, this catfish is perfect. Their care and husbandry, aside from the temperature differences, are exactly like the "Raphael Cats."

Platydoras costatus / Striped Raphael Catfish

LINNAEUS 1758

Natural Range: Widely distributed over much of northern South America.
Size: 10" (25 cm) TL.
Water Chemistry: Tropical; otherwise not critical.
Behavior: Generally peaceful, but will swallow smaller tankmates.
Dietary Requirements: Scavenger; will accept nearly all edibles.

Remarks: The Striped Raphael Catfish is the other choice when walking through your local pet shop in search of that perfect scavenger for your aquariums. Keep in mind that they grow considerably larger than most other "community" fishes, so your community aquarium will have to have larger specimens. Otherwise, their care is identical to the Spotted Raphael Catfish.

Oxydoras niger small adult

Oxydoras niger adult

Platydoras armatulus

Platydoras armatulus

Platydoras costatus

Platydoras costatus

643

Hoplias malabaricus

ERYTHRINIDAE

WOLF FISHES

These are the infamous wolf fishes of South America. About ten species comprise this family, and only three are popular in the aquarium trade. They are large, aggressive fishes with a huge appetite and can consume fishes—and other things—that are about half of their own body length.

In aquariums, they should be kept alone or with others fishes of equal, or slightly larger, size and attitude. Large, fast-moving fishes such as Silver Dollars, Tinfoil Barbs, and *Leporinus* are usually ignored, and hobbyists report that the movements of those types of fishes actually calm the reclusive wolf fishes. Regardless, tankmates should be selected with caution.

Their care and husbandry in aquariums is rather easy once you get beyond the issue of suitable tankmates. Famous fish breeder and master aquarist Hiroshi Azuma has even bred these fish, so reproduction is possible, although it was surely not easy. Their water chemistry requirements are near zero—as long as extremes are avoided, of course. In their native habitats, they seem to prefer deeper waters with good current, so consider providing supplemental circulation. Otherwise, most strong filters and large aquariums will make them happy fishes for years.

Hoplerythrinus unitaeniatus / Aimara

AGASSIZ 1829

Natural Range: Widely distributed over much of Central and South America.

Size: 16" (40 cm) TL.

Water Chemistry: Tropical; otherwise not critical; avoid extremes.

Behavior: Very aggressive.

Dietary Requirements: Feeds on fishes and invertebrates as well as any other meaty foods offered.

Remarks: While not a true tankbuster in size, their attitudes negate the need for a large aquarium that is preferably all their own. In nature, this species inhabits swamps and creeks with little current—quite the opposite of their larger cousins. Their aquariums should be darkened by filtering the water through peat.

Hoplias malabaricus / Trahira

BLOCH 1794

Natural Range: South America: Amazonas, Guyana, Suriname, and French Guiana.

Size: 30" (75 cm) TL; this species' size may exceed size stated.

Water Chemistry: Tropical; otherwise not critical; avoid extremes.

Behavior: Aggressive towards other fish.

Dietary Requirements: Fishes and invertebrates.

Remarks: This wolf fish grows large, and tankmates may be difficult to keep. Provide with good, strong filtration and supplemental circulation.

Hoplias sp. "Shuyo"

UNDESCRIBED TO DATE

Natural Range: Northern South America.

Size: Unknown, but probably no smaller than 12" (30 cm) TL.

Water Chemistry: Tropical; otherwise not critical; avoid extremes.

Behavior: Aggressive.

Dietary Requirements: Live fishes, invertebrates, and other meaty foods.

Remarks: This attractive species of wolf fish is sometimes available in small numbers through exporters in northern South America. While predatory in nature, some specimens may actually live peaceably with others that are too large to swallow. Use caution when handling these fish in a net—they may bite!

Hoplerythrinus unitaeniatus

Hoplerythrinus unitaeniatus

Hoplias malabaricus with young

Hoplias malabaricus profile

Hoplias sp. "Shuyo"

Hoplias sp. "Shuyo"

Esox lucius

ESOCIDAE
PIKES AND PICKERELS

Esocidae is a small and primitive family consisting of only one genus (*Esox*, LINNAEUS 1758) and five species. One of these, *Esox americanus*, has been divided into two distinct subspecies: *Esox americanus americanus* and *Esox americanus vermiculatus*. In the future, and now with the use of DNA for phylogenetic studies, we may see these subspecies rise to full species status. Meanwhile, the status of the other members in *Esox* is solid and unlikely to change.

These fishes are distributed widely over North America and the cooler parts of Eurasia. The Northern Pike, *Esox lucius*, has been widely introduced in many countries. Some of these have reported adverse ecological impacts after introduction. Additionally, *Esox* can tolerate a wide degree of variation in water chemistry parameters, though they avoid extremes. Those waters that contain high nitrogen compounds are generally devoid of *Esox*. Such an attribute allows their range to be wide and expansive, with many habitats being used.

Esox are quite easily identified by even the most novice of fish enthusiasts. Generally speaking, all species are long, slender fishes that have a duckbill-like snout. Their tails are relatively small and deeply forked (caudal rays number between 40 and 50). The other fins are also small and set far back on the body, with no hard spines. An adipose fin is absent.

Esox americanus / Grass Pickerel

LESUEUR 1846

Natural Range: Widely distributed over much of North America and Canada.
Size: 19" (50 cm) TL.
Water Chemistry: Temperate; soft and acidic conditions are preferred.
Behavior: May be aggressive towards smaller fishes and conspecifics.
Dietary Requirements: Small fish and worms.

Remarks: This species lives among dense vegetation in backwaters and lakes. In the aquarium, they prefer cooler water with a high level of dissolved oxygen. Tankmates are not recommended, as this species is solitary in nature, and tankmates may prove to be too stressful for them to deal with.

Esox lucius / Northern Pike

LINNEAUS 1758

Natural Range: Widely distributed over much of North America and Canada.
Size: 49" (125 cm) TL.
Water Chemistry: Temperate; prefers soft and acidic conditions.
Behavior: Aggressive and solitary.
Dietary Requirements: Live fishes, frogs, and crayfish.

Remarks: While young, this species is highly cannibalistic, and may prove to be so throughout its life. Adults seem to be less concerned with fishes that are too small to be worth the effort of a hunt and will actively pursue larger prey such as larger fishes, small mammals, and even ducklings. While in the aquarium, this species will not eat artificial foods with any regularity.

Esox niger / Chain Pickerel

LESUEUR 1818

Natural Range: Widely distributed over much of North America and Canada.
Size: 35" (90 cm) TL.
Water Chemistry: Temperate; prefers soft and acidic conditions.
Behavior: Aggressive and solitary.
Dietary Requirements: Live fishes, insects, and crayfish.

Remarks: The Chain Pickerel is found close to the banks when young and spends a considerable amount of time in deep, cool water as an adult. Their care and husbandry in aquariums is somewhat of a mystery, but specimens that are well cared for apparently live for many years.

Esox americanus americanus

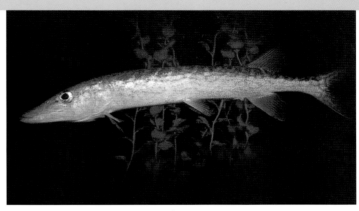

Esox americanus vermiculatus

Esox lucius

Esox lucius

Esox niger

Esox niger profile

651

Gasteropelecus sternicla

GASTEROPELECIDAE
FRESHWATER HATCHETFISHES

These unique small fishes make wonderful additions to community aquariums containing other small and peaceful species. They do, however, have one nasty habit—they are accomplished jumpers who will frequently leap right out of your aquarium. Other than that, they seem to do very well in most setups.

Many hobbyists have stated that these fishes are difficult to care for and seem to be very intolerant of poor water quality. For the most part, this is true, but this is mainly because even today, many of the hatchetfishes that are available in pet shops are wild collected. Apparently, they are quite difficult to spawn, and the fry are also difficult to rear.

Hatchetfishes are widely distributed over Central and South America. There are approximately nine species within the family, but only three of them are profiled herein. Of course, with the influx of new species being discovered and imported annually, we should see new hatchetfishes in the upcoming years.

Carnegiella marthae / Blackwing Hatchetfish

MYERS 1927

Natural Range: Rio Negro and Rio Orinoco basins.
Size: 2" (5 cm) TL.
Water Chemistry: Tropical; slightly soft and acidic is best.
Behavior: Very peaceful, but will jump; keep a tight-fitting lid on the tank.
Dietary Requirements: Small live foods such as *Daphnia*, as well as all types of floating prepared foods.

Remarks: The Blackwing Hatchetfish is probably the least commonly encountered species of the three that are profiled herein. Their care and husbandry is very similar to that of similar-sized tetras.

Carnegiella strigata / Marbled Hatchetfish

GUENTHER 1864

Natural Range: Amazon River basin, including the Rio Caqueta in Colombia.
Size: 2" (5 cm) TL; may not grow as large in nature.
Water Chemistry: Tropical; slightly soft and acidic is best.
Behavior: Very peaceful, but will jump; keep a tight-fitting lid on the tank.
Dietary Requirements: Small live foods such as *Daphnia*, as well as all types of floating prepared foods.

Remarks: The Marbled Hatchetfish is very popular among hobbyists that are looking for something truly different or unique. They are an easy-to-care-for species that does well in small aquariums that are kept warm. Tankmates should be peaceful and less boisterous to help prevent the hatchetfishes from leaping from the aquarium.

Gasteropelecus sternicla / Silver Hatchetfish

LINNAEUS 1758

Natural Range: Guianas, Brazil, Peru, and Venezuela.
Size: 2" (5 cm) TL.
Water Chemistry: Tropical; slightly soft and acidic is best.
Behavior: Very peaceful, but will jump; keep a tight-fitting lid on the tank.
Dietary Requirements: Small live foods such as *Daphnia*, as well as all types of floating prepared foods.

Remarks: This species and *G. levis* are often referred to as the Silver Hatchetfishes. Both species are silver in color but come from differing areas. Additionally, both species grow slightly larger in aquariums than in nature. This is probably due to a greater availability of foods that are high in nutritive value. Their care and husbandry are similar to the other hatchetfishes.

Carnegiella marthae

Gasteropelecus sternicla for comparison

Carnegiella strigata

Carnegiella strigata

Gasteropelecus sternicla pair

Gasteropelecus levis for comparison

Chriopeodon late... li

GOODEIDAE
SPLITFINS

These interesting and peaceful small fishes can be kept in most aquariums without much difficulty. There are approximately 40 species, and they have a broad distribution, from Nevada and the southern United States through western and central Mexico.

Fertilization is internal, and the fishes give birth to live young. Their body forms and feeding habits are diverse and vary from population to population, even within a given species. They are generally not as colorful as many of their closely related cousins of Poeciliidae. However, their care and husbandry are remarkably similar. In fact, it is often quite common to see aquariums containing members of both families living quite peaceably together.

Feeding these fishes is often very easy, as they accept nearly all types of floating foods. Of course, small insects are their favorite, and those species that grow large enough will even take larger insects such as crickets or mealworms. In fact, any fish that is able to consume insects should be offered to them, since more than likely, that is what they feed upon in nature.

Ameca splendens / Butterfly Splitfin

MILLER & FITZSIMONS 1971

Natural Range: Mexico.
Size: 3" (7.5 cm) TL.
Water Chemistry: Tropical; otherwise not too critical; avoid extremes.
Behavior: Generally peaceful, but may nip fins.
Dietary Requirements: All types of small prepared foods work well.

Remarks: A small, somewhat colorful species, the Butterfly Splitfin does well in small aquariums that contain other peaceful fishes. As with other fishes of the family, be sure to watch them closely, since they sometimes have a nasty habit of fin nipping.

Characodon audax / Bold Characodon

SMITH & MILLER 1986

Natural Range: Mexico.
Size: 2" (5 cm) TL.
Water Chemistry: Tropical; otherwise not critical; avoid extremes.
Behavior: Generally peaceful, but may nip fins.
Dietary Requirements: All types of small prepared foods work well.

Remarks: This interesting little species is not widely available in the hobby, but makes an appearance from time to time. Of course, species such as this one are more commonly available from hobbyists who specialize in their care and husbandry.

Characodon lateralis / Rainbow Characodon

GUNTHER 1866

Natural Range: Mexico.
Size: 2" (5 cm) TL.
Water Chemistry: Tropical; otherwise not too critical; avoid extremes.
Behavior: Moderately aggressive; best kept alone or in pairs.
Dietary Requirements: All types of small prepared foods work well.

Remarks: The care and husbandry of the Rainbow Characodon is identical to that of the Bold Characodon.

Ameca splendens

Ameca splendens

Characodon audax

Characodon audax

Characodon lateralis

Characodon lateralis

659

Ilyodon furcidens / Goldbreast Splitfin

JORDAN & GILBERT 1882

Natural Range: Central America.
Size: 3" (7.5 cm) TL.
Water Chemistry: Tropical; otherwise not too critical; avoid extremes.
Behavior: Moderately aggressive; best kept alone or in pairs.
Dietary Requirements: All types of small prepared foods work well.

Remarks: These small fish are actually quite active and peaceful. Just as with other members of the family, watch them in the community aquarium, because they can be prone to fin nipping.

Skiffia francesae / Golden Skiffia

KINGSTON 1978

Natural Range: Mexico.
Size: 2" (5 cm) TL.
Water Chemistry: Tropical; otherwise not critical.
Behavior: Moderately aggressive; best kept alone or in pairs.
Dietary Requirements: All types of small prepared foods work well.

Remarks: A unique and interesting small fish, *S. francesae* is perfectly at home in a community aquarium with other livebearers. Keep as others within the family.

Xenotoca eiseni / Redtail Splitfin

RUTTER 1896

Natural Range: Central America.
Size: 2" (5 cm) TL; may grow slightly larger.
Water Chemistry: Tropical; otherwise not critical.
Behavior: Moderately aggressive; best kept alone or in pairs.
Dietary Requirements: All types of small prepared foods work well.

Remarks: The Redtail Splitfin is an interesting livebearer that is a little more robust when compared to others. They are easily identified by their flashy red tail. Depending on their diet and condition, their tail may be fire red or, more commonly, a dull orange. Regardless, they are a great community fish for small to medium-sized aquariums.

Ilyodon furcidens

Ilyodon furcidens pair

Skiffia francesae

Xenotoca eiseni female for comparison

Xenotoca eiseni male

Xenotoca eiseni pair

Lepisosteus oculatus

LEPISOSTEIDAE
GARS

Gars are chiefly freshwater fishes that may occasionally be found in waters that have a brackish water influence, although this is usually due to tidal surges. Sometimes, certain species may move into full strength seawater, but this move appears to be only temporary (perhaps to relieve their ganoid scales of external parasites).

Members of this family are easily recognized by their elongated jaw, which contains sharp, needle-like teeth. These teeth are used to hold captured prey—usually in the form of small fishes—until a more suitable position can be achieved for their swallowing.

The family's distribution is broad and expansive, covering nearly all of eastern North America with one or more species. Specific distribution is usually overlapping.

In captivity, these gentle giants have the ability to turn on the attitude in a heartbeat. They frighten easily, however, and should not be kept with fast-moving or boisterous species. This is especially true if they are inadvertently being housed in an aquarium that is too small for them, as they will surely bang up their snout. Injured snouts become infected very easily, and while these fishes are more primitive than many other popular species, they will still succumb to infection from these wounds. In the end, nearly all of the Gars are really only suitable for the largest of home aquariums or public aquarium display tanks.

Atractosteus spatula / Alligator Gar

LACEPEDE 1803

Natural Range: United States and Mexico.
Size: 120" (305 cm) TL.
Water Chemistry: Subtropical; otherwise not critical.
Behavior: Aggressive.
Dietary Requirements: Live fishes and crustaceans.

Remarks: This is a very large predator that is better-suited for public aquariums and not the home aquarium.

Lepisosteus oculatus / Spotted Gar

WINCHELL 1864

Natural Range: North America.
Size: 44" (112 cm) TL.
Water Chemistry: Subtropical; otherwise not critical.
Behavior: Aggressive.
Dietary Requirements: Live fishes and crustaceans.

Remarks: Spotted Gars are found in small and large clear rivers and lakes and may also be found in brackish waters.

Lepisosteus osseus / Longnose Gar

LINNAEUS 1758

Natural Range: North and Central America.
Size: 78" (200 cm) TL.
Water Chemistry: Subtropical; otherwise not critical; avoid extremes.
Behavior: Aggressive.
Dietary Requirements: Live fishes and crustaceans.

Remarks: The Longnose Gar occurs in rivers and lakes and is usually found among vegetation. The roe of this species is reported to be poisonous. Just as with the Alligator Gar, the Longnose Gar grows far too large for all but the largest of home aquariums.

Atractosteus spatula

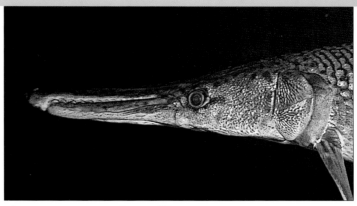

Atractosteus spatula profile

Lepisosteus oculatus young

Lepisosteus oculatus pair

Lepisosteus osseus

Lepisosteus osseus

Lepisosteus platyrhincus / Florida Gar

DEKAY 1842

Natural Range: Florida and Georgia, United States.
Size: 51" (132 cm) TL.
Water Chemistry: Subtropical; otherwise not critical.
Behavior: Aggressive.
Dietary Requirements: Live fishes and crustaceans.

Remarks: The Florida Gar is found amongst vegetation in slow-moving backwaters of rivers and lakes. Like the Tropical Gar, the Florida Gar will prefer slightly warmer temperatures than many of it congeners.

Lepisosteus platostomus / Shortnose Gar

RAFINESQUE 1820

Natural Range: North America.
Size: 34" (88 cm) TL.
Water Chemistry: Subtropical; otherwise not critical.
Behavior: Aggressive.
Dietary Requirements: Live fishes and crustaceans.

Remarks: This species likes to make its home amongst wood structures and vegetation. Generally, they live in the slow backwaters of rivers and in lakes.

Lepisosteus platyrhincus

Lepisosteus platyrhincus pair

Lepisosteus platostomus small adult

Lepisosteus platostomus profile

Copella arnoldi

LEBIASINIDAE

As with so many other families of fishes—both fresh and seawater—this group needs some revision. Currently, there are approximately 60 valid species contained in Lebiasinidae, and possibly many more are awaiting revision. They have a broad range of sizes, as well as diverse natural distribution, although many of the species herein are found in South America, specifically in Amazon River drainage.

All species within exhibit a cylindrical body shape with rather large scales. An adipose fin may be present or absent depending on the genus. Most species are found in clear to tea-stained water at higher elevations. They can tolerate cooler water temperatures, but they should still be maintained as tropical fishes and kept in the mid- to upper 70s F.

In the aquarium, these fishes are generally mild mannered and tolerate tankmates well. Each one has a slightly different reproductive method, and separate research should be done to learn more about them individually. Feeding is simple: They all seem to do best with small live foods such as *Artemia* and *Daphnia*, but many of the smaller prepared foods, especially granules, work well, too. Space is not overly important, and most 15- to 20-gallon aquariums can house a few of these fishes, along with some other small tankmates. As with any fish, of course, be sure to provide good filtration and stay on top of the water quality by performing regular water changes.

Copella arnoldi / Splash Tetra

REGAN 1912

Natural Range: Lower Amazonia.
Size: 2" (5 cm) TL; usually slightly smaller.
Water Chemistry: Tropical; neutral to slightly acidic with moderate hardness.
Behavior: Peaceful, but should be kept in a well-covered aquarium because of their jumping ability.
Dietary Requirements: Small live foods such as brine shrimp, black worms, and insect larvae are preferred, but may accept most standard aquarium fare, too.

Remarks: We have seen many odd methods of reproduction in aquarium fishes, but this species probably has the oddest. In nature, a pair will seek out an overhanging leaf and together leap out of the water and cling to the leaf long enough to paste several eggs to it. They will repeat this many times, until about 100 eggs are laid on the leaf. The eggs do not hatch until three days later, during which time the male remains under the leaf and splashes water on the eggs with his tail every 15 minutes or so to keep them from drying out.

Copella nattereri / Spotted Tetra

STEINDACHNER 1876

Natural Range: Amazon basin.
Size: 2" (5 cm) TL; may grow slightly larger.
Water Chemistry: Tropical; slightly acidic with moderate hardness.
Behavior: Another peaceful fish that needs a well-covered aquarium.
Dietary Requirements: Small live foods such as brine shrimp, black worms, and insect larvae are preferred, but may accept most standard aquarium fare, too.

Remarks: There is a simple beauty to this fish. Not flashy in color, *C. nattereri* is possessed of a subdued warm coloring that is highlighted by occasional bright spots of red and lavender. The most striking of these spots lies immediately between the gill covers and the pectoral fins. All in all, *C. nattereri* gives the impression of refined elegance, especially if it is kept with fishes that are stubbier in form, for then the streamlined charm of the Spotted Tetra is most pronounced.

Nannostomus beckfordi / Golden Pencilfish

GUNTHER 1872

Natural Range: Northern South America.
Size: 2" (5 cm) TL.
Water Chemistry: Tropical; slightly acidic with moderate hardness.
Behavior: Generally peaceful.
Dietary Requirements: Small live foods are best.

Remarks: The Golden Pencilfish is fairly well distributed through most rivers and waterways in northern South America, especially the Guianas. They are fairly easy to breed, but the young are difficult to rear. This is mainly because of their tiny mouths; delivering food to them proves to be a daunting task indeed. Most pencilfishes have a unique characteristic: at night, their coloration changes markedly. This behavior is common in fishes, but only those inhabiting coral reefs change as drastically as the members of *Nannostomus*.

Copella arnoldi

Copella arnoldi

Copella nattereri

Copella nattereri

Nannostomus beckfordi

Nannostomus beckfordi pair

671

Nannostomus eques / Brown-tailed Pencilfish

STEINDACHNER 1876

Natural Range: Guyana and Orinoco basin.
Size: 2" (5 cm) TL.
Water Chemistry: Tropical; prefers soft and slightly acidic conditions.
Behavior: Generally peaceful.
Dietary Requirements: Small live foods are best.

Remarks: This species generally inhabits slower-flowing, heavily vegetated waters that are mildly acidic and very soft in chemistry. They feed heavily on insects and insect larvae on the upper layer or surface of the water. As with other pencilfishes, they are relatively easy to breed, provided they have a small, warm aquarium to themselves.

Nannostomus marginatus / Dwarf Pencilfish

EIGENMANN 1909

Natural Range: Guyana to Colombia.
Size: About 1.5" (3 cm) TL.
Water Chemistry: Tropical; slightly acidic with moderate hardness.
Behavior: Generally peaceful.
Dietary Requirements: Small live foods are best.

Remarks: It is best to keep this fish in a species-specific aquarium in small groups numbering five or more individuals. They are very small, and only the smallest of foods will be taken. When possible, feed them heavily on copepods or baby brine shrimp. This species will not usually do well with larger, more boisterous fishes.

Nannostomus trifasciatus / Oneline Pencilfish

STEINDACHNER 1876

Natural Range: Upper Amazonian region.
Size: 2" (5 cm) TL.
Water Chemistry: Tropical; slightly acidic with moderate hardness.
Behavior: Generally peaceful.
Dietary Requirements: Small live foods are best.

Remarks: Most hobbyists who keep pencilfishes consider *N. trifasciatus* the beauty of the group, and are usually unanimous in expressing the opinion that this species is the most difficult to spawn. Strangely enough, in their native habitat, they are found almost everywhere. They are happiest in a well-illuminated aquarium with a number of other specimens of their own kind.

Nannostomus eques

Nannostomus eques

Nannostomus marginatus

Nannostomus sp. for comparison

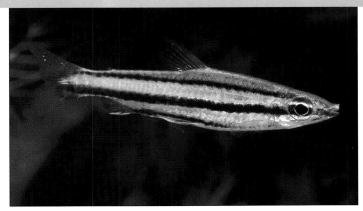

Nannostomus trifasciatus

Nannostomus trifasciatus

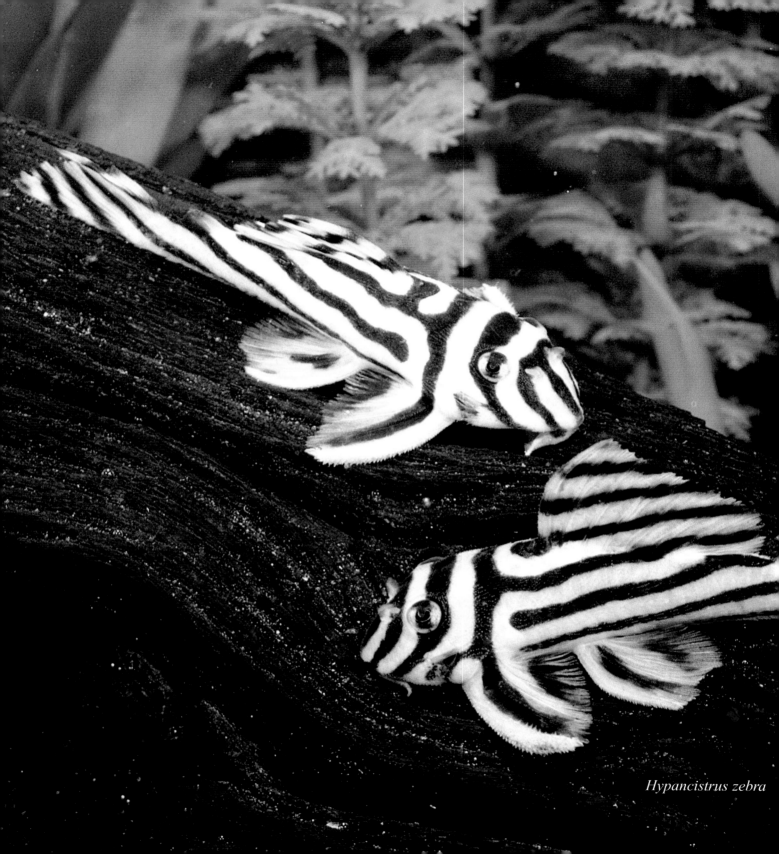

Hypancistrus zebra

LORICARIIDAE
ARMORED CATFISHES

This family has a special place in the heart of many hobbyists. Often, these fishes are big, bold, and beautifully-colored. Additionally, they are long-lived if their needs are both understood and met. The family Loricariidae is composed of approximately 550 species. Thankfully, through the efforts of captive breeding programs, a good number of the more colorful types are available to tropical fish hobbyists around the globe.

Perhaps the most common mistake that people make when adding these fish to their aquariums is offering them too much of the wrong foods. Even though nearly all of them are referred to as "plecos" and plecos are commonly associated with eating algae, many species within Loricariidae need to consume large portions of animal materials. In general, worms and other meaty foods that readily sink to the bottom of the aquarium will suffice. Occasionally, larger specimens may even trap and eat smaller fishes in the aquarium's corners or within decorations. Of course, a piece of zucchini or cucumber attached to a sinking item, such as a small rock or piece of bogwood, will be readily accepted, too.

Acanthicus adonis

ISBRUCKER & NIJSSEN 1988

Natural Range: Lower Tocantins River, Brazil.
Size: 10" (25 cm) TL.
Water Chemistry: Tropical; slightly acidic with moderate hardness.
Behavior: Generally peaceful but may quarrel with other members of Loricariidae.
Dietary Requirements: Omnivorous; accept both plant and animal matter.

Remarks: These beautiful catfish have long, thin extensions on the caudal fin that are quite distinctive and unique. Generally peaceful, these fish may even learn to recognize their owners and approach the aquarium's front glass during feeding time. Additionally, they are often long-lived and hardy.

Acanthicus histrix

SPIX & AGASSIZ 1829

Natural Range: Amazon basin, Brazil.
Size: 20" (50 cm) TL; usually far smaller.
Water Chemistry: Tropical; slightly acidic with moderate hardness.
Behavior: Generally peaceful but may quarrel with other members of Loricariidae.
Dietary Requirements: Omnivorous; accept both plant and animal matter.

Remarks: This giant is truly spectacular in a large aquarium. Recently, there has been some confusion as to whether this species is synonymous with *A. Adonis*, but we will treat them as distinct species herein. As with *A. adonis*, they can become quite tame and may approach the glass during feeding time. This species may also capture and kill smaller tankmates. In nature, they are opportunistic feeders and need some meaty foods in their diet.

Ancistrus claro

KNAACK 1999

Natural Range: Rio Paraguay River drainage.
Size: 4" (10 cm) TL; more commonly smaller.
Water Chemistry: Tropical; slightly acidic with moderate hardness.
Behavior: Generally peaceful but may quarrel with other members of Loricariidae.
Dietary Requirements: Omnivorous; accept both plant and animal matter.

Remarks: As with nearly all species of Ancistrus, *A. claro* appreciate good water flow and plenty of hiding places. Breeding males may quarrel, so keeping only one male with multiple females is best. Be sure to feed some animal matter as well as a variety of plant-based products.

Acanthicus adonis

Acanthicus adonis

Acanthicus histrix

Acanthicus adonis for comparison

Ancistrus claro

Ancistrus claro

Ancistrus ranunculus / Bristlenose Catfish

MULLER, RAPP PY-DANIEL, & ZUANON 1994

Natural Range: Xingu and Tocantins River basins.
Size: 6" (15 cm) TL.
Water Chemistry: Tropical; slightly acidic with moderate hardness.
Behavior: Generally peaceful but may quarrel with other members of Loricariidae.
Dietary Requirements: Omnivorous; accept both plant and animal matter.

Remarks: Another species of the Bristlenose Catfishes is *A. ranunculus*. This species does not grow quite as large as the other members of the genus but is still robust. They prefer to live among roots and rocks where they hide from the strong current. In aquariums, be sure to provide plenty of hiding places.

Ancistrus temenicki

VALENCIENES 1840

Natural Range: Saramacca, Suriname, and Maroni River basins.
Size: 4" (10 cm) TL.
Water Chemistry: Tropical; slightly acidic with moderate hardness.
Behavior: Generally peaceful but may quarrel with other members of Loricariidae.
Dietary Requirements: Omnivorous; accept both plant and animal matter.

Remarks: This small but pretty species is not always offered for sale in the aquarium trade, but occasionally they are imported from exporters in Guyana. The main reason for their scarcity is that Suriname does not currently allow the exportation of fishes from their country.

Baryancistrus sp. / Gold Nugget Pleco

UNDESCRIBED TO DATE

Natural Range: Northern South America.
Size: 4" (10 cm) TL is most common, may grow slightly larger.
Water Chemistry: Tropical; slightly acidic with moderate hardness.
Behavior: Generally peaceful but may quarrel with other members of Loricariidae.
Dietary Requirements: Omnivorous; accept both plant and animal matter.

Remarks: These beauties are found in various regions throughout Amazonia. Perhaps the most notable feature of these fish is their diversity in spotting and coloration. Two distinct color morphs are represented here.

Ancistrus ranunculus

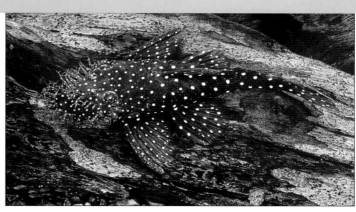

Ancistrus sp. for comparison

Ancistrus temenicki

Ancistrus sp. aff. *temenicki* with young

Baryancistrus sp. L-177

Baryancistrus sp. "Xingu large spot"

Farlowella acus / Whiptail Catfish

KNER 1853

Natural Range: Lake Valencia and Torito River basins, South America.

Size: 8" (20 cm) TL.

Water Chemistry: Tropical; slightly acidic with moderate hardness.

Behavior: Generally peaceful but may quarrel with other members of Loricariidae.

Dietary Requirements: Omnivorous; accept both plant and animal matter.

Remarks: *F. acus* are best kept in small groups numbering five or more individuals. Sadly, they are often sold as singles and many perish a short time later. They also need to be fed a certain amount of plant material, usually in the form of sliced zucchini, which they will consume very quickly. Additionally, this species seems to appreciate good water flow.

Farlowella knerii

STEINDACHNER 1915

Natural Range: Upper Amazon River drainage, Brazil and Peru.

Size: 8" (20 cm) TL.

Water Chemistry: Tropical; slightly acidic with moderate hardness.

Behavior: Generally peaceful but may quarrel with other members of Loricariidae.

Dietary Requirements: Omnivorous; accept both plant and animal matter.

Remarks: Aside from distribution and pattern, *F. knerii* are nearly identical in all other ways to *F. acus*.

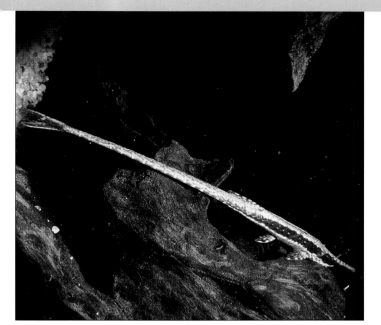

Farlowella acus

Farlowella acus profile

Farlowella knerii

Farlowella sp. for comparison

681

Guyanancistrus niger

NORMAN 1926

Natural Range: Oyapock River basin.
Size: 8" (20 cm) TL.
Water Chemistry: Tropical; slightly acidic with moderate hardness.
Behavior: Generally peaceful but may quarrel with other members of Loricariidae.
Dietary Requirements: Omnivorous; accept both plant and animal matter.

Remarks: *G. niger* need good water flow and a high level of dissolved oxygen in order to thrive in aquariums. They require good algae growth on the tank's décor but may adjust to feeding on plant materials, too. This species does not appreciate any dissolved nitrogen compounds in their water, so a good filter is essential for their well being.

Guyanancistrus sp.

UNDESCRIBED TO DATE

Natural Range: Northern South America.
Size: 6" (15 cm) TL is most common, may grow larger.
Water Chemistry: Tropical; slightly acidic with moderate hardness.
Behavior: Generally peaceful but may quarrel with other members of Loricariidae.
Dietary Requirements: Omnivorous; accept both plant and animal matter.

Remarks: Not much is know about the other members of *Guyanancistrus* aside from what is reported under *G. niger*.

Glyptoperichthys gibbeceps / Sailfin Pleco

KNER 1854

Natural Range: Amazon and Orinoco River drainages, Northern South America.
Size: 20" (50 cm) TL, usually far smaller.
Water Chemistry: Tropical; slightly acidic with moderate hardness.
Behavior: Generally peaceful but may quarrel with other members of Loricariidae.
Dietary Requirements: Omnivorous; accept both plant and animal matter.

Remarks: The Sailfin Pleco is one of the originals of the hobby. Years ago, the closely related *Hypostomus plecostomus* was the common suckermouth catfish and this species was the "rare" and "unusual" one. Today, *G. gibbeceps* is offered as pond-raised stock and even comes in an albino form. Regardless, they make a flashy addition to any aquarium containing large, peaceful fishes.

Guyanancistrus niger

Guyanancistrus niger

Guyanancistrus sp. "Tocantins"

Guyanancistrus sp. "Xingu"

Glyptoperichthys gibbeceps

Glyptoperichthys gibbeceps "albino"

683

Hypancistrus inspector

ARMBRUSTER 2002

Natural Range: Venezuela.
Size: 6" (15 cm) TL; usually far smaller.
Water Chemistry: Tropical; slightly acidic with moderate hardness.
Behavior: Generally peaceful but may quarrel with other members of Loricariidae.
Dietary Requirements: Omnivorous; accept both plant and animal matter.

Remarks: *H. inspector* are absolutely striking catfish that do well in aquariums as long as the specimens are initially healthy. Notoriously difficult to treat when ill, these fish must be maintained in a well-balanced aquarium to prevent disease outbreaks.

Hypancistrus zebra / Zebra Pleco

ISBRUCKER & NIJSSEN 1991

Natural Range: Rio Xingu, Brazil.
Size: 3" (7.5 cm) TL.
Water Chemistry: Tropical; slightly acidic with moderate hardness.
Behavior: Generally peaceful but may quarrel with other members of Loricariidae.
Dietary Requirements: Omnivorous; accept both plant and animal matter.

Remarks: The Zebra Pleco has taken the aquarium world by storm over the last decade or so. There has been such a demand for this species that Brazil has imposed collection laws to help prevent the demise of wild populations. Unfortunately, they do not reproduce well in captivity, so the vast majority that are in captive care are wild collected.

Hypoptopoma gulare

COPE 1878

Natural Range: Amazon River drainage, Brazil.
Size: 6" (15 cm) TL.
Water Chemistry: Tropical; slightly acidic with moderate hardness.
Behavior: Generally peaceful but may quarrel with other members of Loricariidae.
Dietary Requirements: Omnivorous; accept both plant and animal matter.

Remarks: This unique little fish is somewhat of an oddball in the aquarium industry. Many people do not recognize them so they pass up the purchase. What they don't realize is that they are passing up the opportunity to obtain a great fish that is very interesting to observe and quite different.

Hypancistrus inspector

Hypancistrus sp. L-174 for comparison

Hypancistrus zebra juvenile

Hypancistrus zebra adult

Hypoptopoma gulare

Hypoptopoma gulare profile

Hypoptopoma sp.

UNDESCRIBED TO DATE

Natural Range: Northern South America.
Size: 6" (15 cm) TL; may grow larger.
Water Chemistry: Tropical; slightly acidic with moderate hardness.
Behavior: Generally peaceful but may quarrel with other members of Loricariidae.
Dietary Requirements: Omnivorous; accept both plant and animal matter.

Remarks: There are a few species of *Hypoptopoma* that are available in the aquarium trade, and all of them have nearly identical care and husbandry requirements. It is quite safe to say that they can all be kept in a very similar fashion to *H. gulare*.

Hypostomus margaritifer

REGAN 1908

Natural Range: Upper and middle Parana River basin.
Size: 14" (15 cm) TL.
Water Chemistry: Tropical; slightly acidic with moderate hardness.
Behavior: Generally peaceful but may quarrel with other members of Loricariidae.
Dietary Requirements: Omnivorous; accept both plant and animal matter.

Remarks: Large and attractive suckermouth catfish *H. margaritifer* are perfect additions to the community aquarium containing similar-sized fishes. This species is well suited to housing in aquariums that contain moderately aggressive species due to their heavily armored body.

Hypostomus plecostomus / Suckermouth Catfish

LINNAEUS 1758

Natural Range: Northern South America.
Size: 20" (50 cm) TL; usually far smaller.
Water Chemistry: Tropical; slightly acidic with moderate hardness.
Behavior: Generally peaceful but may quarrel with other members of Loricariidae.
Dietary Requirements: Omnivorous; accept both plant and animal matter.

Remarks: This is another large suckermouth catfish species that needs a big tank and good water quality. As with many other species within Loricariidae, *H. plecostomus* are very capable of trapping and killing smaller tankmates. While they are primarily herbivorous in nature, they will greedily accept most meaty foods as well.

Hypoptopoma sp.

Hypoptopoma sp "Peru"

Hypostomus margaritifer

Hypostomus sp. aff. *paulinus* for comparison

Hypostomus plecostomus

Hypostomus plecostomus

Hypostomus sp.

UNDESCRIBED TO DATE

Natural Range: Northern South America.
Size: 20" (50 cm); usually far smaller.
Water Chemistry: Tropical; slightly acidic with moderate hardness.
Behavior: Generally peaceful but may quarrel with other members of Loricariidae.
Dietary Requirements: Omnivorous; accept both plant and animal matter.

Remarks: There are many species within *Hypostomus* that are yet to be described and studied in captivity. Regardless, it is safe to say that this fish can be maintained just like *H. plecostomus*.

Leporacanthicus galaxias

ISBRUCKER & NIJSSEN 1989

Natural Range: Southern tributaries of the Amazon River, Brazil.
Size: 10" (25 cm) TL.
Water Chemistry: Tropical; slightly acidic with moderate hardness.
Behavior: Generally peaceful but may quarrel with other members of Loricariidae.
Dietary Requirements: Omnivorous; accept both plant and animal matter.

Remarks: This widespread species of Loricariid does well in most well-balanced aquariums. Their water chemistry requirements are not as stringent compared to requirements for other members of the family, but they cannot tolerate a high level of nitrogenous wastes in the water either.

Leporacanthicus heterodon

ISBRUCKER & NIJESSEN 1989

Natural Range: Rio Xingu, Brazil.
Size: 6" (15 cm) TL.
Water Chemistry: Tropical; slightly acidic with moderate hardness.
Behavior: Generally peaceful but may quarrel with other members of Loricariidae.
Dietary Requirements: Omnivorous; accept both plant and animal matter.

Remarks: Care in captivity is identical to *L. galaxias*.

Hypostomus sp.

Hypostomus punctatus juvenile for comparison

Leporacanthicus galaxias

Leporacanthicus galaxias

Leporacanthicus heterodon

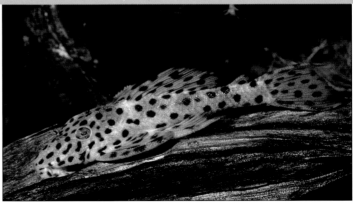

Leporacanthicus heterodon

Leporacanthicus joselimai

ISBRUCKER & NIJESSEN 1989

Natural Range: Tapajos River system, Brazil.
Size: 4" (10 cm) TL; may grow slightly larger.
Water Chemistry: Tropical; slightly acidic with moderate hardness.
Behavior: Generally peaceful but may quarrel with other members of Loricariidae.
Dietary Requirements: Omnivorous; accept both plant and animal matter.

Remarks: Care in captivity is identical to *L. galaxias*.

Loricaria filamentosa

UNKNOWN TO DATE

Natural Range: Northern South America.
Size: 6" (15 cm) TL is common but may grow twice that.
Water Chemistry: Tropical; slightly acidic with moderate hardness.
Behavior: Generally peaceful but may quarrel with other members of Loricariidae.
Dietary Requirements: Omnivorous; accept both plant and animal matter.

Remarks: This attractive species of Loricariid may actually be misidentified. While popular literature lists such a species, scientific literature does not seem to recognize it. Care and breeding is probably very close to if not exactly like *L. simillima*.

Loricaria simillima

REGAN 1904

Natural Range: Northern South America.
Size: 8" (20 cm) TL.
Water Chemistry: Tropical; slightly acidic with moderate hardness.
Behavior: Generally peaceful but may quarrel with other members of Loricariidae.
Dietary Requirements: Omnivorous; accept both plant and animal matter.

Remarks: *Loricaria simillima* have gained popularity in recent years with the increase in shipments of wild-collected fishes from Venezuela. Their requirements for care in captivity are very basic—good water quality, strong filtration, and a balanced diet.

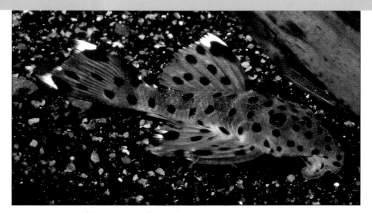

Leporacanthicus joselimai

Leporacanthicus joselimai

Loricaria filamentosa

Loricaria filamentosa profile

Loricaria simillima

Loricaria simillima

691

Megalancistrus parananus

PETERS 1881

Natural Range: Southern tropical Amazonia.
Size: 24" (60 cm) TL; usually far smaller.
Water Chemistry: Tropical; slightly acidic with moderate hardness.
Behavior: Generally peaceful but may quarrel with other members of Loricariidae.
Dietary Requirements: Omnivorous; accept both plant and animal matter.

Remarks: While still tropical in nature, *M. parananus* are capable of tolerating fluctuations in their water temperature. Otherwise, their care is identical to the requirements for *Hypostomus*.

Otocinclus sp. "zebra"

UNDESCRIBED TO DATE

Natural Range: Northern South America.
Size: 2" (5 cm) TL.
Water Chemistry: Tropical; slightly acidic with moderate hardness.
Behavior: Generally peaceful.
Dietary Requirements: Mostly herbivorous but may accept animal matter as well.

Remarks: These little jewels are new to the hobby. Their exact collection locality is not yet fully known, but shippers from Venezuela have begun exporting these little herbivores very recently. It is probably safe to assume that they hail from the Rio Orinoco drainage based on the other fishes that are being exported with them.

Otocinclus vestitus

COPE 1872

Natural Range: Amazon and lower Parana River basins.
Size: 1.5: (3.3 cm) TL.
Water Chemistry: Tropical; slightly acidic with moderate hardness.
Behavior: Generally peaceful.
Dietary Requirements: Mostly herbivorous but may accept animal matter as well.

Remarks: While small in size, the job they perform is huge in importance. *Otocinclus* catfishes are accomplished algae eaters that make perfect candidates for small aquariums with peaceful species. They do best if the aquarium is allowed to cultivate some algae before you add them. This way, there should be a constant growth at all times for them to graze on.

Megalancistrus parananus

Megalancistrus gigas for comparison

Otocinclus sp. "zebra"

Otocinclus sp. "zebra"

Otocinclus vestitus

Otocinclus vestitus

693

Otocinclus vittatus

REGAN 1904

Natural Range: Widespread over South America.
Size: 1.5" (3.3 cm) TL.
Water Chemistry: Tropical; slightly acidic with moderate hardness.
Behavior: Generally peaceful.
Dietary Requirements: Mostly herbivorous but may accept animal matter as well.

Remarks: Aside from differences in distribution, the care and husbandry requirements of *O. vittatus* are essentially identical to those for *O. vestitus*. At certain times of the year, one species seems to be more prevalent than the other in the aquarium hobby.

Panaque nigrolineatus

PETERS 1877

Natural Range: Orinoco and middle to lower Amazon River tributaries.
Size: 18" (45 cm) TL.
Water Chemistry: Tropical; slightly acidic with moderate hardness.
Behavior: Generally peaceful but may quarrel with other members of Loricariidae.
Dietary Requirements: Omnivorous; accept both plant and animal matter.

Remarks: Most members of Loricariidae really only quarrel with other members of their family or sometimes only other members of their genus. Unfortunately, this species is not one of them. Watch all *Panaque* species with other fishes since many tend to be pushy, especially during feeding time

Panaque sp. "L-90"

UNDESCRIBED TO DATE

Natural Range: Peru.
Size: 8" (20 cm) TL.
Water Chemistry: Tropical; slightly acidic with moderate hardness.
Behavior: Generally peaceful but may quarrel with other members of Loricariidae.
Dietary Requirements: Omnivorous; accept both plant and animal matter.

Remarks: This undescribed species of *Panaque* is referred to as "L-90" or "Loricariid-type number 90." It is often available by its L-number designation and usually commands a hefty price. The care and husbandry requirements of this species are identical to those for *P. nigrolineatus*.

Otocinclus vittatus

Otocinclus vittatus

Panaque nigrolineatus

Panaque nigrolineatus juvenile

Panaque sp. L-90

Panaque sp. L-90 profile

Panaque sp. "Colombia"

UNDESCRIBED TO DATE

Natural Range: Colombia.
Size: 8" (20 cm) TL; may grow slightly larger.
Water Chemistry: Tropical; slightly acidic with moderate hardness.
Behavior: Generally peaceful but may quarrel with other members of Loricariidae.
Dietary Requirements: Omnivorous; accept both plant and animal matter.

Remarks: Another undescribed species of *Panaque* that is also quite distinctive with its black striping on a cream-colored background. Care and husbandry requirements in the aquarium are identical to those for *P. nigrolineatus*.

Panaque sp. "Brazil"

UNDESCRIBED TO DATE

Natural Range: Northern Brazil
Size: 8" (20 cm) TL; may grow slightly larger.
Water Chemistry: Tropical; slightly acidic with moderate hardness.
Behavior: Generally peaceful but may quarrel with other members of Loricariidae.
Dietary Requirements: Omnivorous; accept both plant and animal matter.

Remarks: There is much pattern and color differentiation between this species and *P.* sp. "Colombia." However, they are collected many, many miles apart from each other. Care and husbandry requirements in the aquarium are identical to those for *P. nigrolineatus*.

Panaque sp.

UNDESCRIBED TO DATE

Natural Range: Amazon and Orinoco River drainages.
Size: 8" (20 cm) TL; may grow slightly larger.
Water Chemistry: Tropical; slightly acidic with moderate hardness.
Behavior: Generally peaceful but may quarrel with other members of Loricariidae.
Dietary Requirements: Omnivorous; accept both plant and animal matter.

Remarks: There are several other undescribed species of *Panaque* not mentioned within this text. However, the information above can be safely applied to the two species pictured on the right.

Panaque sp. "Colombia"

Panaque sp. "Colombia" juvenile

Panaque sp. "Brazil" juvenile

Panaque sp. "Brazil" adult

Panaque sp.

Panaque sp. profile

697

Panaquolos spp. "L-200" & "L-232"

UNDESCRIBED TO DATE

Natural Range: Amazon River drainage, Brazil and Peru.

Size: 8" (20 cm) TL; either species may grow significantly larger.

Water Chemistry: Tropical; slightly acidic with moderate hardness.

Behavior: Generally peaceful but may quarrel with other members of Loricariidae.

Dietary Requirements: Omnivorous; accept both plant and animal matter.

Remarks: Describing taxonomy of these two fishes is really just a stab in the dark. In the future, we hope to see this worked out because it may provide some more data on their care and husbandry in aquariums. They seem to do best when cared for in a fashion similar to the other members of *Panaquolos*.

Parancistrus sp. 1

UNDESCRIBED TO DATE

Natural Range: Northern South America.

Size: Probably 6" (15 cm) TL or slightly larger.

Water Chemistry: Tropical; slightly acidic with moderate hardness.

Behavior: Generally peaceful but may quarrel with other members of Loricariidae.

Dietary Requirements: Omnivorous; accept both plant and animal matter.

Remarks: This interesting, medium-sized catfish is sometimes offered for sale from exporters in Brazil, Venezuela, and Peru. Their care requirements are identical to those of other "*Ancistrus*" species.

Parancistrus sp. 2

UNDESCRIBED TO DATE

Natural Range: Northern South America.

Size: Probably 6" (15 cm) TL or slightly larger.

Water Chemistry: Tropical; slightly acidic with moderate hardness.

Behavior: Generally peaceful but may quarrel with other members of Loricariidae.

Dietary Requirements: Omnivorous; accept both plant and animal matter.

Remarks: This species is very similar in distribution, care, and husbandry to *Parancistrus* sp. 1, even though they look quite different.

Panaque sp. L-200

Panaque sp. L-232

Parancistrus sp. 1

Parancistrus sp. 1 var.

Parancistrus sp. 2

Parancistrus sp. 2 var.

Pseudacanthicus sp. "L-25"

UNDESCRIBED TO DATE

Natural Range: Rio Xingu, Brazil.
Size: 14" (35 cm) TL.
Water Chemistry: Tropical; slightly acidic with moderate hardness.
Behavior: Generally peaceful but may quarrel with other members of Loricariidae.
Dietary Requirements: Omnivorous; accept both plant and animal matter.

Remarks: This species is very distinctive in coloration. As they grow older, their colors intensify even more, and when they are viewed from a distance they appear very unique. These are fairly easy to keep in aquariums and may live for years. They may also become quite belligerent with tankmates, so watch them carefully. They may eat small fishes.

Peckoltia vermiculata

STEINDACHNER 1908

Natural Range: Middle and lower Amazon River basin.
Size: 6" (15 cm) TL.
Water Chemistry: Tropical; slightly acidic with moderate hardness.
Behavior: Generally peaceful but may quarrel with other members of Loricariidae.
Dietary Requirements: Omnivorous; accept both plant and animal matter.

Remarks: This species and *P. vittata* are often referred to as "Tiger Plecos" because of the striping pattern that alternates from black to orange. Their care should be identical to that of the members of *Hypancistrus*. Many species that were once *Peckoltia* now belong to that genus.

Peckoltia vittata

STEINDACHNER 1881

Natural Range: Middle and lower Amazon River basin.
Size: 6" (15 cm) TL.
Water Chemistry: Tropical; slightly acidic with moderate hardness.
Behavior: Generally peaceful but may quarrel with other members of Loricariidae.
Dietary Requirements: Omnivorous; accept both plant and animal matter.

Remarks: These "Tiger Plecos" may end up either as a subspecies of or synonymous with *P. vermiculata*. Specimens from multiple regions appear very similar to *P. vermiculata* and hybridization between the two species is a possibility where their distribution overlaps.

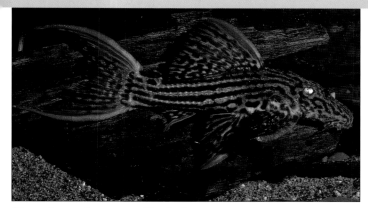

Pseudacanthicus sp. "L-25"

Pseudacanthicus sp. "L-25" profile

Peckoltia vermiculata

Peckoltia sp. L-134 for comparison

Peckoltia vittata

Peckoltia vittata

Sturisoma aureum

STEINDACHNER 1900

Natural Range: Magdalena, San Jorge, and Cesar River basins; South America.
Size: 10" (25 cm) TL.
Water Chemistry: Tropical; slightly acidic with moderate hardness.
Behavior: Generally peaceful but may quarrel with other members of Loricariidae.
Dietary Requirements: Omnivorous; accept both plant and animal matter.

Remarks: The long, rigid fins and body make the members of *Sturisoma* very interesting in aquariums. They generally feed on plants and roots in nature, but in captivity they do well on an assortment of fresh greens, such as zucchini and leaves of romaine lettuce. It is best to supplement their diet with occasional small offerings of live *Tubifex* worms.

Sturisoma festivum

MYERS 1942

Natural Range: Lake Maracaibo basin, South America.
Size: 8" (20 cm) TL.
Water Chemistry: Tropical; slightly acidic with moderate hardness.
Behavior: Generally peaceful but may quarrel with other members of Loricariidae.
Dietary Requirements: Omnivorous; accept both plant and animal matter.

Remarks: Like *S. aureum*, *S. festivum* appreciate occasional offerings of live *Tubifex* worms in addition to their normal diet, which should consist of plant materials. Unlike *S. aureum*, *S. festivum* is geographically isolated to the Lake Maracaibo basin in South America.

Sturisoma rostratum

SPIX & AGASSIZ 1829

Natural Range: South America.
Size: 8" (20 cm) TL.
Water Chemistry: Tropical; slightly acidic with moderate hardness.
Behavior: Generally peaceful but may quarrel with other members of Loricariidae.
Dietary Requirements: Omnivorous; accept both plant and animal matter.

Remarks: *S. rostratum* are easily identified by their snout, which is slightly longer than in other members of the genus. Otherwise, their care and husbandry are normal and typical of the genus.

Sturisoma aureum

Sturisoma aureum

Sturisoma festivum

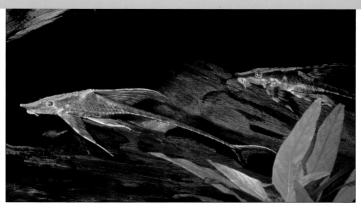

Sturisoma sp. for comparison

Sturisoma rostratum

Sturisoma rostratum

Mastacembelus erythrotaenia

MASTACEMBELIDAE
SPINY EELS

The spiny eels are an interesting and unique group of fishes. Primarily found in tropical regions, they inhabit a broad range of habitats. Generally they can be found in the faster-moving portions of streams, rivers, and creeks, as well as deep within the crevices of rocks in large lakes. They feed mainly on small, benthic invertebrates and crustaceans but will swallow small fishes if they have the opportunity.

In aquariums, they should be given ample hiding places and clean water. Their scaleless bodies are prone to infection should the bacteria count in the aquarium rise to lethal levels. Larger specimens can be paired up by adding several of them to an aquarium, and the ones that are most compatible will begin sharing a cave together. Breeding, although very rare, has been observed in the aquarium with multiple species.

Macrognathus circumcinctus

HORA 1924

Natural Range: Thailand and Indonesia.
Size: 6" (15 cm) TL; may grow slightly larger.
Water Chemistry: Tropical; avoid extremes.
Behavior: Generally peaceful but will swallow small fish whole.
Dietary Requirements: Crustaceans, worms, small fishes, and benthic insect larvae.

Remarks: This small species of spiny eel is very interesting to keep in an aquarium. They will often back themselves into a crevice or hole—as do nearly all spiny eels—in the tank's décor and wait for feeding time. Even though this species is much smaller than many of their counterparts, they can still eat large meals. Watch when placing in an aquarium with smaller fishes, such as many of the barbs or tetras.

Macrognathus pancalus

HAMILTON 1822

Natural Range: Bangladesh, India, and Pakistan.
Size: 10" (25 cm) TL.
Water Chemistry: Tropical; avoid extremes.
Behavior: Generally peaceful but will swallow small fish whole.
Dietary Requirements: Crustaceans, worms, small fishes, and benthic insect larvae.

Remarks: These medium-sized spiny eels are found in slow-moving, shallow estuaries throughout their native range. As with nearly all species within the family, the males are generally smaller and more slender while the females appear more robust. A good aquarium fish that is long-lived.

Mastacembelus armatus / Zigzag Eel

LACEPEDE 1800

Natural Range: Pakistan to Viet Nam and parts of Indonesia.
Size: 30" (75 cm) TL; may grow slightly larger in nature.
Water Chemistry: Tropical; avoid extremes.
Behavior: Generally peaceful but will swallow small fish whole.
Dietary Requirements: Crustaceans, worms, small fishes, and benthic insect larvae.

Remarks: Zigzag Eels are found in streams or rivers with fast-moving water over a pebble substrate where they find refuge in bogwood or rocks. They feed mainly on aquatic invertebrates, such as shrimps and insect larvae, but they certainly won't hesitate to snap up small fishes, too.

Macrognathus circumcinctus

Macrognathus circumcinctus

Macrognathus pancalus

Macrognathus pancalus

Mastacembelus armatus

Mastacembelus armatus

Mastacembelus erythrotaenia / Fire Eel

BLEEKER 1850

Natural Range: Asia.
Size: 40" (100 cm) TL.
Water Chemistry: Tropical; avoid extremes.
Behavior: Generally peaceful but will swallow smaller tankmates.
Dietary Requirements: Crustaceans, worms, small fishes, and benthic insect larvae.

Remarks: In nature, Fire Eels inhabit the slower-moving areas of deep rivers and their tributaries where they prey on a wide variety of organisms. In the aquarium, they are generally peaceful toward fishes they can't swallow, although some may show a slight degree of intraspecific aggression when older.

Mastacembelus sp. "Cameroon"

UNDESCRIBED TO DATE

Natural Range: Cameroon.
Size: 24" (60 cm) TL.
Water Chemistry: Tropical; avoid extremes.
Behavior: Generally peaceful but will swallow small fish whole.
Dietary Requirements: Crustaceans, worms, small fishes, and benthic insect larvae.

Remarks: Although these spiny eels are not actually described, they have been around the hobby for some time. This species is often imported into the United States and Canada, as well as other regions throughout the world, along with shipments of more common West African fishes such as characins and cichlids. Occasionally, you will see them listed as Tire Track Eels, but don't be confused, as that is a separate species, although their care is remarkably similar.

Mastacembelus erythrotaenia

Mastacembelus erythrotaenia

Mastacembelus sp. "Cameroon"

Mastacembelus sp. "Cameroon"

Melanotaenia trifasciata

MELANOTAENIIDAE

RAINBOWFISHES

Rainbowfishes are some of the most colorful freshwater fishes available to hobbyists. Generally, they are peaceful, except for the larger ones, and make excellent additions to a community aquarium. Some of the larger species may become belligerent with members of the same species and possibly even members of a similar species. Regardless, a large aquarium full of plants and bogwood is really accented by the addition of a small group of these fishes.

Fishes within Melanotaeniidae are widely distributed over northern and eastern Australia, New Guinea, and many adjacent islands. One species, the Madagascar Rainbowfish (*Bedotia geayi*), is found on the island of Madagascar off the coast of eastern Africa. This species is not actually in the family Melanotaeniidae, but they are usually compatible with fishes that are.

Many hobbyists attempt to breed their rainbowfishes. Usually, with a concerted effort, they are successful and often raise several generations from only a handful of adults. Hobbyists have reported that it is best to have only one species in the aquarium, and a single male with several females usually produces the best results.

Glossolepis insignis / Red Rainbowfish

WEBER 1907

Natural Range: Lake Sentani in Indonesia.
Size: 6" (15 cm) TL.
Water Chemistry: Tropical, hard, basic water.
Behavior: Very active schooling fish; males will spar with each other.
Dietary Requirements: Will take all normal aquarium fare.

Remarks: These beautiful rainbows have glittering silver females and iridescent scarlet males. A large school makes a wonderful display in large aquaria. It is, like most rainbowfish, a continuous spawner, laying a few eggs each day. A floating spawning mop harvested weekly provides an easy way of propagating the species.

Glossolepis multisquamata / Sepik Rainbowfish

WEBER & DE BEAUFORT 1922

Natural Range: New Guinea.
Size: 6" (15 cm) TL.
Water Chemistry: Tropical; found in fairly soft, slightly acid waters.
Behavior: Unknown in nature but generally peaceful in aquariums.
Dietary Requirements: An invertebrate feeder; will take appropriate aquarium foods.

Remarks: The only rainbowfish known to inhabit floodplain habitats.

Iriatherina werneri / Threadfin Rainbowfish

MEINKEN 1974

Natural Range: Southern New Guinea and northern Australia.
Size: 2" (5 cm) TL.
Water Chemistry: Tropical; neutral with moderate hardness.
Behavior: Timid, schooling fish.
Dietary Requirements: A micropredator by nature. Appropriately sized live foods are best.

Remarks: Despite their delicate appearance, these are fairly hardy aquarium fish. They are always found in heavy vegetation, and the tank should be well planted. Keep these fish in schools.

Glossolepis incisus pair

Glossolepis incisus

Glossolepis multisquamata

Glossolepis sp. profile

Iriatherina werneri

Iriatherina werneri pair spawning

Melanotaenia affinis / North New Guinea Rainbowfish

WEBER 1907

Natural Range: New Guinea.

Size: 5.5" (14 cm) TL.

Water Chemistry: Tropical; neutral with moderate hardness.

Behavior: Typical large, schooling rainbowfish. Watch with smaller fishes.

Dietary Requirements: Will take all normal aquarium fare.

Remarks: Although they are rather drab in coloration, *M. affinis* are perfect additions for a medium-sized community aquarium. They will add a touch of vigor to the tank with their constant back-and-forth swimming and may even act as a dither fish for larger, shy species. As with all other rainbowfishes, keep this species in a small group.

Melanotaenia boesemani / Boeseman's Rainbowfish

ALLEN & CROSS 1980

Natural Range: Known only from lakes in the remote Vogelkop Peninsula, Irian Jaya.

Size: 4.5" (11 cm) TL.

Water Chemistry: Tropical; moderately hard and slightly alkaline water.

Behavior: Typical large rainbowfish; males spar with each other.

Dietary Requirements: Will take any aquarium foods.

Remarks: Reminiscent of some coral reef fishes, this rainbow is two-toned; the front half of the body is silvery blue, and the rear half is orange. In males this coloration is intense; in females it is indistinct.

Melanotaenia goldiei / Goldie River Rainbowfish

MACLEAY 1883

Natural Range: New Guinea.

Size: 5.5" (14 cm) TL.

Water Chemistry: Tropical; found in moderately hard, basic water.

Behavior: Typical large rainbowfish; males spar with each other.

Dietary Requirements: Will take any aquarium foods.

Remarks: This is one of many rainbowfish species that specialist aquarists strive to propagate in pure lineages.

Melanotaenia affinis female

Melanotaenia affinis male

Melanotaenia boesemani

Melanotaenia boesemani

Melanotaenia goldiei

Melanotaenia goldiei

Melanotaenia herbertaxelrodi / Lake Tebera Rainbowfish

ALLEN 1981

Natural Range: New Guinea.
Size: 4.25" (11 cm) TL.
Water Chemistry: Tropical; found in moderately hard, basic water.
Behavior: Typical large rainbowfish; males spar with each other.
Dietary Requirements: Will take any aquarium foods.

Remarks: Like many of New Guinea's rainbows, this species has a limited distribution. With the exception of a single specimen found about 20 miles north of Lake Tebera, all others of this species have been caught in the lake.

Melanotaenia irianjaya / Irian Rainbowfish

ALLEN 1985

Natural Range: Irian Jaya.
Size: 4" (10 cm) TL.
Water Chemistry: Tropical.
Behavior: Typical large rainbowfish; males spar with each other.
Dietary Requirements: Will take any aquarium foods.

Remarks: This beautiful species has highly reflective scales that appear pink or red in coloration. Sparring males show their best colors as they spin around each other violently, but seldom is any real damage done. *M. irianjaya* are smaller rainbowfish and seem to do best in aquariums with lush plant growth.

Melanotaenia lacustris / Turquoise Rainbowfish

MUNRO 1964

Natural Range: Lake Kutubu, New Guinea.
Size: 5" (12.5 cm) TL.
Water Chemistry: Tropical; moderately hard and basic water.
Behavior: Typical large rainbowfish; males spar with each other; should have hiding spaces or a planted tank.
Dietary Requirements: Omnivorous; will take usual aquarium fare.

Remarks: The males have beautiful iridescent blue backs and silvery bellies. Their care and husbandry requirements in aquariums are similar to those for others of the genus.

Melanotaenia herbertaxelrodi male

Melanotaenia herbertaxelrodi

Melanotaenia irianjaya

Melanotaenia irianjaya

Melanotaenia lacustris

Melanotaenia lacustris male

Melanotaenia nigrans / Black-banded Rainbowfish

RICHARDSON 1843

Natural Range: Australia.
Size: 4" (10 cm) TL.
Water Chemistry: Tropical; freshwater and brackish water.
Behavior: Typical rainbowfish; shy and generally peaceful.
Dietary Requirements: Omnivorous; will eat filamentous algae.

Remarks: This species is found both in rainforest streams and in coastal brackish areas. Their tolerance of some salt in the water makes them ideal tankmates for brackish water fishes such as *Scatophagus*.

Melanotaenia parkinsoni / Parkinson's Rainbowfish

ALLEN 1980

Natural Range: New Guinea.
Size: 5" (13 cm) TL.
Water Chemistry: Tropical; neutral with moderate hardness.
Behavior: Typical rainbowfish; shy and generally peaceful.
Dietary Requirements: Will take any aquarium foods.

Remarks: This fish has blue and orange coloration but not demarcated, as in *M. boesemani*.

Melanotaenia praecox / Dwarf Rainbowfish

WEBER & BEAUFORT 1922

Natural Range: Mamberamo River in Irian Jaya.
Size: 2.5" (6 cm)
Water Chemistry: Tropical; neutral with moderate hardness.
Behavior: Typical rainbowfish.
Dietary Requirements: Will take any aquarium foods.

Remarks: Males and females are colored alike, except for the intensity of color in their fins. This species makes a good choice for hobbyists wanting a school of rainbows in a smaller setup.

Melanotaenia nigrans

Melanotaenia nigrans

Melanotaenia parkinsoni

Melanotaenia parkinsoni

Melanotaenia praecox

Melanotaenia praecox

Melanotaenia trifasciata / *Banded Rainbowfish*

RENDAHL 1922

Natural Range: Australia: Northern Territory and Queensland.

Size: 4.25" (11 cm) TL.

Water Chemistry: Tropical; neutral with moderate hardness.

Behavior: Typical rainbowfish; shy and generally peaceful.

Dietary Requirements: Will take the usual aquarium foods.

Remarks: Here is another rainbowfish that is not the most brilliantly colored species but does well in a community aquarium. If nothing else, they provide the hobbyist with something different and interesting to look at.

Melanotaenia trifasciata

Melanotaenia herbertaxelrodi for comparison

721

Synodontis multipunctatus

MOCHOKIDAE
SYNODONTIS CATFISHES

Africa holds a vast number of species of fishes. Among them is Mochokidae—the *Synodontis* catfishes. There are approximately 150 species of these unique and often very popular catfishes. Also called squeakers or upside-down catfishes, the most popular members of Mochokidae that are recognized by hobbyists all belong to the genus *Synodontis*.

These fishes vary greatly in size and temperament, among other attributes, but their suitability in aquariums is generally high. Nearly all of them will eat standard fare for aquarium fishes, such as pellets, flakes, and wafers. Of course, the addition of some meaty foods like bloodworms and shrimp won't hurt either—unless fed in excessive quantities.

Their aquariums should have some cover in the form of rock caves or overhanging shelves and cliffs. Additionally, they seem to like the undersides of bogwood and anything else that provides shelter from the aquarium's illumination.

Nearly all *Synodontis* are either crepuscular or nocturnal, but they are often seen during daylight hours if that is when feeding occurs. They are gluttons who will eat until they burst, so be sure that your other fishes are getting their fair share as well. If properly cared for, these catfishes may live for significant amounts of time, and specimens living for nearly 20 years are not uncommon.

Synodontis angelicus

SCHILTHUIS 1891

Natural Range: Congo basin.
Size: 22" (55 cm) TL; usually far smaller.
Water Chemistry: Tropical; very adaptable to pH and hardness values.
Behavior: A typical *Synodontis* cat, but it may get aggressive as it matures.
Dietary Requirements: Omnivorous; will eat all aquarium foods.

Remarks: An extremely beautiful and sought-after aquarium fish, but one which requires large tanks, especially if you want to try keeping more than one. Plenty of dark hiding spaces should be provided to prevent territorial competition. Like all catfish, these will make noise when netted, leading to their common name of "squeakers."

Synodontis brichardi

POLL 1959

Natural Range: Lower Congo drainage.
Size: 8" (20 cm) TL.
Water Chemistry: Tropical; very adaptable to pH and hardness values.
Behavior: A typical *Synodontis*; best enjoyed in groups on a large tank; generally will not bother other fish.
Dietary Requirements: Primarily herbivorous; feed on filamentous algae.

Remarks: This species has been popular in the hobby for years. Even today, nearly all of them are collected in the wild and command premium prices. This species is very sensitive to medications, so be sure your aquarium is healthy and stable.

Synodontis decorus / Clown Squeaker

BOULENGER 1899

Natural Range: Congo basin.
Size: 15" (32 cm) TL.
Water Chemistry: Tropical; very adaptable to pH and hardness values.
Behavior: A typical member of the genus.
Dietary Requirements: Omnivorous.

Remarks: One of the most distinguishable features of *S. decorus* is their tall dorsal fin and the black extension off the first fin ray. Their spotting is large and scattered with a concentration of much smaller spotting on their head and nape. While they are capable of growing to 15" (30 cm) in total length, specimens measuring 8" (20 cm) are far more common.

Synodontis angelicus

Synodontis angelicus

Synodontis brichardi

Synodontis brichardi

Synodontis decorus juvenile

Synodontis decorus adult

Synodontis eupterus / Lace Cat

BOULENGER 1901

Natural Range: White Nile; Chad, Volta, and Niger drainages.
Size: 12" (30 cm) TL.
Water Chemistry: Tropical; very adaptable to pH and hardness values.
Behavior: This is one of the species that regularly swims upside down.
Dietary Requirements: Omnivorous.

Remarks: Like its congeners, this fish is an easygoing, peaceful, nocturnal scavenger. Provide them with a large aquarium and peaceful tankmates.

Synodontis granulosus

BOULENGER 1900

Natural Range: Endemic to Lake Tanganyika.
Size: 10.5" (27 cm) TL.
Water Chemistry: Tropical; very hard and alkaline is preferred.
Behavior: Aggressive, but only over territory—a sufficient number of caves will keep things peaceful.
Dietary Requirements: Will take any and all aquarium foods; not picky.

Remarks: The coloration of this fish is quite variable, with some individuals showing no spots at all. All specimens will show the granular fleshy pattern on the head that gives the species its name.

Synodontis multipunctatus / Cuckoo Catfish

BOULENGER 1898

Natural Range: East Africa, including Lake Tanganyika.
Size: 11" (28 cm) TL.
Water Chemistry: Tropical; very adaptable to pH and hardness values.
Behavior: Generally peaceful with fishes it cannot swallow; males may quarrel.
Dietary Requirements: Most standard aquarium fare is accepted with offerings of shrimps and worms preferred.

Remarks: This species and perhaps a few close relatives are the only fish known to be brood parasites. These catfish lay their eggs at the same time as various cichlids lay theirs. The female cichlid will take up the catfish eggs with hers. The baby cats hatch out very large and very early and then eat the cichlid eggs or fry. They have been bred using cichlids as hosts, including Malawi mbuna! (*S. multipunctatus* does not occur in Lake Malawi.)

Synodontis eupterus

Synodontis eupterus

Synodontis granulosus adult

Synodontis granulosus

Synodontis multipunctatus

Synodontis multipunctatus

727

Synodontis nigriventris

DAVID 1936

Natural Range: Congo basin.
Size: 4" (10 cm) TL.
Water Chemistry: Tropical; very adaptable to pH and hardness values.
Behavior: Spend much of their time swimming upside down.
Dietary Requirements: Omnivorous.

Remarks: A group of these will take up residence in a cave, and when food is placed on the surface of the water, they will rise up, upside down, and vacuum the surface, then scurry back into hiding.

Synodontis notatus / Onespot Squeaker

VAILLANT 1893

Natural Range: Eastern Africa.
Size: 12" (30 cm) TL, usually smaller.
Water Chemistry: Tropical; hard and alkaline conditions preferred.
Behavior: Generally peaceful with fishes it cannot swallow.
Dietary Requirements: Meaty foods such as clams, squid, shrimps, and fish meat along with standard aquarium fare.

Remarks: These beautiful catfish have a single dark-colored spot on either side of their body. This spot appears smaller as the fish grows, and occasionally there is light ring around the spot.

Synodontis ocellifer

BOULENGER 1900

Natural Range: Senegal, Gambia, Volta, Chad, and Niger drainages.
Size: 20" (49 cm) TL.
Water Chemistry: Tropical; hard alkaline conditions preferred.
Behavior: Typical *Synodontis* cat, only bigger than most others.
Dietary Requirements: Will take any aquarium foods.

Remarks: This fish sports larger and fewer spots than *S. multipunctatus* or *S. petricola*.

728

Synodontis nigriventris

Synodontis nigriventris

Synodontis notatus

Synodontis notatus profile

Synodontis ocellifer adult

Synodontis ocellifer juvenile

729

Synodontis petricola

MATTHES 1959

Natural Range: Endemic to Lake Tanganyika.
Size: 4.5" (11 cm) TL.
Water Chemistry: Tropical; very hard, very basic water as is suitable for Tanganyikan cichlids.
Behavior: Gregarious and active *Synodontis* catfish.
Dietary Requirements: Largely carnivorous; will take any and all aquarium foods.

Remarks: These comical cats are perfect additions to a Tanganyikan cichlid tank—the larger the better, to see their rapid cruising scavenging. Although nocturnal, they will quickly learn to come out for feedings, and they will take food wherever it is, feeding upside down from the surface, catching food in mid-water, or vacuuming it out of nooks and crannies in the gravel or among the rocks. Despite its similar appearance to *S. multipunctatus*, this species does not practice brood parasitism.

Synodontis schoutedeni

DAVID 1936

Natural Range: Central Congo.
Size: 7" (17.5 cm) TL.
Water Chemistry: Tropical; otherwise not too critical, avoid extremes.
Behavior: Typical *Synodontis* catfish; generally peaceful.
Dietary Requirements: Will take any aquarium foods; not picky.

Remarks: These exquisitely and variably marked catfish are rarely available and command a high price. They are highly desirable, and some specimens are colored gold or high yellow.

Synodontis petricola juvenile

Synodontis petricola adult

Synodontis schoutedeni juvenile

Synodontis schoutedeni small adult

731

Gnathonemus petersii

MORMYRIDAE
ELEPHANTNOSE FISHES

Widely distributed over much of tropical Africa, Mormyrids are gentle and peaceful fishes that often do well in aquariums. There are approximately 200 valid species within the family. Of these, only a handful ever make their way into the aquarium trade, and of this small number, only a few are considered popular and regularly available. Three of these species are profiled herein. Of course, new species are being discovered all the time, and in the future, we may see many more Mormyrids available to us on a regular basis.

In general, all elephantnoses require very similar care and husbandry in aquariums. Their biggest downfall is their sensitivity to medications. For this reason, it is imperative that they be maintained in aquariums that are stable and healthy. Even shifts in pH or nitrogen compounds, such as nitrates, can cause major health problems and disease breakouts. Another problem, albeit highly avoidable, is their willingness to attempt to explore outside their aquariums. Unfortunately for them, they are exceedingly effective at this, and hobbyists often find their prized Mormyrid on the floor in the morning. To prevent this, house them in a tank with a very tight-fitting cover.

Campylomormyrus tamandua / Worm-jawed Mormyrid

GÜNTHER 1864

Natural Range: Volta, Niger, Chad, Shari, and Congo drainages.

Size: 17" (43 cm) TL.

Water Chemistry: Tropical; neutral with moderate hardness is best.

Behavior: Electric fish that do not tolerate others of their own kind well. These fish are intelligent and curious.

Dietary Requirements: Carnivorous; worms, shrimps, and other meaty foods are best.

Remarks: This species is not often seen in the hobby, but shipments from the Congo region are becoming more regular.

Gnathonemus petersii / Elephantnose Fish

GÜNTHER 1862

Natural Range: Niger to Congo River drainages.

Size: 14.5" (35 cm) TL.

Water Chemistry: Tropical; neutral with moderate hardness is best.

Behavior: Electric fish that do not tolerate others of their own kind well. These fish are intelligent and curious.

Dietary Requirements: Carnivorous; may require live foods.

Remarks: One of the most commonly encountered mormyrids. this is the species that made this family a hit with tropical fish hobbyists.

Mormyrops engystoma / Torpedo Mormyrid

BOULENGER 1898

Natural Range: Chad drainage.

Size: 6" (15 cm) TL.

Water Chemistry: Tropical; neutral with moderate hardness is best.

Behavior: Electric fish that do not tolerate others of their own kind well. These fish are intelligent and curious.

Dietary Requirements: Carnivorous; may require live foods, especially just after importation.

Remarks: This species is raised in ponds in Southeast Asia, and many of today's specimens are from these pond-raised stocks. Occasionally, wild collected specimens are available also but usually as adults or subadults.

Campylomormyrus tamandua juvenile

Campylomormyrus tamandua adult

Gnathonemus petersii

Gnathonemus petersii profile

Mormyrops engystoma

Mormyrops longirostris for comparison

735

Chitala chitala

NOTOPTERIDAE

KNIFEFISHES

There are eight species of knifefishes currently within Notopteridae, of which three are profiled herein. They are chiefly found in freshwater with some specimens occasionally venturing into brackish water estuaries or lagoons throughout their native range.

The most popular species are found in Asia and Africa, where they inhabit rivers, lakes, and small ponds (during the dry season). All knifefishes are predatory and require feedings of live organisms, such as fishes, shrimps, and worms, to do well in captivity. Of course, as with nearly all predatory fishes, they may be trained to accept non-living foods as well. Occasionally hobbyists have even been able to get their knifefishes to accept prepared foods in the form of large sinking pellets that are traditionally formulated for carnivorous cichlids, puffers, and the like. The author (Scott) has personally found that these formulations are very beneficial and greedily accepted if they have blood meal as a primary ingredient.

As with other predatory fishes, feed knifefishes a few times per week until there is a slight bulge in their sides. They do not get the traditional rounded-belly appearance as most other fishes do, and if they are overfed, they may become stressed and die. Be sure to keep up on the water quality of their aquarium as well, since too much food, especially if it's live food, will foul the water after a while.

Chitala chitala / Clown Knifefish

HAMILTON 1822

Natural Range: India
Size: 48" (122 cm) TL.
Water Chemistry: Tropical.
Behavior: Often intolerant of conspecifics; will eat most other tankmates.
Dietary Requirements: May be hard to wean off live foods.

Remarks: Although this species is commonly sold, few aquarists have the appropriate setup to house these 4-foot fish. The eggs, which are usually laid on a stake or stump in a flooded area, are ferociously guarded by the males.

Chitala ornata / Clown Featherback

GRAY 1831

Natural Range: Thailand; Cambodia; Vietnam.
Size: 40 inches (100 cm) TL.
Water Chemistry: Tropical.
Behavior: Often intolerant of conspecifics; will eat most other tankmates.
Dietary Requirements: May be hard to wean off live foods.

Remarks: These fish are hard to distinguish from *C. chitala* without the trained eye of an ichthyologist who has studied them in detail. There is considerable confusion over the taxonomic standing of this species and they may prove to be synonymous with *Chitala chitala* in the near future.

Xenomystus nigri / African Knifefish

GÜNTHER 1868

Natural Range: Widespread in African river systems.
Size: 12" (30 cm) TL.
Water Chemistry: Tropical; slightly soft and acidic conditions seem to be best.
Behavior: Like most knifefishes, these are nocturnal predators that use electrical fields to navigate and find prey.
Dietary Requirements: May require live foods but will take frozen bloodworms, brine shrimp, and sometimes sinking pellets with blood meal as an ingredient.

Remarks: Quite a bit less colorful than most other knifefishes, this species is routinely found in the hobby. Beware not to include the African Knifefish in aquariums containing small fishes, such as rasboras, barbs, and tetras, as they will be eaten.

Chitala chitala young adult

Chitala chitala uniquely patterned

Chitala ornata young

Chitala ornata

Xenomystus nigri

Xenomystus nigri

Betta Splendens

OSPHRONEMIDAE
BETTAS & GOURAMIES

Bettas and Gouramis are widely distributed over much of Asia. They are most commonly recognized by the often elongated rays of their pelvic fins. Some species, like those within *Betta*, are very aggressive toward conspecifics and sometimes even congeners. While many species are bubblenesters, some actually practice mouthbrooding, similar to cichlids.

In the aquarium, these fishes are often popular and easily obtained. They readily feed on most standard aquarium foods that one would offer community fishes, and recently there have even been specially formulated foods directed at those hobbyists wishing to keep their Bettas in bowls or small aquariums. Many Gouramis will also consume these foods, and from a nutritional standpoint, they are often very suitable.

One of the most important aspects of keeping these fishes in captivity is gaining an understanding of their behavior and what you can and cannot get away with. This topic is crucial, and unfortunately we are not able to expand much upon it here, so make sure to research the unique behavior of these fishes further before you purchase them as additions to your community aquarium. What may appear a beautiful and hardy species may turn into a terror and destroy many of its tankmates.

Betta anabatoides / Giant Bettafish

BLEEKER 1851

Natural Range: Borneo.
Size: 5" (12 cm) TL.
Water Chemistry: Tropical, very warm (80° to 86°F); soft and acidic conditions are preferred.
Behavior: Unknown in nature, but fairly peaceful with other, similar sized fishes; aggressive towards other males and females of same species.
Dietary Requirements: Small invertebrates are its natural diet.

Remarks: A mouthbrooding species that does well in aquariums. They are best kept alone or in pairs, but males may be very aggressive towards females.

Betta bellica / Slim Bettafish

SAUVAGE 1884

Natural Range: Indonesia and Malaysia.
Size: 4" (10 cm) TL.
Water Chemistry: Tropical; neutral to slightly acid with moderate hardness.
Behavior: Peaceful with other species.
Dietary Requirements: Small invertebrates are its natural diet.

Remarks: A bubblenesting species that needs warmer temperatures in order to do its best in aquariums.

Betta brownorum

WITTE & SCHMIDT 1992

Natural Range: Indonesia and Malaysia.
Size: 1.5" (3.8 cm) TL.
Water Chemistry: Tropical; soft, acidic conditions are preferred.
Behavior: A small, shy bubblenester.
Dietary Requirements: Small invertebrates are its natural diet.

Remarks: This is one of the small, red bettas with an iridescent blue-green blotch on the side. Like most rainforest species, this fish prefers cooler temperatures.

Betta anabatoides

Betta akarensis pair for comparison

Betta bellica

Betta bellica pair

Betta brownorum

Betta brownorum

Betta coccina / Wine Red Betta

VIERKE 1979
Natural Range: Indonesia.
Size: 2" (5.6 cm) TL.
Water Chemistry: Tropical; very soft and very acidic conditions preferred.
Behavior: A small, shy bubblenester.
Dietary Requirements: Small invertebrates are its natural diet.

Remarks: This is another one of the small, red bettas with an iridescent blue-green blotch on the side.

Betta foerschi

VIERKE 1979
Natural Range: Indonesia and Borneo.
Size: 2.75" (7 cm) TL.
Water Chemistry: Tropical; very soft and very acidic conditions; temperatures in the 70s are best.
Behavior: A generally peaceful mouthbrooder.
Dietary Requirements: Small invertebrates are its natural diet.

Remarks: Like most rainforest species, this fish prefers cooler temperatures.

Betta imbellis / Crescent Bettafish

LADIGES 1975
Natural Range: Malaysia and Indonesia.
Size: 2" (5.5 cm) TL.
Water Chemistry: Tropical; otherwise not too critical; avoid extremes.
Behavior: It was named *imbellis* because, compared to *B. splendens*, it was not as aggressive towards conspecifics. More than one pair can be housed together. A standard bubblenesting species of *Betta*.
Dietary Requirements: Small invertebrates are its natural diet, but most specimens will take regular aquarium fare.

Remarks: This fish is widely used to cross into domestic betta strains for particular fin and color traits.

Betta coccina *Betta coccina*

Betta foerschi *Betta foerschi*

Betta imbellis normal var. *Betta splendens* male shortfin fighter for comparison

Betta macrostoma / Spotfin Bettafish

REGAN 1910

Natural Range: Indonesia.
Size: 4.5" (11 cm) TL.
Water Chemistry: Tropical; neutral to slightly acidic with moderate hardness.
Behavior: A mouthbrooder.
Dietary Requirements: Small invertebrates are its natural diet.

Remarks: This is one of the larger betta species, reaching almost 5 inches.

Betta picta / Spotted Bettafish

VALENCIENNES 1846

Natural Range: Indonesia.
Size: 2.5" (6 cm) TL.
Water Chemistry: Tropical with temperatures in the 70s; otherwise not critical.
Behavior: A mouthbrooder.
Dietary Requirements: Small invertebrates are its natural diet.

Remarks: *Betta picta* is one of the less colorful species within the genus. They come from high mountain streams and therefore prefer cooler temperatures.

Betta pugnax / Penang Bettafish

CANTOR 1849

Natural Range: Malaysia and Singapore.
Size: 4.75" (12 cm) TL.
Water Chemistry: Tropical; otherwise not critical, avoid extremes.
Behavior: Shy; needs plenty of plants in which to hide.
Dietary Requirements: Small invertebrates are its natural diet.

Remarks: A rather drab mouthbrooding betta.

Betta macrostoma female

Betta macrostoma male

Betta picta mouthbrooding!

Betta picta pair

Betta pugnax

Betta pugnax

Betta smaragdina / Blue Bettafish

LADIGES 1972

Natural Range: Thailand.
Size: 2.75" (7 cm) TL.
Water Chemistry: Tropical; quite adaptable to varying pH and hardness.
Behavior: Fairly peaceful, but males cannot be kept together.
Dietary Requirements: Small invertebrates are its natural diet.

Remarks: This is another species that has been crossed into domestic betta strains to introduce certain colors.

Betta splendens / Siamese Fighting Fish, Betta

REGAN 1910

Natural Range: Thailand.
Size: 2.5" (6.5 cm) TL.
Water Chemistry: Tropical; quite adaptable to pH and hardness, but should have temperatures in the 80s.
Behavior: Peaceful, except towards conspecifics; this is one of several species used for fighting sport.
Dietary Requirements: Small invertebrates are its natural diet, but it will likely take any standard aquarium foods.

Remarks: The original short-finned fish has been selectively bred in a rainbow of solid colors, and furthermore into combinations of colors and in many fin types, including double tail and crown tail, in which the rays of the caudal fin are greatly extended beyond the webbing. Despite popular trends, the fish should not be kept at room temperature, which is much too cool for this species.

Betta taeniata / Borneo Bettafish

REGAN 1910

Natural Range: Borneo.
Size: 3" (8 cm) TL.
Water Chemistry: Tropical; quite adaptable to pH and hardness.
Behavior: A typical shy mouthbrooding betta.
Dietary Requirements: Small invertebrates are its natural diet. It may take prepared foods.

Remarks: The female retrieves the eggs and spits them at the male, who takes them up into his buccal pouch. After spawning is complete, the female guards the male, who incubates the eggs and broods the young in his mouth.

Betta smaragdina pair

Betta smaragdina male

Betta splendens female

Betta splendens male

Betta taeniata female

Betta tussyae male for comparison

Colisa lalia / Dwarf Gourami

HAMILTON 1822

Natural Range: India, Pakistan, and Bangladesh.
Size: 3.5" (8.8 cm) TL.
Water Chemistry: Tropical; otherwise not critical.
Behavior: Very peaceful, good community resident.
Dietary Requirements: Will take all normal aquarium fare.

Remarks: Coloration is sexually dimorphic. In addition, several domestic color variants have been established. The male is more tolerant of the female after spawning than most other Gouramis are. A great deal of plant material is often incorporated into the bubblenest.

Macropodus opercularis / Paradisefish

LINNAEUS 1758

Natural Range: Taiwan, China, and Vietnam.
Size: 4" (10 cm) TL.
Water Chemistry: Subtropical to tropical; otherwise not critical.
Behavior: Males may be aggressive, and they will fight with conspecific males.
Dietary Requirements: Will eat any aquarium foods, and appreciates small insect larvae as a treat.

Remarks: The first "tropical" fish in Europe—1869. An extremely adaptable fish, it is found naturally in habitats from stagnant ditches to large rivers and can tolerate just about any water conditions. An easily spawned bubblenester that is highly recommended for beginners.

Osphronemus goramy / Giant Gourami

LACEPÈDE 1801

Natural Range: Sumatra, Borneo, Java, the Malay Peninsula, Thailand, and Vietnam. **Size:** 28" (70 cm) TL.
Water Chemistry: Tropical, freshwater, brackish.
Behavior: Aside from its size, a typical, lethargic Gourami.
Dietary Requirements: Truly omnivorous; will eat aquatic plants.

Remarks: Too large for most home aquaria, this fish is kept by some people in huge tanks, where they become quite the pet.

Colisa lalia male

Colisa lalia turquoise var.

Macropodus opercularis male

Macropodus opercularis spawning

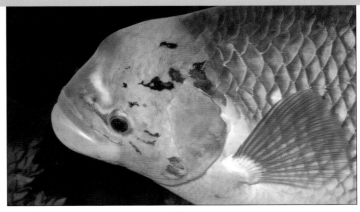

Osphronemus goramy

Osphronemus goramy profile

Osphronemus laticlavius / Giant Red Tail Gourami

LACEPÈDE 1801

Natural Range: Malaysia, Indonesia.
Size: 21" (55 cm) TL.
Water Chemistry: Tropical; otherwise not too critical, avoid extremes.
Behavior: Aside from its size, a typical, lethargic Gourami.
Dietary Requirements: Completely omnivorous.

Remarks: Their care and husbandry in aquariums is extremely similar to *O. goramy*.

Parosphromenus deissneri / Licorice Gourami

BLEEKER 1859

Natural Range: Indonesia.
Size: 1.5" (4 cm) TL.
Water Chemistry: Tropical; prefers soft, acidic conditions.
Behavior: A tiny, shy fish that lives among aquatic plants.
Dietary Requirements: Will usually take standard aquarium fare.

Remarks: For small planted community tanks, this fish is fine, but it cannot compete with larger or more boisterous species.

Parosphromenus filamentosus / Spiketail Gourami

VIERKE 1981

Natural Range: Borneo.
Size: 1.5" (4 cm) TL.
Water Chemistry: Tropical; keep warm, and provide them with water filtered over peat.
Behavior: A tiny, shy fish that lives among aquatic plants.
Dietary Requirements: Will usually take standard aquarium fare.

Remarks: Very similar to *P. deissneri* in all aspects, except perhaps in coloration. Many of these smaller Gouramis do best in small to medium-sized aquariums where they can become intimately familiar with their surroundings.

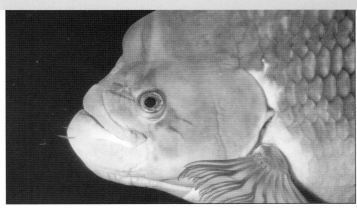

Osphronemus laticlavius

Osphronemus laticlavius

Parosphronemus deissneri

Parosphronemus deissneri for comparison

Parosphronemus filamentosus spawning

Parosphronemus sp. for comparison

Sphaerichthys osphromenoides / Chocolate Gourami

CANESTRINI 1860

Natural Range: Indonesia, Malaysia.

Size: 2.5" (6 cm) TL.

Water Chemistry: Tropical; extremely soft and acid (pH 4 to 6) conditions are best.

Behavior: A surprisingly aggressive but shy mouthbrooder.

Dietary Requirements: Omnivorous in nature, and may require some live foods.

Remarks: This fish has a reputation for being delicate and very hard to spawn. Much of that is related to its intolerance of hardness and high pH, and to its propensity to fight among conspecifics unless kept in sufficiently large groups.

Trichogaster chuna / Honey Gourami

HAMILTON 1822

Natural Range: India and Bangladesh.

Size: 2.75" (7 cm) TL.

Water Chemistry: Tropical; otherwise not too critical.

Behavior: Peaceful.

Dietary Requirements: Will take all aquarium foods.

Remarks: Very similar to *Colisa lalia* in habits. This species is also sexually dimorphic, with the male having brighter coloring. When ready to spawn, he develops a dark head and ventral region.

Trichogaster labiosus / Thick-lipped Gourami

DAY 1877

Natural Range: Southern Burma.

Size: 3.5" (9 cm) TL.

Water Chemistry: Tropical; soft and acidic conditions are best.

Behavior: A typical, peaceful gourami.

Dietary Requirements: Will take the usual aquarium fare.

Remarks: This species is a bit shyer than many of its congeners. Providing them with their own aquarium may make their keeping a lot easier—especially for the beginner, should they choose to care for this species.

Sphaerichthys osphronemoides

Sphaerichthys osphronemoides pair

Trichogaster chuna male

Trichogaster chuna

Trichogaster labiosus

Trichogaster labiosus

Trichogaster leerii / Pearl Gourami

BLEEKER 1852

Natural Range: Malay Peninsula, Thailand, and Indonesia.
Size: 4.75" (12 cm) TL.
Water Chemistry: Tropical; neutral to slightly acid with moderate hardness.
Behavior: Shy, peaceful, and retiring.
Dietary Requirements: Omnivorous, and should be given a wide selection of staple aquarium foods.

Remarks: This fish has understated beauty, with healthy specimens having an almost violet glow. It is an excellent larger fish that is still safe in a community with small tetras and the like.

Trichogaster microlepis / Moonlight Gourami

GÜNTHER 1861

Natural Range: Thailand, Cambodia, and Vietnam.
Size: 6" (15 cm) TL.
Water Chemistry: Tropical, on the warm side, and soft, acidic conditions are best.
Behavior: Peaceful.
Dietary Requirements: Omnivorous, and should be given a wide selection of staple aquarium foods.

Remarks: Even though quite large, this fish is still safe for most community setups; watch carefully, though, just in case they get an appetite for any small fishes that may be sharing the aquarium with them.

Trichogaster petoralis / Snakeskin Gourami

REGAN 1910

Natural Range: Laos, Thailand, Cambodia, and Vietnam.
Size: 10" (25 cm) TL.
Water Chemistry: Tropical; soft and acidic.
Behavior: Surprisingly peaceful for such a large species.
Dietary Requirements: Omnivorous, and should be given a wide selection of staple aquarium foods.

Remarks: Although this is the largest of the regular aquarium species, it can still be considered a community fish. They also do well as tankmates for some of the larger cichlids such as Oscars and Waroo. Of course, keep an eye on them just to be safe.

Trichogaster leerii

Trichogaster leerii male

Trichogaster microlepis

Trichogaster microlepis pair

Trichogaster pectoralis

Trichogaster trichopterus for comparison

Trichogaster trichopterus / Blue Gourami

PALLAS 1770

Natural Range: Much of Southeast Asia.
Size: 6" (15 cm) TL.
Water Chemistry: Tropical; otherwise not too critical.
Behavior: Peaceful, but may become quarrelsome, especially two males kept together.
Dietary Requirements: Omnivorous, but will take the usual aquarium fare.

Remarks: This species is available in a number of domestic color varieties, as well as occasionally as dyed or painted specimens, which should be avoided. Extremely easily spawned; a good choice for a first anabantid breeding attempt.

Trichogaster pumila / Pygmy Gourami

ARNOLD 1936

Natural Range: Thailand and Laos to Indonesia.
Size: 2" (5 cm) TL.
Water Chemistry: Tropical; soft and acidic conditions are best.
Behavior: A very timid, tiny gourami.
Dietary Requirements: Eats small invertebrates in the wild; may need live foods.

Remarks: The pretty little fish in this genus are called Pygmy, Sparkling, or Croaking Gouramis. They are completely peaceful, but their tankmates must be chosen with care, as they are easily intimidated and kept from feeding.

Trichogaster schalleri / Threestripe Gourami

LADIGES 1962

Natural Range: Mekong drainage.
Size: 2.25" (6 cm) TL.
Water Chemistry: Tropical temperatures are required for this species; otherwise, soft and acidic conditions are best.
Behavior: A very timid, tiny gourami that is similar to *T. pumila*.
Dietary Requirements: Eats small invertebrates in the wild; may need live foods.

Remarks: These fish are completely peaceful, but their tankmates must be chosen with care, as they are easily intimidated and kept from feeding.

Trichogaster trichopterus normal var.

Trichogaster trichopterus gold var.

Trichogaster pumila

Trichogaster pumila profile

Trichogaster schalleri

Trichogaster schalleri profile

Scleropages formosus "red"

OSTEOGLOSSIDAE
AROWANAS

Arowanas are a group of tropical freshwater fishes indigenous to the neotropics of South America, Southeast Asia, and Australia and New Guinea. All are predatory and mainly consume small live fishes, although other animals are taken if they can be easily swallowed whole. Osteoglossids are very similar in form and function to the arapaimatids and were, until recently, placed in the same family. In this book, we still have both families listed under Osteoglossidae, as we feel that this grouping will be easier for hobbyists to understand.

Their successful care in aquariums depends on several factors. The first and most important factor is space. The next would be diet and nutrition, while the third would have to be water quality. Of course, these "special" factors are basically the same for all living organisms, whether they're fish or otherwise, but large fishes such as these are particularly sensitive.

As many of you already may know, arowanas are accomplished jumpers, and just like hatchetfishes (Gasteropelecidae), they seem to be able to find the smallest possible hole on the aquarium's canopy and then leap through it. The big problem, though, is that a hatchetfish weighs about an ounce as an adult, whereas a large arowana might weigh ten pounds or more! Needless to say, make sure your aquarium has a well-fitting lid on it at all times.

Arapaima gigas / Pirarucu, Arapaima*

SCHINZ 1822

Natural Range: Amazon River basin, Brazil, Guyana, and Peru.
Size: 177" (450 cm) TL.
Water Chemistry: Tropical; otherwise not critical.
Behavior: Aggressive.
Dietary Requirements: Fish and birds in the wild. In aquaria, they accept most meaty foods and pellets.

Remarks: One of the largest freshwater fishes in the world, the Arapaima has the potential to grow up to 13 feet in length. Its long, powerful body is covered with huge scales that are green and blue in color and feature brilliant red edges towards the rear of the fish.

* Due to its enormous size, the Arapaima is only suited for the very largest aquariums or ponds and should only be purchased if you are willing to provide such enclosures.

Osteoglossum bicirrhosum / Silver Arowana

CUVIER 1829

Natural Range: Amazon River basin, Rupununi, and Oyapock Rivers.
Size: 48" (120 cm) TL.
Water Chemistry: Tropical; otherwise not critical.
Behavior: Aggressive towards conspecifics, particularly as juveniles; generally tolerant of other species.
Dietary Requirements: Most meaty foods are accepted, including shrimp, fish meat, earthworms, crickets, and commercial pellets. Primarily a surface feeder.

Remarks: The Silver Arowana is a truly elegant fish. The distinctive pair of barbels at the tip of the lower jaw allows them to sense and capture prey on the surface of the water, even in total darkness. In addition, their keen vision allows them to see above water and enables them to leap out of the water and accurately strike insects in overhanging branches. Keep in very large aquariums and provide a tight, heavily weighted cover to protect against the powerful jumping ability of this fish.

Osteoglossum ferreirai / Black Arowana

KANAZAWA 1966

Natural Range: Rio Negro basin, Brazil.
Size: 40" (100 cm) TL.
Water Chemistry: Tropical; otherwise not critical.
Behavior: Aggressive towards conspecifics, particularly as juveniles. Generally, they are tolerant of other fish species.
Dietary Requirements: Most meaty foods are accepted, including shrimp, fish meat, pellets, earthworms, crickets, and other live insects. Primarily a surface feeder.

Remarks: The Black Arowana is not as commonly available in the hobby as its silver cousin. However, its unique coloration makes it worth seeking out. Babies are a beautiful jet black with a striking white/yellow stripe running the entire length of the body. Milder in temperament than the Silver Arowana and sometimes timid, they benefit from ample cover in the form of floating plants.

Arapaima gigas tank-raised adult

Arapaima gigas profile

Osteoglossum bicirrhosum juveniles

Osteoglossum bicirrhosum adult

Osteoglossum ferreirai adult

Osteoglossum ferreirai profile

Scleropages formosus / Asian Arowana

SCHLEGEL & MULLER 1839-1844

Natural Range: Indonesia, Malaysia, Thailand, Cambodia, and Vietnam.
Size: 36" (90 cm) TL.
Water Chemistry: Tropical; otherwise not critical.
Behavior: Aggressive towards conspecifics.
Dietary Requirements: Feed meaty foods, including shrimp, fish meat, pellets, earthworms, crickets, and other live insects.

Remarks: Known as the Dragonfish in Asia due to its large scales, barbels, and dragon-like shape, the Asian Arowana is a truly majestic and awe-inspiring presence in the aquarium. Several locale-specific variants exist, including golden, red, and green color forms. High demand has resulted in over-fishing, and the species is now endangered in the wild. Fortunately, commercial breeding operations have been successfully established, and farm-bred specimens are readily available to the hobby in most countries under strict CITES regulation.

Scleropages jardinii / Australian Arowana, Pearl Arowana

SAVILLE-KENT 1892

Natural Range: Northern Australia and New Guinea.
Size: 36" (90 cm) TL.
Water Chemistry: Tropical; otherwise not critical.
Behavior: Very aggressive.
Dietary Requirements: Feed meaty foods, including shrimp, fish meat, pellets, earthworms, crickets, and other live insects.

Remarks: The Australian Arowana is probably the most aggressive species of arowana. If two or more specimens are kept together, intense fighting usually occurs. In addition, they are often intolerant of other fish and will attack tankmates. However, their assertive personalities also make them wonderful fish to keep in the aquarium. They are very keen and observant and can be highly interactive with their keepers.

Scleropages leichardti / Spotted Arowana, Southern Saratoga, Spotted Barramundi

GUNTHER 1864

Natural Range: Fitzroy River system of North Eastern Queensland , Australia.
Size: 36" (90 cm) TL.
Water Chemistry: Tropical; otherwise not critical.
Behavior: Aggressive.
Dietary Requirements: Feed meaty foods, including shrimp, fish meat, pellets, earthworms, crickets, and other live insects.

Remarks: The Spotted Australian Arowana is a less-well known species in the hobby, and as a result is not commonly available. However, they are a beautiful fish, featuring a light blue/silver body color with a red spot on each body scale and red spots within the fins. In Australia, they are a favorite angling species among sports fishermen due to their spectacular jumping abilities. In the aquarium, heavily weighted or secured covers are required to guard against their natural propensity to jump out.

Scleropages formosus

Scleropages formosus "red"

Scleropages jardinii

Scleropages jardinii

Scleropages leichardti

Scleropages leichardti profile

Heterotis niloticus / African Arowana

CUVIER 1829

Natural Range: Western and Central Africa.
Size: 40" (100 cm) TL.
Water Chemistry: Tropical; otherwise not critical.
Behavior: Aggressive towards conspecifics, but generally peaceful towards other species.
Dietary Requirements: Plankton and microorganisms in the wild. In aquaria, they accept frozen brine shrimp, frozen bloodworms, live blackworms, flake food, and softened sinking pellets.

Remarks: Although the African Arowana is not often available to the hobby, its unusual appearance and fascinating behavior make it a worthwhile fish to seek out. The elongated body is gray, olive, or bronze in color, and the head features bony plates with unusual grooves and indentations. They are most remarkable for the fact that they are filter feeders and use an epibranchial organ to concentrate small food particles. Keep in large tanks with tight and heavy covers.

Heterotis niloticus juveniles

Heterotis niloticus young adult

Merodontotus tigrinus

PIMELODIDAE
LONG-WHISKERED CATFISHES

It is quite fitting that the next family to be represented herein is made up of another group of fishes that commonly grow to huge proportions. Of course, this is not always the case, but it's surprising to see how many species in the family Pimelodidae grow to tankbuster sizes.

Probably the most common and easily recognized species within Pimelodidae is the Redtailed Catfish (*Phractocephalus hemioliopterus*). In actuality, this fish should not even be kept in home aquariums, and even many public aquarium personnel have stated that they are not able to give them the space that is truly required of such an adult.

Regardless, people still keep these fish, as well as many others that grow entirely too large for their aquariums. If you are one of these people, then the best thing that you can do for them is to spare no expense in purchasing the largest container that is possible for them. Strangely, many of these huge catfishes have quite a personality and even recognize their owners—perhaps by the footsteps as you enter the room?

One way to help control the rate at which your large catfish grows is by their feeding schedule. While we certainly do not recommend any type of schedule that can be misconstrued as starving them, we can say that feeding small amounts of a good-quality meaty food every other or every third day is probably the best regimen for still allowing good, steady growth but not growth that is out of control. Remember that these fishes are generally gluttons and will basically eat whatever you place in their tank that they can swallow. Use caution and commonsense with these big, bold, and beautiful fishes!

Brachyplatystoma flavicans / Dorado Catfish

HUMBOLDT 1821

Natural Range: Major rivers of the Amazon River basin, South America.

Size: 48" (120cm) TL.

Water Chemistry: Tropical; otherwise not critical; avoid extremes.

Behavior: Predatory towards any species that will fit in its mouth; may be shy and may damage head when frightened; adults require very large aquariums.

Dietary Requirements: Piscivorous; will eat fishes, shrimps, and sometimes mollusks.

Remarks: This is a beautiful large catfish for experts with large tanks. In nature, the species may migrate to spawning sites in the rapids of major rivers. Very popular food fish in the Amazon. The long filaments and smooth skin may be injured by aggressive tankmates.

Brachyplatystoma juruense / Alianza Catfish

BOULENGER 1989

Natural Range: Major rivers of the Amazon River basin, South America.

Size: 48" (120 cm) TL.

Water Chemistry: Tropical; otherwise not critical; avoid extremes.

Behavior: Predatory towards any species that will fit in its mouth; may be shy and may damage head when frightened; adults require very large aquariums.

Dietary Requirements: Piscivorous; will eat fishes, shrimps, and sometimes mollusks.

Remarks: There are two distinct color forms of this catfish, with a more grey or yellow background color. Juveniles and adults can damage each other and should only be kept together with adequate space provided.

Merodontotus tigrinus / Zebra Shovelnose Catfish

BRITSKI 1981

Natural Range: Rio Huallaga and Peruvian Rio Amazonas, Rio Madeira in Brazil, South America.

Size: 36" (90 cm) TL.

Water Chemistry: Tropical; otherwise not critical; avoid extremes.

Behavior: Predatory towards smaller fishes, adults require very large aquariums and are highly aggressive towards conspecifics and sometimes other large fish.

Dietary Requirements: Piscivorous, will eat fishes, shrimps, and sometimes mollusks.

Remarks: A much sought-after species in the aquarium trade that commands high prices. The long filaments and smooth skin may be injured by aggressive tankmates.

Brachyplatystoma flavicans

Brachyplatystoma flavicans profile

Brachyplatystoma juruense adult

Brachyplatystoma juruense profile

Merodontotus tigrinus juvenile

Merodontotus tigrinus adult

Phractocephalus hemioliopterus / Redtail Catfish

BLOCH & SCHNEIDER 1801

Natural Range: Amazon River Basin, South America.
Size: 60" (150 cm) TL.
Water Chemistry: Tropical; otherwise not critical; avoid extremes.
Behavior: Predatory with all tankmates; adults require very large aquariums and will certainly outgrow any aquarium.
Dietary Requirements: Piscivorous; will eat fishes, shrimps, and sometimes mollusks. Will also eat birds and small mammals in nature.

Remarks: The attractive juveniles of this species make the fish frequently available in the trade. The species is not an aquarium fish!

Pimelodus pictus / Pictus Catfish

STEINDACHNER 1876

Natural Range: Amazon and Orinoco River Basin, South America
Size: 10" (25 cm) TL.
Water Chemistry: Tropical; otherwise not critical; avoid extremes.
Behavior: Predatory towards smaller fishes, this fish's constant activity, especially at night, may disturb quiter tankmates.
Dietary Requirements: Omnivorous; will eat all prepared foods, small fishes, shrimps, and sinking tablets

Remarks: A popular aquarium fish that is somewhat sensitive to Ich because of its scaleless body. Members of this species are voracious eaters and will out-compete many other aquarium fishes for food.

Pimelodus maculatus

LACEPEDE 1803

Natural Range: Amazon and Orinoco River Basin, South America
Size: 12" (30 cm) TL.
Water Chemistry: Tropical; otherwise not critical; avoid extremes.
Behavior: Predatory towards smaller fishes, this fish's constant activity, especially at night, may disturb quieter tankmates.
Dietary Requirements: Omnivorous; will eat all prepared foods, small fishes, shrimps, and sinking tablets

Remarks: Rarely seen species that is less attractive than other species of the genus. Members of this species are voracious eaters and will out-compete many other aquarium fishes for food.

Phractocephalus hemioliopterus adult

Phractocephalus hemioliopterus small adult

Pimelodus pictus adult

Pimelodus pictus

Pimelodus maculatus

Pimelodus albofasciatus for comparison

Pimelodus ornatus

KNER 1858

Natural Range: Amazon River Basin, South America
Size: 10" (25 cm) TL.
Water Chemistry: Tropical; otherwise not critical; avoid extremes.
Behavior: Predatory towards smaller fishes, this fish's constant activity, especially at night, may disturb quieter tankmates.
Dietary Requirements: Omnivorous; will eat all prepared foods, small fishes, shrimps, and sinking tablets

Remarks: A striking mid-sized catfish that is, unfortunately, not often seen. Members of this species are voracious eaters and will out-compete many other aquarium fishes for food.

Platystomatichthys sturio / Sturgeon Catfish

KNER 1858

Natural Range: Amazon River Basin, South America
Size: 24" (50 cm) TL.
Water Chemistry: Tropical; otherwise not critical; avoid extremes.
Behavior: Predatory towards smaller fishes, this shy fish with the extremely long whiskers must be kept with non-aggressive fishes.
Dietary Requirements: Piscivorous; will take frozen foods, small fishes, and shrimps.

Remarks: A fantastic sight in roomy aquariums. The fish should never be caught with a fine-mesh net, as the spines easily get stuck in the netting and take a long time to heal.

Luciopimelodus pati / Pati

VALENCIENNES 1836

Natural Range: Rio de la Plata and Rio Parana, Argentina
Size: 36" (90 cm) TL.
Water Chemistry: Subtropical; otherwise not critical; avoid extremes.
Behavior: Predatory towards smaller fishes; a very active and interesting species that can be kept in small groups as juveniles.
Dietary Requirements: Piscivorous; will eat some frozen foods, small fishes, and shrimps.

Remarks: Differs from all other species of the group because of the absence of hard spines in the dorsal and pectoral fins. Juveniles have a wonderful metallic blue background color.

Pimelodus ornatus

Pimelodus ornatus profile

Platystomatichthys sturio juvenile

Platystomatichthys sturio juvenile profile

Luciopimelodus pati small adult

Luciopimelodus pati profile

Lophiosilurus alexandri / Pacman Catfish

STEINDACHNER 1876

Natural Range: Endemic to the Rio Sao Francisco, Brazil, South America.
Size: 24" (50 cm) TL.
Water Chemistry: Tropical; otherwise not critical; avoid extremes.
Behavior: Predatory towards all fishes; will spend all day buried in the substrate and show only seconds of activity to swallow its prey.
Dietary Requirements: Piscivorous; will eat fishes and eventually frozen shrimps.

Remarks: A bizarre catfish species that is not aggressive towards fishes too large to be thought of as prey.

Sorubim lima / Shovelnose Catfish

BLOCH & SCHNEIDER 1801

Natural Range: Amazon and Orinoco River Basin, South America
Size: 18" (45 cm) TL.
Water Chemistry: Tropical; otherwise not critical; avoid extremes.
Behavior: Predatory towards smaller fishes; a good community fish for larger aquariums
Dietary Requirements: Piscivorous; will eat, small fishes, shrimps, and eve*s.

Remarks: The most common shovelnose catfish species.

Goslinia platynema / Slobbering Catfish

BOULENGER 1898

Natural Range: Amazon River Basin, South America
Size: 30" (75 cm) TL.
Water Chemistry: Tropical; otherwise not critical; avoid extremes.
Behavior: Predatory towards smaller fishes; the species likes to stand on its pectoral fins, moving its typical flat whiskers in the current to look for prey.
Dietary Requirements: Piscivorous; will eat, small fishes, shrimps, and occasionally frozen foods.

Remarks: The species lives (like all shovelnoses) in fast-flowing water and needs a well-aerated tank to thrive.

Lophiosilurus alexandri

Lophiosilurus cyclurus for comparison

Sorubim lima juvenile

Sorubim lima adult

Goslina platynema small adult

Goslina platynema profile

777

Pseudoplatystoma fasciatum / Tiger Shovelnose

LINNAEUS 1776

Natural Range: South America: Amazon, Corintijns, Essequibo, Orinoco, and Paraná drainages.
Size: 41" (104 cm) TL.
Water Chemistry: Tropical; any water chemistry.
Behavior: A large predatory catfish.
Dietary Requirements: Feeds on large fish and crabs during nocturnal foraging.

Remarks: Next to the Redtailed Catfish (*Phractocephalus hemioliopterus*), the Tiger Shovelnose Catfish is probably the most popular large pimelodid species. While juveniles and adults are strikingly patterned and show highly variable markings, they are not suitable fish in most home aquariums. They are best left to those who are able to provide them with a large warm water pond or an exceptionally large aquarium.

Pseudoplatystoma tigrinum / Tiger Shovelnose

VALENCIENNES 1840

Natural Range: South America: Amazon and Orinoco drainages.
Size: 51" (130 cm) TL.
Water Chemistry: Tropical.
Behavior: A large predatory catfish.
Dietary Requirements: Piscivorous; may also take crustaceans.

Remarks: Despite the popularity of this and other large predatory catfish, they really have no place in the home aquarium.

Perrunichthys perruno / Leopard Catfish

SCHULTZ 1944

Natural Range: South America: Lake Maracaibo basin.
Size: 24" (60 cm) TL.
Water Chemistry: Tropical
Behavior: A medium-large predatory catfish.
Dietary Requirements: Piscivorous.
Remarks: This pimelodid is small enough to be considered for very large home aquaria.

Remarks: While the juvenile pictured to the right looks innocent, don't be fooled! Their huge mouths are capable of swallowing fishes, and anything else edible, nearly half their own body length. They are, however, suitable for very large home aquariums and do best when given several large caves to hide in during daylight hours. Like most other nocturnally active animals, these catfish will often associate daylight with feeding time and may become very active when the tank is approached while the tank is illuminated.

778

Pseudoplatystoma fasciatum adult

Pseudoplatystoma fasciatum profile

Pseudoplatystoma tigrinum small adults

Pseudoplatystoma tigrinum profile

Perrunichthys perruno juvenile

Paulicea sp. a closely related species

Xiphophorus helleri

POECILIIDAE
POECILIIDS, KILLIES

Members of this moderately-sized family are some of the most popular and recognizable species ever to be kept in aquariums. It includes species such as the Molly, Swordtail, Platy, Guppy, and Mosquitofish, as well as many others. Of these, 12 have been selected and profiled herein due to their overwhelming popularity and ease of recognition by even the most novice of hobbyists.

Poeciliids are distributed in lower altitude regions, from the eastern United States to northeastern Argentina, and may also be found in Madagascar and some areas of Africa. Generally, they are identified by their upward-turned mouths and high pectoral fin placement. A gonopodium is present in males. Additionally, for those who pay attention to the dynamic taxonomy and systematics of fishes, members of Fluviophylacine and Aplocheilichthyinae that were formerly placed in the family Cyprinodontidae are now placed here, thus changing the livebearers to the subfamily ranking of Poeciliinae.

In aquariums, their care and husbandry is probably about as easy as it comes. For many hobbyists, a tank full of guppies is usually their first contact with a wonderful and highly educational hobby. Often, these guppies breed, and the young can be raised with minimal difficulty. Of course, you will need several aquariums all going at the same time to house and raise all of the young. At the end of their poeciliid experiences, hobbyists are usually hooked for life.

Aplocheilichthys normani / Norman's Lampeye

AHL 1928

Natural Range: Widespread in West and Central Africa.
Size: 1.5" (4 cm) TL.
Water Chemistry: Tropical.
Behavior: A peaceful and shy non-annual Killie.
Dietary Requirements: Live foods may be necessary.

Remarks: The lampeyes are non-livebearing poeciliids, named for the iridescent blue pigment on the eye, which is quite visible across a room. Hardy and interesting in the aquarium.

Aplocheilichthys nimbaensis / Mt. Nimba Lampeye

DAGET 1948

Natural Range: Small rivers and brooks in southeastern upper Guinea and northeastern Liberia.
Size: 1.75" (4.5 cm) TL.
Water Chemistry: Tropical.
Behavior: Shy and peaceful.
Dietary Requirements: Live foods are best.

Remarks: Reported not to be an easy aquarium subject, but captive-produced specimens may be easier. Unlike other members of this group, these fish are not recommended for beginners.

Aplocheilichthys spilauchen / Banded Lampeye

DUMÉRIL 1861

Natural Range: Africa: from the mouth of the Senegal River to the mouth of the Congo River.
Size: 2.75" (7 cm) TL.
Water Chemistry: Tropical; freshwater, brackish.
Behavior: Peaceful.
Dietary Requirements: Live foods are best.

Remarks: This lampeye is found in coastal waters, including mangrove swamps.

Aplocheilichthys normani

Aplocheilichthys normani

Aplocheilichthys nimbaensis

Aplocheilichthys pumilis for comparison

Aploceilichthys spilauchen

Aplocheilichthys spilauchen

Belonesox belizanus / Topminnow

KNER 1860

Natural Range: Mexico to Costa Rica, south to Nicaragua.
Size: 5.5" (14 cm) TL.
Water Chemistry: Tropical; freshwater, brackish. Tolerates full marine salinity.
Behavior: An ambush predator of smaller fishes.
Dietary Requirements: Difficult to wean off live foods.

Remarks: Also known as the Pike Livebearer, this fish likes to hang out in aquatic weeds, waiting for small fish to swim by. It then lunges out and captures its prey.

Gambusia affinis / Mosquitofish

BAIRD & GIRARD 1853

Natural Range: North and Central America: Mississippi River basin from central Indiana and Illinois in USA south to Gulf of Mexico and Gulf Slope drainages west to Mexico. Introduced virtually around the globe.
Size: Female 2.75" (7 cm) TL, male 1.5" (4 cm) TL.
Water Chemistry: Subtropical to tropical; freshwater, brackish.
Behavior: Fairly peaceful, but an aggressive feeder that can out-compete even larger fish.
Dietary Requirements: Omnivorous; eats anything.

Remarks: This US native has acquired the pejorative nickname of "Damnbusia" because of the ecological upset that often accompanies its release as a mosquito eater. In many places worldwide, it has pushed other aquatic species towards extinction.

Gambusia holbrooki / Eastern Mosquitofish

GIRARD 1859

Natural Range: United States: from New Jersey to Alabama.
Size: Female 3" (8 cm) TL, male 1.5" (3.5 cm) TL.
Water Chemistry: Temperate; freshwater, brackish.
Behavior: Fairly peaceful, but an aggressive feeder that can out-compete even larger fish.
Dietary Requirements: Omnivorous.

Remarks: This species shares the notoriety of the previous livebearer. Where they are introduced, they seem to prefer eating the eggs and fry of other fish and amphibians to consuming mosquito larvae.

Belonesox belizanus male

Belonesox belizanus pair

Gambusia affinis female

Gambusia marshi for comparison

Gambusia holbrooki male

Gambusia krumholzi for comparison

Lamprichthys tanganicanus / Tanganyika Killifish

BOULENGER 1898

Natural Range: Endemic to Lake Tanganyika.
Size: 6" (15 cm) TL.
Water Chemistry: Tropical; hard; basic.
Behavior: Peaceful and schooling.
Dietary Requirements: A plankton feeder; will take most aquarium foods.

Remarks: This beautiful killifish is a great addition to a Tanganyikan cichlid tank. The neon-blue markings of a spawning-ready male are awe-inspiring. It makes a good aquarium fish, but it is very difficult to ship successfully.

Poecilia latipinna / Sailfin Molly

LESUEUR 1821

Natural Range: North Carolina to Veracruz, Mexico.
Size: 4" (10 cm) TL female, 6" (15 cm) male.
Water Chemistry: Subtropical; freshwater, brackish.
Behavior: A fairly peaceful large livebearer.
Dietary Requirements: Largely herbivorous. Algae or algae-derived foods should make up the bulk of the diet.

Remarks: This is one of the species used to create modern aquarium mollies. They can be kept without salt, but only in very hard, basic water. They can tolerate full marine conditions. The male's courting display with fully unfurled dorsal fin is amazing.

Poecilia reticulata / Guppy

PETERS 1859

Natural Range: Venezuela, Barbados, Trinidad, northern Brazil, and the Guyanas.
Size: 2" (5 cm) TL female, 1.5" (3.5 cm) male.
Water Chemistry: Tropical; freshwater, brackish.
Behavior: A peaceful and lively livebearer.
Dietary Requirements: Omnivorous; will take any aquarium foods.

Remarks: A perennial aquarium favorite, the guppy has been developed in a staggering variety of strains that vary greatly in size, finnage, and coloration. This is another American livebearer that has been widely introduced around the world for mosquito control; like all the others, it has had no measurable effect on the mosquito population, though it has been implicated in the decline of many native fish species.

Lamprichthys tanganicanus female

Lamprichthys tanganicanus male

Poecilia latipinna pair of domesticated strain

Poecilia latipinna domesticated strain

Poecilia reticulata fancy strain female

Poecilia reticulata fancy strain male

Poecilia velifera / Sailfin Molly

REGAN 1914

Natural Range: Southeast Mexico.
Size: 7" (18 cm) TL female, 6" (15 cm) TL male.
Water Chemistry: Tropical; freshwater, brackish.
Behavior: Peaceful.
Dietary Requirements: Omnivorous.

Remarks: Yet another species used in creating aquarium mollies.

Procatopus abberans

AHL 1927

Natural Range: Nigeria, Cameroon.
Size: 2" (5.5 cm) TL.
Water Chemistry: Tropical.
Behavior: Peaceful.
Dietary Requirements: Live foods may be necessary.

Remarks: Like all lampeyes, this fish likes substantial current. A powerhead is perfect for the job. Reported to be very difficult to maintain in the aquarium.

Procatopus similis

AHL 1927

Natural Range: Nigeria, Cameroon.
Size: 2.25" (6 cm) TL.
Water Chemistry: Tropical.
Behavior: Peaceful.
Dietary Requirements: Live foods may be necessary.

Remarks: Like all lampeyes, this fish likes substantial current. A powerhead is perfect for the job.

Poecilia velifera

Poecilia velifera pair

Procatopus abberans female

Procatopus abberans male

Procatopus similis female

Procatopus similis male

Xiphophorus hellerii / Green Swordtail

HECKEL 1848

Natural Range: Mexico to Honduras.
Size: 6.25" (16 cm) TL female, 5.5" (14 cm) TL male.
Water Chemistry: Tropical; freshwater, brackish.
Behavior: A peaceful livebearer, as long as there is only one male per tank.
Dietary Requirements: Omnivorous; likes to browse on algae.

Remarks: Although the wild Green Swordtail is rarely seen in the hobby today, it was the major foundation species for domesticated swordtails, which are multi-species hybrids.

Xiphophorus maculatus / Southern Platyfish

GÜNTHER 1866

Natural Range: Mexico to Belize.
Size: 2.5" (6 cm) TL.
Water Chemistry: Tropical; freshwater.
Behavior: Very peaceful.
Dietary Requirements: Omnivorous; will take all aquarium foods.

Remarks: A very popular aquarium species, at least in its many cultivated forms, most of which are multi-species hybrids. It is commonly called the platy, as is *X. variatus* (and sometimes also *X. hellerii*) and hybrids between these.

Xiphophorus variatus / Variatus Platy

MEEK 1904

Natural Range: Mexico.
Size: 2.75" (7 cm) TL.
Water Chemistry: Tropical; freshwater.
Behavior: Very peaceful.
Dietary Requirements: Omnivorous.

Remarks: This species was used to bring certain traits into domesticated swordtail and platy lines. There are still some varieties that are heavily if not wholly *variatus* in origin.

Xiphophorus helleri wild-type pair (male below)

Xiphophorus helleri male

Xiphophorus maculatus female red var.

Xiphophorus maculatus male hi-fin var.

Xiphophorus variatus

Xiphophorus variatus

Polypterus endlicheri

POLYPTERIDAE

BICHIRS

These interesting and unique fishes are confined to the freshwaters of Africa. There are easily distinguished by their anguillid-shaped body and large, flat heads that are relatively blunt and primitive looking. They also have a symmetrical caudal fin and a long dorsal fin with a series of finlets. Their swimbladder is modified and split into two lobes. The right lobe is more developed compared to the left lobe, which is located ventral to and attached to the fish's esophagus. This modification serves as an accessory breathing organ.

In aquariums, these predatory fishes are rather undemanding. They can be exceedingly aggressive, however, and should only be acquired after careful thought and consideration has been paid to their requirements. They are best-suited to aquariums that contain large peaceful fishes, as hobbyists report that they are not very aggressive towards fishes they cannot eat. Additionally, many experienced polypterid-keepers suggest that these fishes have unique personalities and that they are able to recognize their owners. They may even rise to the surface to greet their owner and feed from his or her hand. As with other large predatory species, be sure to provide adequate filtration and circulation, as well as regular partial water changes

Polypterus senegalus / Cuvier's Bichir, Senegal Bichir

CUVIER 1829

Natural Range: Nile basin and West Africa, including Senegal, Gambia, Niger, Volta, and Lake Chad basins.
Size: 13" (32cm) TL
Water Chemistry: Tropical; otherwise not critical.
Behavior: Generally peaceful. Will eat fish small enough to fit in mouth.
Dietary Requirements: Feed meaty foods such as earthworms, shrimp, beef heart, and frozen fish. Sinking pellets are also accepted.

Remarks: The Senegal Bichir is probably the most prevalent species of bichir in the hobby. There are three subspecies: *P. senegalus senegalus*, *P. senegalus meridionalis*, and an undescribed subspecies from the Nile river basin. Although not the most colorful species, they more than compensate with their outgoing and friendly personalities. As with all bichirs, they are adept at escaping aquariums; tightly sealed tank covers are a must. Their hardiness and modest adult size make them great for beginners.

Polypterus ornatipinnis / Ornate Bichir

BOULENGER 1902

Natural Range: Congo River basin, Lake Rukwa drainage and Lake Tanganyika, Africa.
Size: 24" (60cm) TL
Water Chemistry: Tropical; otherwise not critical.
Behavior: Generally peaceful. Aggressive towards conspecifics. Will eat fish small enough to fit in mouth.
Dietary Requirements: All meaty foods such as earthworms, shrimp, silversides, beef heart, and carnivore pellets are readily accepted.

Remarks: Ornate Bichirs are possibly the most strikingly beautiful species of bichir with their bold, white/yellow spots contrasting sharply against dark marbled lines. However, this species is quite shy and sedentary during the day and only becomes active at night, when they emerge from hiding to prowl for food. Provide hiding places in the form of driftwood, rocks, and sturdy plants to help them feel secure. Long-lived, with documented cases of some specimens living up to 25 years.

Polypterus endlicheri endlicheri / Saddled Bicher, Tiger Bicher

HECKEL 1847

Natural Range: Nile River, Chad basin, Niger River, Volta River, and Bandama River, Africa.
Size: 30" (75cm) TL
Water Chemistry: Tropical; otherwise not critical.
Behavior: Generally peaceful. Can be aggressive towards conspecifics.
Dietary Requirements: All meaty foods such as earthworms, shrimp, silversides, beef heart, and frozen fish are readily accepted.

Remarks: Possibly the most sought-after species by polypterid enthusiasts, Saddled Bichir are extremely attractive, with their wide, distinctive black bands contrasting sharply against a brown/reddish body coloration. In addition, their broad, flat heads and thick bodies give them a fierce and commanding presence in the aquarium. Saddled Bichirs grow to be big and powerful fish, so they must be kept in large tanks. Provide tight, heavily weighted covers to guard against their forceful jumping capability.

Polypterus senegalus

Polypterus congicus for comparison

Polypterus ornatipinnis

Polypterus ornatipinnis

Polypterus endlicheri adult

Polypterus endlicheri

Polypterus delhezi / Armored Bichir

BOULENGER 1899

Natural Range: Congo River, Central Africa.

Size: 15" (40cm) TL.

Water Chemistry: Tropical; otherwise not critical.

Behavior: Generally peaceful. Aggressive towards conspecifics. Will eat fish small enough to fit in mouth.

Dietary Requirements: All meaty foods such as earthworms, shrimp, silversides, beef heart, and frozen fish are readily accepted.

Remarks: An attractive bichir with a marbled body and several thin, dark bands along the dorsal surface. These bands often feature a thin, yellowish border. As with all bichirs, they feature ganoid scales, which are hard, tough scales that hinge rather than overlap. Primarily nocturnal, this species spends most of the daylight hours hiding. Provide their tanks with plants, driftwood, and caves.

Polypterus palmas polli / Marbled Bichir

GOSSE 1988

Natural Range: Lower and central Congo basin, Africa.

Size: 14" (35cm) TL,

Water Chemistry: Tropical; otherwise not critical.

Behavior: Generally peaceful. Occasional aggression towards conspecifics. Will eat fish small enough to fit in mouth.

Dietary Requirements: Feed meaty foods such as earthworms, shrimp, beef heart, and frozen fish. Sinking pellets are also readily accepted.

Remarks: This species was used to bring certain traits into domesticated swordtail and platy lines. There are still some varieties that are heavily if not wholly *variatus* in origin.

Polypterus delhezi

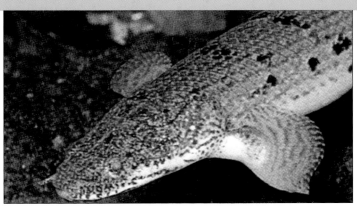

Polypterus delhezi profile

Polypterus palmas

Polypterus palmas

Potamotrygon schroederi

POTAMOTRYGONIDAE
RIVER STINGRAYS

The freshwater river stingrays of the genus *Potamotrygon* are some of the most unique and spectacularly colored fishes available to tropical fish hobbyists. They are often large-growing animals that need very clean water and a soft substrate, if any at all. They are accomplished predators of small fishes, crabs, and other benthic invertebrates. In aquariums, they can be fed a wide range of meaty foods such as squid, clams, mussels, and other seafoods.

Aside from careful attention being paid to the water quality of aquariums containing river stingrays, even more careful attention should be paid to your hands, and where the stingrays are in relation to them, when they are in their aquarium. These animals are capable of providing you with a nasty sting from their tail spine. Additionally, many species are able to strike at potential danger (your hands/arms) from quite some distance away and at some-what odd angles. When servicing their aquarium, it's best to have either another set of eyes watching them while you concentrate on the chore at hand, or have a barrier between you and the stingrays to prevent such occurrences from happening in the first place.

Potamotrygon castexi / Vermiculate River Stingray

CASTELLO & YAGOLKOWSKI 1969

Natural Range: Upper Amazon River basin and Paraná-Paraguay basin, South America.
Size: 32" (80cm) WD.
Water Chemistry: Tropical; otherwise not critical. Avoid extremes.
Behavior: Semi-aggressive. Generally peaceful towards fishes that are too small to eat.
Dietary Requirements: Feed meaty foods such as earthworms, shrimp, and silversides. Live blackworms are also readily accepted.

Remarks: These large, powerful rays are extremely hardy and active. This species has many variants with a wide diversity of disk patterns and coloration, including interesting morphs such as "Otorongo" (Leopard), "Estrella" (Star), and "Motello" (Tortoise). Requires large tanks.

Potamotrygon falkneri / Largespot River Stingray

CASTEX & MACIEL 1963

Natural Range: Paraná-Paraguay River basin, South America.
Size: 20" (50cm) WD.
Water Chemistry: Tropical; otherwise not critical. Avoid extremes.
Behavior: Semi-aggressive towards other rays. Generally peaceful towards fish that are too large to eat.
Dietary Requirements: Live earthworms, blackworms, and ghost shrimp are readily accepted. In time, captive specimens learn to relish non-live foods such as shrimp and silversides.

Remarks: Although this species is not often imported and made available to the hobby due to its area of origin, its attractive pattern and coloration make it a worthwhile stingray to seek out. The dark brown disk covered with many tightly packed orange/yellow spots makes for a breathtaking sight.

Potamotrygon castexi

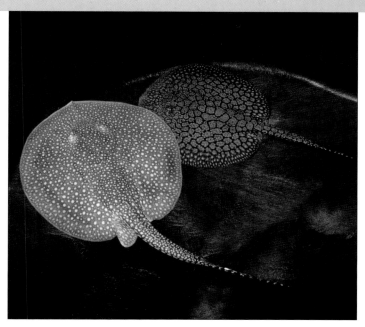

Potamotrygon castexi pair

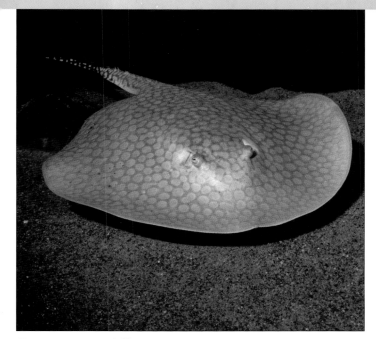

Potamotrygon falkneri

Potamotrygon brachyura for comparison

801

Potamotrygon henlei / Bigtooth River Stingray

CASTELNAU 1855

Natural Range: Tocantins River basin, South America.
Size: 20" (50cm) WD.
Water Chemistry: Tropical; otherwise not critical. Avoid extremes.
Behavior: Semi-aggressive, particularly towards other rays. Generally ignores other fish that are too large to eat.
Dietary Requirements: Feed meaty foods such as shrimp, silversides, and live earthworms

Remarks: This species comes in a variety of subtle variants that range from brown/gray to black disks. Numerous yellow or white spots contrast sharply against the darker background color. Hardy and active.

Potamotrygon leopoldi / White-blotched River Stingray, Polka Dot Ray

CASTEX & CASTELLO 1970

Natural Range: Xingu River basin, Brazil, South America.
Size: 24" (60cm) WD.
Water Chemistry: Tropical; otherwise not critical. Avoid extremes.
Behavior: Semi-aggressive, particularly towards other rays. Generally ignores other fish that are too large to eat.
Dietary Requirements: Feed meaty foods such as earthworms, shrimp, and silversides. Live blackworms are also a favorite food.

Remarks: Polka Dot Rays, with their jet-black disk and brilliant round spots, are one of the most beautiful freshwater rays that are commonly available to the hobby. They are constantly active and have wonderful, outgoing personalities. Once they are accustomed to captivity, they become very responsive and will feed readily (and greedily) from the owner. Extremely hardy.

Potamotrygon henlei

Potamotrygon henlei

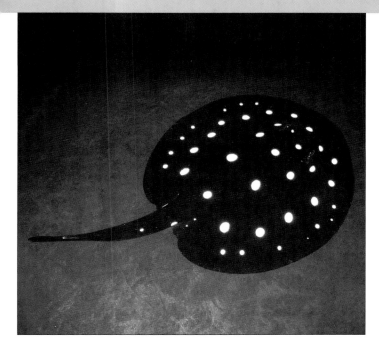

Potamotrygon leopoldi

Potamotrygon leopoldi

Potamotrygon motoro / Ocellated River Stingray

MULLER & HENLE 1841

Natural Range: Uruguay, Paraná-Paraguay, Orinoco, and Amazon River basins, South America.

Size: Size: 20" (50cm) WD.

Water Chemistry: Tropical; otherwise not critical. Avoid extremes.

Behavior: Semi-aggressive towards other rays. Generally peaceful towards fish that are too large to eat.

Dietary Requirements: Most meaty foods such as shrimp, fish filets, and live worms are readily accepted.

Remarks: The Motoro Stingray is one of the most commonly available rays, and is very reasonably priced. They are very hardy and active and make a great starter ray for the first-time stingray keeper. This species comes in a wide variety of attractive colors and spot patterns.

Potamotrygon schroederi / Rosette River Stingray, Flower Ray

FERNANDEZ-YEPEZ 1957

Natural Range: Orinoco basin and Amazon River basin, South America.

Size: 24" (60cm) WD.

Water Chemistry: Tropical: otherwise not critical. Avoid extremes.

Behavior: Aggressive towards other stingrays. Generally ignores other fish that are too large to eat.

Dietary Requirements: Feed meaty foods such as earthworms, shrimp, and silversides.

Remarks: The Flower Ray is probably one of the most beautiful of all freshwater stingrays, with its vibrant golden rosettes, or "flowers," on a deep brown/black background and bold thick stripes all along the tail. This species is quite rare and has only recently been made available to the hobby in small numbers. This ray is a bit more difficult to care for due to its sensitivity to sudden changes in environmental parameters. Therefore, only experienced stingray enthusiasts should attempt to keep this ray.

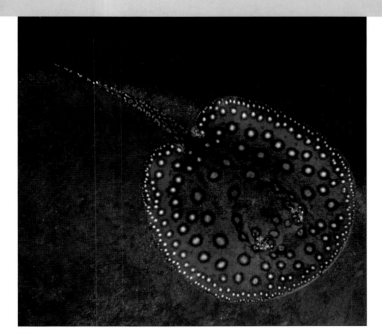

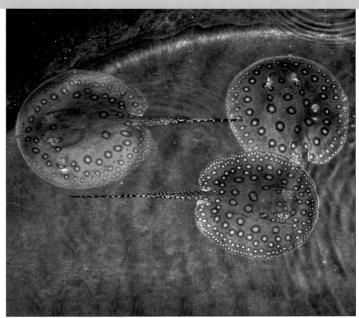

Potamotrygon motoro

Potamotrygon motoro

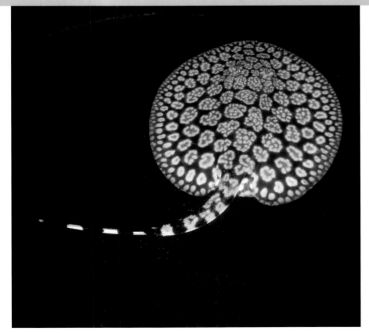

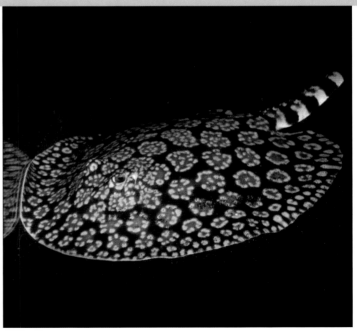

Potamotrygon schroederi

Potamotrygon schroederi

Potamotrygon menchacai / Tiger Stingray

CASTEX & MACIEL 1963

Natural Range: Paraná-Paraguay River basin, South America.

Size: 30" (75cm) WD.

Water Chemistry: Tropical; otherwise not critical. Avoid extremes.

Behavior: Generally peaceful towards fish that are too large to eat. Can be aggressive towards conspecifics.

Dietary Requirements: Live earthworms, blackworms, and ghost shrimp are readily accepted. In time, captive specimens learn to relish non-live foods such as shrimp and silversides.

Remarks: Often referred to as the "King of Stingrays," the Tiger Ray is a large and majestic species. Bold, golden stripes contrast strikingly against the black base color of the disk. Equally beautiful is the extremely long tail with full-height vertical "tiger stripe" bars. Large, mature Tiger Rays move about the aquarium with a regal grace that commands admiration. Considered by many enthusiasts to be the pinnacle of the stingray hobby. Newly captured and imported specimens are often timid and sedentary initially. However, once acclimated and adjusted to captivity, they become quite active and feed aggressively. Not a beginner ray.

Potamotrygon sp. "Pearl" / Pearl Stingray

UNDESCRIBED TO DATE

Natural Range: Rio Tapajos, Pará, Brazil, South America.

Size: 20" (50cm) WD.

Water Chemistry: Tropical; otherwise not critical. Avoid extremes.

Behavior: Aggressive towards other rays. Generally peaceful with other fish that are too large to eat.

Dietary Requirements: Most meaty foods such as shrimp, fish filets, and live worms are readily accepted.

Remarks: Currently the most expensive and rare species of stingray to make its way into the hobby, the Pearl Ray is the Holy Grail for most stingray enthusiasts. Beautiful bright spots, or "pearls," are nestled within black rings, providing these rays with one of the most striking patterns imaginable. Pearl Rays have active and outgoing personalities and tend to be quite domineering when kept with other stingrays. These rays have ravenous appetites and feed aggressively. For those few hobbyists fortunate enough to find and

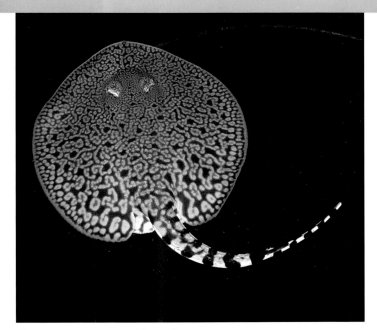

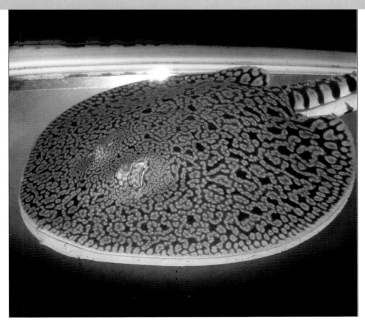

Potamotrygon menchacai

Potamotrygon menchacai

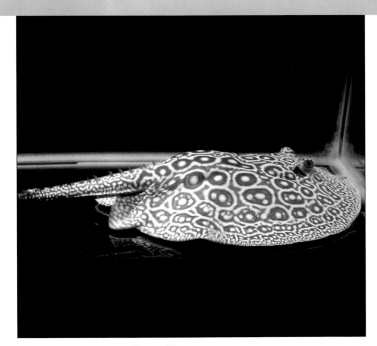

Potamotrygon sp. "pearl"

Potamotrygon sp. "pearl"

Tetraodon miurus

TETRAODONTIDAE
PUFFERS

Pufferfish are cute and can steal your heart, but these are not fishes to be kept by novice aquarists. These exotic creatures require special care and feeding. Puffers are messy eaters and high waste producers—immaculate aquarium upkeep is a must. This means heavy filtration and 50-percent weekly water changes are necessary for the health and well-being of puffers. Puffers must be introduced into a fully-cycled tank. Never cycle a tank with puffers in it—or any other fish, for that matter. With proper care, most should live beyond ten years, with a lifespan in the mid- to upper teens not being uncommon.

Puffers should be considered extremely aggressive, or at least vicious fin nippers. Most puffers are best kept in species-only tanks, and many should be housed as singletons. Extreme caution should be taken when choosing tankmates for them.

One of the most difficult aspects of keeping these special fish is their diet. All puffers are predatory fish and need hard-shelled, meaty foods to keep their teeth trimmed. Like rabbits, their teeth grow constantly and can overgrow enough to cause starvation in the fish. Puffers eat crustaceans in the wild. Foods for smaller puffers are frozen/freeze-dried krill/plankton, gut-loaded ghost shrimp, glass worms, crickets, worms, and small snails (the size of their eye). Larger puffers will eat cut-up pieces of scallops, shrimp, crab legs, whole mussels, clams, oysters, squid, lobsters, and crayfish. They love to hunt down live crayfish, fiddler crabs, and gut-loaded ghost shrimp. Smaller puffers (under 2") need to eat every day, but you can skip one feeding each week. Feed them until satiation. Medium-sized puffers (2–4") should be fed every other day. Larger puffers (4–6") should be fed every three to four days. You may find this schedule difficult, as puffers are very adept at begging for food!

Carinotetraodon lorteti & *Carinotetraodon irrubesco* / Red-eye Puffer

TIRANT 1858

Natural Range: Thailand, Laos, Cambodia, Vietnam, and Malaysia, Asia.
Size: *C. lorteti*, 2" (5 cm); *C. irrubesco*, 1—1 5" (4 cm).
Water Chemistry: Tropical; prefer soft and acidic conditions.
Behavior: Both species exhibit similar appearance and behavior. Intraspecific aggression is less within the *irrubesco* species.
Dietary Requirements: Live or frozen bloodworm, freeze-dried or frozen krill and plankton, and snails.

Remarks: One of the few puffers that are easily sexed. Males are similar in external appearance to the *C. irrubesco*, except the male *C. lorteti* has a blue metallic caudal fin, while the male *C. irrubesco* has a red tail. Females are more difficult to tell apart, and both sport a brownish marbled appearance. These puffers are sensitive to extreme water-condition changes.

Colomesus asellus / Amazon Puffer

MULLER & TROSCHEL 1848

Natural Range: Peru, Columbia, and Brazil, South America.
Size: 3" (7.5c m) TL.
Water Chemistry: Tropical; prefers soft and slightly acidic conditions.
Behavior: These the mildest-tempered freshwater puffers and are constantly on the move. They do well in community tanks with larger or fast-moving fish.
Dietary Requirements: Snails, live or frozen blood-worm, and freeze-dried or frozen krill and plankton.

Remarks: These puffers resemble overstuffed buzzing bumblebees. New inhabitants are extremely susceptible to Ich and velvet. Quarantine of newly-purchased puffers is definitely recommended. Often they come in with internal parasites, which must be treated internally, with an anti-parasitic medication in their food. Once healthy and established, they are very hardy fish. This puffer's teeth grow much more quickly than other puffers'. If not fed a constant daily supply of snails, their teeth will need trimming every four to six months.

Tetraodon biocellatus / Figure Eight Puffer

TIRANT 1885

Natural Range: Thailand, Malaysia, Indonesia, Asia.
Size: 3" (7.5cm) TL.
Water Chemistry: Tropical; slightly brackish water (1.005—1.008 specific gravity).
Behavior: Generally peaceful and lively. Good tank-mates for the brackish water aquarium.
Dietary Requirements: Live or frozen bloodworms, freeze-dried or frozen krill and plankton, snails, gut-loaded ghost shrimp, glass worms, and crickets. Adults will eat shrimp tails and small mussels.

Remarks: Beautiful, bright coloration that improves with age. If kept long-term in fresh water, their immune systems will be compromised and they will be extremely disease-prone. They can live up to 18 years in the proper conditions.

Carinotetraodon loreti

Carinotetraodon irrubesco

Colomesus asellus juvenile

Colomesus asellus adult

Tetraodon biocellatus juvenile

Tetraodon biocellatus adult

811

Tetraodon lineatus / Fahaka Puffer

LINNAEUS 1758

Natural Range: Widespread throughout Africa.
Size: 18" (45cm) TL; may grow larger.
Water Chemistry: Tropical; otherwise not critical, avoid extremes.
Behavior: Extremely vicious, aggressive puffer.
Dietary Requirements: Scallops, shrimp, crab legs, whole mussels, clams, oysters, squid, lobster, and crayfish. They love to chase live crayfish, fiddler crabs, and gut-loaded ghost shrimp.

Remarks: Tanks measuring no less than 48" x 24" x 24" are necessary to house this fish as a singleton. Most will not tolerate tankmates of any kind. Heavy filtration and large weekly water changes are necessary to keep the water clean. Many folks have to net this fish to clean their tank. On the other hand, they are very much like puppies, begging for food and scraping their teeth along the glass when approached. Very personable fish!

Tetraodon miurus / Congo Puffer

BOULENGER 1902

Natural Range: Central Africa.
Size: 6" (15 cm) TL.
Water Chemistry: Tropical; neutral to slightly acid with moderate hardness.
Behavior: A bottom-dwelling, ambush predator. Hides in the sand up to its eyeballs, waiting for unsuspecting prey to swim by, then leaps out and strikes from below.
Dietary Requirements: Although they eat fish in the wild, it is best to get these fish on alternative foods (clams, squid, shrimp, etc.) as soon as possible.

Remarks: Will not tolerate tankmates of any kind! Can be kept in a 20-gallon tank, but because of its messy eating habits and high waste production, 50-percent weekly water changes are recommended. *T. miurus* are found in several colors, but are great at camouflaging to match their surroundings.

Tetraodon mbu / Giant Puffer or Mbu Puffer

BOULENGER 1899

Natural Range: Widespread throughout Africa.
Size: 26" (65 cm) TL.
Water Chemistry: Tropical; otherwise not critical.
Behavior: These puffers may or may not accept tank-mates. Some specimens may be gentle, while others will be killers.
Dietary Requirements: Scallops, shrimp, crab legs, whole mussels, clams, oysters, squid, lobster, and cray-fish. Live crayfish, fiddler crabs, and gut-loaded ghost shrimp are good for them to hunt down and eat.

Remarks: The largest and most stunning of all freshwater puffers. Not a fish for average fish keepers. Unless you are prepared to offer this fish a huge aquarium (up to 1,000 gallons), with serious, multiple sources of filtration and heavy oxygenation, you may want to reconsider keeping this monster puffer.

Tetraodon lineatus   *Tetraodon lineatus*

Tetraodon miurus   *Tetraodon miurus*

Tetraodon mbu   *Tetraodon mbu*

Tetraodon nigroviridis / Green Spotted Puffer

MARION DE PROCE 1822

Natural Range: South East Asia.

Size: 6" (15 cm) TL.

Water Chemistry: Mid to high-range brackish water as juveniles (SG 1.010—1.015), full-strength seawater as adults.

Behavior: Fin-nippers—not good community fish.

Dietary Requirements: Frozen/freeze-dried krill/plankton, glass worms, crickets, worms, and small snails. Larger Green Spotted Puffers will eat cut-up pieces of all types of meaty seafoods

Remarks: This is the most commonly sold and most frequently misidentified puffer of all puffer species. Often they are confused with the Freshwater Spotted Puffer (*Tetraodon schoutedeni*, a puffer not seen for sale with any regularity for over 20 years) and the Ceylon Puffer (*Tetraodon fluviatilis*). Although sold in fresh water, it is best to raise Green Spotted Puffers up to high-end brackish water (specific gravity 1.010—1.015) as soon as possible. You must use marine salt.

Tetraodon nigroviridis

Tetraodon nigroviridis

GLOSSARY

Allopatric Speciation – speciation that occurs in different geographical areas or regions.

Amateur Ichthyologist – advanced aquarists who have not had strict professional training in ichthyology on a college-level but who demonstrate skills and knowledge of such.

Anatomical Characteristics – features of an organism's anatomy that allows them to be classified using standard methods of classification.

Aquariology – the science of fish health management.

Aquarium – a transparent container that is usually constructed of glass and is used to hold fishes for viewing purposes indoors.

Aqua-terrarium – a terrarium that contains a large percentage of water as a decorative feature or to satisfy the needs of semi-aquatic animals kept in the enclosure.

Bioactivity – the activity that has either an indirect or direct effect on living organisms.

Biomass – the total amount of living matter in a system.

Bionomic Ichthyologist – a professional ichthyologist who is a specialist in the care, husbandry, and general aquariology of fishes.

Carotenes – any of several orange or red crystalline hydrocarbon pigments $C_{40}H_{56}$ that occur in the chromoplasts of plants and in the fatty tissues of plant-eating animals and are convertible to vitamin A.

Carotenoids – any of various pigments found widely in plants and animals and characterized chemically by a long aliphatic polyene chain composed of eight isoprene units.

Classification – the systematic arrangement in groups or categories according to established criteria. Hierarchal classification is used for higher categories (i.e., Orders, Families).

Ctenii – tiny comb-like projections that are thought to increase the hydrodynamic effectiveness of ctenoid scales.

Ctenoid Scales – scales with tiny comb-like projections along their outer edge (*ctenii*).

Cycloid Scales – flat, rounded scales that are very thin.

Denitrification – the process where a nitrogen-based compound is broken down into its basic elements.

Dermis – the second to outermost layer of skin cells where many blood vessels and nerves are found.

Dichromatism – color differences in organisms.

Dimorphism – differences in body shapes of fishes.

Ecological Speciation – see Sympatric Speciation.

Elasmoid – a more derived version of the ganoid scales that are found on ancient fishes.

Electrophoresis – a technique that is used to translate the genetic code of an individual cell.

Epidermis – the outer layer of skin cells (usually eight cell layers deep).

Fecundity – the overall number of eggs present within the ovaries (combined) of a female fish just prior to spawning.

Fish – any of numerous cold-blooded strictly aquatic craniate vertebrates that include the bony fishes and usually the cartilaginous and jawless fishes and that typically have an elongated, somewhat spindle-shaped body terminating in a broad caudal fin, limbs in the form of fins when present at all, and a two-chambered heart by which blood is sent through the gills to be oxygenated. Singular or plural; when plural, "fish" is used to describe many specimens of *one* species.

Fishes – plural of fish, used to describe specimens of *multiple* species.

Fitness – a measurement of how likely an individual is to have offspring that will also reproduce successfully.

Ganoid – large bony scales that are found on ancient fishes such as sturgeons or gars.

Genus – a group of organisms divided into one or more species.

Gut Loading – the process where food is given to another organism that is intended for feeding to yet a larger organism with the intent of passing along vital nutrients.

Heterocercal – tails where the upper and lower lobes are of different sizes.

Homocercal – tails where the upper and lower lobes are of equal size.

Ichthyologist – a biologist who is devoted to studying fishes.

Interspecific – interaction with other species (interspecific aggression).

Intraspecific – interaction within the same species (intraspecific aggression).

Karyotypes – the chromosomal characteristics of a cell.

Natural Selection – a natural process that results in the survival and reproductive success of individuals or groups best adjusted to their environment and that leads to the perpetuation of genetic qualities best suited to that particular environment.

Nomenclature – an international system of standardized New Latin names used in biology for kinds and groups of kinds of animals.

Osmosis – the movement of a solvent through a semi-permeable membrane into a solution of higher solute concentration that tends to equalize the concentrations of solute on both sides of the membrane.

Physoclistous – swimbladders lacking a connection to the gut.

Physostomous – having a pneumatic duct between the gut and the swimbladder.

Primary Sex Characteristics – body structures specific to reproduction (ovaries and testes).

Reproductive Effort – a measurement of the amount energy or time that is put into the production of offspring.

Round-tailed – fishes whose caudal fins are rounded.

Secondary Sex Characteristics – gender-linked physical traits other than the reproductive organs.

Selective Breeding – breeding individual parent fish in order to enhance certain traits for further development or propagation.

Speciation – the development of a new species through local adaptation and evolution.

Species – a category of biological classification ranking immediately below the genus or subgenus, comprising related organisms or populations potential capable of interbreeding, and being designated by a binomial that consists of the name of a genus followed by a Latin or Latinized uncapitalized name in agreement with the genus name.

Square-tailed – fishes whose tails appear squared off.

Subspecies – a subdivision of a species. A category that ranks immediately below a species and designates a population within a particular geographical region that is genetically distinguishable from other such populations of the same species and capable of successfully interbreeding, and producing viable offspring, where its range overlaps.

Sympatric Speciation – speciation that occurs in the same area.

Systematic Ichthyologist – a professional ichthyologist who has devoted his or her career to taxonomy and the systematics of fishes. Usually holds a PhD.

Systematics – the evolutionary classification and study of organisms with regard to their natural relationships.

Taxonomy – the science behind the studying and classification of organisms.

Teleosts – bony fishes.

Terrarium – a transparent enclosure that is used for raising plants and small animals indoors.

Uroneurals – specialized bones at the end of the vertebral column to provide support for the caudal fin in teleosts.

Vivarium – a terrarium that is used especially for small animals and is set up in a way so as to replicate their natural environment.

BIBLIOGRAPHY

Adler, H.E. (1975): *Fish Behavior: Why Fishes Do What They Do*. T.F.H. Publications, Inc., New Jersey, United States.

Axelrod, H.R. and L.P. Schultz (1990): *Handbook of Tropical Aquarium Fishes*. T.F.H. Publications, Inc., New Jersey, United States.

Axelrod, H.R., et al. (2004): *Dr. Axelrod's Atlas of Freshwater Aquarium Fishes, 10th Edition*. T.F.H. Publications, Inc., New Jersey, United States.

Axelrod, H.R., et al. (2004): *Dr. Axelrod's Mini-Atlas of Freshwater Aquarium Fishes, 3rd Edition*. T.F.H. Publications, Inc., New Jersey, United States.

Brichard, P. (1989): *Pierre Brichard's Book of Cichlids and All the Other Fishes of Lake Tanganyika*. T.F.H. Publications, Inc., New Jersey, United States.

Burgess, W.B. (1992): *Colored Atlas of Miniature Catfish*. T.F.H. Publications, Inc., New Jersey, United States.

Conkel, D. (1993): *Cichlids of North & Central America*. T.F.H. Publications, Inc., New Jersey, United States.

Degen, B. (1995): *Wild-Caught Discus*. T.F.H. Publications, Inc., New Jersey, United States.

Frey, H. (1961): *Illustrated Dictionary of Tropical Fishes*. T.F.H. Publications, Inc., New Jersey, United States.

Glaser, U. and W. Glaser (1995): *Aqualog – Loricariidae: All L-Numbers*. Verlag A.C.S. GmbH, Morfelden-Walldorf, Germany.

Glaser, U. and W. Glaser (1996): *Aqualog - South American Cichlids I*. Verlag A.C.S. GmbH, Morfelden-Walldorf, Germany.

Glaser, U. and W. Glaser (1996): *Aqualog - South American Cichlids II*. Verlag A.C.S. GmbH, Morfelden-Walldorf, Germany.

Glaser, U. and W. Glaser (1996): *Aqualog - South American Cichlids III*. Verlag A.C.S. GmbH, Morfelden-Walldorf, Germany.

Gratzek, J.B. and J.R. Matthews (1992): *Aquariology: The Science of Fish Health Management, Master Volume*. Tetra Sales USA, Virginia, United States.

Konings, A. (1989): *Cichlids From Central America*. T.F.H. Publications, Inc., New Jersey, United States.

Konings, A. (1990): *Ad Konings's Book of Cichlids and All The Other Fishes of Lake Malawi*. T.F.H. Publications, Inc., New Jersey, United States.

Konings, A. (1996): *Back to Nature Guide to Tanganyika Cichlids*. Back to Nature, Jonsered, Sweden.

Kyle, H.M. (1970): *The Biology of Fishes*. T.F.H. Publications, Inc., New Jersey, United States.

Lager, K.F., et al. (1962): *Ichthyology*. John Wiley & Sons, Inc., New York, United States.

Lamboj, A. (2004): *The Cichlid Fishes of West Africa*. Birgit Schmettkamp Verlag, Bornheim, Germany.

Landau, M. (1992): *Introduction to Aquaculture*. John Wiley & Sons, Inc., New York, United States.

Loiselle, P.V. (1994): *The Cichlid Aquarium*. Tetra-Press, Melle, Germany.

Masters, C.O. (1975): *Encyclopedia of Live Foods*. T.F.H. Publications, Inc., New Jersey, United States.

Moyle, P.B. and J.J. Cech (2000): *Fishes: An Introduction to Ichthyology, Fourth Edition*. Prentice Hall, Inc., New Jersey, United States.

Nikolsky, G.V. (1963): *The Ecology of Fishes*. T.F.H. Publications, Inc., New Jersey, United States.

Ross, M.R. (1997): *Fisheries Conservation and Management*. Prentice Hall, Inc., New Jersey, United States.

Schulte, W. (1988): *Piranhas in the Aquarium*. T.F.H. Publications, Inc., New Jersey, United States.

Smith, L.S. (1982): *Introduction to Fish Physiology*. T.F.H. Publications, Inc., New Jersey, United States.

Staeck, W. and H. Linke (1994): *African Cichlids I: Cichlids From Western Africa*. Tetra-Press, Melle, Germany.

Staeck, W. and H. Linke (1994): *African Cichlids II: Cichlids From Eastern Africa*. Tetra-Press, Melle, Germany.

Staeck, W. and H. Linke (1994): *American Cichlids I: Dwarf Cichlids*. Tetra-Press, Melle, Germany.

Staeck, W. and H. Linke (1994): *American Cichlids II: Large Cichlids*. Tetra-Press, Melle, Germany.

Untergasser, D. (1989): *Handbook of Fish Health*. T.F.H. Publications, Inc., New Jersey, United States.

Untergasser, D. (1991): *Discus Health*. T.F.H. Publications, Inc., New Jersey, United States.

Vierke, J. (1988): *Bettas, Gouramis and Other Anabantoids and Labyrinth Fishes of the World*. T.F.H. Publications, Inc., New Jersey, United States.

Weidner, T. (2000): *South American Eartheaters*. Cichlid Press, Texas, United States.

Wildekamp, R.H. (1993): *A World of Killies: Atlas of Oviparous Cyprinodontiform Fishes of the World*. American Killifish Association, Indiana, United States.

Wischnath, L. (1993): *Atlas of Livebearers of the World*. T.F.H. Publications, Inc., New Jersey, United States.

RESOURCES

MAGAZINES

Tropical Fish Hobbyist
The Leading Aquarium Magazine For Over Half a Century

1 T.F.H. Plaza
3rd & Union Avenues
Neptune City, NJ 07753
Phone: (732) 988-8400
E-mail: info@tfh.com
www.tfhmagazine.com

INTERNET RESOURCES

A World of Fish
www.aworldoffish.com

Aquarium Hobbyist
www.aquariumhobbyist.com

Cichlid Forum
www.cichlid-forum.com

Discus Page Holland
www.dph.nl

FINS: The Fish Information Service
http://fins.actwin.com

Fish Geeks
www.fishgeeks.com

Fish Index
www.fishindex.com

MyFishTank.Net
www.myfishtank.net

Piranha Fury
www.piranha-fury.com

Planet Catfish
www.planetcatfish.com

Predatory Fish
http://predatoryfish.net

Tropical Resources
www.tropicalresources.net

ACADEMIC RESOURCES AND SOCIETIES

American Cichlid Association
Claudia Dickinson
Membership Coordinator
P.O. Box 5078
Montauk, NY 11954
Phone: (631) 668-5125
E-mail: IvyRose@optonline.net
www.cichlid.org

American Killifish Association
Catherine Carney, Secretary
12723 Airport Road
Mt. Vernon, OH 43050
E-mail: schmidtcarney@ecr.net
www.aka.org

American Livebearer Association
Timothy Brady
Membership Chairman
5 Zerbe Street
Cressona, PA 17929-1513
Phone: (570) 385-0573
http://livebearers.org

American Society of Ichthyologists and Herpetologists
Maureen Donnelly, Secretary
Florida International University
Biological Sciences
11200 SW 8th Street
Miami, FL 33199
Phone: (305) 348-1235
Fax: (305) 348-1986
E-mail: asih@fiu.edu
www.asih.org

Association of Aquarists
David Davis
Membership Secretary
2 Telephone Road
Portsmouth, Hants, England
PO4 0AY
Phone: 01705 798686

British Killifish Association
Adrian Burge
Publicity Officer
E-mail: adjan@wym.u-net.com
www.bka.org.uk

Canadian Association of Aquarium Clubs
Miecia Burden
Membership Coordinator
142 Stonehenge Pl.
Kitchener, Ontario, Canada
N2N 2M7
Phone: (517) 745-1452
E-mail: mbburden@look.ca
www.caoac.on.ca

Canadian Killifish Association
Chris Sinclair
Membership
1251 Bray Court
Mississauga, Ontario, Canada L5J 354
Phone: (905) 471-8681
E-mail: cka@rogers.com
www.cka.org

Federation of American Aquarium Societies
Jane Benes, Secretary
923 Wadsworth Street
Syracuse, NY 13208-2419
Phone: (513) 894-7289
E-mail: jbenes01@yahoo.com
www.gcca.net/faas

Goldfish Society of America
P.O. Box 551373
Fort Lauderdale, FL 33355
E-mail: info@goldfishsociety.org
www.goldfishsociety.org

International Betta Congress
Steve Van Camp, Secretary
923 Wadsworth St.
Syracuse, NY 13208
Phone: (315) 454-4792
E-mail: bettacongress@yahoo.com
www.ibcbettas.com

International Fancy Guppy Association
Rick Grigsby, Secretary
3552 West Lily Garden Lane
South Jordan, Utah 84095
Phone: (801) 694-7425
E-mail: genx632@yahoo.com
www.ifga.org

Society of Systematic Biologists
47 Runway Road, Suite G
Levittown, PA 19057-4700
Phone: (800) 821-8312 ext. 117
E-mail: ppagano@taylorandfrancis.com
http://systbiol.org

PHOTO CREDITS

In addition to the photos taken by Oliver Lucanus and Horst Linke, this book also contains many pictures taken by other photographers. The authors apologize for anyone who has been accidentally omitted from the list below.

A. Kochetov
A. Stalsberg
Aaron Norman
Ad Konings
American Fisheries Society
Anatoly Noznov
Andre Roth
B. Baymiller
B. Degan
B.M. Barr
Barry Mansell
Bob Allen
Braz Walker
Brian M. Scott
Burkhard Kahl
D. Allison
D. Schneider
Dan Fromm
Don Conkel
Donald C. Taphorn
Dr. Augustine
   Fernandez-Yepez
Dr. Brooks Burr
Dr. Bruce Turner
Dr. D. Terver
Dr. G. Dingerkus
Dr. Gerald R. Allen
Dr. Harry Grier
Dr. Hiroshi Azuma

Dr. J.E. Randall
Dr. Jacques Gery
Dr. Joanne Norton
Dr. K. Knack
Dr. Lawrence M. Page
Dr. Martin Brittan
Dr. Myron Gordon
Dr. Richard L. Mayden
Dr. Robert F. Goldstein
Dr. Stanislav Frank
Dr. W.E. Burgess
Dr. Wolfgang Staeck
E. Purzel
Edward Taylor
Edward Wong
Erhard Rolof
F.P. Mullenholz
Franz Werner
Freidrich Bitter
G. Meola
G. Schmelzer
G.C. Corcoran
Gene Wolfsheimer
Gerald J.M. Timmerman
Gerhard Marcuse
Glen S. Axelrod
Glenn Y. Takeshita
Graham Murray
Gunter Schmida

H. Grier
H. Hansen
H.J. Franke
H.J. Richter
Hans Mayland
Harold Schultz
Heiko Bleher
Heinrich Stolz
HRA
J. Elias
J. Ferdensi
J. Kadlec
J. Lambert
J. Ward
Jeff Rapps
Jeni C. Tyrell
John O'Malley
Jorgen Scheel
K. Attwood
K. Cole
K. Jeno
Ken Lucas
Kenjiro Tanaka
Klaus Paysan
Kurt Quitschau
L. Seegers
Laurence Azoulay
Leo G. Nico
M. Brembach

M. Brichard
M. Chauche
M. Sanford
M.P. & C. Piednoir
Manfred Meyer
Mark Smith
Mervin F. Roberts
Mike Noren
P. Brichard
Preston Lee
R. de Boer
R. Lawrence
R. Wildekamp
Rainer Stawikowski
Rodney Jonklaas
Ruda Zukal
S. Gill
S. Kochetov
Stan Sung
T. Anger
T. Woeltjes
T. Yokoyama
Theirry Brichard
Uwe Werner
Vojtech Elek
Walter Foersch
Wolfgang Sommer
Y.W. Ong

SUBJECT INDEX TO PART I

INDEX TO POPULAR NAMES OF FISHES

INDEX TO SCIENTIFIC NAMES

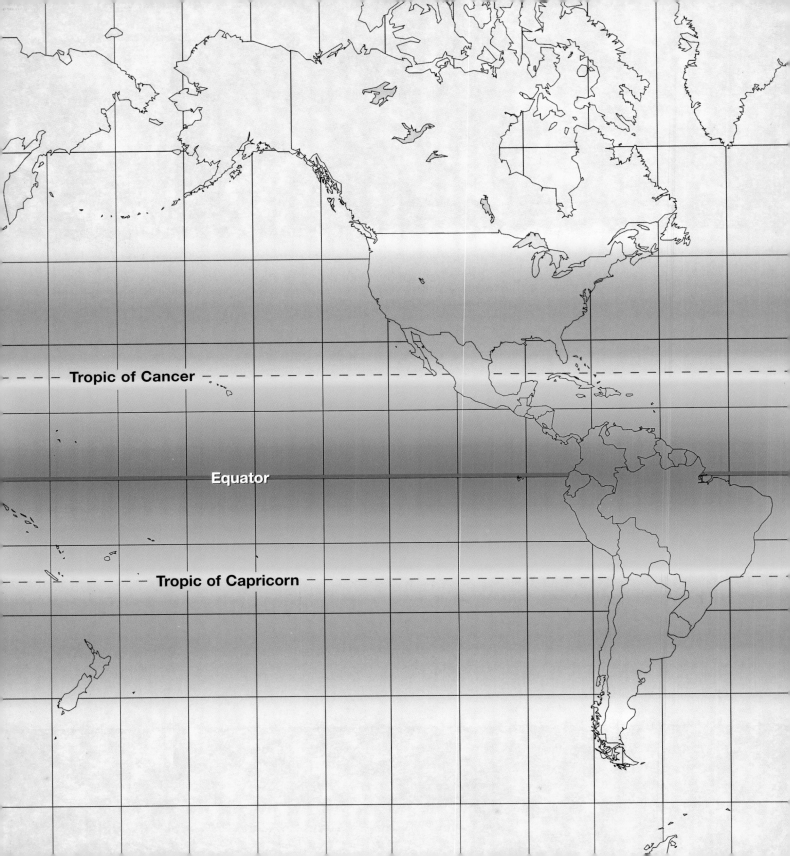

Tropic of Cancer

Equator

Tropic of Capricorn

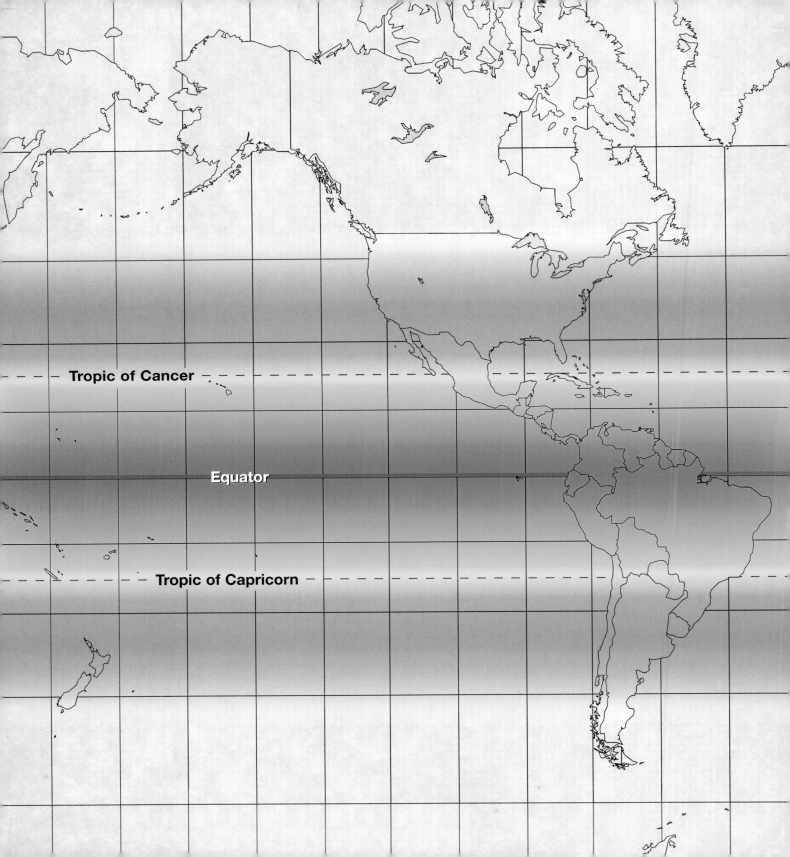

Tropic of Cancer

Equator

Tropic of Capricorn

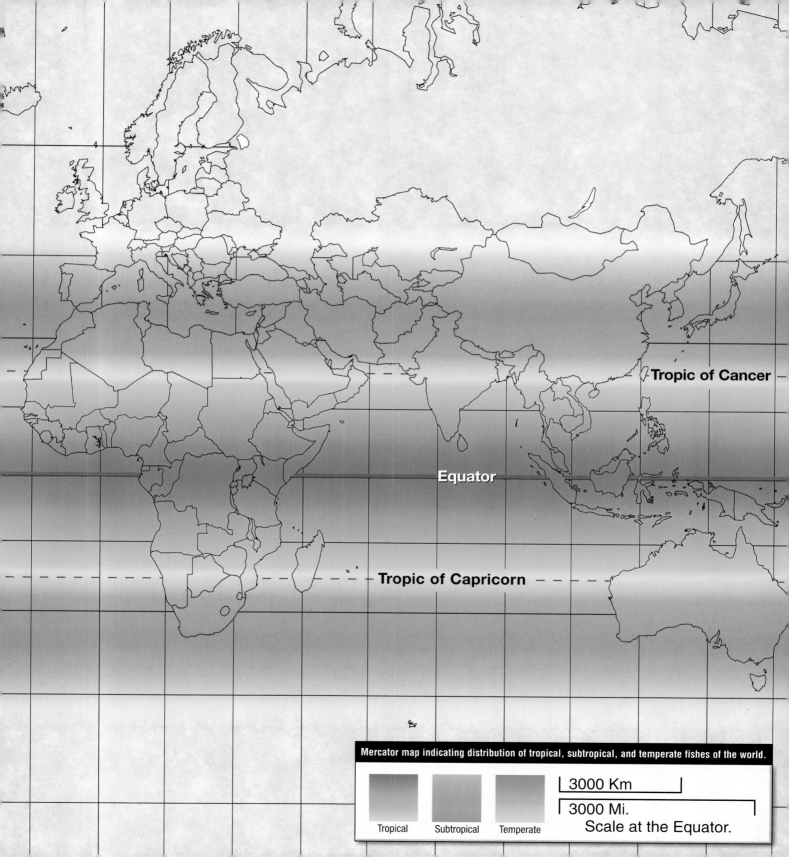

Tropic of Cancer

Equator

Tropic of Capricorn

Mercator map indicating distribution of tropical, subtropical, and temperate fishes of the world.

3000 Km

3000 Mi.

Scale at the Equator.

Tropical   Subtropical   Temperate